A MAN

Sir Mauric

and the

A MAN AND AN INSTITUTION

Sir Maurice Hankey, the Cabinet Secretariat and the custody of Cabinet secrecy

JOHN F. NAYLOR
State University of New York at Buffalo

CAMBRIDGE UNIVERSITY PRESS
Cambridge
London New York New Rochelle
Melbourne Sydney

CAMBRIDGE UNIVERSITY PRESS
Cambridge, New York, Melbourne, Madrid, Cape Town, Singapore, São Paulo, Delhi

Cambridge University Press
The Edinburgh Building, Cambridge CB2 8RU, UK

Published in the United States of America by Cambridge University Press, New York

www.cambridge.org
Information on this title: www.cambridge.org/9780521255837

First published 1984
This digitally printed version 2008

A catalogue record for this publication is available from the British Library

Library of Congress Catalogue Card Number: 83–20930

ISBN 978-0-521-25583-7 hardback
ISBN 978-0-521-09347-7 paperback

Dedicated to the memory
of four men
who awakened and nurtured my interest in history

JOHN L. NAYLOR
EDGAR B. ['DIGGER'] GRAVES
WILLIAM DEMARCUS STARNES
DAVID OWEN

Contents

Preface

The initial stages of my research were funded by the Research Foundation of the State University of New York, for which I am grateful, as I am, in greater measure, to the State University of New York at Buffalo for sabbatical leaves which enabled me to pursue the research and writing of this book. Among debts incurred while in the United Kingdom, I am pleased to acknowledge the co-operation of the staff of the Public Record Office, then housed in Chancery Lane under daunting conditions; I trust that the removal of the Cabinet records to Kew has eased their burdens. In Cambridge, the staff of the Churchill College Archives Centre provided a full measure of support, as did the director, A. J. P. Taylor, and his able associates at the Beaverbrook Library in London. The authorities of the Department of Manuscripts of the British Library and of the National Library of Wales, Aberystwyth, bore with my inquiries for a shorter period of time but with the same consideration. I would like also to acknowledge the assistance given me by the University Library, Cambridge; the Bodleian Library, Oxford; the University of Birmingham Library; the National Library of Scotland, Edinburgh; and the Library of the London School of Economics. In a different, but no less important, vein I am indebted to the continuing hospitality shown me on my sojourns in London by Val and Elizabeth Lewthwaite.

Quotations from government records held in the Public Record Office are Crown Copyright and are used here by the kind permission of The Controller, Her Majesty's Stationery Office. I am also in the debt of the following for permission to quote from copyright materials; where the connection is not obvious, I specify in the parentheses the individual whose papers have been quoted:

Her Majesty Queen Elizabeth II (Lord Stamfordham)
Viscount Addison
Earl Baldwin of Bewdley
The British Library Board (Earl Balfour)
C & T Publications Ltd (Sir Winston Churchill)
The Master, Fellows and Scholars of Churchill College in the University of Cambridge (Sir Maurice, later Baron, Hankey)

Viscount Esher
Baron Hankey
Mrs Susan Hibbert (Sir Lionel Heald)
Hutchinson Limited (readers' reports)
The Trustees of the Imperial War Museum (Field-Marshal Sir Henry Wilson)
The Marquess of Lothian (Philip Kerr, later Marquess of Lothian)
Mr Harold Macmillan
Mrs Mary Moorman (G.M. Trevelyan)
The Warden and Fellows of New College, Oxford (Viscount Milner)
Mr Geoffrey Pike (J. Burgon Bickersteth)
Mr A. J. P. Taylor and the First Beaverbrook Foundation (David Lloyd George)
Baroness White and Tristan Jones (Thomas Jones)

If I have inadvertently infringed copyright in other unpublished materials, I offer my apologies. I would like to acknowledge the permission given to me by Una Maclean Mackintosh and Dr Keith Middlemas to draw upon affadavits submitted by the latter and by the former's late husband, John Mackintosh, in connection with the Crossman legal proceedings in 1975. I am grateful as well to the Baron Bridges for approaching the Cabinet Office to secure permission to quote several extracts from letters written by his father, then Sir Edward Bridges, while Cabinet Secretary.

In the preparation of the manuscript, I have had the benefit of the assistance of skilled typists and good friends: Fran Shayler, Dorothy Ward and Joyce Milligan in the Department of History, and June McMahon and Jackie Ort in the Dean's Office, Faculty of Social Sciences. I owe a major debt of gratitude to those colleagues in the profession who have given me their counsel and criticisms. In Buffalo, Clif Yearley, Paul Guinn and Roberta Dayer have read the manuscript, each at a different stage of its preparation; further afield, Henry Winkler of the University of Cincinnati, Ray Callahan of the University of Delaware and Gaines Post, Jr, of the University of Texas at Austin, have offered useful commentary and encouragement. In England, Donald Cameron Watt, Stevenson Professor of International Relations in the University of London, has shared his knowledge with me so as to inform what I have written in several significant ways. The traditional caveat nonetheless applies: despite these efforts, I alone am responsible for any errors – whether of commission or omission – which remain. A final word of appreciation to those closest to me whose tolerance has extended to my occasional absence, in body or in mind, from the family, in pursuit of 'a man and an institution.' My thanks thus go to my wife, Maiken, and my boys, John and Stephen, both for bearing with me and, on occasion, for diverting me from that preoccupation.

Tonawanda and Eagle Crag Lake, NY — *J. F. N.*
July 1983

Abbreviations

C	Cabinet Minute/Conclusion
CAB	Cabinet records, followed by a suffix indicating the series
CCR	Committee of Civil Research
Cd, Cmd or Cmnd	Command Paper
CID	Committee of Imperial Defence
CIGS	Chief of Imperial General Staff
COS	Chiefs of Staff [Sub-]Committee of CID
CP	Cabinet memoranda
DP[P]	Defence Plans (Policy) Committee
DPRC	Defence Policy and Requirements Committee
DRC	Defence Requirements [Sub-]Committee of CID
EAC	Economic Advisory Council
FO	Foreign Office; when followed by a suffix, Foreign Office document.
HC Debates	House of Commons Debates, preceded by volume number
HL Debates	House of Lords Debates, preceded by volume number
HMG	His/Her Majesty's Government
HNKY	Hankey Papers, Churchill College, Cambridge University
MI 5	Military Intelligence, Department 5, i.e. the Security Service
MP	Member of Parliament
PC	Privy Counsellor
PM	Prime Minister
PREM	Prime Ministers' Private Office correspondence
PRO	Public Record Office
QC	Queen's Council
RAF	Royal Air Force
WC	War Cabinet (1916–19) Minute/Conclusion

Introduction

In the controversy surrounding the publication in 1975 of the first volume of R. H. S. Crossman's *Cabinet Diaries*, which the British government had sought first to discourage and then to proscribe through legal proceedings, contentious questions were posed. Weighed in the balance were such concerns vital to a democracy as the need for secrecy in the highest reaches of government, on the one hand, and, on the other, the right of the citizenry to be informed witnesses and critics of the actions carried out in its name by the government. In the wide-ranging discussion, opposed principles of what in fact constituted the public interest were advanced: for several months, Great Britain engaged in a debate concerning the merits of 'open' and 'closed government.' At law, the Lord Chief Justice of England strove to balance the rival claims, attempting to secure both the desirable ends of an appropriate measure of 'confidentiality' for the business of government and an earlier public accountability for Cabinet proceedings. Whatever the merits of that accommodation – his decision cleared the way for the publication of Crossman's memoirs – the Labour government responded politically by strengthening 'closed government,' in the form of measures which the Cabinet deemed necessary for the effective functioning of government.

Perhaps the most interesting aspect of the proceedings was the attitude evident in official circles, shared by political leaders and preeminent civil servants, to the effect that the citizenry had little business inquiring precisely *how* Britain was governed. By design, the work of the Cabinet, including its delegation of some major responsibilities to select Cabinet committees, remains veiled, although the fact of that veiling is now openly recognized. Her Majesty's Government remain of the opinion that confidential aspects of Cabinet business should not be revealed by those who have taken part for a period of fifteen years; only with the passage of thirty years will the public be granted access to its actual records. Certainly few voices are so reckless as to call for immediate disclosure of the business of the Cabinet, its committees, or the counterpart committees which are staffed by senior civil servants, although a case can be made that an excessive stifling of information about the process of government may mislead the public and impair the functioning of government in present-day Britain.[1] Thus the question persists whether in the name of a better informed, more responsive citizenry measures of 'open government' might secure an understanding of what transpires in the 'corridors of power' and round the Cabinet table.

While that question will receive continued attention in years to come, a related question has emerged from this exchange of views: how, and why, has secrecy come to envelop the practice of modern Cabinet government? It is my purpose to address that question in this book, developing an answer from a variety of records which enable us to gain the necessary historical perspective. In the first place, the vast bulk of the records of Cabinet government now enter the public domain after thirty years, affording an appreciation both of the process and proceedings of Cabinet government at this remove. Secondly, the curtains are parted upon Cabinet secrecy closer to the contemporary scene by a range of ministerial memoirs, culminating in the brightly illumed scene which Crossman depicted for the Wilson administration of 1964–70. Precisely because the government failed to ring down the curtain upon Crossman's disclosures, a limited but informative comprehension of contemporary practices is possible. Since some aspects of government are now closed even to ministerial memoirists, the disclosures made by Crossman bring us closer to the workings of Cabinet government in Britain than we are likely again to approach, unless the government's disposition alters. With this added dimension, the record of the development of canons of Cabinet secrecy very nearly to the present time can be written; that topic constitutes a portion of what I have set about to assess.

Yet I did not have such a theme in mind when first I embarked upon a study of the evolution of the Cabinet Secretariat, an institutional product of the crisis of government in the midst of the First World War which proved more adaptable to peace-time than many of the innovations associated with the war leadership of David Lloyd George. Initially, I anticipated that the scope of this book would be delimited by the regime which Sir Maurice Hankey headed at the Cabinet Office from late 1916 until his retirement as Secretary to the Cabinet twenty-two years later. That period possesses a historical coherence which is reflected in the first six chapters of this work, which deal with the antecedents of the Cabinet Secretariat, the initial organization of Hankey's office, the crisis in the fortunes of the Secretariat which followed upon Lloyd George's fall from power in 1922, and the completion of the process whereby the Secretariat emerged as the central agency for the preparation and disposition of

Cabinet business – a process complete well before Hankey left Whitehall Gardens in 1938. These twenty-two years witnessed the institutionalization both of the Secretariat as an office free from partisan taint and of Hankey as confidant and adviser of successive premiers. Concurrently, Hankey and the Cabinet Office – 'a man and an institution' – discharged a role, never formally defined, as the custodians of Cabinet secrecy. In this last regard, the precedents set before the Second World War frame the post-war debate over the place of such secrecy within a free society.

In an ironic fashion, this last aspect of the present study came into focus with Hankey's struggle to publish his First World War memoirs, based upon a detailed, private diary which he kept while Secretary to the Cabinet. For nearly twenty years, two of his successors and three Prime Ministers refused to sanction the publication of disclosures which they thought destructive of the doctrine of the Cabinet's collective responsibility and of the confidential relationship between ministers and civil servants. Hankey himself fell victim to that concern for the protection of Cabinet secrecy which he had played the major role in formulating. He resisted strongly the proscription of his memoirs, at a time when officially informed memoirs of the Second World War were in full flood, because Winston Churchill, assisted by Attlee's administration, had secured a suspension of the usual canons of Cabinet secrecy. Not until 1961 did HMG grant Hankey his say about Britain's 'Supreme Command' in the Great War, and even then they looked the other way rather than admit the propriety of his diarist's pen. For a full generation after his retirement, the official view of Hankey's memoirs directs our attention to the custody of Cabinet secrecy: restrictions in its name severely limited accounts of the working of British inter-war government written from within by former ministers. Buttressing these conventions was the ubiquitous Official Secrets Act of 1911 and 1920, despite the fact that it had been written for purposes very different from those for which the government threatened its use. In time, however, familiarity with the threat bred contempt, and a discrediting of the Official Secrets Act followed, until it could no longer effectively bear the weight of maintaining Cabinet secrecy.

With the weakening of this prop, accomplished both by governmental abuses and by increasing revelations of 'official secrets' in a procession of post-war ministerial memoirs, the Crossman affair served as denouement: although the government sought to proscribe the detailed record of Cabinet deliberations and the depiction of the processes of government, in which the Cabinet Office is intimately involved, they based the Crown's case not upon the ailing statute but instead upon presumed standards of ministerial conduct. In the legal proceedings, the Cabinet Secretary, Sir John Hunt, necessarily shed light upon the contemporary practices of Cabinet secrecy; thus the Crossman case afforded me a means of pursuing this dimension well within the thirty year period. Yet Hunt and the Cabinet Office succeeded in establishing a legal doctrine of 'confidentiality' as a new weapon in the defence of Cabinet secrecy. To be sure, other duties of the contemporary Secretariat remain masked from public scrutiny; further, the doctrine of 'confidentiality' may well tell in future against any premature disclosures in ministerial memoirs concerning the work of the Cabinet Office. Its activities will – for the foreseeable future – be kept at a remove of thirty years, save for whatever depictions ministerial memoirs may bring our way, perhaps fifteen years after the fact. Whether that genre, particularly in its 'Cabinet diary' form, is likely to flourish as it has in recent years remains problematical.[2]

The final chapter of this book is concerned in the main with the custody of Cabinet secrecy from Hankey's retirement until the recent regime of Sir John Hunt. In its course I offer only a cursory commentary upon the actual workings of the War Cabinet Secretariat of 1939–45 – whose records are available in the Public Record Office – in order to establish the ease of transition from Hankey's peace-time operation to the much more extensive scope of the activities over which his successor, Sir Edward Bridges, presided. The Cabinet Office's role and its procedures clearly had been established in Hankey's time; what demands further exploration, as noted, is the role of the Cabinet Office as custodian of Cabinet secrecy in the post-war years.

How then take the measure of the historical role both of the Cabinet Secretariat and of the man who placed his imprint upon it? An obvious albeit incomplete answer centers upon those very records which Hankey maintained for the Cabinet, which prior to December 1916 functioned without benefit of any record-keeping mechanism. Much more is involved than the best known of those records, the Cabinet Minutes; while useful, in some ways the minutes are among the least revealing sources for a reconstruction of the process of Cabinet government: 'The minutes and conclusions were deliberately prepared objectively and impersonally, and designed to record agreement and not promote controversy; behind many of the decisions lay tensions and influences which are not reflected in the official records.'[3] Nonetheless, the Cabinet Minutes provide an estimable record of decisions, and at times they reveal surprising details concerning policy or individual ministerial attitudes on leading questions. In addition, there exists a vast range of other government records which contributes to a historical evaluation both of Cabinet proceedings and the Secretariat's role; in the latter case, Hankey's office maintained a collection of files which bears directly on its tasks, as regards not only its organization of Cabinet business but also its acquired role as the custodian of Cabinet secrecy. A tightly defined institutional account of the Secretariat affords a detailed explanation of such records: S. S. Wilson's *The Cabinet Office to 1945*, published for the Public Record Office in 1975, is indispensable to an understanding of the mechanics of the organization. Yet such an approach is perforce limited, because the institution itself did not evolve in accord with abstract principles of organization; instead, the Cabinet Secretariat's activities were shaped by political considerations and personal forces which must be taken into account if its role, and that of the Cabinet Secretary, are to be understood. While Wilson's study recognizes Hankey's immense contribution, he does not deal with the shaping influence which the first Secretary had upon the Cabinet Office, nor does he hazard an estimate of his important role as adviser, although in reality that personal contribution is inextricably intertwined with his conduct of office.

Thus a full evaluation of the development of the Cabinet Secretariat must be set in a comprehensive political framework: concerns of foreign and imperial policy occasionally intrude, since they too exercised a significant, albeit short-term, influence upon the extent and style of Hankey's operation. Biographical considerations enter, extending considerably beyond the career of Hankey himself, which Stephen Roskill has assessed in a magisterial fashion. Other civil servants, Hankey's deputy Tom Jones first among them, contributed to the development of the office; politicians, with Lloyd George holding primacy of place, played a vital part in establishing a pragmatic role for the Cabinet Office, which existed on parliamentary sufferance and accommodated to political realities. The Cabinet Secretary's relations with other civil service interests, ably represented by the powerful Permanent Secretary to the Treasury, Sir Warren Fisher, require scrutiny, no less than his dealings with five premiers and scores of influential ministers – in their sum Hankey's dealings with the official and political worlds had a far-reaching impact upon the development of the Cabinet Office. In assessing these constraints upon Hankey's operations, this study deals directly with the nature of British government in the course of our century: it examines the preponderant departmentalism of the pre-war period, which gave way to the fitful, erratic but forceful leadership of Lloyd George; the auxiliary role played by the Secretariat in forwarding his style of government, whether or not it be characterized as 'prime ministerial government'; the concurrent development of a powerful government bureaucracy, which persisted even when Lloyd George's successors sought a return to normalcy; the tightening net of Cabinet secrecy; and finally, the conflict between precepts of 'open' and 'closed government' which built for decades before securing some measure of resolution as a result of the Crossman case. That the Cabinet Secretariat was involved in all these matters is a testimony to its centrality in the processes of modern British government.

The ways in which such a role was assumed are informed by a number of non-official accounts by participants, both on the ministerial side and from within Whitehall Gardens: although these sources are subjective and some are hostage to political or personal interests, they make possible an assessment of the development of the Cabinet Office and the roles played by its principals in the years to 1938. Among these sources, of paramount importance are the diaries maintained – on the whole, consistently – by Hankey and Jones, who retired from government service in 1930; by contrast, Hankey's successors have held it improper to keep any such account of personal commentary on affairs of state. As a result, only for this formative stage in the office's history will we be able to locate the Cabinet Secretary as adviser within the context of the institution. For that reason, and for the information which the diaries contain, I have drawn extensively from those accounts; they possess an immediacy and a force which shed light upon the way in which Cabinet government was carried on, nearly to the outbreak of the Second World War. In utilizing both official and private accounts – published and unpublished, contemporary and reflective – this study seeks to depict the full range of Secretariat activities and to examine the impact of the office upon modern Cabinet government, through the depiction of the institution and the men who in a real sense created it. Such an approach is of course dependent upon the use and interpretation of the written word, more cautiously phrased in government records than in a variety of private forms, but the first generation of those who served in the Cabinet Office is long gone, and their successors are evidently not free to speak in any detail to the issues raised in the last chapter.

There is another important source which should be mentioned in connection with any evaluation of Hankey's own role as adviser, particularly in matters of British and imperial defence policies, where repeatedly he chose to exert his influence. The Cabinet Secretary, ever the man of records, systematically collected important papers, written as part of his official responsibilities, intending subsequently to draw upon these in what he foresaw as his own historical 'Magnum Opus.' Such a volume never materialized – his memoirs, based in the main upon his diary, did not extend beyond the Paris Peace Conference – but the collection eventually passed to the Public Record Office. Readily apparent in these documents are the causes which Hankey served with special fervor and the ways in which he operated as adviser. We have no expectation of seeing the likes of such a collection, maintained by the Secretary to the Cabinet, ever again; his successors in that post have determined upon a far less conspicuous historical role for themselves.

In sum, the career of Sir Maurice Hankey constitutes a remarkable chapter in the development of an institution. While the range of his advice, derived in part from his own military experience, exceeded that which any of his successors have commanded, his person is recognizable in the description of the Cabinet Secretary recently offered by Sir Harold Wilson, following upon his own retirement as Prime Minister:

> The Secretary of the Cabinet is, in a sense, the "prime minister's permanent secretary," to use a phrase of the . . . Secretary's predecessor [Sir Burke Trend] on handing me my first brief in 1964; but his loyalty is, no less, to the Cabinet and the doctrine of Cabinet government . . . He advises also on the practices and conventions about the conduct of ministers in relation to collective Cabinet responsibility, as well as on other matters affecting collective responsibility and loyalty.[4]

Not only did Hankey establish the Secretariat as the agency for the conduct of Cabinet government, but as well he laid out the institutional paths which his successors continue to tread. Ultimately the man and the institution stand as one, together meriting a unified historical treatment, which in turn contributes to an understanding of the ways in which Great Britain is governed.

I

The origins of the Cabinet Secretariat

As the debacle at the Somme ground to a halt in the chilling autumn rains and the squalid muck of the battlefield, the Allied leaders gathered in Paris, in mid-November 1916, to assess the military situation. Two men who shared growing doubts about the British role in the war took a 'stroll' before a morning session of the conference, exchanging views about their country's contribution. One of them was the well-known and controversial politician, David Lloyd George; the other, hardly a public figure, was Lieut Col. Maurice Hankey, a leading military adviser to the government who had served as Secretary to the pre-war Committee of Imperial Defence and during the war as Secretary to the three committees which had, in turn, worked with questions of military policy for the Cabinet. Although a recent appointee as Secretary of State for War, Lloyd George had already become frustrated with the deference consistently shown to the military views voiced by the Imperial General Staff and the British Expeditionary Force exhibited by Prime Minister Asquith, head of a Coalition government.

According to Lloyd George's recollection, Hankey took the initiative and sketched proposals for a re-organization of the British war effort:

> We both felt that nothing in the way of a change in the conduct of the war had been accomplished and that in the absence of some dramatic *coup* things would go on as before until we slide into inevitable catastrophe . . . I was in favour of an immediate resignation [on his own part]. To this Sir Maurice was opposed until some means of effecting a change had first been attempted. I can recall that as we passed the Vendome Column, Sir Maurice paused and said: 'You ought to insist on a small War Committee being set up for the day-to-day conduct of the war, with full power. It must be independent of the Cabinet. It must keep in close touch with the P.M., but the P.M., as the Head of Government, could not manage that. He has a very heavy job in looking after the Cabinet and attending to Parliamentary and Home Affairs. He is a bit tired, too, after all he has gone through in the last two and half years. The Chairman of the proposed Committee must be a man of unimpaired energy and great driving power.'[1]

Although Hankey did not himself record such a striking initiative on his part,[2] he too had grown disillusioned with the traditional ways in which Britain was governed, in the midst of a war grown beyond any nation's control. Nor was he alone in official circles in his dissatisfaction with the direction and vigor of Britain's war effort, which reflected in part the inadequacies of the governmental and institutional framework within which Asquith's regime operated – the legacy of nineteenth-century Cabinet government. Thus the confidences shared by Lloyd George and Hankey revealed anxiety about policy and concern with the mechanism of policy-making: institutions which had served splendidly in the palmy days of Victorian England were by 1916 foundering on the destructive reefs of modern warfare.

No two men did more to bring Cabinet government into the twentieth century than Lloyd George and Hankey: whatever was said on that fateful walk in Paris matters little beside the shared recognition of purpose. Both men sought first and foremost to win the war;[3] that Asquith had to yield his high office after eight years, and an established pattern of government succumb in the wake of his overthrow, is a measure of the dedication and fixity of purpose shown by these critics of the old order. Malaise had seeped into political precincts almost from the very first months of the war, which had witnessed strained relations between civil authorities and the military; in the spring of 1915 the acerbic Lt-General Henry Wilson had retorted to Asquith's ill-tempered jibe that the war had produced no great generals: 'No, Prime Minister, nor has it produced a statesman.'[4] No one could deny that the British war effort ground unevenly: by the autumn of 1915, the failure to break through at the Dardanelles served to provoke a serious government crisis. Lord Milner, nearly a decade in the political wilderness, reflected more than a bruised ego in commenting 'the change of Ministry will not bring us victory without a change in method.'[5] Milner nonetheless recognized the need for changes in the leadership, commenting in August 1915 on the coalition formed in May that only 'the consistent display of qualities which are the absolute antithesis of what we know of Asquith, McKenna, Simon, *et hoc genus omne*, and . . . of A. J. B[alfour], Lansdowne and most of their Unionist colleagues' would save the day – and the nation.[6] That methods of governing and personnel mattered to Milner is clear in his joining with younger Unionist critics, including Leopold S. Amery, F. S. Oliver, and Geoffrey Dawson in weekly meetings of a 'ginger group' whose purpose was stated later by Amery as 'somehow or other to secure a change of government.'[7]

As a result of his public stand, Milner attracted the attention of other critical peers; among them was Lord Sydenham, CID Secretary from

1904 to 1907, who attributed the 'terrible mistakes' in the conduct of the war directly to Asquith's leadership: 'The ragged discussion of the Cabinet. . . lies at the root of our misfortunes.'[8] Since the formation of the coalition, Sydenham had urged the creation of a War Council of some five or six individuals 'with full and complete charge of all matters relating to the conduct of the War'; only such 'a complete change of methods' would sustain a successful war effort. Yet Milner and Sydenham failed at that time to achieve their goal; another year of brutal but inconclusive warfare was required before Asquith fell and 'a complete change of methods' instituted. In the interim, the same flaws which had undercut the Cabinet's first attempt to delegate responsibility for the conduct of the war – a War Council established as 'a supplement to the Cabinet for exploring some of the larger questions of policy rather than as an instrument for the day to day conduct of the war'[9] – hampered the efforts of its successor bodies, the Dardanelles Committee and the War Committee. Changes in personnel alone – the formation of the coalition – had not proved sufficient.

Complicating the Cabinet's role in the discussions of military planning, shared to some extent with those three committees, was its large size and cumbrous deliberations: the military authorities generally and in particular Kitchener, the Secretary of State for War until his death in June 1916, were reluctant, in the latter's words, 'to reveal military secrets to twenty-three gentlemen with whom he was barely acquainted.'[10] Owing to Kitchener's secretive ways – Esher later wrote of his ministerial method that 'he neither argued nor discussed; he simply ignored'[11] – the Cabinet spent most of its time either duplicating the work of its War Committee or engaged in arguments based upon inconclusive military appreciations.[12] A recently published account of Kitchener's insistence on enforcing Cabinet secrecy in a matter openly discussed in *The Times* on the previous day underscores the problem; to such an entreaty Lloyd George retorted that neither he nor his colleagues ought 'stay there 5 minutes if they were not to be trusted with real numbers and requirements.' The War Secretary threatened resignation and took '3 slow, very slow steps to the door,' only to be called back by some but not all of his fellow ministers.[13] Despite such painful exchanges, Kitchener refused to share responsibility with the Cabinet on a number of occasions.

Certainly he had good grounds for protecting military secrets from a government which was disposed to talk rather than to act: gossip concerning military operations was common fare in London; security provisions in official circles were lax, by any standards. *The Times* appeared to specialize in publicizing breaches of Cabinet secrecy, and that body's discussions at times appeared to be public property, for reasons which the politician Christopher Addison adduced:

It is really too scandalous that *The Times* should be able to publish these accounts of Cabinet meetings. But seeing that the whole of the daily discussions and negotiations between Carson, Curzon, Northcliffe, Lloyd George and others are probably at the disposal of *The Times* through various intermediaries, this publication is scarcely to be wondered at.[14]

Additional criticism from outside the coalition regime centered on the Cabinet's discursiveness no less than its laxness: Leo Amery, no friend to the regime, noted Sir Edward Carson's contempt – in words which echo Kitchener's suspicions – 'of the present system of governing by 22 gabbers round a table with an old procrastinator in the chair.'[15]

The massive loss of life on the Somme served to intensify the dissatisfaction with Britain's military ineffectiveness, which in turn raised fundamental questions about the structure and personnel of the government. Such influential Tories as the Earl of Derby and the former premier, A. J. Balfour, were now prepared to withdraw their support from the Asquith-led coalition; as important, they were now prepared to transfer their allegiance to their longtime political foe, Lloyd George, whom Balfour described to King George V in June 1916 as 'out to win the war.'[16] Balfour also recognized the need to alter the 'accustomed machinery' of government, a structure to which the incumbent premier was deeply attached.[17] When events finally led to Asquith's fall, the climate existed for a change in system as well. Other Unionists also noted the growing disparity between Lloyd George's growth in stature and the disarray of the coalition government.[18] In July 1916 Viscount Esher, who tended his political sources closely, drew an obvious conclusion: 'I should not be surprised if Asquith had to go and little L. G. reigned in his stead.'[19] In the meantime, and within the coalition, the Unionist leader, Bonar Law, expressed his own doubts about the system to which Asquith, premier since 1908, adhered in war as he had in peace:

when he joined Asquith's Cabinet [in May 1915] he was astonished at the lack of method, the absence of any agenda or minutes. He told Asquith this. The latter said that everyone who joined the Cabinet made the same observation, but speedily became reconciled to the method of doing business and saw its advantage for the special purposes.[20]

Asquith's refusal to acknowledge that the lack of an official record of Cabinet proceedings accessible to Cabinet members reflected an anachronistic bent which flew in the face of the increasing complexity of wartime government. Even before the war, ministers had had to deal with inter-departmental matters[21] which required co-ordination and consensus at the Cabinet level. Asquith's stubborn refusal to depart from past verities reflected his philosophical disposition become political reality, 'Wait and See.' Yet the Great War waited upon no man nor the traditional methods of governing Britain.

In such a darkening setting, Hankey and Lloyd George – who were not personally close[22] – looked to a strongly centralized, possibly authoritarian, executive as Britain's only escape from ineffective government. Even prior to the Somme offensive, Lloyd George had confided to C. P. Scott, editor of the *Manchester Guardian*: 'We are losing the war if indeed we have not already lost it.'[23] In a parallel fashion, Hankey had in December 1915 despaired of the Cabinet's conduct of the Dardanelles operation; although his advice had been rejected, Hankey was not so much troubled by that rejection as by the Cabinet's inability to come to terms with the issue. After a month's dithering, the continued British presence at Gallipoli (and in yet another peripheral expedition at Salonika) hung in the balance, and Hankey recorded in his diary:

Cabinet met in the morning and decided to evacuate Sulva and Anzac [bases opened in support of the main offensive in the Dardanelles], retaining Helles for the present. No decision as regards Salonika . . . This delay in decision is absolutely fatal . . . The Government are really dreadfully to blame. They put off decisions, squabble [,] have no plan of operation, and allowed themselves to be dragged into this miserable Salonika affair at the tail of French domestic politics. I can see only one solution – to suspend the constitution and appoint a dictator.[24]

Nor, from Hankey's perspective, did the situation improve when the Dardanelles expedition was completely abandoned, because the Cabinet continued to talk to no purpose. The War Committee proved no more successful an agency for war planning than its predecessors, and Hankey noted a succession of its 'dreadful' meetings in early November 1916:

The War Cmt work is hopelessly congested, great questions dealing with Man Power, the [illegible] Board, Food Supply, and Finance all urgently awaiting settlement. Yet I could not get a meeting for tomorrow because Runciman was going for a day's shooting, Lord Curzon for a week-end, and Lord Crawford to address his former constituents. I managed to get a meeting for Monday but the P.M. said 'You won't get anyone.' Today's meeting had to end soon after 1 p.m. to enable Ministers to attend official luncheons. Thus and thus is the British Empire governed at a critical stage of the war. I have done all I can to get meetings; to crystallize woolly discussions into clear-cut decisions, and to promote control – but the task is a Herculean one![25]

To be sure, Hankey's diary contains an element of the self-serving – understandably a characteristic of most such records – but there can be no doubt that his complaints with the War Committee were well-grounded; not even the Prime Minister could dispute its shortcomings, as he perceived them:

The two main defects of the War Committee, which has done excellent work, are (1) that its numbers are too large, and (2) that there is delay, evasion, and often obstruction on the part of the Departments in giving effect to its decisions.

I might with good reason add (3) that it is often kept in ignorance by the Departments of information, essential and even vital, of a technical kind, upon the problems that come before it; and (4) that it is over-charged with duties, many of which might well be delegated to subordinate bodies.[26]

Despite this recognition that the flow of information from the departments had to be improved and regularized, Asquith himself proved to be an obstacle to conveying information in the opposite direction, by failing to give sufficient attention to Cabinet decisions.[27] Reliable, unambiguous information was difficult to secure through institutional means in 1916; political gossip flourished in its absence.

Thus the coalition disintegrated, a victim of its own institutional malaise rather than a political conspiracy engineered by Lloyd George.[28] Yet the Secretary of State for War played the key role – Bonar Law, the Tory leader, confided to Hankey: 'Lloyd George is at the same time the right hand to the P.M. and the leader of the opposition'[29] – and he intended to gain personal direction of a three-man War Committee, which would possess 'full powers, subject to the supreme control of the Prime Minister, to direct all questions connected with the war.'[30] Asquith would retain the right to refer any matter from the committee to the full Cabinet as well as nominal responsibility, but Lloyd George demanded in exchange for his continuance in office nothing less than 'a fundamental reform of the British constitutional machinery for waging war.'[31] At this juncture the War Minister sought not the succession to Asquith but instead the taking of war powers from his indecisive hands.[32] The choice – however disagreeable – remained with the Prime Minister.

Asquith negotiated the terms concerning the scope and powers of the proposed committee with Lloyd George and his Tory associates, and Hankey had a hand in drafting the agreement. Yet Lloyd George was warned to beware of Hankey's actions in the final stages of the gathering crisis, whatever his degree of sympathy for reform; Admiral 'Jackie' Fisher, who knew Hankey well, judged him 'extravagantly loyal to his immediate chief and would sell his best friend in the interest of his chief.'[33] It is clear, however, that Hankey's role in these days was that of a mediator, because throughout he desired Asquith's continuance in office; in fact, he had reservations about Lloyd George's 'dictatorial' bent and regarded his 'publicity and press methods' as 'intolerable.'[34] His loyalty to Asquith, to the moment of his resignation, remained above reproach, but there remained a war to be won.

Mediation between the Cabinet colleagues proved impossible in face of the public discussion of the emasculated role which Asquith had been assigned. In particular, the publication in *The Times* on 4 December of an article which declared that Asquith was acting under duress and could not be considered as master of the government caused the premier to decline the honorific functions which Lloyd George and his Tory colleagues insisted upon. Despite Lloyd George's disclaimer of responsibility for the article, relayed to Asquith in a conciliatory if disbelieved fashion, the Prime Minister chose to resign office; after the Unionist leader, Bonar Law, deferred to him, David Lloyd George assumed the supreme direction of the war effort and the premiership in the bargain. Whether Asquith had hoped to foil the efforts of his colleagues by resigning and in due course emerging as the indispensable man, alone able to sustain a government, is not here the issue; what is of import is that his actions in responding to the *Times*' article signaled an inflexible repudiation on his part of the hard-won progress towards a re-organization of the war machinery.[35] His attitude all but assured a continuance of the old methods, masked by some cosmetic surgery performed on the extant War Committee. From an institutional perspective, the events of the first week of December established that the price of fundamental reform was nothing less than Asquith's deposition: ironic indeed is the fact that Asquith chose to depose himself.[36]

The re-organization of government which Hankey had prepared at Lloyd George's behest – tailored to Asquith's continuance in office – was quickly abandoned. In its place Lloyd George, commissioned to form a government on 7 December, headed a small War Cabinet of five; only Bonar Law among them assumed departmental responsibilities, while Milner – returned from the wilderness – Curzon, and the Labour leader, Arthur Henderson, sat without executive tasks. Authority was vested collectively in the War Cabinet, with whom the Prime Minister would meet on a regular basis; unlike the November proposals, divided responsibility was out of the question. Lord Sydenham might claim some degree of paternity for the principle of the reform, but Milner himself had given even more concrete form to the idea, in recommending to Bonar Law on 2 December that supreme direction of the war effort could not be vested in one man, because of the vast field of operations. What was required was a 'Super Cabinet' of three to five men, although he thought five 'almost too many': 'They are in fact an Autocrat, a Dictator, or Supreme War Lord in Commission, the Prime Minister being the Head Commissioner . . . They must *all feel responsible for the whole of it, all the time* . . . They will have to do a lot of Thinking and Deciding. They should have to do precious little else.'[37]

Lloyd George consulted with Hankey on his very first day in office; the two discussed 'the personnel of the new Govt., the procedure of the new War Ctee., and the future of the war.'[38] Although Hankey turned immediately to prepare a memorandum on the last topic, by the 9th he was in harness as Secretary to the War Cabinet, confronting the task of administrative reform, bringing his experience to bear in building the new to repair the faults of the old system. He was much aided in his efforts that the desire for basic change was shared by men as essentially conservative as Balfour, Derby, Carson, and Bonar Law, who shared with Curzon the sense that 'the country . . . is not merely willing to be led, but is almost calling to be driven' and the conviction that the time for an overhaul of governmental organization was long overdue:

No one will deny that a system, however embedded in the tradition of the past and consecrated by constitutional customs, which was attended by . . . defects, was a system which was destined, immediately it came into contact with the hard realities of war, to crumble into dust at once . . . I do not think that anyone will deny that the old Cabinet system had irretrievably broken down, both as a war machine and as a peace machine.[39]

Curzon's commentary, widely shared during the war, is important in understanding the survival of this reform of Cabinet government when, in the post-war years, much that bore Lloyd George's political mark was discredited and discarded.

While the passing years would reveal Hankey's own conservatism, in December 1916 he stood as Lloyd George's agent in revolutionizing the mechanism of government in the name of winning the war. While he regretted Asquith's departure from Downing Street, he had no hesitation in working with the new regime, although initially he held reservations about the personnel of the proposed War Committee:

The new War Ctee. [i.e., with Asquith remaining as premier] is really ridiculous. Bonar Law is by common consent the poorest figure on the present War Ctee. Carson, on the old Dardanelles Ctee. was positively pitiful and worse than Bonar Law. Henderson is an untried man, and it's scarcely possible that his education can have fitted him for the job. Really it all depends on Lloyd George, who is brilliant but often unsound. The others are merely representatives of the noisiest groups in the House of Commons to prop him up, and there is no member of the House of Lords. No one would say that these four were the wisest hands to win the war – two are really feather heads. It is a mere political expedient of the most transparent kind to tide over a difficult crisis.[40]

Hankey's attitude stemmed from his fear that as Secretary he would be trapped between the Prime Minister and the War Committee, an unwelcome predicament which disappeared with Lloyd George's leadership of the War Cabinet. Though Law and the little known Henderson joined him on that body, Carson was excluded, and in his place two peers eased Hankey's reservation on that score. Yet the inclusion of Milner troubled many, Hankey among them, as he noted: 'I had to see Lord Milner by appointment and spent two hours with him. I have always hated his politics but found the man very attractive and possessed of personality and got on like a house on fire.'[41]

Hankey had every reason to be pleased with the role which Lloyd George gave him in the new regime, involving his counsel in questions of policy as well as appointing him Secretary to the War Cabinet. Given the extraordinary sway Hankey was to exercise in this post over more than two decades, it is well to recall that there were rivals for the position, one at least prominent in the new premier's own Welsh entourage; yet another confidant of Lloyd George, Tom Jones, noted that claim but added 'there is already a something Hankey who has had long experience of such work, and was before the war Secretary to the Committee of Imperial Defence.'[42] Certainly Hankey's appointment proved most important in the creation of a new system of Cabinet government, and what has been described as 'the ending of Cabinet informality' arguably involved the passing of classical Cabinet government.[43] Immediately apparent was the assumption of supreme responsibility by a five-man War Cabinet, replacing a cumbrous structure which had divided planning if not responsibility. Other far-reaching changes in the manner of Cabinet government were less evident: a network of Cabinet committees was instituted to secure the co-ordination of the vast range of war-time governmental activities; at the center of the new machinery, a Cabinet Secretariat had been established to hold the entire operation together. Put in simplest terms, the Cabinet Secretariat was intended to secure full communication between the executive authority vested in the War Cabinet and the departments, which were charged with carrying out Cabinet decisions. Because that flow had proved such a daunting problem during the war years, new arrangements had to be forged if the Lloyd George regime were to avoid the failures of its predecessors. If the informality and 'amateurism' which had characterized nineteenth-century Cabinet government had been thoroughly discredited, could system and 'professionalism' be put at the service of the twentieth-century Cabinet?

To secure such organization of Cabinet business, systematic records of Cabinet proceedings were officially maintained for the first time in British history: not only were the decisions recorded, but often the process whereby those war-time decisions were reached became a matter of record. Not only did these minutes and 'Cabinet papers' regularize the conduct of Cabinet government, but, in a way which no one foresaw at the time, they have become available to inform historical understanding of Cabinet activities, since they were made available at the Public Record Office a half-century later. Prior to the establishment of the Cabinet Secretariat, no attention whatever had been paid to the historical dimension of Cabinet business: no agendas were set, no decisions were recorded, no minutes were circulated or filed.

Some years after this innovation, Hankey was delighted to discover what he viewed as a precedent for the maintenance of Cabinet Minutes. In 1925, the well-known historian, Sir John Fortescue, referred to eighteenth-century 'secretarial' practices in a three-part article published in *The Times* dealing with the papers of King George III. What must have caught Hankey's eye was one short pasage:

> a very frequent occurrence in all of George III's Administration, until Pitt became Prime Minister, was that Ministers sent the King a Minute of Cabinet and forgot to keep a copy of it. Then they asked for it to be returned; and the request, although complied with, was not always unaccompanied by just rebuke. Occasionally the King did not restore it until he had taken a copy with his own hand, on at least one occasion through sheer good nature to save trouble to a harassed Minister, but more often evidently from distrust of his careless habits.[44]

Fortescue elaborated on the form of these 'Cabinet Minutes' in an exchange of correspondence with Hankey: he informed the Cabinet Secretary that George III's Cabinets met only at his behest, alone to deal with questions which he placed before them. In turn they informed the monarch of their deliberations: 'Having met, the Cabinet submitted its opinion in the form of a *Minute of Cabinet*, which began with a list of the members present, place (often a private house), time, and proceeded to the resolution. Such Minutes were drawn up by the Minister for the Department concerned, often so hastily that words were omitted, and often ungrammatically and sometimes almost illegible.'[45] Although these minutes were irregular and sparse in terms of content, Hankey took to them with enthusiasm, extended his research into the medieval period, and concluded that 'Cabinet Minutes' stretched back into the mists of the fourteenth century (for the Privy Council), were revived in the eighteenth century, and did not disappear until Queen Victoria's reign. Hankey used a very selective historical approach for one contemporary purpose: 'Their existence disposes of the argument which followed the institution of the Cabinet Minutes by Mr. Lloyd George that this was such an outrage to tradition as to make Mr. Gladstone turn in his grave!'[46] While Hankey sought remote institutional precedent for the work of his Secretariat, he was unaware that records of Cabinet discussions far closer in style to those minutes which he kept had been maintained, albeit for private purposes, by several ministers in the era of Gladstone and Disraeli.

These records, which possess considerable value for the historian of the Victorian Cabinet – who has very limited documentary sources at his disposal which touch upon the dynamics of Cabinet policy-making[47] – serve to 'lift the veil' from actual Cabinet meetings, in the case of *Lord Carlingford's Journal* in connection with the Gladstone ministry on the verge of collapse in 1885.[48] Similarly, Viscount Sandon's *Cabinet Journal* sheds considerable light upon Cabinet discussion of the Near Eastern crisis of 1878, although Sandon maintained his record only for three months. Ironically, Sandon's glimpse serves to show that the nineteenth-century Cabinet scrupulously avoided keeping records: on 24 May, the

Foreign Secretary, Lord Salisbury, collected the several copies of a memorandum upon which the Cabinet had based its policy, and he 'burnt them with some matches over the grate – and Lord J. Manner's copy was also burnt, he being absent from gout.'[49] Limited in purpose, the journals of Carlingford and Sandon are closer to the type of record maintained by Hankey than are the 'Minutes' which he claimed for precedent, but they constituted no precedent for his role – nor were they known to him.

Yet Hankey's investigation of precedent poses for us one question, namely why had the rudimentary practice of informing the monarch concerning the fact of Cabinet discussion lapsed in the nineteenth century. In truth, it had not, because the 'Cabinet Minute' in no precise fashion metamorphosed into a communication known as 'the Prime Minister's letter.' Hankey thought that the two forms overlapped – he identified the last 'Cabinet Minute' of the eighteenth-century type in Melbourne's hand in 1839 and detected what he called 'a Cabinet letter from the Prime Minister two years earlier'[50] – but the Royal Archives' collection of prime ministerial letters dates only from 1868.[51] The form of the letter differs from the formal character of the 'Cabinet Minute,' but it served to accomplish the same limited purpose: the monarch was informed of the Cabinet's conduct of affairs of state. Its different style is accounted for by the continuing evolution in Cabinet government: a Prime Minister had unquestionably come to head the Cabinet by the mid-nineteenth century, and the responsibility of informing the monarch accompanied such authority; as well, the initiative had by this time passed to the Cabinet, and the 'Prime Minister's letter' reflected the Cabinet's intentions rather than a mere response to matters first raised by the King. With these adjustments, there remains substantial continuity between the two: neither was intended as a record of Cabinet business; the documents were not subsequently available to the Cabinet or the premier, and in that sense they were very much 'occasional' pieces. As a result, Hankey was quite devoid of precedent for the maintenance of formal Cabinet Minutes: the organization of a Cabinet Secretariat represented a radical departure from past practices.

Nonetheless, the letters written by the Prime Ministers afford some otherwise unobtainable information about Cabinet proceedings in the years to 1916. Drafted after each Cabinet meeting, these letters often reflect the personal interests of, and immediate pressures upon, each premier – facing other engagements, possibly preoccupied, perhaps even bored by the convention – as he sat at the table round which the Cabinet had recently gathered, to inform the monarch about Cabinet proceedings. By and large, the leading ministers were not over-generous with information: on one occasion, Gladstone 'padded' his account of proceedings to assuage Victoria's complaint with 'very meagre news' of the previous Cabinet meeting.[52] Nor is 'inform' a description aptly applied to the letters sent to Edward VII by the penultimate premier of the old order, Sir Henry Campbell-Bannerman; the King was often irritated with the lack of information conveyed to him.[53] Campbell-Bannerman's personality may well account for the diffident nature of his letters,[54] but it appears that he 'found the Cabinet discussion tedious and discursive, and [so] he could not manage to manufacture a lucid but specious account for the King.'[55] Retrospectively, Hankey described these letters as less than adequate, citing George V's experiences: 'He told me several times that until he received the Cabinet Minutes and papers . . . he had never been fully informed of what was going on.'[56] Where the letters are relatively full – Asquith's are much lengthier, but other sources (e.g., the *Hobhouse Diaries*) have shown them to be incomplete accounts of Cabinet discussions – the premier's own interests or faulty recollection may intrude. Although particular specimens of 'the Prime Minister's letter' are interesting and useful, the genre communicates only a limited understanding of the dynamic of nineteenth-century Cabinet government.

And of course it served no useful purpose so far as the Cabinet itself was concerned: the result of the lack of any official record had often been either ignorance or confusion, comprising a pattern attested to by a wide variety of ministerial frustrations. Certainly best known, and possibly most telling, among a number of such incidents is the 1882 inquiry of Lord Hartington's Secretary, directed to Gladstone's Private Secretary:

> Harcourt and Chamberlain have both been here this morning and *at* my Chief about yesterday's Cabinet proceedings. They cannot agree what occurred. There must have been some decision, as Bright's resignation shows. My Chief has told me to ask you what the devil was decided, for he be damned if he knows. Will you ask Mr. G. in more conventional and less pungent terms?[57]

The episode gave Philip Snowden cause to ponder practices which he had experienced as a minister with the older approach which he could barely comprehend:

> Everyone who has experience of committee meetings where a large amount of business is considered must know how difficult it is to remember precisely what happened, and members of the committee in the absence of a record of the proceedings carry away with them various impressions. By the time the next meeting is held there are probably as many impressions of what was agreed to as there were members of the committee present.[58]

In the intervening half-century, other ministers had on occasion lamented the difficulty of comprehending Cabinet deliberations under such a handicap, a complaint forcefully registered by Lord Lansdowne, who in 1900 had been distressed by the Prime Minister's claim of Cabinet support for his refusal to publish certain Foreign Office dispatches: 'I was quite unaware of any such decision but our decisions are very often impalpable and perhaps I ought to have been able to construct one from materials afforded by Devonshire's yawns, and casual interjections around the table.'[59] Whatever the political cast of the ministry, such incidents document a type of malpractice common to nineteenth-century Cabinet government, namely the faulty administrative practices of Cabinets sometimes unable to agree whether they had agreed on a given issue. Lord Derby's restrained language of 1877 – 'he understood that the recollection of some of his colleagues was of a different character' – stands as an early epitaph for a lack of system which, at its worst, precipitated unjustified and unnecessary ministerial resignations.[60]

Problems with the Cabinet's resolution of business persisted into the midst of war, as Hankey discovered in one case where he had taken a CID report on the treatment of aliens to the Cabinet, requesting immediate attention; despite persistent inquiries, he had 'never been able to discover whether the Cabinet actually discussed the Report.'[61] He could not judge by the results, because some of the CID's recommendations had been carried out, others not; nor could he get anywhere with Asquith, and attempted instead to turn the premier's flank by raising the question with Balfour.[62] Earlier, Hankey had witnessed at a remove ministerial misunderstanding and the imprecise execution of a Cabinet decision on 29 July 1914 to put into immediate operation measures deemed precautionary in view of the outbreak of war in Europe.[63] Flawed practices continued to characterize Cabinet deliberations to the very last meeting prior to Asquith's resignation; as the war ground on, Britain's margin of tolerance for the foibles of nineteenth-century ways narrowed drastically. Recognition of this basic deficiency moved Lord Curzon in 1918 to speak of the old procedures with an air of incomprehension:

> There was no agenda, there was no order of business. Any Minister requiring to bring up a matter either of Departmental or of public importance had to seek the permission of the Prime Minister to do so. No one else, broadly speaking, was armed in advance. It was difficult for any Minister to secure an interstice in the discussion in which he could place his own case. No record whatever was kept of our proceedings, except the private and personal letter written by the Prime Minister to the Sovereign, the contents of which, in any case, are never seen by anybody else. The Cabinet often had the very haziest notion as to what its decisions were.[64]

What to do with Cabinet decisions posed another set of problems. An errant minister could mislead his own department, which Hankey vouched for in regard to pre-war Admiralty practices, as the First Lord would 'write down his own Minute of the Cabinet decision on the appropriate office file, notifying the Office of whatever it was essential they should know.'[65] According to the sole official inquiry concerning Cabinet procedures from 1900 to 1916, such a regular practice – however subject to misunderstanding – cannot be assumed for all departments: 'In the absence of minutes of [Cabinet] meetings it seems to have been the practice for Ministers to record Cabinet decisions on the appropriate Departmental file, although sometimes the fact that the decision was a Cabinet decision might not be mentioned. On other occasions they no doubt gave their substance orally to their officials.'[66] In other cases, ministers might not recognize the implications which a particular decision might have for their departments.

With such practices, the possibilities for disagreement were manifold: to guard against such misunderstanding, on one occasion a minister secured a formal record of the Cabinet's assent to a number of proposals which he had brought forward against considerable opposition. In this strange episode, the Secretary of State for War, Arnold-Forster, 'got Austen Chamberlain to note down the eight decisions he had obtained, a precaution he had learned from the aptitude of his colleagues to forget his projects.'[67] How many of his colleagues derived the same lesson, in the absence of an authoritative record? Apparently there was no need to disguise the practice of note-taking, at least in the Asquith administration: a new minister noted in his diary that at his very first Cabinet meeting a colleague 'took copious notes of the proceedings.'[68]

In his charge as Secretary to the War Cabinet, Hankey was expected to draft an authoritative record of Cabinet proceedings. While a radical departure from traditional Cabinet procedures, such a practice had important institutional antecedents: the nature of these secretarial tasks did not differ substantially from those he had acquired while serving in the Secretariat to the Committee of Imperial Defence. That record-keeping body, in existence since 1904, had been adapted during the war to serve the needs of the several war committees. Although such techniques as invitations to meetings, agendas, and minutes can be traced back to a predecessor body, a Cabinet Defence Committee established in 1895 carried out its charge for seven years, although little is known of its efforts, because, as a Cabinet committee, it kept no records.[69] In the wake of the Boer War, two criticisms were laid against its performance: one concerned its inadequate use of intelligence sources; the other, its inability to serve the ends of defence planning, namely: 'how to settle the broad principles of national and imperial defence upon the basis of information from all the interested Departments, and then to lay down, again in principle, the size and composition of the military and naval forces necessary in peace to make such a defence policy.'[70] Such a criticism reflected a flaw in the Defence Committee's original charge, as its founders had assumed that such a measure of inter-departmental co-operation and co-ordination could be secured without an agreed-upon record of planning and in the absence of any kind of permanent staff officials; the assumption reflected the style of nineteenth-century government.

Complaints voiced from within the Defence Committee in 1900 pointed to the relationship between the lack of minutes and the failure to apprehend decisions, but these were fended off by the service departments on the grounds that regular organizational mechanisms would turn the committee into a 'Court of Revision.' The Admiralty and the War Office resisted such surveillance of their work by other Cabinet members.[71] Paradoxically, the impetus for the institution of a stronger committee came two years later from the service ministers; but in this case a new First Lord of the Admiralty had concluded that were such a committee to produce convincing evidence that a larger Navy was needed for the defence of the Empire, 'he would have an irrefutable case for asking for enough money to build it.'[72] After initial reservations, the Prime Minister, A. J. Balfour, agreed to the reconstitution of the committee, and a re-organized Committee of Imperial Defence emerged in late 1902; it differed from its predecessor in its regular meetings and limited membership – the Prime Minister, the First Lord, the Secretary of State for War, and their four military advisers, which met at the premier's summons and as his own committee. In such a fashion the CID circumvented 'the established conventions of Cabinet secrecy which, at their worst, made unbusinesslike methods inevitable.'[73] The CID was given a part-time clerk from the Foreign Office staff to keep a record of its proceedings, but his activities were limited to clerking.[74] The product of his efforts, the CID conclusions were sent to the King commencing in March 1903.[75]

Pressures for more formal structure of CID activities came from the report on military re-organization returned by the Esher Committee in December of that year; they recommended the appointment of a civilian secretary and a full-time staff to consider all aspects of national and imperial defence on a continuing basis. Esher personally hoped to strengthen the CID as a 'department under the Prime Minister' which would serve as a 'Great General Staff' for the Empire.[76] In May 1904 the Prime Minister sanctioned the creation of such a department with the organization, bearing the less grandiose title of 'Secretariat.'[77] Such a staff was intended to provide continuity in defence planning regardless of the political composition of the government, amounting in one sense to insurance taken out against a Liberal regime, although phrased circumspectly in the Esher report: 'It is not safe to trust matters affecting national security to the chance of a favourable combination of personal characteristics.'[78] In sum, the re-organization of 1902 and the strengthening of the CID in 1904 established the importance of record-keeping techniques and permanent staffing in defence planning for the United Kingdom and her Empire. More than a decade was required to establish a similar need for the conduct of the business of the Cabinet.

The centralization inherent in Esher's scheme for a Prime Minister's department to oversee defence planning had another profound, if delayed, consequence for nineteenth-century Cabinet government. While Balfour insisted that the CID was an advisory body, its existence transgressed on the departmental concerns of service ministers. Nor was the development unnoted, as Esher remarked in connection with the 'General Staff' analogy: 'The CID Secretariat as a Prime Minister's department became the point d'appui of a significant trend in government which eroded away the departmental autonomy of ministers and the departmentalism of government business, while it enhanced the super-departmental authority of the Prime Minister.'[79] The incursion upon departmentalism, particularly from Downing Street, came to characterize the emerging pattern of modern Cabinet government.

In the shorter run, the keeping of records in the defence sphere proved a significant departure from traditional Cabinet ways: nor is it coincidental that during the same period the question of proper record-keeping had arisen at the Foreign Office, where the clerks had been unable to maintain an ordered flow of paper: 'It became increasingly difficult to locate past papers, and an endless amount of time was consumed in searching for lost documents. The system of keeping records . . . proved totally inadequate.'[80] Changes in personnel and internal organization undertaken at the Foreign Office in the first decade of this century ensured that the days of the office 'as a department of scribes' were past. Across Downing Street, within the ambit of the Prime Minister, the day of the secretary of the CID dawned in 1904; he was to prove no scribe either, nor was his lineal descendant, the Cabinet Secretary of December 1916.

Yet in its dozen years of pre-war experience the CID did not become the powerful agency which Esher hoped to secure in the 1904 reorganization. The reason was structural: Balfour did not insist that CID conclusions should be the basis upon which the War Office and Admiralty shape their roles; thus the CID judgment of 1905 that Britain need not take seriously the prospect of invasion did not influence the services' military planning. So too in Asquith's time: CID inquiries were launched, conclusions were drawn, advice given, but the government did not force the military to plan accordingly.[81] Whatever progress was made between 1904 and 1911 in preparing the Army and Navy for a European war stemmed from departmental initiative.[82] In what proved to be the decisive military planning of the period – the military staff conversations between Britain and France – the CID Secretariat played no part; the parent committee heard nothing of the 'conversations' in the years to 1911.[83] A Liberal War Secretary, Haldane, reported that 'the CID never touches policy. It ascertains facts and supplies technical information.'[84] In the context of strategic planning, the CID failed to resolve – as had been the case with the Defence Committee – the basic dilemma of British pre-war defence planning, 'the conflict between capability and policy.'[85] The Committee of Imperial Defence lacked the institutional strength to undertake such an over-riding co-ordination of defence planning: in that sense, its failure was determined by the departmentalism inherent in the political dynamic of the nineteenth-century Cabinet.

On the other hand, the CID's positive achievements, especially the collection of what Haldane called 'technical information,' ought not be discounted, because that information contributed to Britain's war readiness: paramount among the CID's contributions was the assembling of the War Book, prepared in 1911–13. It detailed and collated departmental plans for a 'Precautionary Stage' when the outbreak of hostilities seemed likely, specifying actions to be taken by departments at that time in the first stages of war; given the departmentalism of the old order, there is no doubt that the War Book provided the means by which HMG moved with some semblance of lock-step into war in August 1914. In after years, Hankey viewed the preparation of the War Book as his greatest achievement.[86] Yet in the event Asquith's inherent disrespect for planning of any sort was evident in his decision to throw open Britain's projected military role in France and the Low Countries to rival strategists, at two extraordinary gatherings of soldiers and statesmen at the very outset of war; possibly only French reliance on these long-established plans prevented what has been fairly called 'a spate of improvisation.'[87] Improvisation was at the core of the traditional Cabinet system, and the method had carried Britain far, but it was unable to sustain her in the First World War.

Improvisation of a sort is apparent in the fact that the CID had planned no role for itself in war: ideas ranged from Haldane's design to transform the committee from an advisory body into the center of an executive control to Esher's resolve that 'in war its doors should be closed: yes, at the very first shot.'[88] Whether or not caught between two such extreme views, the CID had not foreseen how the war effort should be directed, which has been viewed as 'a catastrophic oversight.'[89] Yet one must question whether 'oversight' is the proper term, given the fierce pre-war departmentalism of the War Office and Admiralty: Asquith certainly held no brief for a co-ordinating agency, and the CID – the Prime Minister's own committee – was in no position to project itself as a war directorate-in-waiting.[90] Though the CID studied specific war plans in the last months of 1914, its limited co-ordinating functions had already passed to the War Council, a partly advisory, partly executive body which served Asquith's style well. The CID Secretariat had been placed at the disposal of the War Council, and Hankey brought to that body a secretarial apparatus which went without challenge at the sub-Cabinet level. Yet the Cabinet war committees were unable to secure overall direction of the war effort along the lines of a 'supreme command.' Through the end of 1916, and even into the last year of the war, the government proposed as they might; the military by and large disposed as they pleased.

In this setting, accounts of the 'failure' of the CID exaggerate the possibilities open to the ministers who sat upon it and the officials who staffed it.[91] The deficiency lay instead in governmental organization, which indulged the excessive departmentalism which permitted the service ministries to go their own ways. Esher's 1904 re-organization aimed to secure a measure of control over the services, exercised by a Prime Minister's department in the hands of a senior military planner: Sir George Clarke, later Lord Syndenham, attempted to play such a role, but he was frustrated under Unionist and Liberal regimes alike; Clarke's hopes to preside over a 'Department of National Defence' had vanished before he stepped down in 1907. His immediate successor, Admiral Charles Ottley, accepted the limitation of purpose with the position.[92] Thus with Hankey's succession in 1912 the 'raking in' of technical work for the CID, which functioned as 'an inter-departmental catch all,' amounted to a recognition of what was possible.[93] As a relatively junior officer, Hankey thought it essential not to injure the extant relationship between the services and the CID: where men such as Esher, Balfour, and Clarke had been unable to create an independent status for the Committee of Imperial Defence, Hankey did well to work within the limitations posed by prevailing political attitudes and an ascendant departmentalism.

Thus Hankey built, as in a fashion Ottley had before him, where realities permitted: the CID discharged its technical tasks with an undoubted competence which was not exactly the hallmark of pre-war government; in particular, its secretarial techniques had been tested and sharpened with the passage of a decade. The Cabinet Secretariat possessed a useful institutional antecedent: to be sure, the CID did not function as 'the centre of strategic planning' prior to the Great War,[94] but it did provide an important precedent for the updating of Cabinet government in the midst of war. Along with the wealth of experience and range of acquaintances which Hankey acquired in his CID service, the new Secretary shared in its carefully nurtured non-partisan status. Esher played a role in the committee's deliberations under Unionist and Liberal governments, but most of the credit for keeping CID activities at a remove from partisan politics is owed to A. J. Balfour, who joined in the work of one of its sub-committees while a leading Opposition figure.[95]

Hankey's own training in the Royal Marines had included a keen interest in Intelligence, which helped to qualify him for service at the CID; the attitude of political neutrality acquired there Hankey subsequently cultivated in the Cabinet Secretariat, although Hankey's own neutrality proved less than absolute. Already known to Admiral Fisher through his years in the Mediterranean Fleet, Hankey owed his initial CID appointment to Admiral Charles Ottley, who five years later worked with Fisher to secure the Secretary's post for Hankey.[96] At that time Hankey had not shied from lobbying on his own behalf, showing the same detailed preparation which was to characterize his secretarial labors. Haldane had been asked to interview the candidates, and he pressed Hankey on the question of his age and relatively junior rank; according to Hankey, he replied to the War Secretary that 'at my age he was a Q. C. and a leading member of the English bar (!) (having looked the matter up in *Who's Who*), and I said that so far as I knew there was no other profession (including politics) where a man of 35 would be held too young for a high position.'[97] His gambit successful, Hankey's appointment was generally well-received, although he lacked the reputation which Clarke and Ottley, to a lesser extent, had brought to the post.[98] There is little question that Hankey made his mark upon the ministers with whom he came into contact: Asquith did not hesitate to name him Secretary to the War Council, formed in November 1914. Yet Hankey was not perceived as a threat in military quarters, in part because the CID had in no significant fashion transgressed upon the military's strategic concerns; nonetheless, Hankey had won the soldiers' respect and gained their confidence.[99]

So too did David Lloyd George have good reason to turn to Hankey to help organize what the new premier viewed as 'virtually a new system of Government in this Country.'[100] To secure that reform, the first session of the War Cabinet sanctioned 'the advisability of strengthening the secretariat of the former war committee by the addition of a civil side.'[101] Hankey walked away from that historic meeting – the first 'outsider' to attend a Cabinet meeting to maintain a record of its proceedings[102] – with a massive task at hand. If Sir Edward Carson accurately depicted their mood, the members of the War Cabinet derived a great deal of satisfaction from that meeting; Carson told the editor of *The Times* that 'they had got through more work at the Cabinet on Saturday in seven hours than in all the time he had been a member of it before.'[103] Several months later, Carson expanded on his initial reaction:

in the first instance the absence of collective control by a Cabinet of the heads of the great departments had led to confusion, but [he] said that a system of control had been developed which was now working extremely well and was, for war purposes, incomparably better than the old Cabinet system, though he admitted that after the war, we should have to go back to a Cabinet system, but the Cabinet should be much smaller – 12 or 14.[104]

One senses that Carson thought the old Cabinet far too discursive – hence the success of the smaller version; yet it was also the tendency to duplicate discussion in war committee and full Cabinet which the new 'system of control' had been devised to correct.

What was the basis for that system? Clearly it took its point of departure from Hankey's proposed 'Draft Rules of Procedure,' drawn up for the War Cabinet and subsequently discussed by that body. To facilitate the War Cabinet's conduct of business, the Secretariat was charged with these functions:

(1) to record the proceedings of the War Cabinet;
(2) to transmit relevant extracts from the minutes to departments concerned with implementing them or otherwise interested;
(3) to prepare the agenda paper, and to arrange the attendance of ministers not in the War Cabinet and others required to be present for discussion of particular items on the agenda;
(4) to receive papers from departments and circulate them to the War Cabinet and others as necessary;
(5) to attend to the correspondence and general secretarial work of the Office.[105]

The record-keeping function is clear, but the communication of decisions is every bit as important; as well, the reverse flow of information to the War Cabinet was provided for. Another crucial fact of information-gathering was secured through the appearance before the War Cabinet of ministers and military leaders; in this regard Carson provided a contemporary impression of how the new system functioned:

On the Agenda paper (of some 15 items) there was a rough time-table as an indication to the ministers and others concerned of the time when their presence might be required, though of course the indication was far from precise and, though the War Cabinet worked very hard (straight on from about 11:30 to about 7:30 daily), they could not depend on getting through the whole of the agenda. The persons notified to attend varied from 3 to 4 to about a dozen and generally included the head of more than one of the great departments as well as permanent officials or officers of the services and experts.

The whole arrangement appeared to be effective and businesslike, but I [C. P. Scott, Carson's interlocuter] remarked that it appeared to place the great officers of State in an extremely subordinate position. Carson did not altogether dispute this, but said that on the other hand it relieved them of unnecessary attendances and enabled them to get on with the work each of his own department far more efficiently, particularly having regard to the vast increase of public business owing to the war and to the constant multiplication of departments since the war.[106]

To strengthen the Secretariat's personnel, the War Cabinet approved, on 18 December, the appointments of four Assistant Secretaries: G. M.

Young transferred from the Board of Education; Thomas Jones, for the rest of his life a confidant of the great and their satraps, was posted with Young to the civilian side; Captain Clement Jones and Temporary Captain L. C. Amery, MP, were added to the military staff which was largely carried over from the Secretariat of the late War Committee.[107] Hankey expressed particular enthusiasm for Young's appointment and voiced no concern about those of the two Jones' – both Welsh – but he was less than pleased with Amery's posting; he acquiesced – 'as Lord Milner insists' – but explained to Lloyd George 'I always suspect him of being anti-Russian, and would much sooner see him elsewhere.'[108] It is likely that he feared Amery's close connection to *The Times* and possibly his Milnerite view of the dominions,[109] but the Cabinet Secretary certainly recognized the political nature of these initial appointments.

That of Thomas Jones was to prove the most influential in contributing to the institutional development of the Cabinet Secretariat, since he subsequently became Deputy Secretary, holding that post until his retirement in 1930. With the singular exception of Hankey, no man saw more from the inside of the operations of the Cabinet during these years, and, like the Cabinet Secretary, Jones recorded detailed observations in a diary. The records of the two men afford a unique view of the operation of the new system of Cabinet government. Jones stood on peculiar footing from the first, possessing what he described as 'the privilege of direct access [to Lloyd George] whenever I sought it,'[110] in addition to functional responsibilities within the Secretariat. His first interview with his superior established Jones' style: 'I . . . talked over the sort of work I might do. L. G. had spoken to him. I explained that I didn't want to touch office machinery but rather to act as a fluid person moving about among people who mattered and keeping the P. M. on the right path so far as possible. He quite understood.'[111] From his privileged position Jones noted his first impressions of his colleagues: he found Young, the future historian of Victorian England, 'very much the super-Oxonian and also very ambitious and secretive,' yet the potential rivalry dissipated when Jones received from Hankey functional responsibilities – for Food, Drink, Coal Mines, the Disabled, Propaganda and the study of enemy and neutral countries – which did not overlap with Young's; Jones carefully kept his distance from Amery, 'a politician and a pressman.'[112]

In such an orthodox fashion Jones entered an organization where rumor had him 'a disguised Bolshevik whom Lloyd George had discovered somewhere in a Welsh coalpit'; in fact Hankey had been warned that the former academic was 'a peace-monger and a syndicalist.'[113] However, Hankey took an immediate liking to the man 'despite rather a sly face like Ll. G.'s and I think I could use him on the industrial side.'[114] Any account of the relationship between the two men, which was professional rather than personal, must recognize that their interests were complementary, Hankey on the military side and Jones on the civil; nor did the Cabinet Secretary ever attempt to deny Jones the latitude which the premier had given him.[115] For his part, Jones observed, with the other Assistant Secretaries, Hankey's insistence that their liaison functions should not interfere with department work: 'It is of the utmost importance that the responsibility of the Departments should be in no way weakened or over-ridden by the development of the Secretariat . . . [which] is neither an Intelligence Department nor a General Staff, but a machine for the service of the War Cabinet in co-ordinating the action of the responsible Departments.'[116] Yet the staff of the office did bring information to bear upon War Cabinet discussion, through their individual dealings with its five members.[117]

The Assistant Secretaries played a collective role within the office, as Jones noted in February 1917:

> We are also rather in a flux as to methods of working the Secretariat. This last week we are on a rota, each acting as Editor [of the Cabinet records] for the day. This means being responsible for preparations the day before, a full day at No. 10, and a third cleaning up . . . In addition we help the Editor and attend No. 10 when our own special subjects come up. The work is greatly increased by the uncertainty of the P. M.'s demands; agendas are suddenly scrapped, a meeting called for the afternoon or evening, usually at 5 o'clock. Subjects it was hoped to discuss are not reached and have to be fitted in to a later agenda, etc. etc. Some of the changes are, of course, inevitable because caused by changes in the war position.[118]

Obviously, the Secretariat experimented in order to improve the flow of business, surely sharing – whatever the temporary setbacks – the conviction voiced by Leo Amery to the Prime Minister of Australia that secretarial techniques could overcome the failures of the old order:

> We have in fact swept away altogether the old system which you saw working at the very height of its inefficiency when you were over here of twenty-three gentlemen assembling without any purpose and without any idea of what they were going to talk about, and eventually dispersing for lunch without any idea of what they had really discussed or decided, and certainly without any recollection on either point three months later. Under the new system the Cabinet has definite agenda; there are no speeches but only short, business-like discussions between the four or five Cabinet Ministers or professional experts brought in for the discussion; full Minutes are taken, more particularly of the actual decisions arrived at; these are circulated the same day and unless they are corrected by one of the Cabinet Ministers concerned, the Secretariat assumes that the decisions hold good and makes it its business to see that the Departments are informed of the decisions and carry them out.[119]

Amery marveled at the results of such orderly proceedings: 'The output of energy on the part of the new Cabinet is amazing . . . What is more, at each meeting some, and not infrequently quite a large number of decisions were arrived at.'

Yet for all the change in methods, the war policy of the British government did not much alter. Changes in military leadership were particularly difficult to achieve: not until the spring of 1918 was Lloyd George able to replace the Chief of the Imperial General Staff, 'Wully' Robertson, and even then he dared not move against the commander of the British Expeditionary Force, Sir Douglas Haig.[120] As a result, the war of deadly attrition persisted in France and Flanders. Nor could the military orientation of the Cabinet Secretariat ease the acrimonious relationship between the executive and the military authorities in the formulation and execution of war policy. Though the divisive struggle between war committees and the Cabinet had been ended, the debilitating conflict of politicians and soldiers persisted: in fact, relations between the 'frocks' and the 'brasshats' deteriorated throughout 1917. In some quarters, this problem has been viewed as institutional, as the War Cabinet failed to include any representative of the service departments and could not bridge the differences between the soldiers and the politicians.[121] Much of the same type of criticism is expressed in the assertion that the War Cabinet lacked 'a steady, continuous stream of authoritative advice.'[122] Yet the Secretary of State for War, the First Lord of the Admiralty and their senior officers were in frequent attendance at Cabinet meetings; the flow of information to the War Cabinet was steady. What frustrated the military was that despite their advice the War Cabinet proved less committed to the 'Westerner' approach of Robertson and Haig than the service ministers; in that sense, the War Cabinet questioned the 'continuous stream of authoritative advice.' As early as 26 December 1916 Hankey touched the core of the problem: 'The new War Cabinet are really up against it, as they don't believe in Robertson's "Western Front" policy, but they will never find soldiers to carry out their "Salonica" policy.'[123] The difficulty in reconciling soldiers and statesmen was not institutional, but strategic – and political. As the leader of a Coalition government, Lloyd George lacked the political power directly to confront and reject the military advice which was approved by many of his Tory supporters. Thus the military went their own strategic way until the Prime Minister, intent on out-flanking his service advisers, dared to cry 'Halt!' That moment did not come until the spring of 1918, and even then the Prime Minister knew better than to shout the word to his coalition. Institutional innovation could not serve to reconcile the 'frocks' and the 'brasshats.'

To return to the Secretariat's work, Amery's appointment illustrates an important political dimension of the reforms of 1916, namely the arrival in Whitehall of a band of young, able, and aggressive men who for more than a decade had looked to the lead of Lord Milner, now a member of the War Cabinet.[124] The long years in the political wilderness had ended dramatically, and the Milnerites, 'serene in their conviction that they were better equipped than their fellows to serve the State,'[125] strove to seize places in the new regime. Initially, Hankey feared a Milnerite coup within the office, as two members of the War Cabinet joined with Milner in recommending that Arthur Steel-Maitland should be offered 'the Civil Secretaryship as an equal colleague of Hankey.'[126] The Cabinet Secretary lost no time in approaching Lloyd George, who scuttled the scheme, although Hankey assured him that his objection was to the 'tactless' figure of Steel-Maitland rather than the development of the civil side of the Secretariat.[127] Yet only two days later he informed his wife, 'I am aiming at remaining the sole Secretary.'[128] Having bested Milner's attempt, Hankey proved accommodating in the case of Amery's appointment as an Assistant Secretary, for all the fact that he distrusted Amery's motivations and even a month later referred to his subordinate as a 'scheming little devil.'[129] In short order, Hankey came to appreciate Amery's abilities and interest in imperial affairs, and the two worked well together until the latter assumed similar secretarial labors with the Supreme War Council at Versailles a year later; although the two differed concerning Amery's 'independent' role at Versailles, the Milnerite proved a loyal colleague.[130] Nor, in a wider compass, did Hankey have any quarrel with Milner's professed aloofness from party politics. 'My interests do not run on the lines of Party & if I can help, in however small a way, to carry out the objects I have at heart, I do not care two straws how the politicians are labelled who execute them,'[131] Milner had written in 1893; Hankey, and Lloyd George too, had been pressed to share such sentiments a quarter-century later.

At first Hankey had envisaged a functional division of responsibilities within the Secretariat, drawn along lines of machinery – the process of record-keeping – and what was described as 'ideas'; the civil side of the office had been strengthened to serve these purposes. After discussion with each member of the War Cabinet, Hankey advanced the 'ideas' side as one which would supplement rather than replace departmental initiatives: 'the War Cabinet, composed of selected Ministers without Portfolios, is in a position to view every question from a wider point of view, and to formulate ideas far beyond the probable scope of any Minister engaged in the task of administering a great Government Department.'[132] However, the concept of a collective 'ideas' operation within the Secretariat was short-lived, and the organizational pattern of the Secretariat divided instead along other lines: a military branch was headed by an experienced Secretariat hand, E. D. Swinton, and the civil side first under Young and subsequently Thomas Jones.[133] The War Cabinet Rules of Procedure specified no 'ideas' function for its own Secretariat

Instead, such 'ideas' as emerged were to be collected and discussed within the Prime Minister's Secretariat, an entirely new organization housed in the gardens at No. 10 Downing Street, 'the yard where huts were set up for the overflow of secretaries'[134] late in the month. Headed at first by Professor W. G. S. Adams, the 'Garden Suburb' was organized in a manner not unlike Hankey's operation: each of Adams' four assistants advised on a particular group of topics in which he was knowledgeable, but other problems were investigated as they appeared. Unlike the Cabinet Secretariat, necessarily concerned with routine matters, the Prime Minister's counterpart gave few matters attention for more than a few weeks at a time.[135] Even in such a piece-meal fashion, the Prime Minister's Secretariat quickly claimed a greater role than his Private Secretaries had collectively discharged.[136] With its tasks broadly defined 'to assist the Prime Minister in the discharge of the heavy responsibilities which fall upon him under the War Cabinet system,'[137] the Prime Minister's Secretariat effectively found only discussion of military and naval policy beyond its scope; as it moved freely in other sectors, including foreign policy, conflict with departments was inherent in its operation. Yet an ever increasing number of war-time problems required inter-departmental co-operation, and – to state the case in its behalf – 'the Garden Suburb could work to foster that co-operation, acting as a substitute for "proper channels" which did not exist.'[138] Eventually a much-maligned body, the Prime Minister's Secretariat represented another attempt by the radical innovator, David Lloyd George, to create a means around the departmentalism and traditions of the old order.

The War Cabinet charged the two Secretariats with working in the closest possible collaboration. In that quest Hankey dined in February with the leading figures in the other body, although it is clear that his military proclivities clashed with certain concepts of the 'Garden Suburb': 'They [Professor Adams and Philip Kerr] talked a lot of very academic stuff about Leagues to enforce Peace.'[139] According to Tom Jones, Hankey thought that the other Secretariat had gotten off to a good start and judged that the two organizations worked well together. Apparently the Cabinet Secretary considered an exchange of some personnel, inquiring whether Jones might move over to Downing Street, with Adams joining his office; Jones was not enthused, and the scheme came to nothing. The close co-operation of the two operations served to blur the distinction between them.

Within the 'Garden Suburb' Milner's attempt to place his cohorts met with greater success than it had in Hankey's operation: both Lionel Curtis and Philip Kerr, soon the most prominent of its personnel, were well-known 'Milnerites,' although generally its political coloration is more complex than has usually been depicted. Turner's recent study mandates a discussion cast along lines of the individual concerns and pursuits of its members rather than their 'collegiate' influence.[140]

However, the contemporary impression ran to the contrary, and the co-operation between the two bodies added a Milnerite hue to the Cabinet Secretariat, despite Hankey's efforts to steer clear of political groupings in whatever garb.[141] As the months passed, Hankey grew increasingly discomfited by the activities of the Prime Minister's Secretariat,[142] but it must be added that his own inclusion in a secretarial capacity within British delegations which discussed Allied foreign policy added to the functional overlap between the two bodies. Even more basic was Lord Milner's close connections with the two Secretariats, which served to compound the confusion – at a time when 'Milnerism' was nearly as suspect in Liberal circles as the forces of the Kaiser himself. Until recently, historians had not generally differentiated sufficiently between the two operations; evidence of the actual influence of the 'Garden Suburb' is finally in hand, and its war-time activities have been clarified: its irregular status and ad hoc pursuits are confirmed; the myth of a Milnerite monolith operating in the gardens of No. 10 has been dispelled; and the individual contributions of its leading members carefully evaluated.[143] While 'influence' is difficult to measure, the time for confusing the two operations[144] surely is now past.

Physically, the two were quite distinct: the temporary quarters of the one stand in marked contrast to the Cabinet Secretariat's quarters across Whitehall, in what were by common assent beautiful Regency-style houses next to Montagu House; this cul-de-sac, Whitehall Gardens, where Peel and later Disraeli had lived, has lamentably vanished from the London scene.[145] The Committee of Imperial Defence had been quartered in No. 2, as the government had taken over the site in the early years of the century; with Hankey's new responsibilities, he received from Lloyd George a free hand to commandeer the houses on either side, which had been recently used by the Ministry of Munitions. In early 1917, upon his return from an Allied conference in Rome which the Prime Minister had attended, Hankey discovered that the office was in a state of 'terrible congestion' because the necessary renovations had not yet been accomplished;[146] the Secretariat's facilities mirrored the general confusion from which the new regime attempted to forge order. Still, Hankey reveled in the comfortable spacious houses and their setting, separated from the Embankment and the Thames by long gardens planted with rows of trees: 'With its central situation, close to the principal Government offices, its quiet, and the peep of the river with its endless traffic of small craft there was no pleasanter spot for an office in the whole of London.'[147] History was present in these buildings: Disraeli had lived in No. 2 between 1874 and 1878, and Hankey's operations were based where Cabinet meetings – without benefit of records – had been held in May 1875.[148] Now the intimate record of the British Cabinet's role through the Great War and beyond, nearly to the renewal of hostilities twenty-one years later, was kept in Whitehall Gardens.

In what form were those records to be maintained? Who was to benefit from access to them? Neither basic question was settled with the establishment of the Cabinet Secretariat, but Hankey and his staff strove for answers which would make the new system an effective means of government, while at the same time protecting the integrity of War Cabinet proceedings. Although the records of the Committee of Imperial Defence represented a precedent of sorts, there the pattern of record-keeping had changed considerably over a decade. In its first years, relatively sparse records served primarily to preclude future governments from closing down defence planning through ignorance alone.[149] In the years to the outbreak of the war, with the introduction of the Secretariat and a full-time staff, the CID minutes gradually became fuller, until Hankey's hand on occasion recorded near-verbatim proceedings.[150] Despite this change, there was no formal repeal of the secretarial precepts laid down in 1903 for the 'part-timer who did not pretend to know the job':[151]

> It was agreed that no attempt should be made in the Minutes to summarize the conclusions of the Committee or to record the arguments used during the discussions. The Minutes should only mention the points actually discussed; the conclusions being eventually summed up in the reasoned Memorandum which would be left to place on record, for future reference, the decision arrived at.[152]

Rule and practice had diverged, as rather full records had taken the place of skeletal conclusions: the dilemma of the record-keeper had arisen.

When war came, the precedent of maintaining records in matters of defence planning sufficed to overcome whatever reservations Asquith may have had about violating established traditions, if only at the Cabinet committee level. During his twenty-eight month war leadership, Asquith sought to balance his belief in the collective responsibility of the Cabinet with the need for executive planning of the war effort: three successive committees of the Cabinet assumed the latter task. None succeeded as an executive body, in large measure because the Prime Minister reserved to the Cabinet the effective control of war policy. These committees nonetheless assumed the functions of the pre-war CID and its Secretariat as well. The break with precedent was clear in the minds of those who assumed committee responsibility, and, according to Hankey's account, they were determined upon more efficient practices:

> The Dardanelles Committee . . . [May–November 1915] was itself in theory a Cabinet Committee, and held its first meeting without a Secretary. But Asquith, Balfour, Kitchener and Lloyd George insisted on a Secretary, and I was brought in and succeeded in gradually infiltrating it with the Chiefs of Staff and all the procedure of the CID.[153]

Hankey attended these committee meetings to take manuscript notes from which decisions were extracted and circulated to the departments, although the right of appeal reserved for Cabinet discussion of contentious matters repeatedly compromised the committees' effectiveness.

The minutes and papers preserved for the three committees provide an adequate record of their deliberations, and once again the scope of the minutes gradually widened; for example, there exists a great deal of relevant information concerned with the Gallipoli expedition.[154] The value of these records was underscored for Lloyd George when he began to gather documentation for his assault upon Asquith's war leadership. At his behest, Hankey collected a record of everything which Lloyd George had said at meetings of the three committees; thus armed, the War Secretary had records in hand when he attacked 'the military policy of our advisors' in the final, traumatic meeting of the War Committee on 1 December 1916.[155] When Lloyd George asked Hankey to prepare Cabinet Minutes for the new government, they were meant to communicate decisions to the departments, but as the months passed, a widening in their contents took place. The Prime Minister's own desire for fuller minutes may well provide the explanation, because on several occasions he had protested incomplete or misleading minutes of the War Committee; Hankey had then only been able to protest that his minutes were substantiated by 'a very full Secretary's note of everything that had occurred,' which was available for his examination.[156] It is not likely that Hankey forgot his difficulties, and, whether by inference or direction from the premier, concluded that fuller minutes would be a wiser and more acceptable course in the Lloyd George administration.

Verbatim minutes, however, presented substantial difficulties: Hankey did not use a shorthand technique, although he utilized a form of 'shortened longhand' in compiling his rough record of proceedings, upon which he based the actual Cabinet Minutes.[157] The process enabled him to clarify the issues and to refine the actual language of the final form.[158] Certainly the 'shortened longhand' which he used was vital to the accuracy of his minutes, but other factors contributed to his style: from his CID experiences he learned 'the art of drafting a formula which would satisfy both parties to a dispute.'[159] And many of his acquaintances testify as well to his 'incredible memory,'[160] which surely could be put to short-term use in drafting minutes no less than over the long haul as custodian of records. Yet the pressures for a full record persisted, particularly in certain quarters.

In August 1917 a heated protest from Lord Curzon occasioned a resolution of the matter in a manner which proved decisive for the format of Cabinet Minutes. The irascible peer expressed concern bordering on outrage that his views on the proposed establishment of an Imperial War Museum had not been made a matter of record; while Hankey's minutes attributed views to ministers outside the War Cabinet, there was no sign that he had even spoken! Hankey replied in a reflective vein:

The system of record of Cabinet Minutes has always been a matter of great difficulty to me from the very first day that the War Cabinet was inaugurated. I remember that I raised the question at the very outset. Some Ministers were in favour of no record of arguments at all and merely a bald statement of the Conclusions. There was a good deal of feeling against recording the views of individual members of the Cabinet unless they definitely expressed dissent with a Conclusion. I remember that it was pointed out that the decisions of the Cabinet had to be regarded as the collective decision of its Members, even if some had expressed contrary opinions in the discussion, and that, for this reason, it was undesirable to bring out the individual views of Members.[161]

A year later, Hankey reiterated this concern for the doctrine of collective responsibility: 'Broadly speaking . . . I aim not at giving an accurate account of what everyone said, but a general synopsis of the expert evidence upon which the Conclusion was based, and a general summary of the arguments for and against the decision taken.' The Cabinet Secretary added that such a procedure enabled him to reconstruct the rationale upon which the Cabinet had based its decision, which obviated the need for a *procès verbal*.[162] However, Hankey acknowledged one exception to the precept that the views of individual War Cabinet ministers ought not be recorded: if he spoke upon a certain topic as an expert – he gave the diplomatic example of Curzon on India – then his views were recorded. To prepare a *procès verbal*, he maintained, would cause him to 'lose the grip on the form and the style of the Minutes which I do my utmost to maintain.'[163]

The Cabinet Secretary pointed as well to the use of the minutes as the means of informing the head of a concerned department of the War Cabinet's decision. Thus a concise résumé of the arguments which lead to a decision served important informational needs, but fuller minutes would reveal the individual positions of War Cabinet ministers and could lead to invidious pressures emanating from the departments; in contrast, the résumé protected the Cabinet's collective responsibility and eliminated any susceptibility to individual posturing for the record.[164] In this exercise – valuable for the light shed upon Hankey's constructing the records – the Cabinet Secretary obscured the office's suspicion that Curzon may well himself have been the real problem. Several months earlier, Amery had bluntly characterized Curzon's concern with the Cabinet Minutes: 'He was in a fearful state to begin with because he didn't figure sufficiently in the proceedings. He asked me if I had a personal down on him . . . He has a very comic side.'[165] Confronted by Hankey's full explanation, Curzon yielded, although not without one further egotistical outburst.[166] Yet as had been the case with CID Minutes, so too with Cabinet Minutes, because fuller accounts of deliberations became more common;[167] such a trend may have reflected Hankey's increasing confidence in his mastery over the minutes; on one occasion, confidence ran to excess, because he recorded proceedings of a crucial War Cabinet gathering, despite instructions to the contrary, 'because they had been on the verge of such important conclusions.'[168]

In dealing with Curzon, Hankey had underscored the direct use of Cabinet Minutes in the execution of policy by the departments; thus he had to clarify deliberations which sometimes made an unambiguous decision difficult to discern. In this regard his own talents were brought to bear, according to the description of a post-war Cabinet Office associate, Frederick Leith-Ross:

> He had an uncanny instinct for extracting a decision out of a Cabinet dicussion. However inconclusive it might have been, Hankey was able to jot down at the meeting and subsequently elaborate a conclusion which often had not been expressed in so many words by anyone at the meeting but which was accepted afterwards as representing the outcome of the decision. On one occasion the Chancellor, coming out of the Cabinet, was asked by his Private Secretary what decision had been reached on some item on the agenda. 'I really couldn't tell,' he replied, 'you'll have to wait for Hankey's minute.'[169]

Another significant aspect of directing unambiguous information to the departments was the question of access to the Cabinet Minutes, because most ministers, including the heads of the great departments, were outside the circle of the War Cabinet. While the creation of the small War Cabinet settled the problem of divided responsibility which had felled Asquith's government, communication of information had also suffered.[170] Under the new regime, the War Cabinet required much departmental information, which had to flow in the reverse direction as well; hence the provision of relevant extracts to the departments which were responsible for taking action or were otherwise concerned.

In a more comprehensive fashion, Hankey sent copies of the final draft minutes of the War Cabinet, approved and initialed by the Prime Minister, to its members and to the King, and they received printed copies a day or two later. George V was made privy to far more information than ever he had received before, although his Private Secretary expressed the hope that 'the Prime Minister will adhere to the time-honoured custom of reporting in his own hand the conduct of actual *Cabinet* business, as such reports are the sole record of the proceedings of a Cabinet meeting.' Hankey suggested to Lloyd George that Buckingham Palace make do with the Cabinet Minutes, explaining: 'Personally I hate "time honoured" customs that waste time.'[171] The Prime Minister, whose distaste for written correspondence was lengendary among family and friends,[172] had no troubles in terminating the 'Prime Minister's letter' forthwith. Even on the day that the Treaty of Versailles was signed, Lloyd George was reluctant to put pen to paper to inform the King; although he did so, the premier 'didn't really see why he should write the letter, or where the King came into the matter.'[173] If this experience set a precedent, Cabinet Minutes had rendered obsolete all but the most ceremonial correspondence between monarch and leading minister.

Complete copies of the printed minutes were sent as well to the Secretaries of State for Foreign Affairs, the Colonies, India and War, the First Lord of the Admiralty, the Minister of Blockade, and the President of the Board of Trade; subsequently, the Minister of Munitions and the Minister of Information were added, as was Dr Christopher Addison, oddly 'in his personal capacity.' Both the First Sea Lord and the CIGS received printed copies, Hankey noted, 'as so much of the business of the War Cabinet concerns them that the system of sending extracts was not found suitable.'[174] Beyond deciding which extracts should go to which departments – 'a much more difficult duty than would appear at first sight' – the Cabinet Secretariat had to administer a system for the circulation of full sets which evolved in an ad hoc, even ad hominem, basis. One further complication was mandated by security concerns: minutes for about 150 War Cabinet meetings or portions thereof were not printed in the usual fashion but instead were given a much more restricted circulation in typescript.[175]

Circulation of Cabinet papers – 'the memoranda which were circulated to members of the Cabinet to provide the basis of discussion or to give information'[176] – stood as no innovation, as such memoranda had long been submitted to the Cabinet, albeit in an irregular fashion:

> Foreign Office memoranda were probably circulated in the pouches or boxes containing copies of Foreign Office prints; and it is likely that other Departments were responsible for circulating their own papers, either in separate boxes or in one circulating box. On occasion a memorandum might first be passed through the Prime Minister's hands and circulated from 10 Downing Street.[177]

Prior to 1916, Hankey recollected, 'no large portion of the Cabinet's business was done on the basis of memoranda,' but from that time forward, the Cabinet Secretariat supplied a mechanism both for distribution and central retention of file copies. The standard distribution was restricted – only the King, members of the War Cabinet, and Balfour, in his role as 'elder statesman' rather than as Foreign Secretary, saw them all – but distribution could be quite extensive, because the Secretary was authorized to send particular papers to ministers not in the Cabinet, to the military chiefs of staff and to permanent officials. As a result, routine informational papers – reports from departments or committees, for instance – acquired a wide and regular circulation; on the other hand, memoranda intended to shape War Cabinet 'policy' required evaluation to determine an appropriate distribution. Hankey recognized that for optimal performance 'the Heads of the great Departments . . . [should] be in possession of all the necessary information to enable them to safeguard interests committed to their trust.'[178] For that reason the Cabinet Secretary disliked the invidious distinctions which his office was compelled to draw concerning Cabinet papers, presenting an even more difficult problem than the properly balanced circulation of extracts from Cabinet Minutes.

From past experience Hankey had concluded that excessive secrecy took its own toll on efficient government:

> In matters of war plans, where the fate of the nation, the success of a campaign, and the lives of our soldiers and sailors are at stake, no precautions for the preservation of secrecy can be too great. But secrecy ought not to be carried to the pitch where it interferes with the requisites for forming a balanced judgment or with administrative efficiency . . . the whole machinery of government works more smoothly if the political and professional heads of Government Departments are kept *au courant* with decisions of policy which affect them, whether in the first or second degree. Moreover, with proper precautions the risk of leakage is infinitesimal.[179]

Although it is unclear whether Hankey himself encouraged a gradual widening of distribution or, alternatively, whether ministers pressed for more information, in April 1918 slippage occurred and the Cabinet Secretary informed his staff that 'very serious mistakes' had been made in connection with policy papers. In response, Hankey restricted the authority to circulate a memorandum to ministers other than the select few who received all such documents.[180] Later in the year, however, he felt that the great problem was the undue restriction of the flow of information to ministers outside the War Cabinet: in a draft circulated to his Assistant Secretaries, he proposed to meet the informational needs by sending all ministers of Cabinet rank the printed Cabinet Minutes; he noted that the highly secret 'A' minutes might have to be expanded but he thought that would pose no problem. With as much irony as Hankey permitted himself, he commented: 'Surely, if Minutes are not too secret to print they are not too secret to circulate to Ministers of Cabinet rank.'[181]

About Cabinet papers the Secretary felt much the same, except he recognized that a more limited circulation of those papers dealing with 'naval, military and aerial operations . . . and diplomatic questions' was required; all other memoranda he proposed to circulate to all ministers who received the printed minutes. In such a fashion Hankey intended to close the gap which had opened in the flow of information from the War Cabinet to the departments. Yet he was frustrated in his hope, ironically in this case, by his co-reformer, the Prime Minister, who objected to Hankey's appeal to share more information with the Secretaries of State for the Colonies (1916–18), Walter Long, and for India (1917–22), Edwin Montagu:

> He replied that it was his responsibility and not Walter Long's to keep the Dominions' Premiers informed. My rejoinder was that, even so, he ought constitutionally to be advised by the S. of S. for the Colonies. He did not admit this, but he asked me not to raise the question at present, because he did not trust Montagu. This places me in a difficult position because I am always being badgered by these people about not getting enough information.[182]

In this instance is revealed the 'underside' of Lloyd George's use of the new administrative arrangements to bolster his own standing vis-à-vis his colleagues, even if he invoked constitutional proprieties. Yet Hankey two days later added to the standardized distribution lists the names of Long, 'unless there is some very special reason to the contrary,' and Montagu, whom he noted should receive a large proportion of the 'Special Distribution' telegrams in question. With the impending termination of hostilities, Hankey advised his Assistant Secretaries that 'the rule of the Office in case of doubt is to distribute too widely rather than too narrowly.'[183]

The 'Special Distribution' telegrams, which came from the Foreign Office, represented another source of information for the War Cabinet; it appears as if Lloyd George's own interest in foreign policy predisposed him to restrict the circulation of these telegrams – the operational mechanism of foreign policy – but Hankey did not indulge the premier; instead he secured an agreement from Sir Eric Drummond, Private Secretary to the Foreign Minister, to distribute 'practically all the most secret telegrams' as War Cabinet papers.[184] Telegrams and documents of lesser importance were circulated even more widely, including copies sent to the former premier, Asquith, at Lloyd George's request.[185] All in all, the results were such that Walter Long, who had good reason to be grateful to Hankey, commented on the superiority of the arrangements made by the Secretariat to the older control exercised by the Foreign Office: 'the Secretariat have overcome all sorts of difficulties and have invariably managed their circulation with the most wonderful success.'[186] In such ways Hankey and his staff bridged the information gap which threatened to divide the War Cabinet from the departments; to be sure, the answer lay in mechanical devices, but such a solution served in important ways to harness the government's war effort.

The control of the circulation of Cabinet and allied documents was but one aspect of the greater problem faced by the new regime and particularly by the Secretariat: how to preserve the secrecy of Cabinet deliberations. In the old regime, there had been frequent breaches of government secrecy, both from within and without. In 1889 HMG secured legislation designed to protect official secrecy: according to A. J. Balfour, the incident which provoked this 'important legal reform' dated to 1878, when a resentful temporary Foreign Office clerk, Charles Marvin, secured a windfall by memorizing the text of an Anglo-Russian treaty, which he sold to a London newspaper, the *Globe*.[187] Although Marvin's action proved not to be an offence at law, the government moved to curtail the practice of newspapers transgressing official secrecy. Viscount Sandon recorded that the *Globe*'s editor had paid Marvin £40 for his feat of memory: 'It seems that Captain Armstrong has been boasting at the Clubs that there is no confidential Paper which he cannot buy – a sad affair – which we [the Disraeli government] must try to stop.'[188] Yet it was not for another eleven years that the government moved appropriate legislation. By that time the rationale was cast in terms of espionage and treason: over two decades, only one prosecution brought under the terms of the Official Secrets Act of 1889 dealt with a matter other than military or naval secrets.[189]

The only significant source of information about Cabinet business in the pre-war period proved to be the ministers themselves, although the press remained the recipient of such breaches of secrecy. Already in 1885 the situation was such that Lord Carlingford remarked that the Cabinet 'works in a glass house.' Gladstone himself had harsh words in Cabinet 'first about the "leakage" of the Cabinet which he said was a disgrace, and of bad augury for future governments.'[190] A long succession of diaries and memoirs which often draw upon Cabinet proceedings to which the diarists were not themselves a party point to the persistence of such disclosures, though few of them came to the attention of the public. Another measure of ministerial misbehavior is the restriction of the flow of Foreign Office telegrams by Sir Edward Grey, Foreign Secretary from 1905 to 1916; he hoped to circumvent the radical disputation of his policies which appeared in the pages of the *Manchester Guardian*.[191] Surely he was confirmed in his secretiveness by the occasional instances of leakage which mark the Asquith regime. Even the loquacious Asquith occasionally was exasperated: 'The P. M. began by saying that Cabinet Govt. was impossible if *The Times* was to be able to give a shorthand report of all our proceedings and proposals as it had done yesterday.'[192] To be sure, the creation of a Secretariat could not directly prevent such ministerial indiscretion, which reached alarming proportions in the war period. While the problem eased somewhat with the withdrawal of Asquith and his coterie from government – he and his Liberal colleagues had exhibited an 'extraordinary freedom' in conveying confidential information to families and friends[193] – methods mattered as well as personnel: by insuring that concise, accurate information about Cabinet decisions reached responsible departments, the Secretariat procedures discounted the premium on rumor and gossip in official circles.

Hankey knew that the custodians of Cabinet records had themselves to remain beyond reproach in their custody of government secrets, and he personally was described as 'the man of a million secrets' upon his death in January 1963.[194] His staff too had to be kept up to the mark, because some held that the Secretariat as an institution breached the secrecy of Cabinet deliberations. In a sense that view is accurate, but conclusions drawn from it by contemporaries were not. For example, R. L. Schuyler contended in 1918: 'Under the new system, it has become necessary to devise prompt and intimate communication between the Cabinet and the officers of administration, who are now removed from it; and these in turn have involved the virtual abandonment of secrecy.'[195] The assertion misses the essential point: secrecy continued to cloak Cabinet discussions; the addition of a Secretary did not undermine the freedom of discussion nor the doctrine of collective responsibility. Decisions had after all been communicated to the departments under the old regime, admittedly in an imperfect fashion. Now Cabinet decisions were to be rendered unequivocal and shared with the concerned departments. There was no question of these decisions becoming public, unless HMG chose to inform Parliament. Thus the Cabinet Secretariat had, in effect, been charged with the custody of Cabinet secrecy. The casual approach of the old regime no longer sufficed; system was required to preserve secrecy and to make government effective.

Even prior to his becoming Cabinet Secretary, Hankey had protected the inviolability of Cabinet discussions. In July 1916 he authored a passionately argued memorandum opposing the publication of any papers related to the ill-fated Dardanelles campaign, only to see Asquith waver in the face of parliamentary pressures and agree to an official inquiry. However, Hankey determined to protect the 'Secretary's Notes' which he had kept for the War Council, the committee responsible for the controversial operation, rather than turn them over to the official inquiry conducted by the Dardanelles Commission. Having secured Asquith's instructions to refuse the request to examine these 'Notes' – as opposed to the War Council Minutes – Hankey had nonetheless to withstand the ire of the Commissioners, who had been given the power by the government to compel the production of relevant documents. The dilemma is an obvious one, and Hankey informed Asquith laconically following his own testimony before that body that they had threatened to put someone in the Tower – 'whether this was serious, and whether it was you, or me, or the War Committee, or the Cabinet, that was going to the Tower, I did not gather.'[196] His position, supported by the War Committee, was that the release of the 'Notes' would compromise the collective responsibility of the War Council, a sub-Cabinet body, and its successors; disclosure even to an official commission would 'hamper free discussion at the War Committee in the future if its members were aware that anything they said might, as it were, be used on some future occasion as evidence against them.'[197] While endorsing Hankey's position, the War Committee offered a compromise: the Chair of the Commission could be given access to the 'Secretary's Notes' not as a matter of record but 'so as to satisfy himself that nothing had been held back.'[198] It was left to Lloyd George's War Cabinet to sanction such an arrangement, which may be viewed as a limited victory for the inviolability of certain Cabinet records relating to actual committee discussions.

While Hankey's conduct impresses in its loyalty to the Asquith regime – he presented the government's case, which involved weeks of preparation and days of what amounted to cross-examination by the Commissioners[199] – following upon the events of December 1916 Hankey exhibited an over-riding institutional allegiance. After leaving office, Asquith requested a copy of the self-same 'Secretary's Notes' of War Council meetings, but Hankey only complied after receiving permission from the new premier, whom he assured that his predecessor's interest was defensive.[200] Neither of the two was intent upon recrimination at this time, and thus the request did not divide them. Yet the episode is instructive, because it shows Hankey acting as custodian of the records of past Cabinets as well as the keeper of new and more comprehensive records. In both cases, he was intent upon preserving the collective responsibility of the Cabinet and its committees through the administration of Cabinet secrecy. Surely he did not then foresee that history would ultimately lay claim to these documents, when these records would be used in ways which none of the founders of the new system could anticipate.

Hankey's care to maintain the secrecy of Cabinet deliberations was marred, it appears, only twice during the war years. In mid-1917 Asquith learned, by some means, that Foreign Secretary Balfour had expressed displeasure with Lord Northcliffe's appointment to ministerial rank. At one point Lloyd George's suspicions about the source of this leak centered on his Cabinet Secretary, whom he asked to withdraw along with his assistants during War Cabinet discussion of a very secret item; Hankey took care to reassure the premier about his own role, even accounting for his recent social movements: 'I am very jealous of the honour of my Office, and the War Cabinet.' In a more practical vein, Hankey added that he set himself 'a very high standard in the matter of reticence – never more so than on those occasions (twice only since you came into office) when I run across the Asquiths.'[201] By a strange twist of irony, Hankey lapsed from grace in uttering an ill-advised word to the Asquiths – even a word with Margot could be too much – in May 1918; his information was but a small part, and not a secret one, of an erroneous report that the British might have to evacuate the Channel ports.[202] Yet the incident, minor indeed, strengthened Hankey's recognition of the precarious nature of his position: 'I always lived on a knife edge, with an abyss on either side . . . every day I was continually concerned in questions of such delicacy that anytime I might make a false step and be engulfed.'[203] Hankey's slip had been momentary, and it does not much subtract from the basic probity – 'he has probably never said a foolish thing in his life, betrayed a secret, made a tactless remark or spoken out of turn'[204] – which reflected directly on the organization he headed.

In contrast to the Cabinet Secretary's public persona, Hankey's private maintenance of a full, revealing, and opinionated diary of his activities is at first glance surprising. Admittedly, he guarded his diary closely, keeping it stoutly bound and locked; he never took it abroad and he even discarded his original plan to use his wife, Adeline, as his amanuensis.[205] Instead he made his own entries in a careful hand, normally during free moments in his Whitehall Gardens office, but often in a more summary fashion over the weekend at his home. He opened his diary on 5 March 1915 with a rhetorical flourish, inscribing on the flyleaf of what proved to be the first of four volumes:

> For a long time I had felt that my association with many interesting people, and my experiences as Secretary of the Committee of Imperial Defence ought not to go entirely unrecorded. Now, as Secretary to the Prime Minister's War Council, I find myself directly associated with the central policy of the great European war. Though regretting that I have not commenced this diary earlier I have decided that no further time should be lost, and that, so far as time permits, I will jot down from time to time any incidents of historical, political, military or personal interest with which I may be personally connected.[206]

With the assumption of his even more vital post as Secretary to the War Cabinet, Hankey did not hesitate to carry his diary forward to the new regime. Nor did he doubt the propriety of his record of the Cabinet's innermost secrets, in a fashion which – privately – exposed the useful fiction incorporated in the doctrine of collective responsibility.

Though Hankey's activities were on one level antithetical, apparently he reconciled his pursuits on the ground that all the Prime Ministers whom he came to serve knew of and approved his keeping a diary. In Asquith's time, the diary had served as a record at a time when records were hard to come by, and possibly Asquith's approval came for that reason.[207] Certainly Lloyd George was well aware of Hankey's use of his diary as a supplement to the official records, and he expressed no objection to Hankey's chronicle.[208] As for the diarist, it is clear that in a psychological sense Hankey alleviated or relieved the manifold pressures under which he labored: the occasionally brutal remarks, directed at 'frocks' and 'brasshats' alike, enabled Hankey to deal equably with those who were his 'masters' or those who far outranked him in the military hierarchy, whatever their flaws. Examples of this means of releasing tension abound in the diary, although there is no evidence that Hankey himself was aware of this particular function.[209] His colleagues and subordinates were never given access to the diary, but at some point in the inter-war years Hankey decided upon the eventual publication of the diary, 'after about fifty years.'[210] Following his retirement, Hankey shared information which he culled from the diary with numerous historians of the era; late in his life, he published memoirs, *The Supreme Command, 1914–1918*, which drew heavily from the diary, although largely devoid of the most critical and subjective judgments.[211] Only with the extensive use of many full entries from the diary in Stephen Roskill's biography, published between 1970 and 1974, did the full spectrum of his insights and biases become clear; they have revealed as well a less attractive feature of the diarist's personality, Hankey's overweening if private vanity. His diary entries are replete with admiration for his own largely undisclosed importance in the scheme of things. Such a characteristic may be the well-spring of the diarist, but Hankey's self-righteousness renders him a less appealing if rather more human figure than the Cabinet Secretary who had 'probably never said a foolish thing in his life.'

Since Hankey was ever interested in precedents which cloaked the activities of his organization with what he viewed as historical legitimacy, he would no doubt have welcomed – had he known – the sanction of the record kept between 1880 and 1906 by a preeminent civil servant, Sir Edward Walter Hamilton; in Gladstone's second ministry, Hamilton served as a Private Secretary and for three years, Principal Private Secretary, to the Prime Minister. The editor of Hamilton's diaries has characterized them in words which fit Hankey's endeavor:

> There are throughout the journal – but increasingly so with the passage of time and the development of Hamilton as a civil servant and as a diarist – the astute observations of one in a remarkable position to know men and events, with wonderfully balanced powers of judgment, and possessed of the uncommon perserverance needed to keep a journal alive.[212]

The two diaries, however, are not analogous, because the duties and activities of the two men differed markedly: Hamilton, for example, was not privy to Cabinet deliberations, although on one occasion his presence at a Cabinet meeting proved an exception to the traditional rule that no 'outsiders' were ever admitted.[213] More telling, Hamilton's viewpoint was dependent almost entirely upon Gladstone, and he had not the range of contacts and sources of information which Hankey possessed. Precisely because his diary was by design less 'private' than Hankey's, Hamilton's is a rather pale document in comparison.

Hankey's concern to keep the Cabinet Secretariat free from political entanglements of any sort was well-judged, because there was good reason to demarcate the institution from his own personal role as an adviser and confidant to the British war leadership. Hankey had no control over this latter role, which he had inherited from the Asquith administration, when he had been asked 'to free himself as far as possible from detailed work in order to give his attention more closely to the higher policy of the war.'[214] Already by that time he had gained the confidence of the 'frocks' from the abilities and tact which he had shown in dealing with the Dardanelles operation and, even earlier, by his mastery of the co-ordinated process whereby the departments moved to a war footing, embodied in the War Book assembled by the CID in 1911–13.[215] There had been minor slippages in the meshing of those gears, but Hankey had taken pride in 'pressing my last button'[216] and seeing the completion of his efforts, and the Asquith Cabinet thereafter viewed him as a vital cog in the war machinery.

As a strategist, Hankey had long offered an alternative to the stalemate established on the Western Front; in a lengthy memorandum written on Boxing Day 1914, he had argued for the partial withdrawal of British forces in that theatre in order to force the issue at Constantinople, in conjunction with Greece and Bulgaria. Although Roskill avoids the use of the pejorative term 'Easterner' to describe his strategy – in essence a maritime rather than continental approach – Hankey's memorandum he describes as 'the inception of the Dardanelles venture.'[217] The CID Secretary was among the first, in mid-March 1915, to sense the 'premonition of disaster' in Britain's execution of such a strategy, and four months later Hankey was sent by the government to report on the imbroglio.[218] At first the object of military suspicions, Hankey succeeded in establishing clearly that 'he was anxious only to use his exceptional talents for their good.'[219] When the expedition could not be spared – Hankey was among the last to advise against complete withdrawal from the Gallipoli peninsula – Hankey escaped the stain which blotted the records of nearly everyone connected to the venture; he had not, to be sure, held a line command. Not even the role of 'counsel for the defence' which Hankey played on behalf of the Asquith government in the proceedings of the Dardanelles Commission served to discredit Hankey, or the advisory role which he played, in any important quarters. The change in military command which brought Robertson and Haig, convinced 'Westerners' both, to the fore did not appear to diminish his offering constructive advice which was not without significance in the war effort.[220] Even Haig, in a personal diary rooted in suspicion and steeped in character assassination, expressed confidence in Hankey's friendship and willingness to be of assistance throughout the war.[221]

What helps to account for Hankey's ability to succeed in his advisory capacity is the tact which enabled him to mask from the military leaders, particularly on the Western Front, his deeply felt abhorrence of the policies of those who led, in his savage diary comment, an 'English Army so rotten that it has never achieved one successful offensive in the whole course of the war.' In May 1916, Hankey recorded his belief that 'the Army want a regular orgy of slaughter this summer,' coupled with his regret that the Asquith ministry had yielded, against their better judgment, to the plan for another 'great offensive' conceived 'in the heads of the red-hatted, brass-bound brigade . . . who know little of the conditions at the actual front and are out of touch with real regimental opinion.'[222] The Battle of the Somme rightly served to confirm in Hankey's mind the accuracy of his view, and it caused him to question the war leadership of Asquith, who had acquiesced in such unwise advice. At no time could a man of Hankey's rank hope to contest the generals, save by advocating a change in Britain's supreme command, as he did – finally – in his conversation with David Lloyd George.

In embracing the alternative of Lloyd George's leadership, Hankey proved an indispensable institutional asset to the new regime. He continued to act as the secretary to the British delegation in a number of Anglo-French and other Allied conferences held at London and on the continent, providing records of those proceedings, as he did for the War Cabinet. In his advisory role, he mediated between the soldiers and the statesman, serving as an ill-defined but useful bridge between the two camps: he never played that part to greater effect than in February 1917 when, anticipating difficulties at the Calais Conference – since the Prime Minister sought to place Robertson, Haig, and the British Army under the command of the French general Nivelle – he had prepared in advance a compromise. In fact his suggestions resolved, if only temporarily, a divisive public conflict, and he took credit for a 'great personal triumph' in recording in his diary:

> I tried to frighten him [Lloyd George] by the probable results of Robertson's and Haig's impending resignation, and he was affected, though he swore he was not going to be beaten over this. Then I warned him that he could not fight on the basis of the outrageous French document and he agreed and asked me to draft something on which he could fight. This was the psychological moment to pull my formula out of my pocket. He read it, accepted it, sent for Robertson who accepted it with intense relief and took it to Haig, who accepted it after palaver. Ll. G. then showed it to Briand, Lyautey and Nivelle, who accepted it. All therefore was well . . . all had been effected by my little scrap of paper.[223]

Hankey's mediative role involved foresight no less than tact in this case; consistently he seemed able to gauge with a Bismarckian precision politics as 'the art of the possible.' While he won plaudits for his roles at the great war-time conferences, in peace-time his prominence began to reap resentment for the Cabinet Secretariat. Yet the institution and the man did not have to be differentiated as long as Lloyd George continued in office.

In the meantime, the morass of indecision and inefficiency which hampered the British war effort had in an administrative sense been bypassed by the new secretarial arrangements. Yet the fitful, erratic nature of Lloyd George's leadership led Hankey to record private criticisms of the War Cabinet's occasional inability to discharge its responsibilities in a businesslike fashion.[224] Witness to a number of wasteful and unproductive meetings of Cabinet committees, Hankey saw that adequate records could not always resolve inconclusive discussions. In late 1917, he rued the lengthy discussions of a Cabinet Committee on Manpower, chaired by the Prime Minister: 'They sat all that afternoon, and all day Tuesday . . . but in orbits of much deviation, having covered a lot of ground. On Tuesday evening, having come nowhere near a conclusion, the P.M. turned to me and said "Now Mr. Secretary I think you had better draft a report . . .". It was a desperate job.'[225] 'Desperate jobs' became the lot of the Secretariat, but even such tasks serve to remind of the alternative, the attempt of Asquith's ministries to conduct world war for nearly two and a half years without recourse to system in general and a Secretariat in particular to tend to the flow of business. In December 1916, Britain was fortunate that the new regime could draw upon a decade of experience, at the sub-Cabinet level, in secretarial techniques; no one can say what price the nation may have paid because re-organization of Cabinet business had been so long delayed.

> Gone were the scramble of Ministers to get their pet subjects discussed at Cabinet meetings. Gone were the endless rambling discussions with no one to give a decision. Gone was the exasperating waste of time while the affairs of a department were discussed by people who knew little of the matter and had received no Memoranda on the subject. Gone were the humiliating and dangerous doubts of what the decision was, or whether there had been a decision at all.[226]

Hankey's own verdict rings true: the old Cabinet ways were doomed, long after their time had run out.

2

The Lloyd George regime

The fallen premier, H. H. Asquith, chose not to challenge in Parliament what his successor described as 'the amalgamation of the old War Committee with the Cabinet.' Nor did Asquith express more than his regret that the new regime had abandoned what he described as 'the inflexible unwritten rule of the Cabinet,' namely that the Prime Minister alone took a record of Cabinet proceedings, for the sole purpose of informing the King.[1] In the wake of political crisis, near-universal approbation of the various administrative reforms followed; nor did the establishment of a Cabinet Secretariat loom particularly large in the redefinition of the relationship between Cabinet and Parliament, which was so far-ranging that A. J. P. Taylor has commented that 'parliamentary government, as it had been known for the last century or so, ceased to exist.'[2] Nonetheless, Parliament deferred to Lloyd George's assurances, at least in part because Asquith tacitly acquiesced to the new premier's statement:

> There seems to be a little concern that the new organisation should have the effect of lessening Parliamentary control. I wonder why on earth it should do that. Each Minister answers for his Department exactly in the same way as under the old system. Each Minister is accountable for his Department to Parliament, and the Government as a whole are accountable to Parliament.[3]

While the Opposition Front Bench remained quiet – they had failed to win the war, after all – back-bench critics were not long in detecting a bureaucratic threat to representative government: linking together the two Secretariats they found 'growing up round the War Cabinet a perfect fungus growth of liaison officers and paid secretaries of one kind or another.'[4]

This initial parliamentary criticism echoed press attacks unleashed in the columns of Massingham's *The Nation*, which in February 1917 denounced the imposition of a 'double screen of bureaucrats,' consisting of the Cabinet Secretariat, 'almost a Ministry in itself,' and the *illuminati* in the Prime Minister's own Secretariat; these bodies were interposed between the War Cabinet and the heads of departments. Lloyd George's system threatened parliamentary government and the representative principle. Massingham had no difficulty in locating the source of this assault upon traditional ways:

> Reactionary Imperialism [read, Milnerism] has thus seized the whole body of Liberal and democratic doctrine, and is making off with it under the cover of war . . . the seat of power . . . is being distributed among thousands of office-stools in the jerry-built homes of our new Constitution . . . Mr. George has used Toryism to destroy Liberal ideas; but he has created a Monster which, for the moment, dominates both. This is the new Bureaucracy which threatens to master England, unless England decides in time to master it.[5]

Other journalists accepted the need for improved management of the affairs of state; the Treasury's general supervision, dating to Gladstone's time, had fallen into abeyance. Yet Lloyd George, the *New Statesman* suggested, had gone about re-organization in a mistaken way:

> in creating his Secretariats Mr. Lloyd George has made the double mistake of giving them too large a role and manning them with a personnel of insufficient standing even for the role that they might have legitimately undertaken. Their functions should not have been in any sense a substitute for those formerly discharged by the Cabinet; they cannot do anything which efficiently replaces that regular meeting and consultation between the responsible heads of the Departments.[6]

The comment itself represents a mistaken idea about the Cabinet Secretariat's role, since it had been designed to secure the departmental implementation of the decisions reached by the 'regular meeting and consultation' now vested in the War Cabinet.

Much of the misunderstanding of the functions which Hankey supervised was a product of the overlap between his office and that of the Prime Minister's Secretariat, which he admitted was understandable; however, he added that 'occasionally *I* was attacked for the Garden Suburb's activities – it eventually became a joke between Philip [Kerr] and myself that I was his "whipping boy," but it was a wry joke for me because the War Cabinet Office was an object of suspicion.'[7] The Cabinet Secretary himself supplied another source of confusion through his attendance at meetings which shaped Allied war policy, which underscored his advisory capacity; it was no easy matter for press or Parliament to differentiate his role from Kerr's, who in time became the guiding hand of the counterpart Secretariat. Yet for all the political fervor of *The Nation*'s attack, it proved short-lived: not until March 1918 did the press again question the impact of the new methods. By that time *The Spectator*, which granted the need for re-organization of the Cabinet system, regarded as unproved any contention that 'the new machine has produced results greatly superior to those produced by the old.'[8] Such an assessment was not incorrect so far as the military situation was concerned, because Lloyd George and the military leaders remained at daggers drawn; Hankey continued to play a mediative role between 'frocks' and 'brasshats,' a thankless if necessary task.[9]

Disappointment with the progress of the war effort contributed to a questioning of the Lloyd George reforms, which in perspective ran contrary to 'the Whig theory of British history,' a belief that the pattern of Cabinet government which had operated in the Victorian period represented the culmination of some fifteen hundred years of progress towards representative government. As a result, 'the conventions and practices of the late Victorian period were not considered as merely true for that time, they were regarded as proper or normal. When further changes occurred, they were noticed with reluctance and tended to be regarded as departures from the norm.'[10] Departures from established ways were justified by the exigencies of war, but the burden of proof remained with the reformers, and the events of 1917 had not returned a clear verdict. Yet few would deny the judgment of Hardinge, the crusty but experienced Permanent Under-Secretary of the Foreign Office, that the War Cabinet system stood as 'an improvement over the last administration. It has its weak points, but anyhow decisions are taken.'[11] Such efficiency did not come easily, and for a time Hankey despaired about the War Cabinet's performance; on 18 March he noted in his diary:

> The War Cabinet has met every day this week, but is not working satisfactorily. They never discuss the Agenda Paper at all – in fact they have not done so properly for a fortnight. They invariably allow themselves to be side-tracked into something else – often some parliamentary business, or else Ll. George has an intense longing to discuss something different . . . Consequently, all the work is dreadfully congested – far worse than it ever was under the so-called 'Wait & See' Government. Another difficulty is that Lloyd George will not initial the conclusions (without which they do not become operative), and will not give me a reasonably free chance to act without them, so that all the business of the War Cabinet gets in arrears, and the Departments, tired of waiting for their decisions, get discontented. I have only got the work along at all this week by a wide delegation of decisions to Committees, to which with some difficulty I persuaded Ll. G. to assent.[12]

Grieved that 'Lloyd George's method of doing business is to discuss every subject under the sun except what is on the agenda,' Hankey feared that the premier's disposition would give the War Cabinet and its Secretariat 'a bad reputation.'[13] Periodically the Cabinet Secretary insisted that the War Cabinet clear its congested agenda, noting at the end of May 1917: 'they set to work with a will and with the determination to clear up all arrears in two days . . . They are all rather done up and I felt rather cruel.'[14] For his part, Hankey preferred the delegation of specific items in arrears to individual members of the War Cabinet, a system of his own devising which yielded good results: 'the War Cabinet were actually abreast of their work. I felt like "pilgrim relieved of his burden" and as elated as if we had won the war.'[15] From this time, Hankey maintained close tabs on the pace of Cabinet business, acting forcefully to produce decisions.[16]

While the *modus operandi* of the War Cabinet and its Secretariat evolved in a pragmatic fashion, Bonar Law assured the House of Commons that the new system was functioning well.[17] The House of Lords engaged in a fuller discussion of its effectiveness in June 1918: the major issues were whether the War Cabinet ought to restrict itself to war business and, as a corollary, whether orthodox Cabinet government ought to be restored for all other purposes. The defenders of the new system insisted, in Lord Lansdowne's words, that 'there can be no question of going back to the old system of Cabinet government as we knew it before the war.'[18] Further, Lord Curzon rejected the view that the War Cabinet system was meant only for war: 'We never threw off our shoulders the general responsibility of government. The Ministry were called a War Cabinet because their main function is war, but the idea that they were not held accountable for the administration of the vast number of ideas that ordinarily rest upon the Government of this country never entered our heads.' As he warmed to his cause, Curzon rode roughshod over what was viewed as a delicate point: 'I doubt very much whether there has ever been a war waged by this country in which the military advisers of the Government have had a freer hand in the expression of their views, or in which there has been more deference paid to their opinion.' As for future prospects, Curzon foresaw that the business-like procedures of the War Cabinet would long survive the war which had occasioned them: 'whether our work be good or bad . . . my own opinion is that when the war is over and the history of this time is written, it may be found that we have left a not inconsiderable mark upon the constitutional development of this country.'[19] Curzon awarded Hankey the major credit for 'the successful working of the system,' although he did not acknowledge his own debt to the Cabinet Secretary for the success of his speech! Hankey recorded in his diary that

> on the evening of the 13th I went to coach Lord Curzon on a speech he is to make . . . in defence of the War Cabinet system. I was with him an hour and a half. At the end he was most extra-ordinarily complimentary, and thanked me profusely, expressing astonishment at the way in which I managed to have every subject at my fingers ends. He said that, whatever happened to this or other governments, and whatever happened to the war, I should be indispensable to every Prime Minister.[20]

While the diary entry served Hankey's ego, as well it suggests that the partisans of the new ways recognized the debt owed to Hankey for his efforts in that cause: a product of the Asquith regime, he was clearly identified with the new.

The turn in the fortunes of war associated with the collapse of the German offensive in the spring of 1918 brought to the fore the question of the survival of the war-time reforms in government. The achievements of the Cabinet Secretariat could not, however, be dissociated from Hankey's variegated responsibilities during that conflict: his role had never been one of mere clerk to his chief; rather he served as a trusted adviser to the Prime Minister, but the military never begrudged him such influence. To the contrary, Haig appealed to Hankey in 1919 in an attempt to secure better terms for the Germans at the Paris Peace Conference; he judged the Cabinet Secretary's intervention successful, noting in his diary that 'chief credit is due to General [sic] Hankey.'[21] In fact Hankey was no better able than anyone else to stem the vindictive tide, but he did recognize the key dilemma confronting the peacemakers:

> For some time past I have felt a vague and indefinite uneasiness as to whether the Peace Treaty was developing on sound lines of policy . . . On this exhausted, depleted, crippled and reduced country [Germany] a prodigious indemnity is to be imposed. That Germany ought by every law of justice to pay the penalty of her crimes no reasonable man can deny. The question, however, is whether justice and policy can run hand in hand in present conditions.[22]

Throughout the war, Hankey had never feared to transmit ideas which had contributed, on several occasions in important ways, to winning the war.

Such a role dated to the Asquith regime, although Hankey most often agreed on strategic matters with Churchill and Lloyd George. While it is not particularly pleasant to recall that in February 1915 'Hankey proposed (a) igniting German crops and (b) distributing a "blight" over the crops,'[23] more to his credit is his role in the initial planning of a 'land battleship,' known to posterity as the tank, and in the development of the convoy system later in the war. Hankey's role in overcoming Admiralty opposition to the convoy system has long been recognized as a major contribution.[24] Despite these successes, Hankey thought that his CID duties limited the scope of his innovation, as he confessed: 'I was as keen as mustard on the tank, but with my own overwhelming preoccupations the extent to which I could push it [with the War Office] was limited.'[25] With the change of regimes, Hankey did not cease to advise on military matters, but his other responsibilities as Cabinet Secretary became more time-consuming; it is well to record the wear of the pace which he had to set, as outlined in his diary:

> Every day I work at the greatest pressure from 10 a.m. to 7:30 or 8 p.m. I am at every Cabinet meeting. At present I have in addition the Committee on War Policy, at which I am allowed to have no assistant secretary, with very heavy

consequential work. Although I have decentralized much of the ordinary office work to my assistants I still have to keep a fairly close watch on the work of the War Cabinet, Agenda papers, Minutes &c &c. In addition I have members of the War Cabinet and all the other Ministers stopping in all day and asking me to drop in on them, nearly always to confer about some difficult point, or some great point of policy. On these subjects also I have a vast correspondence. In order to keep up to date I have to read an enormous number of telegrams, Memoranda, letters &c every day and to see a great number of people from the different armies, military attaches, diplomatists &c &c.[26]

His burdens were great, but such constant informal conversations strengthened Hankey's influence upon those in authority. General Sir Henry Wilson, successor to Robertson as CIGS, may have exaggerated in commenting in 1919, 'if you once lost hold of Hanky-Panky, you are done, absolutely done,' for doubtless Hankey saw some of his advice – including the 'Easterner' strategy – go unheeded; nonetheless the process yielded an important result: 'in coming to regard Hankey as indispensable, Ministers must have absorbed many of his views.'[27]

Such was the respect Hankey gained that Lloyd George considered appointing him Secretary of State for War, but Lord Milner – while admitting that 'a great deal' might be written in Hankey's behalf – managed to convey more in his own interest, and five days later he gained the post.[28] Even earlier, Hankey refused to entertain the prospect of becoming First Lord of the Admiralty, explaining that he would be 'quite hopeless as regards parliamentary matters, deputations, etc., in regard to which I had no experience.'[29] Although Hankey's ministerial experience was deferred to another war, his ministerial career does not put the lie to such a self-assessment. With the conclusion of the First World War, his name was mentioned as a possible successor to Hardinge at the Foreign Office, but George V objected, on the grounds that his position at the Cabinet Office was more important.[30] Even the mention of Hankey's name in connection with such leading posts, political and civil service alike, serves as testimony to his standing in the eyes of contemporaries.

His name also figured prominently in any discussion of those individuals who were most responsible for winning the war. In August 1918 the press magnate Lord Riddell secured the premier's agreement to Hankey's strategic contribution:

Hankey is also entitled to a share, and a large share [Riddell claimed] of the credit for the convoy system, which saved the nation. He had the idea and, in the face of fierce opposition, continually urged its adoption.

L. G.: Yes, quite correct. For the moment I had forgotten. Hankey is one of the great figures in the war.[31]

The experienced elder statesman Balfour rated Hankey highly for his able role in ensuring communications within the Lloyd George coalition;

for this and other reasons Balfour declared in after years: 'I tell you that without Hankey we should not have won the war!'[32] According to Hankey's own testimony, his Sovereign's praise was even more pronounced:

> He then reminded me that early in the war he had warned me that, if I confined myself to my job, and avoided all temptation to make suggestions and get power into my hands, I should be a great force in the war. He said I had followed his advice, with the result that, in his opinion, I had done more than any other person towards winning the war. He added that Lloyd George and Asquith had independently said this.[33]

While Hankey acknowledged that George V exhibited mistrust for Lloyd George, it impresses as odd that he did not recognize that such a bias had likely contributed to his own elevation in his monarch's eyes. It also deserves recording that Lloyd George entered his own claim to a place of primacy in winning the war, when in 1939 he acidly explained his own exclusion from Neville Chamberlain's war coalition: 'Neville put Hankey into the War Cabinet instead of me because he thought it was Hankey who had won the war.'[34] One cannot begrudge the aged and embittered figure his resentment, but even more to the point, Hankey never questioned the towering contribution of David Lloyd George. Late in his life, Hankey challenged the assertion that his erstwhile chief would live on in history as the greatest of British war ministers, save only for Sir Winston Churchill: 'If you take the war as a whole, including its preparation, its course, the extent of the victory, and the condition in which it left our country, our Empire, and the peace of the world, I venture to say that Lloyd George comes out first and Churchill second.'[35]

In more practical terms, with the termination of hostilities there arose the matter of rewarding Hankey for his efforts, since sizeable grants were awarded the military leaders. As post-war Secretary of State for War, Churchill declared that 'his brilliant services deserve exceptional recognition,' and he suggested that Hankey be made a Privy Counsellor and given a grant of £20,000;[36] the Cabinet proved more generous, agreeing upon a sum of £25,000, 'without a dissentient voice,' the Cabinet Secretary noted. Although he was troubled by Lloyd George's refusal to accept anything whether from public funds or private subscription for his services, Hankey felt that he could not afford to follow such an example, describing himself as a 'poor man.' Although financial concern played a part in his decision, it appears that on another level Hankey could not bear the prospect of his service going unrewarded: 'I did as much to win the war as any of the Admirals and Generals. I have no doubt whatsoever of this.' He then spelled out in his diary two pages of his war-time achievements to bolster his deserving status.[37] That account, incidentally, reveals Hankey's own belief that his contributions were basically two-fold, as the organizer of the new Cabinet system, and as military adviser and ministerial confidant. Thus the fortunes of the Cabinet Secretariat in its early years must be assessed in the totality of Hankey's achievements: the institution cannot be severed from the man, because the Cabinet Secretariat evolved in pace with Hankey's contribution. When Curzon remarked in the House of Lords that the Cabinet Secretary 'had been more responsible than any other individual for what he [Curzon] claimed to be the success of the system,' he had established that inter-relationship.

In the course of the war, Hankey applied the procedures which were established by the Cabinet Secretariat to other new bodies created to improve and co-ordinate the war effort. Both the Imperial War Cabinet and the allied Supreme War Council were served by mechanisms modelled on the original Secretariat model.[38] Although there is no need to explore the functions of these bodies, records of the proceedings of both were handled along familiar lines, and Hankey personally sat to keep the minutes of the former, which attached the dominion Prime Ministers visiting London to the War Cabinet deliberations concerning imperial matters. The British section of the Supreme War Council's Secretariat was housed at Versailles and staffed largely by Army officers, but it operated under the control of the War Cabinet Office.[39] Hankey's methods of operation were taken up as well by the French and American governments, the latter at the insistence of that keen observer Col. House.[40] Thus the dissemination of practices based upon the Cabinet Secretariat's procedures was widespread within the allied camp.

No one recognized more clearly than Hankey that the major work, and indeed the success or failure, of the Cabinet Secretariat lay with the performance of the War Cabinet. At the conclusion of the war, he spoke along those lines to his staff:

> We have recorded the decisions, we have been the link between the War Cabinet which took the decisions and the Departments who were responsible for giving effect to them. We have turned [sic] the machine up to the pitch, when, I am sure, an absolute minimum of time has been occupied in translating these decisions into actions . . . On the prompt transmission of these masses of orders the whole success of the Government policy has again and again depended. You cannot lose time in War.[41]

He predicted that the secretarial system evolved to meet the needs of war would survive to serve the nation's needs in peace, the settlement of whose terms HMG now confronted. Dealing with Allied statesmen was for Hankey nothing novel, even in the Asquith regime; now the War Cabinet established an office in Paris, upon the opening of the peace conference in January 1919; the Foreign Office and other departments concerned with the peace negotiations also established missions.[42]

Hankey served as Secretary to the British Empire Delegation, which caused some consternation in the Foreign Office, although it seems that Hardinge, the Permanent Under-Secretary, was not particularly troubled.[43] The tell-tale signs of the Hankey method were soon evident: never – it would appear unqualified – did he fail to lay his hand upon a paper required for some or other discussion; the utility of such readily accessible records was established when Hankey alone got the tangled affairs of Yap straightened away.[44] Whatever the failures of the Paris proceedings, Hankey's 'methods of recording minutes, circulating papers and dealing with other procedural and secretarial matters were adapted by the international secretaries of this and later conferences.'[45]

His own services were conspicuous in their absence: the glacial rate of progress in the Council of Ten led to private negotiations among the heads of government, although a stumbling block soon arose; Lord Riddell offered an explanation – and a solution – to Lloyd George on 24 March 1919:

> he ought to have Hanky-Panky with him. The trouble is that the four [heads of government] meet together and think they have decided things, but there is no one to record what they have done. The consequence is that misunderstandings often arise and there is no definite account of their proceedings and nothing happens.[46]

Records for the Council of Four, formally constituted on 27 March, date from that time, with Hankey's hand in evidence.

As Lloyd George's right-hand man, Hankey earned considerable notice at Versailles; his advisory role was clear. Leo Amery has illustrated the type of influence which the methodical Secretary exercised over the mercurial premier, who was known to propose spontaneously some particular policy which the British delegation had already decided to oppose; Hankey would pass along a note which Lloyd George would quickly assimilate, without a pause in his remarks.

> Presently he would blandly explain that he thought he had done full justice to a view which however the British Government did not share, and would now expound our own real attitude. Meanwhile Hankey would draft a resolution which Lloyd George would then read out as representing the fully considered proposal which he had brought with him.[47]

Hankey's impact upon the conference mechanism and the quality of his advice to the premier account for the unusual accolade conferred by his chief, who rarely took the time to write to those with whom he was in daily contact: 'Your work has been beyond the praise of words.'[48] Yet Hankey, for all the fact that he had discharged duties which he described with a touch of hyperbole as 'Secretary of the Cabinet of the World,' came away from those proceedings disappointed: the final terms of the treaty troubled him, as had the course of the negotiations. In fact, he resolved to turn down the post as Secretary General to the fledgling League of Nations, because he doubted the strength and soundness of the League, especially in regard to the Covenant's provisions for automatic sanctions, which he thought mistaken.[49] Advice from the likes of Curzon and Esher reinforced his own fears, and in April 1919 he refused to let his name go forward, explaining that a number of developments had run contrary to his expectations; among unsettled questions he cited what he had 'always regarded as an essential condition, namely the certainty of the acceptance of the Covenant by the United States of America.'[50]

In such a fashion Hankey opted against becoming the chief servant of the new international order; instead, he remained on in London, buoyed by his view that 'the British Empire is worth a thousand Leagues of Nations.' Alas, the British Empire, like the League, was to fall upon fallow days, and Hankey was to live to suffer the dénouement at Suez. Upon returning to Whitehall Gardens, the Cabinet Secretary entertained hopes that the British Empire staff assembled at Versailles might be transformed into a body serving the activities of a post-war Imperial War Cabinet and leading to 'a real Imperial Cabinet Office' on a permanent basis.[51] In his absence, the Cabinet Office had been ably run by his deputy, Tom Jones, in a fashion that might be viewed as 'on guard for the Prime Minister.' At one point Churchill had attempted to settle the principle of the continuance of compulsory military service in the War Cabinet, before referring the matter to Lloyd George in Paris. Jones had quickly informed Hankey, who had gone to the Prime Minister; according to Hankey, Lloyd George was 'much annoyed about Churchill's proposal and has written him to stop it' without mixing Jones' name in.[52] Such plain dealing between Hankey and Jones eased the Cabinet Secretary's initial suspicion that the deputy might covet his position; though the two men were not personally close, there were no signs of professional envy.[53]

The activities of the Cabinet Secretariat and the role of the Cabinet Secretary were known in any detail only to a few in the inner circles of government. Some attention – whether or not welcome – had been directed their way in press and Parliament, and official commentary had been offered both in Parliament and in the innovative *War Cabinet Reports* for 1917 and 1918, although the latter broke no new ground so far as the Secretariat's activities were concerned; it noted that the major administrative development of 1918 was the assumption of responsibility by Cabinet committees in dealing 'with groups of questions which previously had tended more and more to come within the range of subjects dealt with by particular members of the War Cabinet.'[54] The service of such committees, along with the co-ordination of government business in order to ensure the maximum utilization of the country's productive resources, had become major activities of the Secretariat, as important as the keeping of the record of War Cabinet meetings.[55] The *War Cabinet Reports*, which addressed these administrative practices, were on one level 'accounts of stewardship, setting out the administrative work of the new government and concentrating on the new developments and on constitutional innovations such as the War Cabinet itself.'[56] On another level, the *Reports* were intended to advertise and promote the government's efforts; probably for that reason, they were drawn up by the Prime Minister's Secretariat, but there is evidence that a Cabinet Secretariat functionary was so appalled by the lack of 'literacy' in the draft that he had his subordinates rewrite it.[57] In any event, the Cabinet Secretariat had nothing whatever to fear from the *War Cabinet Reports*.

The continued existence of the War Cabinet system of government was called into question with the Armistice of November 1918: how long could it remain intact when its purpose had been realized? Hankey had labored to make the system function in war-time, because he had seen that the traditional methods would not suffice; he became the 'task-master' of the new regime, striving to keep the War Cabinet on the mark. On one occasion, in the Prime Minister's absence, Bonar Law had proposed that the War Cabinet go no further in settling business:

> I then spoke out and said I thought it my duty to warn the War Cabinet that their work was badly in arrears; that many questions were awaiting decision; and that there were at least three questions on the Agenda paper that they could settle without the Prime Minister. This shamed them into continuing. But, by this time, I found that Mr. Balfour, Lord Derby, Sir Eric Geddes and Adl. Jellicoe, all of whom were concerned in these questions, had slipped out of the room. So I ran out into the passage . . . and said 'look here, you must not blame me if your department affairs at the Cabinet get in arrears. There are questions on the Agenda which concern you all, and here you are all bolting off.' So they all filed back, and we got a good deal of business done.[58]

The Cabinet Secretary entertained no doubts about the value of the system he had managed, but he foresaw several alternatives as far as the configuration of the Cabinet in the post-war period was concerned: these ranged from a large Cabinet of the pre-war type to a small Cabinet composed mainly of ministers without portfolios, with several possibilities between the two. Assuming that Lloyd George intended to propel 'a great scheme of reconstruction and social reform' with the energy committed to winning the war, Hankey preferred the small Cabinet:

> if efficiency only is taken into account, the War Cabinet system is by far the best. One of the principal reasons for the success of the War Cabinet system was undoubtedly the small number of persons with whom the final decision rested, coupled with the elasticity which enabled the arbiters to hear all sides of the case.

The moment the numbers become larger, and more particularly the moment the Heads of Department become final judges on questions in which their Departments are interested, the power of decision will become weaker.[59]

Hankey anticipated the objections which would be raised to what he advised calling the 'Reconstruction Cabinet'; to meet these, he recommended weekly or fortnightly meetings of all ministers to hear and question the premier, and he advised full circulation of the Minutes of the Cabinet and its committees.

Lloyd George himself had already intimated that 'in some form or other he wants to keep the War Cabinet system after the war.'[60] To be sure, he took political factors into account, and Esher spelled these out to Hankey at the end of 1918:

Having broken up the Party system, it is childish to revert to a formula which was the outcome of that system. This is bed rock. So is the deduction, that you must let the principle of Evolution work freely: and without obstruction. The War Cabinet – as you well know – was not a sudden inspiration but the natural corrollary [sic] of a Committee within the Cabinet etc. dating from Gladstone's time. If the P. M. goes back to the old inane system, he is done for.[61]

Support for an extension of the new ways came from another quarter, as the Milnerites strove to strengthen the imperial fabric, in the main by the establishment of a post-war Imperial Cabinet every bit as important as its domestic counterpart. Amery took the prospect of two distinct Cabinets seriously, although his lengthy memorandum has all the flavor of a period piece:

The Prime Minister should, in fact, be the only common link between the two Cabinets, associating with himself, to prevent his being overloaded by the burden of work, a trusted lieutenant on each side, in the one case the Dominions Minister, in the other the Leader of the House of Commons. As far as possible the two Cabinets should be kept clearly separated . . . In this way a tradition against dragging Imperial affairs into local party politics might very rapidly grow up . . . The whole aim, in fact . . . is to attain as far as possible the clear separation of Imperial and domestic policy.[62]

Hankey was personally sympathetic to such a bifurcation, although he informed Amery that despite his advocacy to Lloyd Geroge, the premier had yet to commit himself. For that reason, the Cabinet Secretary suggested a different approach: he 'had suggested to L. G that if he wasn't prepared to go as far as that, he should have a Cabinet of 22 or so and at their first meeting inform them that he didn't intend to meet them as a whole body but would formally divide them into Imperial and Domestic Cabinets.'[63]

Unwilling to contemplate the restoration of the old Cabinet system, which simply could not sustain the pressures of contemporary government, Amery agreed with Hankey the small Cabinet was much preferable. Yet his thoughts about the Secretariat did not echo Hankey's, because Amery foresaw that

> when ordinary party conditions return, this secretariat would become to some extent a political body and include a certain number of young politicians who were definitely put in to study administration and other problems from the point of view of the policy of the party in power . . . the Prime Minister might delegate the general control of the Home Cabinet secretariat to the Leader of the House of Commons.

Such a step would involve the fusion of the distinct secretariats which Lloyd George had established, and it gave every appearance of disengaging from civil service principles. Despite this difference concerning the Secretariat of the future, Hankey and Amery agreed that increasing the numbers of departmental ministers within the post-war Cabinet gravely increased the risk of inefficient and discursive government, reducing that body to a rag-tag debating assembly. Perhaps both underestimated the ability of the secretarial mechanism to cope with larger numbers in Cabinet assembled, since peace-time Cabinets have generally included twenty or so members; on the other hand, it is possible that the greater numbers paradoxically enabled the Prime Minister to distance himself from his Cabinet colleagues and to strengthen his role at their collective expense.[64]

In the meantime, Lloyd George managed to finesse the question of the size and type of the post-war Cabinet. Ministerial changes within the coalition brought the question to the fore in January 1919, but the Prime Minister accepted a compromise, suggested by Bonar Law, which called for the continuation of the War Cabinet for the duration of the Peace Conference: Austen Chamberlain remained a member of that body in a personal capacity, although he became Chancellor of the Exchequer at this time.[65] The small War Cabinet gained another ten months' life, and constitutional principles were wholly ignored; what had transpired has been described accurately as 'the casual outcome of a compromise adopted largely on personal grounds to meet a particular political situation.'[66] The irregularity of the proceedings illustrated anew Lloyd George's contempt for traditional ways, whether in peace or in war. Of course the conclusion of the Paris Conference removed the last prop buttressing the existence of the War Cabinet; political revolt ensued in the House of Commons, where the government sustained a defeat. Bonar Law immediately moved for adjournment, 'the only possible course open to us under the circumstances.'[67]

When the Commons reassembled four days later, the Cabinet had been re-structured along pre-war lines: the heads of the great departments of state again graced the councils of the Cabinet, and the action of the Commons symbolized the termination of its deference to the centralized executive incorporated in the War Cabinet model. The question of the size of the Cabinet had been discussed on the 23rd of October by Lloyd George, Bonar Law, Churchill, Walter Long, and Hankey; the quintet was well aware that the Machinery of Government Committee had recommended as optimum a range of ten to twelve members for the post-war Cabinet, while acknowledging that 'a rearrangement of the supreme direction of the executive as it formerly [i.e., prior to 1916] existed has been rendered necessary, not merely by the war itself, but by the prospect after the war.'[68] Hankey judged that his own intervention had been decisive in disregarding the 'optimum' size and instead reverting to a figure of about twenty; his appeal for the larger number reflected a political calculation that with only a half-dozen Cabinet ministers 'all those left out would be discontented, and the Coalition would be weakened.' Nonetheless, the Cabinet Secretary recognized that his own labors would be complicated:

Of course, impossible to write down conclusions only, because what actually happens in a Cabinet of 20 is that someone drops a suggestion, later on someone else reverts to it and perhaps amplifies it, and then it becomes the conclusion. No one knows exactly what the conclusion is, and the Secretary only discovers it by piecing together the bits.[69]

No doubt it mattered more to Hankey that the Secretary was still around 'to piece together the bits.' The Machinery of Government Committee, chaired by Haldane, had favored the continuation of the Cabinet Secretariat.[70] Thus its institutional survival came as no surprise, and its peace-time functions were modeled directly on its war-time activities, 'subject to the cessation of the extraneous war duty of preparing reports on foreign and overseas matters.'[71] However, the Haldane Committee had added a cautionary note concerning the role of the Cabinet Secretary as an adviser to the Cabinet, suggesting in rather labored terms that if that body were not considering executive actions, 'the participation of a Secretary in the proceedings is not put forward as being applicable to meetings of this character.' Lloyd George honored no such distinction for the whole of his premiership.

By inference, the Machinery of Government Committee had rejected a more comprehensive scope proposed for the Cabinet Secretariat by Prof. W. G. S. Adams of the Prime Minister's Secretariat, who thought the former body should incorporate 'a staff. . . particularly alive to the whole trend of development, not only in the administration, but throughout the country. It should be a very quick Intelligence Department. . . closely in touch . . . with the whole field of foreign development, with the progressive forms of administration in other countries.'[72] Consistently resistant to 'intelligence' activities within his own bailiwick, Hankey had kept his distance from the other Secretariat, even in testimony given to the Haldane Committee.[73] Adams' proposal that a Prime Minister's staff merge the activities of the two Secretariats did not find favour in the *Report* of the Machinery of Government Committee, and the functional distinction between the two bodies was preserved for the balance of Lloyd George's premiership.[74] Thus Hankey's Secretariat had survived, virtually intact, and without unwelcome additions; nor had Hankey's own advisory role been compromised.

He had every reason to be satisfied with the ease with which his operations had been adapted for peace-time purposes; subsequently he saw in the events of October 1919 the formal confirmation that the Secretariat afforded an essential means by which

> the great mass of Cabinet business [could] be handled. Every day the Cabinet was faced with novel and complicated problems arising out of the war, out of the peace treaties, out of demobilisation, or out of the difficult industrial and labour positions created during the war. Nearly all these problems were inter-departmental in character.[75]

Nonetheless, the question remained whether heads of departments sitting in Cabinet could discharge both ministerial and Cabinet responsibilities. In this regard Frederick Leith-Ross contended that the volume of Cabinet business forced ministers to rely more on their civil servants, which altered the mode by which the Cabinet did its business; his comments deserve recognition, as novel procedures confronted a 'traditional' Cabinet:

> It has been claimed that this procedure, and the recording in the Cabinet minutes of the decisions taken, made for a more orderly system of administration. It may be so, but it also made the system much more complicated. The papers to be circulated became longer and more frequent until often a Cabinet Minister would receive a box containing enough reading matter to keep him busy for a week. So he generally glanced through the papers and handed over to his private secretary anything that did not interest him specially. The private secretary would pass the papers on to the department and obtain their comments and these eventually came back to the Minister. They related mostly to details of the proposal, but the Minister usually felt bound to raise any of them that seemed to him relevant. So the Cabinet tended to get immersed in discussions of detail which took up too much time. In order to relieve the pressure on the Cabinet, therefore, the papers were referred to an inter-departmental committee of officials, whose duty it was to sift out the various proposals or counter-proposals put forward and if possible arrive at an agreed recommendation for the Cabinet. Thus there was a proliferation of committees.[76]

Such a complication may well have been the price which Cabinet government paid for moving from an 'age of hum-bug to an age of hum-drum.'[77]

When Bonar Law informed the Commons about the continuance of the Cabinet Secretariat, his announcement encountered some parliamentary criticism. In response to a query concerning the presence of a Secretary compromising Cabinet secrecy, the Prime Minister intervened to brush the point aside: 'The secretary to the Cabinet is trusted in precisely the same way as the secretary of the Committee of Imperial Defence was trusted in the past.'[78] Interestingly, Hankey recognized that such 'trust' left him freer than the Oath of the Privy Counsellor, as he had not after all been given that status:

> It seems to have been decided not to make me a Privy Counsellor . . . Of course I shall respect this confidence, in or out of office, so long as is necessary for the safety of the country, or for the stability of the Government, but I do not regard myself or my heirs to be bound by an oath that I have never been asked to take, and my memoirs will be the more interesting for my not having taken the Privy Counsellor's Oath. Otherwise I am not sure that I should feel free to keep this diary.[79]

To be sure, Hankey did not mask his keeping a diary, which he had used in his governmental activities: proof of his openness is contained in a letter informing the Prime Minister that he could not settle the latter's query by the Cabinet records; nonetheless, Hankey continued, a particular interpretation 'is confirmed by the following extract from my private diary for May 22nd 1918,' quoting some twelve lines in the process.[80]

Press reaction generally favored the reversion to the 'traditional' Cabinet, although *The Spectator* thought that such a modification as the Secretariat had been justified: 'all we ask is that there shall be no Spenlow and Jorkins business between the Cabinet and the Secretariat. It will not do for the Cabinet to say they have been misled by the Secretariat or that the Secretariat has acted beyond its authority. The Secretariat must be the intelligent servant of the Cabinet, but the Cabinet must always be responsible.'[81] Such advice represented a reasonable cautionary note, as the enlarged body of customary size undertook collective responsibility for the spectrum of government business.

Among the first items on the agenda, the new Cabinet took up a 'Set of Instructions to the Secretary of the Cabinet,' which they discussed, amended and approved at a meeting on 4 November; no 'Spenlow and Jorkins' relationship could ensue if these regulations were observed. Some deviation from war-time practices is evident: thus the Secretary was instructed to keep a record of Cabinet proceedings, 'confined to conclusions similar to those circulated recently in connection with the War Cabinet discussions.'[82] In this connection, Hankey was convinced that the minutes had become 'inordinately long' during his absence in Paris and had recently made strenuous efforts to shorten them.[83] As if to underscore the purpose of the record, in August 1919 the description 'Minutes' no longer stood at its head; 'Conclusions' had taken its place.[84]

The Cabinet Secretary recognized full well the difficulty of separating 'Conclusions' from the give-and-take of Cabinet discussion: 'As a matter of fact I work the whole of the important points of the discussion into the Conclusion . . . Churchill attacked me for taking full notes the other day, and I had to explain to him, but I told him I would destroy my pencil notes, which is now being done.'[85] As well, his own burden was increased, because from October 1919 Hankey was no longer permitted to keep an Assistant Secretary in the Cabinet room – though the practice soon revived. The reason seemingly lay in a desire to demarcate the Secretary's unique institutional responsibility: 'The Secretary thus, besides being the Permanent head of the Office, has direct personal responsibility to the Prime Minister for all arrangements connected with the Meetings of the Cabinet . . . [including] Minutes of Meetings &c.'[86]

During the war, Hankey had relied on a relay system among his assistants, with each responsible for a particular item in his turn: Lawrence Burgis began a long association with the office in January 1918, and late in his life he recalled the helping hand that Hankey had extended to him when he was faced with his first minute:

> it was my job to record their discussion and, afterwards, turn my notes into a minute. My first scribbles made no sense at all, but when my time came to depart and another Assistant Secretary took my place, Hankey beckoned me to him and handed me a sheet of paper on which, in his spidery handwriting, was a record of the discussion and the decision arrived at. He said 'this might help you.'[87]

Although Hankey would appear to be in need of aid given the reversion of the Cabinet to its pre-war size, he was left on his own, facing a task which the Tory minister Walter Long viewed as daunting in the best of circumstances: 'I don't know,' he had remarked to Burgis, 'how you make any sort of record with all that talk going on.' At the same time, the Cabinet decided upon a change in format for the Conclusions, which were no longer to be printed but instead reproduced in typescript. Perhaps this was an economy, but there had been another kind of problem as recently as February, when Tom Jones had reported to Hankey: 'we have stopped printing the Minutes for a few days until these lightning strikes are over as I got a hint from the F.O. that some of the men were Trade Unionists first and citizens afterward.'[88] Fewer hands were involved with typewritten Conclusions.

The secrecy of Cabinet proceedings was served by the circulation of complete copies only to the King, the Prime Minister and the Leader of the House of Lords. Although the monarch may well have preferred a resumption of the Prime Minister's letters, Hankey demonstrated that George V had been fully informed by the new procedures.[89] Whatever wistful visions may have preoccupied Buckingham Palace, traditional ways were not about to be revived because of the War Cabinet's demise.

Specific conclusions were sent to concerned departments, which were accountable for their implementation.[90] Such a pattern derived directly from war-time practices, although at that time a larger number had received full sets; other ministers had received extracts, in some cases for 'Action,' in others for 'Concern,' and in some instances 'For information only.'[91] In contrast to the record of proceedings, all memoranda and other documents prepared for the Cabinet were to be circulated to the Cabinet, unless the Prime Minister ruled to the contrary. Hankey had sought such a wider circulation in the last months of the war, and he was now given discretion to circulate some documents to ministers outside the Cabinet and to Permanent Secretaries. However, certain Cabinet papers regarded as 'exceptionally secret' were to be circulated under 'Lock and Key' procedures:

> only one copy is sent to each Cabinet Minister, and the issue, without express sanction, of duplicate copies is forbidden. Moreover, the copies themselves are sent in sealed envelopes addressed to the respective recipients; these envelopes bearing the printed instruction 'To be opened only by the person to whom addressed.' These envelopes are in turn placed in 'red boxes' and then circulated.[92]

In other procedural matters, the Cabinet decided that records of Cabinet committees 'shall as a rule be kept on the same principles as are laid down for Cabinet records'; normally they were circulated to all Cabinet members. However, in the case of one important committee, Home Affairs, full minutes soon became the norm, serving a useful purpose attested to by Austen Chamberlain in 1922:

> I am accustomed to look through the conclusions of the Home Affairs Committee and not infrequently to read the discussion in order to elucidate one or the other of those conclusions. The rather full Minutes of this Committee, which constantly deals with proposed legislation, are useful to me in considering the business of the House and they are, of course, the only source of information which the Cabinet as a whole possesses of the doings of a Committee which is almost a Cabinet within a Cabinet . . . I think that some little indication of the arguments leading up to these conclusions is in this case necessary.[93]

In sum, the Cabinet Secretariat continued its ways following the government re-organization of 1919: in short order, Hankey even prevailed – likely upon the Prime Minister – in securing assistance at Cabinet meetings; on a dozen occasions between March and July 1920 he was accompanied by Thomas Jones, and Jones, in Hankey's absence, had an Assistant Secretary helping. Not until Lloyd George's fall from power in 1922 did a single Secretary chronicle Cabinet business.[94] Jones confessed his pleasure in another device which facilitated the premier's control of government business: 'We also have what we call Conferences of Ministers when it is not desired to bother the Cabinet as a whole. To these Conferences Ministers are invited according as they are likely to be interested in the subject of the Agenda. It is a convenient device, some would suggest, for excluding Ministers!'[95] Yet another mechanism which strengthened the premier's hand in dealing with his colleagues was the control of the Agenda, which could be used to ensure Cabinet disposition of items which he wished settled, or – as important – avoided.[96] More troubling for Hankey's staff was the need to determine the distribution of the Conclusions, a burden which the Secretary remarked upon in 1922: 'The selection of these Departments [to receive extracts] was a matter which required, in the case of every separate Conclusion, the most careful consideration on the part of myself and my principal Assistants.'[97]

In another aspect of the procedures, Hankey had not gotten his way in 1919: he was baulked in his quest for stricter long-term custody of Cabinet secrecy, hoping to recover in the Cabinet Office the minutes and papers circulated on behalf of the Cabinet. To that end, the draft 'Instructions' which he had surely drawn up had stipulated that 'Cabinet Minutes and Papers are not the personal property of members'; the Secretary was charged with regaining custody in the event of the resignation or death of a minister. Yet the Cabinet deleted this provision; hardly disinterested parties, they held that secrecy was 'safeguarded by the rule that no-one is entitled to make public use of Cabinet documents without the permission of the King.'[98] In effect, the Cabinet provided their own files for future reference. Hankey did not indicate whether he was concerned with the possible publication of such materials, as a result of the inclusion of several such documents in the memoirs of Field-Marshal Lord French, *1914* – published earlier in the year; his stated concern was instead the regathering of all Cabinet papers in order to protect the secrecy of Cabinet proceedings.[99]

For his part, the Cabinet Secretary thought ample precedent existed to warrant the collection of official materials. The Committee of Imperial Defence had decided in 1908 that no private files of CID papers ought to be maintained; any access would have to come through the committee's own file, but Hankey's account gives good reason to think that the rule had been stretched.[100] However, the War Council, the Dardanelles Committee and the War Committee had accepted the rule; the question came to the fore with Arthur Henderson's resignation from the War Cabinet in August 1917, since the CID precedent clashed with what Hankey admitted had been the 'immemorial custom' of the Cabinet, whereby Cabinet papers remained 'the personal property of Cabinet Ministers on their vacating office.'[101] In making his case for recovery, Hankey differentiated between peace-time conditions and those under which the War Cabinet labored, particularly the fact that 'there is no comparison between the amount of secret information placed at the disposal of the War Cabinet now and before the present Government assumed office.' Carefully avoiding the Privy Counsellor's Oath, which prohibited public disclosure of Cabinet documents, Hankey convinced the War Cabinet to vest property in such materials in His Majesty's Government. Documents dating to the formation of the government were to be returned to the Cabinet Office, where ex-ministers would be allowed access to them, should the need arise.[102] Henderson and Austen Chamberlain both complied with the decision.

On 4 November 1919 the Cabinet disregarded the war-time precedent, and Hankey noted, 'the Secretary's proposals for continuing the practice of the War Cabinet were deliberately over-ruled by the Cabinet itself, and he was thus relieved of the difficult and invidious task of pursuing ex-Cabinet Ministers with request for the return of all their papers.'[103] The CID held to established practices, and some retiring ministers handed over their papers to their successors; on the other hand, Hankey later noted in high dudgeon, 'instances could be given . . . of Ministers who, on retirement, have required a pantechnicon to remove their Papers from their Offices.' Why had the post-war Cabinet so acted? Obviously some of its members, Lloyd George and Churchill included, foresaw writing memoirs of the period. In all fairness to those two, both had already felt the heat of concerted military and naval criticism, ample reason for them to break the War Cabinet's precedent now that military secrets mattered for less. Lloyd George's own stance became even clearer to Hankey when in 1922 the Cabinet Secretary informed him that the embittered former Secretary of State for India, Edwin Montagu, intended to take nearly all his Cabinet papers with him – perhaps for political purposes: the premier refused to stay Montagu's hand, and he chose not to take the matter up with his coalition Cabinet.[104] It is difficult not to conclude that Lloyd George was concerned with his own cache of Cabinet papers rather than with Montagu's more limited store; and it is conceivable that the premier thought that he might soon have some use for his own collection: the political going for the coalition was noticeably rougher, and he had received 'very big offers' for his memoirs.[105] The Prime Minister's files included some rare specimens; Frances Stevenson recounted subsequently how he had handed her the Articles of Agreement for the Irish Treaty of 1921 with the instruction, 'Lock it up carefully.' She did just that, and the Treaty remained with his papers until claimed by the Cabinet Office in 1945, after his death: 'The amazing thing was that during all that time it had never been asked for.'[106] More fitting testimony to Lloyd George's determination to provide for his own records, or to the transitory nature of Anglo-Irish agreements?

Frustrated with regard to the custody of Cabinet records, Hankey asked the Cabinet to consider the question of the possible publication of official materials, admitting that 'we have not had very much experience . . . The majority of our Reports have been of a secret nature and unsuitable for publication, but there have been exceptions.'[107] Strict rules for the use of such materials in the Official Histories, written in a branch of the Cabinet Office, had been drawn up,[108] but 'unofficial' accounts written by participants who had kept certain government records were bringing the issue to the fore: 'There were notorious cases where the policy of Ministers had been attacked by partial and misleading quotations from Cabinet Papers, and [the post-war Cabinet felt] general sympathy . . . with the desire of Ministers to be allowed to use official papers to defend themselves in such circumstances.' In short order, Lloyd George had a researcher loose in the War Cabinet records – while still in office, he contracted to write memoirs – and with the fall of the coalition in 1922, Bonar Law continued the arrangement: 'The [Army] Officer in question reads the Papers in the Cabinet Office and takes notes, but does not take copies or take them away.'[109] Lloyd George's coalition had gone no further towards resolving the problem than to appoint a committee, which had not met before the government disintegrated. The successor Conservative administration appointed a Committee on the Use of Official Material in Publications, chaired by Lord Curzon,

> to prepare for consideration by the Cabinet a code of rules for the future guidance of Cabinet Ministers and other public servants and Departments in regard to the following matters:
>
> a) The circumstances in which it is permissible in any publication to refer to proceedings of the Cabinet, having regard more particularly to the Privy Counsellor's oath;
> b) The circumstances in which it is permissible in any publication to use or quote from Cabinet or Department documents, however obtained;
> c) The rules to be observed by Departments in dealing with applications from ex-Cabinet Ministers or other public servants for permission to have access to or quote from official documents in connection with personal memoirs or other publications.[110]

The scope of its inquiry exceeded the question of ministerial access. Hankey, appointed as Secretary to the Cabinet sub-committee, observed that the Official Secrets Act could be brought to bear, although it had not been drafted to cover Cabinet documents; nonetheless, the legislation could be invoked in the event of unauthorized publication of government documents by anyone if 'it appears that his purpose was . . . prejudicial to the safety or interests of the State . . . unless the contrary was proved.'[111] With guilt presumed until innocence was proved, HMG had a powerful weapon at their disposal, and so the Official Secrets Act was to prove for decades to come.

In contradistinction, a cautionary note was brought to the committee's attention by the Permanent Secretary to the Admiralty, who warned that the public would have to play a role in determining the degree and even the type of secrecy which the government might maintain, within the scope of the Official Secrets Act:

> the ex-Minister, the retired Naval Officer and the retired Civil Servant are alike free to publish official information in their possession, subject to their being no infringement of the Official Secrets Act, and subject also in the case of the ex-Ministers to the special obligation as to actual Cabinet proceedings. [Though in theory the government might prohibit] . . . anything dealing with their exercise of their official position [such action would] . . . go beyond what is necessary in the public interest, would not be supported by the public, and would never really be observed or enforced.[112]

Officially informed reminiscences, in other words, were very different from official documents. Whether this sensible document dampened Hankey's enthusiasm for some rules it is impossible to say, but the Curzon Committee, like its predecessor, never met; there is no trace in the files of the abandonment of its mission. The situation remained as it had, and officially informed publication flourished, though there remained the risk – however dimly perceived – of violating the Official Secrets Act.

As well as the survival of the Cabinet Secretariat, the year 1919 had witnessed a significant strengthening of the Treasury's role; the relationship between the two was to prove Hankey's most daunting problem in the immediate post-war years. In September of that year, the Permanent Secretary to the Treasury had been named as well the official Head of the Civil Service, implicitly recognizing the 'General Staff' function which the Treasury discharged for the government.[113] Although Treasury stalwarts claimed to trace the devolution of such a role for the Permanent Secretary to 1867, the re-organization of 1919 formally specified the responsibility, which a new and able Permanent Secretary, Sir Warren Fisher, seized upon as a means of improving the quality and efficiency of the Civil Service.[114] Such a re-organization was in no way directed towards Hankey's responsibilities in the Cabinet Secretariat: 'It would be constitutionally wrong to assume that for general government matters, as distinct from financial affairs, the permanent Head of the Treasury had been in any measure supplanted during the inter-war years by the development of the office of Secretary to the Cabinet.'[115] Hankey had at no time entered a claim to administer 'general government matters,' and the official spheres in which he and Fisher moved were quite distinct, although on occasion they did intersect. Yet that separation will not admit to Greaves' view that the Secretariat emerged as 'that off-shoot from the Treasury,' because no such process had occurred; its roots lay elsewhere.

In considerable measure, Fisher's appointment as Head of the Civil

Service was designed to resolve a particular problem which concerned some leading members of the regime, namely the impending retirements of a number of leading civil servants who headed 'traditional' departments anxious to maintain or to regain their independent standing.[116] Through Fisher's involvement in senior appointments, the coalition sought to escape the departmentalism inherent in the Civil Service, which the new Head personally detested; his exercise of such a role over two decades and his outspoken manner – reflected in 'sweepingly condemnatory remarks' about those civil servants who fell shy of his high standards – earned Fisher a number of enemies and account for his still controversial reputation.[117] Yet another important aspect of his appointment deserves mention: his enlarged responsibilities strengthened the role of the premier and were crucial in the turn towards what has been called – with some exaggeration – 'prime ministerial government,' with the Prime Minister standing at the apex of a centralized administrative structure.[118] Thus, if the establishment of the Cabinet Secretariat is viewed as the first major administrative departure from 'traditional' Cabinet government, then the bureaucratic centralization inherent in the Treasury re-organization is the second. Both were restraints upon the departmentalism of the old order, and both enhanced the authority – and the powers – of the premier. Representatives of reform, Fisher and Hankey proved to be occasional rivals as well as allies in that cause. For long periods they went their separate ways, but Hankey had no difficulty in honoring aspects of 'Treasury control' which had atrophied during the war. In December 1919 the Chancellor, Austen Chamberlain, proposed that a member of the Treasury staff be seconded to the Cabinet Secretariat – serving under Hankey and available for general services – 'to resume the old-established arrangement under which Public Departments were accustomed to thresh out with the Treasury – from the outset – proposals which may involve charges upon the Exchequer.'[119] Hankey welcomed the proposal, and the Cabinet, accepting Chamberlain's contention that the principle had yielded to the press of business during the war, agreed with him that the Treasury role should be restored.[120]

In one regard, however, Hankey questioned the Coalition government's view of the relationship between the Secretariat and the Treasury, as he opposed in vain a Treasury-initiated proposal which in April 1921 shifted the budgetary provision for what was known as the Cabinet Office from a category within 'Treasury and Subordinate Departments' Vote' to a separate status.[121] Hankey himself wished to keep his operation at a remove from direct review, as he contended that 'the delicate day to day functions of the Cabinet Secretary were difficult of adequate exposition in Parliament.' He viewed the Prime Minister as the Head of the Cabinet Office as well as First Lord of the Treasury and argued that he should have only one department, accepting a view of the Treasury as a 'foster parent' of the Secretariat.[122] Curiously, he was prepared to forego theoretical autonomy, apparently because the alternative was in 1921 more threatening: Hankey must have feared that the Cabinet Office could be thrust into the political arena by the new arrangements, with the Prime Minister directly responsible for the conduct of the office; the confusion between the two Secretariats was in the process increased.

The Cabinet Office had successfully made the transition to the post-war period, although the deaf ear which Hankey turned to another proposal indicates his caution lest the Secretariat encroach upon the departments. To a proposal that the Secretariat include an organization to which the public might turn with complaints about departmental administration – the forerunner of the Scandinavian ombudsman – Tom Jones took first objection: 'To have this work done well requires persons able to weigh the complaints and able to set in motion appropriate action, or in serious cases, to call the P. M.'s personal attention.'[123] Despite Lloyd George's initial enthusiasm for the 'Ministry of Complaints,' Jones and Hankey convinced him that any action would have to be taken in his own name, rather than that of the Secretariat, and the premier chose to go no further with the concept, whose time had not yet come.

In structural terms, the post-war Cabinet Office incorporated the Cabinet Secretariat, a much smaller Secretariat for the Committee of Imperial Defence, a small branch charged with the publication of Official War Histories and another responsible for all communications dealing with the League of Nations. Functionally, however, Cabinet Office responsibilities were divided into two main branches, dealing with home and external affairs, although there was both overlap and close co-ordination between the two.[124] The Home Affairs Branch was led by Tom Jones; the Imperial, Foreign, and Defence Branch was renamed in 1922 the Committee of Imperial Defence Branch, although it continued to serve non-CID Cabinet committees dealing with defence matters or foreign affairs. Its principal Secretaries were seconded from the War Office, the Admiralty and the India Office; the Treasury representative sat with the Home Affairs Branch. Hankey was personally pleased with the renaming of the other branch, which symbolized the revival of the CID proper, as no one had worked harder than he to revive that organization once the war was over. He encountered a good deal of prime ministerial foot-dragging, but the CID met at the end of June 1920 – its first meeting in more than five years.[125] Yet while the coalition survived, the CID did not flourish; indeed, Lloyd George's refusal to use the CID to gain a realistic military evaluation of developments in the Near East contributed to his downfall.

The existence within the Cabinet Office of a branch dealing with the publication of the Official Histories was natural, considering that the Secretariat had been the repository of all Cabinet documents dealing with the Great War. Yet the charge of writing authorized history was delicate, not least in the need for the branch to avoid any direct quotation of Cabinet documents. Hankey had never been fully comfortable with the inclusion of the Historical Section in the CID ambit, in part because as Secretary he had greater claims upon his time: 'Consequently, it has always been, to a considerable extent, a separate organization.'[126] Nonetheless, in May 1921 he gained Cabinet approval of guidelines for the Official Historians lodged in his office: these sought to bar the use of such descriptive terms as War Council, Dardanelles Committee, War Cabinet, and the like, instead mandating a decision 'by the Government'; as well the Official Historians should 'on no account give any indication of the views expressed by any individual member' of those bodies, except where accounts published by the Dardanelles and Mesopotamia Commissions had already done so.[127] Guidelines which implicitly stressed collective responsibility were one thing, but selection of materials and facts is inherent in the writing of history. Winston Churchill vented his displeasure on this score with the first volumes of Sir Julian Corbett's *Naval Operations*, which in some thousand pages,

> adduce almost every essential fact, and cites or quotes all the important telegrams . . . All these telegrams were approved in writing by me and the bulk of them are my own drafts. Anyone who chooses to read the late [he had died in 1922] Sir Julian Corbett's text and compare the lengthy summaries of the telegrams with the actual texts, will see how extremely unsatisfactory and how unintentionally unfair this method of citation is.[128]

Regardless of the merits of Churchill's complaint, the episode illustrates that someone's historical standing is always at stake, even where Official Histories are involved – perhaps more so because of the authoritative connotation – and those governmental bodies which are associated with such work cannot wholly avoid the cross-fire. Interpretation is open to objection, as when in 1924 a Foreign Office-sponsored confidential history of the Paris Peace Conference accused Lloyd George of bad faith in the matter of reparations; Hankey challenged the allegation, and commented generally to Balfour, Foreign Secretary at the time of Versailles:

> If confidential histories are to be written, no one is safe. There may be at this moment chapters of Mr. Headlam-Morley's [the author of the work in question] history which damn your reputation or mine, of the very existence of which we have no knowledge. They may have been lying, for two or three years in the Foreign Office without our knowledge. Some years hence they will probably be handed over to the Record Office and accepted by the world as a correct account.

The obvious remedy appears to be that they should be communicated to all concerned.[129]

Such 'confidential' histories were produced by the departments, outside the watch of the Cabinet Office; the Official Histories were at this time written within the branch for publication, although the process proved to be a lengthy one. The branch proved to be as durable as the Cabinet Office.

However, the attachment of a League of Nations Branch proved of far less duration. At first, Hankey had betrayed no particular enthusiasm for the inclusion of such a function within his office; however, in 1920 the Cabinet decided that the Cabinet Office should serve as the distributing office for League business, without executive or advisory authority. The Cabinet Secretary informed the premier that such an arrangement would not work, because of overlap between the branch and a Foreign Office staff official; instead, he secured the agreement of Balfour and Hardinge to an amalgamation in which that official would be transferred to the Cabinet Office in order to handle all communications with the League.[130] Lloyd George agreed, and expressed his pleasure that the consolidation had made for greater efficiency at no increased price; he noted the Foreign Office's satisfaction that their own man headed the League operation. For his part, Hankey now welcomed the clear lodging of responsibility for the conduct of League affairs within the Cabinet Office,[131] although he subsequently had cause to regret the move.

Given such a diversity of tasks, the Cabinet Office personnel – exclusive of the Historical Branch – remained near the war-time complement, at a time when stringent economies were called for by the government: while CID ranks declined from 27 to 14 in peace-time, Cabinet Office staffing stood at 123 in 1922, only a score less than in 1919. Such staffing levels may have engendered skepticism among those who were told the office was engaged only in the task of keeping Cabinet records. Hankey's own salary, which had risen sharply over a decade to one of the highest of all government salaries, may have occasioned some envy among senior civil servants.[132] Certainly some criticism followed upon the Cabinet Office's assuming League of Nations work, which appeared to confirm the alleged encroachment of the Secretariat upon the preserves of the Foreign Office. In Parliament, fears of a bureaucratic loss of control were voiced by a former Secretariat assistant, Ormsby-Gore: 'I speak with some knowledge . . . I know what it is and how well it works – very largely because it is a small Department. The whole secret of Sir Maurice Hankey's success was, I believe, because the office was kept small and under his own personal supervision in every corner of it.'[133] An as yet unknown MP, Oswald Mosley, spoke in much harsher terms of the abuses of a 'vicious system' of which the Cabinet Office was an integral part: 'The Prime Minister to-day surrounds himself with a staff of amateurs who improvise settlements in a European situation of peculiar difficulties and complexity, and the relationship between the expert Foreign Office staff and this band of amateurs is highly anomalous.'[134] Mosley – whether or not deliberately – confused the two Secretariats, although Hankey and the Cabinet Office had not eschewed 'foreign policy' altogether. The Cabinet Office was staffed by competent administrators, some of whom were seconded from the departments, but the 'system' of government which had replaced the old departmental order sustained a major assault in 1922; its repercussions were severely felt in Whitehall Gardens.

The Cabinet Secretariat's crisis was a direct result of the fall of Lloyd George's Coalition government in the autumn of that year; political collapse was rooted in conservative distrust of and some antipathy towards the Prime Minister's supposedly reckless leadership. Directly at issue was the conduct of British foreign policy, particularly in the unsettled situation in the Near East. Yet dispute over policy took place in a wider setting, namely the decline of the Foreign Office as the sole institution for the formulation as well as execution of foreign policy. For a number of reasons, institutional and personal, the Foreign Office had, even prior to the deposition of Asquith, entered into the shadow of eclipse,[135] which deepened with the exclusion of Foreign Secretary Balfour from the War Cabinet. Lloyd George's well-known disregard for traditional institutions, and his preference for private rather than official advice, predisposed him to turn to the Prime Minister's Secretariat, and to a lesser extent and in a personal fashion to Hankey, instead of to the Foreign Office.[136] Though not a leading sinner, Hankey no doubt provoked resentment within the tradition-bound Foreign Office because 'he was qualified and, indeed, willing to offer advice and to give his opinion on all aspects of war policy.'[137]

The inclusion of the Foreign Secretary in the post-war Cabinet and the succession of Curzon to that post improved the prospects for a revival of the institution, particularly since Balfour had shown no inclination to lead. Yet Lloyd George had no particular difficulty in getting his way with Curzon, for all the latter's bluster; moreover, hopes entertained in the Foreign Office for a reversion to the ways of the period before 1914 were delusive, for the same reason that any return to the pre-war Cabinet system was impossible: foreign affairs could no longer be kept in a watertight compartment, separate and distinct from other concerns;[138] instead, the conduct of British external policy had to be co-ordinated at the Cabinet level. Though the war had thrown up myriad problems with external and domestic aspects – shipping, blockade, manpower, food supplies among others – in the post-war era the question of reparations alone serves to illustrate the inability of the Foreign Office to 'go it alone.'

Understandably, however, the Secretariats remained foci of discontent as agencies for Lloyd George's intrusion into areas reserved until a few years earlier for 'experts.' For some the prominent role Hankey played in British deputations abroad was an affront, although the Cabinet Secretary was satisfied in his own mind that his secretarial presence was as justified at such conferences as within the Cabinet:

> These Conferences are concerned with business that is just as much interdepartmental as international. . . Moreover, the interdepartmental questions dealt with at these Conferences are essentially of the order of Cabinet questions and it is convenient that they should be handled in their secretarial aspects by the same office which handles them secretarially for the Cabinet. By these means a continuous and fully indexed record has been built up of all the international Conferences from the beginning of the war until to-day. Moreover, the Cabinet Secretariat has acquired an experience of secretarial work and of co-ordination in international, imperial and national affairs, which is certainly unique and of considerable value in facilitating the transactions of the business of our widespread Empire.[139]

Since the Secretariat possessed no executive or advisory functions, Hankey contended its role was beyond suspicion, but he did not reflect upon his own advisory capacity; in that sense he differentiated between the man and the institution, but his critics did not. And the man engaged in personal diplomacy, although he protested his inclusion on a special mission with Lord d'Abernon and General Radcliffe to investigate the Polish frontier dispute in 1920.[140] Further, Hankey badly miscalculated the resolution of this confrontation with Bolshevik Russia; he thought the Poles 'were absolutely done and a hopeless people altogether,' and thus was very much surprised by their recovery.[141] Hankey's role has been strongly criticized, in the main because he 'possessed the habit of saying what he was expected to say' and presented biased and ill-informed information which confirmed Lloyd George in his determination to avoid entanglement in Poland.[142] Clear flaws in his reportage can be cited, stemming in appalling measure from Hankey's interest in phrenology, seemingly never stronger than during the Polish mission; yet the other members of the Inter-Allied mission fared no better, and Hankey, the Secretary, 'had nothing to do but watch the successive failures of his colleagues.'[143] From the perspective of the Foreign Office, the mission, regarded from the outset 'as the prime minister's private outfit,'[144] served as an illustration of Lloyd George's errant diplomacy; they had good reason to consider the Cabinet Secretary among the knights errant.

On the other hand, the Prime Minister had his own complaints about the traditional conduct of British foreign policy, which he thought partly responsible for the outbreak of the war. Writing about the years from 1906, he asserted:

There was a reticence and a secrecy which practically ruled out three-fourths of the Cabinet from any chance of making any genuine contribution to the momentous questions of foreign policy then fermenting . . . Direct questions were answered with civility but were not encouraged . . . we were not privileged to know any more of the essential facts than those which the ordinary newspaper reader could gather.[145]

In his post-war administration, Lloyd George on occasion reversed the process, as Curzon and many of his colleagues were ignorant of the premier's personal diplomacy: if Clemenceau regarded war as too important to be left to the generals, his British counterpart viewed foreign policy as too significant to be consigned to the diplomats. Even Balfour had grown impatient with the premier's use of Philip Kerr in high-level negotiations at Versailles, but Lloyd George believed that 'open diplomacy' obviated the need for the traditional agencies and methods of foreign affairs.[146] Critics of Lloyd George's *modus operandi* objected to the same flaws which those who had denounced the 'old diplomacy' had earlier pointed to: 'The tortuous mentality, secretive methods and exclusive loyalties of which the Diplomatic Corps was . . . suspected can rarely have been so blatant as in the behaviour of Lloyd George's personal representative [Hankey] in Poland.'[147]

Contemporary hopes ran high that Curzon, an experienced hand, would restore Foreign Office primacy, but in the event he did not contest Lloyd George for supremacy in the making of foreign policy.[148] Although he did threaten his own resignation periodically, he apparently enjoyed office too much to follow through; he reasoned as well that his own resignation would leave no significant check upon the premier's mistaken ways.[149] Several of his close friends sustained him in the acceptance of personal humiliation as a patriotic virtue.[150] Despite the personal strains between the two men, it is important to recognize that they were not in basic disagreement about the general outlines of post-war British foreign policy. The Foreign Secretary was fully prepared to defer to the premier's lead on a number of issues, and on others he was given what Harold Nicolson has described as 'perfectly unrestricted scope, or subjected to perfectly normal management.'[151] One problem persisted: 'It was only on the Eastern question, on the question of the Turkish settlement, that his more expert opinion was deliberately ignored.' With this important exception, substantive matters were not the crux of the deteriorating relationship; instead, Lloyd George's cavalier treatment of the Foreign Secretary and Curzon's distrust of an irresponsible cabal round the Prime Minister fed upon each other. For all Curzon's bluster and bombast, those who witnessed the struggle between the two felt some sympathy for the Foreign Secretary, perhaps because the contest was not an even one. Hankey thought that Lloyd George 'bullied' his Foreign Secretary, adding: 'He always bullies those Ministers who have little popular following.' When Curzon was rebuked in a Cabinet meeting, Bonar Law spoke to the premier, who pointed to this very factor; Hankey recorded Law's response: 'Still, he is a very big man, and his colleagues will not stand to have him treated like this.' The Cabinet Secretary himself thought that Lloyd George indulged himself in 'a touch of swelled head,' although he judged that the premier remained 'much the biggest man among them.' Even in its early stages, the dispute threatened the unity of the coalition, Hankey noted in his diary, confident that Bonar Law shared his doubts about its long-term survival.[152] Neither may have fathomed the smoldering resentment which Curzon felt with the pattern of prime ministerial involvement in the widely heralded post-war alternative to the 'old diplomacy,' namely the new-fangled 'diplomacy by conference,'[153] conferences, alas, from which the Foreign Secretary was often excluded. In his words: 'When I reflect that the P.M. is alone at Genoa with no F.O. to guide him . . . and when I recall the whole trend of his policy for the past three years – I can feel no certainty that we may not find ourselves committed to something pregnant with political disaster here.' An element of consolation occurred to Curzon after the failure of the Genoa Conference: 'I hope that this will be the last of these fantastic gatherings which are really only designed as a stage on which he is to perform.'[154] For Curzon, the 'lines' spoken on that stage mattered not so much as the fact that Lloyd George took them all himself.

At a time when an occasionally distraught Foreign Secretary held less than firm command over British foreign policy, the Near Eastern crisis came to a head in September 1922. Under the able leadership of Mustapha Kemal, Turkish resistance to the terms of the Treaty of Sèvres – incorporating territorial gains for Greece at Turkish expense – strengthened; France and Italy preferred concessions rather than armed confrontation with Turkey. Despite such waverings by the Allies, Lloyd George remained adamant in his support of the pro-Greek terms, even accepting the restoration of the notoriously pro-German King Constantine late in 1920; invoking British naval and imperial concerns, the premier yielded no quarter to the traditional pro-Turkish protestations of his Tory colleagues. Buoyed by support from such a powerful quarter, Greece carried well into Asia Minor the military attempt to enforce the terms of Sèvres, provoking a formidable resistance which was compounded by French defection from the effort in October 1921. Kemal regrouped and chose his opportunity to take the offensive well: so complete was the resulting rout of the Greek forces that by September 1922 only an outnumbered contingent of British forces, encamped at Chanak on the southern shore of the Dardanelles, stood between the Turkish Army and its reconquest of the lost European provinces of the

Ottoman Empire. A crossing of the Straits threatened a renewal of war; the British Cabinet met on 15 September to consider a further course of action, including an appeal for assistance to the dominions.

In view of the past differences over the merits of conflicting claims, the Cabinet emerged from that meeting surprisingly united and clearly resolute. Supported primarily by an experienced quartet – Balfour, Birkenhead, Austen Chamberlain, and Churchill – Lloyd George secured a Cabinet warning to Kemal to respect the allied zone of occupation at the Straits; the French premier, Poincaré, agreed, not without misgivings, to the warning. The Cabinet also solicited dominion support, albeit in a clumsy fashion which won backing only from the governments of New Zealand and Newfoundland. Unfortunately, most dominion leaders learned first of the warning from a press communiqué issued from Downing Street rather than directly from the British government. That communiqué, issued on the following day, was so strongly worded that the French government backed off again; only the diligent efforts of the Foreign Secretary, dispatched forthwith to Paris, persuaded Poincaré to maintain even the façade of Anglo-French solidarity. The experience was a wrenching experience for Curzon, who commented about the French premier: 'I can't bear that horrid little man.'[155] Given his lengthier frustrating exchanges with the British Prime Minister, he might well have used the plural. The explosive situation in Asia Minor did not ease until mid-October, when what Churchill described as the worst moment of Anglo-French relations in the twentieth century[156] had passed – alas, he was to preside over worse. In the Chanak crisis, Lloyd George carried with him a reluctant Cabinet and an equivocal Foreign Secretary, at the risk of renewed war; indeed, there are those who have found in these events 'the last occasion on which Great Britain stood up to a potential aggressor before the outbreak of the Second World War.'[157] Yet the price paid by Lloyd George was the fall of his government and his loss of office, which he never regained.

Even informed contemporaries marveled at this conjunction of events, as in Leo Amery's noting that 'a great many people abroad and in the Dominions and not a few at home will be puzzled as to why the crisis should have arisen just at the moment when the Govt has on the whole covered itself [sic] with credit by its handling of the Eastern situation.'[158] The explanation lies in the tenuous dynamic of coalition government: within the Cabinet Lloyd George claimed to feel that he was 'the only Liberal left, the only upholder of the Gladstonian policy.'[159] In recent years Lloyd George had encountered strong opposition to his pro-Greek stance. With the sole exception of Balfour,

> all the others have done their best to obstruct & the W.O. have behaved abominably. However D. [Lloyd George] has got his way, but he is much afraid

lest the Greek attack should be a failure, & he should be proved to have been wrong. He says his political reputation depends a great deal on what happens in Asia Minor.[160]

The domestic dimension of the Chanak crisis is found in its use to fell a leader whose style of leadership had become unacceptable to a number of his Tory allies. Stanley Baldwin, for example, held the mores of the leading members of the coalition in contempt:

You can't imagine the impression the meetings of the Cabinet made on me. I had been in business for years . . . In business you discuss a thing and decide whether to do it or not, but as I watched L. G.'s Cabinet – watching each of its members under a microscope – I felt I was in a thieves' kitchen. Nobody seemed to have any principles. There was the most awful cynicism. Perhaps it was all due to a reaction after the war.[161]

Surely the strain of nearly six years of governing had taken its toll, because the administration was gripped by malaise: the Prime Minister's Secretariat was in near-chaos, with no effective head; the Cabinet was divided, although – ironically – perhaps less so over the Near East than on other issues; even the Court was disturbed by its cavalier treatment at the hands of the regime.[162]

Lloyd George entertained the hope that by giving a strong lead – in a matter which extended the epic struggle of the Great War – others would be compelled to follow, as in fact his Cabinet did; yet he may have mistaken his ability to prevail over opposition within his Cabinet as the key to political developments. Such a key did not turn other important constituencies in his behalf: the public remained indifferent, the press hostile, and vocal sections of Parliament were critical of 'aggressive' actions in the Near East.[163] Yet there is no evidence that the Prime Minister carried on a secret pro-Greek policy behind his Cabinet's back; the Foreign Secretary lost the contest in open Cabinet rather than to a secret cabal.[164] Lloyd George deceived himself that his ability to carry the leading Conservative coalitionists would breathe new life into his administration. In fact he and his Unionist Cabinet colleagues reckoned up the political 'risk' incorrectly, since the rank-and-file remained as determined as ever to break with his leadership.[165]

His critics were particularly appalled by the Cabinet communiqué of mid-September, which was widely viewed as a reckless document.[166] Cabinet records confirm that it was but one product of a Cabinet meeting which reflected 'many ideas but few decisions . . . in the end the Cabinet decided to try something of everything,'[167] including this document, a draft telegram for the dominion premiers, drawn up by Winston Churchill. Neither in its language nor in its tardy dispatch to the dominions did it prove a particularly good idea, and the response was distinctly cool; Mackenzie King sounded the most cynical note in recording in his diary, 'All were inclined to feel whole business "an election scheme" of Lloyd George and Co.'[168] Some of the resulting criticism incorporated the notion that the Cabinet Secretariat had a devious role in the Chanak crisis, an indictment given a place of prominence in the correspondence columns of *The Times*. Alleging that the manifesto of 16 September was 'presumably, due to the existence of the Cabinet Secretariat – an institution unknown to the Constitution, and the sole creation of the present Prime Minister,' J. G. Swift MacNeill judged that the document 'ought to be the death warrant of the Cabinet Secretariat.' Such unfounded allegations were disputed in other portions of the press; the *Yorkshire Post* labeled as 'misapprehension' the belief that the Cabinet Secretariat had acted as a 'pro-war agency' in the Near Eastern crisis; on the contrary, its role was to keep the records of Cabinet deliberations.[169]

Those records – which include a near-verbatim account of the meeting of 15 September – establish that Hankey's office had nothing to do with the fateful communiqué. In the Cabinet, Curzon had been an active, albeit defeated, participant, and ultimately he expressed no dissent from the Cabinet's agreement to take diplomatic and military steps 'to safeguard the neutral zone of the Straits against the Turkish menace.'[170] Although there were no specific instructions given for the issuance of a communiqué/manifesto, both the content and even the tone of the document of 16 September are consistent with the gravity of the measures agreed to by the entire Cabinet. On the following afternoon, Churchill – who had hitherto opposed Lloyd George's pro-Greek predilections but now refused, in his words, 'to scuttle at the approach of armed men' – drafted, at the behest of the premier and his principal colleagues, Curzon excepted, a press communiqué which in brusque language depicted the Turkish menace to the peace.[171] Of the provenance of the document, there could be no question, and Hankey was outraged that his office should reap criticism for Churchill's effort.

> The issue of a statement of this kind is no part of the duty of the Cabinet Secretariat. As a matter of fact, no member of the Cabinet Secretariat saw the statement before reading it in the public press. The allegation . . . that this statement was the result of deliberation at the Cabinet at which the Secretary of State for Foreign Affairs was not present is entirely without foundation.[172]

The latter point arose because Curzon had protested the communiqué drafted in his absence – he had withdrawn to the country following the Cabinet meeting – but Lloyd George retorted that the Foreign Secretary's behavior had been 'extraordinary' and that the Foreign Office functioned only 'sometimes.'[173] The two men were thereafter thoroughly disaffected with one another; Curzon saw in Lloyd George's action confirmation of a pattern of events, although he spared Hankey from his criticism: 'I have suffered as you know terribly from the encroachment of Downing Street but never from yours. You have always been a model of constitutional propriety and personal consideration.'[174] What Curzon characterized as 'the encroachment of Downing Street' led directly to the rupture within the coalition, despite the successful resolution of the Chanak crisis.

Curzon did not press his case in the Cabinet, but he did summarize his case against Lloyd George's 'system' in a letter written on 3 October but characteristically never sent to the premier:

> Thus there has grown up a system under which there are in reality two Foreign Offices: the one for which I am for the time being responsible and the other at Number 10 – with the essential difference between them that, whereas I report not only to you but to all my colleagues everything that I say or do, every telegram that I receive or send, every communication of importance that reaches me, it is only by accident that I hear what is being done by the other Foreign Office; and even when I am informed officially of what has passed there, it has nevertheless been done, in many cases without the Foreign Office, for which I am responsible, knowing that the communication was going to be made or the interview take place . . . There cannot be a doubt that public opinion has not merely condemned this procedure as unconstitutional and improper, but has clamoured without a dissentient voice for its cessation.[175]

While Curzon's particulars were self-serving, Lloyd George's 'system' had troubled others too, for reasons judiciously stated by Harold Nicolson: 'The implication is not that the Prime Minister's methods [in foreign policy] were ever consciously evasive or misleading; the implication is that they were personal, forensic, imprecise, variable, conceited and far too private.'[176] Yet such irregular ways required the confidence of his coalition colleagues and parliamentary supporters.

Such confidence was undermined by the divisive events of autumn 1922, but the Prime Minister could hardly be expected to mend his ways, because a personal approach to affairs of state was the only way in which he could lead.[177] By nature a maverick politician, Lloyd George's politics of improvisation were all too readily equated with a sheer lack of principle. Indeed, he recognized such a criticism of his methods, even if – as in 1922 – he underestimated the gravamen of the charge. In this vein he once remarked to Bonar Law: 'Bonar, you know, I can conceive of circumstances arising in which I might be compelled to act on principle myself – but you can't say that of FE Smith [later Lord Birkenhead] or Winston can you?'[178] Yet he could not afford to look humorously upon the political situation, because with the passage of time the unanswered question of the 1919 General Election – whether the Unionists needed Lloyd George more than he needed them, in order to govern – had been resolved in their favor: the Prime Minister had lost much of his Labour support because of his industrial policy, and he had forfeited some of his

Liberal and radical backing through his Irish policy, despite the settlement of 1921.[179]

Unionist MPs had accepted his war leadership, but, a few Tory leaders aside, 'the Conservatives had never viewed him with trust or affection; and, what was more important, they had never suggested that they meant to remain his allies once he had served his immediate purpose.'[180] Although the leading members of the Cabinet were not prepared to turn the premier out, others were sincerely troubled; Baldwin, of course, was particularly concerned with what he thought the corroding effect of Lloyd George upon his colleagues' moral susceptibilities, and he found in the premier's actions 'a profound threat, made more serious because of the wide appeal which apparently easy, authoritarian solutions had over the slow processes of democracy.'[181] The list of grievances was a long one, but principal items included 'the close conspiracy, the leaks to those papers whose support he needed, the muzzling of the rest of the press, the discussion of Cabinet secrets with Beaverbrook and Rothermere, the prostitution of judicial office and the sale of honours.' Yet it may be argued that Lloyd George's abuses were not so out of step with those of his own contemporaries: his practices differed from those of his time in degree rather than in kind, although his methods were far from circumspect. While his involvement in the sale of honors was evident, he defended his actions with reference to the practices of the time, contending that it was better to sell honors than policies, as he claimed the Tories and Labour regularly did.[182]

Yet when that defence is entered, his idiosyncratic refusal to heed the conventions of the business at hand made for a difference in the method of his operations, if not in the content of his policies. Fittingly, Stanley Baldwin articulated such instinctive feelings at the decisive moment in Lloyd George's fall from power, the meeting of the Unionist MPs at the Carlton Club. The fact remains that Lloyd George's alleged 'adventurism' in the Near East did not precipitate the Tory desire to have done with his leadership; rather the events of the autumn 1922 supplied reinforcement for ousting a leader who no longer fulfilled an essential purpose.[183] According to Beaverbrook, Lloyd George recognized that the changing tides of politics had eroded his ability to lead; he had the option of resigning office, with the Chanak chapter successfully closed, thereby opening the way for the resumption of party government. Why did he not?

> There is only one explanation – infirmity of purpose . . . He knew he was damaging his own best interests by refusing to surrender power for a time. The glitter of his supreme office held him in chains and he could not bear to give up power and patronage, even for a few months or a year or even two, with the prospect of a return to his high office. It was weakness and he knew it was weakness . . . the will had gone.[184]

Politics for Lloyd George had become a means to the end of retaining office: success at Chanak meant power in Westminster. Whether or not aware that 'the communiqué of September 16 had been a stroke of reckless genius justified by the result,'[185] the premier may well have convinced himself that the coalition would survive. Certainly the leading Cabinet ministers stood with him to a man, and even Curzon had been cowed once again into submission. In fact, the Chanak 'success' disposed the Tory coalitionists to push their rank-and-file critics into a corner on the issue of another coalition electoral venture, led by Lloyd George.[186] At this juncture a dispute erupted between the leadership and other groupings within the party – not only back-benchers, but as well a 'revolt of the Under-Secretaries'[187] – and the coalition fell as a result.

Along with the Unionist leaders, Lloyd George failed to take into account political forces below the Cabinet level; Bonar Law, from without, hazarded an explanation which time and the proliferation of government bureaucracy has added force to: 'My experience is that all Prime Ministers suffer by suppression. Their friends do not tell them the truth; they tell them what they want to hear. It was so with Asquith . . . George also was misled. People are always apt to think that what had been will be.'[188] The Lloyd George regime came to its end. What would be the fate of the 'system' which he had forged in war-time to energize the forces of government? Would administrative practices revert to the 'time-honoured' customs which had served his predecessors? Had that 'system' insulated the Prime Minister from political reality, serving to the premier's detriment as an agent of what Bonar Law feared as 'suppression'? It is no exaggeration to state that the fate of the Cabinet Secretariat hinged on Bonar Law's attitude to such questions, since the political succession was his.

3

Crisis 1922

For the Cabinet Secretariat, the political crisis of the autumn of 1922 occurred at a time when, along with the Lloyd George 'system,' the body had sustained mounting criticism. The *Daily Express* had swung into action late in the previous year, and in the course of 1922 both the *Sunday Express* and *The Economist* had joined the fray.[1] In June the well-informed Viscount Esher was sufficiently concerned to write to the Prime Minister that 'Beaverbrook and Co seem in full cry after Hankey and are not easy to whip off.' He suggested that Lloyd George ask two former premiers, Balfour and Asquith, and the titular leader of the Labour party, Adamson, to discuss with him 'the future of a Cabinet Secretariat,' if possible limiting the conversation to 'the necessity for some such body.'[2] Apparently nothing came of the suggestion, although it indicates that Esher once again looked with favor upon Hankey's endeavors; only two years earlier, he had written to Tom Jones in a vein which suggested that a less attractive characteristic of the Lloyd George regime had rubbed off on the Cabinet Secretary: 'When Hankey digs the Secretariat in far deeper than he has at present, it will, as far as its personnel is concerned, disappear with any change of Ministers. The virtue goes out of some men when success touches the hem of their garment. I fear Hankey is one of these.'[3]

The pace of the criticism of the institution quickened in June 1922, when Parliament launched upon its most extensive debate since 1918. On a motion to reduce the parliamentary estimate of the Cabinet Secretariat, Sir Donald Maclean opened for the Liberal Opposition by acknowledging that constitutional usage varied from generation to generation; thus the relevant tests were whether the Secretariat was a useful body and whether its functions conflicted with vital aspects of Cabinet government. On the latter point, he lamented the transfer of power from the Cabinet to the Prime Minister, which characterized Lloyd George's 'system': 'I say that it is not in the interests of the nation that more power should pass into the hands of the Prime Minister. Otherwise, what will happen? We shall, inevitably, be driven to an imitation of the Presidential system.' Turning to the Secretariat, Maclean suggested that it interfered with the Foreign Office and the Civil Service, without any success in discharging its liaison tasks: 'Perhaps the Cabinet Secretariat has this in its favour, that without it things might have been much worse. All that I can say is that it would be rather difficult to have things much worse in many respects than they are.'[4] As had others before him, Maclean confused policy formulation with the mechanism needed for its implementation, but he properly suggested that any such system had to be measured by its results, which were held against the Secretariat's performance. Concern with the Secretariat's anomalous role in the machinery of government was voiced even by coalition supporters; Lord Eustace Percy, for example, granted that the Secretariat possessed no executive machinery, yet he held that in fact it discharged executive functions, which produced 'a constant chopping and changing in the locus of responsibility.' As for the result: 'administrative and executive execution is muddled and weakened and divided and distributed between multifarious agencies.'[5] Authority should be restored to the Cabinet, he concluded.

An outspoken back-bencher viewed a nefarious design behind the confused picture which Percy had depicted:

> [The Secretariat] seems to me rather to be a machine whereby the Prime Minister has brought about . . . what amounts to a revolution in our system of government, a revolution involving a great breach of our Parliamentary traditions and a very great blow at our historical safeguards . . . I believe that many of our present discontents are due to this system of personal Government, which has displaced collective Cabinet responsibility. I believe that this system has been able to grow up only by means of this Cabinet Secretariat.[6]

In the course of the debate, lesser grievances were added to the Opposition's bill of particulars – including the expense of maintaining the Secretariat – but the focus of criticism remained upon the agency which it seemingly provided to enable Lloyd George and, to a lesser extent, his colleagues to evade the pre-war mechanisms of parliamentary scrutiny and accountability. In response, Austen Chamberlain defended the Secretariat and the administrative methods which stood in marked contrast to 'the old unbusinesslike system which nothing but the comparative simplicity of the matters to be dealt with in those days rendered possible at all.' Chamberlain countered the points which had been claimed against the Secretariat: he accepted parliamentary accountability for the ministry, which the existence of a Secretariat did not compromise; he defended the Secretariat's supervision of League of Nations business, which was not alone a Foreign Office concern; he rejected the notion that Britain had accepted 'prime ministerial government.' In sum, the work done at Whitehall Gardens served the Cabinet's collective responsibility:

> So far from the effect of having this record taken being to increase the power of any individual minister, be it the Prime Minister himself, it is an essential feature for the preservation of control by the Cabinet as a whole over the general affairs of the nation. The Cabinet Secretariat has no executive function, has no administrative function, displaces no other Department and does the work of no other Department . . . they are not themselves authorised to take the initiative in any matter of administration, in any matter of legislation, or in any matter of executive action.[7]

Such a blanket disclaimer of abuses revealed the considerable gap – not merely politics – in the perceptions of the role of the Cabinet Secretariat: its defenders looked alone to tightly defined secretarial functions, necessitated by modern demands upon government; its critics instead feared its executive functions and its exercise of influence in undefined ways. It must be added that the Prime Ministers closest to the changes, Asquith and Lloyd George, made no attempt to reconcile the divergent views or to ease the burgeoning acrimony of the exchange. The former premier refused to credit the need for practices which had not been required by the likes of Gladstone, Disraeli, and Salisbury, nor by his own regime: 'The system was neither slovenly nor unbusinesslike, nor in practice, did it lead to misapprehension or confusion.'[8]

Even more regrettably, Lloyd George made no attempt to bridge the gap nor to remove the Secretariat from the harsh glare of politics. The man most responsible for the new system denied that personal government was secured through the agency of an irresponsible department: 'No man who knew anything at all about it could possibly talk like that. They are a communicating Department, they are a means of transmitting to Departments the decisions.' Choosing the example of reparations, Lloyd George contended that the need for co-ordination was self-evident where half-a-dozen departments were concerned to nearly an equal degree. But talk of more than a limited function he rejected: 'The Cabinet Secretariat has nothing whatever to do with any question of policy. It is purely a recording machine . . . This is a machine which is an improvement upon the past. It is a machine which, I venture to predict, no responsible Minister, when he has got the chance, will cast away.' Throughout his speech, Lloyd George took the offensive against his critics, and at its conclusion he inflamed the debate by linking 'the good old dignified ways' to 'the cataract of 1914': 'the world wants a change from the old methods. I am making no comment upon any particular Minister or otherwise – I am simply contrasting one system with another.'[9] In this sense, Lloyd George tied the Cabinet Secretariat to his 'system'; of course, he was correct, but whether he was wise is another matter. If the institution were to survive his own regime, other men would have to disentangle it from his personal methods of governing. Hankey had good reason to be disappointed with the nature of Lloyd George's defence, since he had briefed the premier – as he had Curzon on an earlier occasion; the premier had clearly exceeded that brief in warming to the challenge mounted by the Opposition, which predictably lost its parliamentary appeal.[10]

The bulk of Lloyd George's remarks was derived from a memorandum which Hankey had prepared for him; the Cabinet Secretary had eschewed contentious references to past practices, arguing instead that there was no analogy whatever between pre-war and post-war governmental responsibilities: as inter-departmental problems now constantly arose, there was need for careful co-ordination of the activities of many departments. How much more apt are his concluding sentiments than those with which Lloyd George inflamed the debate:

> The Cabinet is a Committee in continuous session to which are brought from day to day the most baffling and perplexing problems . . . the solution of which requires the most carefully concerted action between a number of Departments and authorities. Surely then the Cabinet is entitled in the present arduous times to such Secretarial assistance as its members require and as experience has shown to be necessary.[11]

Hankey's common sense approach possessed merit: surely the members of the Cabinet should themselves decide how their business was to be carried on – what had sufficed for Gladstone and Disraeli need not dictate the patterns for their successors.

In the wake of the parliamentary exchange, the press examined the Cabinet Secretariat even more closely, although not necessarily more accurately. Thus *The Spectator*, an outspoken opponent of the Lloyd George regime, criticized Hankey's operation for failing effectively to define the government's policy:

> We cannot recall a time when policy was as shifting and as incalculable as it is now. It is never the same from day to day. There are unceasing adaptations, accommodations, surrenders. The Government say that they will never consent to something or other and within a few days they consent. The Secretariat, we are told, is necessary to bring clarity to the work of the Government, but what we see is not clarity but confusion.[12]

Clarity of policy demanded certainty of purpose on the Cabinet's part; for a Secretariat to impose a contrived unanimity upon a divided coalition would have required the office to function in ways which its critics decried. Yet *The Spectator* would not accept the contention that the Secretariat was only a record-keeping body: if that were its purpose, the journal reasoned, then 'surely some member of the Cabinet could be trusted to jot down in ten or twenty lines the decision reached. The record could then be countersigned by the Cabinet, or by the Prime Minister acting on behalf of the Cabinet, when the minute had been read out.' Such a technique would surely have often re-opened discussion, and Cabinet business as a result may never have been concluded, let alone the decisions implemented. For the most part, press notice duplicated criticism voiced in the Commons; in one case, an MP, Sir Henry Craik, reiterated in the debate what he had already written about, at great length in the June issue of *Nineteenth Century*. Admitting that past practices could not bulwark a case against the Secretariat, Craik feared that Secretariat officials would become major figures of state[13] and endanger the balance of Cabinet government: 'And is it not quite possible that in this new and very powerful machinery an ambitious Prime Minister might find a very convenient instrument by which to exercise an authority in even wider spheres, to issue ukases to the Press, and to manipulate to his own purposes the stream of public opinion?'[14] Despite a disclaimer, this cloth was cut to the figure of David Lloyd George. In some quarters, constitutional questions were raised in the name of preserving traditional ways: for example, the editors of the *Law Times* found a structural flaw in the new arrangements: 'The presence of a stranger at a Cabinet meeting divests that meeting of its character as a meeting of the Cabinet, having regard to the oath of a Privy Councillor, by which the obligation of secrecy is imposed as to what happens in the Cabinet.'[15] The point does not impress as a weighty one – Cabinet secrecy had if anything been strengthened through its administration – and one wonders if there were no better constitutional case to be made.

More telling was the argument centering on the size and expense of the Secretariat, especially since the period had been marked by government economies; Hankey had already responded to such pressures, reducing both items from the 1921–2 levels. Maclean had questioned the number required for a record-keeping operation, and the press was even less kind to 'Hankey's Beauty Chorus,'[16] numbering in addition to its principals some forty-seven clerks, twenty-two typists, twenty messengers and fourteen charwomen. The *Weekly Dispatch* was at least novel in explaining the last contingent: 'Three competent officials could do all that is required. The others are writing unnecessary minutes and memoranda, which explains the need for 14 charwomen.'[17] Even George V drew the line at charwomen and excessive numbers, although he left no doubt of his preference for 'the modern Cabinet system with a secretariat.' Oddly, only the curmudgeonly Treasury expressed its assurance that such numbers were required for the operations of the Cabinet Office.[18]

Hankey had conveyed to Lloyd George the information that the

Secretariat had prepared the agenda for, taken, and circulated the minutes of some ninety-three Cabinet meetings in 1921, as well as servicing the meetings of fifty-three Conferences of Ministers, twenty-two meetings of the Home Affairs Committee, seven of the Finance Committee and one hundred and sixty-four meetings of various other Cabinet committees. In the month of January 1922 the Cabinet Office supplied the Secretariats for four major conferences – the Irish, another at Cannes, the Washington Naval and the meeting of the Council of the League of Nations. 'Three men' would have been stretched rather thin! And as well a case could be made for the numbers involved in 'Hankey's Beauty Chorus':

> Throughout the [inter-war] period the ratio of subordinate to senior staff was high, and is largely explained by two factors: first, in the interests of security a good deal of clerical work was involved in recording the distribution and whereabouts of papers; and secondly, as many matters tended to reach the Office when they were at crisis point, a margin of staff had to be available to handle urgent work by day and by night, particularly in the duplication of papers and in their prompt dispatch to the recipients.[19]

The calm elaboration of such practical concerns could well have eased the criticisms directed towards the Secretariat, but Lloyd George chose to do otherwise.

More problematic throughout the 1922 collapse of the regime was the continued close relationship with the Prime Minister's Secretariat, which had over the years caused Hankey concern. The Downing Street 'irregulars' remained highly visible, in marked contrast to the precepts proclaimed in the less frenetic environs of Whitehall Gardens, as subsequently enunciated by Hankey's deputy, Tom Jones: 'The Private Secretary does not seek public power, he nurses instead a passion for anonymity and secret influence. He would be horrified to see anything attributed to his own initiative.'[20] Yet the Prime Minister's Secretariat remained a part of Lloyd George's post-war *modus operandi*,[21] and Hankey had no choice but to co-operate with it: he tacitly acknowledged the role which the premier had assigned to Philip Kerr in the formulation of foreign policy by reporting to him concerning a conversation which he had had with the Italian statesman Sforza.[22] Kerr had come into his own as an adviser to Lloyd George during the Paris Peace Conference, and thereafter his reports were frequent but by no means sinister, and no attempt to undermine the role of the Foreign Office is in evidence.[23] Confronted with a health problem, Kerr concluded in early 1921 that the post-war work which Lloyd George had asked him to undertake was finished, and he thought the same might be said for the work of the Prime Minister's Secretariat:

As to my successor, I cannot find anybody with quite my experience . . . unless you have someone else in mind, I rather think the best plan is to close the Secretariat altogether, economy!!! and divide its functions between Hankey's office and J. T. [Davies]. The Cabinet Office is really your Secretariat and has all the knowledge and experience I can supply. And the other work, now that you have drawn out of the active management of Foreign Affairs, can I think be done by an intelligent Private Secretary under J. T. Davies.[24]

Kerr remained on until May, but Lloyd George disregarded his advice and kept the Prime Minister's Secretariat, now headed by Sir Edward Grigg (later Lord Altrincham). Even from without Downing Street, Kerr continued to discharge an advisory role,[25] a strong indication that for the premier it was not the institution which mattered but instead the men around him and the ways in which he could put them to good use.

In the first post-war years, the advisers in Downing Street functioned as they had in the war, discharging tasks which Frances Stevenson has described as 'a great deal of preliminary work in arriving at decisions . . . beforehand sift[ing] the facts and prepar[ing] memoranda and often convey[ing] messages from him to his Ministers. Such procedure was most distasteful to some Ministers who preferred the old-fashioned etiquette.'[26] In particular, as noted earlier, Curzon and the Foreign Office disliked intensely the goings-on at No. 10, although they extended a grudging tolerance to the counterpart Cabinet Secretariat, to some degree compromised by Hankey's tendency to become 'secretary of everything that mattered.'[27] In the Prime Minister's Secretariat, Grigg took up where Kerr had not quite left off: he paid close attention to the press and tackled a range of detailed tasks which were hardly the stuff of epic policy-making; he did play an advisory role in several spheres of foreign policy, including both the Near East and the daunting question of an extension of the Anglo-Japanese alliance.[28] Grigg was very much his master's servant, but the Prime Minister's Secretariat never won any standing with the departments, precisely because Lloyd George used the institution to fend off ministers intent on dealing with the Prime Minister himself.[29] In addition, the Prime Minister's Secretariat recruited 'outsiders' with a relative lack of knowledge of the internal workings of what is called 'British Central Government.'[30] The Cabinet Secretariat had brought a similar war-time recruitment policy much more into line with orthodox procedures, but Hankey's steady attendance at foreign conferences continued to blur the distinction between the two bodies.

Yet it is difficult to credit the extraordinary degree of journalistic confusion alone to misapprehension: to assert in 1922 that the Cabinet Secretariat was otherwise known as the 'Garden Suburb'[31] required malice, rather than ignorance. With Beaverbrook in pursuit of Hankey, the *Daily Express* merged the Cabinet Secretariat with the 'Downing-street Garden City' and questioned 'why its members are still retained to do work which many people think was just as efficiently done before the war without them.'[32] The Cabinet Office file of press clippings bulges with cases of mistaken identity, most reflecting unfavorably upon its work, but a few editors saw through the welter of confusion. The *Glasgow Herald* properly viewed Lloyd George's system in terms of institutional evolution: 'the introduction of the new [Cabinet Secretariat] system during the war, by an Act of the Executive, illustrates at once the flexibility of the British constitution, and our national preference for the reception of innovations as accomplished facts rather than as theories.'[33] Precisely because the Opposition lacked a constitutional case against the 'accomplished facts,' they chose 'to pose as champions of the authority of the House against an ambitious minister.' Above all else, both Secretariats owed their existence to Lloyd George – and opinions passed on his leadership reflected on them – although insiders knew enough to distinguish between the two. By 1922 an MP, Field-Marshal Sir Henry Wilson, knew both operations well, and he noted in his diary after leaving the debate: 'I could have knocked Lloyd George and his quibbles [sic] with ease, but not without using my inside knowledge, which I did not think was fair. The truth, of course, being that Hankey and his Secretariat are essential, whereas Philip Kerr, Ned Grigg, etc., are poisonous.'[34] Such a view of the Downing Street operation is exaggerated – in light of the historical evidence – but the Cabinet Secretariat had shortly to share with its counterpart the fruits of that 'poison,' which for a time looked very nearly fatal.

In the meantime, how well had the Cabinet Secretariat served its primary function, the maintenance of a record-keeping apparatus for Cabinet government? Certainly the casual but widespread leakage of Cabinet business had been stemmed with the reforms of December 1916; not until 1920 did the Cabinet again take notice of what were described as minor leakages to the press, cautioning 'all persons engaged in publicity on behalf of the Government' that no publication of Cabinet business could be arranged without prior ministerial approval. Nor was this alone a matter of the Prime Minister's Secretariat, as Hankey explained: 'So many Departments nowadays have publicity sections of their own that leakage is much more likely than in the past. The publicity departments, in order to secure a good press, must be strongly impelled to communicate information and I think that this is one source of leakage.'[35] However, ministers were not beyond fault, Hankey added, as on one past occasion he had located the source of a leak in a Cabinet Minister 'attacked by journalists in Downing Street itself on leaving a Meeting.' In his own operation, Hankey had determined to sever all connections with the press, a policy incorporated in 'a standing office order dated December 7, 1921 which lays down that no member of the Cabinet Secretariat Staff is to give interviews or official information of any kind to representatives of the Press in any circumstances whatever.'[36] Clearly, Hankey's hope was to keep the Secretariat beyond even the suspicion of consorting with the press.

In November 1920, the Cabinet Minutes recorded 'a scandalous instance of leakage in editions of the Press issued comparatively early in the afternoon of the previous day, of information regarding the discussion of the Cabinet on the same morning on the subject of Russia, some indication having been given even of the views expressed by individual ministers.'[37] No one could flaw secretarial procedures in this case, because at the Prime Minister's instruction the minutes of this contentious meeting had been drafted so as to reveal no details of individual views; even in that fashion, they had not been circulated until well after the papers involved had gone to press. The guilty parties – and there could not have been much doubt about their identities – were duly cautioned to exercise 'the utmost reticence' along with their colleagues in commenting about Cabinet business.

A little more than a year later, another leakage led to a re-ordering of Secretariat procedures: at a Cabinet meeting on 8 March 1922, the Minister of Labour, Macnamara, complained that proposals which he had earlier presented to the Cabinet had appeared in some detail in the press on the previous day; Churchill, Secretary of State for the Colonies, noted that 'practically the very words he had used in the [Cabinet] discussion in regard to Russian relief' had also been quoted; the Prime Minister himself observed that the first notice of the topics for this Cabinet meeting had come not from the agenda paper but instead from the daily press.[38] Here was unequivocal evidence that several Cabinet documents had fallen into – or been placed in – the hands of the press, and the Cabinet inquired whether the Secretariat could reduce the numbers of Cabinet papers in circulation, particularly those sent to ministers outside the Cabinet. Hankey attempted to reduce the volume and to restrain the flow of such materials, although the restriction did not prove long-term.[39] At this time, the Cabinet also resolved upon a much more stringent circulation of Cabinet Conclusions, which placed complete copies only in the hands of the King and the Prime Minister, with another in the custody of the Secretary; as a result, Hankey had to write personal letters to every minister who had either to implement a Cabinet decision or take it into account – perhaps twenty such letters.[40] This curtailed pattern of vital information remained in effect for the balance of the coalition's existence.

The great value of preserving the confidentiality of Cabinet proceedings is evident in an incident which involved disagreement within the Coalition Cabinet in July 1922. Lloyd George authorized the Secretary to make a full note of the discussion, including specific reference to dissent from several ministers; Austen Chamberlain protested the practice, which 'appeared to him to be at variance with the constitutional rule that ministers were corporatively responsible for all Cabinet decisions.' Arthur Balfour countered that such a convention was rooted in 'the importance of preserving an unbroken phalanx in the face of the public and . . . he did not consider that it was infringed by the confidential record of a dissent.' Chamberlain quickly deferred to his colleague's 'high authority and long experience,'[41] and such important records of dissent – revealing the dynamics of Cabinet government – surface on occasion in the Cabinet records;[42] unintentionally, they serve to inform history, which is indebted to the Secretariat's protection of the confidentiality which ensured freedom of discussion.

The achievements of the Cabinet Secretariat do not address the question which troubled Lloyd George's contemporaries in 1922, namely whether the two bodies primarily served the Prime Minister's personal ends. 'Prime ministerial government' was objectionable enough in many quarters, but the announcement in August 1922 that the Prime Minister intended to write his war memoirs 'by way of reply to the criticism of his direction of the war which were constantly appearing in articles, pamphlets and books'[43] likely reinforced suspicions concerning the use of the Secretariats in such a venture: how else could an incumbent premier accomplish such a daunting project? Though Lloyd George's anger was genuine, a direct response to what he regarded as the misstatements and lies found in the war memoirs of 'Wully' Robertson and his ilk, some of those close to him advised against such an activity while holding office.[44] Along with the misrepresentations in the popular press, the climate of suspicion which gripped British politics in 1922 must be taken into account in any understanding of the Cabinet Secretariat's difficulties. Why such a parliamentarian as Sir Henry Craik should fear for the continuity of personnel in Whitehall Gardens with a change in regimes is otherwise inexplicable, but, in contrast to departmental civil servants, Craik found them

> a body of officers, who have shared the most confidential secrets of one body of ministers, and who be called in turn to share equal confidences with another body of ministers fundamentally differing in regard to every political principle. Even to the well-trained adaptability of our civil servants this transference of service and of intimate confidence must surely present some difficulty.[45]

Nor did Craik have much confidence that a new government could resist using the 'candid records' of a predecessor regime in a partisan fashion. Ironic that a staunch defender of parliamentary government had so little trust in the men who governed, politicians and civil servants alike, but such was the climate of 1922. The *Westminster Gazette*, a staunch Liberal journal, asserted flatly that 'no Cabinet will be willing to go forward with the secretariat of its predecessor.'[46]

In this hostile light, little if any regard was paid to the contention that the new system was required to cope with the gathering pace and complexity of twentieth-century government. Certainly Lloyd George intended to centralize governmental power in his office, and both the War Cabinet and the Cabinet Secretariat were devices to overcome the departmentalism of the old order. Yet to combat departmentalism is not necessarily to overthrow the Cabinet's collective responsibility.[47] However, as a result of the winning war effort mounted by his regime and – it must be added – the premier's instinct for the limelight, he stood head and shoulders above his Cabinet colleagues. By reputation towering above all rivals – even as the political base of his coalition eroded – Lloyd George utilized the Cabinet Secretariat to serve his unorthodox, idiosyncratic ways of resolving government business. The point remains that the premier had not attained his domination of the Coalition Cabinet through the use of the Secretariat to undercut his colleagues; rather, his strength and stature enabled him to use the Secretariat as he did: 'There is no doubt . . . that in the last analysis the Cabinet Secretariat was an auxiliary rather than an agent of power.' Hankey pointed to a mechanism which militated against the premier's use of the Secretariat to arrogate power from his colleagues: 'If anything, the Secretariat would seem to act as a check upon individual action, as it is its duty to communicate the decision to the minister who is called upon to act.'[48] As had been endlessly repeated, the Cabinet Secretariat had no executive functions, but Lloyd George's role, and his influence, could not be so neatly confined. Whatever mechanistic explanations were offered, the association of premier and institution remained: in its inception and development, the Cabinet Secretariat was so much a part of Lloyd George's 'system' that it could not escape criticisms directed at his policies, his practices, or his person.

In sum, the entire question of Lloyd George's 'presidential' style of government has very little directly to do with the functions of the Cabinet Secretariat. Yet that style has been so widely commented upon that the connection cannot be altogether eschewed. Several observations seem to be in order. Even those who contest the concept of the development of prime ministerial 'Caesarism' admit that the Lloyd George regime was an exception: Ian Gilmour, for example, depicts the Welsh radical launching the only attempt to increase the powers resident in Downing Street between the time of Salisbury and Churchill; to achieve such an end, he had to protect himself from the specialist preoccupations of all government departments. Thus 'the Cabinet Office has not pushed the Prime Minister far ahead of the field; it has enabled him to keep up with it, to retain the place he formerly held. Without a Cabinet Office, a Prime Minister would be at the mercy of the Departments.'[49] Certainly the trend to specialization has accelerated since Lloyd George's time, but departmentalism was undoubtedly a force which he had to take into account and attempt to combat. A second critic of the concept of the development of 'prime ministerial government' acknowledges the direction of Lloyd George's intention, but Gordon Walker points to his attempt as an aberration, since decline in the premier's authority ensued. With the subsequent revival of the concept, Gordon Walker identifies Attlee and Eden as premiers who took major decisions without full Cabinet approval. With their actions, the trend resumed, but their procedures reveal that 'partial Cabinets . . . not Prime Ministerial Government, have become an accepted and established part of the Cabinet system.'[50] In a fashion, the precedent had been established in the autumn of 1922: although at that time the whole Cabinet decided policy, a 'partial Cabinet' carried the day, and an even smaller group actually was involved in drafting the communiqué which proved decisive in the Chanak crisis. Yet throughout the entire incident Lloyd George worked within the limits upon 'prime ministerial government' which Gordon Walker insists remain in place: 'The Prime Minister can exercise his greatly enhanced powers only if he carries his Cabinet with him.'[51] Lloyd George managed that; what he lacked was the means to carry the Tory junior ministers and the back-benchers, whose support was required to sustain the coalition in power.

In the other camp, those who see the tides of twentieth-century politics running towards 'prime ministerial government' – Richard Crossman, John Mackintosh, Frank Stacey, and Humphrey Berkeley among more recent commentators[52] – do not describe the Cabinet Secretariat as the agency whereby power has been transferred to Downing Street. Stacey's description is typical: 'the Cabinet Secretariat has grown steadily in importance and has helped to enhance the efficiency of the Cabinet, both as a decision-making body and as a means of co-ordinating the whole Government machine.'[53] Agreeing that the institution provides a kind of 'mantle' which strengthens politically weaker premiers, they attribute the development to Lloyd George: he transformed the powers which he 'exercised by virtue of his personality . . . into an institutional basis by setting up the Cabinet Office.'[54] Despite the continuing dispute concerning a 'presidential' system, there is general agreement that the Cabinet Secretariat, in its formative years, did not provide the means by which Lloyd George won accretions of power at the expense of the traditional collective responsibility of the Cabinet. The point is speculative, but without the Cabinet Office Lloyd George's successors might well have been harder pressed to lead their regimes, lacking as they did the personal dynamism of the Welsh maverick. There is a massive if seldom remarked-upon irony in his making possible a more highly centralized and efficient government for his less persuasive successors, several of whom decried the system which he had forged. The difference remains: Lloyd George's approach to a 'presidential' system was the threat of one individual;[55] the subsequent threat consists instead in the weight of bureaucratic centralization vested in the office. Nonetheless, it must be said of Lloyd George that he had given the office a different working relationship vis-à-vis the Cabinet, but throughout his tenure the Cabinet remained – as was its right – the most important body which he consulted; indeed, it is clear that he had to carry the Cabinet with him in order to make what his critics called his 'personal' policy.[56]

In March 1922, one former member of the Coalition Cabinet denounced the premier's flaunting of collective responsibility: Edwin Montagu, Secretary of State for India since 1917, had published – without consulting the Cabinet – a telegram from the Viceroy criticizing the Cabinet for favoring Greek interests in Asia Minor and Constantinople. Montagu had acted on his own in order to quiet Moslem alarm in India. In the ensuing furor over his action, Montagu resigned his office; he had little choice, because Austen Chamberlain had dissociated the Cabinet from an action taken on a minister's sole responsibility.[57] Montagu reacted bitterly to his colleagues' censure by attacking Lloyd George:

> an accusation of a breach of the doctrine of Cabinet responsibility from the Prime Minister, of all men in the world, is a laughable accusation . . . The head of Government . . . has demanded the price which is within the power of every genius to demand – and that price has been the total, complete, absolute disappearance of the doctrine of Cabinet responsibility ever since he formed his Government.[58]

Montagu was technically in the wrong for acting as he had, although he was angered that the technicality was but a pretext for his removal, as Lloyd George sought to appease the Tory 'Die-hards' in forcing him out; as for invoking the concept of collective responsibility against him, Montagu was stunned: 'The wizard . . . from his cupboard where he has locked his doctrine, brings it out conveniently and makes me the victim of this new creed . . . Cabinet responsibility.'[59] The Cabinet displayed no sympathy for his action, nor, more important, for his criticism of the premier. In an informal discussion presided over by Austen Chamberlain during a suspension of a Cabinet meeting, senior Cabinet ministers agreed that despite regular Cabinet meetings, much more of its work was carried on by Cabinet committees; Balfour thought that 'the whole machine is worked harder than formerly.' Drawing upon his long experience, he defended Lloyd George's activism: 'All Prime Ministers in my time have been charged either with being figure-heads run by abler men or tyrants. There has never been a middle position.' Chamberlain added that the Prime Minister had been careful in putting Cabinet members of divergent views on Cabinet committees, apparently concluding that such a practice dictated against his dominating those committees or excluding proper deliberation. In sum, the Cabinet informally scoffed at the accusation brought against the system of government, namely that, in Chamberlain's phrase, it embodied 'autocracy tempered by disorganisation.'[60] Perhaps more concerned than the Cabinet, Hankey pursued the matter, inquiring privately of Balfour whether he discerned less collective responsibility in the present Cabinet than in its predecessors: 'He absolutely scouted the idea that the sense of Cabinet responsibility is any less now.'[61] The political crisis of autumn 1922 brought to the fore the question of how the Cabinet would discharge its collective responsibility; by that time Hankey's concerns were with the survival of the Cabinet Secretariat, midst the wreckage of the Lloyd George system of government.

Even before the dust had settled at the Carlton Club, Hankey shared with Tom Jones his thoughts on how the Cabinet Office would have to adapt to the fall of the coalition: 'Thinks drastic reduction of staff inevitable . . . The first thing to be shed will be our responsibility for foreign conferences. This will go to the Foreign Office. Next we will shed our relations with the League of Nations. Next restrict as far as possible our responsibilities for committees.'[62] On that same afternoon, Lloyd George commented: 'Hankey, you have written your last Minutes for me,' but not until the next day did he assure the Cabinet Secretary that he should remain on to serve Bonar Law, insisting that 'he would never allow anything to pass that would embarrass me in my loyalty to my new chief.'[63] Although Hankey did not hesitate to sever his official relationship, his actions leave no doubt that a genuine personal affection survived. His emotions rarely surfaced, save in his diary, but he permitted himself a strong expression in inviting, some months later, the former premier to dine with the Cabinet Office staff: 'My dear Chief – that was and I hope one day is to be.'[64] Did he share with Tom Jones the latter's paradoxical – and yet incisive – verdict about Lloyd George: 'one could say fifty things of L. G. that might appear to be contradictory and all would be true'?[65] Never the most consistent of politicians, Lloyd George had revealed himself to Hankey in all his faults and strengths, and the Cabinet Secretary warmed to a man from whom he was temperamentally very different.[66] Above all else, however, Lloyd George had gotten the job done – in war to greater purpose than in peace – and Hankey, time would reveal, did not again encounter his like.

The immediate concern for Hankey and the Secretariat lay in the need to accommodate to a Prime Minister who was very different from his predecessor; in fact, his success in that office depended in part upon his ability to differentiate his style of government from the coalition. Yet Bonar Law had himself been an important figure in that regime, until his own resignation – for reasons of health – in March 1921; indeed, he had been in the chair at the third meeting of the War Cabinet, in those distant days in 1916, at which time the distribution of the Cabinet Minutes had been decided upon.[67] Would four years of service as Lloyd George's loyal second dispose him favorably to the reforms of that period? Or would his new Cabinet colleagues, men who for the most part had rejected Lloyd George's lead, prevail upon him to discard the new machinery of government, as they had removed its founder?

The initial signals of his attitude were ambivalent, but throughout Hankey showed a determination to salvage the Secretariat in a struggle which he had to wage on two fronts: in the political arena, he had to win Law's support for the Secretariat; in the institutional setting, he had to withstand what amounted to a take-over bid from Sir Warren Fisher, Permanent Secretary to the Treasury, who wanted to absorb the Secretariat within his own central department of government. The survival of an independent Cabinet Secretariat was by no means assured, and Hankey's handling of its defence impresses as masterful, given the strong current running against Lloyd George's 'system.' As noted, he was very much aware of the institution's vulnerability, confirmed at a gathering in the Guildhall on 20 October, when 'several people asked me half chaffingly whether I had resigned and alluded to "superfluous" officials.' Directly he secured Lloyd George's approval to place the Secretariat at Law's disposal, while he was still forming his Cabinet. Hankey secured an interview with the Tory leader, and he drew up 'a list of the really urgent questions before the Cabinet on which he could not long defer a decision.' Hankey worded the note carefully, taking particular care not to assume that there would be a Cabinet Secretary, let alone his continuing in the post.[68] In contrast to his willingness to help, Hankey discerned a move from his opponents when he learned that 'the usual batch of Foreign Office telegrams' had not been sent to his office: 'This looked ominous, as I had read in the newspaper that Lord Curzon had been seeing Bonar Law, and it rather looked as though this was a sign that the insistent and much repeated newspaper stories were true and that they had decided to scrap the Cabinet Secretariat.' Yet it transpired that Lord Curzon had stopped the entire Cabinet circulation at a time when 'there was practically no Cabinet,' and the Permanent Under-Secretary immediately arranged to send the usual papers through to the Cabinet Office.

Despite the false alarm, Hankey decided to yield gracefully to the Foreign Office what would otherwise likely be summarily taken, although he reasoned that in so acting he would immediately effect 'big economies' in expenditure. Thus he informed the Permanent Under-Secretary, Sir Eyre Crowe, that he would propose to Law that

> the League of Nations section should be handed over to the Foreign Office, and . . . that the Cabinet Secretariat should drop out of all International Conferences. I pointed out that I had long favoured both courses, as he knew, and that it was Lloyd George and Balfour who had always insisted on my doing this work. I also recalled that in fact I had never interfered with the advisory functions of his office, and had never had any quarrel with him or the Foreign Office in fulfilling my secretarial functions, but I thought that in principle it was only right that for the future he should undertake both functions.[69]

Not surprisingly, Crowe agreed to absorb these activities, 'even if they did not at first do them so well.' Hankey found Crowe very complimentary; nonetheless, one wonders if the Permanent Under-Secretary credited the entire conversation, given Hankey's involvement – whether or not voluntary – in past incursions upon Foreign Office preserves. For his part, Hankey turned to the main business at hand, namely Bonar Law's attitude, calling upon him at his home:

> he asked me point blank if I was prepared to serve him as loyally as I had served Lloyd George. I replied that, if he wanted me, I would serve him as loyally as I had served Asquith and Lloyd George and that the latter was quite prepared that I should do so. 'That is the answer I had expected', he said, 'and you can help me at once because your experience in these [constitutional] matters is unique.' [Subsequently, Hankey asked him] point blank if he intended to have a Cabinet Secretariat or to scrap it. He at once replied that he intended to continue the system of recording Cabinet conclusions, which he thought essential to businesslike procedure. But he thought it essential that the cost should be curtailed. I said I would work out the plans for this, if he would decide the broad lines, and I could suggest the lines to him in three minutes.[70]

With Stanley Baldwin joining in the conversation, Hankey outlined the abandonment of Foreign Office business and proposed some personnel cuts on the Cabinet side of the office business, which his new masters thought 'a great help.' On such a positive note Hankey took his leave after informing Law and Baldwin that he could give them 'a defence' against criticism of the Secretariat.

Yet the crisis was far from over, although the Cabinet Secretary immediately set about 'save[ing] the ship by chucking ballast overboard' in implementing the economies promised to Bonar Law: he found the business of sacking some of his assistants 'very trying,' although one individual took the action so unpleasantly that the Secretary did not after all regret his departure.[71] Hankey was particularly anxious to retain Tom Jones, having raised the matter at his meeting with Law. Clouds continued to gather round the Cabinet Office, as Hankey noted in his diary on 25 October:

> I have been fighting all day with my back to the wall for my position. I am up against the whole hierarchy of the civil service, who have taken advantage of Lloyd George's fall to try and down me. Luckily their representative was Warren Fisher, a personal friend and a gentleman. I think I have succeeded in retaining all essentials.

The Cabinet Secretary took the care to dictate a fuller account of these proceedings which exposes the inadequacy of this diary entry.[72] Far from acting as a representative of an irate Civil Service, Fisher is depicted as intent upon incorporating the Secretariat within the Treasury: after the initial skirmish with Fisher, Hankey learned from Law that his statement of the principles for the re-organization did not 'quite conform' with Fisher's understanding of the arrangements which he had struck with the Cabinet Secretary at that meeting.[73] Hankey was taken aback when Law asked him to agree on a 'formula' for the status of the Cabinet Secretariat, so that he might make reference to it in an address scheduled for Glasgow on the 26th. The dispute centered on the status of the office: Hankey wished to regain its position 'under the War Cabinet system, when it appeared for parliamentary scrutiny on the general vote of the Treasury' – as had been the case until 1921 – but Fisher had looked to its becoming 'in effect . . . a branch of the Treasury.'[74]

When Fisher and Hankey sat down for another discussion, the Cabinet Secretary protested what he described as the 'planting' of 'a scheme of this kind (which, he afterwards admitted) had been maturing for a long time without talking it over beforehand.'[75] He learned that the Cabinet Secretary would be quite unaffected in his work under Fisher's scheme, as he would retain direct access to the Prime Minister, but Fisher would not guarantee that his successors would accept such a special arrangement. Even more pressing for Hankey was the status of his office in the eyes of the Whitehall community, politicians, and civil servants alike:

> the prestige of the post of Secretary of the Cabinet and Committee of Imperial Defence would be largely lost and . . . the Secretary's position with other Departments would be seriously weakened if they regarded him as they would be entitled to regard him, merely as a Treasury official. Cases often arose where the Treasury was in conflict with other Departments and these were brought to the Cabinet or the Committee of Imperial Defence, and the Cabinet Secretary, though possessing no advisory duties, ought to be entirely unbiassed.

With careful argumentation, Hankey persuaded Balfour – whose counsel he sought, although Balfour was no longer in the Cabinet – that such a position was unacceptable, and the elder statesman advised him that, should Fisher press his point, Hankey should resign as Cabinet Secretary but remain on as Secretary of the CID. Returning to the fray with Warren Fisher, Hankey again heard the latter's view that 'the Treasury is the central Department of the Government and for that reason he considered it essential as part of Treasury control (though he did not like the word) that the Cabinet Secretariat should become an integral part of the Treasury.' In reply, Hankey admitted that such an approach 'might or might not be logically defensible and if he was starting a Cabinet Secretariat afresh as a new scheme, it might or might not be the right way to do it.' Yet in reality Hankey's own experience mattered, and he had run the office in an autonomous fashion. He would not undertake to run it in Fisher's fashion; without attaching undue importance to matters of form, Hankey claimed he could not function effectively without 'that shred of prestige that attached to a semi-autonomous position.' He might have used stronger if less personal language, for it is clear that Hankey looked to the Cabinet, not to the Treasury, as his masters.

The thrust of Hankey's admitted 'personal appeal' went home: Fisher agreed to concede what Hankey desired, although he considered the fate of the Cabinet Office after Hankey quite a different matter. Thus the two administrators hammered out a proposed statement for Bonar Law:

> Part of the work of the Cabinet Secretariat is being distributed among other Government Departments. I have already given orders for all work connected with the League of Nations and International Conferences to be handed over to the Foreign Office. The remaining secretarial work required by the Cabinet and the Committee of Imperial Defence will be retransferred to the Treasury vote.

Though 'retransferred' impresses as a curious turn of phrase, Hankey deliberately resorted to it instead of the word which Fisher had sought to use, namely 'transferral.' The Cabinet Secretary sought to underscore the reversion to the position which had operated prior to the Cabinet Secretariat's separate parliamentary vote, which dated only to March 1921.[76] Such a mechanism would create the 'semi-autonomous' status which he sought for the Cabinet Office, even if it involved the 'foster-parentage' of the Treasury.

Yet the struggle was not yet over, because Bonar Law's Glasgow speech displayed a hostility to the size and the autonomy of the Cabinet Secretariat:

> We [the Cabinet] have decided to bring the Cabinet Secretariat in its present form to an end (Cheers.) Now that does not mean that everything connected with it has got to go. I wish to make that quite plain . . . There are two things which we must retain, and I believe honestly that no man who has tried both systems will have any doubts about it. We must have an agenda at our meetings, and we must have a

definite record of our decisions . . . But there is no need, I am sure, of the big body, which I believe was necessary during the war and immediately after it, but which can come to an end now. I am convinced that the work can be done as efficiently, and far more economically, by having the Cabinet Secretary . . . and whatever help he needs treated as part of the Treasury, which is the central department of government.[77]

Bonar Law noted the assumption of some Secretariat responsibilities by the Foreign Office, which would realize economies and, more important, encourage a resumption of traditional patterns in the conduct of foreign affairs. The speech caused Hankey grievous disappointment, not only with the Prime Minister's failure to stress the 'retransfer' arrangements contrived with Fisher but also with the tenor of his campaign oratory:

He had managed to convey the impression that we were to be absorbed into the body of the Treasury, which was exactly what I wished to avoid. Moreover he had omitted to do what I had begged him to do, and to say something which would make clear that we had in fact not encroached on other Departments, and had done our work efficiently and well. In fact, as Lord Esher said in a telegram he had conveyed the impression that all the allegations against the office were true.[78]

Hankey pursued his dissatisfaction with Warren Fisher, proposing an inquiry to settle the question of the Secretariat's role: 'I could not honourably or loyally accept the new post until I had removed the stain from the office in regard to my previous administration.' After considering the request, Fisher refused to agree: 'There was no precedent in the case of the civil service, and there were many precedents to the contrary. Civil servants were supposed to be anonymous, and it was their business to put up with attacks until Ministers defended them in Parliament.'[79]

Finessing the point that in this case the attack came from a minister – indeed the first minister – Fisher suggested that in lieu of an inquiry he accept a statement made in Parliament refuting such charges; Hankey temporized, but the Permanent Secretary continued with what Hankey thought an 'extraordinary' proposal,

that in addition to continuing [as Secretary of the Cabinet and CID] I should also become Clerk of the Privy Council – practically a sinecure. The post will shortly be vacant as Sir Almeric Fitzroy, the present Clerk, has been convicted of bothering women in the [Hyde] Park, and even if he wins his appeal, will probably have to retire. The proposal of course eases everything. The Cabinet [is] constitutionally a Committee of the Privy Council, as the C.I.D. is of the Cabinet. The whole arrangement is symmetrical and logical, but one that I have often thought of. Fisher then astonished me by saying it had been in his mind throughout.[80]

With good reason, the Cabinet Secretary thought the proposal a *volte face* on Warren Fisher's part, and he disbelieved the latter's claim to have had such a scheme long in mind; instead, Hankey thought that his demand for an inquiry had placed the Treasury and Bonar Law 'in a cleft stick': 'If they granted an impartial inquiry, I should get such a flaming report that everyone would say – " Why on earth did you abolish it? " If they refused an inquiry people would say they were afraid of it.' Hankey recorded in his diary that Fisher did not dispute his comparison of the war-time achievements of the Cabinet Secretariat to the utter failure of the central department of government, the Treasury:

It had shown neither foresight nor imagination nor organising capacity, and had plunged the country into something like administrative chaos until the War Cabinet machine came to the rescue. This he did not dispute, and even strengthened what I said. He must have realised that if I developed this case before an impartial tribunal the Treasury [would] look rather silly.[81]

A curious conversation, this: there is no reason to doubt that Hankey's dislike of the Treasury was deep and intensely felt; but would Hankey go out of his way to attack its performance at precisely the time when the tide appeared to have turned; would Fisher meekly agree to a disparagement of the institution which he headed, although only since 1919?[82] Yet so reads Hankey's record, to which he appended his own suspicion that Fisher was prepared to take the post as Cabinet Secretary, if Hankey had to step down; Hankey associated this possibility with 'a long dated civil service cabal' to force his departure, but there is no evidence to confirm either notion.[83] In either event, Fisher and Hankey parted with the understanding that the latter would consider the proffered parliamentary 'whitewash' along with the Clerkship.

The Cabinet Secretary informed his staff of these recent developments: Tom Jones and his anxious associates thought the notice of absolution in Parliament as much as civil servants could hope for, but they were very much taken aback as Hankey continued enthusiastically about the Clerkship:

Hankey told us that whenever he had seen Sir Almeric [Fitzroy] he had said to himself: 'There goes me.' 'The Cabinet was a committee of the Privy Council; what more proper than that the Secretary of the Cabinet and the Committee of Imperial Defence should also be Clerk to the Privy Council. Besides it would restore the relations with the King which he enjoyed in the pre-L. G. days when after each meeting of the CID he reported in person to the King. It would enhance the prestige of the office to be thus in touch with the Sovereign.'[84]

The Secretary's enthusiasm for the symmetry of the arrangement and the prestige attendant to it did not carry over to his associates; Tom Jones recorded that he 'relapsed into a painful silence,' apparently fearing for Hankey's integrity, and according to him, Rupert Howorth commented that 'Only Dumas could do justice to the events of this day!' The Deputy Secretary's suspicions were misplaced: the Cabinet Secretary had already taken care to protect Jones' post – although his associations with Lloyd George had been close – and generally he looked to spare his senior staff.

Yet Hankey might have been more convincing had he advanced at this time the explanation that his appointment as Clerk solved a continuing problem, reflected in criticisms voiced by 'self-styled constitutional authorities' that the presence of a Secretary not sworn to secrecy violated the secrecy of Cabinet meetings: the Clerk in fact subscribed an oath very similar to that of the Privy Counsellors.[85] A constitutional point to be sure, but it was not one which much preoccupied the press, which continued to question both the need for, and the performance of, the Cabinet Secretariat.

Bonar Law's Glasgow speech was widely reported in the midst of the electoral campaign; *The Times* endorsed his call for a return to 'normal procedure in methods of government.' In its first leader, the prestigious journal inexcusably fostered the confusion of the two Secretariats by claiming that Hankey's body 'in practice became a Prime Ministerial Department for the conduct of important national affairs apart from, or even in subversion of, well-tried constitutional practices and safeguards.'[86] Confident that the quarry was in their sights, the Beaverbrook and Rothermere newspapers went to even greater lengths: the *Daily Mail* asserted that 'Sir Maurice Hankey's share in the direction of the country has been distinctly unconstitutional'; Beaverbrook's *Evening Standard* engaged a man whom Hankey had once dismissed from his staff to write a lengthy article describing the Secretariat as 'simply an expansion of Sir Maurice Hankey,' which was involved in 'issue[ing] orders to all the Ministers, who become mere subordinates.'[87]

At his next meeting with Bonar Law, on the 29th, Hankey responded in a direct way to the Prime Minister's raising matters of Cabinet business, replying that he could not do so unless he knew that he would be able to continue on as Cabinet Secretary. As well, he had prepared what he described as a 'resigning document for publication if necessary' which he handed to the Prime Minister, recounting the concerns which he had previously raised with Warren Fisher:

> He [Bonar Law] read it, said I was too sensitive, and then promised to meet me everywhere – a statement in Parliament refuting the foul accusation against the Cabinet Office, i.e. encroachment on Foreign policy; the statement of Sept. 16th; overstaffing and extravagance; and interference with the press. Bonar also promised that we should revert to the position of a subordinate dept. of Treasury and should not be swallowed by the Treasury, and that I should have my own staff, which I volunteered to reduce to a minimum.[88]

The Prime Minister also indicated that he had spoken to Wickham Steed of *The Times*, protesting the recent criticisms of the Cabinet Office. Although pleased with Bonar Law's position, Hankey still harbored suspicions about the designs of Warren Fisher: 'The Treasury began by trying to swallow us from the head. The mouthful was too big. Now they will try to swallow us from the tail.' The Cabinet Secretary resolved not to accept his 'vital clerical machine' being put on the Treasury vote, since that would entail control by someone else.[89] Since that someone was likely to be the Treasury, Hankey once again committed to paper, within his diary, an angry indictment of that 'so-called Central Department of the Government [which] has failed as regards the past, present, and future.'[90]

Further meetings between Fisher and Hankey followed, and the Permanent Secretary to the Treasury gave way:

> [he] said I should have my staff on my own vote as a subordinate Dept. of the Treasury . . . He said he would put forward a Minute to the effect that in his view the logical plan was the absorption of the Cabinet Office into the Treasury; that owing to my personal position he would not press it and would agree to the Cabinet Office being a subordinate Dept. of the Treasury; that there was a minor question as to which vote the clerks and typists etc. should be on, in which we also disagreed, but he did not think it necessary to quarrel over it and would therefore agree to let me have my way.[91]

Fisher had very little to show for his efforts, for there is good reason to think that he was intent upon the absorption of the Secretariat: far from the Cabinet Secretary serving as a fourth Treasury Controller, Fisher had secured only Hankey's 'consent to leave Whitehall Gardens and to go to the other side of Whitehall, where . . . [he] should be under the same roof as the Prime Minister.' The Cabinet Secretary had anticipated such a move[92] – in fact he personally never made the trip, although he served nearly another sixteen years in his post. Even this rumored shift won the new regime little more than laughter at Lloyd George's hands: in a speech replying to the serious allegations which his successor had endorsed, Lloyd George attacked the lack of concrete proposals – he could find only two – masking as the new government's electoral program. One such proposal, he noted, involved no more than putting 'Sir Maurice Hankey, the Cabinet Secretary, into a pantechnicon van and transfer[ing] him from one side of the street to the other.'[93]

Nonetheless, Sir Warren Fisher held out for a continuation of the Secretariat's status only for the duration of Hankey's tenure of office, which angered the Cabinet Secretary, who considered this a remarkable gloss on Fisher's willingness to accept Hankey's case.[94] Yet Fisher had deferred to Hankey's 'personal position,' and thus his new proposal represented a skilled withdrawal, albeit a defeat for his design. For his part, Hankey objected to any inference that the Secretariat would one day be 'swallowed' whole into the Treasury; he maintained that any declaration of principle concerning the distant future of the Secretariat would elicit a similar declaration of interest on his part. Rather than continue the exchange of views, Fisher settled for the abstract principle that the Treasury was 'the natural body to provide for the secretarial needs of the Cabinet,' wording which Hankey agreed to in the joint draft at long last agreed to on 7 November.[95] With his post securely in hand, and his office possessed of an effective autonomy, Hankey noted in his diary on the following day: 'I hope the matter is closed.' And so it was, except for a renewed struggle when Hankey stepped down as Secretary to the Cabinet in 1938; although the two men disputed the succession at that time, the independence of the Cabinet Office had been won in 1922. In the years that followed, Hankey and Fisher worked closely together, in an especially significant way with regard to the vital question of British rearmament in the 1930s.

What had their fortnight of such civil but determined strife concerned? For Hankey's part, the issue was no less than the survival of the Cabinet Secretariat as it had developed in war and peace, beholden to no master save the Cabinet. In this sense, Hankey sought to conserve the mechanism which he and Lloyd George had forged to bring order and efficiency to the increasingly complex business of government. Sir Warren Fisher stood for reform, in the name of the central department of government, but reform to what end? Hankey and his Secretariat stood as a formidable obstacle to the further centralization of the bureaucracy under the Treasury upon which Fisher was intent: whether his immediate purpose was to transform Hankey into a Treasury official or to replace him with a 'regular' civil servant,[96] Hankey's operation remained outside the circle of 'Treasury control.' Yet there was more than administrative centralization to Fisher's conception of the Civil Service: Horace Wilson has pointed to his distaste for the corruption of the Lloyd George regime, his dislike of the Garden Suburb and the inefficient administrative arrangements around the person of the Prime Minister. The new premier could tend to the political operation centered in Downing Street, but Fisher could hardly ignore that auxiliary of power, the Cabinet Secretariat, under the direction of a civil servant who was not accountable to the central department of government. Such an anomaly must have troubled Fisher, since the reorganization of 1919–20, including the designation of the Permanent Secretary as Head of the Civil Service, had gained for the Treasury 'a completed circle of control . . . at no time in the past had the relationship of Treasury control with the machinery of government been so logically formulated or so clearly enunciated.'[97] Very likely in Fisher's mind, that 'circle' was not quite complete, and thus the 'take-over' bid of 1922 is readily understood.

Nonetheless, Fisher consistently held that the re-organization 'made no change so far as the position of the Secretary to the Treasury in his relationship to the [Civil] Service is concerned,' contending that a Treasury Blue Note of 1887 had alluded to the dual functions which he discharged. In fact, Stanley Baldwin had to admit in Parliament that while the association of the two functions dated to 1867, the file containing the official Treasury Minute and certain related papers had been missing for more than fifty years.[98] Though a source of embarrassment for the Treasury, the missing file essentially made no difference, as Fisher was able to sustain the association of the two; one of his successors noted that the re-organization of 1919–20 'substituted for a rather vague informal arrangement something clear, precise, and formal.' However, this successor, Sir Edward Bridges, acknowledged that in one matter Fisher had outreached himself, commenting that because 'the Cabinet Secretariat serves all Ministers, it is right that it should not be absorbed into the Treasury.'[99] Bridges had served both as Cabinet Secretary and as Permanent Secretary to the Treasury, and his testimony bears directly upon the soundness of Hankey's insistence upon institutional autonomy.

Yet in all fairness to Fisher, his desire to absorb the Cabinet Secretariat was but a part of a greater campaign to insulate the Civil Service from partisan politics, so that with the Army, Navy, and Air Force the Civil Service would constitute 'one Service of the Crown with four Divisions.'[100] Concurrently, he sought to abolish the distinction between the Foreign and the Home Civil Service; here too his over-riding concern was the efficiency of the public service, reflecting an intention 'so to reform the Civil Service as to make of it a single efficient entity, a unified machine in which advancement came by merit, whose standards of conduct were of the highest and whose administrative capabilities would not be impeded by jealousies or red tape.'[101] In considerable measure Hankey sympathized with Fisher's design, since he had been sufficiently discomfited by the activities of the Downing Street 'irregulars' to welcome the maintenance of professional standards. At the same time, Hankey would surely have agreed with Thomas Balogh's judgment, based upon the experiences of two world wars, that such professionalism encourages the development of a mandarin caste, superb in the execution of policy but woefully deficient in the ability to formulate new policies. In the context of war, Balogh argues, 'whenever any effort had to be organized, indeed palpably threatening disaster averted, outsiders had to be recruited to take charge.'[102] In such a context, Balogh viewed Fisher's formal appointment as Head of the Civil Service as 'total victory' for the bureaucrats in the struggle with the 'outsiders' whom Lloyd George had used to bypass administrative obstacles to a successful war effort. Yet Warren Fisher was no orthodox 'mandarin,' since he was from the first a reformer intent upon the eradication of departmentalism and the unification of the Civil Service.[103] On the other hand, Hankey – despite his military background and experience as CID Secretary – must be ranged with the 'outsiders,' among the most important innovators of the First World War. Thus his resistance to Fisher's scheme represented a defence of progressive innovation in government, undertaken in order to enable the Cabinet and the Prime Minister to cope with the increasing complexity of twentieth-century government.[104] Like Fisher, Hankey feared a revival of departmentalism, although the Cabinet Secretary had in mind a massive exercise on the part of the Treasury, at the expense of effective government. Though the two men were reformers, Hankey had accomplished his and wished to protect it; Fisher wished to close his 'circle' in 1922. Much had been at stake as they clashed: in fact the survival of the Cabinet Secretariat, cast along lines laid down in the Lloyd George era, serves as proof that Hankey had waged his struggle against Fisher's design and Law's apparent indifference in a worthy cause which time has sustained.

An immediate task for Hankey was settling with the new Cabinet the way in which its members wished him to handle its business. Already by the 30th of October, the Cabinet Secretary summed up for Bonar Law the procedures followed by the coalition, as amended since the time he had left that body; he took care to spell out an exception to a general rule concerning the contents of the minutes:

> The record under each heading is as short as possible, unless the Cabinet itself desires a full record. Sometimes a Minister who has to make a speech has asked for a full record. If new facts are introduced during the meeting, such as a telegram which has not been circulated, a short precis of the reasons for a decision is given, but this precis is anonymous and the views expressed by individual Ministers are only occasionally recorded at their request.[105]

On the following day, Hankey drew up 'Draft Instructions to the Secretary of the Cabinet,' which, slightly revised and provisionally approved, became the guidelines for the new administration.[106] At the first meeting of the new Cabinet on 1 November, the Secretary was charged with preparing the Agenda Paper in accordance with the premier's wishes and with attending Cabinet meetings to record conclusions; Hankey personally was buoyed by the 'many flattering tributes' paid him by members of the new Cabinet.[107] Further, the Cabinet reaffirmed recent practices of the Secretariat with regard to succinct minutes – 'in the absence of instructions to the contrary the record is to be as short as possible, and, apart from the conclusion itself, should normally be limited to such explanation as is indispensable to render the conclusion itself intelligible.'[108] Provision was made for the expression of individual dissent, again confirming recent practices. A departure was effected in the Cabinet's willingness to widen the circulation of Cabinet Minutes, in their entirety: ministers retained the responsibility for communicating relevant decisions to their own departments.[109] No doubt Hankey welcomed a procedure which freed him from an onerous process of selection; an additional benefit was the underscoring of the Secretariat's liaison function, because no ministers could be bypassed, so far as Cabinet records were concerned. These procedural decisions reveal that campaign oratory aside, Bonar Law, who was familiar with the Secretariat's work, recognized the utility of the institution. While Hankey had readily yielded work which gave the appearance of encroaching upon departmental responsibilities, the core of his operation was intact.

Bonar Law tempered his campaign criticism in short order: where previously he had not countered the charge that the Secretariat was overstaffed and too expensive, on the 2nd of November he reminded his audience of the conclusion of the Geddes Committee, namely that the size of the body was proportionate to the work of the office. He insisted that the changes within the Secretariat were of a piece with the change in regimes:

> It is not . . . that it has been an extravagant and wasteful department. I have made that change with the approval of my colleagues, because I think that now the whole system ought to be altered if we are to get back to the old customs regarding the essential machinery of government . . . The Romans, politically, were a very wise people. They had a different system in peace and war . . . During the war we set up a War Cabinet. You had to have things centralised. That was right in war, but now we have come back to normal times. Let us do as the Romans did; let us get back to normal machinery.[110]

Law himself sought a different role from that of his predecessor, who had settled major matters by himself: 'That is not my idea. My idea is that of a man at the head of a big business who allows the work to be done by others and gives it general supervision. That is my idea of the work of the Prime Minister.' In Bonar Law's mind, Lloyd George had too often beaten the drums of war; his aim was to tidy up the latter-day Roman Empire. As 'businessmen' had taken up the tasks of government, the collective responsibility of the Cabinet prevailed over the dominance of a single individual. Yet the Tory government recognized that the patterns of secretarial work could be altered to accommodate the different needs of the post-war period.

One further eruption occurred within those ranks: in this unnecessary instance, the censure of 'the too powerful and too numerous Cabinet Secretariat'[111] came from an individual, Lord Curzon, who had as recently as 23 October promised to defend the Secretariat publicly. Curzon's censure was doubly gratuitous, as Hankey recorded with distaste verging on contempt:

> He had actually asked me to lend a stenographer to report the [electoral] meeting and I sent Owen my best man. After the meeting Owen came to me very depressed and read the passage. Then I got a message that Curzon particularly wanted the

speech today. Previously he had said tomorrow would do. I tried to borrow some 'dictatees' from the F.O. but their people had all gone, so poor Owen had to work to 9:30 p.m. to reproduce it. How nice? You abuse us like that and then sponge on our efficiency because the rotten Foreign Office cannot provide an efficient stenographer.[112]

The Cabinet Secretary immediately remonstrated with the Foreign Secretary both about his remarks – Curzon could hardly claim to having been misquoted – and the abuse of his staff:

I pointed to the difficulty of maintaining the morale of the office when they were asked to work late to record the false charges made by a Minister whom we had regarded as a friend. Lord Curzon was frightfully upset. Said his words had been hasty and unpremeditated and delivered on the spur of the moment. I made him feel, he said, that he would never deliver another speech again.[113]

Proffered a public apology, Hankey declined rather than call attention to what *The Times* had not after all printed, but instead he called together his staff, pledged them to secrecy and read them Curzon's recantation of 'words which were certainly never intended to convey any hostile criticism.'[114]

Yet the bitterness felt within the Secretariat did not dissipate forthwith, as Lawrence Burgis many years later recollected the Foreign Secretary's 'double-faced action . . . he was the champion fence-sitter of all time.'[115] Hankey's own feelings were as acute, as Tom Jones recorded barely a week after the episode:

He mentioned the Curzon incident and had by this time realized how contemptible Curzon's action had been. I said L.G. would never have done that and that in fact in any crisis of this kind he was much the greater gentleman than the noble Marquis. He agreed and said the same was true of Balfour. As to Bonar Law's public utterances on the subject he felt he had been very tepid in his treatment of us and had not erred on the side of generosity.[116]

There is ample justification for Hankey's feelings towards the premier and his Foreign Secretary in the events outlined above, but Hankey's disposition could not have been improved by the repeated failure of the Cabinet Secretariat to disappear as a campaign issue when the general election drew to a close. Bonar Law's words with Wickham Steed did not prevent *The Times* from listing 'Abolition of the Cabinet Secretariat' among the planks of the Unionist platform.[117] The Tories were confirmed in office by the electorate, and the reversion to a more evident pattern of collective responsibility persisted, although Hankey's operation represented a survival of war-time 'reform.'[118] Once the dust of the campaign had settled, the Prime Minister announced, on 27 November 1922, that his government would retain the Cabinet Secretariat 'to provide such secretarial service as the Cabinet requires to facilitate the transaction of its business.'[119] At the same time he noted a reduction in the number of staff and a transfer – or in Hankey's terminology, 'retransfer' – of its estimate to the Treasury and Subordinate Departments vote. Though no encomiums were addressed to Whitehall Gardens, Hankey could take satisfaction from the subsequent clarification of his own position: 'The Cabinet Secretary is, like any other, a permanent Civil Servant, and I think his experience with one Government would be of value to the next.'[120] Stanley Baldwin announced that the Secretariat staff, which on 1 October had numbered 102, had been reduced to 63, with another 23 declared redundant and put on notice.[121] A Cabinet Secretariat reduced in size and shed of ancillary responsibilities had assumed a permanent status.

Government spokesmen insisted that the Cabinet Secretariat now had no scope for policy-making. Such a description recalled Hankey's own involvement in international conferences: between November 1921 and May 1922, the Cabinet Secretary had spent seven months in attending the Washington Naval Conference and the Genoa Conference, although Balfour's praise of Hankey's role left no doubt of his secretarial contributions: 'What on earth should we have done if you had not developed your admirable machinery for extracting the required needles from the large bundles of hay which accumulate round any prolonged conference?'[122] To be sure, no evidence that Hankey actually formulated 'policy' exists, although his influence upon the likes of Balfour and Lloyd George cannot be gainsaid.[123] Perhaps such ambiguity accounts for Baldwin's inept handling of a parliamentary question whether 'the former practice of using the Secretariat for conducting foreign negotiations' had ceased; he replied 'absolutely,' although he continued – when pressed by Austen Chamberlain – that to the best of his knowledge the Secretariat had not been used for that purpose.[124]

Nonetheless, Hankey had already been informed – on 30 November, when Bonar Law had delimited the Cabinet Secretary's role to the keeping of Cabinet records[125] – by the premier himself that he would be associated in the 'conduct' of foreign policy negotiations in the immediate future:

> To-day Bonar Law astonished me by saying that he wants me to undertake the secretarial work for the big conference which is to meet in London next week on reparations – Poincaré, Mussolini, Theunis etc. I urged that the Foreign Office should undertake it, but he said he thought I should have to, as the F.O. were already strained in providing a secretariat at Lausanne. I was vastly tickled at this request, after the speeches he and Curzon have made to the effect that never again shall the Cabinet Secretariat take part in International Conferences. Even if I do not act as Secretary it is very humourous that I should have been asked to do so.[126]

At the conference, which centered on the conversations of the four premiers, Hankey found himself, 'once more in the familiar role of secretary to a meeting of Prime Ministers.'[127] In the meantime, Thomas Jones, for whose continuation as Deputy Secretary Hankey had appealed to Bonar Law, had been pressed into service writing speeches for the new premier, as he had for Lloyd George.[128] Thus the two leading figures in the Secretariat were asked to play personal as well as institutional roles within the new regime, whatever the talk about the Cabinet Office serving only the record-keeping needs of the Cabinet.

In institutional terms, Hankey was quite content with the developments since the first Cabinet meeting, although these were not without irony, as he recorded on 26 November:

> My work is proceeding on nearly the same line as in the past. I attend all meetings of the Cabinet and keep the Minutes exactly as before.[129] My relations with Bonar Law are very nearly the same as my relations were with Lloyd George. In spite of all the talk of 'Conferences of Ministers' and 'Cabinet Cmtees' being unconstitutional, force of circumstances has compelled the new Government to adopt this method of transacting its business. We have had two Conferences of Ministers presided over by the Prime Minister this week, and the Cabinet has already set up Cabinet Committees to deal with Home Affairs, Ireland, Mesopotamia, Unemployment, and the Air question. I cannot supply secretaries for all these from my reduced staff and I have 'farmed out' the Unemployment Committee to the Ministry of Health[!] and 'Ireland' to Lionel Curtis of the Colonial Office, who took the corresponding Committee under the late Government. We do the distribution of documents but not their reproduction. It is amusing to observe that owing to departmental jealousy there are now two Secretaries, one from the Ministry of Health and one from the Ministry of Labour, both highly paid officials, with a third man to take the Minutes. All this was done single-handed by Wicks of my office, who drew £700 a year and did other work as well, when we supplied the secretary![130]

Hankey's comment, which of course is not without its bias, suggests that the 'economies' effected through the reduction of Secretariat staff were illusory, since the work concentrated in the Secretariat would be done less efficiently scattered among the departments. The reduction in staff did not much compromise the Secretariat's vital role in co-ordinating government policy, linking together the Cabinet's proposing and the departments' disposing. Certainly the profile of the Cabinet Office was lowered with the departure of Lloyd George, and it may have receded from what has been called 'the limelight,' but it is well not to exaggerate its withdrawal from the stage, whether serving the Cabinet or nearly two dozen international conferences of the inter-war period.[131]

Yet little remained known of the activities of the Cabinet Office, and less about its origins, after the flurry of interest – in the main, politically motivated – in the year of its crisis, 1922. A decade and a half later, from within the well-informed circles of Cambridge academia, G. M. Trevelyan confessed ignorance in writing to Hankey:

I want to get one point right – even the latest edition of Anson's *Law of Constitution* throws no light. When did the Cabinet first have a Secretary and regular Minutes? I gather the change happened during the war, and has obtained ever since? . . . Was there a Secretary *of the Cabinet* as distinct from the *War Cabinet* between 1916 and 1919?[132]

Absent from 'the limelight' after 1922, in reality the Cabinet Secretariat had weathered the storm and remained on course.

4

The Secretariat in the 1920s: policies and procedures

Hankey's presence at the first gathering of European statesmen in which Bonar Law took part led him privately to question the widely heralded distinction between the ways of Lloyd George and those of his successor:

> Bonar Law is more tricky than I suspected . . . he asked to meet the Belgians (Theunis and Jaspar) alone, and asked them to Downing St., and for some reason he did not want Poincaré to know they were conspiring. (Vain thought! Foreigners always tell!) I met them all coming downstairs together. Theunis and Jaspar entered the Cabinet room by the usual entrance from the hall. Bonar came in through another door from the private secretary's room. Seeing M. Poincaré in the Cabinet room he turned to the Belgians (whom he had just left at the bottom of the stairs) and greeted them effusively, *shaking them by the hand*. And the *Morning Post* and other papers this morning are contrasting the 'straightness' of Bonar Law with the obliquity of Ll. G.! The latter would not have done this, I feel sure. It makes me suspect that Bonar was behind Warren Fisher all the time.[1]

Despite his resentment with the recent treatment of the Cabinet Secretariat and his suspicions of his new Tory masters, Hankey soon came to their service in a fashion which demonstrated unequivocally the value of scrupulous record-keeping. His role was ironic, as it turned upon his defence of Curzon's past actions from an attack mounted by partisans of Lloyd George. Yet it was in Beaverbrook's *Sunday Express* that there surfaced in December 1922 a letter sent to Curzon earlier in the year by the-then Greek premier, Gounaris, calling the British Foreign Secretary's attention to the faltering strength of Greek arms in the struggle with Turkey; he had warned that unless British arms and money were forthcoming, Greece would have to withdraw from Asia Minor. Nor was this warning an isolated instance, because the letter was part of a lengthy correspondence which the two leaders had carried on. The implication was clear: throughout 1922, Curzon had been apprised that the Greek army in Turkey stood on the verge of disaster.

Adding tragic force to this revelation was the execution in Athens in late November of Gounaris and five of his colleagues, in what amounted to an updating of Voltaire's maxim, 'pour encourager les autres.' In this climate, several of Curzon's coalition colleagues claimed that they had never been shown Gounaris' warning, because the Foreign Secretary had failed to circulate to the Cabinet a document of grave import.[2] Ever a partisan and now among the Tory 'outs,' Lord Birkenhead criticized the poor judgment and secretive ways of his former Cabinet colleague, using as his text Curzon's reply of 6 March to Gounaris' warning, an exchange which Beaverbrook had published:

> What was said by the noble Marquess was that he had confidence that the historic martial qualities of the Greek Army would suffice to meet the needs of the next few weeks and of the campaign that was so soon to follow.
>
> If that advice did not mean: 'Stay, at least for the present,' I do not understand the meaning of words, whether they be employed in diplomacy or for any other purpose, and I most deeply deplore that we in the Cabinet were not allowed an opportunity of examining this letter for ourselves, and giving our opinions upon it, and of seeing whether there might not have been evolved from Cabinet discussions, with the collective gravity of responsibility, an advice which might have saved the lives of these Ministers.[3]

In pressing the attack on Curzon and those who had criticized the 'adventurist' policies of the late administration, Birkenhead acted impetuously, even recklessly: trusting to his own memory, shared by his political associates, he failed to consult either the Cabinet records or their custodian, Sir Maurice Hankey. The Cabinet Secretary had no trouble in locating in Cabinet files a copy of the Gounaris letter in question, which had in fact been circulated to the Cabinet by the Foreign Office. A search of the Cabinet Minutes revealed that 'the telegram had never been considered by the Cabinet,' he informed Bonar Law, but the point remained that the Cabinet had been given access to the information.[4] While Birkenhead lamely protested that he had queried nearly every colleague of 'first-class importance' on the matter, the evidence was such that he apologized to Curzon for a statement made with every confidence but 'which, when the facts are fully examined, is found to be without foundation.'[5]

Thus passed within a weekend what had initially appeared as a budding political crisis, and the episode must have been instructive, particularly for those in the new regime who had no direct experience of the Secretariat's role: the utility of Cabinet records had been demonstrated, and Hankey had shown himself master of the situation, in part at the expense of his former chief, Lloyd George. If Hankey's impartiality had once been a concern, surely it could be no longer. As well, the incident served to underscore the desirability of a clear separation between the Cabinet Secretariat and the Prime Minister's own staff of Private Secretaries: had the former been absorbed by the partisan staff in Downing Street, any such arbitration of disputes among former Cabinet colleagues would have been highly unlikely. Could any government trust 'records' maintained by political appointees of predecessor regimes?[6] Continuity in record-keeping would certainly have been adversely affected.

Although Bonar Law's Cabinet had settled upon a scheme for maintaining such Cabinet records, they did not confront directly the question of the use to which official materials could be put in personal memoirs, a matter which Hankey feared as a likely source of leakage of Cabinet secrets. Their coalition predecessors had decided in January 1922 that former ministers would be allowed to publish official documents in order to vindicate their actions, provided such publication did not compromise current public interest: in the case at hand, Winston Churchill had secured this right of direct quotation, in order to rebut criticisms directed his way in a number of officially informed accounts, most conspicuously in Lord Esher's *The Tragedy of Lord Kitchener*, published in 1921.[7] The former First Lord proved liberal in his use of this ministerial right in the second volume of his war memoirs, entitled *World Crisis, 1915*. Hankey played no discernible role in the discussion concerning Churchill's publication, although the materials which he collected for the Cabinet Committee on the Use of Official Material in Publications suggest that his own concern was to prevent similar use of post-war Cabinet papers; towards this end, he hoped to regain custody of ministerial files of Cabinet papers from those ministers who had been free since 1919 to retain individual copies.[8]

The Cabinet Secretary likely recognized that the stream of war-time revelations could not be dammed, because too much concerning the conduct of the war had already been published, particularly by military figures critical of HMG's conduct of the war; nor were the 'frocks' disposed to deny themselves the right of informed reply, as Churchill's attitude confirmed: 'The question . . . is not whether disclosures are to be made, but whether partial disclosures are to stand; not whether all persons concerned in these historic events are to preserve a life-long silence, but whether only certain persons are to be indefinitely prevented from stating their case.'[9] Although he had carried that question in the Coalition Cabinet, Churchill now perceived a threat to his freedom in the statements Bonar Law had made in the House of Commons; on 15 February, the premier acknowledged that the present First Lord had granted Churchill authority to publish 'certain Admiralty orders issued to the Fleet during the war,' adding that 'it is of course an obligation upon Ministers and officials not to disclose confidential State or official papers or information without the previous approval of His Majesty's Government for the time being, or in the case of Cabinet information, without the consent of His Majesty.'[10] This statement did not satisfy Churchill's critics, who pressed the matter further; Law seemingly refused to be drawn beyond his previous statement, until asked whether such revelations constituted a breach of the Privy Counsellor's Oath, to which he tersely replied: 'I have taken the oath and personally I think I should consider it a breach.'[11] Yet the Prime Minister refused to consider any formal proceedings: HMG would take no measures beyond reiterating the rules applying to such publications.

Although on holiday, Churchill disliked the implications of Bonar Law's statement and he was concerned with the Cabinet's recent establishment of a Committee on the Use of Official Material in Publications; he took counsel with Lloyd George, implicitly suggesting a common front against any attempt to restrain them from publishing their own accounts, drawing upon the official papers which each retained.[12] In the event, that front persisted until both men had completed their memoirs of the First World War, in Lloyd George's case more than a decade later. Churchill protested shortly to Bonar Law that he had 'in no way trespassed beyond the limits which have frequently been used by Ministers in defending, on the platform or in the country, themselves, their departments or the Government to which they belonged.' Yet – in contrast to others whose memoirs had drawn upon official documents – Churchill advised Law that he had 'consulted the Prime Minister of the day (Mr Asquith) in regard to every reference, however general, which I made to Cabinet proceedings.' Since no formal arrangements for official scrutiny of ministerial memoirs existed, Bonar Law's diffidence is easily understood. Drawn into the discussion by the Prime Minister, Hankey accepted the main lines of Churchill's argument; he characterized Churchill's involving Asquith as 'a new factor of great interest.'[13] In time, this 'factor' became institutionalized, and thus Winston Churchill's procedure gave birth to the official 'vetting' of ministerial memoirs.

In future, Churchill submitted to an official review of his memoirs: with the completion of the third volume, he asked both Lloyd George and Hankey to 'vet' it, using the latter's approbation in approaching the former, Prime Minister for much of the period: 'Hankey, who is no fair weather friend of yours, has read it all and thinks it is scrupulously fair. Of course I bulk very largely in it all, but then it is I who am telling the tale. I hope you will tell yours when the time comes.'[14] Some years later, the former war leader told his tale, and he too turned to Hankey to read and 'vet' his memoirs, although the Cabinet Secretary pointed out his own unofficial role in such proceedings:

> I have, of course, no status to give you official permission to publish official documents. I can, on my own authority, exempt you neither from the Privy Counsellor's Oath nor from the Official Secrets Act.

I am no lawyer, but I think that the only way in which you can proceed in absolute security is to ask for official permission through the proper channel, viz the Prime Minister.

At the same time I am not suggesting that this procedure has invariably been followed. There are precedents both ways.[15]

Certainly Hankey had begun to function as an informal censor of Cabinet memoirs by this time; such a role came naturally to the Cabinet Secretary, in part because of his knowledge of the inside history of the Great War but also because of his impartial status. There can be no doubt that he discharged a rather thankless task in a conscientious fashion, showing great compassion for those whom he suspected history might treat unkindly; he thought it regrettable that men who had served their country faithfully, if controversially, should reap harsh criticism. In the 1930s, when the political wheel of fortune had revolved against Churchill, he urged Lloyd George to temper a particular criticism which was 'frightfully damaging':

Although Churchill is my friend, I am not pleading for him on that ground. At the present time he is rather down on his luck and this passage [in the third volume of Lloyd George's memoirs] will hit dreadfully. It will always be quoted against him if he is ever in, or aspires to get into, office again . . . I ask myself whether it is really to the public advantage that our national heroes should be hauled off their pedestals.[16]

From the Cabinet Secretary's perspective, 'vetting' ministerial accounts of service afforded Hankey a means of maintaining a cloak of secrecy over Cabinet deliberations for nearly the whole of the inter-war years, although little could be done to stem the reports of war-time strife between 'frocks' and 'brasshats.' Hankey had precisely this distinction in mind in urging Churchill in 1926 to conclude his *World Crisis* with the Armistice of November 1918, although he advanced other reasons in urging Churchill to delete post-1918 chapters from the last volume of his memoirs:

Chapter XXV contains a most brilliant description of the end of the war on a note of triumph. It concludes, if I can remember right, with a thought-compelling query as to whether these things are to happen again. On that note I would end the volume. 'The Aftermath' is too much of an anti-climax. Instead of ending with wedding bells or, shall we say, joy bells, it takes us into the squalid circumstances of a poverty-stricken marriage. I think that 'The Aftermath' would come better as the first chapter of a future book on the reconstruction – the time for which is not yet ripe.[17]

Here, at any rate, is the genesis of the separate volume which Churchill published only three years later, with an expression of thanks to Hankey for his assistance in its preparation;[18] Churchill regarded the volume as a continuation of his 'contemporary contribution to the history of the Great War,'[19] concluding with a treatment of the Chanak crisis of 1922.

He utilized some post-war Cabinet documents, for the most part those which he had written, but the license afforded those ministers who had written about the war was extended to Churchill's foray into the early post-war years.

Hankey's unofficial role was reinforced by his functional responsibilities in connection with the Official Histories, which were researched and written by a branch within the Cabinet Office.[20] The Secretariat had absorbed the Historical Section of the Committee of Imperial Defence, which had undertaken such historical inquiries because Lord Esher had contended in 1906 that War Office and Admiralty accounts failed to perceive military operations, together with political considerations, as a whole: the 'Official History of the War in South Africa' had been completed in four volumes by 1910, and a history of the Russo-Japanese war, in which Britain had not been a belligerent, occupied the whole of its attentions until the onset of war in 1914. Even in Esher's eyes, the operation had become suspect, and in 1913 a sub-committee of the CID recommended that the Section revert to 'research work,' maintaining a permanent staff of but one officer and one clerk.[21] Thus the First World War brought new life to its operations, as the Historical Section was charged with the 'tabulation of information of historical importance in regard to the war,' and in short order pressures mounted for an official history of a more popular and general character than had been the case in the past. Although the CID's Historical Committee, which oversaw the operations of the Section, quickly selected two authorities, John Fortescue and Julian Corbett, respectively to write accounts of a 'Military History' and a 'Naval History,' the Treasury posed a financial obstacle to the venture, insisting that previous publications had been 'appallingly costly and practically unsaleable.' Hankey deftly countered that 'the fallacy of the Treasury objection lay in the attempt to measure their value by the test of receipts, and that if such a test were applied to other scientific works it was probable that scientific research would come to an end. A history was essentially a work of reference and education.'[22] Through the advocacy of the CID Secretary,[23] Treasury resistance was overcome, and Asquith announced in June 1916 that official histories would be undertaken; before the war had ended, the widening scope of the project necessitated the hiring of additional historians.[24]

In the minds of its practitioners, official history possessed an educational value and an objective status denied to other historical accounts. E. Y. Daniel, Secretary of the Historical Section, warned of the risks of leaving the study of war to private hands:

> if widely read it owes its popularity to the amount of secret information which the author has divulged, or to the extent to which he has entered into personal controversies. It would be morally wrong to leave either the public or the services to such guidance; as it is a matter of honour and common sense that the country's

unprecedented effort between 1914 and 1918 should be analysed, and its efforts made clear . . . it is the object of the government to place before the public an absolutely reliable and impartial account of what occurred.[25]

Yet the belief, which Hankey shared,[26] that the official historians were a breed apart in their impartiality no less than in their sources was belied by experience directly within the Historical Section. Fortescue had not worked well within the harness of the Historical Section: his publication of a review of Lord French's *1914* in October 1919 led to a severing of his relationship with the 'Military History,' as Hankey explained to him: 'The Government consider it highly important that the Official History, when published, should be recognized as thoroughly impartial. While expressing no opinion upon the merits of the controversy, they feel that the character of your article makes it impossible for you to continue your association with the History without compromising its impartiality.'[27] 'Impartiality' was in turn conferred upon Brigadier-General J.E. Edmonds, who found it necessary to rewrite practically the entire Fortescue narrative for the first volume.[28]

'Naval Operations' had proved as difficult to launch; although the Admiralty had insisted upon a prefatory note placing the responsibility for content solely upon the author, the former First Lord, Churchill, quickly took exception both to Corbett's selection of official documents and to his treatment of particular episodes. Several months and much effort was required in meeting Churchill's objections – although it is unlikely that he was ever satisfied with Corbett's version[29] – and Hankey was given ample cause to reflect whether official histories of recent and controversial events could be successfully accomplished. No one, he thought, could have been more 'discreet' than Corbett, yet his judgments were bound 'to reflect on one leader or another, on this department or on that.' Pessimistically if not inaccurately, Hankey admitted: 'There is not the smallest reason to suppose that the other distinguished historians engaged on the Official Histories will be more successful.'[30] He warned the Cabinet that the Official Histories in aggregate might prove troublesome, but he pointed out in their behalf that 'the education of the professional officer' and 'the enlightenment of the public' would be served by the prompt historical utilization of official materials which could not be placed at the disposal of the general historian, over whom the government could exercise no control. In fact, Hankey continued, government had a significant stake in such a venture: 'There is the consideration that an antidote is required to the unofficial histories, which habitually attribute all naval and military failures to the ineptitude of the Government, to say nothing of the accounts of individual officers, frequently ill-informed and partisan in character, which are apt to mislead public as well as service opinion.'

Despite Hankey's endorsement of the project, the Cabinet gave only a hesitant approval to the publication of Corbett's first volume, along with the initial installments of two other series; the Historical Section was informed that 'the preparatory work of collecting and collating material . . . should continue but the actual writing of these [subsequent] volumes in their final shape should not be taken up, and nothing should be set in type until the Cabinet decides that they should be proceeded with.'[31] In so advising, the Cabinet were endorsing the recommendations of a Conference of Ministers, at which the decision to sanction publication of the first volume of 'Naval Operations' hung in the balance.[32] To a man, the several designated authors protested the Cabinet's warning that the government were in no way committed to eventual publication of further volumes, but Hankey informed Daniel that the Cabinet had acted deliberately: 'We shall evidently have a devil of a row if we don't continue publication, but I think the Cabinet realised that they would have to stump up if they shut down these books.'[33] Daniel's Historical Section thus manifested more than cursory interest in critical reaction to Corbett's venture, and a very favorable collection of reviews and clippings enabled him and Hankey to secure Cabinet authorization first for the extension of the 'Naval History' and in due course for other series of the Official History.[34] In May 1921, the Cabinet approved publication of the initial volumes in the important series dealing with the military and air histories of the war;[35] at this point the Official Histories can be regarded as well established, although no one would have suspected that before the various volumes dealing with the Great War were completed, another and arguably greater war would have supervened. Although the Official Histories were Daniel's charge, Hankey played a role in the choice of authors for the series: in the case of the 'Air History,' he rejected several candidates with a journalistic background, expressing a preference for 'technical' rather than 'literary' Official Histories.[36]

Throughout this undertaking, the Cabinet Secretary insisted upon the protection of his major charge, Cabinet secrecy: proceedings of the Cabinet and its committees were to be masked, as were individual contributions to Cabinet discussions, 'subject of course to reference to the Prime Minister or other Ministers in cases of doubt or difficulty.'[37] Other procedural guidelines were involved, with departmental scrutiny provided for; thus the Official Historians were cautioned that 'in any matters affecting our diplomatic relations [i.e., involving past foreign policy] the proofs should be sent to the Foreign Office.'[38] Departmental scrutiny could become a daunting experience: one volume was sent to no less than 799 recipients for critical commentary![39] The Prime Minister gave final sanction, although it appears that nothing more than notification of publication was in fact involved.[40] Thus a near-moribund operation had developed into a formidable tool for the education of the nation; in the process, the Historical Section of the Cabinet Office won itself a place as an adjunct of Cabinet government. When in 1922 Warren Fisher suggested that the Section be transferred from the Cabinet Office to a less conspicuous location, such as the British Museum, Hankey promised only to canvass the notion, which came to nothing.[41] Official Histories were in time published concerning the Second World War, although the claim to an inherently superior account was abandoned: 'The term ["Official History"] did not imply that the work gave an official view, or that it gave a full and complete story, or that it could be expected that all its conclusions would stand in any long-term perspective.'[42] Distinguished though a number of them were, the official historians were after all not a breed apart, save in their earlier access to the sources.

Where the Historical Section pioneered, the Foreign Office followed: after the fall of the Labour government, the new Foreign Secretary, Austen Chamberlain, confirmed the decision taken by his predecessor, Ramsay MacDonald, to publish a collection of 'the official documents bearing on the general European situation out of which the war arose.'[43] Editorial responsibility was entrusted to G. P. Gooch and H. W. V. Temperley, and Chamberlain commented that 'the reputation of the editors offers the best guarantee of the historical accuracy and impartiality of their work.' Published over a thirteen year period, the eleven volumes of *British Documents on the Origins of the War* testify to the wisdom of the choice of respected historians from outside the Foreign Office. Nonetheless, the British government had been among the last European powers to commission such an undertaking, yielding reluctantly to the valid fear voiced by R. W. Seton-Watson that 'slowly but surely very serious injury is being done by the continued silence of the British Government.' A campaign in the correspondence columns of *The Times* had brought official acknowledgment that historians were 'gravely handicapped when they come to deal with the charges and insinuations directed against British policy in the period preceding the war.'[44] A war later, Britain proved quicker off the mark in determining upon the publication of *Documents on British Foreign Policy* in order 'to forestall a German version of events, which might otherwise get in first (as after 1919) and "sell" the German case to all the innocent pedagogues and publicists here and in America.'[45] Thus the practical importance of prompt publication of documents 'as a result of which the war is being fought' had this time been recognized in official circles; Oliver Harvey even argued in terms of the public's 'moral' entitlement to examine the record.[46]

In his continuing defence of Cabinet secrecy, Hankey did not have recourse in the immediate post-war years to the Official Secrets Act, which in 1920 had been revised to strengthen earlier legislation designed originally to combat espionage but already in 1911 widened in scope. Government attempts to forestall unauthorized use of official documents – usually to secure some financial gain – stretched as far back into the Victorian period as 1858, but only in 1889 had Parliament passed legislation designed to protect military and naval secrets; with a single exception, this legislation had been directed against British citizens disclosing secrets rather than foreign nationals 'spying' in England.[47] With the German threat as backdrop, in 1911 Parliament enacted an Official Secrets Act which, for all the government's stress upon its amending the 1889 legislation, broke new ground. Though the first section of the 1911 Act was directed wholly against espionage activities, section 2 construed as an offence the action of any person who, 'having in his possession any information . . . which he has obtained or to which he has had access owing to his position as a person who holds office or has held office under His Majesty . . . communicates the information to any person other than a person to whom he is authorised to communicate it.' Further, although the legislation is less than clear on the point, the 'commonly accepted interpretation . . . is that when official information has been communicated in contravention of section 2, the recipient commits an offence if he in turn communicates that information without authority.'[48] While prosecutions were brought during the war under the terms of section 2, only in 1919 did the courts rule that it applied to any information – rather than only to secret data – obtained by a person through his official position.[49] In such a fashion section 2 came into its own, and to this day it has lost neither its prominence nor its notoriety: 'a law whose original purpose was the limited and acceptable one of fighting espionage has been widened in scope so as both to diminish the effective working of Government and to harm society in general.'[50]

For all the fact that section 2 was not once mentioned in the cursory Parliamentary debates of 1911, the Franks Committee maintained in its 1972 review of the legislation that the broad provisions of section 2 had a deliberate design:

> Although surviving official papers are incomplete . . . those who drafted the 1911 Bill . . . clearly intended it to operate as a general check against civil service leaks of all kinds. Official papers show that from 1889 to the present day the Civil Service has always seen this as one of the objects of the Official Secrets Act, and has never regarded the Acts as being confined to matters connected with the safety of the State.[51]

Whether ministers of the era thought the Official Secrets Act binding upon them is much more doubtful: although Asquith's remarks in the House of Commons in 1915 appear to point in that direction,[52] his own private revelations of Cabinet business and those of a number of his colleagues point in quite the opposite direction.[53] Neither Asquith's war-time regime nor that of Lloyd George earned particularly high marks for the observance of secrecy in matters touching their work, although improvements came with the systemization of War Cabinet business through the Secretariat. Yet the Official Secrets Act did not enter the picture, nor was it invoked to stem the flood of post-war memoirs based upon official information. Indeed, Bonar Law's reference to Churchill's possible breach of the Privy Counsellor's Oath suggests that the Official Secrets Act did not operate in ministerial quarters.

Whatever the past concerns with civil service leaks, the 1920 amendment incorporated further provisions against espionage: the Franks Committee claimed that espionage was 'almost entirely' its concern, citing the Attorney-General's remarks to the effect that the whole of the 1911 Act, including section 2, had been directed at spying.[54] Alas, the Attorney-General, Sir Gordon Hewart, had spoken in an ambiguous, even confusing, fashion. On the one hand, he specifically disclaimed the contention that the revision of 1920, like the legislation of 1911, dealt only with spying: 'it deals also with certain other things . . . the improper communication of official documents, a provision due to the fact that information of a secret nature is too often obtained from or through indiscreet persons.' Hewart stressed two linked facets of an offence against official secrecy: first, 'retention [of official documents] for some purpose prejudicial to the safety or interests of the state,' a forceful clause because a servant of the Crown may submit such a contention without challenge in an English court;[55] and second, the unauthorized use of such an official document. On the other hand, the Attorney-General continued that the use of such an 'official document' had nothing to do with materials frequently mentioned earlier in the debate, namely 'a circular, a Cabinet paper, a memorandum, or something stamped with a statement that it is the property of His Majesty's Government.' Having excluded the entire range of Cabinet papers, Hewart offered a description of official documents: 'We are dealing, and dealing only, with passports, passes, permits, certificates and the like.'[56] Such documents were the very stuff of espionage, but for some reason Hewart refused to label them as such, and thus clearly to limit to espionage the application of the Official Secrets Act. The product was the confusion which the Franks Committee remarked upon a half-century later:

> We found section 2 a mess. Its scope is enormously wide . . . The drafting and the interpretation of the section are obscure. People are not sure what it means, or what kinds of action involve real risks of prosecution under it . . . There is a widely held view that the Official Secrets Act should be concerned only with spies and traitors.[57]

The emergence of such a 'widely held view' is in major part a product of the promiscuous use of the Official Secrets Act, 1911 and 1920, by

HMG during the inter-war years, in a fashion inconsistent with legislative intent; the Cabinet Secretariat came in time to use the 'catch-all' provisions of section 2 to protect the secrecy of Cabinet proceedings. Yet the legislation had not been initially directed against the likes of Churchill, as we have seen, nor was it mentioned in 1923, when Bonar Law failed to respond to a proposal that the Prime Minister make it a condition of acceptance of ministerial office that 'no ex-Minister, until he has been out of office for 15 years, shall be permitted, when writing articles or books for monetary consideration, to make use of information of a confidential character acquired during his period of office.'[58] Lloyd George's coalition had accepted no such self-denying ordinance when the Cabinet had resolved upon ministerial retention of official papers upon leaving office, nor did successor governments alter the situation for another decade. Although since 1934 ministers supposedly have not retained comprehensive collections of Cabinet papers, their memoirs have remained outside the scope of the Official Secrets Act; only one exception, discussed below, mars that generalization and in that case the former Cabinet minister himself was not prosecuted. As countless volumes of ministerial memoirs testify, section 2 ultimately could not be sustained against ministerial recollections, despite the attempt of Hankey's Cabinet Secretariat to utilize the 1920 legislation in the custody of Cabinet secrecy.

The history of the short-lived Bonar Law government had little further significance for the Cabinet Secretariat: its initial reforms had reduced the staff and the scope of the latter's activities. The new premier, consistent with his own intentions, functioned in a different fashion from Lloyd George, for example conducting the affairs of his own office through Private Secretaries, dispensing with the structural remains of Lloyd George's Secretariat.[59] Bonar Law, stricken with throat cancer, resigned his office, and the Tory succession passed unexpectedly into the hands of Stanley Baldwin in May 1923.

Hankey was not privy to the tangled events culminating in the 'emergence' of the new Tory leader, although it is unlikely that the Cabinet Secretary relished the prospect either of his succession or the widely expected appointment of Lord Curzon. His diary is silent on these events; not until 11 November 1923 did Hankey speculate on recent events, and even then at no great length: 'I have passed without note Bonar Law's retirement, Baldwin's succession and Bonar Law's death. Poor Bonar never had the nerve for the job of Prime Minister. The responsibility preyed on his mind and, I feel sure, hastened on his cancer. Baldwin has nerve but scant capacity and I fear will not last long.'[60] Setting aside Hankey's psychosomatic view of Bonar Law's terminal illness, his prediction was not inaccurate in the short term, but in the long run Baldwin was a better survivor than anyone foresaw. Nor did he have any reason to hope for a long tenure on Baldwin's part, because the two men had no strong feelings for each other; Roskill's description is retrospective but instructive: 'From Hankey's personal point of view the accession to power of Baldwin was a disaster. All observers of the contemporary scene agree that, of all the Prime Ministers whom he served, Baldwin was the one with whom he was least in sympathy. Nor is there any doubt that the lack of sympathy was reciprocated.'[61] Whether the situation was so stark in 1923 is problematic, because in the years that followed the two men worked together effectively and, at times, cordially. In 1923 it may suffice to remark that the Cabinet Secretary may well have preferred Curzon – for all his faults – because he might have wielded greater influence, although it should not be suggested that he was devoid of influence over Stanley Baldwin.

Nonetheless, Hankey's diminished personal impact upon the premier did not sever the Prime Minister's informal links to the Cabinet Secretariat; instead, Hankey's deputy Tom Jones emerged as a leading confidant of Baldwin, and their relationship persisted long after Jones left the Cabinet Office in 1931. Although one could reasonably surmise that his loss of informal standing at No. 10 would trouble the Cabinet Secretary, there is no sign of any animosity on Hankey's part towards Jones, in the main because in the minds of those who knew him well, Jones was not self-serving. From within the Secretariat, Lawrence Burgis had direct experience of Jones' behavior, which rebutted any notion that he was an intriguer, seeking 'to advance some kind of action that will accrue eventually to his own advantage.'[62] Within the Cabinet Office, Hankey's authority remained unquestioned, and his loyalty to his new chief was beyond doubt.[63] Thus the lack of intimacy between the Prime Minister and the Cabinet Secretary, a function of their personalities, seemingly troubled no one, because it left their professional relationship untainted.

Hankey was troubled by Baldwin's decision to call a snap general election on the issue of Protection, although he witnessed it from afar; when Baldwin made clear to his Cabinet his decision to go to the polls on 23 October, several ministers remained after the conclusion of the meeting 'to continue the discussion,' and at that time, as Jones noted, 'the P.M. gave Hankey a clear indication that he was not wanted.'[64] A strange experience for Hankey, but the business of the Cabinet had been concluded: thus the incident ought not to be exaggerated, as Patrick Gordon Walker did by intimating that Hankey had been asked to remove himself from a Cabinet meeting.[65] Nor was the experience novel, because early in his tenure the Cabinet Secretary had twice been asked to withdraw, once for a discussion of the Secretariat and once when he was in temporary disfavor with Lloyd George.[66] Apparently not again until Attlee's premiership, and then only on several occasions when party matters were discussed, has the Cabinet Secretary been asked to leave.[67] Harold Wilson recalled 'two or three occasions' between 1964 and 1970 when the Cabinet met without Secretariat officials, in the main to consider the timing of elections; on those occasions, the Prime Minister himself provided 'a short, usually uninformative, note for the Cabinet records.'[68]

The 1923 incident illustrates Hankey's exclusion from an advisory capacity, even in the limited fashion of preparing the government for a controversial electoral issue, which Tom Jones puzzled over in his own diary:

> How the P.M. came to put forward his proposals in the sudden way he did, at the time he did, is still wrapped up in mystery . . . Hankey and I were given no opportunity of putting out red lights. We could have told the P.M. with what careful preparation L.G. paved the way for the Safeguarding of Industry Bill.[69]

One suspects that Baldwin would not respond to advice couched in these terms, and indeed he rejected the advice even of such confirmed protectionists as Leo Amery in deciding upon an early general election.[70] In the ensuing campaign, by a strange twist of fate Tom Jones was given leave to place caution lights in the flow of Baldwin's speech-making:

> Throughout the campaign I was in the closest touch with the P.M., saw him almost daily – every day when he was in town . . . I would . . . tell him the main features in the speeches of the previous day and any gossip I had heard. I would indicate the sort of line to take, the points to combat or avoid. He never attempted to explain to me how protection would cure unemployment. I told him several times that all my instincts and training were dead against his policy and that I thought that he would corrupt our politics still more. I had undertaken at the start to do my utmost to help him, as he had asked me to help, and this I did.[71]

Perhaps Jones was drawn to Baldwin in a personal fashion[72] but as a civil servant he could rationalize his conduct; it is unlikely that he forgot that his own survival in the 1922 reforms of the Cabinet Office had been 'a damned close run thing,' and his position vis-à-vis Baldwin marked a continuation of speech writing which Bonar Law had asked of him.[73] Nor, in the matter of protection, did Jones find writing speeches contrary to his own views an impossible assignment.

Hankey limited his own consternation with the way in which Baldwin had conducted the affairs of state to the privacy of his diary, having discovered that 'the Tariff Reform decision has been taken without consulting a single official,' despite a wealth of information readily available in a number of departments. An even more troubling aspect of the Baldwin 'Follies' of 1923 concerned his own office:

The most extraordinary feature of the election was that almost the whole of all the Prime Minister's speeches was written by Tom Jones, my no. 2, who is a passionate Free-Trader, an intimate and trusted friend of Lloyd George, voted Liberal, and at the 1906 Election was engaged as Professor of Economics at Glasgow University in supplying pablum for the Free-Trade campaign. Nowadays Tom Jones is a Civil Servant, and is supposed to have no politics. Moreover he is the most loyal creature under the sun, and sweated blood for Baldwin. Still no one could believe that he would be chosen to write the P.M.'s election speeches in a Tariff Reform campaign. It shocks me inexpressibly that the P.M. should have his speeches written for him.[74]

Though Hankey registered 'shock' at this turn of events, there is an element of disingenuousness in his comment, since he had on a number of occasions prepared speeches for the likes of Curzon and Lloyd George, although the Cabinet Secretary had not been involved in electioneering.[75] His anger would be more plausible had he contrasted the way in which the Deputy Secretary to the Cabinet was being pressed into service with the expressed intention of the Tories to limit the Secretariat to record-keeping functions; the danger of politicizing the institution was now as real as at any time during the coalition's existence. In the light of Hankey's strong feelings, it is all the more surprising that his own relations with his deputy did not suffer – as did Baldwin's majority in the calculated if maladroit General Election of 1923 – but the two appreciated the need to adapt their responsibilities to the desires of their new masters. Not even in the privacy of his diary did either complain of the other's actions, although Jones expressed some reservations with Hankey's tight-fistedness in Cabinet Office salaries.[76]

Under Unionist administrations, Hankey continued to function much as he had in the past, for example in his efforts to ensure secrecy for the gatherings of European statesmen, sometimes in the face of difficulties posed by the cupidity of his counterparts. Meetings with the French were particularly prone to leakage, and a revealing incident centered on Bonar Law's dissent from French policies, expressed at a meeting which according to Baldwin's close friend and political colleague, J. C. C. Davidson, was held under conditions of 'absolute secrecy':

the whole of the discussion, with all the best things Bonar said omitted, appeared at lunchtime in an evening paper. An inquiry was held by Hankey, and I was kept informed on Bonar's behalf. It turned out that the Permanent Under-Secretary of the French FO admitted that he had to give a scoop occasionally to the press, as he was paid a ridiculously low salary and was expected to live like a gentleman, dress well and entertain.[77]

Davidson's own role raises a question concerning the heralded abolition of the Prime Minister's Secretariat in 1922, because its work went on: Baldwin's biographers remark on the functions discharged by

Davidson's serving as the Chancellor of the Duchy: 'his office at the Duchy of Lancaster was very much Baldwin's own Garden Suburb.'[78] The implication is clear: any premier needed a mechanism to discharge a variety of political tasks which were outside the purview of the Cabinet Secretariat, whatever it was called and wherever it was lodged; it appears that Baldwin would have served the Cabinet Office well by seeking his speech writer for the election of 1923 in that other office.

In the domestic sphere, Hankey eagerly hoped for a revival of the Committee of Imperial Defence: since shortly after the Paris Peace Conference, he had worked for its reactivation.[79] Lloyd George had other matters to occupy his time, although in June 1920 the CID met for the first time in more than five years. At that time a Standing Defence Sub-Committee was charged with surveying the nation's defence commitments, and in effect this group carried on the CID's business until the fall of the coalition. On his own, Hankey had already undertaken the revision and up-dating of his most favored project, the War Book, but under the increasingly infirm Balfour, the sub-committee made no progress in what its Secretary described as 'the serious and complete stagnation as regards the business of the CID.' While Hankey did succeed in convoking a full CID meeting in July 1922, the Greek misadventure – in part a result of inadequate military intelligence – strengthened in his mind the case for a revivified CID, a matter which he quickly raised with Lord Salisbury when the latter assumed responsibility for the Standing Defence Sub-Committee in the Bonar Law government.

On 17 November 1922 Hankey proposed a full agenda for a meeting of that group, although in fact it did not begin to function until March 1923, when it undertook a review of the co-operation and co-ordination of the three Fighting Services. We need not follow in detail the work of that Salisbury Sub-Committee,[80] but no study of the Cabinet Secretariat can forego entirely Hankey's deep involvement in military affairs for the whole of his time in Whitehall Gardens; his role was unique, and as well it affords an understanding of the ways in which Hankey worked and of the causes which he served. Two results of the labors of the Salisbury Sub-Committee are relevant to this limited purpose: first, that body spun off yet another sub-committee, chaired by Balfour, to adjudicate the volatile question whether the Navy would gain complete control of the Fleet Air Arm or, instead, whether that force would remain a part of the RAF, as had been the case since 1918. In an attempt to resolve this dispute, Hankey – whose personal sympathies were '"mildly pro-Navy"'[81] – strove through his impartial conduct as Secretary to the parent Salisbury Committee to win the confidence of the RAF chiefs, especially Air Marshal Hugh Trenchard. In July 1923 the Balfour Sub-Committee returned a verdict favoring the newest of the services, and the Salisbury Sub-Committee in its turn endorsed that decision, although not without some ministerial dissent. Predictably, the Admiralty proved unreconciled to the separation of the Air Arm from the Fleet;[82] Hankey continued his efforts to secure a more lasting compromise, but the proposal of the Balfour Sub-Committee did not long survive. Although bad feelings between the Admiralty and the RAF persisted, Hankey's mediative efforts were nowhere resented, and his impartial conduct was everywhere recognized.

The second important result of the Salisbury Sub-Committee's work was its recommendation that, to secure improved co-ordination, the Chiefs of Staff of the three services constitute a committee of the CID:

> each of the three Chiefs of Staff will have an individual and collective responsibility for advising in defence policy as a whole, the three constituting, as it were, a Super-Chief of the War Staff in Commission. In carrying out this function they will meet together for the discussion of questions which affect their joint responsibilities.[83]

The COS Sub-Committee acquired functions of co-ordination in defence policy which had once been intended – but never secured – for its parent, the CID. In this important re-organization of British defence several factors deserve mention: Hankey played a leading role in creating the new mechanism and secured a key post as its Secretary in the process. The COS Committee – as it came to be known – represented a victory for Trenchard, who had worked since 1919 for a forum in which he might deal in a direct fashion and on an equal footing with his counterparts at the War Office and Admiralty.[84] Thus Trenchard had good reason to acknowledge his debt to Hankey, who in fact drafted the report of the Salisbury Committee, in close consultation with the three chiefs.[85] From the time of its first meeting on 17 July 1923 Hankey once again sat at the very center of defence planning, acquiring what his biographer characterizes as 'powerful influence . . . if only because Chiefs of Staff came and went, while he went on, seemingly, forever.'[86] Yet Hankey's influence did not result from the periodic change in military leadership alone: rather he provided an important link between those leaders and their civilian chiefs in the Cabinet, and his long experience in civil–military relations represented a positive asset for the COS Committee.

With the establishment of the COS Committee and the revitalization of the CID, Hankey regained in institutional terms the personal influence with the premier which he had lost with Baldwin's succession; and although he lacked decisive influence on Baldwin, he did possess the confidence of that other inter-war figure who 'went on, seemingly, forever.' In fact, Hankey had little to complain of in his dealings with the Tory leader, as recounted by Baldwin's biographers:

Yet if there never was complete sympathy, there was complete confidence and trust on both sides. Hankey's loyalty was total, his efficiency a bye-word. His administrative value was too great to neglect . . . He found in Baldwin a readiness to listen and a willingness to act, if he were once convinced; and within certain limits they became friends . . . Hankey's influence at least ranked with that of Warren Fisher and probably exceeded it where defence problems were concerned; and it counted for considerably more than that of many Cabinet ministers.[87]

While it is true that Baldwin checked Hankey's advice against that of others, so too had Lloyd George, whom Hankey had by no stretch of the imagination dominated; thus the professional nature of the relationship between the two did not differ markedly from those developed by Hankey with other premiers whom he served, but the personal aspect of the dealings between the two was simply less intense.

While Hankey did much to forward the institution of the COS Committee, part of the impetus stemmed from his aversion to any proposal to establish a Ministry of Defence, which organization he viewed as superfluous in light of the co-ordinating mechanism afforded by the CID. In evidence offered to the Salisbury Sub-Committee, Hankey argued that defence was too comprehensive a concern to relegate to a single ministry:

the means of co-ordination in the C.I.D. apply not only to the Service Departments but to every Department of State which has any action to take on the outbreak of war. In the larger questions of policy the Treasury, Foreign Office, Colonial Office and India Office are involved only to a slightly less extent than the Service Departments . . . In the widest sense of the term this Committee [of Imperial Defence] may be said to fulfill many of the functions of a Ministry of Defence.[88]

There is no reason to question Hankey's conviction that the CID afforded a means of ensuring that Britain's defence organization 'should be sufficiently elastic in character to focus . . . all the resources of Empire,' but his assurance is all the more remarkable, coming as it did at a time when the CID was barely functioning. His skill in characterizing the work of a Defence Ministry as narrower in scope than that of 'defence by committee' should also be remarked upon. Personally, Hankey did not admit to the possibility of much tinkering with the extant defence mechanism; when in 1926 Lord Esher weighed suggesting that the task of co-ordinating the work of the CID be transferred from the premier to the Lord President, Hankey objected that no other Cabinet member could have the former's authority in dealing with his colleagues. Even more telling was his belief that 'if ever we have a war, the Prime Minister and nobody else must undertake the supreme direction, and if he is to do that he must educate himself up to it. The CID is the only means of education we have.' To Esher's contention that the Prime Minister no longer had the time to undertake such responsibilities, Hankey *qua* Cabinet Secretary retorted that he had 'at least as much leisure as the Prime Minister before the war,' provided he did not take on another office as well. Because of his own combining two secretarial posts, Hankey continued: 'the opportunities of discussing Cabinet business are equally available for the discussion of C.I.D. business. This I can say definitely, that for once I saw Asquith in pre-War days I see Baldwin twenty times in post-War days.' Nor for the last time, Hankey specified his own unwillingness to serve any other defence organization: 'In fact I should not hesitate to go if there was any considerable change.'[89]

The CID Secretary thus poured his efforts into making a success of the COS 'troika,' in the face of constant inter-service rivalry for declining defence expenditures – an understandable conflict exacerbated by War Office and Admiralty resentment with the 'extravagance' of Trenchard's commitment to the doctrine of strategic air bombardment. In all this strife, the service chiefs were at least talking with one another, no mean accomplishment; thus Hankey found value in their meetings, even if he had yet another set of minutes to supply, and complaints to resolve about their form. Pressed by Trenchard for a fuller version, Hankey professed his willingness to supply 'the sort of record which the Chiefs of Staff would themselves like to have,' although he added that only the briefest of records could be kept for any discussion of war plans. He proposed a two-tiered system for other discussions, with full minutes going to the COS and a shorter version sent to those on the distribution list of the parent CID.[90] Hankey, it appears, recognized the likely contentiousness of the fuller version,[91] but over the years such a format won out, and the records of the COS Committee serve above all to depict the disagreements of the chiefs as they struggled to shape a comprehensive policy which fitted the priorities of their respective services.[92]

With the defeat of the Tories in December 1923, Hankey's thoughts gravitated to the vital issue of the attitude which a Labour government would take to the existence of the CID; nor for that matter could he take for granted acceptance of the Cabinet Secretariat. To resolve these questions, Hankey called upon Ramsay MacDonald even before Baldwin's defeat in the House of Commons. Some months later, he recollected the details of that meeting, in a diary entry which indicates gathering doubts about the propriety of such a record as he had kept for nearly a decade:

My journal lapsed for nearly a year, partly because I had an attack of writer's cramp at that time, partly because I cannot write of what happens at Cabinet owing to my Oath as Clerk of the [Privy] Council, partly because I am still trying in a desultory way to continue my work on the Higher Command in war, but mainly from sheer laziness.

Although these concerns collectively weigh upon the contents of his diary, he periodically collected his reflections on happenings in a fashion which suggests that the Oath taken in 1923 was not decisive.[93] For the moment, he recorded 'a number of peculiar circumstances' attending the likely formation of a Labour government, including such ironies as the need to name MacDonald a Privy Counsellor before he could be asked to form a government. He noted as well the substantive matters in his first conversation with the Labour leader:

After discussing the Privy Council arrangements I passed on to the Cabinet Secretariat. I said I did not know whether he proposed to have a Cabinet Secretary, but that in any event I recognized it to be a very personal matter, and if he wanted someone else I begged him not to consider my personal feelings. I should not take umbrage if he appointed someone else. He replied very frankly that he had made many personal inquiries about me, and had heard nothing but good of me, and he begged me to remain, and added that he hoped we should become friends as well. After describing in some detail the work of the Cabinet Secretariat I passed (with some trepidation) to the Committee of Imperial Defence. Rather to my surprise he displayed a good deal of interest, and, pointing to his bookshelves, he told me that General Smuts had said that he possessed one of the best military libraries in London. He promised me every support in the C.I.D. He then went on to discuss very frankly his difficulties in finding Labour Ministers suited to take charge of the three Service Departments, and in particular pressed me for details as to how far as Prime Minister he could expect to control their policy. I told him through the medium of the C.I.D. he could do a good deal.[94]

Hankey could not have hoped for a better light in which to view the activities of the CID, surely an exhilarating experience in view of the possibility that the best-known pacifist of a decade earlier might reject outright the idea of military planning.[95] And in fact MacDonald followed through, taking the chair at the first meeting of the CID under his administration; while the press of other business would prevent his acting frequently as chair, he announced that 'the interests of Imperial defence would be adequately safeguarded by the appointment [in his stead] of Lord Haldane, who, as the Committee well knew, possessed unique experience in matters of this nature.'[96] Since the Prime Minister attended only two of the subsequent nine meetings during his first administration, Haldane's appointment was from Hankey's point of view crucial: 'I feel sure you must feel glad that you took the plunge and entered the Labour Government,' he wrote in August 1924; 'had you not done so, I believe that we would have had something like disaster on the defence side.'[97] The survival of the CID helps to explain Hankey's enthusiasm for the succession of Ramsay MacDonald, which otherwise can be explained only in terms of the Cabinet Secretary's being 'taken in by MacDonald's eloquence and personality.'[98] Even if that be the case, Hankey was neither the first nor the last to succumb.

On 22 January 1924 MacDonald was asked by George V to form a government, and the Cabinet Secretary discussed the 'brave new world' of Court etiquette with the Labour leaders that very day. When he learned that the new premier had made no dinner arrangements, Hankey proposed dinner at the United Services Club, to which he belonged; he obviously enjoyed the ensuing scene:

> As it chanced, the only vacant table was in the far corner of the big dining room. We had to walk past a number of tables occupied by retired Colonels and Admirals of highly correct Tory politics. Many of them looked at us open mouthed, pausing twixt cup and lip as I filed down the room followed by the tall, frock-coated figure of the new and sinister Labour Prime Minister. That he should dine in their club on his first night in office![99]

Hankey's wry sense of humor is in evidence, and in fact the military had very little to fear from a minority Labour government. Nor had Hankey anything to fear from MacDonald, and the two men took readily to one another: in effect, he and Tom Jones exchanged places as the premier's personal confidant. Hankey was delighted with the 'excellent personal relations,' visiting MacDonald at Chequers as he had often done with Lloyd George, but Jones was downcast by the turn of events. For his part, Jones hoped to secure 'one of the big Permanent Secretary-ships,' most likely at the Board of Education, for which he was well qualified. However, his role as speech writer for Baldwin was no secret,[100] and as recently as November 1923, *The Times* had printed a picture of the Deputy Secretary walking through the fields with Baldwin at Astley House, his Worcestershire residence; Jones' diary entry is a candid one: 'Pleased but also rather vexed [with the publicity] because I have a first-rate record for anonymity during the seven years of work for the Prime Ministers. Then so many, especially in Wales, will not understand how a Civil Servant does his best for his Chief, whatever the politics of the said Chief.'[101] Though Hankey did not record the incident, surely he thought it conveyed the wrong impression, given his insistence upon the Cabinet Office avoiding the attention of the press.[102]

Disappointed by his failure to secure such a post, Jones held Hankey partly accountable, although he recognized that the Treasury heads – he specified Warren Fisher, who advised on such appointments – had been 'dead against' his going to the Board of Education. Yet by Jones' own account, based upon what Hankey told him, his chief had mentioned his aspirations to the King and twice to the Prime Minister, although the latter did not 'rise' to the proposal. When Jones learned from his chief that MacDonald had concluded that he ought to continue at the Cabinet Office, he rather petulantly, and inaccurately, noted in his diary that

Hankey had not 'lifted a finger to help . . . The result is that I revert to the post I had when I came here, of being Secretary to Cabinet Committees, and, as I understand, have nothing to do with the new Prime Minister.'[103] Jones' subsequent enmeshment in the tortuous but interesting Irish boundary negotiations eased his accommodation to the new pattern, and in any event MacDonald did not long remain in Downing Street.

Despite the collective inexperience of the new Labour ministers, the formalities of their accepting office proceeded to Hankey's satisfaction, although the Webbs claimed to discern 'a hitch' in the arrangements which he had made.[104] From the first, the Cabinet Secretary's relations with the formidable Webbs were strained, although Beatrice Webb marked well those qualities which enabled him to discharge his responsibilities, following upon his week-end visit at Passfield Corners:

An attractive personality, trusted and liked by all Cabinets in succession for the good reason that he likes them and is absolutely loyal and amazingly appreciative of the different statesmen he serves. A simple-minded soldier of the conventional type, devout Christian, a puritan in habits, a perfect gentleman in manners. He *assumes* that the men he serves are public-spirited however they may differ in opinion and capacity. He has plenty of shrewd intelligence, but no intellect; abundance of good temper but no wit; irony or sarcasm would, I think, be inconceivable on his own part and somewhat unintelligible in others . . . Hankey, like other simple-minded persons, mistakes *power* over other people for real distinction of thought and feeling. But this lack of censoriousness – this slightness of critical facility, combined with absolute integrity, kindliness and loyalty and quickwittedness, make him an ideal secretary to Cabinets. If ever a man was perfectly suited to his job it is Maurice Hankey.[105]

The condescension for which Beatrice Webb was well known is apparent in her description of Hankey's intellectual shortcomings, but it is unlikely that the Webbs would care to discuss those matters – in a word, defence – about which Hankey thought deeply and possessed a critical facility which far outpaced 'simple-mindedness.' That Hankey was at the least uncomfortable in the company of the Webbs is apparent in a pained note to his wife, who had sought his instruction concerning another social engagement: 'I think you had better accept the Sidney Webbs, though I shall hate it.'[106] Incidentally, Tom Jones fared no better at Beatrice Webb's hands, despite his Fabianism and genuine interest in education and research; all his experience 'has not given him any insight into public affairs, superior to that of the clever student or professor of public administration. Of course he can give you tid-bits of political gossip; but with regard to the *problems themselves* he knows less than many persons who are excluded from the inner circle.'[107]

The Labour government showed no hesitation in accepting the mode of secretarial arrangements evolved by predecessor regimes: the Cabinet instructed its Secretary to record Conclusions only, 'with such explanatory notes as are essential to render the Conclusions intelligible.'[108] Ministers were responsible for communicating relevant decisions to their own departments. Labour did innovate in requesting the Secretary to give to the press a list of ministers present 'as soon as the Cabinet has assembled.' A week later, that charge was broadened to include the Secretary's taking 'the instructions of the Prime Minister as to the issue of a Communique to the Press in regard to the business discussed.'[109] It appears that the Labour Cabinet had concluded that an official statement of Cabinet business was preferable to the possibly inaccurate summations of a score of ministers, many of whom had no experience in dealing with the press in an official capacity. In view of these developments – Hankey had to dislike them, because he had altogether eschewed dealings with the press – his memory played him false when he recalled, a quarter-century later, that only one minor innovation had marked Labour's accession:

> The old [Cabinet] convention was 'No Smoking before lunch.' It was observed until 1924 when MacDonald renewed it at the outset of his first meeting. But J. H. Thomas came in later and knowing nothing of the rule, continued to smoke. Soon others lit their pipes, and the rule vanished – to the intense discomfort of non-smokers.[110]

Despite the centralization of Cabinet contact with the press, ministers went their own way, and several leakages occurred: already in February, press reports of naval matters caused the premier to appeal to his colleagues to exercise their 'gravest discretion'; in the following month, an apparently deliberate leakage took place at the Admiralty, whose service personnel were distressed by the government's aversion to the construction of a great naval base at Singapore.[111] In due course, such matters as plans to deal with Communist propaganda, a draft of the Unemployment Insurance Bill and CID discussion of the Channel Tunnel were aired in the press, moving MacDonald to repeated pleas for what was the need for 'utmost discretion.'[112]

Convinced of the soundness of the 'very elaborate precautions . . . taken in this office to comply with the instructions of the Cabinet on the subject,' Hankey concluded that the problem of leakage stemmed from the loss of close control when Cabinet Conclusions passed into departmental hands. Despite a repeated prohibition of the practice, indiscriminate reproduction by concerned departments Hankey thought in the main responsible; he recommended the Treasury practice of circulating 'the Minute round to the few heads of [internal] departments who must see it, in a special box.'[113] Nonetheless, the Cabinet Secretary continued to acknowledge that secrecy at the departmental level could be overdone: 'Effective administration depends so often not only on knowledge of the decisions, but of the policy behind the decisions, which may react into ever so many questions. If your officials do not know the policy they will not be good administrators, and will often fail to give advice consistent with the broader policy.'[114] Hankey's pragmatism, even in regard to Cabinet secrecy, led him to accept the Treasury's request in 1924 that two sets of Conclusions be sent, because the Chancellor, Churchill, liked on occasion to take them with him, leaving the office 'embarrassed by not being able to ascertain what decisions have been taken.'[115] Three years later, he favored similar treatment for the Foreign Office, but he added that any other requests ought to be turned down, because leakage had in the past stemmed from too many departments receiving additional copies.[116] On one point the Cabinet Secretary was adamant: Cabinet Conclusions were not sent abroad to ministers.[117] For all his care, Hankey could not control the 'political' aspect of Cabinet leakage: in any Cabinet, differences of opinion exist, despite the doctrine of collective responsibility. Such differences yield to political pressures in disregard of the principle of Cabinet secrecy, with the press serving as conduit for the information: 'The result is that Government and Opposition leaders recognise the need to disregard up to a point in practice the principles of secrecy; while dissidents are only too anxious to do so.'[118] From this reality, there is no escape for the Cabinet Secretariat.

Hankey strove as well to improve the procedural practices of Cabinet government. Labour's Attorney-General, Sir Patrick Hastings, called to his attention the fact that the Law Officers were not adequately consulted about the legal aspects of government bills brought to Parliament; after Hankey's mediation, the Cabinet agreed that whenever a minister intended to submit 'an important question of policy involving legislation,' he should arrange prior notification of the Law Officers. Further, at the Prime Minister's invitation, they might be brought into Cabinet for the discussion of the proposal, and, in any event, they were to receive copies of the relevant Conclusions.[119] In less than a month's time, a procedural anomaly of some significance had been laid to rest. The first Labour government undertook another step in regularizing Cabinet procedure: in April 1924 the Cabinet ruled that, with only the most pressing exceptions, 'a question should be placed on the Cabinet Agenda providing the Minister initiating a subject has circulated his Memorandum at least 5 days prior to the meeting of the Cabinet.'[120] These memoranda should deal with parliamentary considerations and pass the scrutiny of the Home Affairs Committee before they were circulated to the Cabinet. When the Conservatives returned to office later in the year, they accepted these arrangements, subject to the Prime Minister's approval; thus they were satisfied with the effectiveness of these guidelines, which had been violated consistently only by the Foreign Office. In November 1924, a Treasury Minute codified the sequence whereby ministerial initiative secured Cabinet approval: the Secretariat would distribute memoranda only 'after their subject matter has been fully examined between [sic] the Departments from which they emanate, the Treasury, the Law Officers where contentious Bills are involved, and other Departments concerned, and these documents will bear on the face of them a specific statement that this examination has taken place.'[121] In sum, a short-lived Labour regime had contributed significantly to Cabinet procedure.

Such developments help to account for Hankey's pleasant discovery that the personnel of the Labour government composed a 'more business-like Cabinet' than any he had ever worked with:

> They read their papers and get up their subject, and, on the rare occasions where they do not complete their agenda, meet either the same afternoon or next day to finish up. There is never any accumulation of Cabinet business, and it is the first time I have ever known such a state of affairs in the seven years I have been at this work.[122]

The Cabinet Secretary credited Labour's use of Cabinet committees to deal with specific problems; he recognized that the Labour leaders were drawing upon their experience in serving upon similar committees established by party headquarters to examine various subjects.[123] Hankey assigned much credit directly to MacDonald, who had proved 'an admirable head of the Cabinet,' although the Cabinet Secretary questioned his assumption of too great a responsibility: 'The trouble is . . . that no man, or super-man, can really carry the affairs of two such heavy Offices as Prime Minister and Secretary of State [for Foreign Affairs], at any rate while Parliament is sitting . . . Moreover, the signs of overwork in our Prime Minister are at times rather distressing.'[124] His initial enthusiasm for the Labour leader had been reciprocated, as MacDonald queried Hankey's views on a range of topics and encouraged him to resume his private diary.[125]

That activity occupied Thomas Jones too, and his diary, like Hankey's, has become a valuable source for the study of the period in which he served as Deputy Secretary. Delighted to discover that Hankey kept a diary 'in a stoutly bound locked book, the first I had ever seen,' Jones claimed a functional rationale for his diary: 'I was sometimes involved in confidential exchanges with opposed parties during labour and other disputes, or in secret conversations with Ministers. I then felt the need for written proof that I had faithfully interpreted the instructions of my principals.'[126] Neither man disguised the fact that he was keeping a private record of his public activities; Hankey claimed, later in life, that all the Prime Ministers whom he served knew of and encouraged his keeping a diary.[127] The conclusion is inescapable: what a later generation of civil servants viewed with extreme distaste was sanctioned within the context in which Hankey and Jones operated. That the precedent Hankey forged has been disavowed by others ought not to weigh against his valuable record.

In the meantime, Hankey's role deepened when MacDonald – his own Foreign Secretary – turned his attention to the settlement of German reparations as a step towards general European stability. In deciding first to summon the former Allied powers to the London Conference on Reparations, MacDonald hoped to reach an agreement which would in turn be presented to the Germans. The Prime Minister valued Hankey's experienced hand in dealing with such deeply rooted problems; when the Foreign Office insisted that Hankey serve as Secretary-General, he was bound to work closely with MacDonald:

> I became what I had not intended to become – the principal adviser and counsellor to Ramsay MacDonald. I had gone to the [United Services] Club to stay during the Conference, as I could not keep my grip on all its activities at home – and the family had gone to St. David's in August. Ramsay's family had also gone to Scotland; his cook went off, and thereafter we had all our meals together at the Club. Thus it came about that we were thrown together in great intimacy. When Parliament arose his colleagues left town and I was almost the only friend he had left. For the last ten days of the Conference we were almost inseparable. MacDonald worked in almost as irregular a way as Lloyd George – often seeing people early in the morning and late at night. The Foreign Office men, working from 11 a.m. to 7 p.m. and then going home, were not much use to him for his erratic methods. I, having nothing else to do, living at the Club, feeding with him and fully in his confidence naturally became his assistant and abetter. This was all the more so since he and Snowden, the Chancellor of the Exchequer, who was his principal colleague in the Conference, did not hit it off and could not work together. Thus it happened that, while the Foreign Office people did the technical part on Committees and so forth very admirably, the more delicate diplomatic negotiations on points of high policy, and on irreconcilable differences of opinion, passed more and more into my hands so far as MacDonald let go at all.[128]

Hankey's role had come full circle: less than two years after the Cabinet Secretary had been relegated to secretarial tasks, he had re-emerged as a close confidant to the Prime Minister, working at a considerable remove from his formal responsibilities. If the crisis of 1922 had contained a lesson, there is no sign that Hankey perceived the wisdom of avoiding conference responsibilities, nor of maintaining a certain distance from the Prime Minister.[129] To the contrary, he was willing again to function as a right-hand man. At the same time, he had again claimed a central role in defence planning: Sir Maurice functioned both as man and as institution, a formidable combination. While the Cabinet Secretariat may have eschewed the 'limelight' in the wake of 1922, the Cabinet Secretary himself did not seek obscurity in the wings.

Yet the 'honeymoon' period for MacDonald and Hankey began to dissipate – unnoted at the time – during the Reparations Conference. His confused, evasive, and misleading response to the unfolding scandal of the Campbell case – 'the silly little issue of the Campbell prosecution' was Beatrice Webb's rueful description[130] – discredited and ultimately felled the first Labour government. The proceedings raised a question about Ramsay MacDonald's fitness for high office; Hankey discovered behind the hale exterior of the man risen from the people some troubling traits. The Cabinet Secretary loyally served MacDonald upon his return to Downing Street in 1929, but the deep disappointment cannot have been forgotten.

Only certain features of the Campbell case can be treated, because our concern remains with the implications for the Cabinet Secretariat of the actions on the part of the Prime Minister and his colleagues. On 25 July the Communist party newspaper, *Workers' Weekly*, published an 'Open Letter' to the Fighting Services, steeped in revolutionary rhetoric and appealing for class solidarity.[131] Asking for the organization of 'committees in every barracks, aerodrome, and ship,' as a first step in concerting 'a common attack upon the capitalists and [to] smash capitalism for ever and institute the reign of the whole working class,' the party letter came to the attention of the military authorities, who urged an appropriate response. The Director of Public Prosecutions and the Attorney-General, Sir Patrick Hastings, agreed that statute law had been broken by the appeal, and the DPP secured a warrant for the arrest of the person responsible for the issue in question, one John Campbell.[132] Even before Campbell's arrest, the episode was raised in Parliament, when the Under-Secretary for Home Affairs was asked how HMG intended to respond to a document possessing 'a subversive character and calculated to disturb and undermine discipline in His Majesty's Service.'[133] With the arrest of Campbell, acting editor of the *Workers' Weekly*, several days later, the government took a flow of questions from the Labour left; noting that Campbell had accepted responsibility for a breach of the law, the Attorney-General admitted surprise with the vehemence of the questions from that quarter; as a result, he consulted with a spokesman for the Labour left, James Maxton, learning only at that time that Campbell was only acting editor and that he personally had an outstanding war record. In the light of this conversation, Hastings regarded his initial decision 'an unfortunate mistake' because prosecution of a political nature 'entails the consideration of a great many elements, not the least being the personality and antecedents of the individual to be charged.'[134]

Nonetheless, formidable obstacles stood in the path of dropping the charges: Hastings had first to inform MacDonald of this change of opinion, suffering criticism from the Prime Minister both for the initiation of proceedings and the willingness to abandon prosecution, once undertaken.[135] Notwithstanding MacDonald – he explained later –

deferred to the Attorney-General, who as a Law Officer bore the responsibility in the case and who had himself taken the initiative in the proceedings. He invited Hastings to a Cabinet meeting later in the day, 6 August, because the Campbell case had assumed political importance. Since Hankey was involved in the work of the Reparations Conference, Thomas Jones took the minutes of that Cabinet meeting, and his several accounts leave little doubt that following a full but rambling discussion, the Cabinet was persuaded by the Attorney-General's review of the case.

The Attorney-General said he took full responsibility for proceeding with the case, which disclosed a bad criminal offence, but inasmuch as it transpired that the person charged was only acting temporarily as Editor and was prepared to write a letter to that effect, steps could be taken not to press the prosecution in the circumstances against this particular offender, if the Cabinet so desired.

After considerable discussion of the procedure which had led to action being taken in the Courts without the knowledge of the Cabinet or the Prime Minister the Cabinet agreed:

(a) that no public prosecution of a political character should be undertaken without the prior sanction of the Cabinet being obtained.

(b) that in the particular case under review the course indicated by the Attorney-General should be adopted.[136]

So much for the Cabinet decision, but in this matter – because Jones preserved the notes which he took during the discussion – we are far better informed than is usually the case; although these notes are not free from some internal confusion, they are quite consistent with the Conclusions.[137] Prior to the Attorney-General's entering the meeting, MacDonald complained that Hastings ought to have consulted him in an obviously political matter; for his part, Hastings admitted that 'in case of great importance' he ought to consult the Prime Minister – the unstated implication was that he had not perceived the Campbell proceedings in this light. Noting the extenuating circumstances which he had recently uncovered, the Attorney-General informed the Cabinet that there existed 'a possible way out if you desire it against this man.' MacDonald countered with a different preference: 'I'd rather go through once started than show white feather. If you stop prosecution you will be asked all round what [you are] going to do.' At this point, the Cabinet decided to instruct the Attorney-General to secure its prior approval for political prosecutions.

The Cabinet discussion then returned to Campbell's offence, and Hastings reiterated the extenuating circumstances, including: 'Man arrested [Campbell] prepared to write a letter say he was [editor] only few days.' On this point, according to Jones' notes, a decision was apparent:

Attorney-General: I'll accept his letter – reply being that we had to take cognisance reluctantly.

Henderson [*the Home Secretary*]: More questions tomorrow.

Attorney-General: Steps have been taken. Nothing to add [presumably to such questions as were raised in the House of Commons].

(Attorney-General authorised)[138]

'Authorisation' in this context almost surely implies the Cabinet's agreement to drop the prosecution, in response to Campbell's 'letter,' but such an item apparently never existed, and thereafter it disappears entirely from Hasting's account. Nonetheless, such a document had been a premise upon which the Cabinet had accepted Hasting's 'possible way out'; on this point the Cabinet Minute is deficient,[139] although surely the Attorney-General personally bore responsibility for its subsequent collection. In the absence of further information, one may speculate that James Maxton had suggested that such a 'letter' could be secured, which gave the Attorney-General a rationale for his reversal of field.[140] Yet another puzzling feature is that the Prime Minister apparently abandoned his fear of showing the 'white feather' as the discussion abruptly ended; perhaps for him too the alleged 'letter' represented the 'way out.'

How to explain the Cabinet's action? While one may question the thoroughness of the discussion and resulting minute, there appears to be no reason to challenge the explanation adduced three weeks later by the Home Secretary, Henderson:

the Cabinet as a whole felt that proceedings against Campbell . . . would do more harm by advertising the Communists than any harm which would follow the publication of the article, and that it would appear that far more importance was attached to the views and activities of the Communists than in fact they deserve. This would have been the attitude taken by the Cabinet had it been consulted before the proceedings were launched. It was recognized that a withdrawal of the prosecutions would not leave the matter in the same position as if the prosecution had not been started; but on the whole it seemed better to adopt this course rather than let the trial of Campbell proceed to a conviction.[141]

While the Cabinet asserted its right to intervene in a legal proceeding, Hastings did not protest the action, nor did the Cabinet over-rule him, as he had already reversed his position.[142] Management of the proceedings again fell to Hastings, who properly assigned the task of informing the court to a Treasury Counsel, Travers Humphreys, who did not care in the least for his brief. Convinced that the grounds for withdrawal advanced by Hastings were each deficient, Humphreys chose the least weak among them, namely that the intent of the letter was not to seduce men in the services from their duty, an interpretation bolstered by Campbell's own military record. On 13 August he moved withdrawal of the charge, accepting representations that Campbell intended only to comment against the state's use of armed military force to suppress industrial disputes.[143] Since Humphreys did not publicly link those 'representations' to the queries voiced by the Labour left in the House of

Commons at the end of July, the CPGB seized upon his statement to suggest that the 'representations' had been made by such Labour leaders as MacDonald, Henderson, and Clynes, who feared that they would be called as defence witnesses because of their own past statements on the use of military force in industrial disputes.[144]

Against this backdrop of ambiguous 'representations' *The Times*' leader of 15 August deplored any such action on the part of a Minister, which would

> constitute an interference by the Executive with the course of justice which should not be tolerated by the people of this country. To arrest a man on a grave charge and then to refuse, at the instance of someone, presumably in authority, to disclose the evidence when the accused professes to have a good defence, is not consistent with British ideas of justice. It undermines the confidence of the public in the procedure of our Courts of Law.[145]

Among those who expressed an interest in the case was George V, and in the course of answering his inquiry, MacDonald learned of the Home Office's insistence that they had no official knowledge of the reasons for the withdrawal of the prosecution, because the Cabinet had acted. On 13 September the premier sought further information from the Attorney-General, although his own secretarial staff apparently had not consulted the Cabinet records in the interim.[146] Hastings promptly responded to this second request, informing the Prime Minister that he had decided against the prosecution of Campbell; he did not mention the Cabinet's agreement to the action.[147] Armed with the information that Hastings had throughout acted on his own authority, MacDonald chose to challenge the Cabinet Minute in question, when it came to his attention.[148] No coincidence, then, that on 22 September MacDonald, in the presence of a number of Cabinet ministers, asked Hankey to show him the Cabinet Minute dealing with the prosecution of the editor of the *Workers' Weekly*; according to Hankey, 'on reading the minute, the Prime Minister at once challenged its accuracy, more particularly in regard to conclusion (b).'[149] As the Cabinet Secretary, who had not attended the meeting in question, recorded no response to this allegation, MacDonald may have concluded that his challenge had been sustained.[150]

When the House of Commons reassembled a week later, MacDonald's angered but impetuous response to a hostile parliamentary query transformed an embarrassing incident into a budding parliamentary crisis:[151] 'I was not consulted regarding either the institution or the subsequent withdrawal of those proceedings. The first notice of prosecution which came to my knowledge was in the press. I never advised its withdrawal, but left the entire matter to the discretion of the Law Officers.'[152] MacDonald's words left the impression that he had been in no way involved, which his colleagues and the Cabinet Office knew was inaccurate, although Hankey put a finer edge on the proceedings by commenting that his statement was '"a bloody lie".'[153] The Cabinet Secretary's use of what was for him a strong expletive was matched by a resolute course of action, based upon a source which MacDonald likely knew nothing about – Jones' own rough notes of the Cabinet meeting at issue. Hankey's practice was to destroy such notes when the agreed version of the Conclusions appeared, in order to ensure the secrecy of what was said in Cabinet; in this case at least, Jones had acted differently:

> [On] . . . 2 October, when Howorth told me that he understood that the Prime Minister was challenging the accuracy of the Minute I had written on the subject I dug out my rough notes on which the Minute was based, had them typed, and went with them to see Hankey. He told me that on 22 September the P.M. had said to him that the Minute was inaccurate. I asked him in what respect, and Hankey could not tell me. He and Howorth read my rough notes and agreed that on the evidence before them, the Minute was, if anything, an understatement. In particular I had down 'A. G. authorised', whereas in the Minute I had used our usual formula 'The Cabinet agreed.'[154]

Strengthened by this particular phrasing – though the distinction is puzzling – Hankey decided that he had sufficient evidence to press the premier to make an exculpatory statement, thereby heading off a censure debate. Concurrently, he sought to protect the integrity of Cabinet record-keeping by attaching to the Cabinet Minutes for 6 August a note of the Prime Minister's subsequent challenge.[155] The political storm clouds gathering round the Labour government threatened to engulf the Cabinet Secretariat: if MacDonald were to convince the Opposition parties that he bore no responsibility for the handling of the Campbell case, that success could come through his challenge to the credibility of Cabinet Minutes.

To obviate that possibility, Hankey carefully compiled an account of the way in which Cabinet Conclusions generally, and the Campbell Conclusion in particular, were approved. To MacDonald's protestation on 2 October that he could not remember having seen the minute in question, Hankey reconstructed the events of 6–7 August in such a way as to convince the premier that he must have seen it. According to Hankey, Jones sought immediate approval of the draft minutes, since the Cabinet was on the point of dispersing for holiday; Hankey's account of what ensued illustrates the care with which the Cabinet Office operated:

> Mr. Jones, however, was rather anxious about the particular Minute relating to the *Workers' Weekly*, and he handed me a Note . . . in the following terms: –
>
> 'Secretary.
>
> For Prime Minister's approval. If he cannot look at all perhaps he would look at No. 5 (*Workers' Weekly*).
>
> T. J. 11.40 a.m.'

. . . I have no precise note of the moment at which I obtained your approval. My strong recollection is that this occurred at the House of Commons on the conclusion of the Meeting of Heads of Delegations [to the Reparations Conference] at 11 a.m.; that is to say, just before lunch. In fact, it must have been so . . . there is a note in the Office that the draft Minutes actually left this Office for circulation to the Cabinet at 3.20 p.m. Allowing over an hour for the final clerical and manipulative stages of the reproduction and circulation of the rather long Minutes of this Meeting, the office must have had authority to circulate somewhere about lunch-time. I do not think there is the smallest doubt that I did show you this Minute [in a footnote asterisked at this point, Hankey added, 'Mr. Tom Jones tells me that this entirely confirms his recollection, which is that at the time I definitely informed him that the Prime Minister approved this particular Minute.']. It is true that on some occasions, especially when I think there is no matter of a doubtful or controversial character in the Minutes and you are very preoccupied, I issue them on my own authority. But in this case a special form of notice is attached to the draft, which indicates that they have not yet been submitted for your approval. In the present instance, however, I have on the file a duplicate of the notice which accompanied the Minutes. It is the normal notice for an occasion on which the Prime Minister has seen the draft, and is couched in the following terms:

> 'The attached draft Conclusions are circulated by direction of the Prime Minister. It is requested that any corrections may be communicated to the Secretary not later than 12 Noon on Friday, 8 August 1924.'

No corrections were received. The fact that this form of notice was issued is a proof that I was satisfied that you had read and approved the draft Minutes.

I would draw your attention to the form of the above notice. It invites every member of the Cabinet to send corrections. The Distribution List shows that it was sent, along with the Minute on the *Worker's Weekly*, to the Attorney-General and the Solicitor-General. Neither of them criticized the Minute, nor did any member of the Cabinet.[156]

While Hankey's primary concern was the defence of his own operation, his exercise also afforded MacDonald a means of dignified retreat from his self-imposed dilemma. Hankey took care to cite the events which had occupied the premier's attention, expressing his sympathy with 'an observation of a general character which I have often heard you make . . . that you objected to having documents pushed into your hands for approval at a time when your mind was full of other matters.'[157] Was the Cabinet Secretary suggesting in a tactful way that the Prime Minister plead press of other business by way of apology for a faulty recollection? To be sure MacDonald had complicated matters by his denial of involvement, coupled to his challenge to the Conclusion, but an admission of error – plausible in light of the Jones notes – could well have cleared the political atmosphere. Certainly the Tory and Liberal leaders would have been hard pressed to bring down a minority government because of the Prime Minister's faulty memory: such grounds would not give the appearance of a popular electoral issue.[158]

Unwilling to admit his error, the Prime Minister chose to regard a Liberal attempt to substitute an inquiry for the Conservative censure motion as equivalent to a vote of no confidence in his administration; when the Tories chose to support that parliamentary tactic, the doom of the Labour government sounded. Even in the wake of the Conservatives' return to power, Ramsay MacDonald professed to view the Campbell incident as an 'extraordinary series of muddles,' lodging the responsibility elsewhere: the Attorney-General had misunderstood his own assertion that he must carry through any political prosecution, once launched, and the Cabinet had shied from any attempt to intervene – although they had discussed the matter 'from various points of view.' The Cabinet Secretariat had played what was perhaps the key role, he informed C. P. Scott some months later:

> Hankey, the usual Cabinet Secretary, had been unable to attend and a substitute had been employed to take the minutes who took them all wrong. When Hankey brought them to MacDonald to be initialled he was in the midst of an important discussion . . . on a proposed London Agreement. MacDonald scolded him for bringing them at such a time, contrary to his instructions, but Hankey persisted and said he thought he should look at item 5. MacDonald, still impatient, said, 'Well, is it all right?' [to a man who had not attended the meeting] and Hankey replied, 'Yes, I think so.' 'So I just initialled it,' said MacDonald and thought no more about it. (The other members of the Cabinet all saw the minutes and no one called them in question.) In fact, said MacDonald, they did not read them.[159]

Apart from the slur on Hankey's role and that of the unknown 'substitute,' MacDonald's self-pleading does not convince: that no member of the Cabinet, even on the eve of summer holiday, would read the minutes exceeds the bounds of credibility. Yet MacDonald admitted that his belated attempt to correct the minute appeared to be an afterthought: 'There is only my word for it that it was not, which people can believe or not as they please.'[160] Examined in the detail which the existence of Cabinet records and the Jones notes make possible, it is no longer possible to 'believe,' and MacDonald's attempt to extricate himself from muddles and misunderstandings in which he had played a leading role does not constitute a creditable chapter in his long political career. The point remains that his actions indicate that he was prepared to discredit the Cabinet Secretariat for errors committed by the Executive.

Nearly on the eve of their defeat in the Commons, the Labour Cabinet expressed some bitterness with Cabinet Minutes, which was understandable if misjudged. Hankey shared their sentiments with Jones, who recorded them in his diary:

> They [the Cabinet] have been greatly worried not only about my Minute and my rough notes on which the Minute was based but also on the fact that the Minute had become widely known in some Departments. Apparently it was 'Roneoed', i.e. multiplied. One Civil Servant who had seen it and seen the Prime Minister's reply in the House of Commons . . . had gone to the 1st Lord and said the P.M. was lying. This has naturally caused much fear and trembling . . . In future I gather even the summary of the discussion is to be dropped [it was not], and this

conclusion is not to be circulated but is to be paraphrased by the Minister to the officials of his Department concerned. That was the view yesterday, but Henderson prompted by Hankey urged the Cabinet not to scrap the present system [because] they had got into trouble over a Minute and not to do so anyway on almost their last day.[161]

The Prime Minister too seized upon the circulation of the Cabinet Minute dealing with the Campbell prosecution in his subsequent chronicle of the sad affair, and he once more depicted the Cabinet Secretariat's role as inept, explaining to C. P. Scott:

some military business had been dealt with [at the Cabinet meeting] and the custom is that where any Departmental matter is dealt with a copy of the minute relating to it should be sent to the Department concerned. On this occasion the communication was sent to the Admiralty, but instead of the particular minute alone the whole of the minutes were communicated including the erroneous one about the Campbell affair. The Admiralty circulated them among the Navy and Army chiefs and so the matter came to be known.[162]

While internal procedures with regard to Cabinet Minutes at the Admiralty left much to be desired, the balance of MacDonald's remarks are nonsense, viewed in the context of Secretariat practices: in the first place, the military authorities had a vital interest in the case, since they had first called the *Worker's Weekly* appeal to the attention of the Law Officers; surely the War Office and the Admiralty would be informed concerning the disposition of proceedings. Even more tellingly, Hankey commented that neither of the Law Officers criticized the terse minute 'nor did any other member of the Cabinet,' which could only mean that the relevant Conclusion was routinely sent to all members of the Cabinet, including the First Lord; indeed the whole of the Cabinet Minutes were sent to all Cabinet ministers at this time. Ramsay MacDonald sought sympathy at the expense of the truth.

On the day the first Labour government fell, Hankey oddly absented himself from Whitehall Gardens, and thus Tom Jones wrote to him, suggesting that he use his influence with the King to deny MacDonald the dissolution which he was intent upon: 'Don't you think in as much as (1) we have a minority government and (2) no-one (except some Labour men) wants an election, that the King should refuse a dissolution until he has exhausted such alternatives, i.e., seen Baldwin and Asquith?'[163] In the event, time proved too short for Hankey to play the role for which Jones cast him, but it is not likely that the Cabinet Secretary would have been well advised to intervene in a matter with weighty political overtones. Nonetheless, it is interesting that George V felt as did Tom Jones, privately recording his dismay that another election would be so soon required.[164] Probably the basis for Jones' appeal was a conversation with J. H. Thomas, who opposed such an election; as well, the Colonial Secretary, 'with the aid of the lurid language of which he is such a master, declared that unfortunately "Mac" had gone beyond the truth and we had got to try and pull things together.'[165] In the Campbell affair, no one could accomplish that feat.

One other exchange with the Prime Minister may have been unsettling for the Cabinet Secretary, although Hankey had no choice but to take his chief's instructions. On 22 September, the occasion when MacDonald challenged the accuracy of Jones' record, he did so at a gathering which Hankey thought a Cabinet meeting, with the premier in the chair and a goodly number – though far from all – of Cabinet members in attendance. Unable on the next day to gain access to the premier, Hankey circulated draft minutes, only to earn the retort from MacDonald, written across the first page: 'This was not a meeting of the Cabinet at all and no record shd. be made.' Yet the Prime Minister also took the trouble to read and comment upon the minutes which Hankey had made, raising the possibility that the meeting became a non-event because MacDonald wanted no record of what had been talked about. Beside one suggestion made with regard to parliamentary tactics, MacDonald asserted: 'This was a joke.'[166] No one has ever accused Hankey of an excess of levity in the maintenance of Cabinet records, but it remains improbable that he would not recognize intentional humor within the Cabinet. The Cabinet Secretary recovered all but one copy of the 'Minutes,' but the Secretariat copy remained in the files; although one must treat this singular episode with some care, its timing suggests that Hankey was determined to maintain a record of the meeting – whether or not a Cabinet gathering – authenticated by the premier's own hand, despite instructions to the contrary. Nothing ranked higher in the Cabinet Secretary's precise mind than the integrity of Cabinet Office operations.

With MacDonald's subsequent willingness to use the Secretariat's 'blunders' to excuse his handling of the Campbell affair, Hankey's concerns surely mounted: what transpired in these months was far from the overt, well-publicized attack which the institution had withstood in 1922, but in a covert and ill-managed way a premier gave the appearance of discrediting a body which deserved better of him. Precisely for the reason that the Secretariat might well have suffered had MacDonald not been bested by an unequivocal 'record,' Hankey's defence of procedures must be regarded as a significant victory for an agency of Cabinet government neither tied to party nor hostage to a premier. In this sense, the events of 1924 confirmed the independence of the Cabinet Office.

In the course of the ensuing electoral campaign, Ramsay MacDonald was ill-served by senior civil servants within the Foreign Office. Although the Cabinet Office was in no way involved – in fact, Hankey took his holiday abroad, at a complete remove from the events centering on the publication of the 'Zinoviev letter' – the fullest record of the

Cabinet's reaction occurs in Tom Jones' diary. On 10 October a copy of a letter purportedly signed by President of the Comintern, Grigory Zinoviev, and two of his associates on its Executive Committee was received in the Foreign Office; addressed to the CPGB, the letter sought ratification of the Anglo-Soviet trade treaties, an appeal couched in appropriate revolutionary rhetoric. Despite its clearly controversial nature, the bureaucratic mills ground slowly over the weekend, and four days passed before the Northern Department received the copy.[167] In due course it was forwarded, along with other papers, to Ramsay MacDonald, who was electioneering; he rightly asked, on 17 October, for senior Foreign Office officials to confirm its authenticity. Yet views differed: the head of the Northern Department advised that it could not be easily authenticated and advised against its publication; the Permanent Under-Secretary, Sir Eyre Crowe, thought it genuine and dispatched to MacDonald his draft of an official protest to Russia. MacDonald revised that draft, which he returned a week later to the Foreign Office, but without his own initials, which he claimed to withhold until he granted final approval. In the interim, another copy came into the possession of the *Daily Mail*, which threatened publication if the government failed to take action. With the elections only days away, Crowe decided, on his own authority, that immediate publication was the least dangerous course open to HMG, explaining in a letter to MacDonald:

> What would have been the impression if – as would inevitably happen – it was discovered that the Foreign Office had been in possession of the incriminating document for some time, but had concealed this fact and had refrained from all action? Would it not have been said that information vitally concerning the security of the Empire had been deliberately suppressed during the elections, which were meanwhile to be affected by Bolshevik propaganda?[168]

So convinced was Crowe on the need for immediate publication that he published the 'Zinoviev letter' and the British protest simultaneously, without again consulting the Prime Minister.[169] Throughout this period, the communications between MacDonald, on the hustings, and Crowe, in Whitehall, were poor, although the Prime Minister later claimed that at the time Crowe decided upon publication he was available on the telephone. Yet Crowe's 'anti-Russian mentality' carried the day: 'He had no intention of being disloyal,' the Prime Minister commented, 'indeed quite the opposite, but his own mind destroyed his discretion and blinded him to the obvious care he should have exercised.'[170] Although MacDonald was prone to find others responsible for matters to which he was a party, in this instance his depiction of his victimization is persuasive: 'Nobody in the F.O. had 'phoned or wired,' he informed his Cabinet, 'or in any way communicated the fact of publication to him . . . "I felt like a man sewn in a sack and thrown into the sea".'[171]

And for two days MacDonald sank silently in that 'sack,' although he defended his inaction by claiming that, at this remove from the Foreign Office, he lacked the information upon which to base a public explanation.[172] As the Tory opposition fell upon what had come to be known as the 'Red Letter' in a flurry of patriotism, the Labour leader gave his party no lead at all; only on the following Monday did he declare that the British protest had been mistakenly issued, but by this time Labour's electoral campaign had ground to a halt.[173] Although the degree to which this variant on the post-war 'Red scare' influenced the election must remain an open question, there is little doubt that the Labour Cabinet were grievously disappointed with the results, which restored to the Conservatives a firm majority in the House of Commons. From the suspicion that Labour had been done in by its opponents among the Civil Service emerged the desire for an enquiry into recent events:

> A group of the Cabinet, led by Parmoor, were . . . all the time demanding an inquiry which would table all the available evidence and expose our Secret Service . . . Haldane insisted that if Parmoor had his way the result would be the assassination of some of the instruments of the F.O. It is plain that Trevelyan [yet another dissident] believed that Crowe and Gregory had stooped to a mean political trick in order to damage the Labour Party, but the Prime Minister rebutted any such suggestion with energy. He was certain that there had been no bad faith. Subsequently the Prime Minister urged the importance of distinguishing two questions:
> a) The conduct of the Civil Servants;
> b) The authenticity of the letter.[174]

In an angry meeting, MacDonald resisted an examination of the first matter, but a Committee of Haldane, Parmoor, Henderson and the Prime Minister took up the second; Jones was instructed to make no reference in the Cabinet Minutes 'to the Civil Service aspect of the business.' The enquiry was pursued by the successor Tory regime; in mid-December the Foreign Secretary, Austen Chamberlain, informed the Opposition in an assured fashion that the 'Zinoviev letter' was genuine beyond a doubt: 'It is suggested that the Foreign Office was hoaxed by some vulgar imposture such as have been fabricated in various parts of the world. The Foreign Office and our Secret Service have probably a closer knowledge of these manufactories and manufacturers of forgeries than even hon. Members opposite. We know them, and the fact that we know them is a guarantee that we are not taken in.'[175] Yet the controversy simmered, and in 1927 the Baldwin administration requested the Attorney-General, Sir Douglas Hogg, to investigate the matter anew. So sensitive was the question of authenticity that Hogg submitted no written report, and Hankey recorded Hogg's conclusions in his own hand and kept that sparse record in a highly secret category of Cabinet papers. Citing circumstantial evidence, the Attorney-General expressed his opinion that 'the information was genuine,' although it could not be produced in a Court of Law.[176] Obviously HMG relied upon secret sources of intelligence.

Yet that 'official' view of the authenticity of the 'Zinoviev letter' remains in dispute, although the recent emergence of variegated sources – but not the actual records of the intelligence organizations – has served to narrow the scope of historical disagreement concerning related matters. While authenticity remains necessarily unproved, there is no longer room for doubt that 'the political bomb which exploded in the last days of the Labour government was planted by the intelligence community'[177] – past and present, acting in a common cause. In sum, the 'Zinoviev letter' was deliberately manipulated by a number of hands to secure a political end, namely Labour's defeat at the polls. Yet Foreign Office officials, with several exceptions, and the successor Tory ministry found their belief that the document was an intercepted Russian missive confirmed in November 1924, by a confluence of independent sources of intelligence. Officials of the Conservative Central Office likely found their rush to publish the document justified; without apparent hesitation, they had arranged a staggering payment from party coffers to the informant who had supposedly placed a former MI5 official, Donald im Thurn, on the trail of this piece of Bolshevik infamy.[178] Thus from a historical perspective, the shocking aspect of the sordid electoral proceedings is the joint intrigue of the intelligence community with leading Tory party officials, including the chairman, Sir Stanley Jackson, and the treasurer, Lord Younger, to ensure the publication of a document bound to influence the latter stages of the campaign. Since the Tory officials believed that the 'Zinoviev letter' was authentic, doubtless they concluded that the use of party funds was an investment in the national interest. Nonetheless, their machinations – two years after their party had forced Lloyd George from office in part because he had flouted standards of political morality – struck at those democratic institutions which they feared the Bolsheviks would subvert.

The concern which gave rise to 'Red scares' accounts for the enthusiastic acceptance of the 'Zinoviev letter,' and the Bolshevist menace preoccupied the watchdogs of MI5 and Scotland Yard throughout the early 1920s. Fear that a General Strike would produce the kind of anarchy and chaos in which Communism would flourish led the Baldwin government 'to protect the people against any attempt at direct action by revolutionary methods to put in an anti-democratic body to control the people.'[179] Placed in charge of appropriate measures was Baldwin's close political associate, J. C. C. Davidson, Chancellor of the Duchy, who drew up measures which, in the case of a General Strike, placed a Commissioner in charge of maintaining essential public services in each of twelve districts. The scheme was a closely guarded secret, which with the fall of Baldwin's first government posed a problem, namely whether a Labour ministry could be taken into confidence concerning the work of the Supply and Transport Committee. A potentially divisive situation could eventuate:

> the Chief Civil Commissioner [of the scheme], appointed under that government, might well be a prominent trade unionist . . . In this event, whoever was appointed would at once become acquainted with all the machinery for quelling that very crisis which he himself, when in opposition, may have done his best to foment. In these circumstances, it is for consideration whether the organisation had not better be wrapped in temporary obscurity and silence.[180]

To circumvent the problem, the file of papers could be handed over to a civil servant, rather than to Davidson's political successor, 'leaving it to Hankey to raise the question of your successor [as Chief Civil Commissioner] with the Home Secretary of the new government.' Such a conspiracy of silence Davidson wisely resisted, and he informed his successor as Chancellor of the Duchy, his old friend Josiah Wedgwood, that 'whoever was in power, it was his duty to protect the Constitution against a Bolshevik-inspired General Strike.' He appealed to Wedgwood not to destroy what he had done, nor to inform his Cabinet. The former pacifist and radical Labour MP agreed not to interfere with the work which had been done, and in November 1924 returned the plans to Davidson: 'I haven't destroyed any of your plans. In fact, I haven't done a bloody thing about them.'[181] Whatever the wisdom of Wedgwood's acquiescence, Davidson's refusal to use such highly placed civil servants as Hankey to hide information and contingency plans from members of a suspected regime is commendable.

The Cabinet Secretary could not have welcomed one of the Labour government's final actions, when the Cabinet agreed to adhere to past procedures regarding the custody of Cabinet papers: 'Ministers should retain such Cabinet documents as they desire, on the understanding that as ex-Ministers they could have access to Cabinet minutes and other documents issued during their term of office.'[182] By this time, Hankey had on several occasions lost what he considered to be a vital element in the preservation of Cabinet secrecy, although he noted that CID documents fell into 'a different category' and were to be recovered. As for his role during the Labour administration, he continued to function as an ad hoc censor in the publication of official documents, advising in one case against a Foreign Office desire to publish two documents dating from the Paris Peace Conference in a projected Blue Book.[183] The authority of the Cabinet Office went unchallenged in the historical realm of Cabinet government.

The 'muddles' of the Campbell case and the hysteria associated with the 'Zinoviev letter' ought not to leave the impression that Labour had proved unable to conduct the affairs of government, but all was not orderly in the last months of the regime – in contrast to the first few. What has been described as 'a dangerous lack of administrative and political cohesion' had been revealed by an investigation which Hankey was asked to undertake into the proceedings of the Home Affairs Committee. In particular the Law Officers were on occasion lost in the shuffle of Cabinet business, but the root cause was political rather than administrative.[184] On balance, Hankey's initial satisfaction with the business-like ways of MacDonald's Cabinet is confirmed in several sources; the most experienced member, Haldane, commented that the Cabinet worked hard and was well prepared: 'They made their points briefly and forcibly, trained to do so by Trade Union discipline, and MacDonald was an excellent President. We always got through our business.'[185] Sidney Webb credited the circulation of memoranda in advance of the Cabinet meeting with the positive effect upon discussion and deliberation: 'This practice, no doubt facilitated and developed by the existence of a Cabinet Secretariat, has very largely relieved the Cabinet from speech-making, and apparently enlarged its capacity for getting through business.' Yet Webb's credit was tempered by a description of the Cabinet Secretary which illustrates well how to damn with faint praise:

> Hankey was admirable in every way; but not quite perfect. He made the Cabinet minutes too full, putting in more than the bare conclusions come to; and not completely realising the danger of their coming to light in politically hostile hands. His knowledge of procedure and constitutional forms, though extensive and ready to hand, was not quite complete. When he did, privately, make a suggestion on policy, it was sometimes quite extraordinarily inept.[186]

Implicit is Webb's dissatisfaction with the Secretariat's role in the Campbell case, but no one knew better than Sir Maurice Hankey the need to preserve secrecy for Cabinet documents, nor did anyone do more to protect useful Cabinet Minutes from falling into the wrong hands. As for his policy recommendations, several in the defence sphere failed to persuade his Labour masters, but as we shall see they were hardly ineptly prepared or argued.

With the return of the Tories to office, there is little need to comment on Cabinet procedures, as these men had not yet been a year in opposition: they were fully aware of the ways in which the Secretariat operated, and in their initial meeting Baldwin's Cabinet specified that the Secretariat should continue under the procedural instructions in effect since October 1922. The regime was hostile to one of Labour's recent innovations, deciding that 'the Cabinet should revert to the earlier procedure of issuing only a list of names of those present, without any particulars of the subjects discussed.'[187] In fact, Hankey had brought the press communiqué to the new government's attention, stating forcefully in a memorandum that he did not share MacDonald's belief that publicizing the topics which the Cabinet had considered served a useful purpose. On the contrary, 'in practice it was hardly ever found possible to do more than list the subject discussed, but, even so, the list was often defective or misleading – serious trouble could be caused in India or Egypt just by mentioning the fact that they had been discussed. The meagreness of such communiqués defeated their purpose and engendered criticism.'[188] Hankey's memorandum secured its desired end.

Baldwin's second administration had to resort to unorthodox means to deal with an undesirable compromise of Cabinet secrecy, rooted in the propensity of a prominent Cabinet member to supplement his income by writing signed articles for the press. While a member of Lloyd George's coalition, the Lord Chancellor, Birkenhead, had written numerous signed articles, but Bonar Law's ministry had frowned upon the use of public office for private gain and 'agreed to refrain from the practice indulged in by certain members of recent Cabinets, of writing signed articles on current topics to the press during their tenure of office.'[189] The Labour government did not contest the validity of the precedent, although they were content to declare that all ministers should 'use their discretion as to what they say whether speaking or writing publicly.'[190] Perhaps Birkenhead's keen legal mind fastened upon such an opening, but he did resume the practice of contributing articles on a variety of current topics when he assumed office as Secretary of State for India in 1924. Questions were asked in the House of Commons, and Baldwin reiterated the convention that ministers were disbarred from writing about public affairs; nonetheless, Birkenhead published further articles, seemingly in direct defiance of the Prime Minister. Baldwin accepted these as historical articles which the minister had already contracted to write, and Birkenhead grudgingly agreed to bring his literary venture to an end: 'Birkenhead yielded with an ill grace and nourished an abiding grievance . . . He was prepared to submit to the ruling against political articles, but failed to understand why Cabinet rank should disbar him from writing on general subjects.'[191] Although his biographer-son recognized that Birkenhead was motivated principally by the fact that 'he had always spent more money than he had earned,' apparently he was unaware that the arrangement struck with Baldwin had a financial aspect, namely that since Birkenhead had to give up the £5000 pension to which he was entitled as a former Lord Chancellor, Baldwin arranged to compensate him with a sum of £10,000 from the ever-ready Conservative party treasury.[192] Two payments were made in the course of 1926, yet in the spring of 1928 he published an article declaiming against any extension of female suffrage, a topic of current interest and controversial nature. Baldwin managed to fend off parliamentary criticism by acknowledging to an 'error of judgment' on Birkenhead's part, but the latter had grown tired of office and politics, and in October 1928 he resigned his last Cabinet post.[193] The immediate problem was eased, but the members of Baldwin's Cabinet subsequently refused to disbar themselves from replying to articles published by Opposition leaders, dealing with domestic political concerns, so long as these 'supplemented means already used for enlightening the public in regard to measures before Parliament and other administrative measures.'[194] Since specific reference was made to the 1923 Cabinet decision, we may infer that such articles were not to be written for remuneration.

While Baldwin's second administration opted for Secretariat continuity, one particular innovation may have become institutionalized at this time. Writing in 1927, Tom Jones asserted unequivocally: 'Although Hankey writes a letter offering his resignation as Secretary of the Cabinet when the Government changes, his resignation has never been accepted. Hankey is an established Civil Servant but thinks it right to do this, owing to the intimate personal relations which must exist between a Cabinet Secretary and the Prime Minister.'[195] As Hankey's own diary records no formal written letter of resignation either in 1922 or January 1924 – he had orally announced his willingness to leave – the offer must be associated with Baldwin's return to office. Documentation that such an offer constituted a precedent binding upon his successors is unavailable. One final item serves to link the deliberations of MacDonald's short-lived Cabinet and its successor of much longer duration: on 3 December the Tory Home Secretary, Joynson-Hicks, asked the Cabinet to determine 'to what extent (if any) he and the Attorney-General could make use of the Cabinet Minutes of the previous Government, and other documents in which this Minute was referred to,'[196] in the event that the 'Campbell case' was raised in Parliament. The Cabinet agreed that 'it was highly undesirable and would furnish a most unfortunate precedent, to make public in any form the text of the Cabinet Minute.' Here is the likely genesis of the precedent that a ministry's papers were domestic only, closed as a matter of course to its successors; as recently as 1966 Prime Minister Harold Wilson applied the convention in noting that his government could not even inquire concerning the existence of documents dating to 1956, involving the possible collusion among the British, French, and Israeli governments in the Suez invasion: 'the Government can have no knowledge of any engagement of this kind which may have been made by a previous Administration but which, in the nature of things, can no longer be valid or operative.'[197] Yet with regard to the Campbell prosecution, Hankey honored the instructions given him by the late premier, MacDonald, to the effect that he should show his successor certain papers related to the minute of 6 August if that particular minute were discussed by a subsequent government; Baldwin himself read those papers.[198] Apparently MacDonald had no notion that his administration's Cabinet papers would as a matter of course be closed to successor regimes, but surely the Conservative Cabinet's creation of a convention was sound: to record Cabinet deliberations as grist for future governments to mill for political purposes was not what record-keeping was all about.

At this December Cabinet meeting the Baldwin government also overturned their predecessors' hasty decision that prosecution of offences of a political character could not be undertaken without the Cabinet's prior sanction. The Home Secretary was instructed to convey this revocation of 'certain instructions of their predecessors affecting the freedom of action of the Attorney-General' to the concerned parties.[199] To the House of Commons, Baldwin criticized the partisan character of the Labour Cabinet's position: 'Such an instruction, in the opinion of the [present] Government, was unconstitutional, subversive of the administration of justice and derogatory to the office of Attorney-General.'[200] In the crucible of this heated parliamentary exchange there was forged what has been characterized as 'the modern exposition of the constitutional position of the Attorney-General.'[201] Thus the otherwise lamentable Campbell proceedings had the unforeseen but salutary effect of clarifying the position of the Attorney-General within the administration and in regard to the enforcement of the criminal law: 'In exercising these duties he is wholly independent of the Government, and is responsible only to Parliament.'[202]

For Hankey personally, the change of regimes opened anew the problems of dealing with Stanley Baldwin other than on an official basis: his deputy, Tom Jones, took his place as the premier's principal adviser.[203] Yet the official relations between the Prime Minister and the Cabinet Secretary showed no signs of strain: although he lacked direct influence on the person, Hankey played a prominent role in the organization of the nation's defences, in the main through the Committee of Imperial Defence. Secretariat practices were by this time well established, and the institution secure. One slight change in practices centered on the occasional initiative taken by Baldwin's Private Secretaries, instructing the Cabinet Secretary to place certain items of business on the Cabinet Agenda; Hankey continued to maintain that Agenda, and the change reflects no more than requests in lieu of the daily contact with Downing Street which he had hitherto maintained.[204]

Baldwin was prepared to use the Secretariat in irregular ways; for example, the Prime Minister smarted under the criticism by some Tory

MPs that he had acted weakly in the events centering on 'Red Friday.' While defending his actions at a party meeting, at the same time he sought to use the Cabinet Secretariat for what could be called either educational or propagandistic purposes. Whitehall Gardens was asked 'to prepare a campaign to educate the country concerning the real issues involved in a general strike.'[205] Since Hankey eschewed contact with the press, his reluctance to involve the Cabinet Office must be assumed; because there is no evidence of a 'campaign' mounted from those quarters, the collapse of this particular project also appears likely. In the following year, the industrial scene darkened, a General Strike took place, and the Secretariat played only a minor role in countering the resort to industrial action. While protracted negotiations were carried on by the mine owners and the coal miners, Hankey had been at work drafting 'Emergency Regulations 1926,' which were issued by royal proclamation at the end of April, when negotiations collapsed. As the Trades Union Congress called for strike action at midnight on 4 May, HMG responded with an implementation of the measures which J. C. C. Davidson had developed for the Supply and Transport Committee. Although these measures were drawn up 'very much on the lines of Hankey's famous War Book,'[206] the Cabinet Secretary played no part in their development. In his official capacity he was thoroughly occupied, taking three crucial Cabinet meetings on 2 May.[207] Personally he showed an open mind on the justice of the miners' case, but the resort to industrial action found him resolute, if hardly Churchillian, in his attitude: 'It is going to be interesting seeing if we can beat these fellows. I think we can, but it involves a big effort.'[208]

Where Hankey's involvement was throughout functional, Thomas Jones became deeply involved in the abortive negotiations, and subsequently he attempted to influence Baldwin to moderate any governmental over-reaction, such as he detected in the proposed Illegal Strike Bill:

> I told him that in my belief Eccleston Square [TUC headquarters] was already beaten, and knew it was beaten, that it had taken some time to get the country to appreciate what the General Strike was, but this new Bill would come as a thunder-clap on the country which was utterly unprepared for it, and would greatly confuse its mind.[209]

In broadening his effort to avoid forcing a profound change in 'the quiet peaceful temper of the men now on strike,' Jones contacted a number of influential people, including Sir Warren Fisher and Hankey; the latter 'in his unemotional way said he rather felt the thing was being hurried, but told me that Saturday's Cabinet was unanimous.'[210] Nonetheless, the Cabinet did not proceed to immediate legislation, but instead adjourned discussion for three days, in the meantime stating the belief that existing law made any general strike illegal. With more legal force, Mr Justice

Astbury made much the same point in Chancery on the 11th, and within a day the General Council of the TUC withdrew support from the General Strike, although the miners carried on their courageous albeit futile struggle for many months. For all his centrality in the Baldwin administration, Tom Jones preserved a sense of humor and a perspective on those with whom he dealt, 'warts and all,' on a daily basis; these features lend a human aura to his dealings and to his diary:

> If only I could take myself so seriously [as had Col. House in his published account] I might persuade posterity of my importance in the scheme of things. But I can't – that is why there are so many and such long gaps in this story. I have been consulted in the making of Cabinets. Indeed I am consulted by the present Prime Minister almost every day on matters small and great . . . I've discussed matters of State in lavatories with three Prime Ministers [MacDonald, it appears, excluded]. If I scratch my head long enough, I shall be able to recall quite a number of momentous happenings.[211]

Yet his diary supplies such events no less than the every-day business of government and stands as a vital source for those years when he was close to the premier.

During the second Baldwin government, a novel form of 'leakage' threatened the Cabinet Secretariat, as two burglaries of Whitehall Gardens were attempted; Hankey recorded the apprehension of the culprit in the second instance,[212] possibly to acquaint the Cabinet with the need for improved security. Certainly the curiosity of the press posed the graver threat to Cabinet secrecy, and Hankey still viewed the individual 'indiscretion' as the most likely source. For him, Lord Beaverbrook and the *Daily Express* were prime suspects: in February 1926, Hankey was confronted with a leakage which led him to query the President of the Board of Trade: 'Where did Lord Beaverbrook spend his weekend?'[213] The corollary is clear: 'And with which Cabinet Ministers did he spend it?' Yet another threat to Cabinet secrecy stemmed from revelations of past Cabinet discussions by former ministers, which the Cabinet Secretary had attempted to stem for the post-war period. In 1927, however, there arose a current issue, namely the question of British rearmament, which had led to the resignation from the Cabinet of Viscount Cecil. Convinced of the correctness of his action, the great League of Nations advocate was determined to justify his resignation by publishing a letter which drew upon recent Cabinet discussions. Hankey viewed Cecil's draft letter with extreme misgivings, concerned that it would damage the present government as well as compromise the absolute privacy within which Cabinet business ought to be conducted.[214] Typically, Baldwin was reluctant to intervene, but he permitted Hankey to discuss his views with the elder statesman, Balfour. Encouraged in that corner, Hankey assumed the responsibility for checking the several successive drafts composed by Cecil to meet the Cabinet Secretary's criticisms. After several go-rounds, Cecil decided to forego a discussion of Cabinet deliberations; Hankey was momentarily disappointed because he was certain that the government reply, which Baldwin had left in his hands, along with those of the Foreign Secretary, Austen Chamberlain, would have 'smashed Cecil's whole case to smithereens,' but he recognized that Cecil's expurgated version should be accepted 'in the public interest.'[215] Securing the King's permission to publish the exchange, Hankey brought the untidy incident to a satisfactory – albeit temporary – conclusion. Austen Chamberlain perceived the difference between Hankey's resoluteness and the Prime Minister's inaction: 'I can only say that Hankey was a brick as always, but I do not think it fair of the Prime Minister to leave a matter of this personal character to be dealt with by others.'[216]

Hankey maintained a full record of the events surrounding Cecil's resignation, anticipating that the latter might use the traditional forum for an oral explanation of his resignation, when Parliament reassembled. From Hankey's point of view, that privilege ought to have ruled against Baldwin's permitting Cecil to submit a letter of resignation; Balfour had agreed with the Cabinet Secretary, contending that 'the proper course was for a Minister to give the reasons for his resignation in Parliament where he could be answered if necessary.'[217] While Baldwin evaded the force of that argument, he did take the trouble to commend Hankey for his efforts in terms which are not typical of the exchanges between the two men: 'Your delightful letter gave me great pleasure, increased, if possible, my respect for you, and certainly made me more than ever grateful, I left you a most tiresome task and nobly have you accomplished it.'[218]

With the Secretariat nearly a decade old, Hankey and the Cabinet Office derived satisfaction not only from its survival and development but also from the expressions of interest voiced from abroad. Following such a show of interest by the French government, Hankey drew up in July 1925 a memorandum on the work of his body, in order to enable the French to develop a mechanism to ensure liaison among ministries. In recommending that the Prime Minister approve the dispatch of Hankey's memorandum, which was couched in generalities, Austen Chamberlain felt impelled to add his own views about the success of the British prototype, in which he paid warm tribute to the Cabinet Secretary:

> The continuance of the Cabinet Secretariat after the war led to some criticism, but this has entirely ceased. Successive Governments have experienced its utility and become convinced of its necessity in the ever-growing pressure and complexity of the work of administration. But the question of its success in the

initial stage was largely a question of personality. The Secretary of the Cabinet is now recognized by all Departments as a friend who helps to get their business properly considered and promptly decided, and by the Prime Minister as an agency without whose help it would be impossible for him in present-day conditions to maintain his general right of supervision and control over all aspects of Government policy. The secret of this success has lain in the fact that the Secretary 'is never in the way and never out of the way!' He never obtrudes an opinion unasked and is always helpful when consulted.[219]

Baldwin endorsed Chamberlain's 'admirable description,' which became a part of the cover letter sent to the French along with the memorandum. Results followed quickly, as *The Times* reported on 5 October that a reform of the personal secretariat of the President of the Council of Ministers 'will make it an exact replica of the British Cabinet Secretariat in Whitehall-gardens.'[220]

Two years later, Hankey and Jones conferred with J. Burgon Bickersteth, an associate of Canadian Prime Minister Mackenzie King, concerning the establishment of an office to assist the premier in his duties. When Jones noted that his functions included speech writing for the Prime Minister – nearly all save what he described as Baldwin's literary speeches – Bickersteth pointed to the desirability of 'the distinction between the Cabinet office or Secretariat and the Prime Minister's personal staff,' a distinction substantially blurred by Jones' own role as confidant. Hankey did not concern himself with the anomaly; instead he stressed the need for any such Secretariat to win the confidence and co-operation of the government departments, specifying the 'extreme care which must be exercised to prevent Permanent Under-Secretaries of the various departments from thinking that the Secretariat were unduly influencing the Prime Minister or other ministers.'[221] But Bickersteth remained unconvinced about the speech writing role, unswayed by Jones' lame assertion that someone had to write speeches for a modern-day premier. For his part, the Canadian academic decided against assuming 'a post new in Canada . . . which might be described as Executive-Assistant to the Prime Minister.'[222] In declining the post, Bickersteth confessed his personal preference for the British model, which he thought superior to what the Canadian premier had in mind.[223] Owing to his reaction, Mackenzie King's project lapsed at this time, but in 1939, under King's aegis, a body was established much closer to the British model in its conception. Reviewing his correspondence with Bickersteth at a later date, Jones noted in the margin: 'It was the war which made this possible in the same way as the *first* war made possible in England the first Cabinet secretariat.'[224]

Since the reform of 1922, the Cabinet Office had remained a small, tightly knit body under Hankey's direct supervision. To save on staff, he had introduced a procedure of co-opting departmental officials for the work of Cabinet committees, a practice initially used for serving the Committee of Imperial Defence. Many Cabinet committees had joint secretaries, one from the Cabinet Office and the other from the department most closely concerned with the committee's charge. Economies were effected, but, as important, departmental suspicion of the work carried on at Whitehall Gardens was alleviated: ideally, the Cabinet Secretariat provided for the co-ordination of the committee's work, and the departmental representative supplied the technical expertise.[225] In terms of staff, the reforms of 1922 had bitten deeply, since the complement of the Cabinet and CID Secretariats numbered 44 in 1925, by comparison to some 123 only three years earlier.[226] Yet in the process, the departments had been made responsible for preparing the requisite number of copies of memoranda for Cabinet committees, and the Cabinet Office had resumed the printing of documents with large circulations – the Cabinet Minutes did not fall into this category. Frequently, Hankey looked elsewhere for support: 'On the occasion of a big international Conference or an Imperial Conference we sometimes expand into quite a large Department, with reinforcements from other Departments.'[227]

In organizational terms, the work of the Cabinet Office at this time was divided into three distinct operations: Hankey of course headed the Committee of Imperial Defence, where he was aided by four Assistant Secretaries, seconded from the Admiralty, War Office, Air Ministry and the India Office. A second responsibility involved the work of Cabinet committees, some few permanent but most transient, responding in an ad hoc fashion to perceived problems; in 1925 two Assistant Secretaries were assigned. Serving the secretarial needs of these two operations were nine stenographers, twelve clerks and nine messengers, directed by an Establishment Officer. The third function was self-contained, namely the maintenance of Cabinet records: either Hankey or Jones alone attended Cabinet meetings, and the minutes were prepared by one confidential short-hand writer and another typist; Hankey's personal secretary was also included in the staff of the Private Office.[228] Nor was there any significant growth in staff during the ensuing Baldwin regime.[229] There were two advantages in such a small-scale operation: within the Private Office the value of tight control in stemming non-ministerial leakages is obvious; and generally the numbers at Hankey's disposal were not such as to suggest involvement in policy formulation. The Cabinet Secretary constantly underscored the latter point: 'The function of the Cabinet Office is essentially one of machinery of Government and not of policy. It cannot be too strongly emphasized that the Cabinet Secretary has no duty of offering advice in any matter of policy or of interfering in any way with the functions of responsible Departments in this respect.'[230]

A novel, and fourth, responsibility was assigned to the Cabinet

Secretariat in June 1925, under the supervision of the Deputy Secretary, Tom Jones. Initially called the Committee of Civil Research, the operation was patterned closely on that of the CID, designed to function neither as a conventional Cabinet committee nor as a department:

> It is not the first because it can do nothing but investigate and recommend; it is not the second because it has no fixed numbers or rigid procedures. No executive officer is under its authority. No department is in obedience. No man sits on it as of right except the Prime Minister and those who attend on his invitation.[231]

Its charge was simply stated yet wide-ranging, namely 'giving connected forethought from a central standpoint to the development of economic, scientific and statistical research in relation to civil policy and administration and it will define new areas in which enquiry will be valuable.'[232] This acceptance of such a responsibility by government had been foreshadowed in the *Machinery of Government Report* of 1918, for which Haldane was in the main responsible; thus it was no coincidence that the project was revived during the Labour regime, when MacDonald's Cabinet established a Committee of Economic Enquiry, to ensure that 'national problems were actually . . . being faced and thought out in advance on a basis of fact.'[233] Yet the short life of the government and the disposition of the premier meant that Haldane's ideas were not put to the test; MacDonald took no action to make a reality of what the Cabinet and the Treasury had endorsed.[234] With Baldwin's succession, the initiative for the development of a research organization passed into the hands of A. J. Balfour; not only was the former premier well acquainted with the elastic nature of the CID, but he also was a patron of science and a pioneer in the co-ordination of governmental scientific research. Under his leadership, the Committee of Civil Research strove to combat the harsh realities of Britain's post-war economic problems: 'Industrial research ought not to be regarded as a desirable luxury like good motor roads,' he commented to Hankey; 'can we afford *not* to spend the sums on research which the general economic policy of the government and our national position among world producers seem to require?'[235]

Between 1925 and 1929, the main Committee met twenty-six times, investigating a dozen topics, including such major concerns as the Iron and Steel Industry, Overseas Loans, Electrical Development and Unemployment in the Coal Industry; either the Prime Minister or Lord Balfour chaired these meetings, and a half-dozen ministers attended with some regularity, although invitations varied with the scope of each inquiry. In addition, some eighteen sub-committees were established to investigate technical matters, ranging from the Tsetse Fly to Radium Supplies; the membership of these bodies usually consisted of distinguished authorities unconnected with the government, and such 'experts' were on occasion co-opted by the main committee.[236] Despite such activity, the CCR's Secretary, Jones, regarded the analogy to the CID as 'apt to mislead,' and he recognized that it failed to realize the high hopes of its founders in its first years of existence. A re-organization in 1930 pointed very clearly to deficiencies in the relationship of the CCR to the executive departments.[237] Yet its existence, within the Cabinet Office, incorporated a measure of 'constitutional innovation': 'Conceptually, it was the first attempt to create, along the lines suggested by Haldane and Balfour, a "research department" at the highest level, able to recruit economic and scientific specialists to tackle problems outside the jurisdiction of particular government departments.'[238] Admittedly, there developed a considerable gap between the concept and the practice, which another Labour regime attempted to narrow in 1929.

Hankey's own hand did not loom large in the work of the Committee of Civil Research, and his biographer's assertion of his 'great interest' in its labors must be viewed as an uncharacteristic exaggeration.[239] Surely he regarded the use of the CID analogy as a compliment, and he expressed the hope that the CCR would be useful in strengthening imperial bonds.[240] We do not know if Hankey relished the lodging of such an operation – minute though its scale – within the Cabinet Office, which contradicted the Tory demands to restrict the scope of his operations voiced only several years earlier. His operation continued to discharge a number of responsibilities in the co-ordination of Cabinet government. While the Treasury remained the central department of government, the Cabinet Secretariat had maintained its function as the primary agent of the Cabinet.

5

Twin institutions

During the second Baldwin administration, Hankey remained a leading military adviser, whose counsel was nearly always sought albeit not in all cases heeded. Nor did Hankey shy from obtruding that advice where he thought the national interest at stake. Generally he maneuvered with his fabled tact, as we shall see in our conspectus of Hankey's activities: Hankey had himself become an institution, above and beyond the Cabinet Secretariat. As his contemporaries could not separate the twin institutions, some account of his personal involvement is needed to supplement consideration of his secretarial labors. While Hankey as Cabinet Secretary influenced ministers who were now, by and large, far less experienced in affairs of state than he, his own institutional strength derived from his position as Secretary to the Committee of Imperial Defence, which co-ordinated the defence arrangements of the United Kingdom and the British Empire. We need recall Hankey's own assertion, dating to 1927: 'I do in fact give more time to the affairs of the C.I.D. than to the Cabinet,' an allocation of time and effort which he preferred.[1] Hankey's involvement with the CID stemmed at least in part from the lessened scale of Cabinet activity in Baldwin's regime; since Hankey continued to take Cabinet Minutes unless otherwise occupied, he had more time for other concerns than had been the case during the Lloyd George coalition.[2] Yet the major reason for his priority remained his interest in military and defence questions; whether as mediator or, on occasion, as an activist, Hankey strove to prevent any relative weakening of Britain's overall military posture and strength.

Of course, Hankey's fears that a Labour government would undermine the CID's work had not been realized: from the first, MacDonald had assured the committee that 'there would be no break in the harmony which had previously existed.' He observed that differences of opinion concerning details of expenditure might arise, but more ominously, the Labour leader suggested that 'public opinion was as important as military considerations in formulating sound strategical plans.'[3] Granted that the force of 'public opinion' may have represented novel input for the military leaders; nonetheless, its impact might well be blunted by the assuring presence of Haldane presiding over the CID in the Prime Minister's absence. For his part, Hankey quickly acquainted the new members of the CID, which remained the Prime Minister's own, with the work carried out by its standing sub-committees, and he addressed the problems which the CID had to confront.[4]

The Admiralty first felt the force of 'public opinion' when the Labour government refused to carry on construction of the Singapore naval base. The Colonial Secretary, J. H. Thomas, acknowledged a 'most admirable case' made from a strategic perspective, but the Cabinet gave priority to the concern for 'international co-operation,' hoping that Britain's evident restraint would contribute to 'the creation of conditions which will make a comprehensive agreement in limitation of armaments possible.'[5] As an advisory body, the CID could do no more than review the broad implications for British naval dispositions east of Suez posed by Labour's commitment to test the waters of disarmament.

In the course of announcing to the House of Commons the Singapore decision, MacDonald appeared to call into question the role of the CID in co-ordinating defence policy; he inferred that the committee was too narrowly based to reflect a balanced view of British interests:

> I put in a plea for a wider co-operation of national policy with national defence schemes. . . Sooner or later this country will have to devise some means by which that co-ordination is to affect our defensive military manoeuvres. So far as Singapore is concerned I say that we have created a Defence Committee with the Prime Minister as Chairman [i.e., the CID]. That is an excellent idea, and an excellent machine if it could work. But it cannot work! It shows certain weaknesses . . . the extension of Singapore is one of the most magnificent test cases demanding that wider co-operation of any that has happened in our lifetime.[6]

Hankey immediately protested what he regarded as aspersions upon the CID: 'There may or may not be weaknesses in our present system of co-ordination, but I submit that Singapore is about the worst case that can be taken to illustrate them . . . no question has been more exhaustively studied in the last twenty years.' The CID Secretary maintained that the Singapore base had been abandoned because of Labour's 'foreign policy'; such a rationale, he insisted, did not invalidate decisions taken by previous governments, nor did it point to faulty co-ordination. His passion was such that he had recourse to a tactic which had worked to the Cabinet Secretariat's advantage two years earlier, suggesting an enquiry, 'if only in justice to those who have been trying, as they thought with success, to make it work.' MacDonald eschewed any such investigation, nor did he avail himself of Hankey's offer to review the CID records himself; instead, he commented lamely that 'the weakness is in the P.M. himself and that is what I had in mind . . . I shall have a talk with you one day soon. Meanwhile leave it where it is.'[7] The exchange was private, but Hankey had vindicated the committee as the agency for the co-ordination of defence.

Admiralty anger with the Singapore reversal was somewhat assuaged by the Cabinet's decision to proceed with the construction of five large cruisers, although that decision owed more to Labour's preoccupation with relieving high unemployment in ship-building centers. Hankey accommodated himself to these Labour initiatives – his sympathies lay with the Admiralty throughout – and his influence was not forceful, save in defending the CID. Almost certainly Hankey had decided not to press his new masters, but in general he preferred what his biographer has rightly called 'the method of indirect approach' to attain his ends.[8] Indirection requires time, and Hankey was inclined to patience: time was, after all, on his side. With the return of the Conservatives to office, Hankey's need to defend the CID lapsed, and he found Curzon, Haldane's replacement, 'extraordinarily prompt in dealing with business,'[9] no small virtue in his book. As encouraging was the interest which Stanley Baldwin showed in the CID and in defence problems, as Hankey recorded in March 1926: 'he is taking as great a personal interest in the Committee as any Chief I have ever had . . . since he has been in office, he has, I think, missed only one Meeting. In addition to this, he sees me every day.'[10] In this coupling of an official role and a personal presence, Hankey exercised an influence over ministers which reminds one of Bagehot's description of the rights of a constitutional monarch, namely to be consulted, to encourage, and to warn.[11] No monarch he, but Hankey followed the institutional route to influence, and his centrality in defence matters was the result.

In the mid-20s, Sir Maurice not only recorded the proceedings of the COS Committee of the CID, but he also mediated the tension-laden meetings of that body, in which the three service heads maintained an intense rivalry. Nonetheless, they were charged with giving collective advice, and Hankey exercised his conciliatory talents in helping to forge some twenty 'joint appreciations'; by no means did he reconcile the senior services to the extravagant claims of the RAF concerning its role in any future war,[12] but relations among the services would likely have been noticeably worse had it not been for his efforts.[13] Hankey's mediative skills were also fully extended by the willingness of the Conservative regime to delegate to the CID the taxing question of 'the rate at which the Singapore base should be proceeded with,' since they had agreed on renewed construction. A sub-committee was appointed, ultimately under

Baldwin's lead, with Hankey as secretary: the services disagreed about the type of fortifications desirable for the base and Hankey dealt with the conflicting claims advanced by the Admiralty, the Air Staff, and a Chancellor intent upon economies, Winston Churchill. Hankey's efforts to achieve a compromise foundered on the prejudices of the rival services: with the Treasury's opposition added to the balance, the Admiralty had to settle for substantial reductions in expenditures.[14] Influence, in short, did not always produce the desired results; Singapore is a case in point.

Naval expenditures proved another contentious topic, because Churchill was anxious to curb excessive expenditures, assuming, as he did, that there was no serious prospect of war with Japan within his lifetime. In this matter Hankey engaged in an exchange of divergent views with his deputy, Tom Jones, revealing the gap which had opened between the two. The Cabinet Secretary advanced an economic rationale for armaments expenditure, which in the past had constituted 'a gigantic subsidy' which met the overhead expenses not only of the armaments firms but also of a vast network of suppliers. Cuts in defence spending undercut this subsidy, and, in Hankey's view, 'the consequence is that in all the centres of our vast shipbuilding industry and of the other connected industries, thousands of men are walking the streets and half-starving on the deadly demoralizing dole.'[15] In a memorandum sent to the Prime Minister, Jones bluntly disagreed with Hankey's thesis: '*Disarmament is not a root cause of unemployment*. It is a contributory cause in particular centres and temporary circumstances.' Nor were there simple solutions to the problem of unemployment:

> There is only alleviation. The real issue is: Which is the less harmful way of alleviating – building battleships which by hypothesis are not wanted and would rapidly disappear or increasing our permanent productive assets by constructive measures of alleviation. We can spend the money either way but which would have the more beneficent reaction is obvious.

What was obvious to one was contested by the other: 'Expenditure on Defence is better than Doles . . . which rot the morale of the people and promote the interest of the shirker.'[16] Strong disagreements these, as two nominal civil servants contested for influence upon the Prime Minister: in the era of Hankey and Jones, the Cabinet Secretariat was not a bloodless bureaucratic institution.

Through these years, the CID had re-emerged from wartime eclipse, once again to play a dominant role in defence: the Labour party in opposition expressed concern that it constituted a hindrance to the exercise of democratic government.[17] MacDonald had direct experience of its operation, but he nonetheless queried Hankey concerning the subordination of the CID to the Cabinet. Hankey reminded the former premier that the CID shunned the word 'decision,' since its 'conclusions' or 'recommendations' would 'always be brought to the Cabinet.' Admittedly the CID might resolve technical matters, but with regard to policy the Committee remained a consultative body; in fact what Hankey referred to as 'the improved organization for the transaction of Cabinet business' ensured that recommendations concerning policy had to come before the Cabinet. Although MacDonald accepted the description forthwith, Hankey took further pains to compile a lengthy memorandum, based upon the experiences of the late Labour government, demonstrating that 'the strength or weakness of the CID at any moment is entirely under the control of the Prime Minister and the Cabinet.'[18] Characteristically, Hankey asked only that his own name be kept out of whatever use MacDonald might choose to make of the document; again we see him moving behind the scenes, following the 'indirect approach,' in order to defend the defence organization with which he above all others was directly identified.

The point of departure for Hankey's exercise of influence in defence policy lay in his functional responsibilities as Secretary of the CID: on any such issue, Hankey could establish a preliminary direction of inquiry, through his circulation of relevant materials from two decades of the committee's deliberations. While memoranda could be drawn up anew, often they were simply updated for the occasion; in either case the conservative basis of materials reflecting above all else experience remained intact. In councils of defence, whatever the forum, Hankey could bring his vast experience and sets of records quickly to bear upon the discussion. His 'expert' status was denied by no one; however, where defence concerns intersected with foreign policy, Hankey had to move more warily, because military considerations were but one source which the Cabinet had to take into account. Not only might suspicions based upon past criticisms of the role of the Cabinet Secretariat resurface, but also party ideology could be placed above the most thoroughly researched defence inquiry: Singapore underscores the point.

Given these limitations, what attitudes did Hankey show towards issues of foreign policy in the post-war era? How did he bring his influence to bear in matters where he was not conceded 'expert' status? It is instructive to compare his reaction to the proposed Geneva Protocol with his subsequent posture towards the Locarno pacts. In the former he played a role, precisely because he was able to establish a functional responsibility, which he discharged with conviction and vigor. The Labour government had wrestled with but had failed to resolve the question of Britain's adherence to the Geneva Protocol, and so it was left to Baldwin's Cabinet to settle; from within, Lord Cecil pressed, with the conviction of the true believer, to secure British assent. To do otherwise, he argued, would undermine British obligations under the Covenant of the League of Nations; in particular, the continental nations looked to Article 16, which stipulated automatic sanctions, as the 'sheet anchor' of peace. Hankey dissented from British acceptance of such 'impracticable' commitments, which history – and the American refusal to join the League – had outpaced: 'My own fear is, and always has been, that the League may become discredited by these repeated efforts to achieve the impossible, and that the priceless work it is doing in the direction of peaceful settlement of disputes and the creation of a better feeling in nations may for this reason be hampered.'[19] Cecil was not deflected from his advocacy of the Protocol, although he must have been disheartened by his exclusion from a CID sub-committee – chaired by Sir Maurice Hankey – appointed in December 1924 to consider amending the Protocol. In its deliberations, Hankey minced no words with fellow leading civil servants who comprised the sub-committee: automatic sanctions carried with them nothing less than the 'surrender of the rights of national sovereignty.'[20]

Yet in this instance the CID Secretary did not carry his colleagues to the point where he could sign the sub-committee's report; however, the Baldwin government took the position which Hankey had advocated in rejecting British participation in the Geneva Protocol. They had then to deal with the unresolved problem of European security. Talk of a security pact among Britain, France, Germany, and Belgium persisted with the Foreign Office, but Hankey lobbied the contrary case with the former Foreign Secretary, Lord Curzon, as well as with Lord Balfour and Stanley Baldwin: 'I pointed out that the average Englishman . . . would never consent to guarantee the German frontier against France, because this could never be really a British interest.'[21] He believed that there was no substantive reason – save the need to remain on cordial terms with the French – to support a four power pact.[22] Curzon's death removed his principal ally from the scene, but Hankey approached the Foreign Secretary, Austen Chamberlain, who had in the interim convinced the Cabinet to negotiate such a pact. In this case, Hankey's post as Cabinet Secretary secured him access to Chamberlain, whom he asked to approve minutes of a Cabinet meeting at which the latter had presided, and he proceeded

> to point out that the question had not been considered from the point of view of [military] commitments . . . Some day the cheque might be presented, and we should have to honour it. Had he considered the desirability of having the question of the commitments involved in his policy considered by the [Fighting Service] staffs and the CID?

The tactic is familiar: Hankey hoped to re-open the question of a security pact within a military context. Chamberlain, however, did not take the bait:

He thought that by this quadruple pact he might secure a permanent peace, and get rid of the war spirit which is so rife in Europe. If he failed he thought that Europe would inevitably drift in time into another war. He did not wish to wreck his policy on the technicalities of military considerations. Military men were bound to look at the question from rather a narrow point of view – and so forth.

Hankey had to settle for Chamberlain's willingness to enlist the 'good will' of the COS in this course, but such an outright dismissal of 'the technicalities of military considerations' troubled Hankey, and he confided to his diary: 'I am unhappy about this Four Power Pact. It is not as bad as the Geneva Protocol, but it will be unpopular . . . But I have done as much as I ought, and shall now leave them to work it out.'[23] In this episode, Hankey had recognized the limits to his influence and steered within them: where the issue was not a military one, he could proceed no further than his influence would take him. As far as the four power pact was concerned, Chamberlain was not prepared to be diverted; he had embarked on the diplomatic path which led to Locarno.

Since Hankey could welcome the absence of compulsory military sanctions in the Locarno pacts, he came to support those arrangements.[24] As well, he commended Chamberlain's efforts in a way which came readily to him: 'I have been something more than a spectator of all the efforts made since the war to bring about a durable peace, and I know that very soon after you took office you drew your course on the chart and that you have pursued it unerringly to your destination.'[25] Doubtless the compliment was an honest one, but Hankey, at the same time, cultivated future influence where he had been unable on this occasion to exercise it.

The era of Locarno produced insistent demands for substantial reductions in British armaments, but in no quarter more strongly than Lord Cecil's. Hankey kept a measured distance from Cecil, even in the latter's service as chairman of a CID Sub-Committee dealing with disarmament.[26] In 1927 Cecil came into sharp disagreement both with the Admiralty and a number of his Cabinet colleagues, in a dispute whether Britain had accepted the principle of parity in the cruiser category at the Washington Naval Conference in 1922.[27] When the successor Geneva Conference broke up in August 1927, Cecil resigned, owing to his belief that the Cabinet was opposed to additional measures of naval disarmament. Frustrated in his attempt to force the issue by a letter addressing the Cabinet discussions, Cecil chose the occasion of Parliament's reassembly to speak his mind; his revelations far exceeded the bounds within which Hankey had attempted to maintain the secrecy of Cabinet deliberations. As a result, the Cabinet Secretary prepared a lengthy memorandum which cited the various distortions, misleading statements, and inaccuracies which Cecil had, in his view, inflicted upon the House of Lords; it is difficult to determine whether the disclosures or the inaccuracies disturbed Hankey more, but Baldwin took no further action.[28] Hankey's several exchanges with Cecil serve to strengthen an understanding of Hankey's own beliefs, which amounted to a philosophy of what could be called 'military necessity'; for instance, he wrote to the dedicated pacifist in August 1925:

> I confess that I cannot go all the way with your view that war is necessarily evil in itself . . . War is one of the forces by which the powers of evil have been combatted. But my earlier paper was not written as an opposition to peace, as you suggest. I tried to show that, whatever you do, war will come sooner or later, and, if you carry disagreement too far and crush the military spirit, your civilization will go under . . . My argument, then, is not for war, but for caution, lest we bring down civilization with a crash.[29]

In truth, Hankey was no opponent of peace, but even in the Locarno years, the menace of war confronting an unprepared Britain was ever present in his mind.

Throughout the period, Hankey remained a firm opponent of any idea involving the creation of a ministry of defence: CID files swelled with accumulated arguments against even such a variation as an amalgamation of the supply services of the forces. He contended that the COS Committee of the CID determined priorities which would facilitate the Treasury design to impose a maximum figure for all defence spending, writing to Churchill: 'For modern war we have to organize the whole resources of the nation. At the CID this has been done to a considerable extent, and the process is going on without involving any special expenditure.'[30] In 1928 Hankey had to defend the extant defence organization from the views of his former chief, Lloyd George, who suggested that a single minister could impose 'a much more cost-effective system.'[31] Fearing for the independence of the CID with a defence minister in place, Hankey couched his impressions of Lloyd George's scheme in terms that it appears were designed to catch Baldwin's eye, advising him that the proposal was not necessarily 'impossible or unworkable . . . but it rather assumes the "super-man" – a dangerous assumption.'[32] Since the Prime Minister did not look with any favor upon that *rara avis*, Hankey blunted the force of Lloyd George's criticism and held the fort for the CID, very nearly to the end of the Baldwin era.

Secure in the military sphere, Hankey maintained throughout the decade a successful defensive perimeter in an issue with foreign policy repercussions, namely the projected construction of a Channel Tunnel: he wanted no part of any scheme which would directly threaten Britain with a continental incursion. Defence considerations in fact carried the day when Prime Minister MacDonald and an all-party committee supported by some four hundred MPs favored its construction.[33] On one extraordinary occasion in July 1924, four former premiers – Balfour, Asquith, Lloyd George, and Baldwin – met with the CID in order to remove the issue from the realm of partisan politics. Military opinion, past and present, ran heavily against a continental connection, to which Hankey appended his own conclusion: 'there appears no room for doubt that the existence of a Tunnel would be bound to add something to the anxieties of those responsible for national defence, to our commitments, and to our expenditure.'[34] MacDonald reluctantly accepted the unanimous view of the CID, although he thought that the 'military mind . . . has got itself and the country as well in a rut where neither fresh air nor new ideas blow.'[35] Hankey remained ever vigilant against a revival of the hoary proposal, exulting in 1930 that the 'weak and sickly' project had been 'killed,'[36] as it had – at least for his lifetime.

On another matter Hankey felt so strongly that he would not entertain compromise, despite the fact that what its partisans called 'Freedom of the Seas' involved much more than what Chamberlain had dismissed as 'the technicalities of military considerations.' Hankey's aversion to any compromise of Britain's long-standing claim to 'Belligerent Rights' stemmed from pre-war CID doctrine that, in the event of war with Germany, 'the utmost possible economic pressure' should be brought to bear. When in February 1915 Col E. M. House raised the question of 'Freedom of the Seas,' Hankey minuted Asquith 'not to take any action which would fetter our use of the weapon of starving Germany unless overwhelming advantages are to be gained thereby.'[37] His feelings did not abate with the years, as a torrent of memoranda written in 1927–8, when the matter was re-opened, indicate: the Cabinet Secretary strove to counter the contention that Britain ought to improve her relations with the United States through the surrender of portions of her claim to 'Belligerent Rights.' When Austen Chamberlain appeared to be so inclined, Hankey – ill and absent from London – mounted one of his 'campaigns':[38] not only did he write Chamberlain, but he also urged his deputy, Tom Jones, to intercede directly with the Prime Minister in order to impress upon him that:

(1) Austen's paper ought not to be taken by the Cabinet until the Admiralty have been given time to prepare something.
(2) If the Cabinet decide upon an inquiry it should be a CID inquiry, as the matter is vital to Imperial Defence.
(3) My experience in this matter is so unique that I ought to be a *member* of the CID inquiry.

I decided years ago that if ever 'Freedom of the Seas' went through I should resign, as Imperial Defence would then become a sham.[39]

Remanding the question to the CID was the usual tactic, but the depth of Hankey's commitment quite exceeds that of the other causes which he served;[40] he found it ironic that this sad state of affairs should come about with the 'patriotic' party in power.

Tom Jones immediately called Hankey's views to Baldwin's attention, although in a fashion which the Cabinet Secretary likely did not anticipate:

Saw the P.M. alone. I gave him Hankey's letter on blockade to read, remarking that it seemed to me a wrong conception of a Civil Servant's function to threaten resignation on policy and that in any case there was no immediate danger of a change of policy by the Cabinet. The P.M. agreed to the latter remark, and added, 'After all, the Cabinet must discuss issues of this kind.'[41]

Since Hankey had not specified that his letter should be shown to Baldwin, in one sense he was not threatening resignation; on the other hand, he would expect Jones to convey the strength of his convictions to Baldwin. Thus Roskill's judgment that the incident 'was not exactly a display of loyalty by Hankey's deputy'[42] impresses as harsh: it was not exactly a display of disloyalty, either. Nonetheless, Jones' comment that Hankey held a 'wrong conception' of the civil servant's role seems gratuitous, because no one knew better than he that such frank confidences were the rule, not the exception, in the exchanges between premiers and leading Secretariat personnel. After all, Baldwin apparently registered no surprise – let alone outrage – that Hankey had written in such terms. Nor was such passion novel among the major government advisers of the inter-war period, whatever glossy fictions may be advanced concerning the neutrality of civil servants: Hankey's advocacy of 'Belligerent Rights' remains a particularly telling example.[43]

Nor did Hankey make any effort to mask what he described as his 'bias' from those who knew him well.[44] Though he was not appointed a member of the Belligerent Rights Sub-Committee of the CID, chaired by Salisbury, Hankey was given status as an 'expert assessor,' with the Prime Minister's authority 'to depart from the usual rule of not offering comment on matters before the Cabinet.'[45] Although this body continued its discussions for the balance of the Baldwin regime, at no time did it forward recommendations to the CID or the Cabinet. Hankey's position throughout was to maintain in an absolute fashion Britain's claim to 'Belligerent Rights,' avoiding any discussion of the matter which in itself posed a danger: 'the nations of the world,' he wrote, 'would be well advised at the present time to leave alone the international study of war and its rules (which are apt to prove a cause of friction and irritation) and to devote their energies to the promotion of peace, security and disarmament, which when accomplished, will render war and its rules a thing of the past.'[46] In this advice, Hankey conveniently suspended his own belief that nothing could render war an anachronism: if during peace there was no discussion of the 'rules' of war, Britain would be free in time of war to impose a blockade of her enemies.

Discussions of Britain's naval role served as well to focus Hankey's thoughts concerning relations with the United States, another matter in which he and Tom Jones differed. In October 1928 Hankey wrote caustically that a recent 'offensive and provocative' communication from Washington had accepted the notion of 'special needs' for the French and Italian navies, while ignoring altogether those of the British Empire. In replying to his chief, who was abroad at the time, Jones disclaimed any expertise in naval matters but contended that the British position was difficult to comprehend; Hankey's own views he thought in effect ignored America: 'It is idle to pretend that America isn't there, or is not ten times richer than we are, and that in a struggle the behaviour of the Dominions would at least be doubtful. But this will seem awful tosh to you so I'll switch off.' And 'tosh' it proved to Hankey, who revealed in his reply a deepening animus towards America:

> We have been practising your policy for 10 years, and it has been a dead failure. We have played up to America over the Covenant of the League, abandonment of the Japanese Alliance, Washington Treaties, debt settlement, Irish settlement, liquor treaty (limit of territorial waters); always making concessions and always being told that the next step would change their attitude. Yet they are, as the result, more overbearing and suspicious against us than anyone else.
>
> I am, of course, not for an aggressive attitude. But I would make no more concessions to the Americans, and I am convinced we cannot 'square yardarms' over the naval agreement . . . You can't do business with them.

Hankey reminded Jones that Britain had unique naval responsibilities: 'Our communications, vital to our existence, run through the deep seas and the narrow seas. We must be able to defend either. Global tonnage parity is therefore impossible to us.'[47] The 'special needs' of the British Empire, in sum, dictated for Hankey a superior Fleet.

Hankey's comments, to be sure, came at the nadir of Anglo-American naval relations in the inter-war years, and his dislike of American conduct must be viewed in that context. On the other hand, the tides of history were running against Hankey's vision of the world order, and he shared the strategic astigmatism which Tom Jones detected in the Foreign Office: 'The F.O. is still dominated by the 19th Century tradition of dealing with Europe through France and forgetting the existence of the U.S.A.'[48] Hankey had not forgotten the United States, but he gave the impression of not forgiving America its emergence as a world power.

The question of naval relations remained an open one when, in June 1929, Ramsay MacDonald again exchanged places with Stanley Baldwin; the Labour leader lost little time in agreeing to preliminary conversations in Washington. Since informality was to mark the discussions, Hankey was left behind because, he explained to his son, he was considered too much 'the pundit' in defence matters.[49] Alas, Hankey's suspicions about the Americans were reinforced by the events across the Atlantic:

First, MacDonald is told in June that the question 'Belligerent Rights' is off. Then he comes to Washington and gets a tremendous reception. When drunk with success he is brought to the lumber camp [of President Hoover], and without any experts to consult with – for there was an understanding that he should take no experts to Washington – the question is sprung on him in a most acute and contentious form.[50]

Hoover had proposed the issuance of a communiqué, announcing 'conversations to be begun on Belligerent Rights . . . and . . . the hope that foodstuffs would . . . be excluded from the scope of blockade, foodships being treated like hospital ships.' In London there was consternation with this turn of events: the Chancellor of the Exchequer, Philip Snowden, was 'intensely irritated.' For his part, Hankey resorted to a familiar tactic: he rallied the Chiefs of Staff, conferred as well with Snowden and the other leading ministers in London, and personally warned MacDonald that danger flags were flying as a result of what he characterized as 'in 21 years at the C.I.D. . . . the most controversial subject of all: . . . a storm would arise if the food paragraph appeared; . . . the national support he was receiving would disappear and be replaced with a sharp controversy.'[51]

In receipt of what Hankey thought 'a pretty hot telegram,' MacDonald denied that he had agreed to the exclusion of foodstuffs from the act of blockade; whatever the reality, his confreres had advised that no mention of blockade be made, less 'tacit acquiescence' be attributed to MacDonald's role in the discussions. When the much-feared communiqué was issued on 10 October, those paragraphs which had provoked London were nowhere to be seen: Hankey even checked the contents of the communiqué as it appeared in *The Times*, and its absence there as well produced a state of euphoria in the dyspeptic Snowden, who according to Hankey was 'astonished at his own success in getting the objectionable paragraphs deleted.'[52] To consolidate the position, Hankey subsequently sought to convince MacDonald that the topic of 'Belligerent Rights' ought not to be raised at the forthcoming London naval conference, in view of the *contretemps* at Washington.

To this point Hankey's actions fell within his adviser's role, but so deeply did he feel about the matter that he took a nearly unprecedented step, in order to complete the rout of the American position: he agreed to an interview with a newsman from *The Times*, sent to him by the editor 'to ask my views, which, for the first time to a newspaperman, I gave. As a matter of fact he was quite sound on the subject and the Times leader was admirable.'[53] The Cabinet Secretary had every reason to be pleased with *The Times*' contribution to the cause, since the journal wrote in an optimistic vein about the likely success of the London conference, precisely because Hoover and MacDonald had created a favorable atmosphere in their discussions. One conclusion in particular represents vintage Hankey: 'No one can discuss belligerent rights unless he is in imagination already at war, and therefore too easily a prey to the old ideas and the old temper.'[54]

So vital did Hankey judge Britain's right to blockade that he violated a self-imposed rule of the office, namely that the Cabinet Secretary 'never communicates with the press in any shape or form.'[55] Hankey clearly knew what he was doing, because his identity was masked in the leader. At the same time, Hankey abandoned the 'indirect approach' which usually marked his dealings with ministers. In effect, MacDonald remarked upon Hankey's departure from the civil service role in directing a remark his way in the presence of the Cabinet: 'Here is Sir Maurice Hankey,' he commented in apparent good humour, 'as long as he remains in office there are two institutions which are quite safe. One is monarchy. The other our Maritime Belligerent Rights.'[56] Seemingly the Prime Minister bore Hankey no animosity for having mustered the forces which brought him to heel: perhaps he thought that a function of advisers.

In fact there was a very close connection between the institutions which MacDonald rightly perceived Hankey's determination to uphold, because George V was equally insistent concerning 'Belligerent Rights': the monarch had expressed 'violent' opinions about Hoover's proposal, and he showed great confidence in Hankey's judgment in matters associated with Britain's claim to exercise such rights.[57] Yet the Cabinet Secretary's adherence to a policy – however meritorious his commitment to the maintenance of Britain's naval strength – impresses as essentially ministerial, rather than bureaucratic, in nature. By present-day standards, Hankey exceeded the bounds for civil servants. Yet the point remains that Hankey's activities served in his own time to define what was proper for him as a civil servant, so long as the Prime Minister and the Cabinet accepted such a role for him, or for other servants of the Crown, such as Tom Jones, whose wide-ranging functions were definitely not unique.[58] Neither Baldwin nor MacDonald challenged such activities on the part of leading civil servants: for that reason, Hankey's role must be viewed as constitutionally proper.

With a modest electoral swing to the left in 1929, MacDonald once again led a minority government; no questions were raised about the survival either of the Cabinet Secretariat or the Committee of Imperial Defence. With the Prime Minister's approval, Hankey circulated a Memorandum on Cabinet Procedure to the relatively inexperienced Labour ministers, and the Cabinet agreed that the responsibility for effecting Cabinet decisions lay solely with ministers: thus, at each department the minister alone could open the envelope which contained Cabinet Minutes, with full responsibility for preserving secrecy devolving upon him. Yet such a practice could not be sustained, as the information required to implement Cabinet decisions could not be so drastically curtailed: at the second Cabinet meeting of the new regime, the Prime Minister was given authority to instruct the permanent head of a department to communicate to that department a relevant decision.[59] Three weeks later, ministerial discretion widened: ministers were henceforth free to take the senior permanent officials and the Principal Private Secretary into full confidence, after 'warning them of the particular importance of secrecy in regard to Cabinet proceedings.'[60] Clearly more officials had a 'need to know' than the Labour Cabinet had first recognized. At no point did Labour attempt to re-introduce the detailed press communique of 1924; they accepted instead the Baldwin practice of releasing to the press the names of those who had attended. Almost surely with the events of 1924 in mind, the relationship of the Law Officers to the Cabinet was redefined by a stipulation that Cabinet proceedings would be reported to the Attorney-General and the Solicitor-General only through the person of the Lord Chancellor; they were to be advised prior to the circulation of memoranda which involved legal matters, as was the case with the Treasury and new expenditures. The distinction between the legal functions of the Law Officers and the political concerns of the Cabinet was ensured by this procedure.

The Cabinet also agreed that the Cabinet Minutes (they were once again so characterized) were 'to avoid any reference to opinions expressed by any individual and to limit the Minutes as narrowly as possible to the actual decisions agreed to.'[61] As a result, the Cabinet Minutes for the two successive MacDonald ministries, through 1935, are the most austere, even sparse, for the whole of Hankey's tenure: with the ironic exception of several periods when Hankey was abroad while the Cabinet met regularly, Cabinet Minutes of this period lack the flesh of individual contributions: ministerial titles disappear, and references to conflicting views are masked by such phrases as 'after considerable discussion.' Only in the case of ministers who had circulated a Cabinet memorandum is the notice given that they initiated discussion of the topic.

Hankey's assistants apparently paid less regard than he to these strictures about identification of individual views: while Tom Jones remained at the Cabinet Office, he sometimes recorded specific attributions of comments made in Cabinet.[62] Following Jones' retirement in 1930, he was succeeded by Rupert Howorth, Deputy Secretary until 1942, who recorded more comprehensive minutes for the important Cabinet proceedings of August 1931. Yet Hankey maintained the lean style until, with Baldwin's succession in 1935, he began again to record the views of individual ministers. Why the terse style during

MacDonald's return to Downing Street? That he desired to maintain the 'ridiculous fiction . . . that Cabinet decisions were invariably unanimous'[63] is far from sufficient, in light of the public breach of Cabinet collective responsibility dating to that period.[64] Surely the explanation is that MacDonald's memory ranged back to 1924, when the existence of fuller Cabinet records, supplemented by Jones' draft notes, had from the Prime Minister's perspective contributed directly to the fall of his first government. The point remains: Hankey prepared the minutes in accordance with MacDonald's wishes.

Nonetheless, the Cabinet Secretary continued to maintain a separate file of Cabinet Minutes dealing with sensitive matters; those minutes, few in number, are fuller both with regard to the range of discussion and attribution of individual views.[65] At no time was the accuracy of Cabinet Minutes challenged; thus, the complaints with present-day Secretariat practices voiced so strongly by R. H. S. Crossman lack any parallel in Hankey's tenure.[66] Nor in any accounts or documentary collections is there any allegation that Hankey engaged in a practice which Crossman attributes to Sir Burke Trend's operation, 'constantly transform[ing] the actual proceedings of Cabinet into the form of the Cabinet minutes (i.e. it substitutes what we should have said if we had done as they wished for what we actually did say).'[67] In the years from 1929 to 1935, only one instance of a requested alteration in the wording of a Cabinet Minute has come to light, which very nearly confirms the recollection of Hankey's Secretariat associate, Lawrence Burgis, that 'never once in my experience was a draft decision questioned or not acted upon.'[68] Crossman's observations are those of one contentious observer and will require substantiation, but the integrity of Hankey's operation withstands historical scrutiny.

In the memorandum which Hankey circulated to the Labour ministers concerning Cabinet procedures, he went to some lengths to outline the work of the various Standing Committees which had functioned under the predecessor regime. Since MacDonald had played a key role in what had been formally constituted in 1925 as the Committee of Civil Research, Hankey's review of its work, first among Standing Committees, does not appear coincidental. Basically, his treatment of the CCR as analogous in structure and procedures to the Committee of Imperial Defence was valid, because both were advisory bodies with no administrative or executive functions.[69] However, one senses in Hankey's description an equivocal view of its actual achievements, though some of its sub-committees clearly had made advances within limited areas of scientific inquiry. In co-ordinating diverse scientific projects, Thomas Jones had served ably as the CCR Secretary, but his contemporaries were agreed that the CCR had not evolved in such a way as to encourage those who hoped to develop a mechanism along the lines of an 'economic general staff.'[70] Far from functioning as an overseer of the relations among government, industry and science, the CCR's work remained fragmented from the first. Indeed, any claim to synoptic planning emanating from within the Cabinet Secretariat would have been strongly resisted by the Treasury.[71] That the shortcomings of the CCR were evident is clear in the comment of the Labour premier in November 1929: 'when we came into office we found absolutely nothing of the least use to us – no statistics prepared, no experience codified.'[72] As clearly, Hankey's description of its activities had not hidden the fact that as an agency of co-ordination, the CCR left everything to be desired.[73]

The Cabinet Secretary continued his review of the work of Standing Committees by noting that during the Baldwin administration the Home Affairs Committee had assumed a functional responsibility 'to examine, particularly from the legal point of view, Government Bills and other important Bills, and to make recommendations to the Cabinet on drafting the other questions of detail, reserving all major questions of policy for Cabinet decision.'[74] Hankey's thrust was to establish that the Home Affairs Committee did not function as an inner Cabinet but rather provided a technical scrutiny which he judged particularly valuable in removing by committee discussion 'difficulties . . . which would otherwise involve considerable departmental correspondence, loss of time and Parliamentary embarrassment.' As an aid to the Cabinet, the full minutes and recommendations of the committee were printed and circulated to all its members: these items were subsequently placed upon the Cabinet's Agenda, and each formed the subject for a distinct Cabinet Conclusion. In 1928 the committee had met thirteen times to discuss between forty and fifty draft bills, but certain of the new ministers inferred that its functions had been unduly narrowed to the point where it was deficient in preparing the Cabinet's business. In December 1929, Beatrice Webb noted that Arthur Henderson had lamented 'the lack of any organization of Cabinet business especially with regard to finance. Ministers come, one by one, with demands for money to successive Cabinet meetings – There is no kind of survey of their respective demands with a view of discovering which of the proposals are most important.'[75] Since 'Treasury control' supposedly operated with regard to such expenditures, it is not clear why Henderson expected the Home Affairs Committee to operate in a policy-making fashion, but economic problems were to plague the second Labour government to the end of its days.

A product of such dislocation was the standing Unemployment Committee, first constituted in August 1920 and reappointed by each successor government; adopting the procedures of the Home Affairs Committee in circulating full minutes and recommendations, its members had been drawn from departments grappling with aspects of the problem. The second Baldwin government had approached the problem differently, establishing a number of specialized Cabinet committees, and as a result the Unemployment Committee had not met since the autumn of 1925. To this small number of Standing Committees the Baldwin government had added a Naval Programme Committee to consider such questions as fleet construction, fleet manning, and oil fuel supplies; after issuing several reports, it had been reconstituted as a CID sub-committee, and thus its survival as a Cabinet committee appeared problematic. Still on the books was an Expenditure Committee, charged in 1925 with 'review[ing] the estimates of National expenditure with the object of making substantial reductions of the charges on the tax payer.' As this group had not met since 1927, its existence too was tenuous. Nonetheless, along with the CID and the Committee of Civil Research, which were not strictly speaking Cabinet committees, these five standing bodies represented the institutional inheritance of the Labour regime.[76]

That administration reconstituted the Home Affairs, Unemployment, and Civil Research Committees, although the Prime Minister's dissatisfaction with the last led to a re-organization; the Expenditure Committee was quietly interred, and a new Committee on the Fighting Services established, although this innovation did not encroach upon the activities of the CID. As had been the case with its predecessors, MacDonald's second government appointed a number of ad hoc, short-lived committees to consider specific problems: some led an active existence, some few never met. In the period 1923–39, some 379 Cabinet committees have been enumerated, along with 275 CID and 70 for the CCR and its successor.[77] Obviously, their work, and their demands, were variegated, but each represented a charge upon the Cabinet Office, and the burden surely was considerable, especially with the proliferation of committees examining aspects of foreign policy in the later 1930s.

Labour accommodated itself with ease to the Secretariat routine, which renders MacDonald's subsequent conduct in the House of Commons, at first glance, puzzling. In response to a question concerning the role of the Cabinet Secretary, the Prime Minister announced that Hankey's appointment had been continued and that no alteration was planned in his duties; what ensued reads strangely, for Macdonald replied to a supplementary question whether the Cabinet Secretary 'attends Cabinet meetings and makes out the minutes': 'I am very much obliged . . . The statement appeared in some newspapers the other day, and it is absolutely without foundation.'[78] If MacDonald's reference was to the *Morning Post*'s assertion that the Secretary no longer attended Cabinet meetings, his statement can be explained: such an explanation is plausible in view of the lack of any reaction among politicians or journalists, who knew better.

Hard pressed by economic events for which they had developed no solutions, the Labour government exhibited nagging difficulties in meeting the procedural requirement that Cabinet memoranda be circulated with ample time for ministerial deliberation. Again and again the Prime Minister complained about the circulation of documents on the very eve of a Cabinet meeting, 'in entire disregard of the rules laid down by the Cabinet itself.'[79] Hankey moved to tighten procedures by circulating a Treasury Minute dating to April 1924 which mandated a Treasury review of any proposal involving new expenditures, although the problem persisted.[80] While MacDonald protested the hasty submission of Cabinet memoranda on at least three occasions in the following year, his colleagues claimed that 'the exigencies of political life' often made it impossible to comply with the terms of the minute; the Chancellor of the Exchequer countered that release from its terms could come only from the Prime Minister.[81]

From time to time the Labour regime was troubled by ministerial indiscretions, which exceeded in scope the information conveyed in the Cabinet Minutes. Tom Jones recorded such an instance in his diary, pointing to a source within the Cabinet: 'Cabinet had, on November 3rd 1929, discussed retirement Pensions and on December 24th an accurate record appeared in the *Manchester Guardian* and the *Yorkshire Post*, though there had been no detailed record in the Minutes. No action, warning to Ministers to behave themselves.'[82] Several months later, Jones cited an example that such leakage could be inadvertent as well as intentional or self-serving: the unwittingly Home Secretary, J. R. Clynes, enabled the press to conclude that the government had decided to arrest Gandhi, the Indian nationalist leader, some forty-eight hours before the fact. His lack of circumspection in handling press queries after a Cabinet meeting merited the embarrassment which he must have felt in ascertaining through unofficial channels from the proprietor of *The Daily Telegraph* that 'he had better call off his sleuths' because the Home Secretary himself was the source of the 'leak.'[83]

In some cases, however, leakage was clearly deliberate, and recrimination followed, as Jones noted in May 1930:

> The Report of Snowden's Committee on Unemployment turning down the famous Oswald Mosley Memorandum [Mosley was at this time Chancellor of the Duchy of Lancaster] has got into the *Daily Herald* and the Lord Privy Seal [J. H. Thomas] indicated the suspicions he held of his three colleagues [Mosley; Lansbury, the Commissioner of Works; Thomas Johnson, with Mosley not a Cabinet Minister] as being implicated, at which Lansbury lost his temper. At this stage Hankey put his pencil down, and took no notes.[84]

Lansbury's close ties to the *Daily Herald* were known to all his colleagues, and the leakage of the contentious memorandum does not appear an accident. By 1931, following a rash of disclosures concerning the break-up of the Labour government, Hankey had grown sufficiently concerned with leakages to take a new tack by attempting to deal with the problem in a humorous vein. Acting at the Prime Minister's behest, Hankey compiled a collection of classical aphorisms and exhortations that might well have been entitled 'On the Need for Cabinet Secrecy.' Perhaps the most incisive reminder came from Bacon's essay, 'Of Counsel': 'But let Princes beware that the unsecreting of their affairs comes not from themselves. And as for Cabinet counsels, it may be their motto "Plenus rimarum sum" (I am full of leaks): one futile person, that maketh it his glory to tell, will do more hurt than many, that know it their duty to conceal.'[85] The Cabinet was amused, and possibly instructed, but George V queried upon reading his copy whether it would have any effect; Hankey too must have entertained doubts about the leaky barque of state.

The year 1929 did not pass without another personal triumph for Sir Maurice Hankey, who played a central role at The Hague Conference, which seemed at the time to portend a final settlement of the reparations problem. Initially, Hankey had protested his inclusion in the British delegation, explaining that he had forgotten 'the tricks of the trade'; he expected that 'in these days the F.O. would take it on themselves.'[86] Involved in the British contingent at the urging of the Chancellor, Snowden, and the Foreign Secretary, Arthur Henderson, Hankey was appalled to discover that the Foreign Office had not acquired any expertise: 'I only had a week's notice,' he explained to his son Robin, just beginning a long association with the Foreign Office, 'and found the F.O. had done nothing: – no organization, no interpreters, no [illegible] stenographers, no roneo machines, no accommodations booked, no nothing.' Mechanical difficulties were one matter, but Hankey recognized that a more intractable problem could prove to be the relations between the leaders of the British delegation:

> Snowden and Henderson are not only rivals politically, not only are they personally uncongenial to one another; not only have they poor ideas of team-work; but in addition they were diametrically opposed on the policy to be adopted at The Hague . . . The officials were ranked behind their respective chiefs, and were barely on speaking terms . . . I conceived my main job to be to keep our Delegates together and to make them work as a team.[87]

Hankey foresaw a task not unlike that which he regularly played within the Chiefs of Staff Committee; he ensured that he would be able to influence the Prime Minister, on holiday in Lossiemouth, by asking Tom Jones to abandon his vacation and return to the Cabinet Office, from which post he would have ready access to MacDonald.[88]

At The Hague, Hankey's helping hand soon became a guiding one, since the Dutch were no better prepared to host than the Foreign Office was to participate; still it was his mediative, rather than his organizational, talents which were stretched thin: as Secretary-General of the conference and within the British deputation, Hankey strove to establish productive relationships. Ironically, one of the most difficult to secure was that between Snowden and his absentee premier: 'Temperamentally he and Snowden are poles asunder and neither could possibly conduct the affair on the same lines as the other . . . I set myself to support Snowden for all I was worth . . . This meant long letters to the P.M. to try and keep his nose straight.'[89] Thus Hankey found himself in a position to influence Britain's diplomatic stance, and, characteristically, he chose the approach which reflected his passionate belief that Britain's world role could yet be restored. Nor was his support of Snowden's posture simply of the moral variety, as he worked diligently to free the Chancellor from the shackles of a Cabinet mandate which threatened the success of the conference.[90] As his view prevailed in London, and Snowden persisted in his hard line at The Hague, Hankey could subsequently exult: 'we turned the corner last night we did': Britain secured terms which Snowden considered equitable, although the major beneficiary was the Weimar regime.[91] Since Hankey again bestrode the international stage as he had in the time of Lloyd George, it was appropriate that he revived a 'Welsh connection' in order to defeat any Dutch attempts to intercept phone conversations: a Welsh-speaking Foreign Office staffer at The Hague accounted for that end, and Tom Jones took the line in London.[92] Hankey took the extra precaution of asking that all Welsh or Welsh-speaking tourists then in Holland be investigated for security purposes, 'through channels we do not mention.' Such precautions, which extended to sending his letters concerning proceedings to his wife in the diplomatic pouch, reflected the determined hand of the preserver of Cabinet secrecy.[93]

In the meantime, the long association of Hankey and Jones was drawing to a close; the latter spent much of his last year in government service re-organizing the Committee of Civil Research, whose efforts MacDonald had recently criticized. MacDonald's intention 'to examine the proposals . . . for an Economic General Staff somewhat on the analogy of the Chiefs of Staff Sub-Committee of the Committee of Imperial Defence' Jones thought a misleading model: 'Preparing for the next ten years of economic life requires different methods.'[94] Hankey was if anything less impressed with the possibility of such staff work within his small office: 'It looks to me like a feckless duplication of work already being done quite efficiently by departments. I hope the Cabinet Office will be able to keep clear of it.'[95] He cautioned that an expert body independent of the departments could produce another, undesirable, analogy to the early days of the CID, when it had stepped on departmental toes: 'The result was something approaching a boycott of the Committee, which I found in full operation when I joined the Secretariat in 1908.' Instead he proposed that the so-called Economic General Staff be composed of the permanent heads of all departments concerned with the economic side of national life, which would have at its disposal 'the vast administrative machinery of the British Government.'

After a series of meetings attended in the main by outside 'experts,' Jones concluded that the outlines of an 'Economic General Staff' were emerging, albeit not on the lines which Hankey had advised. Instead, a nucleus of civil servants would meet frequently with an advisory committee of outside 'experts' – economists, industrialists, trade union leaders – together constituting a body which, in the Prime Minister's words, 'does more to co-ordinate Departments . . . not a super Department . . . We should learn by the experience of the CID.'[96] MacDonald insisted throughout on the parallel, but in fact the new body arose from what its historians characterize as 'the experience of a wide spectrum of serious observers of the economic scene throughout the 1920s.'[97] The re-organization accomplished, the Economic Advisory Council began to function early in 1930. Jones briefly served as Secretary, and his views on the new body were these:

> It will differ from the CCR in that there will be, in addition to a group of Ministers primarily concerned with economic policy, six or eight outsiders who will be full members. Then I, as secretary, shall have with me a small staff of trade economists whose activities will be directed by the Council and who will report to the Council on the situation. I am all for this development but I cannot expect from it as much as the P.M. does. The amount of prediction possible in economics is not great and it is even less in politics.[98]

Such 'predictions' did not much help as Britain's economic picture darkened in 1930: unemployment mounted, Snowden's Treasury policy remained steadfastly orthodox, and the Economic Advisory Council proposed no solution for the problems stemming from the collapse on Wall Street. Thomas Jones grew disenchanted with its role, a factor which contributed to his decision to leave government service later in the year, when he marked his sixtieth birthday. Marginal topics came the way of the EAC, but there was little direct liaison with the departments; Oswald Mosley described it as 'a discussion group revolving ideas in a void.'[99] Jones himself stopped just short of making the same observation to MacDonald, because he found the Labour government 'dodged the points' of the 'brass tacks' which the Council was beginning to insert in the political landscape.[100]

As to some degree Jones' functions had deviated from those of his chief, Hankey, so too had his preoccupations. Nonetheless, when they worked in tandem – Hankey at The Hague, Jones in London – there is no sign of anything less than teamwork; to read the confidences which the two exchanged is to survey a relationship of trust and tact. Their political sympathies were by no means close: Hankey walked warily where Labour's policies were concerned, and Jones, although a confidant of Stanley Baldwin, remained unimpressed with Tory domestic policies, especially with regard to the working class.[101] These political differences were not often articulated – an incident dates to 1925 – and their relations appear not adversely affected by the few exchanges. In this light, it is difficult to understand why Sir Maurice Hankey, who nearly without exception tendered a courtesy to those who left government service or retired from public life, failed to convey any written tribute to his own deputy, in contrast to the sentiments of Ramsay MacDonald:

> In the public service you have won a very distinguished place – and not only that, but also the most sincere personal regard of all those with whom you have come into contact and whom you have served. With me, you have played many parts . . . You go and leave a vacancy which cannot be filled up.[102]

Hankey's biographer observes that the two had not been intimate friends and had drifted apart on political and defence issues.[103] True enough, but the whole truth encompasses more: the two men had, over the course of nearly a decade and a half, moved in step on administrative matters; together they had accounted for the institutional development of the Cabinet Secretariat. What bonded them together was far stronger than the forces which pushed them apart. Yet in 1930 Jones left the scene, and the absence of Hankey's regrets impresses one who has chronicled their interdependent relationship as altogether odd. The two exchanged little correspondence for the balance of Hankey's tenure of office, and their meetings after 1930 – judging by their respective diaries – were few in number.[104]

Hankey's defence interests did not slacken in these years; of particular concern was the convening of the London Naval Conference in late January 1930. In his efforts, Hankey stayed well within the lights by which he had steered since the conclusion of the war twelve years earlier: he defended Britain's world-wide naval role and the continued exercise of her rights upon the high seas, although he did not fare well with his Labour masters in regard to the construction of the vast and expensive naval base at Singapore, a development cancelled by the first Labour government but renewed by their Tory successors. With Labour's return to office and what MacDonald characterized as their 'general re-examination of the problem of defence in relation to the political state of the world,' he had concluded that the possibilities of naval agreements loomed large. While eschewing any policy which aimed only at 'hasty "scrapping"' of British forces, MacDonald informed the CID that 'as security is found, stage by stage by the establishment of sure means of peaceful settlement, so military organization will accommodate itself to the new circumstances.'[105]

Though Hankey immediately countered with reminders of strong dominion support for the base – including the promised defraying of nearly half its total cost – MacDonald and his colleagues were not deterred: the Cabinet chose, in October 1929, to slow down the pace of construction wherever possible and to embark upon no new work. Buoyed by the agreements reached at the London Naval Conference, the Labour government confirmed the 'all engines slow' signal to the Admiralty in May 1930, pending a permanent settlement of the question, to be reached with the dominions at a forthcoming Imperial Conference.[106] Hankey found the Labour scheme 'a bitter pill,'[107] but there remained the imperial gathering. In preparation for that meeting, the Oversea Defence Committee of the CID circulated to the dominions what the Prime Minister described as 'the history of the undertaking' at Singapore.[108] That Hankey had personally prepared the accompanying memorandum is unlikely, but he judged that the document neither made a case for nor against the base.[109] Consequently, he did not in the least expect a strongly worded assault on the credibility of the CID memorandum, which came from a dangerous quarter, namely Downing Street. C. P. Duff, Private Secretary to MacDonald and an experienced hand, minuted to the Prime Minister that the conflicting positions had not been equitably stated: 'the large space given to recommendations of the CID or its sub-Committee in regard to the arming of Singapore, etc., definitely load the dice against the Labour Party Govt's decision in 1924 and even against the decision to go slow in 1929.' Duff tempered his outspokenness in writing to Hankey that the Prime Minister was displeased with the paper, which 'gave rather a pro-Singapore impression'; he suggested the deletion of much of the detailed historical review. Hankey countered that to delete the arguments which had in the past been advanced on behalf of the base would bias the paper wholly in favor of the present government's position. A bit tartly, Hankey reminded Duff that 'during the last eight years the Conservative Party has been in power about four times as long as the Labour Party, and it is therefore inevitable, in any historical review covering the period, that there should be more decisions made by the former party than the latter, to be recorded.'[110]

Hankey's view had much to recommend it: it is difficult to find anything in the body of this 'colourless résumé' to which legitimate exception could be taken; on the other hand, a heavy-handed 'Annexure' was a different matter, because it quoted portions of a speech made by Lord Curzon in 1925 in favor of the base, which played directly to dominion sentiments. Duff weakened his case by failing to take specific exception to these opinionated paragraphs. More tellingly, perhaps, Hankey established that the memorandum had been approved by the government before its dispatch to the dominions; its withdrawal would pose serious questions. In procedural terms, Hankey was fully in the right, as Duff admitted that the Prime Minister had 'ticked it off without comment when it was first circulated as an Imperial Conference paper.' Without admitting to a *faux pas*, MacDonald minuted: 'As the paper has been issued it must stand.'[111] Whatever satisfaction Hankey may have derived from the capitulation was of little account balanced against the Labour determination to reduce expenditures upon the Singapore base. And for his part Hankey had reason to recognize that a shot had been fired across his bow and that of the CID. Duff's complaint proved a harbinger of criticism to come, directed against Britain's higher defence organization.

At the London Naval Conference, where complex multi-lateral negotiations among Britain, the United States, Japan, France, and Italy aimed at carrying forward the work undertaken nearly a decade earlier at Washington, Hankey again served as Secretary-General. What transpired in due course was that America and Britain settled their long-standing differences first; Japan subsequently accepted a compromise to broaden the base of agreement to three powers; however, France and Italy remained in fundamental disagreement concerning any extension of the Washington ratio system to categories of warships other than those specified eight years earlier. As a result, the London agreement prescribed new limitations in size and type of armament only for the three leading naval powers. For Britain, the price of the three power agreement consisted of a 'paper' reduction in the number of cruisers carrying eight-inch guns from seventy to fifty, at a time when Britain actually manned only forty-five such ships. Although the Sea Lords resisted the scaling-down of the cruiser program, the Labour government insisted; the Board of Admiralty extracted a commitment to cruiser construction and acceded to the arrangement. Nonetheless, they maintained their position that '70 cruisers present the minimum for our full [imperial] defence requirements,' while accepting the lesser number 'for a strictly limited period.'[112]

Beyond criticism were the organizational mechanisms which Hankey supervised; in contrast to the recent conclave at The Hague, the arrangements were well-prepared and fully satisfactory. Four separate series of conference proceedings constitute a full record of the cross-currents at St James's Palace, and Hankey supplemented these with a record of informal discussions among the several parties.[113] At its conclusion, the Secretary-General received both public and private praise from its chairman, MacDonald, who referred to him as the 'master engineer.'[114] His advisory role is open to question, nonetheless: Hankey either failed to recognize or discounted the fact that British naval strength had declined as a result of the agreement, a conclusion underscored by the Admiralty soon after the conference ended: '[The] treaty will result in an increase in the relative strengths of the U.S.A. and Japan as compared with us. French and Italian programmes also foreshadow considerable increases. Great Britain is reducing her strength as compared with the others.'[115]

The agreements encountered strong parliamentary criticism from former First Sea Lords, most conspicuously Winston Churchill, whose attack in the House of Commons reads oddly in view of the naval economies mandated during his recent tenure at the Treasury. Yet his criticism centered on the strategic consequences of abandoning 'the long and hitherto carefully guarded interests of the country.' Churchill contended that the agreements denied Britain 'not supremacy, for that has been given up, but even the right to have a navy equal to that of any other great power.'[116] Moderate enough in contrast to Churchill's better-known philippics later in the decade, Churchill's bewilderment with the course of events serves to raise the question whether Hankey lost sight of those British naval interests which he had so long and ably defended. Roskill remarks that his activities indicate a concentration of all his powers of organization and of persuasion 'on reaching an agreement – at almost any price.' Thus Hankey failed to utilize the 'indirect approach' to warn the Labour government of the grave risks inherent in 'the immediate and the longer-term consequences of the agglomeration of compromises reached in order to achieve a treaty.'[117] What the biographer cannot comprehend, others can only speculate about, but might it be that the dramatic détente in Anglo-American naval relations – after a decade of rift – contributed to Hankey's willingness to accept a relative weakening in Britain's naval strength? Only a year earlier, he had expressed skepticism about America's willingness to negotiate in a conciliatory fashion; thus he likely found in the provisions of the three power pact a commitment hitherto lacking on the part of the United States government. Such is a likelier explanation for his posture than the alternative, namely that he yielded to the Labour government's determination to pursue a conciliatory path in international relations; Hankey had recently shown that he could stand against that tide. Whatever the rationale, there is no reason to doubt that Hankey understood and, at the least, tacitly approved the three power pact of 1930; otherwise, his opposition would be a matter of record. If Hankey's acquiescence is to be deplored – pace Roskill – surely that criticism cannot ask him to take into account the rise of Hitler, nearly three years and the economic collapse of

1931 removed from the last phase of this era of European conciliation.[118] The naval threat lay elsewhere, in the Far East, but even there the Japanese did not move against Shanghai until early 1932.

Two other major concerns occupied Hankey in the sphere of defence policy in the early 1930s. In one, he deployed forces to protect what might be called a defensive perimeter; in the other, he took the first steps in what was to prove a major campaign. In the latter effort, spurred by reports reaching the Foreign Office and there assembled by Sir Robert Vansittart, Hankey circulated to the CID in May 1930 a document which questioned the Weimar regime's continued acceptance of the restrictions placed upon German armaments at Versailles. In a talk later in the year with Vansittart, Hankey's fear that Germany was intent upon rearmament he found fully confirmed; nor did he think that the forthcoming Disarmament Conference would provide a solution: 'it appeared the very reverse. It was unlikely that France would disarm down to anything approaching the German level, or allow Germany to arm up to her level.' The likely result was German rearmament, and for Hankey the conclusion was inescapable: 'the outlook in Europe was very much worse than it had been ten years before the late War, and to base our Imperial Defence on a ten-year date advancing from day to day appeared to me to be living in a fool's paradise.'[119] From this pessimistic conversation stemmed Hankey's effort to repeal the Ten Year Rule, which dated to 1919, had been reformulated on a self-perpetuating basis by the CID in July 1928 and had been validated by that body as recently as June 1930. To document his case, he prepared a survey of military developments in Germany and sent his tightly argued twelve page review to the Prime Minister in January 1931; three weeks later, he received a far from encouraging reply from that office, informing him that although MacDonald did not dissent from his conclusions, he felt that no action should be taken, pending the work of the Disarmament Conference.[120]

Frustrated in his initial effort, Hankey next undertook to ascertain whether the outbreak of war in the Far East dictated the cancellation of the Ten Year Rule. The COS argued it should; they also sought provision for purely defensive commitments, with the Far East given first priority; and they also warned that their recommendations ought not be held hostage to the outcome of the Disarmament Conference. On 22 March 1932 the CID accepted the recommendations of the COS, 'at least in theory.'[121] Yet in short order the Cabinet drastically compromised these recommendations: they insisted that the acceptance of the COS report could not justify increased expenditures on defence without regard to the depressed economic and financial situation which the country still faced; second, they mandated further exploration of the relationship to disarmament prospects. As a result, twenty months passed before the COS recommendations were put into effect, in the main because the National Government held that national finances posed a greater threat to security than did foreign aggression.[122] The period between March 1932 and November 1933 was doubtless a frustrating time for the CID Secretary: in theory the Ten Year Rule had been abandoned, but in practice its constraints were operative.[123]

He did not shy from the struggle: as the situation 'in the Far East and Europe crumbl[es] before our eyes,' Hankey carried the case for rearmament directly to the Chancellor, Neville Chamberlain. At this time he expressed particular concern with the 'moribund' state of the British armaments industry: 'Unless . . . action is taken fairly soon to place more Government orders foreign orders would seem indispensable to its survival.'[124] While Britain's capacity to rearm stood as a genuine concern, one senses that Hankey followed such an approach because he recognized that the Cabinet was unlikely to endorse rearmament in its own right. If this surmise is correct, Hankey practiced the 'indirect approach' with regard to yet another issue.

The events of 1933 – Hitler's emergence, and the dwindling hopes for disarmament at Geneva – proved decisive in altering the British government's calculation of the priorities of financial and external threats: in November 1933 the Cabinet formally accepted the COS recommendations, and at the same time authorized the CID to establish a Defence Requirements Sub-Committee which would prepare a program for repairing the 'worst deficiencies' in Britain's armed forces, measured against the military commitments addressed in the COS Annual Review of October 1933.[125] That latter report had not differentiated among the priorities of those commitments, and thus the DRC, composed of the three Chiefs of Staff, Sir Warren Fisher of the Treasury, Sir Robert Vansittart of the Foreign Office and, as Chair, Sir Maurice Hankey, began to sort through the various short-comings in Britain's arsenal. While the Cabinet reserved the right of ministerial review which was to cause further delay, Hankey had nonetheless won a powerful forum for the pleas which to this point had gone unheeded.

In the meantime, Hankey had held firm to the belief that the mechanism afforded by the CID held decisive advantages for the organization of defence efforts over the suggestions which surfaced from time to time concerning a ministry of defence. In 1931, he developed a novel brief for the CID, contending to the cost-conscious members of the May Committee on National Expenditure that the CID was inherently more efficient than a large department:

> Beyond a certain point over-centralization defeats its own object. The head of the Department and his principal officials lose their grip and there is loss both of efficiency and economy . . . From personal experience . . . I can say that there is a

limit to wise rationalization in a Government Department. In my opinion that limit would be passed by an attempt to fuse the three Service Departments into a single Ministry of Defence.[126]

While the May Committee recommended a reduction in benefits paid to the unemployed, they did not find reason to advise the creation of a defence ministry as an effective economy. In a novel fashion, Hankey had once again prevailed as an advocate for the *status quo* in defence.

The appointment of the May Committee reflected both the pressing economic problems which beset Britain in 1931 and the inability of the minority Labour government to deal successfully with them, since they had been required to accept such an independent inquiry as the price of parliamentary survival. The May Committee reported at the end of July, when Parliament had already risen for the summer recess; the committee's deflationary recommendations were viewed by a number of Labour ministers as draconian. We need only consult the Cabinet Minutes – which were kept by the Deputy Secretary, Rupert Howorth, until Hankey returned to London at the very end of the political crisis – to establish the divided reaction of the Labour government to the proposals of the May Committee. The full Cabinet did not meet until the 19th, by which time the Prime Minister and the Cabinet's Economy Committee had met with interested parties, most contentiously with trade union leaders; at that time, MacDonald discovered that, in Howorth's words, 'the Cabinet were not prepared to entertain the main recommendations of the May Committee in regard to Unemployment Insurance, including the proposal (rejected by the Cabinet Committee) for a 20% reduction of benefits, and also a suggestion that persons who have fallen out of insurance should be handed over to the Public Assistance Committees.' Two days later, however, the Cabinet agreed, at MacDonald's behest, to continue the search for economies sufficient 'to restore public confidence.'[127]

The conflicting pressures, from financial circles on one hand to the Labour movement on the other, are not here relevant, although they are clear in Howorth's rather full minutes. The result is relevant: on the evening of 23 August, MacDonald decided that the Cabinet's refusal to agree to economies less than those proposed by the May Committee left him with no choice but to resign as the leader of the Labour government. He concluded his remarks by stating that he would tender the government's resignation and 'assist in the formation of a national Government on a comprehensive basis for the purpose of meeting the present emergency,' but his colleagues had no reason to anticipate that his 'assistance' would take the form of his continuing on as premier of a coalition. By midday on the 24th, MacDonald – responding to a belief that party loyalty had to yield to the higher national interest of saving sterling[128] – had taken the fateful decision to accept the King's commission to form a National Government, and shortly thereafter, he conveyed the news to his Labour comrades, many dismayed, and one at least shocked beyond words.[129]

Setting aside the question of the political upheaval of 1931, what role did the Cabinet Secretariat and Hankey, who returned to London only hours after the course of events had been decided, play in working once again with a Coalition government? The Cabinet Secretary certainly was influenced in his dealings with the new regime by his own sympathy for what MacDonald and his counterparts in the Tory and Liberal parties had done, in major part because he did not doubt that the drain on British resources had proceeded 'catastrophically'; he accepted as reasonable the conditions for a loan set by the American bankers, 'who were most anxious to help.'[130] His basically benign view of the role of the financial community in the events which had led to political crisis in fact reinforced the hopes which Hankey had entertained of attacking the problem of unemployment which had for so long plagued Great Britain. Nearly a year earlier he had pointed to the need to overcome 'defeatism' about unemployment as a step towards Britain's recovery of her world standing: 'All classes must tighten their belts and discipline themselves to live and enjoy a cheaper, though not necessarily a lower, standard of living.' An analogy had come to his military mind at that time:

> The problem of unemployment is like that of the submarine campaign in the war. It was not defeated by any single measure – though the adoption of the convoy system was the turning point. The facts were put plainly before the nation, and disaster was averted by a vast national policy in which every individual played his part by accepting temporarily the lower standards consequent on reduced imports, rationing . . . and so forth. If unemployment is faced in that spirit . . . we can win through.

In August 1931 Hankey was disposed to view the formation of the National Government as potentially the 'turning point' in Britain's struggle for recovery, since he had maintained that no one political party could prevail against unemployment: 'It could only be done by a national agreement on principle.'[131]

How appropriate, then, that Hankey was asked to draft a statement of principle concerning the sole purpose of the new coalition; it was not his fault that the near ten year existence of the National Government made a mockery of his pen:

> The specific object for which the new Government is being formed is to deal with the national emergency that now exists. It will not be a Coalition Government in the usual accepted sense of the term, but a Government of co-operation for this one purpose. When that purpose is achieved, the political parties will resume their respective positions.[132]

The new regime set to work, meeting in Cabinet for the first time on 25 August, but its Secretary was organizing its activities in the hope that the 'turning point' was at hand: describing himself as 'desperately busy,' Hankey recalled the days of yore: 'It is a Cabinet of Ten with a lot of outside Ministers, and has to be run like the War Cabinet, but I am allowed to send the Minutes to most of the outsiders.' In fact, a procedural anomaly had occurred at its outset, when a Conference of Ministers held less than an hour before the first meeting of the new Cabinet decided that the Cabinet would follow established procedures: men who were not themselves in the Cabinet helped to determine how the Cabinet would function.[133] Prepared to defer to the small Cabinet, the Conference nonetheless specified that each Minister was to receive all Cabinet Minutes and Agenda, thereby 'enabling Ministers who were outside the Cabinet to notify if their Departments were concerned with any subject on the Agenda Paper and to raise for consideration any question on which they required a Cabinet decision.'[134] Under the circumstances – Hankey described the new Cabinet, drawn from three parties, as an 'awkward machine' – such a procedural arrangement made good sense, but the manner of settlement appears constitutionally dubious: only a Cabinet, possessed of collective responsibility, ought to decide its procedures.

The Conference of Ministers also asked the Cabinet Secretary to circulate a memorandum dealing with Cabinet procedure and committees, as had become customary. At this time, Hankey was still flush with the discoveries of Sir John Fortescue, and so cited the irrelevant eighteenth-century precedents for the work of the Cabinet Secretariat.[135] In other respects, the form of this informative memorandum had not significantly altered since 1929, although new materials were added concerning the Economic Advisory Council, which had recently acquired responsibilities new to those Conservatives and Liberals joining the MacDonald administration. Yet the transition from one government to another is not complete, in procedural matters, without some decision on the part of the outgoing ministers as to the disposition of Cabinet papers. At Labour's final meeting, they had agreed to adhere to what was described as 'the procedure of their predecessors in regard to Cabinet documents: that is to say, Ministers should retain such Cabinet documents as they desired, on the understanding that as ex-Ministers they should have access to Cabinet Minutes and other documents issued during their period of office.' The precedent cited was that of the Labour government in 1924, because the recent Baldwin government had not held a 'final' meeting after their electoral defeat in 1929 – Howorth, who took the 1931 minutes, added a note stating that there was no reason to think that Baldwin's Cabinet would have acted differently. Finally, the second Labour Cabinet went so far as to request that each Cabinet minister retain his own copy of two highly secret memoranda dealing with financial matters; the rationale was that any minister, lacking these documents, would have difficulty in establishing his degree of commitment to the economy proposals which had divided and brought down the government.[136] Since these controversial documents had already been returned to the Deputy Secretary precisely because of their nature, this late Cabinet decision involved the deliberate dissemination of volatile materials, although the Cabinet certainly had the right so to act. The result of the decision was that erstwhile colleagues in government, now turned political foes, had armed themselves to continue in Parliament the rancorous argument hitherto confined to the Cabinet. Hankey had good reason to fear for the secrecy of Cabinet deliberations, when the next, public, round was fought in a few weeks' time.

A decision taken by the new government also deserves note, since it was concerned with Cabinet procedure: the question was raised whether a minister who was not in full agreement with the Cabinet in a particular matter should be allowed to record his dissent in the minutes. MacDonald, perhaps recalling that such a practice had been sanctioned as his Labour regime had begun to unravel, argued that such a record was a sign of Cabinet weakness; the Cabinet 'accepted the view of the Prime Minister that the recording of notes of dissent or reservation was contrary to the general principle of Cabinet unity.'[137] In so asserting, MacDonald acted as if the whole of the Cabinet was greater than the sum of its coalition parties, because they had been unable to agree on an electoral program to put forward in the name of the National Government; at that time the Prime Minister instead asked for a 'doctor's mandate.'[138] Although he soon had to abandon the pretense of Cabinet unity, MacDonald's attempt may well have been regarded as a precedent: whatever the source, in August 1950 the Secretary to the Cabinet, Sir Norman Brook, refused to record Aneurin Bevan's professed 'opposition' to measures of rearmament, explaining that such a term undercut the Cabinet's collective responsibility.[139]

In short order, the National Government divided over the question of the fiscal measures needed to combat the adverse balance of trade; Hankey had done his best to prevent such a rupture in October 1931, through the expedient of slowing down the circulation of Cabinet Minutes.[140] In so acting, the Secretary played a political role, albeit in the hope of preserving both Cabinet unity and the government. Three months – and an immensely successful general election – later, the arguments centering on the imposition of a revenue tariff resumed. Though the Cabinet recognized that collapse from within would have deplorable consequences, that spectre did not suffice to produce agreement. In the impasse, Viscount Hailsham suggested that 'in the exceptional circumstances of the day some relaxation might be made of the ordinary rule of collective responsibility.' Those who did not agree with the majority's revenue tariff would record their dissent and express freely their opposition to the policy. Precedent Hailsham dismissed as of no moment: 'That [National] Government having, by its formation, provided one new precedent, need not be afraid of creating a second.' The rationale was specious – whatever the talk of special character, the National Government was another Coalition government – but Hailsham's proposal, seconded by an appeal to the minority by Sir John Simon, proved decisive: the minority agreed to retain ministerial office, their political consciences spared by the agreement that 'members of the Cabinet should be entitled to record their dissent from Conclusions of the Cabinet.'[141] The waiver applied only to import duties and cognate matters; on this point Philip Snowden and three Liberals – Samuel, Sinclair, and Maclean – availed themselves of the opportunity.

What was at issue here was not the recording of dissent in Cabinet Minutes – that had been done in the past, and MacDonald's earlier plea against the practice had proved inefficacious – but the breaching of the doctrine of collective Cabinet responsibility. In this regard, the National Government's action departed from past practices, although it was within the Cabinet's prerogative, provided Parliament did not object. The Labour Opposition, reduced to minuscule proportions in the General Election of 1931, properly if futilely challenged this departure from collective responsibility. In attacking a government whose leader had commented that when his Cabinet ceased to work 'as a whole' it ought not to continue,[142] the Labour leader, George Lansbury, reminded the minority in the Cabinet that the doctrine of collective responsibility involved more than words: 'no one can absolve another person's conscience. The fact that 16 people have told these four other right hon. Gentlemen what they can do, does not absolve them from responsibility.'[143] Lansbury's appeal to political conscience proved, predictably, in vain, and the now-divided National Government went their several ways, in the process establishing a precedent invoked as recently as 1975.[144]

In the first weeks of its existence, the National Government had been ably served by the Cabinet Secretary, whose actions reveal why ministers, particularly the premier, had come to rely upon him. Even before the reassembly of Parliament, Hankey had foreseen that problems might well arise when embittered members of the Labour Opposition faced their former leader across the floor of the House; he confided to his wife that 'there are going to be frightful reactions when Parliament meets.'[145] As the coalition had not yet resolved on calling an election, the

Labour Opposition was still formidable, and Hankey took the initiative in consulting with other leading civil servants and several ministers to calculate an agreed impact upon Britain's world standing of any abandonment of the gold standard, which the government had been formed to uphold. As early as 28 August, Hankey sought the Prime Minister's approval for his co-ordinating the parliamentary defences of the government, 'to ensure that the Departmental brains will be at work on the subject but that material will be collected and will be available whenever you or the Cabinet decide to ask for it.' He noted the talk in Labour ranks of a 'bankers' ramp' and advised MacDonald that 'if... it can be shown beyond dispute, first, that the crisis was imminent and second, how serious it effects would have been, I believe that half your difficulties will vanish.'[146] The Prime Minister was appreciative: 'Most grateful. Make these suggestions into official instructions.' While Hankey sincerely believed in the correctness of MacDonald's actions, his taking the initiative reveals again his personal and institutional value to any government he served.

He had anticipated correctly as well, because Labour leaders strongly attacked the government's economy proposals when Parliament re-assembled. There was however, an initial lack of recrimination between MacDonald and his former colleagues: the concept of MacDonald's 'betrayal' was not immediately voiced by the Opposition. In the course of debate on the government's Economy Bill, J. H. Thomas, one of a handful of Labour politicians who had followed the premier's lead, sought to expose what he regarded as the false issues of choices among various cuts in expenditure: 'No one liked the cut, no one desired the cuts, but the choice was not teachers', a cut in police pay, the unemployed cut; the choice was whether we would take the responsibility of a certain cut or of a disaster to the working classes that would have been irretrievable.'[147] To bolster his case, 'Jimmy' Thomas had recourse to what politicians like to describe as 'the record,' in this case Cabinet Minutes dealing with the late Labour government's attempt to impose economies. Lansbury challenged Thomas' account of those proceedings,[148] and the combative Dominions Secretary retorted in a way which posed a problem for the custodian of Cabinet secrecy. Hankey's diary entry reflected his own ambivalence, because he found the Opposition's attempt to dissociate themselves from most of the economy measures 'disingenuous,' designed 'to curry favour with the electorate.'

The Prime Minister had to show this up... and J. H. Thomas hammered it home with overwhelming power in winding up Friday's debate and discomfited the opposition to an extent such as I have never before witnessed in Parliament. Unfortunately he had to base himself on the Cabinet Minutes of the late Government and this produced great indignation. Both the Prime Minister and I had seen him separately and urged him to be discreet. He accomplished this (a) by sticking to points which Henderson had been the first to refer to . . . (b) by mentioning only matters which had been communicated by decision of the late Cabinet to the other party leaders. Still, he sailed very near the wind in his very remarkable speech, and I am nervous for the whole secrecy of Cabinet Minutes.[149]

Thomas' speech was hardly 'discreet,' and in certain particulars he exceeded the limitations which Hankey had likely urged. The Cabinet Secretary's anxieties were not realized, as the partisan use of Cabinet Minutes faded into insignificance in the midst of angry and personal recriminations loosened, in part, by those disclosures.

In early October, the new government decided to appeal to the nation, ironically enough in view of the failure to maintain the gold standard which they had undertaken to defend little more than a month earlier. The political calculation was shrewd, although their claim to stand as something other than a coalition 'in the usual sense of the term' was no longer valid, save for the fact that MacDonald, virtually bereft of party backing, was deeper in parliamentary bondage to the Tories than ever Lloyd George had been. The staggering parliamentary majority given the government removed the last obstacle to what Hankey had personally sought, namely a 'national agreement on principle,' and Hankey's thoughts in September 1931 were consistent with those he had held for years:

While our fighting strength had been reduced by repeated 'cuts' – relatively to foreign nations – there has been an orgy of extravagance on social reform. Old age pensions have both increased and extended; widows' pensions have been adopted and absorb the whole of the money accruing from the diminution of war pensions; wages have risen . . . and are much higher than they are abroad; the cost of education has been prodigiously increased; unemployment has risen to about $2\frac{3}{4}$ million; but the doles have been increased by the Labour Government and the precautions against fraud reduced.

In reflecting on Britain's downward spiral since 1919, Hankey associated the items of Britain's economic faltering and the dole as if the latter were the cause of the former, rather than the other way round; he also deplored 'our insistence on maintaining a much higher standard of living than our economic circumstances justify.'[150] All of this incorporates an orthodox, deflationary approach to complex economic matters. Though no economist, Hankey was very much a man of his times: the long lines of the unemployed shuffling towards the dole did not impress him as a problem rooted in the capitalist economies of the west. There is no point to lamenting his narrow vision; what is of import is that these views disposed him to co-operate closely with a National Government whose arrival upon the scene Hankey had to invest with the character of a 'turning point.'

His biographer remarks upon what we might describe as the social sclerosis which had set in by this point in his career, insisting that it was not a question of capacity:

> no visible sign of any decline in his astonishing stamina and vitality had yet become apparent . . . Intellectually he was still at the peak of his powers . . . Yet something of warmth and spontaneity in his feelings and reactions, not to mention the compassion he felt for suffering – notably that of the soldiers of World War I – is no longer so evident . . . he never seems to have appreciated what to-day appears to be the astonishing patience of the vast army of the unemployed of the period, or to have understood how very hard the economies introduced in 1931 hit those who were least able to withstand the shock.[151]

Hankey, it is clear, had lost his ability to empathize, particularly outside the military sphere. Yet even in that domain, where Hankey once had been a force for change, in the 1930s he appeared to many to be the opponent of reform. Obviously, Hankey discharged his duties in pointing the country towards rearmament in a meritorious fashion, but even within the CID there was criticism of his 'inaccessibility,' a product of the fact that he had 'far too many irons in the fire.'[152] Testimony exists that Hankey was resistant to proposals to improve the 'system' of CID record-keeping: 'It is all very well to rely on people's memories, as is mostly done here. However good the memories, that is not a system . . . I am told Hankey is utterly averse to all change in anything, that he wouldn't consider for a moment any system for the whole office.'[153] Four years later – at a time when any margin for error had narrowed greatly – Hankey failed to respond to criticism from within the committee that coverage of the economic situation abroad was inadequate.[154] If there is an explanation for Hankey's distance, even aloofness, surely it is that as a person – a man of fifty-odd years – and as Cabinet and CID Secretary he had become an institution: governments came and went, but Hankey remained, careful not to exceed his charge but determined to serve vital national interests. Yet institutions tend to lose contact with popular concerns and common people, and Sir Maurice Hankey proved no exception. In the 1930s Hankey dealt with issues and judged men through the lens of his own vast experience; not surprisingly, he lost his mastery over men.

One such issue which Hankey was bound to deplore was the development of pacifism in the post-war years, because it led to a weakening of patriotism domestically and of prestige abroad. Such manifestations of weakness as the past efforts to secure disarmament and the dangerous plight of the RAF had, according to Hankey, convinced foreigners that Britain suffered not from an excess of idealism, but rather 'our realisation of our exhaustion and economic weakness.'[155] In such a fashion he tied together his hopes for a reversal of the drift and weakness of Britain's foreign policy with his conviction of the need for 'belt-tightening' domestically. That association led to an unusual expression of his sentiments, when in 1931 he cast his first ballot since the war, on behalf of a National Government candidate; even odder, Hankey's vote was canvassed by none other than his monarch, George V, in a conversation which illustrates the peculiar flavor of 1931:

[Hankey]: 'As a matter of fact, since the war I have rather made a point of not voting. I have my views, of course, but I like to keep a very detached point of view.' 'But this time it is different' said his Majesty 'I want the National Government to get every vote possible.' 'Is that a command, sire?' I asked. 'Yes. You really ought to vote.' 'Very well, Sire.'[156]

The sentiment, we have noted, was widely shared: even Tom Jones, late of the Cabinet Secretariat and never a Tory sympathizer despite his relationship with Baldwin, admitted to a departure from form: 'I voted Conservative for the first time in my life . . . Labour had to be thrashed, but it cannot be destroyed.'[157]

In the wake of the 'thrashing,' the Cabinet Secretary, closeted with the Prime Minister, turned his hand again to Cabinet-making, both in general and in specific. As for the former, he advised against MacDonald's passing the leadership of the House of Commons to Baldwin, since a similar transfer had not worked well for Lloyd George. Further,

I also strongly advised him to have a large Cabinet again. After the huge number of Conservatives had been elected, he could hardly keep his three [National] Labour colleagues in a Cabinet of 10, but could do so in a Cabinet of 20. He agreed and said he had come to the conclusion that this country could not be governed permanently with a Cabinet of 10.[158]

Concerning the specifics, he directed strong remarks against the possible appointment of Walter Runciman as Chancellor of the Exchequer; nor could his approach in this case be described as anything but direct, even blunt:

I recalled Kitchener's verdict that Runciman was always very impressive in Cabinet, but failed to deliver the goods. I added that Ll. G. (who, of course did not like Runciman) often quoted this. I added from experience R. was not an easy man in a Cabinet. He was, like McKenna, Donald Maclean or Samuel (to a lesser extent), that hard uncompromising radical mind that bases itself on principle, and is not easily moved.[159]

Strange criticism to voice to the war-time pacifist leader and socialist premier, but Hankey must have known his master by this time; he tempered his criticism with reference to Runciman's 'gift of exposition' and 'competence,' but there was nothing improper about his advice so long as the Prime Minister accepted it, as he did. Nor did Runciman secure the coveted post, which instead went to Neville Chamberlain, whom Hankey recognized as 'an extreme Tariff Reformer.' Tariff reform followed in his stead, much to the discomfiture of the 'hard uncompromising radical minds' who stood, as we have seen, for Free Trade.

Although no major changes were made in the way in which the Coalition Cabinet conducted its business, the procedural problems which the Cabinet Secretariat had to deal with in the years when MacDonald headed the National Government are instructive. Hankey won one major victory in this period, although his gaining Secretariat possession of Cabinet papers will be treated in the next chapter. For the most part, in the Secretariat it was 'business as usual': the tardy circulation of Cabinet memoranda proved a nagging, if minor, irritant. With such incidents in mind,[160] MacDonald acknowledged that the Cabinet was unlikely ever to adhere entirely to the practice of adequate prior circulation; nonetheless he sought an even earlier submission of most memoranda by setting the Cabinet Agenda six days before the scheduled meeting. Strict observance of the rule that memoranda should be circulated at least five days prior to the publication of the Agenda – in other words, eleven days prior to the Cabinet meeting – became more difficult, which is likely why the Prime Minister could not expect full compliance.[161] Where Treasury consent was involved – in February 1934 MacDonald specified that no proposal for defence expenditure should be submitted to the Cabinet until it had been discussed with the Chancellor[162] – the cycle took a considerably longer period of time before coming to the Cabinet.

The leader of the coalition personally felt the pressure of the vast range of topics covered by the Cabinet papers; when Hankey was informed that MacDonald had too much reading to do, Hankey replied that the problem stemmed entirely from the practices of the present government rather than, as had been maintained, a proliferation over the years in the volume of Cabinet business.[163] MacDonald did not mend his ways or those of his regime, according to word which had come Tom Jones' way:

> Ramsay was feeling the pressure last week [November 1932] also and . . . dictated a Memoir of protest at the number of Memoranda sent up to the Cabinet by the Departments, and suggested that no Memorandum should be put up without his first reading and approving. And this with his eyesight! It was sent to Hankey who told him, politely, that it was nonsense. He has never really had the charge of a Department.[164]

Whatever Hankey's reaction, MacDonald's request was not cavalierly dismissed: Hankey's instructions with regard to Cabinet procedures hereafter advised that it was usual for any minister 'to consult with the Prime Minister and to send him an advance copy' before circulating any memorandum to the Cabinet.[165] For his part, MacDonald, ever beset by such memoranda, insisted that a memorandum in which a minister did no more than signify his agreement with the views already expressed by a colleague was, in a word, unnecessary.[166]

Two distinct categories existed for the classification of Cabinet papers, although the vast majority – more than nineteen in twenty – were circulated as had been the case since the inception of the Secretariat, with multiple copies sent to ministers and senior civil servants; in 1934 circulation of such Cabinet papers averaged 400 copies. Much more limited circulation and far stricter control was given to Cabinet papers dealing with 'specially secret and confidential matters,' a determination made by the Deputy Secretary, Sir Rupert Howorth, who for many years had been responsible for the circulation of Cabinet documents.[167] Papers classified as 'exceptionally secret' bore a label including the inscription in red print placed upon each of the forty copies:

> This Document is the Property of His Britannic Majesty's Government
>
> TO BE KEPT UNDER LOCK AND KEY
>
> It is requested that special care may be taken to ensure the secrecy of this document.

Only one copy was sent to each Cabinet minister; departmental duplication of the memorandum, for internal purposes, was specifically forbidden. Each copy was placed in a sealed envelope addressed to the recipient and bearing the printed instruction, 'To be opened only by the person to whom addressed'; these envelopes in turn were placed in locked 'red boxes.' Such time-consuming controls were placed upon only 2–3 per cent of all Cabinet papers, by Howorth's estimate.[168]

The circulation of Cabinet Minutes was tightly controlled, although not quite to the extent which marked 'exceptionally secret' Cabinet papers. MacDonald cautioned his colleagues to warn any departmental personnel who were given access to the minutes that 'they must be confined within the narrowest possible circle consistent with administrative efficiency.'[169] It deserves notice that in one especially sensitive matter, the Chancellor's Budget speech, no Cabinet record was made of the proposals: though the Cabinet was informed about and, in fact, approved the budget before the annual announcement in the Commons, his remarks to the Cabinet went unrecorded.[170] Though Baldwin's return to the premiership in 1935 brought slightly fuller Cabinet Minutes, Hankey resisted efforts to increase their circulation significantly for the balance of his term as Cabinet Secretary.

The secrecy both of Cabinet Minutes and Cabinet papers had been challenged during the early years of the National Government, and in both instances Hankey rose to the defence of the established arrangements. Oddly, the first challenge had come from the man who with

Hankey had done so much to forge the system, David Lloyd George, who was prepared to breach the secrecy of Cabinet Minutes in order to make political points at the expense of certain Tory leaders. The former premier took exception to the claim by Sir Robert Horne, who had been sent to Washington by Lloyd George's coalition to discuss debt settlement, that he had possessed 'full discretion' in the negotiations; not so, according to Lloyd George, because Horne was bound by the Cabinet to base any settlement upon the Balfour Note's principle of all-round repudiation of war debts. In joining the fray, Lloyd George quoted verbatim from the Cabinet Minute in question, justifying his use of that document because Horne had already raised the matter in a letter to *The Times*; he completed a parliamentary rout of Horne's position by revealing that Horne had been one of two Cabinet members who had initially dissented from the Balfour Note. Horne protested: he had not disagreed with its substance, only from the manner in which the coalition chose to send that note 'out to the world,' which he had thought would irritate America. To judge this claim, Lloyd George called for the relevant Cabinet papers, and Horne agreed to their publication; more important, he secured Stanley Baldwin's agreement that 'the whole of the discussions of the American Debt' should be published.[171] In a calculated way, Lloyd George had taken a major stride towards securing 'a full note' of what had transpired in Cabinet, which had decided upon a full record precisely because 'the discussions were of such vast moment.' The former coalition leader recognized the need to secure the consent of the present Prime Minister and the King for publication, but surely Baldwin was in a position to influence both.

Hankey quickly recognized the audacity of Lloyd George's proposal, and Baldwin himself had second thoughts, because on the following day – without prompting from the Cabinet Office, according to Hankey – he assured the Cabinet Secretary that 'I could feel assured that the Cabinet Minutes would not be published.' Given this assurance, Hankey assembled a legal case intended to prevent Lloyd George from himself publishing the materials, as he threatened now to do without consent, if need be.[172] Hankey also contacted his former associate, A. J. Sylvester, now Lloyd George's secretary, to convey the word that publication would render his old chief liable to prosecution under the Official Secrets Act as an illegal act contrary to the public interest. MacDonald exercised moderation in conveying word unofficially to Lloyd George that 'he was actuated by no hostile motives . . . but that it would be a deplorable precedent; that there would be a dozen questions on which publication of Cabinet Minutes might be demanded if this precedent were set.'[173] Lloyd George persisted to the point of asking Baldwin in a parliamentary question whether the government were prepared to publish the Cabinet

Minutes relating to the debt settlement, but the latter replied on behalf of the Prime Minister, 'the custodian of Cabinet archives,' that he was not prepared so to advise the King.[174]

Having failed to achieve his coup, Lloyd George claimed to derive satisfaction that he had called attention to the 'reality' of the Balfour Note, nor could he resist chaffing Hankey about the threat directed against him, as he turned to a journalist, in Hankey's presence, and remarked, 'in a bantering way, "if I give you the Minutes of the Cabinet to publish you will be subjected to the most terrible penalties".'[175] He was less amused, however, when what amounted to a review of the incident occurred in the debates of his old bugbear, the House of Lords. His threat to publish was the implicit subject of an inquiry raised by Lord Rankeillour 'whether the business of the King's Ministers . . . shall be conducted under an implication of secrecy or not.' Although Rankeillour recognized that the character of modern government made secrecy more difficult to maintain, he insisted that it was essential to preserve secrecy of Cabinet deliberations by recording only Cabinet decisions, and not any opinions or divisions within the discussion.[176] Another peer went further: the Marquess of Salisbury insisted that any record at all compromised the essentials of Cabinet government, namely 'freedom of discussion, freedom of opinion and freedom of decision, formed upon that freedom of opinion and discussion.'[177]

In responding for the government, Viscount Hailsham pointed to the lesser danger of keeping a record only of Cabinet Conclusions, as at present, but he added that he 'should be very sorry if a system of keeping Cabinet minutes were ever to grow up.' Contending that the recent episode was a product of certain 'misunderstandings,' he accepted the view that full records would stifle what Salisbury had referred to as 'freedom of discussion':

> It would be an intolerable position if in discussions in the Cabinet individual Ministers had to remember that whatever they said in the course of a discussion, the thoughts which they may have expressed aloud on matters which they had not thoroughly thrashed out, and opinions which they had put forward for discussion and consideration, would be allowed to be brought up against them with charges of inconsistency if they departed from them.[178]

While Hailsham's remarks blunted the force of any nostalgia for a resumption of pre-1916 Cabinet practices, they did not serve to establish that the real problem was not the record itself – whether full or spartan – but rather the use to which such a record might be put. MacDonald's government had, after all, acted to ensure that the full records would not be used to fan the embers of a political controversy only a decade in the past. Nor did Hailsham take into account the fact that a Cabinet was free to choose whatever style of record-keeping it wished: the Lloyd George coalition had wished a full record of their deliberations on the American debt settlement.

For his part, Lloyd George was infuriated with the aspersions cast his way by way of 'misunderstandings,' and he informed the House of Commons that the present government's position was distorted:

> The question is not whether a Minister is entitled to give publicity to what happens inside a Cabinet. The question is, when a Minister or ex-Minister does publish a one-sided account of a transaction [e.g., Horne's letter to *The Times*], whether the other Ministers concerned are not entitled to publish the whole of the proceedings in order to make quite clear what did happen . . . especially if there is documentary proof.

What then, the war leader inquired, if the Sovereign, who was constitutionally obliged to take the advice of his chief minister – 'bound to be more or less partial in the matter' – refused permission to publish? 'The person who is damnified, as it were, by the partial disclosures has no remedy at all – none.' Lloyd George threatened in such a case to proceed independently: 'if partial disclosures of this kind are given again of transactions which occurred during the time when I was at the head of a Government I should, without any hesitation, take the responsibility of publishing the whole transaction.'[179] Thus the threat to reveal Cabinet deliberations persisted, even if only in one well-informed quarter.

Yet Hankey could look upon the incident as a closely contested victory for the secrecy of Cabinet proceedings, since Lloyd George had not pressed his case to the point of publishing Cabinet Minutes. Perhaps more symbolic for the Cabinet Secretary was his discovery, in the midst of the incident, of Sir Robert Horne 'refreshing his memory for the second time on the Cabinet Minutes'[180] held at Whitehall Gardens. The Cabinet Office was precisely the location where Hankey wished to lodge all Cabinet documents, for one and all former Cabinet ministers, and shortly Hankey was to renew his efforts to secure that control in the name of Cabinet secrecy.

On the other hand, Lloyd George's threats to publish must have been associated in Hankey's mind with the criticisms he had articulated concerning the partial, distorted, misleading, and occasionally false memoirs and autobiographies written by military leaders in the attempt to vilify the civilian war leaders, most conspicuously himself: he had oft times announced his intention to write war memoirs in order to correct the record left by others. And now Lloyd George was bringing to fruition the decade-old project of writing those memoirs: his interest, which had been sporadic, revived during his illness in 1931 – intimation of mortality? – and he had instructed several of his assistants to begin to prepare materials for the first volume.[181] It is clear that the passage of time had not lessened the hostility and contempt which Lloyd George felt for those memoir warriors who for fifteen years had directed against him 'a stream of criticism polluted with much poisonous antagonism . . . the books published by Generals and Admirals and their minions have all quoted – or summarized very unfairly – official secret documents. My shelves here [at Churt] groan under their mutilated, bowdlerised, distorted quotations.'[182]

In view of the former premier's commitment 'to tell the entire truth,' Hankey's involvement in 'vetting' these memoirs proved to be a sensitive task. Although the Cabinet Secretary's view of Lloyd George as 'the man who had won the war' had held firm,[183] he had to protect what tatters were left of the secrecy of war-time Cabinet deliberations, if only to bolster the case for the preservation of post-war Cabinet privacy. Second, Hankey was sincerely anxious, as we have seen, to spare the historical reputations of all Cabinet ministers from attacks by their former colleagues; he deprecated the practice of hauling 'national heroes' from their pedestals. For this reason, he had urged Winston Churchill to temper his criticism of Lloyd George in his memoirs; now in a sense he returned the favor, since it was at Hankey's behest that Lloyd George revised some passages in the third volume of his memoirs which were critical of Britain's future leader, producing what Lloyd George called 'a refurbished Winston.'

Hankey's criticisms of the six volumes of war memoirs show his close attention to the text, his careful checking of documentation against records and recollections, and his scrupulous attempts to secure a fair measure of objectivity in Lloyd George's memoirs: very nearly all his influence was concentrated on the 'official' dimension of the memoirs, for the over-riding purpose of 'vetting' was to protect Cabinet proceedings. The interpretive aspect of the war memoirs was another matter, but Hankey hazarded criticism, in the main to temper some outburst on Lloyd George's part. Then too, he supplied some aid, in the form of documents lacking in Lloyd George's extensive collection, for clarification of certain matters; Hankey asked only that certain CID papers which he forwarded be returned, since they were file copies. One discovers these in the Lloyd George Papers with a sense of irony![184] For all his efforts, the Cabinet Secretary played only an advisory role, and Lloyd George had to seek release from the Privy Counsellor's Oath and guard against violation of the Official Secrets Act.[185]

MacDonald's refusal to publish a post-war Cabinet Minute may have raised a question in Lloyd George's mind concerning official approval of his memoirs, but there is no evidence that any obstacles were placed in his path; nor is there any reason to think that MacDonald himself played anything other than a pro forma role in approving publication. In fact, Stanley Baldwin assumed the responsibility of approving the memoirs, although he deferred to Hankey's scrutiny; nonetheless, Baldwin's comment upon reading the first volume captures the mixture of official propriety and personal animus which consistently marks Lloyd George's work:

I agree with Hankey: for him it is restrained. But there are plenty of back-handers in it. Grey is evidently one of his bete-noires, and he has a nasty chapter on him. McKenna is another, and he gives a good claw. The Brass Hats get it all through. His chapter on Bonar is good and very fair. He has been quite judicious in the use of State papers and again I agree with Hankey that he has used nothing to which exception can be taken. Others have sinned more in that respect.[186]

Keeping Lloyd George on the straight-and-narrow was not without difficulties, Baldwin informed Tom Jones a year later: 'Hankey is having an acrimonious, no, not acrimonious, correspondence with L.G. over the third volume of the *Memoirs* – they are friendly, of course, but Hankey is trying to keep him to the facts.'[187] After he became premier, Baldwin continued his official scrutiny, and although Lloyd George became even more contemptuous of the military leadership – '"The soldiers are getting it in the neck on every other page"' Baldwin commented about the fifth, penultimate volume[188] – he did not transgress the bounds of propriety. Nor did the severe tightening of Cabinet Office control of Cabinet papers, accomplished by Hankey in 1934, pose any problem for Lloyd George, although he had feared at first that his use of documents, which were usually incorporated within his account without indication of quotation or even attribution,[189] would be curtailed; in that event, Lloyd George had in mind 'taking all the stuff abroad and publishing it there.'[190]

The Secretariat's recovery of Cabinet papers, described below, did serve to make more prominent the King's ultimate sanction in publishing official papers, which Hankey had hitherto taken quite for granted, assuming that 'when the Prime Minister gives permission without submission to the King, such permission is in effect being given on His Majesty's behalf.'[191] MacDonald, however, took the royal sanction as a literal requirement,[192] and although Lloyd George felt differently on that point, he did submit to George V a chapter, written at Hankey's diplomatic request,[193] concerning the King's contribution to the war effort. That effort sat well with George V, but he was less than pleased with certain derogatory references to MacDonald's war role and requested that the offending passages be deleted; Lloyd George, according to Frances Stevenson, was

furious and says he will certainly not do this, and that H.M. has no right to make the request. The only effect of the King's interference is to make D. rewrite the passage on R.M. in the chapter on Labour Unrest, and strengthen the case against Ramsay in doing so – make it more hostile and more vehement.[194]

Royal sanction did not translate into royal influence over David Lloyd George.

Hankey served his former chief in another unofficial way by suggesting that he invite a military authority, Basil Liddell Hart, to review his manuscript from the standpoint of strategy and tactics; at Lloyd George's expense, Liddell Hart worked with the war leader for several years. Since Lloyd George's memoirs have drawn historical scorn – and they no doubt contain significant errors of commission[195] – Liddell Hart's opinion is interesting, and it is very probable that Hankey would not have disagreed with Liddell Hart's view:

> the data for his war memoirs was extraordinarily full and accurate – far superior to that of his critics. Its presentation in final form was his own, but I saw so much of the process of composition at close quarters . . . as to appreciate that it had deviated far less from the trend of the evidence than most of the memoirs produced by statesmen and soldiers, while providing a much more solid basis of factual evidence on the great decisions.

Why then the controversial nature of the *War Memoirs*? Liddell Hart thought the problem Lloyd George's inability to use 'restrained language': 'It was the pungency with which he drove home his points that produced such violent reactions both during his ministerial career and when he came to write his account of the war.'[196] Of course Lloyd George had the advantage of utilizing official materials within the text, so long as they were not identified as such; such was by no means an even-handed practice, because those who had been outside the Cabinet, yet figured in the war events, lacked any means of access to the former premier's source.

The first former official to complain of such discriminatory treatment was the erstwhile Treasury adviser, John Maynard Keynes, who protested the inclusion, in Lloyd George's second volume, of extracts from a memorandum attributed to him and allegedly circulated to the Cabinet in September 1915; he noted that he possessed no copy and had 'little or no memory of its contents.' Keynes insisted that he was entitled to a copy: 'Since it has been quoted from fairly extensively in print, and made the basis of an attack on a Civil Servant by a Cabinet Minister of the day, presumably it is regarded as a public document.'[197] Hankey sidestepped that issue, explaining that no government had come to terms with it, but he showed little sympathy for Lloyd George's old detractor: 'The War Cabinet Office was not started until December 1916, and although I have had our records searched, I can find no trace of the document you mention. I suggest you try the Treasury.'[198]

Evidently Keynes fared better there, since he showed a familiarity with the document when, a month later, he aired his grievance in *The Times*: Keynes protested that Lloyd George had excerpted a 'few sentences of a lengthy document, detached from their context and from the setting of the facts to which they were directed.' His own hands were tied, since an ex-civil servant was free 'neither to publish nor to defend what he wrote in an official capacity,' despite the fact that a former premier had quoted from it. Keynes did not dispute the soundness of the principle involved, which he thought 'in the interests of the Civil Service,' but he contended that the government had created an anomaly by publishing memoranda signed by civil servants among Foreign Office papers.[199] Now the situation had worsened: 'The publication . . . by an ex-Prime Minister with abusive comment of a selected extract from official advice given by a Civil Servant to another Minister seems to carry the doubtful precedent somewhat farther.'[200] The anomaly persisted: cries of discrimination, whether voiced by interested parties – former civil servants – or by disinterested historians, both denied access to documents used by former ministers in the preparation of their memoirs, fell upon deaf ears for another thirty-odd years. As for Keynes' foray, Lloyd George did not spare him when, later in the decade, he turned his historical attention to the Paris Peace Conference. While 'vetting' that particular book, Hankey conveyed the Treasury desire that reference to Keynes by name ought to be avoided, explaining that 'Keynes was discharging his duties as an official; that as such he was bound to do his best to comply with the general wishes of Ministers; and that he had a right to official anonymity.' Yet he failed expressly to add his own weight to that request: 'I expect that your reply to this would be that Keynes forfeited his privilege as a former official by hastily retiring to write his book.'[201] The specific reference stood.

Whatever criticism may be directed against Lloyd George for his partisan use of official documents, there can be no doubt that he drew more extensively upon the full range of war-time Cabinet documents than did anyone else, Churchill included, and his mastery of those sources was not rivaled until Hankey himself published his memoirs of the war years – and Hankey, by what proved to be a bitter irony, was denied permission until 1961 to publish his account. Ultimately, however, the opening of the Cabinet papers afforded historians a similar opportunity to draw upon relevant sources in order to assess the conduct and concerns of the British government during the Great War.

6

Hankey's last years

If Sir Maurice Hankey needed a reminder that a recurrence of the disclosure of Cabinet business which had followed the Great War would undermine the secrecy built round that body in the post-war years, the exchange with Lloyd George surely served that purpose. Yet during that time his attempts to gain Cabinet Office custody of the papers of outgoing administrations had met with frustration. In 1934 the story proved to have quite a different ending, as the National Government acted upon the Secretariat's request to regain custody of those Cabinet papers. Though Hankey of course needed Cabinet approval to initiate his 'paper' campaign, the mandate for governmental secrecy generally had strengthened of late: in particular, the Official Secrets Act had emerged from the shadows of its post-war revision – in 1920 undertaken almost entirely as a means of combating espionage and terrorism – as legislation with broad implications for the maintenance of government secrecy.

On one occasion in 1925, the Home Office had threatened prosecution, citing section 6 of the Official Secrets Act, brought against the author of a book about the Anglo-Irish patriot, Roger Casement, executed for treason in 1916; the book was based in part upon diaries which the government refused to allow publication, then and for decades to come. The Home Secretary, Sir William Joynson-Hicks, cited the situation in Ireland as the rationale for his decision; when the would-be author countered that future Home Secretaries might feel differently, 'Jix' countered with a determination that his successors were to share for a half-century: 'but the Act remains.'[1] Yet the regime which changed the tenor of the Official Secrets Act was MacDonald's second Labour government, which had recommended its ad hoc use for purposes removed from the Act's original intent. The Labour leader of the House of Lords, Parmoor, explained in this regard:

> After an act has been passed, on the question as to what it means, how it should be interpreted and how it should be used we are guided by the words of the Act itself

and not by statements made by either one side or the other at the time the Bill was before your Lordships' House or another place.[2]

Whatever the legalistic merits of this approach, shared by successor regimes, it is in sharp conflict with the principle that criminal law ought not be adapted for purposes for which it was not originally intended.[3]

Nonetheless, the Official Secrets Act of 1911 and 1920 became law widened by usage; in 1932 its terms were directed at the well-known man of letters and former British intelligence agent, Compton Mackenzie. Since Mackenzie had previously published two volumes of war memoirs, he had no reason to fear that a third volume – dealing with intelligence coups and fiascos – would be received differently by the authorities; rather naively, he anticipated that he would be warned if that were the case, since his intentions had been announced in advance; he acknowledged that much of the third volume amounted to first-time revelations.[4] Even after a summons was served in rather an off-hand fashion – his prosecution had first been announced to the press – Mackenzie did not take too seriously the prospect of facing a jury, but the good humor rapidly dissipated as he was enmeshed in the absolute rigor of the Official Secrets Act: on advice of counsel, he pleaded guilty, as there was no question but that, at law, he had committed an offence. Subsequently, he was told in several quarters that the government had used his case 'in order to warn Lloyd George and Winston Churchill that they can go too far in using information they could only have acquired in office'; Harold Nicolson wrote to Mackenzie that he had been victimized as 'a scape-goat . . . to cover the potential crime of others in the future.'[5]

Mackenzie learned as well that the Secret Service had deeply resented the damage which his memoirs had rendered its reputation and had initiated the actions taken against him, but the warning was clear to those who might proceed to compromise government secrecy: the Official Secrets Act had seriously to be reckoned with.[6] Embittered by the experience Mackenzie wrote in 1939

that the tendency of our democratic rulers moves steadily towards repression, and the Official Secrets Act is a convenient weapon for tyranny . . . there is no clearer sign of the decay of statesmanship in this country than the eagerness of second-rate politicians to preserve the secrecy of their own place-hunting and time-serving.[7]

These comments of Mackenzie mark a dawning recognition, widely echoed in the years after the Second World War, that the Official Secrets Act, once intended to combat espionage, could be invoked for purposes less worthy than the protection of the state.

To return to the concerns of Hankey in connection with the business of the Cabinet: in 1933, a son of Lord Lansdowne sought permission to publish a Cabinet document which shed light upon his father's famous 'peace letter' of 1917. While Hankey credited himself with 'a rather latitudinarian view' in connection with the events of the war years, he advised consultation in this case both with the Foreign Office and the War Office; the latter ministry objected to the publication of the document because of several direct references to the advice of the-then CIGS, 'Wully' Robertson; Hankey agreed with the War Office that such references were 'unfair to the C.I.G.S.'s successors for they are entitled to feel that the advice that they give to a Cabinet is given for the information of the Cabinet alone.'[8] Of course the irony is that, for the most part, the military leaders had not hesitated to publish such advice as they had given, but Hankey looked only to the protection of sources of information given to the Cabinet. Thus the case was very different from that raised by Lloyd George, but the two together had strengthened the concept of Cabinet secrecy and extended its scope.

So far as the recovery of Cabinet documents was concerned, events played directly into the Secretariat's hands. An article printed in the *Manchester Guardian* of 6 March 1934, 'Last Labour Cabinet: Papers Disclosed . . .' caught the eye of the Deputy Secretary, Sir Rupert Howorth. The anonymous columnist assessed the import of the biography written about Labour's leader, George Lansbury, by his son Edgar:

> The difficulties, internal and external, of the Labour Cabinet of 1929–31 are a matter of history, and of well-known history at that. In spite, however, of the extensive leakages, so far none of the Cabinet documents bearing on the dissensions, not even the Mosley Memorandum, has been disclosed. Mr. Edgar Lansbury . . . gives long extracts from memoranda submitted to the Cabinet by the First Commissioner of Works [his father], which cast a little light on its internal struggles.[9]

The implications for Cabinet secrecy were obvious, and Howorth immediately collated the extracts cited in the *Guardian* article with their sources in the Cabinet papers; he discovered that one document had been classified as 'strictly secret and confidential,' because of its sensitive nature. Howorth knew from the article that Lansbury had lent certain papers and letters to the son but had not himself seen the manuscript of the book: whether or not willfully, Edgar Lansbury had breached the bastion of Cabinet secrecy.[10]

In reacting to what he viewed as a grave offence, Howorth expressed a rigorous point of view concerning the use of Cabinet documents:

> While no formal rule has, so far as is known ever been given [presumably a legal opinion] the customary, well established and well recognised practice has been that the contents of a Cabinet document must not be disclosed to any unauthorised person without the consent, both of the Prime Minister in Office when the document was prepared, and of the Prime Minister in Office at the time of the proposed disclosure . . . The practice has been uniformly followed in

modern times and, as a rule, when consent has been asked for it has been given, the last time being in October 1933, when the present Lord Lansdowne obtained permission . . . to publish one of his father's War Cabinet memoranda.[11]

Howorth's brief did not record the long-held distinction between the use of such documents for the war years, which Hankey had viewed as *sui generis*, and the post-war era; yet this lapse may be explicable because Churchill's memoirs had served to regularize the procedures involved. More conspicuous is the absence of any reference by the Deputy Secretary to the fact that in 1927 Stanley Baldwin had voiced a 'formal rule' by informing the Commons that those who had held high office under the Crown were obliged to consult the government of the day 'upon the publication of any confidential matter of which they may have acquired official knowledge which may affect the public interest.'[12] It is improbable that Howorth acted in ignorance of this convention; more likely is an unspoken determination to afford the protection of the Official Secrets Act to the preservation of Cabinet secrecy. Such a suspicion is strengthened by the language which Howorth used in his reference to 'any unauthorised person,' a concept drawn from the Official Secrets Act. Baldwin's convention apparently no longer sufficed, if a formal law of official secrecy could be brought to bear, given the Lansbury disclosures.

In this instance, the Deputy Secretary was convinced that permission to publish would have been out of the question: 'The subjects discussed in these two memoranda deal with extremely controversial issues of very recent date and still very much alive.' That question aside, the publication of verbatim extracts involved a breach of George Lansbury's Privy Counsellor's Oath and an infringement of the Official Secrets Act, committed in common with his son, the publishers, and the *Manchester Guardian*.[13] Immediate action was imperative, 'either under the Official Secrets Act or in some other way,' if a further compromise of Cabinet secrecy were to be prevented. Hankey responded with alacrity, and within a day, at the Prime Minister's behest, Howorth had held conversations with the Attorney-General.

In contrast to a number of accidental leakages since 1919 – some forty instances in all, most due to 'a combination of unguarded conversation, and sharp ears supported by astute questioning'[14] – Howorth had argued that the present case was qualitatively different, although not unprecedented. A 'flagrant' leakage had occurred once before, when with the break-up of the Labour government in 1931, the *Daily Herald* had not only summarized the fateful Cabinet meeting but had given the names of those ministers who had voted against the reduction in unemployment benefit. At that time, he had informed Hankey: 'I think that the Prime Minister knows the name of the person who, there is the strongest reason to believe, must bear responsibility for this act.'[15] Howorth surely had then alluded to Lansbury, who had a long and passionate relationship with the *Daily Herald*: throughout his career the Labour leader had displayed naiveté, a characteristic evident three years later in his allowing unrestricted access to his Cabinet papers. While Howorth did not specify an unequivocal connection between the two flagrant violations of Cabinet secrecy, surely he and Hankey recognized that Lansbury represented the weakest link in the chain of post-war Cabinet secrecy forged over the years.

The legal wheels were set in motion: at the instigation of the authorities, the publishers of the Lansbury biography recalled all copies, and Edgar Lansbury in short order was convicted on two misdemeanor counts under the Official Secrets Act. The Attorney-General, Sir Thomas Inskip, did not suggest that he had sought to do anything 'contrary to the interests of the country,' but Inskip held that he had received information 'with reasonable ground to believe when he received it' that it had been given him in contravention of the Act. The Crown also contended that a failure to prosecute would be irresponsible: 'It is obvious that . . . the Official Secrets Act must either as far as possible be enforced or it must be treated as a dead letter.'[16] The latter argument impresses as specious, since the prosecution was designed to extend the scope of the Official Secrets Act by judicial interpretation: it had survived for three decades without such an application.

The presiding magistrate found for the Crown, assessing a fine of £20 and court costs of 25 guineas attached to mark 'the seriousness of the offence'; he left no doubt of the implications of the case, remarking that 'the main object of this prosecution is to establish the principle that Cabinet documents . . . are confidential documents, and must not be disclosed to any persons other than members of the Cabinet.'[17] Yet an anomaly persists in these proceedings: why was George Lansbury not in the dock with his son? Perhaps the problem was legal, because the Act nowhere defines who is empowered to authorize 'communication.'[18] Possibly political concerns were decisive: might HMG have been embarrassed at the sight of a former Cabinet minister and present Leader of the Opposition prosecuted by his political foes? If, as appears to be the case, the legal action was undertaken solely to establish a legal framework for the protection of Cabinet secrecy, the conviction of Edgar Lansbury served the purpose. Whatever the rationale, the selective prosecution constituted a precedent which has held over the years: no former Cabinet minister has ever suffered the weight of the Official Secrets Act.[19] The threat of such prosecution nonetheless remained; for its part, the Secretariat had clearly won a 'formal rule' on behalf of secrecy.

In short order, the Lansbury leakage was turned to a purpose which Hankey had long held in mind, namely Secretariat retention of all Cabinet documents. Howorth prepared a memorandum on the topic for the

MacDonald Cabinet: he reviewed the historical dimension, noting that the Committee of Imperial Defence papers had since 1908 been recovered from ministers who were leaving office; further, the War Cabinet had, in effect, decided that upon leaving office ministers should either hand their Cabinet papers to their successors or return them to the Cabinet Secretariat. However, the first post-war Cabinet had abandoned that practice in November 1919, and since then the various administrations had retained their papers upon vacating office, although the actual practice varied among ministers:

A small minority retain no Papers and return all their Papers to this Office, either periodically when in Office, or in bulk when they leave Office. The usual practice, however, is for Ministers to return certain Papers and to retain others; the retained Papers being as a rule those of the greatest importance and of the greatest interest to the particular Minister. It is, however, by no means usual for Ministers to retain *all* their papers, and this practice seems to have been generally followed by the Ministers in the late Labour Government.

Howorth examined what he described as the 'only argument advanced for the retention of Papers,' namely the convenience of ex-Ministers in referring directly to the records, but he countered that such convenience was better served by the use of the Secretariat records, with its indices, cross-references and general system; he advanced as a case in point Lloyd George's reference to those records, despite his own collection.

Having dismissed ministerial convenience as an issue of substance, the Deputy Secretary mounted an array of arguments against the practice of retention:

(1) There is no certainty, even in the lifetime of an ex-Cabinet Minister, that his papers may not fall into wrong hands and be put to improper uses. The Lansbury case is a striking example of what may happen with the acquiescence of the ex-Minister himself. In some cases, no doubt, an ex-Minister will be able to arrange for the satisfactory safe custody of his Papers, but in many cases this will not be done, and there is a grave risk of Cabinet Minutes and other extremely secret documents getting by accident, theft, or design, into the possession of unscrupulous persons who would have no compunction in selling them to the highest foreign, or other bidder. Many of these Papers would fetch very high prices from foreign agents, newspapers, and others, and when, as is bound to happen sooner or later, it becomes generally known that they are held in large numbers by ex-Ministers (or their representatives) in their homes, there will be a loss of Papers, a grave public scandal, and the public interest may be acutely prejudiced.

(2) Every precaution is taken to safeguard the secret character of these Papers so far as this Office and the Departments are concerned. Elaborate measures are taken to secure that, even after very many years, these Papers will not be available for public inspection with other Government records preserved in the Record Office. The object of these safeguards will be wholly frustrated if other copies of the Papers are to be left in the hands of private persons unable to protect them.[20]

Of particular interest is Howorth's untroubled assurance that Cabinet records were not, in contradistinction to other government records, to be made available, but rather would remain permanently closed; in fact, the prohibition held through 1966.[21] Howorth as well pointed to 'the difficult question of the outstanding Papers in the possession of living ex-Cabinet members, all of whom will have taken them away under the express authority of the Cabinets of which they were members.' In short, the Cabinet Secretariat hoped – with the provocation of the Lansbury case – that the National Government would undo what its predecessors over a period of fifteen years had agreed upon.

The Deputy Secretary did not underestimate the difficulty of that task, what with the numbers and the diverse personalities of those men who had served in Cabinets since 1919; he acknowledged that some would 'doubtless refuse,' but he thought that most would gladly shed the burden, and, as a result, 'the area of possible mischief would be reduced.' Howorth underscored the fact that the numbers refusing would be reduced given the non-partisan nature of a request from the National Government, which would also constitute a precedent for any future party government. On the day after Edgar Lansbury's conviction, after a short discussion, the Cabinet asked Hankey to request all living members of post-war Cabinets to return to the Cabinet Office all Cabinet papers in their possession and to do the same with the representatives of deceased Cabinet ministers; that the Lansbury case was decisive is clear in the Cabinet Minute: 'No doubt . . . difficulties must be expected in carrying out the present proposals. The moment, however, was considered opportune for taking action owing to a recent case in the Law Courts.'[22] The Cabinet specified that its ministers were free to retain documents while they occupied office.

Despite the swift success in a matter which had frustrated Hankey since 1919,[23] his office was concerned with several cognate matters. In a note which followed the Cabinet's decision, Howorth commented that 'it seems very desirable to know what is the precise legal position in regard to the property in these [Cabinet] documents,' in view of the practice since the war of heading them: 'This document is the Property of His Britannic Majesty's Government. Secret, Cabinet.'[24] In 1931, however, certain 'inter-departmental discussions' had led to a ruling by the Law Officers which strongly suggested that such a heading had legal deficiencies, because the two had jointly opined:

> We are of the opinion that the statement that a document is the property of His Majesty is more accurate in law than the statement that it is the property of His Majesty's Government. We think that, from the point of view of possible proceedings under the Official Secrets Act, the words 'Secret and Official' would be the most satisfactory to employ.[25]

Yet no action had been taken to implement this opinion, and no change had been made in the heading of Cabinet documents. The conventional heading had not been questioned when prosecution was brought under the Official Secrets Act, but Howorth now thought that the matter should be explored. Hankey, however, was not sympathetic, because he had throughout resisted the notion that a change in phraseology was needed. Characteristically, the Cabinet Secretary thought that the practices of some thirty years' duration constituted sufficient sanction, and he added: 'it is better to leave sleeping dogs lie.'[26] Howorth could not arouse the dormant beasts in 1934, and the conventional heading survived as long as Hankey held office as Secretary to the Cabinet, and, in fact, beyond.[27]

A more unsettling discovery was the fact that the Cabinet's pronouncement could not be enforced, because the National Government lacked the legal power to recover Cabinet papers from former ministers. The Law Officers ruled that the minute adopted at final Cabinet meetings of all post-war governments save Baldwin's second 'entitled Ministers to retain possession of the documents if they exercised the right of retention.' However, only the minister personally possessed the right, and any attempt on the part of an executor or an heir to retain the documents constituted an offence under section 2 of the Official Secrets Act[28] – yet another example of its enlarged scope. Apparently this latter point constituted the rationale for the seizure of George Lansbury's Cabinet papers nearly a decade later, although in defending that seizure Clement Attlee remarked that the papers were 'Crown property' – a position belied, as we have seen, by the heading attached to all Cabinet documents for the inter-war years. George Lansbury himself misjudged the property of these documents in assuring his biographer that they were 'the property not of the Crown but of the Government of the day, [and] no legal question could arise.'[29] The question of property in these documents certainly befuddled contemporaries, but what does seem certain in these events of 1934 is that Cabinet papers in no sense can be regarded as the 'property' of individual Cabinet ministers, to dispose of as they wished; nor were they free to utilize them in publications.

Despite the legal barrier to enforcement, the Cabinet Office nonetheless mounted a campaign to secure all outstanding Cabinet papers; the Cabinet were not informed of the Law Officers' opinion, although Baldwin knew, and likely as well the Prime Minister and the Lord High Chancellor, through whose office the Law Officers dealt with the Cabinet.[30] In fact, the distinction between the rights of former Ministers and their heirs was tacitly incorporated in the texts of the two letters which were sent out from the Cabinet Office, respectively 'inviting' the former and 'requesting' their executors to co-operate in the recovery of Cabinet documents. In nearly all other regards, the letters were identical, as Howorth generously characterized the recent decision of the National Government, in light of the legal situation: 'the Cabinet in fact decided that members of former Cabinets shall continue to have the right of access to the record copies of all Cabinet Minutes and Papers issued to them during the time they were members of the Cabinet.' As a result, he wrote to former ministers, 'these records will always be available to you at this Office, where they are kept in convenient form and properly indexed.'[31] Nowhere did the Deputy Secretary's misleading letter note that the present regime lacked the right to reclaim the papers of previous governments, so long as former ministers lived; instead, by inferring that former ministers had no right save access, Howorth left no choice save compliance.

Though Hankey and the Cabinet had anticipated 'difficulties' in the recovery of Cabinet papers, resistance to their request was initially scattered and on a small scale. Resistance had been expected in quarters which were the likely sources of future disclosures, as they had been of past; for this reason, Howorth was particularly concerned with Lloyd George and Churchill, not for disclosures about the war, but rather because 'Mr. Lloyd George continues to produce volumes, and, for all I know, Mr. Churchill and others may follow his example and may not confine themselves to the war, but may endeavour to disclose and publish Secret post-war material.'[32] While he acknowledged that both sought permission to publish, the news that both refused to co-operate in the recovery effort could not have been welcome, in part because others looked particularly to the former premier for a lead in responding to the request. The former Liberal minister, Christopher Addison, had written to Lloyd George immediately, noting his own belief that 'if a man is trustworthy enough to be a Cabinet Minister he is trustworthy enough to treat his papers decently,' but deferring to the other's seniority: 'I should be glad if you will tell me what your view is and what action, if any, you propose to take. I can imagine what Winston said.'[33] Abroad at the time of Howorth's request, Churchill replied in November that in his case the Secretariat's concern was misplaced: acting as had his father before him, Churchill had provided for his papers under a deed which specified that no state papers might be published without the consent of 'the Government of the day.' He saw no need to alter his practice.[34] For his part, Lloyd George replied to Addison: 'I am in no mood to surrender them.'[35] In time, Howorth became aware that in certain quarters reluctance verged on refusal: he had also encountered a less than universally favorable response among 'the members of the late Socialist Government [who] wish to discuss the matter among themselves before taking any action.'[36]

The 'difficulties' assumed a more formidable guise when the

Secretariat's recovery effort was reported in the *News Chronicle* of 5 October; Howorth, in charge of the office during Hankey's absence on a Commonwealth tour, protested the 'outburst' with which that paper had cast suspicion upon the National Government's action.[37] Surely some former minister had sought to enlist the *News Chronicle* in an effort to resist the attempt and question the government's purpose: 'Is it an attempt to muzzle criticism of the complicated political moves of 1931? Or is it intended to prevent former Cabinet Ministers from using official documents for the purpose of memoirs and newspaper articles?'[38] Confronted with public suspicions, Howorth moved to inform press and public of the real purpose of the action – the protection of the secrecy of Cabinet deliberations. To accomplish this end, Howorth had recourse to the extraordinary device of meeting the press, a means which Hankey had utilized on only three occasions.[39] The Acting Secretary contravened a 'standing order' of the Secretariat in meeting with the press to explain – though without direct attribution – the true purpose of the recovery attempt and to inform them that 'by far the greater number' of ex-ministers had already willingly complied. In remarking that 'no Minister has refused to comply with our request,'[40] Howorth's enthusiasm outpaced reality, as Addison had already indicated a tentative refusal. He disputed the notion that the request was directed against the preparation of memoirs, noting that the Official Secrets Act already guarded against undue disclosure of official materials.

For his newly acquired audience, Howorth stressed that the issue was the prevention of state papers falling into strange hands:

> While there is no suggestion of imperilling national safety or anything romantic like that, it is obviously not in the public interest that State papers should, for instance, find their way to the stalls of second-hand book dealers.
>
> That has happened more than once. Usually the responsible Minister has died, and either his executors have not recognized the importance of official documents or have not looked after them properly [paragraph in boldface type].
>
> All the well-known book dealers in London and the provinces know what to do with such papers when they are found. On several occasions this department has been extremely grateful to London book-dealers for promptly returning to us State papers which have inadvertently come into their hands.
>
> At other times when State papers have been seen lying on second-hand bookstalls reports have been sent to us, and officials of this department have had to go and get them back. In one or two instances they have actually bought official documents for a few coppers [sentence in boldface type].

Oddly, this explanation had not surfaced in any of Howorth's earlier memoranda concerning Cabinet documents, nor had it entered into the Cabinet's deliberations. The ring of 'coppers' is implausible in view of the apparent legal title to documents clearly headed 'Property of His Britannic Majesty's Government.'[41] Whether Howorth had tailored his rationale for a mass audience is problematic, but certainly he hoped to secure public understanding of the Cabinet's action: why else talk to the press? The likelihood that the Deputy Secretary was consistently loose with the facts is increased in view of his attempt to scuttle the notion that the recent Lansbury biography had 'prompted' the action; even the Cabinet knew better. At the very least, Howorth had shifted the grounds for the recent decision, although the press clippings which he kept indicate that public interest was neither wide-spread nor long-lasting: *The Times* afforded the interview virtually no coverage, as its parliamentary correspondent remarked only that 'dissatisfaction has been felt for a long time by members of the present Cabinet at the use which has apparently been made of Cabinet documents.'[42] The Deputy Secretary had made no impression in this key forum.

Notwithstanding Howorth's efforts, the *News Chronicle* persisted in its speculation about the appeal, commenting that 'the intention is to clip the claws of Lord Snowden and Lloyd George, both of whom are writing their memoirs.' The journal did report restrained reactions from several former Labour ministers: J. R. Clynes wished only to know 'whether this demand has been made to all ex-Cabinet Ministers irrespective of party,' as was the case, and Arthur Henderson accepted the government's explanation, although he had not taken any action about his papers; the outspoken former Chancellor, Philip Snowden, reportedly welcomed the relief from responsibility afforded by the call,[43] a good omen for the Secretariat in view of the potentially controversial character of his memoirs. Fittingly, it remained to George Lansbury to denounce in strong terms the action which he had done so much to precipitate:

> This Cabinet has no moral or legal right to tell the members of previous Cabinets what they shall do with their papers or to interfere with the discretion of previous Governments with regard to public documents. I have not the slightest intention of complying with the request. Parliament is the only authority which has the right to decide on such an issue.[44]

Though Lansbury's initial assertion was, unknown to him, borne out by the opinion of the Law Officers, the latter reference appears to be to the Official Secrets Act, which he had reason to acknowledge. His determination to resist was unequivocal, but there exists no evidence to establish that the Labour leader concluded an agreement with the equally resolute Lloyd George to defy any demands from the Cabinet Office for the return of Cabinet papers still in their possession.[45] Nor was there any agreement between Lloyd George and Churchill, although their secretaries had arranged for the two men to meet to discuss the question upon Churchill's return from abroad.[46] The three men remained individually adamant, with very different results ultimately.

Churchill and Lloyd George, at least, prevailed, retaining custody of their Cabinet papers to their deaths and beyond; contrary to the 1934 opinion, their executors were evidently not required to return inter-war official documents to the Cabinet Office upon their death. Only the Irish Treaty, a document of considerable historical importance, was recovered from the hoard of Lloyd George's papers.[47] At the time when those papers were incorporated into the holdings of the-then Beaverbrook Library, a representative of the Cabinet Office took a note of the holdings of official documents, 'ticked' against a list of Cabinet papers, but no request to transfer those items followed.[48] Of course the availability of Cabinet papers at the Public Record Office since 1966 has made the question of the Lloyd George holdings academic, and the same consideration applies to the Churchill papers, now in private hands. Churchill himself had resisted the importunings of the Cabinet and Secretariat with a mixture of diversionary tactics and ill humor directed MacDonald's way, although in April 1936 Hankey thought that he had managed to secure the return of 'the whole of the Minutes which he had retained,' but he was to be disappointed in that regard as well as in his hopes 'to recover a great part, if not all, of the Cabinet Papers in due course.'[49] In the latter quest, Hankey deputed his own secretary, Lawrence Burgis, who as a near-neighbor of Churchill was invited to luncheon and a monologue at Chartwell: 'I had arrived at 12.45 and it was now 2.45 and I had not mentioned those damned papers – the collection of which was the object of my visit. At last I summoned up courage to do so and all I got was "Don't you bother about them my dear boy; I'll give you the abridged version of my World Crisis instead."'[50]

Though these several collections proved elusive, Howorth had every reason to be pleased with the results, which he reviewed about a year after the initiation of the recovery attempt: with regard to 'the safeguarding of the public interest,' he judged the situation 'infinitely better' than earlier. Following upon an initial calculation of likely removals of Cabinet papers, the Secretariat had addressed some eighty-seven inquiries, seventy-one to living ex-ministers and the balance to the representatives of their deceased colleagues. In the latter category, resistance had come only from Lady Curzon, who had not replied to official inquiries; since it was thought unlikely that Curzon had held any post-war Cabinet documents at the time of his death, the request was not pressed.

Among living former ministers, sixty-two had agreed to the request, and papers were being recovered from all but seven of these, who had accepted the principle but had not yet begun to deliver their holdings. The 'difficulty' had come to center on nine individuals, and as one of these, Clement Attlee, had not served in the Cabinet and held only certain 'unimportant' Cabinet Committee documents, Howorth recounted the attitudes of the eight hold-outs:

Mr. Arthur Greenwood. No reply has been received to the original circular or to the reminders which had been sent to him. It is inferred that he is unwilling to co-operate.

Dr. Addison has written declining to co-operate.

Lord Cecil. After the whole position had been fully explained to him in correspondence, Lord Cecil declined to co-operate.

Mr. Lloyd George. At an interview with Mr. Lloyd George's private secretary some months ago, it was learned that, while Mr. Lloyd George was willing that his papers should be returned after his death, he was not prepared to surrender them during his lifetime. There is no reason to think that Mr. Lloyd George will reconsider this decision.

Mr. George Lansbury. Apart from a bare acknowledgement no reply has been received, but statements have appeared in the newspapers to the effect that he has no intention of returning his papers.

Mr. Lees Smith has declined to co-operate.

Mr. Winston Churchill, after considerable correspondence, has in effect declined to give up his Papers.

Lord Moyne has declined to give up his Papers.[51]

Only Lord Moyne, who as Walter Guinness had served as Minister of Agriculture in Baldwin's second government, lacked ties either to the Lloyd George post-war coalition or to the second Labour government. Even with the refusals, Howorth found solace in the fact that 'the majority are probably as fully safeguarded against improper access by unauthorised persons as if they were in official custody' – a qualification which had gone unmentioned earlier. He suggested that no further action be taken while these men lived, which impresses as a gratuitous suggestion, although the papers should be recovered following their deaths. The Cabinet shortly approved the report.[52]

In this manner, the Secretariat had very nearly realized Hankey's design upon custody of post-war Cabinet papers; as well, Howorth reported that in most cases current Cabinet papers were being returned periodically to Whitehall Gardens. Such did not prove to be a universal practice, as some ministers preferred to maintain their own files of Cabinet papers: with the change of regime in 1935, by and large the ministers who had remained on in the new Baldwin government took such files as they had accumulated to their new ministries; two years later, the incoming ministers of the Chamberlain administration generally took over the official papers left behind by their predecessors in office, e.g. Chamberlain inherited the file maintained for Baldwin at No. 10.[53] The latter practice corresponded roughly to that in use at the Committee of Imperial Defence, where about a dozen files were maintained on what was described as a permanent basis by military functionaries and Permanent Under-Secretaries; others, including Cabinet ministers who were sent

CID papers in connection with a particular meeting, were required to return those papers forthwith.[54]

In the course of his inquiry, Howorth had identified a related problem which deserved consideration, namely the historical reputation of a deceased minister: how could authoritative biographies be undertaken without access to the official records, which came as a matter of right to surviving colleagues? In the course of a lengthy memorandum, Howorth contended that no simplistic formula would justly resolve the dilemma; he advised that no rules be set down, but that each case should be judged on its merits. To do nothing would mean treating the dead less fairly than the living, but any alternative posed 'constitutional and legal questions of no small complexity.' Yet his illustration reflected politics more than these:

> should Mr. Harold Nicholson [sic] be given access when writing a Life of Lord Curzon? If so, should Lord Beaverbrook (who I believe was the executor of Mr. Bonar Law) be given similar access if he wishes to write Mr. Bonar Law's life? If access is to be given in the latter case, where could any line be drawn? And if it is not to be given, on what grounds is the refusal to be justified?[55]

Given Beaverbrook's past hostility to the Secretariat[56] – to say nothing of his standing as a press magnate – the notion of his using the facilities of the Cabinet Office could not have appealed to Hankey; Howorth had aptly pointed to the tangles of the issue.

The hypothetical question was not taken to the Cabinet, but that body had shortly to consider an actual appeal for access to the Cabinet records on the part of the widow of the deceased War Cabinet Minister, Lord Milner. Again, Lloyd George had served as catalyst, since in his War Memoirs he had quoted a lengthy paragraph from a memorandum which Milner had written, giving the former premier grounds to allege Milner's failure, while in Russia, to perceive and warn the British government of the impending outbreak of the November Revolution.[57] Lloyd George had, to be sure, secured official sanction for the extract's publication. Lady Milner inquired 'whether she might be allowed to see the documents in question in order that if she saw fit she might reply to Mr. Lloyd George's observations in a further Volume of Lord Milner's Life, now in the course of publication.' Hankey determined that the Foreign Office did not object and took the matter to the Cabinet for a decision on the principles involved, and he took care to detail what would likely constitute 'a precedent in future similar cases':

> the view was expressed that very great care should be exercised in authorising the publication in the first instance by ex-Ministers of Cabinet documents, having regard to the possible reactions of such publication resulting, as in the present case, in the claim of non-official persons to inspect the documents. It was suggested that a distinction should be drawn between cases where a historian or a

biographer wished to see Secret Papers in order that he produce a better book, and cases, like the present, where a person with good title to vindicate the memory of a deceased Statesman desired to see the Papers in order that he might defend the memory of the deceased against criticism made by some other person who had published extracts from the document with authority. In the former class of cases access should, as a rule, be refused, as the historian or biographer should not be placed in any better position than an ordinary member of the public, and should therefore only get access to the documents if and when they became available in the Record Office. In the latter class of cases, however, it would be very difficult to refuse access to an aggrieved person of a document, the publication of which by another person had been duly authorised.[58]

In light of the discussion, the Cabinet granted access in this instance and, generally, 'to any person who has a good title to vindicate the memory of a deceased person and who claims that the memory has been injured by the [prior and authorized] publication in question.' Three conditions required to be met:

(a) That the documents must contain nothing the publication of which would be prejudicial to the public interest.
(b) That in each case the proofs of anything proposed to be published by the vindicator should be submitted to the Cabinet Office for approval before publication.
(c) That the specific sanction of the Prime Minister of the day as well as of the Prime Minister in office when the Secret documents were actually produced and circulated, must be obtained before access is given by [to] a non-Official person.

The Cabinet decision provided a means for the defence of dead statesmen from attacks based on official documents; its 'vindicator' rationale stemmed from Lloyd George's own complaint about the use of 'garbled' extracts no less than from his own criticism of a dead colleague. In no way did the action facilitate the publication of 'official' biographies based upon Cabinet papers, however, and in this regard surviving ex-ministers possessed a formidable advantage over would-be biographers. As well, one must note the animus against the 'better book' incorporated in the Cabinet decision, although Hankey at least foresaw the distant possibility that Cabinet records might be treated as were other government records. Clearly, the Milner decision was consistent with the defence of Cabinet secrecy. Since Lady Milner failed subsequently to secure general access to Milner's Cabinet papers for an 'authorized' biographer, and because no other 'vindicators' came forward before 1945, the importance of the case lies in the future use which Hankey made of the precedent forged at this time.

Later in the year, the Acting Secretary examined the extant precedents and the recent Cabinet decisions, likely in the hope of bringing system to the treatment of Cabinet papers. Several points were of import: Howorth specified that sanction to use and to publish a Cabinet document was dependent upon both departmental and Secretariat scrutiny before the premiers, present and past, were involved; as only Bonar Law among post-war Prime Ministers had died, Howorth did not address the question of how to approach a request dating to the regime of a deceased premier. He noted as well that 'informal consultation has . . . on occasion taken place with the King's Private Secretary,' an oblique reference to the fact that MacDonald had recently insisted that the role of the Sovereign ought to be strengthened. Hankey's deputy expressed the hope that war memoirs, which had posed problems over the years, were a 'dying class' which would require treatment on a case-by-case basis. His present concern was directed to the three categories of future utilization of Cabinet documents: first, publication by former ministers; second, the 'vindicator' category; and third, the rare need for administrative access to the documents of a preceding regime for official purposes, not partisan political concerns.[59] Howorth proposed that henceforth the King's consent ought to be secured, through his Private Secretary, for any publication in the first two categories; MacDonald's wish was to be honored.

The Prime Minister, however, raised another matter upon reading Howorth's memorandum: he inquired about the continued access of 'official historians' to Cabinet papers, which was – oddly – nowhere specified in the document. In fact, such access had regularly been given, since 1921, under conditions laid down by Hankey to preserve secrecy and to protect collective responsibility. Howorth had assumed that the official historians were under no obligation to secure special consent, and, privately at least, he regarded the inquiry as irrelevant, remarking that 'it would be very undesirable to disturb the existing arrangements which I imagine work most successfully from every point of view.' MacDonald expressed a desire to review with Hankey the questions of access to and publication of Cabinet materials upon his return from abroad, but no changes in the arrangements codified by Howorth emerged from any such discussion.

In the matter of the Official Histories, Howorth sought to leave well enough alone; a decade and a half after the conclusion of hostilities, these volumes continued to chronicle Britain's far-flung military and naval role. After initial vicissitudes, the Historical Section had gone its own way within the Cabinet Office, and there is no indication that Hankey was at all burdened by its activities since its existence had been sanctioned by a Cabinet Committee in late 1922: 'The Committee are satisfied that the Official Histories fulfil a useful purpose and that their preparation ought to be continued. Several of these histories . . . are required for the education and instruction of officers and consequently their preparation should not be unduly delayed.'[60] At the same time, the committee recognized that the publication of certain volumes could compromise the national interest, and thus advised that the Historical Section should be supervised by a permanent sub-committee of the CID.[61]

Such a committee was established in November 1923, composed of representatives from the Treasury, the Admiralty, War Office and Air Ministry, the Secretary of the CID, and the President of the Board of Education, whose ministry retained the chair until the committee was suspended in 1939.[62] Its supervision was exercised only annually, and thus the Historical Section stood autonomous in all but name.[63] At its inter-war peak, no fewer than eight Official Historians were employed, with a maximum staff of forty in 1925. The tasks of its long-time Secretary, Colonel E. Y. Daniel, were described shortly before his retirement: 'to censor every volume; to ensure that no political indiscretion that might create difficulties found its way to the public, and to maintain touch with other Government Departments, most of which are concerned, one way or another, with the histories.'[64] While there is no doubt that the Official Histories constituted what had been called a 'National Memorial,' Hankey's description, courtesy of the father of military historians, Thucydides, applied equally well, namely that these were essays written not 'to win the applause of the moment, but as a possession for all time.'[65] In truth, little applause was heard from the public, surely in some measure because of the time-lag between the events and publication of the volumes. Initial critical reaction had been favorable, but the sale of the later volumes in each of the major series – 'Military Operations (Western Front),' 'Naval Operations,' and 'The War in the Air' – fell off considerably from those of the first volumes; the minor series, in a relative sense, did not sell well at all.[66] Whether or not in this sense the expectations of the Historical Section had been disappointed, the end seemed to be in sight: in 1939, the section hoped to wind up its activities by 1944–5.[67] Though the judgment of its accomplishment is best left to students of military history, the Historical Section fitted so silently into the structure of the Cabinet Office that Hankey's successor as Cabinet Secretary had to inquire whom he should approach in order to pay a courtesy call upon the operation.[68] Such a query is surely an unmistakable hallmark of institutional autonomy.

Midst the attention given to the strengthening of Cabinet secrecy in these years, the Secretariat could take pleasure that recent events had not been lost on George Lansbury, who in 1934 proved more discreet in his use of Cabinet papers than had his son. Howorth's description makes it clear that the former Cabinet minister had not submitted his manuscript to the Secretariat prior to publication, but scrutiny of Lansbury's *My England* revealed that no objection could be taken: 'No documents are quoted and little, if any, information is given which is not already public property.'[69] Cabinet secrecy stood intact. Yet Howorth's satisfaction on this score was tempered by Lansbury's strong criticism of all 'experts,' civil servants generally and Treasury officials in particular. Also troubling was Lansbury's inference that some, though not all, leakage of Cabinet secrets emanated from other than politicians: 'The Cabinet secretariat,' Lansbury had written, 'with its staff of typists, printers [the Cabinet Minutes had not been printed since 1919] and others, also all see the Minutes and most other documents connected with national business.' And yet, he continued, leakages which appeared on paper to be serious hardly ever mattered; in this light, he proposed a radical departure from past Cabinet procedures.

> In a Socialist Government all this make-believe of secrecy would be abolished. Nothing that happened in the Labour Government in its dealings with the unemployed and the proposed cuts in 1931 could injure the well-being of the nation if revealed. The publication of the bare [they were fuller than he recalled] Minutes of the proceedings in the Labour Cabinet during the four or five days before we broke up might make me and others appear in some respects in an invidious position. Even so, I would be quite content to have the whole published.

Yet this did not represent a new position: already in February 1932 Lansbury had criticized the artificial secrecy of Cabinet proceedings, proposing instead the immediate publication both of the Cabinet Conclusions and the Minutes kept by the Cabinet Secretary.[70]

In this forlorn quest Lansbury now invoked the public's 'right to know': 'In a democratic state, all this effort to maintain secrecy should be abolished. Cabinet Minutes should be public property, and they should be fuller and clearer than now. The Minutes should record everything.'[71] While democracy's defenders could point to problems inherent in Lansbury's suggestion, his views on the place of Cabinet secrecy afford a marked counterpoint to those which the National Government had that same year endorsed. It may well be a reflection of Lansbury's naiveté in political proceedings that the debate over the need to maintain them in secrecy has never been joined in Great Britain.

Instead, the strict views which Hankey and Howorth secured in 1934, involving among other matters the denial of access to Cabinet records to those interested only in 'better books' – that is to say, those seeking to write an informed political history of twentieth-century Britain – prevailed for a period of thirty years after the codification of 1934. Yet in the middle of this period, a massive exemption was granted for the war years: War Cabinet papers were made available on a selective basis, only to those ministers who had served in Winston Churchill's coalition. Both this waiver for the period of the war and its implications are relevant to this investigation of the administration of Cabinet secrecy, a concern which transcends Hankey's years at the Secretariat. The figure responsible for the suspension – contravention would not be too strong a word – of the 1934 rules clearly was Churchill himself; in Whitehall circles, Churchill's 'Personal Minutes' had long been suspected as likely material for the war memoirs which were expected from his pen.[72] Yet the Prime Minister did not formally signal his intentions until he proposed that a paragraph be added to a memorandum which the Cabinet Secretary, Sir Edward Bridges, had drafted to facilitate the transition from the War Cabinet to a successor government. Churchill sought to specify that

> Ministers are entitled to keep all telegrams, minutes or documents circulated to the Cabinet which they wrote and signed themselves . . . These must be regarded as their personal property except that they will be bound by the rules governing the use of official papers which are well established. To these should be added, in the case of the Prime Minister, correspondence with Heads of Government.[73]

When the Secretary failed to establish this point with sufficient emphasis, Churchill's secretary returned to the point in a more succinct fashion, noting to Bridges that the Prime Minister desired 'a much shorter draft . . . contain[ing] in as few words as possible an instruction that they [ministers] keep all official papers which they have written themselves but must return the remainder.'[74] Bridges apparently deferred to rank; his Note specified that 'such documents may not be quoted or published without the permission of the Government of the day,' but he foresaw that Churchill would prevail, remarking: 'After the last war substantial latitude was given [more accurately, taken] in this matter.'[75] In effect, Churchill had redefined the concept of 'property' in Cabinet documents: however clouded that issue had been in 1934, no one had advanced a claim to personal property residing in official material! In refusing to accept any other notion, Churchill secured a radical departure from the 1934 conventions, and his War Cabinet routinely approved his initiative on the day the great coalition broke up. Although that decision overthrew the 1934 conventions, the War Cabinet acted only in regard to its own papers, in exactly the same fashion as had governments from 1919 to 1931: Churchill's own bias notwithstanding, the War Cabinet was returning to traditional ways. In any event, although it is unlikely that Churchill had anticipated that he would be turned out of Downing Street in the ensuing general election, he had provided well for alternative employment.

When Churchill, out of office, began to prepare his memoirs, the Cabinet Secretary, Bridges, recommended to the Labour government policies to deal with the memoirs of a period made exceptional, he contended, by the requirements of war-time military security. Essentially, Bridges sought to limit the damage which could follow from the

Cabinet Office's loss of custody of certain documents; thus, he sought continuing protection of 'information whose disclosure would be injurious to us in our relations with other nations, including . . . a potential enemy': and of 'information the publication of which would be destructive of the confidential relationships on which our system of government is based.' These proved to be concerns which the Cabinet Office was persistently to defend in the years after the Second World War, albeit without much success for the latter principle of 'confidentiality' so long as the flood of post-war military memoirs rolled on. Bridges strove to keep most Cabinet papers beyond the pale of publication, while accommodating his office to the usage upon which Churchill was intent: 'the publication *in extenso* of official documents otherwise than by the Stationery Office should only be allowed in very exceptional cases; and then only when the document is in some sense personal to the writer.' Further, he insisted upon the maintenance of the procedures which had evolved for 'vetting' memoirs based on official materials.[76]

Attlee's government approved the terms of Bridges' memorandum on 23 May 1946, and two months later the House of Commons was informed of the guidelines. The Home Secretary, Herbert Morrison, spelled out the responsibility for war-time ministers and others to consult the government of the day in regard to the publication of 'any unpublished information which they have obtained by virtue of their official position and to obtain formal permission in any doubtful case.' He specified the differential standards which would apply:

> In dealing with such applications His Majesty's Government will distinguish between the position of a former Minister, who has been responsible to Parliament and subject to public criticism, and other former Crown servants, who had not had a Minister's responsibilities. Further they will bear in mind that during the war information that would ordinarily have been published had to be kept secret for reasons of military security; they will therefore be disposed to allow the greatest practicable freedom in the use of official information about the events of the war period and defence themes in the years immediately preceding the war, subject to no matter being disclosed which would be clearly contrary to the public interest, or would impair the confidential relationships which subsist between Ministers, or between Ministers and their advisers.[77]

Morrison spared the Commons much of the detailed historical commentary which Bridges had developed in his memorandum; nor did he inform the House that the war-time ministers had won a significant exemption from a decade-old practice, although the war years, he noted, had been granted a different status.

The other distinction which Morrison sought to make between politicians and advisers proved very difficult if not impossible to maintain: whether or not grounded upon official materials, military memoirs of the war certainly addressed the question of the 'confidential relationships' which the Secretariat had attempted to proscribe. Thus while Churchill surely had his full say in six volumes replete with official materials, his critics had theirs as well. The Second World War breached most of the bulwarks of Cabinet secrecy as the First had before it. Distinctions there were, so that the inter-war efforts to codify procedures and to protect the concept of Cabinet secrecy had not been expended in vain: even Churchill's own prime ministerial papers were ultimately held to be state property, and, unlike his earlier Cabinet papers, the 'complete' collection was many years later, in 1972, made available at the Public Record Office.

Those whose government service dated to the inter-war years were discouraged from publication of memoir-type records drawing upon Cabinet documents. Hankey had recognized from the first the implications for his own literary future and that of his past associate, Tom Jones. Indeed, in March 1935 he wrote to his former deputy, who had recently contributed a biography of Bonar Law to the *Dictionary of National Biography* – Hankey judged it 'a little more laudatory than I really think he deserves' – to seek 'reassurance' from Jones that he had not drawn upon secret Cabinet records in describing a particular Cabinet meeting: 'I imagine that these accounts of what happened at the Cabinet have already appeared in one or another of the Memoirs. You have been so discreet that I expect you could give an authority other than records which are still Secret.'[78]

The Cabinet Secretary acknowledged that his own prospects for a memoir account of Britain's war-time Supreme Command would be affected; already in 1930 he had briefly considered resignation in order to devote his time to what he foresaw as a 'tremendous epic,' even if he felt 'considerable repugnance in withdrawing the veil from even a portion of . . . [his] official Life.'[79] Despite Lloyd George's encouragement to write the book, Hankey stayed on at Whitehall Gardens, and in 1935 he confessed a weakening in his resolve eventually to publish his own war memoirs; he cautioned Lloyd George's secretary to 'keep quotations from the Cabinet Minutes down to a minimum. I find the position here has hardened in this respect.'[80] How formidable that 'hardening' would prove for Hankey's own efforts gradually emerged, as Hankey had to persist some twenty-six years in order to gain no more than a tacit acquiescence in the publication of his own memoirs. True that Hankey was hoist on his own petard, because three premiers and several Cabinet Secretaries held against his account what he had deprecated in other memoirs, namely the inclusion of materials dealing with the relationships between individuals: 'Unfortunately the practice of doing so started immediately after the war, with the result that much secret material has been used, which, in the public interest, it would have been far better not to have published.'[81] Hankey's invocation of the public interest in time was directed by others against his own revelations.

The first former minister to encounter the new regulations was J. H. Thomas, who had fallen upon hard times, his reputation tarnished by his forced retirement in the wake of his inept disclosure of budget secrets in April 1936. His political reminiscences came to the Secretariat's attention when Thomas requested that Cabinet papers relating to five major incidents, including the crisis of 1931, be sent to his Sussex home; Howorth saw no objection to meeting this request or that of any ex-minister who 'for reasons such as ill-health or old age could not conveniently come here.' Yet the Deputy Secretary was troubled by the substance of the request, which entailed the 'first occasion on which we have been told by an ex-Cabinet minister that he proposes to make use of *post-war* Cabinet documents in an autobiography and the case will therefore constitute a precedent.'[82] 'Jimmie' Thomas may have been down on his fortunes, but he remained a controversial figure whom HMG had declined to prosecute under the terms of the Official Secrets Act for his budget disclosures,[83] and Howorth thought it essential that Thomas should be asked 'to avoid giving the impression that the information contained in his book had been derived in some way from secret official documents.'

Hankey, however, took a harder line to Stanley Baldwin, who agreed to resolve the matter in Cabinet. The Cabinet Secretary contended that the 'right of access' spelled out in 1934 meant that the Cabinet Secretariat must at all times exercise 'control and supervision' over the Cabinet papers; now he asked for a sanction,

> namely that I am precluded by the express instructions of the Cabinet from parting, even temporarily, with documents entrusted to the Cabinet Office for safe custody: and that this entitles an ex Cabinet Minister to inspect the Papers in question at the *Cabinet Office*, but not to ask that the Papers should be sent to him at his home or elsewhere.[84]

Hankey defended such a proscription in terms of the increased risk of the papers falling into 'wrong hands,' but neither did he show any sympathy for handicapped former ministers, for instance the physical disabilities of Philip Snowden or the psychological problems which Thomas suffered at this time.[85] In his memorandum, Hankey refurbished the Milner case to suit present purposes: the actual Cabinet Minute had simply ruled out access to 'non-official persons' concerned with 'ordinary historical, biographical or other similar work,' but Hankey now asserted that 'in spirit this Cabinet Conclusion is definitely directed against use being made in ordinary work of Cabinet and other secret documents, whether the authors of such works are Ministers or ex Ministers, or other persons.' Hankey may well have pressed the 'spirit' because the 'letter' was lacking: the 1934 decision had not engaged with the permissible content of ministerial memoirs; ministers had to this point been free to publish what they wished, subject only to the strictures of the Official Secrets Act. Of course a court had held against the direct quotation of extracts from Cabinet documents, but references to Cabinet proceedings had not been the issue, in the Lansbury case, the Lloyd George memoirs, or elsewhere.

Nonetheless, the Cabinet Secretary recommended in 1936 that the former Cabinet minister be placed in a position which had been reserved for 'non-official persons,' namely that he had not the right 'to use the documents to give his version of the various contentious issues with which they [the documents] are concerned.'[86] Only if his reputation had been attacked could the former minister refer to the specifics. Thus the right of access, as Hankey now described it, served the minister only the purpose of 'refreshing his memory'; he had not the option 'to refer in his autobiography to proceedings in the Cabinet, still less to quote from Cabinet Minutes or other post-war Cabinet documents, and . . . it would be desirable if he could avoid giving the impression that the information in his book had been in any way derived from secret official documents.' Likely Hankey distorted the Cabinet's earlier decision because he feared the one case which would provide an ignoble precedent to loosen the floodgates of post-war disclosures; for J. H. Thomas to write about Cabinet controversies would

> start a new and most embarrassing series of post-war memoir cases. Other ex Ministers . . . will claim the right to reply to Mr. Thomas, and for that purpose will insist on having access to the same documents which he used [a right they already possessed]. The War Memoir cases have shown how mischievous and embarrassing is the practice of using Cabinet documents, whether the necessary consent for their use have been obtained or not. If this practice is now to be extended to the post-war documents the consequences must be very grave indeed, and in any case must be highly detrimental to the public interest.

If Hankey thought that the most likely spark would be found in the events of 1931, he may have chosen to raise the matter specifically in the context of the Thomas appeal. Nonetheless he did advance a further justification for his stance, namely a belief that 'the reason and justification for the Cabinet document system is to facilitate the efficient conduct of public affairs, and . . . to make use of the system for the writing of memoirs, etc., is to divert it from its proper purpose to a purpose for which it was never designed, and to bring the system into disrepute.' Surely the latter need not follow upon the former: though Hankey may have vaguely feared the future use of Cabinet materials, the creation of a secretarial mechanism was not a substantive issue unless he resisted enabling posterity to examine the workings of Cabinet government.

In a sense, Hankey's reaction serves to underscore his growing inability, noted above, to empathize with a point of view which he did not share; a hardening of his attitudes had set in by the early 1930s. Yet there is no sign that he had any difficulty in carrying Baldwin or the Cabinet with him; not even MacDonald, who was absent from the meeting, saw any alternative to the rejection of Thomas' request and the codification of Hankey's views.[87] Care was taken – at his old colleague's urging – to explain the position to J. H. Thomas,[88] who accepted the handicap and agreed as well to submit the relevant portions of the manuscript to the Cabinet Secretariat, where Hankey read the chapter dealing with the 1931 crisis with gathering dismay, because he judged that 'in certain not unimportant details, and particularly in the sequence of events, your account materially differs from our records.'[89] In this assertion, Hankey parted company with MacDonald, who had given the chapter his approval, but the Cabinet Secretary pressed to remove the inaccuracies and an account of the proceedings 'at a comparatively recent meeting of the Cabinet, including statements made at the Meeting, attributed to particular members.'

Hankey noted drily that the former minister 'ought not to be allowed to describe what actually happened and was said in the Cabinet – even if his account is not correct.' Beyond the principle of Cabinet secrecy, Hankey had pragmatic grounds to object, because some of those former colleagues whom Thomas had criticized had not returned their Cabinet papers and were in an excellent position to denounce the inaccuracies and to provoke what the Cabinet Secretary foresaw as 'a demand for publication of the Cabinet records which might even become difficult to resist.' Thomas had, after all, once before 'sailed very close to the wind' in referring to Cabinet deliberations,[90] and Hankey required that, with a squall on the horizon, he trim his literary sails. He took a positive tack in suggesting that Thomas use as a model the brief reference to the events of 1931 which Philip Snowden had made in his *Autobiography*, compressing a four page description to several sentences. Lest the Snowden parallel be taken too far – the former Chancellor had questioned MacDonald's motivations in the 1931 crisis[91] – Hankey added in a hand-written note appended to his letter: 'You could include . . . a sentence, as I understand you want to do, to explain that Mr. Ramsay MacDonald made every possible effort to save the Government but without quoting what he actually said in Cabinet.'

The Cabinet Secretary also asked Thomas to delete an account of a conversation with the late Arthur Henderson: he invoked the precept which he had upheld in 'vetting' war memoirs, namely that 'nothing should be said or done or written which might have the effect of lowering the status and prestige of Cabinet Ministers and Privy Counsellors in the eyes of the public.' Although Hankey merely requested the deletion, he likely held in reserve the support afforded his request by the language of the Official Secrets Act, which prohibited the disclosure, without authorization, of such official information as a person obtained or to which he had access by virtue of his position as a Crown servant.[92] From the events of 1934 and the formidable shadow of the Official Secrets Act, Hankey had constructed a fortress to protect Cabinet secrecy; Thomas yielded to the criticism, expurgated his account[93] and published a memoir of negligible value. Hankey's 'ukase,' based on the 1934 rules and sanctioned by the Cabinet, possessed enormous significance: it is not an exaggeration to comment that those men who held ministerial office in the inter-war period were until recent years ill-served by the restriction of access to and the use of their Cabinet papers.

Only lately have sympathetic studies of the likes of Baldwin and MacDonald emerged which have been partly based on official papers; whatever their particular merits, these statesmen and their first advocates were handicapped by the revised rules and severe interpretation which the Cabinet Secretariat insisted upon. Several examples show the absolutism which the Cabinet Office brought to the task: the biographer of such a minister, Sir Walter Long, was in effect refused permission to publish a memorandum which Long had written in 1920; furthermore, the author, Sir Charles Petrie, was called to Whitehall Gardens to yield up the document – Long's executors had assured HMG that all his Cabinet papers had been destroyed – and to confirm that no other Cabinet documents were in his possession. In return Petrie received not leave to publish, but rather Howorth's statement that 'it appeared to us that this would be a case in which it would be to the highest degree improbable that sanction for publication in any form of the draft . . . would be given.'[94]

Although it might be argued that Britain's war-time search for 'Guilty Men' stood Baldwin and Neville Chamberlain in sore need of 'vindication', the latter's biographer, Keith Feiling, was given no access to Cabinet materials; he was asked to delay publication of the book, based upon a diary and private papers, because of the official concern that 'a number of caustic remarks about America, Russia and certain living people . . . would certainly cause ill feeling and might do definite harm' and to excise certain of Chamberlain's personal diary entries which referred to Cabinet proceedings.[95] The end of the war apparently eased the concern for diplomatic relations, and permission to publish was given in little more than a year's time, but the deletion of references to Cabinet deliberations stood. Such proceedings had to be masked, but Feiling utilized both the diary and correspondence in such a way as to shed some light upon the 'official information' which had come to Chamberlain as a minister and as premier. Of course Hankey was no longer Cabinet Secretary, and Bridges, his successor, may have felt differently about the propriety of such revelations, or he may have deferred to Prime Minister Attlee's observation that 'the only point on which I am entitled to take any action is the protection of the secrecy of Cabinet meetings etc.'[96]

Stanley Baldwin, unlike Chamberlain, survived to see his reputation brutally assaulted, and he turned to the Cabinet papers as a likely line of defence, inquiring of the-then premier, Winston Churchill, whether his biographer, G. M. Young, could have access to his official papers. Baldwin recalled the restrictions imposed in 1934, but he thought the rule 'subject to the Prime Minister's dispensing powers' and thus inquired whether Young might go on his behalf to the Cabinet Office to examine the files, concluding: 'It would be some small comfort to see in writing the truth as I see it set out, however long publication may be delayed.'[97] The list of the Baldwin Papers supplies no evidence of a reply – the request may not have been sent – and G. M. Young's biography reflects the lack of any official papers for the administration of 1935–7 within Baldwin's own collection of papers.[98] Although Young's own predisposition colored his account of Baldwin's life as much as the paucity of official information,[99] Baldwin had posthumously nearly a quarter-century to await the publication of a massive biography informed by those sources, until what Baldwin might have perceived as 'the truth' emerged.

Memoir activity was not altogether closed down, as Lloyd George continued to publish, without exception seeking permission, and Hankey played his counter-part role into his last months as Cabinet Secretary.[100] In 'vetting' official materials, Hankey played a contemporary role on one occasion, since he was asked to write a decorous 'finis' to the dispute between Chamberlain and his Foreign Secretary, Anthony Eden, which had led to the latter's resignation in 1938. Eden had commented upon those policy differences in the House of Commons following his resignation, but he had still to address his constituents when he turned to Hankey: 'he rang me up to ask my help over his speech, so as to avoid saying anything to exacerbate the situation. I saw the P.M.: fixed up an agreed formula on the two most difficult issues: vetted the speech. I was successful. To-day the P.M. told me that the speech was admirable.'[101] Hankey's Cabinet Secretariat remained a formidable bulwark against disclosure of Cabinet deliberations or differences, whatever the setting.

In fact, Hankey's success accounts in significant measure for the caution and, alas, the lack of detailed political and diplomatic information in the rather commonplace memoirs written by the statesmen of the 1930s. Simon and Halifax both inclined to the Thomas model, adhering closely to the strictures laid down by the Cabinet Office. Viscount Samuel observed proper silence concerning the substance of Cabinet proceedings, although he did include an account of the role of George V in the negotiations which led to the formation of the National Government, and he discussed the attitude of the coalition Liberals both with regard to the 'agreement to differ' and their subsequent resignation from the National Government – much if not all of which had been public knowledge at the time.[102] Duff Cooper took the novel approach of recording the burgeoning differences between Chamberlain and Eden which led in early 1938 to the latter's resignation, although the Cabinet had *not* been kept informed at the time; he related the events which led to the Munich crisis, which precipitated his own resignation, largely from a diary, which he quoted extensively. Although he did not attribute opinions expressed by ministers within the Cabinet room, Duff Cooper's approach was not well received at the Cabinet Office, which looked askance at the use of his diary in connection with Cabinet proceedings.[103] While writing a fuller memoir than most of his colleagues save Duff Cooper, Sir Samuel Hoare defended his own contribution to the policy of appeasement, but without direct reference either to Cabinet proceedings or to a diary.[104] Lord Londonderry attempted during the war to set the record straight concerning his years at the Air Ministry between 1931 and 1935, but the Cabinet Office protested and he made a number of amendments, although not entirely to Edward Bridges' satisfaction, before publishing. Yet Churchill was sympathetic to Londonderry's request, for reasons which are not difficult to discern: the Prime Minister acknowledged that quotations from official documents could be barred on the grounds of the public interest, but he added: 'a bona fide interpretation of the public interest must prevail. The precedents in favour of a fairly free publication after the war are very numerous – see my own voluminous writings.' Churchill had also held out the hope of publication after the war of a volume of Lord Chatfield's memoirs, in which the former First Sea Lord and, from January 1939, Minister for the Co-ordination of Defence attacked government defence policies of that era; publication was denied in 1941, nonetheless, on the premise that the volume would weaken the sense of national unity and impair the war effort.[105] In sum, the regulations of 1934 severely handicapped the statesmen of that period and, as well, the initial biographers of men who either did not live, or choose, to write memoirs – such as Baldwin, MacDonald and, to a lesser extent, Neville Chamberlain. At what price their initial – and perhaps lasting – historical reputations?

While these men operated under restrictions, none was treated with anything approaching the severity with which the Cabinet Office dealt with the estate – and historical standing – of the deceased Labour leader, George Lansbury, whose misadventure with Cabinet papers had set these events in train. Although in the midst of the Second World War the economic problems of the second Labour government were of no great moment, in 1944, four years after Lansbury's death, the Cabinet papers which in life he had refused to yield were summarily confiscated. According to his biographer son-in-law, Raymond Postgate, who held custody of Lansbury's papers – including 'several boxes apparently containing mostly official papers'[106] – both the Deputy Secretary to the Cabinet, Norman Brook, and a Treasury Solicitor brought pressure to bear upon him and Lansbury's executor to turn over '"a dozen or at most a score"' of particularly secret papers which legally, they held, must be returned to the Cabinet Office. Since Postgate was at this time on active service in North Africa, he accepted the Treasury Solicitor's offer that a government official collect the papers and extract the few documents at issue, returning the remainder.[107]

The contents of some thirty boxes of Lansbury's papers vanished in short order, as Postgate ruefully recollected in 1951: 'In the first place, *all* the papers that I sent were seized. So far from a dozen being kept, nothing whatever was returned. I was sent, it is true, a set of signed applications to subscribe to the *Labour Gazette* in 1893; but if this was an official's jest or what I have never fathomed.' Among the confiscated items were political correspondence which Lansbury had engaged in before the First World War; the writ of 1934 had assumed a shocking if ad hoc dimension at the very time when the Prime Minister was intent upon forging an entirely novel concept of 'personal property' in official documents. The irony of the situation was not lost upon Postgate, when he discovered that correspondence had been exchanged between his father-in-law and Churchill's secretary in 1934 to resist the National Government's attempt to recover Cabinet papers.[108] At no point was Postgate apprised that the Law Officers had drawn a distinction between ministers themselves and their heirs or executors. Thus he pressed for the return of Lansbury's papers, but in 1951 Attlee's Labour government denied the request. Further, in the comments which Postgate addressed to the confiscation in the Preface to the biography, he was refused permission to quote from HMG's correspondence.[109] With this action the Cabinet Office exhibited a determination to ensure the continuing application of the 1934 rules to the inter-war period, although the arbitrariness of the action taken against Lansbury's reputation cannot be defended. Postgate drew a general lesson from these events: 'the story raises the question of how far Ministers, as public servants, are entitled to withhold the records of what has been done in the service of the public.' What he did not know was how singularly Lansbury had been treated: as far as can be ascertained, only in his case did the Cabinet Secretariat resort to outright confiscation: Lloyd George was treated very differently, and Churchill too. Whether the estates of any of the other half-dozen recalcitrants of 1934 were exposed to similar pressure, let alone confiscation, is unknown, as are the reasons for claiming Lansbury's papers.[110] Surely though, the successor regimes to Hankey's had attempted to strengthen their institutional role as the custodian of Cabinet secrecy.

A decade later, the Cabinet Office took a further step, in attempting to close the papers of Viscount Milner, at New College, Oxford, because the publication of Richard Ullman's *Intervention and the War*[111] had revealed that Milner's collection was replete with Cabinet papers and Foreign Office correspondence.[112] Since the war period had long been regarded as *sui generis*, this attempt may be explained by Ullman's intention to treat the post-war period as well – Milner held ministerial office until 1921. Under the leadership of Sir Norman Brook, third Cabinet Secretary, the office reached the apogee of its efforts to hold inviolate Cabinet secrecy for the years after 1919. It is also alleged that at this time an attempt was made to persuade the authorities at the Bodleian Library to remove from the Asquith papers copies of his letters to the King concerning Cabinet proceedings, although the majority came from the pre-war period; further, it appears that at least for a short period of time the Cabinet Office held that records of Cabinet proceedings should never be disclosed and were exempt from the provisions of the Public Records Act of 1958 which stipulated the delivery of most official papers to the Record Office after fifty years had elapsed.[113] Fortunately for those with an interest in modern British government, such an absolutist construction could not be sustained.

At the time when Howorth had moved to recover Cabinet papers, he had been acting in Hankey's absence, though doubtless with his concurrence. The Cabinet Secretary spent the latter months of 1934 touring South Africa, Australia, New Zealand, and Canada in order to discuss British defence planning with the dominion leaders; although ostensibly on a private visit, Hankey carried out official conversations which normally would have been assigned to a minister.[114] Such an undertaking by a civil servant serves not only as a reminder of Hankey's imperial associations but also of his deep involvement in defence planning. In his stead at Whitehall Gardens were Howorth as Acting Secretary to the Cabinet and Wing-Commander John Hodsoll in a similar role at the Committee of Imperial Defence; such a division of responsibilities raised within the office speculation whether any successor would combine the two tasks.[115] In the little more than three years left in his combined post, Hankey continued to pursue relentlessly large-scale measures of British rearmament. To follow those activities in great detail would be superfluous in light of Roskill's biography and the attention which has at last been given to the British rearmament effort,[116] but Hankey's continuing influence upon defence activities cannot be wholly severed from a study of the institutional development of the Cabinet Secretariat. The man and the institution remained one, and not even the creation of a Minister for the Co-ordination of Defence in March 1936 substantially affected his centrality in defence deliberations. In a physical sense, the minister, Sir Thomas Inskip,[117] worked within the defence organization at Whitehall Gardens, but his activities were closely attended to by Sir Warren Fisher – who has been described as 'virtually . . . Inskip's permanent under-secretary'[118] – as well as by Hankey. Devoid of ministerial resources, Inskip functioned within the extant system, in effect serving as a Treasury deputy for defence expenditure.[119] Hankey of course kept close counsel with Inskip, but prior to that time he concentrated his efforts to achieve rearmament within the CID and the newer forum of its Defence Requirements Committee.

In examining the defence establishment's 'worst deficiencies,' Hankey differed from his counterparts Fisher and Vansittart in awarding the highest priority to the defence of the Empire in the Far East, which dictated naval construction; in RAF circles, Hankey was suspect – as recently as May 1932, he had entertained the prospect of abolishing all military and naval air forces, but the attempt to secure an Air Convention along these lines had gotten nowhere, either with the French or Prime Minister MacDonald.[120] In their collective efforts, however, the three accepted the priorities developed by the Fighting Services – whose military heads sat on the DRC – rather than attempt to adjudicate priorities among the Services; such a process produced unanimity within the DRC but assured that those priorities would be contested at the level of Cabinet review. Fisher in particular worked upon the Chancellor, Chamberlain, to ensure that air preparations directed against the German threat received a higher priority than naval measures against Japan.

Hankey thought the Treasury-backed air proposals mistaken, and he succeeded in achieving minor changes in the configuration of the deficiency program, but the Cabinet, in June 1934, actually increased the expenditure which the Chancellor sought.[121] Concurrently, the Cabinet, at Chamberlain's behest, cut the Army's deficiency appropriation in half and left the Admiralty's share open to further negotiation with the Treasury.[122] Thus a program which Hankey and the COS had viewed as a 'balanced allocation of resources between [sic] the services,'[123] incorporated in the DRC report despite the reservations of Fisher and Vansittart, was redeployed in recognition of Britain's inability to counter an air threat. Curiously, the role of the civil servants in preparing the report and of the Treasury in re-directing Britain's deficiency program far outstripped the contributions made by the military leaders; nor was the irony lost upon officials within the CID and certainly not on the civil servants themselves.[124]

As Hankey left for the dominions in August 1934, he had personal reason for dissatisfaction with the British defence stance: despite his painstaking work to produce a unanimous DRC report, the government had chosen 'to look beyond the menace of Japan to Germany and pronounce her the ultimate political enemy against whom long-range defence policy must be planned.'[125] To Pacific dominions concerned above all with the menace of Japan, Hankey carried the news of a British defence posture geared primarily to the German threat. The Cabinet Secretary had been selected in February of that year to visit Australia, in part to acquaint its government with Britain's 'trend of thought' in defence matters; subsequently Hankey was charged with conveying the tenor of ministerial review of the DRC report; the report prepared by the ministerial committee had not been sent to the dominions precisely because it had left open the question of Britain's naval program. Although Hankey thought that he had succeeded in 'papering over the cracks' in British policy in the Far East while on his mission, the Australian authorities concluded that objectives had been stressed but that means to those ends had not been resolved.[126] For all Hankey's efforts, the 'cracks' could not be hidden from view.

Late in his life, Hankey recollected that while crossing the Atlantic to complete his Empire tour, he wrote an initial draft of what became in due course the 1935 White Paper on Defence.[127] While there seems to be no corroboration of his work while on shipboard, it is clear that upon his return in January Hankey joined in an effort to educate the public about defence policies, a need all the greater for mounting evidence that German air rearmament already by November 1934 had outpaced Britain's deficiency program. Fisher and some other senior civil servants who had worked on that scheme were again involved.[128] The Prime Minister remained to be won to the issuance of such a statement, which would provoke parliamentary debate; Hankey secured his assent to a draft which MacDonald amended in no significant way.[129] In the Cabinet, however, some amendments were made, which Hankey and Fisher thought weakened the White Paper, published in March 1935.[130] Once a pacifist, the Prime Minister now witnessed the highly unusual personalization of this key state paper on the road to rearmament, namely the use of his initials, 'J.R.M.,' below the final paragraph. Much speculation was provoked, but no authoritative explanation followed; only recently has MacDonald's own comment emerged: 'by accident my initials were put on to indicate that the document I last saw was the authentic copy to be put in order.'[131] Thus MacDonald's role was inadvertently featured, but the entire incident again shows Hankey's use of the 'indirect approach': frustrated both by the pace of HMG's reaction to developments abroad and the decisions made by the Cabinet, he and his cohorts – Warren Fisher most prominent – enlisted the Prime Minister in order to gain public attention for their pleas.

Meanwhile, the international situation deteriorated, as the Germans introduced conscription in March 1935: several months earlier, Fisher had received intelligence of massive German borrowing for rearmament, an ominous development by any standards. As the COS had not yet accepted as final the ministerial recommendation and Cabinet decision to overthrow the 'balanced' advice of the DRC, that committee was reconstituted and charged to report about the deficiency program as a whole to a ministerial committee, the Defence Policy and Requirements Committee (DPRC), at this time acting as an agent for the Cabinet; the DRC's recommendations were to be made in the light of recent military developments, but attention was to be given to financial co-ordination as well. An Interim DRC Report of 24 July pointed to the inescapable conclusion that Treasury orthodoxy would have to be compromised by the institution of a defence loan. Although the DPRC refused for the moment to commit the Cabinet 'as to the methods by which the programmes of the Defence Services were to be financed,' the ministerial committee in short order gave the DRC license to consider the state of readiness which the Services should attain by 1939.[132] Once again the initiative – and an awesome responsibility – lay collectively with Hankey, Fisher, Vansittart, and the Chiefs of Staff.

The content of the Third Report of November 1935 is not here at issue: suffice it to reiterate that the concept of repairing 'worst deficiencies' had now given way to what N. H. Gibbs has characterized as 'an urgency to complete programmes unhampered by traditional methods, especially of finance.'[133] Of course further ministerial review was required, but on this occasion the Treasury had to yield to other desiderata of national security: in March 1936 another *Statement Relating to Defence* confirmed that Britain had embarked upon a massive scheme of rearmament.[134] 'At long last,' Hankey and his colleagues would have been justified in commenting, because they had labored mightily to bring HMG to recognize the danger of developments abroad at a time when the fear of a much misunderstood 'pacifism' influenced ministerial thought.[135]

In that process, the senior civil servants had differed sharply among themselves: Hankey and Fisher were both angered by Vansittart's enthusiasm for the Foreign Office-sponsored air convention initiative of early 1935, objecting not only to substance but also to contravention of established civil service procedures.[136] The Cabinet Secretary had a year earlier remarked acidly to his CID deputy, Pownall, that Warren Fisher's papers were on occasion 'astonishing, long tirades far removed from the point and irrelevant.'[137] For their part, Fisher and Vansittart had contested Hankey's sense of priorities in developing a response to external threats. Despite the differences among these strong-willed civil servants, together they dominated proceedings of the DRC and performed an estimable service in the cause of rearmament. Despite his part in this effort, Warren Fisher, nearly a decade later, was among those who felt the sting of criticism that Britain had not prepared earlier and more comprehensively for war.[138] Although Hankey rejected the harsher charges about Fisher, he did comment unfavorably about his colleague's excessive interference with Britain's rearmament efforts.[139] Yet it is clear that Hankey – whatever memories he may have held of struggles within the DRC, the ministerial committees, and the Cabinet – exempted Fisher from the substantive criticism which he directed against the 'dead hand' of 'Treasury control,' which in its 'extravagant interpretation' had 'militated against the efficiency of our defences.'[140]

Fisher's role at the Treasury is now far better understood than only a few years ago, let alone 1943, and his contribution to rearmament – even in this brief compass – cannot be disputed, even taking into account his insistence upon curbing defence spending for economic reasons.[141] Ultimately, the Treasury Secretary, like his Cabinet counterpart, exercised influence, but neither could claim power.[142] Whether the institution within which Fisher moved to influence the course of events damaged Britain's war readiness is a more contentious matter: a long succession of military commentaries advanced 'Treasury control' as the culprit, and Hankey had no doubts; recent accounts, firmly grounded in the records, incline against such a monocausal explanation.[143] On the contrary, argues G. C. Peden, because 'Treasury control' 'forced ministers and military men to come to decisions about priorities, and thereby ensured that essential elements in Britain's defences were completed first.'[144] Yet the point remains that the Treasury's exercise of financial control over rearmament left next to no margin for error in the choice of those priorities. The 'fourth arm of defence,' it appears, shed constraints of fiscal orthodoxy all too slowly, and the nation paid a price in the events of 1939–42.[145]

While Sir Warren Fisher insisted that the Fighting Services could not independently make the best use of Britain's financial resources,[146] in other quarters – most prominently a small but vocal parliamentary group – complaints were lodged against the co-ordinating mechanism supplied by the CID. Hankey was unable to persuade these Tory MPs that the higher organization of defence was all that it should be.[147] For several years Hankey fended off the suggestion that a full-time deputy at the CID would lighten his own burden. Several times mentioned as a possibility for such a post, the respected military commentator Basil Liddell Hart was dismayed by Hankey's failure to respond to proposals for improved defence planning, noting after a conversation in March 1935: 'He mentioned that he became Secretary of the C.I.D. at 34 and was now 58. This explains much – why a man of such alert mind and ideas is clearly, as I have noticed, becoming more complacent with things as they are.'[148]

Liddell Hart concluded that the opposition to a Ministry of Defence came from Hankey and the civil heads of the Fighting Services: 'A Minister of Defence with a combined General Staff would be likely to impair their present degree of authority.'[149]

Hankey's defence of the status quo weakened when his former colleague from the COS Committee, 'Boom' Trenchard, urged publicly that the secretaryship of the Cabinet and the CID ought to be divided, with the latter becoming a full-time post.[150] Written 'in sorrow but not in anger,' Hankey's private reply described the suggestion as 'deplorable.' Yet as press criticism of the status quo mounted in early 1936, not even his defence of the defence organization could be sustained; a parliamentary debate on 14 February forced Hankey to admit that changes would have to be made – though he claimed to hold in reserve his own resignation if those changes were too severe. Already he had warned the Cabinet about the dangers inherent in establishing even a Minister of Defence, *sans* ministry, because such a course would pose the dilemma of 'dual control, not only between the Prime Minister and the Minister of Defence, but between the Minister of Defence and the Fighting Service Ministers.'[151] He acknowledged the unsatisfactory condition of the present planning for 'supplies in time of war' but contended that the cause of this deficiency was external, a product of the now-abandoned Ten Year Rule.

Although in the past Hankey had voiced reservations concerning the difficulties which a minister co-ordinating defence might have in Cabinet with his Service colleagues, he capitulated to the appointment of a minister as a defence deputy to the Prime Minister. He could hardly do otherwise in view of Baldwin's feelings:

> This [the appointment] was forced upon them [the Cabinet] if for no other reason than by the P.M. saying he did *not* have adequate time to go properly into defence questions. In ordinary times perhaps he could, but now that Defence has become a major issue and a really close watch will be needed over the carrying out of the programmes he can't do the job. So that settled the point.[152]

And on that point Hankey finally lost his struggle to preserve the Committee of Imperial Defence as the sole agency for the co-ordination of Britain's defence planning. Yet the question arises whether Hankey, having lost the battle, won the war, because the selection of Sir Thomas Inskip for the position, an appointment widely criticized at the time, did not place an experienced student of military affairs at Hankey's shoulder.[153]

Surely it is no coincidence that Hankey chose this time to strengthen the organization of the CID through the appointment of a senior officer as Deputy Secretary, noting laconically that such a post had 'existed for some years after the war and was dropped for reasons of economy.' The appointee, Colonel Hastings 'Pug' Ismay, did not assume the post until

August 1936.[154] Another key CID appointment was that of Major L. C. Hollis as a full-time Secretary to the Committee of Deputy Directors (Planning), an action which strengthened the Joint Planning Committee and accelerated the business of combined planning, so vital when war came.[155] In these particulars, the 'flexible' CID structure which Hankey had so long defended admitted of change, although that change has been characterized as 'conservative in intention and . . . equally so in effect.'[156] Clearly the Committee of Imperial Defence remained entirely Hankey's type of organization as long as he continued in his post.

Nor did the structural changes in defence organization associated with Inskip's appointment affect Hankey's own role in defence planning. The role of the Minister for the Co-ordination of Defence was not cast in independent terms, but he did not lack influence, and influence mattered in defence planning.[157] True that Inskip was chosen by Chamberlain to 'involve us in no fresh perplexities,'[158] but he did join in the preparation of the country for war. Particularly consequential was his challenge to the traditional strategic doctrine of the Air Staff which held that because victory lay only in air attack, construction of heavy bombers mattered above all else. Countering that 'German bombers . . . could be better destroyed over Britain by a fighter force than by bombing her aerodromes and factories,' Inskip carried in the Cabinet his proposal that the RAF fighter force should be strengthened and provided with full reserves.[159] Thus Scheme 'K,' in whose development Inskip was directly involved, gave priority in air rearmament to the defence, a trend which intensified in the months before the outbreak of war. Generally, Inskip worked closely with the new Prime Minister, Chamberlain, and his successor as Chancellor, Simon, in the last major pre-war review of Britain's defence preparations in the winter of 1937–8, a review in which the Treasury again exerted its force, for fear that, in Fisher's words, 'we are rapidly drifting into financial chaos and are in danger of undermining ourselves before the Boche feels it desirable to move.'[160] This review assured that priority went to provision against air and sea attack, which accorded with Hankey's own predilection to place island and imperial defence above military support for Britain's allies on the continent.[161] Inskip's contribution may best be understood as an extension of 'Treasury control' within Whitehall Gardens, but Hankey took care not to neglect his ministerial associate, because Inskip was susceptible to influence, and he possessed Chamberlain's confidence.[162]

Inskip personally caused Hankey no problems – the Cabinet Secretary saw himself and the minister as 'twin brothers' – although the relationship imposed 'a lot of rather thankless and unremunerative work' on him, in connection with Inskip's parliamentary responsibilities. On balance, however, Hankey concluded that 'the Government . . . are not doing enough even now and not doing it quick enough,'[163] and he speculated with less than total certainty that had he been left in charge of the DRC, the rearmament program might have been moved along more quickly. To the end, the defence re-organization of 1936 remained no more than a 'marriage of convenience': his heart and mind remained of the old persuasion.

Nor did Hankey part company with the geo-political considerations which marked his inter-war views; if anything, the developments of the 1930s confirmed his assumptions. All along he had viewed the League of Nations as a thin and undependable reed, unable to sustain the fervid hopes of its partisans. Too much could not be asked of that body, but in 1935 the British government attempted to use League sanctions in order to curb Mussolini's territorial designs upon Abyssinia. The Cabinet Secretary used his influence directly upon the new Foreign Secretary, Samuel Hoare, as a full diary entry reveals:

> Hoare said this abandoning the sanctions would be letting down the League. Public opinion would not stand it. I disagreed. All the official world, outside the F.O. (and many within it) are against sanctions, and especially the oil sanction. Most intelligent people outside that I had met felt the same. He said, in effect, that the official world had 'cold feet' about it.
>
> I replied in effect that we knew the facts.
>
> . . . Hoare said my policy was really a confession that we were not prepared to support the League. We might as well scrap it at once. That was what my policy came to.
>
> I said 'No'. I have never been opposed to the League. I regarded it as a great organ of conciliation, with immense possibilities for the future. We ought to keep it. But with four of the seven Great Powers outside, and with the only effective one of the three remaining Powers (France) lukewarm we ought not push economic sanctions to the point where force might be invoked. It was too dangerous. And it was making the League an instrument of war instead of an instrument of peace.[164]

Hankey's position was consistent if narrow: his 'support' for the League was predicated upon a drastically altered Covenant, as his thoughts on Britain's defence posture in mid-1936 make unequivocal:

> Articles 10 and 16 must be put into cold storage outside these limits [a purely defensive commitment on behalf of France, Belgium, and Holland], so far as we are concerned. There they are likely to remain, for the reason that men and women are unwilling to incur the horrors and dangers and exhaustion of modern warfare except for the immediate defence of their own country.[165]

Such a view, strongly put to the Foreign Secretary in November 1935, may have contributed to Hoare's change of face, which led him in short order to conclude his ill-fated pact with Pierre Laval.

In so advising the Foreign Secretary, Hankey represented the views of the COS, who had earlier held that while Britain was sufficiently strong to prevail in the Mediterranean, losses would result from the Fleet's lack of full preparation for such warfare; further, they viewed reaction abroad, particularly in the Far East, as a complicating factor which also dictated a refusal to challenge Mussolini.[166] Following HMG's implementation of such advice, Chatfield, the First Sea Lord, pithily reflected the view held throughout military circles: 'Collective security showed itself to be a heavenly dream, as it was the British sailor's nightmare.'[167] Hankey was at home amidst such sentiments, but he could not have been more off the mark in his assertion that public opinion would sanction Britain's scuttle from a pro-League stance; in fact his notion that public opinion followed that of the 'official world' indicated how out of touch Hankey had become, although the politicians who had recently won an election fared no better. However, in Hankey's case, there is a rare cynicism in his assertion that 'the Government had won the election decisively. They no longer had to angle for votes from the left wing and could do what they wished.'[168] Within a month Hoare lost the Foreign Office because in good measure he could not do as they wished – their electoral pledges on behalf of what appeared a genuine League policy had been taken seriously.[169] Though the direct weight of 'public opinion' precipitating Hoare's resignation may have been exaggerated – ironically by the government and Hoare himself – Conservative MPs realized that their commitment to collective security could not be casually abandoned.[170]

It must be remarked that in the context of HMG's pro-League statements in 1935, Hankey deluded himself in thinking that he was 'pro-League': in fact he referred to a very different League of conciliation, shorn of the automatic sanctions which from a military perspective he greatly feared.[171] The supreme irony remains that the actions of Hankey, his military cohorts and the British government helped to maim the ailing but real League of Nations, whatever their claims to uphold it. It may be argued that a long-term consequence of the Hoare–Laval Pact was to foster the very notion of Britain's irresoluteness and weakness which the government hoped to overcome; ultimately Hitler's belief that Britain would not defend any interests save her own influenced his attack upon Poland, bringing about the Second World War. Whether or not a true collectivist policy, organized through the League in 1935, might have discouraged the dictators from their piece-meal acquisitions of 1935–9 cannot be settled; indeed the question serves as an interpretative watershed for the historian of Britain, and Europe, in those years. Yet one matter is clear: Britain's leaders, civilian and military, never gave the collectivist policy a chance to succeed. If that be a failing, Sir Maurice Hankey embodied the flaw.

Since Britain's leaders had no illusions – in their own eyes – about the viability of a League policy, their determination to secure more effective means of rearmament mattered above all else; until that time, they were intent upon avoiding conflict before Britain's defences were in place. Hankey himself put a fine edge to that sentiment in April 1936: 'The essential thing is to stave off war and to strengthen ourselves in case one day we can stave it off no longer – which God forbid.'[172] The effort, as we have seen, was bounded by the structure of 'defence by committee': questions were raised particularly about the proliferation of CID committees in the years of rearmament,[173] but as late as May 1938 Hankey insisted that only through such committee work could 'the large mass of inter-Departmental business on which principles, policy, plans and preparation for war . . . be settled.'[174]

Yet confusion was engendered by the creation of a number of senior ad hoc committees: with the establishment in early 1937 of a standing ministerial committee designated as a CID Sub-Committee on Defence Plans (Policy), there existed three such top-level committees, namely the CID, the DPRC – concerned mainly with the supply question – and the DP (P). In the judgment of the official historian, 'all, to some degree, were independent of each other, and yet dealing with defence questions with no clear line of demarcation between them. There was a good deal of overlap, and one committee took work which more properly belonged to another.'[175] The conclusion cannot be avoided that with duplication of effort came loss of time. A further question remains: had a monolithic structure been forged, could Britain's pursuit of rearmament have assumed a heightened tempo? In view of recent scholarship examining the external constraints to which the Treasury as an institution and the Cabinet as a political body answered, defence organization does not appear as a consequential restraint upon rearmament. If responsibility be personalized for what can be called Britain's 'grand strategy' in these years, then Neville Chamberlain occupies center-stage no less than he did in the conduct of foreign affairs after becoming Prime Minister.[176] Hankey recognized that the dictators were rearming 'ohne hast und ohne rast,'[177] but a democracy moved by consensus no less than by committee.

Sufficient arms would not be in hand until 1939, and nothing in the interim should detract from realization of rearmament programs. Thus the COS feared above all the simultaneous 'hostility, open or veiled, of Japan in the Far East, Germany in the West and any power on the main line of communication between the two'; further, they could not foresee the time when Britain's defence forces would be sufficiently strong 'to safeguard our trade, territory and vital interests against Germany, Italy and Japan at the same time.'[178] These fears define the strategic context for appeasement, but however defensible the design, its execution proved to be a frustrating if not humiliating experience, particularly for the Foreign Office – which accepted the strategy.[179] Nonetheless, such a rare success in curbing belligerent acts as occurred at the Nyon Conference in September 1937 served to intensify the frustration felt in circles within the Foreign Office at the undue pessimism which marked the stance of the COS. Hankey shared the military posture and pressed upon Vansittart the need to 'make friends with Italy.'[180] In this unpopular quest, Hankey revealed how his patience with contradictory counsel had been stretched taut: 'We take far too much notice of the yapping of little dogs.'[181] Where others were frustrated, Hankey remained fearful of the possibility of a premature war, touched off in the Mediterranean; on the other hand, Eden and some of his cohorts in the Foreign Office viewed such a policy of accommodation as a bribe to an aggressor power, likely to encourage other claims to territorial change.[182]

In this embittered exchange, Hankey was a central figure who, in Pratt's view, 'used every opening to press his influence.' Hankey's own travels in Italy during September 1937 served to strengthen his feelings both about the country and its regime, which supplied an ideological reinforcement for his strategic thought.[183] In working on these grounds for accommodation with Italy, Hankey welcomed Eden's resignation in February 1938, concluding that the Foreign Secretary had constituted a barrier to the kind of understanding which Chamberlain sought, a settlement which for the Cabinet Secretary transcended the designs of the dictator: 'It is the world situation and our armaments situation that trouble me more than the Mediterranean.'[184] One may properly note that Chamberlain's search for an accommodation was grounded in part on 'the fallible opinion of very fallible men' such as Hankey, but it is idle to deny that a significant debate informed the policy-making process.[185] The decision ran against Eden, but the predominant view was based not on 'complacency' but dread of provoking a war before Britain's defences were in order. The shortcoming in British defence planning, in sum, was not 'structural' but rather attitudinal. It may well be that the missing element in the calculations of those who counselled military inaction on all fronts was the effect that such a policy of disengagement had upon the thinking of the dictators.

Despite the fact that Hankey backed Chamberlain's initiative, he had not welcomed the prospect of his succession to Baldwin in 1937; two years earlier, he had recalled Balfour's opinion, voiced late in his life, that Chamberlain's judgment could not be trusted.[186] In January 1937 he had complained to Inskip that he personally had little hope of securing from Chamberlain, still Chancellor, a decision about the Army's role: 'probably [he] views me, as Chairman of the Defence Requirements Committee, as one of the "old gang" on this subject. Anyhow, he has never asked my opinion on it, so I do not suppose he wants it.'[187] Hankey's immediate concern was to upgrade the Army's rearmament effort, but he held as well to the opinion that a balanced effort for the three Fighting Services had to be attained. To the RAF assurances that the next war would be won, or lost, in the air, he noted tartly: 'In spite of their immense value for innumerable purposes, I do not think that anyone had claimed that they were able to replace armies either in attack or in defence.' Hankey's own view of the air role had undergone an evolutionary change in the decade, in view of the German threat. Yet the doctrine of the strategic offensive espoused by the Air Staff no longer went unchallenged: the air war in Spain had indicated that the defence was beginning to catch up with the attack in important ways.[188] British military thought looked increasingly to defence against air attack as the most pressing priority, in part because the temptation to score a 'knock-out blow' appeared to be the only reason why Germany would choose to go to war in 1938. Inskip, Hankey, and Fisher agreed that Britain need only survive the initial phase of a war; thereafter her sea power would inevitably be brought to bear. Treasury support was given Hankey's suggestion of December 1937 that air planning should substitute 'a larger proportion of light bombers and medium bombers for our very expensive heavy [four-engined] bombers.'[189] Fisher took solace in an idea which strengthened the Treasury desire to control defence spending and so maintain the 'fourth arm of defence' as a barrier to German aggression. Treasury and COS records of these discussions undermine the claim that Hankey was the first authority to propose a reduction in bomber strength in favor of fighters.[190] In fact, the Air Staff disputed Hankey's suggestion, and the minister, Inskip, ignored his proposal to alter the bomber 'mix': he temporized on that matter but did agree to the full increase in fighter squadrons sought by the Air Staff. Nonetheless, the Minister denied parity in bombers to the RAF and stressed the defensive role which the air arm would play in the initial phase of a war.[191] The claim to Hankey's initiative advanced by his biographer cannot be sustained, but the crucial episode does illustrate the free interchange of ideas between military leaders and the senior civil servants: the decisions of Inskip and the Chamberlain Cabinet were taken upon a stage carefully set for them.

Since Hankey sympathized intensely with Chamberlain's efforts – in the absence of an agreement with Germany – to strike an accommodation with Italy, there is no indication of tension in the dealings between the two men, despite reservations which Hankey had once entertained; in the Prime Minister's conflict with the Foreign Office, Hankey's sympathies were with Chamberlain, and he welcomed Eden's resignation in February 1938:

> Fond as I am of him on personal grounds, I woke this morning with a strange feeling of relief. I am sorry to say that generally I wake on how we are to provide for some horror in the next war. Today I felt there was just a possibility of peace. I only hope I am right.[192]

Now the Prime Minister was free to base his conduct of British foreign policy upon the risky grounds of his personal determination to come to terms with Italy and Germany, crowning his hopes in the Munich gathering of September 1938. By that time, Hankey had taken his leave of the Cabinet Secretariat – a year after his sixtieth birthday – but Hankey agreed with the Prime Minister's quest for peace. The two had not grown close together in the brief direct association, but the mutual determination to avoid war in 1938 is not in doubt. For Hankey the reasons have been already advanced; for Chamberlain, the rationale lay in his positive intention to avoid war, though not at all costs, rather than in the dread of the likely outcome of a war fought before Britain was fully prepared.[193] Hankey does not stand in the ranks of the 'appeasers' round the premier, because for the Cabinet Secretary the policy was a diplomatic mask designed to disguise the inability of British arms yet to sustain any other foreign policy. Hankey conciliated from a conviction of weakness rather than a sense of mission, although no one had labored harder than he to overcome defence deficiencies.

The measure of Hankey's achievement in securing Britain's war readiness is a difficult one to ascertain, because his voice blends into a chorus, although the attempt has been made to delineate his 'line' from that of those with whom he worked in a collaborative fashion. In his last years, British policy moved in the direction he desired, though not at the pace he hoped: in this sense, his influence was insufficient to overcome the political and economic pressures which his masters had to take into account in accepting the case for rearmament. Given these constraints, it is altogether possible that no one, Churchill included, could have advanced the defence program with more speed than did Hankey's experienced hand. Deficiencies remained in September 1939, but Britain in short order made a successful transition to conditions of total war in such a way as to belie the contention that she was unprepared for war at its inception. Though the official historian of the rearmament effort shies from apportioning credit, alone 'the name of Sir Maurice (later Lord) Hankey would spring to most minds.'[194] Quite rightly, Hankey's contribution is linked to the higher organization of defence: 'at the level of administrative planning Britain had never been better prepared for a major war than she was in September 1939.' The question might be posed, could Hankey reasonably have been expected to accomplish more? Specifically, did the hardening of his views adversely affect his contribution, because his biographer detects in Hankey 'severe physical and mental strain . . . weaken[ing] his normally limitless tact and patience' in his last several years in office?[195] Perhaps more tact would have yielded better results, but British rearmament was slowed by factors over which Hankey, and indeed the defence organization, had little if any control.

Indeed, the damage from Hankey's hardening mental cast was visited upon his close associates and himself, above all else. The most regrettable product of Hankey's strain was a quarrel with Winston Churchill, for which Hankey was to pay heavily, as Churchill slowly but surely eased him out of ministerial office in his war-time regime. Over the years, the two had maintained correct if not cordial relations: however, Churchill's pursuit of economies in the Fighting Services during his term at the Treasury had taken their toll not only of the Estimates but as well of Hankey's forbearance.[196] Then too Churchill had played a leading role in giving final form to the Ten Year Rule, which complicated Hankey's subsequent official life enormously. In the 1930s, Hankey recollected Churchill's 'special responsibility' for what was 'perhaps the root cause of our accumulation of deficiencies.'[197] Yet Churchill was by this time becoming a leading critic of the government's defence measures, an irony which did not amuse those who had formerly wrestled with his formidable presence at the Treasury. In 1936, Churchill's persistent criticism of the Baldwin administration's response to German aircraft production had raised the question whether secret papers should continue to be given to him in his capacity as a member of the CID Sub-Committee on Air Defence Research. Hankey attempted to finesse the question, and as a result Churchill did not realize how hard pressed Hankey, Swinton, the Air Minister, and Inskip were in their dealings with him.[198] The problem was compounded by their realization that generally in the British air effort 'the need for push and drive . . . has not penetrated very far below those who hold immediate responsibility.'[199] Another complication was a continuing flow of Air Staff information to Churchill, supplemented by the sources cultivated by Desmond Morton, Chairman of the Economic Intelligence Centre.[200]

From any perspective, the air imbalance worsened early in 1937, and Churchill and Hankey discussed these developments in a strained conversation: Hankey was irritated by Churchill's threat to circulate among his own 'friends' the latest information which had come his way, if he were not given the Air Staff's reaction to those figures. In fact the Air Staff disputed Churchill's conclusions, but the Cabinet Secretary did not want to share with Churchill 'specially secret information' which the Air Staff had used to refute his claims. Churchill held his fire for the moment, although he informed Hankey – for the second time in less than a year[201] – that he possessed 'no separate source of information,' which the latter had inquired about.

Churchill took umbrage at the proposed visit of German Air General Milch and a deputation, scheduled for the autumn of 1937. Layers of intrigue envelop this episode – Vansittart suspected that Milch had in the past done his best to lull his British informants into a false sense of security[202] – but Churchill derided the 'sham show' mounted for Milch's benefit. In an appeal addressed to Hankey, he included a letter from 'a high Staff officer of the RAF' who had written of the prospects for the visit in scathing terms.[203] Although Hankey did not dispute Churchill's 'pretty shrewd knowledge of the situation,' he was angered by Churchill's access to such information, cleverly supplemented by his reference to Hankey's actions in the Great War: 'I remember how you played an essential part in saving the country over the convoy system, and how when young officers came to you and told you the truth, against Service rules, you saw that the seed did not fall on stony ground.'[204] Registering his belief that 'a most shocking state of affairs' operated in the Air Force, Churchill sought to enlist the CID Secretary in remedial action: 'you have a great responsibility – perhaps on the whole second to none – and therefore I leave the matter for the moment in your hands.'

Hankey summarily rejected Churchill's appeal and denounced his approach as 'all wrong, that the thing is infectious, and subversive to discipline and that the damage done to the Services far outweighs any advantage that might accrue.' In this instance, he intimated, the 'unofficial' route was contaminated by Churchill's involvement: 'It shocks me not a little that high Officers in disciplined Forces should be in direct communication with a leading Statesman who, though notoriously patriotic beyond criticism, is nevertheless in popular estimation regarded as a critic of the Departments under whom these Officers serve.' Nor did Hankey need a reminder of his own responsibilities, and he declined to discuss the substantive matters raised by Churchill without ministerial authority. While he hoped to retain Churchill's 'goodwill,' his letter impresses as brusque, even brutal, and Churchill's succinct termination of the correspondence was merited: 'I certainly did not expect to receive from you a lengthy lecture when I went out of my way to give you, in strict confidence, information in the public interest.' The point of the exchange is not whether the Air Staff or Churchill's network was better informed about the actual dimensions of German air construction,[205] but rather why had Hankey committed what his biographer views as 'perhaps his worst tactical error'? As a rule, he burned no bridges to former ministers and sought no unnecessary enemies, especially among unquestioned patriots. Why the unwise and damaging outburst, when Hankey had so long exercised restraint? The action was wholly out of character,[206] and it is explicable only in terms of Hankey's exhaustion from the ever-accumulating weight of duty; his patience with criticism had worn thin and, confident of Churchill's errant ways, Hankey attacked by way of compensation for all the problems Churchill had posed over the years. His lapse was regrettable, but it may well have been necessary.

Of far less consequence to Hankey's future was a needless quarrel with Lawrence Burgis, his Private Secretary of many years' standing, which serves to confirm Hankey's exhaustion. The details of this rupture are not germane,[207] and although Hankey himself protested that 'there are always two sides to every question,' opinion within the Cabinet Office swung against Hankey's harsh handling of a trivial dispute; Henry Pownall related the dispute to his general concern about Hankey: 'The fact is I suppose he's showing the strain of all his many years of hard work and his nerves are beginning to jangle.'[208] The strain, we have witnessed, was cumulative, but in his last months Hankey encountered the agonizing prospect that Chamberlain's search for an agreement with the dictators – if successful – might 'weaken, and perhaps destroy, his efforts in the rearmament field.'[209] Perhaps it was this uncertainty that two projects which he wholeheartedly supported might serve to cancel out each other which haunted Hankey, although there is no direct evidence. Nonetheless, it is well to keep in mind that the complexities of the last three years of peace were in some ways harder to bear than the simplicities of war, a point made by Hankey's CID deputy 'Pug' Ismay: 'The . . . years from 1936 to 1939 were more difficult and anxious than the three years of almost uninterrupted disaster which followed them.'[210] Hankey left Whitehall Gardens uncertain that Britain would prevail, and that – above all other uncertainties – weighed heavily upon him.

In his understandable preoccupation with defence, the administration of Cabinet business did not much concern Hankey in those years, although he continued to take the minutes of all Cabinet meetings, and he involved himself with some Cabinet committee work as well. He worked within the system which had evolved over the years, adapting procedures to suit the style of the incumbent premier: when Baldwin took over in 1935, the Cabinet Minutes regained some substance, occasionally taking the form of the attribution of individual views. The Cabinet Secretary felt free to maintain something approaching a verbatim record of Cabinet deliberations in vital matters, for example the discussion prior to Hoare's resignation in December 1935. In informing the Prime Minister about the existence of such a record, Hankey noted that only one copy existed, partly in his own hand – the ministerial comments bearing upon that resignation Hankey had not given to a typist – and that he proposed to keep it, under seal, with the Cabinet archives. Curiously, the minute was examined on one occasion before the entire file of Cabinet Minutes was sent to the Public Record Office: in June 1946, the Cabinet Secretary, Norman Brook, had some reason to examine it, and he then replaced it in a cover marked 'TOP SECRET – To be opened personally by . . . . . .,' filling in 'The Secretary of the Cabinet.'[211]

Nor did the circulation of Cabinet papers prove in Hankey's last years to be the problem it once had been. Some modifications were made in the lists of those to whom certain categories of documents were circulated, but the matter was handled routinely. In April 1937 the Cabinet agreed to the request of the new monarch, George VI, that copies of Cabinet memoranda should be sent to the Duke of Gloucester, who would become Regent in the event of George's death; copies of Cabinet Minutes and Cabinet committee papers were excluded from the arrangement. However, the scheme represented an adaptation of arrangements made late in the reign of George V to send a very limited selection of Foreign Office and Dominions Office telegrams to the Prince of Wales and the Duke of York. The old king had expressed 'the greatest misgivings' even about that arrangement, maintaining that their duties did not include access to such materials, but he had yielded.[212] When the Prince of Wales became Edward VIII, his Secretary, Hardinge, likely was a party to the screening of certain Foreign Office papers from him, on security grounds: allegedly the action was taken because no staff accompanied him on his forays to Fort Belvedere.[213]

In the wake of Eden's resignation, complaints were voiced from Buckingham Palace that communications had broken down between George VI and his government; Hankey was chided by Hardinge, but he quickly established that the Prime Minister's Office was the accepted channel of communication. In fact, the blunder had occurred in the King's staff, and nothing more was heard from Hardinge.[214] To the end, Hankey was not caught in a procedural *faux pas*. Greater problems were posed by documents emanating from the Committee of Imperial Defence, whose efforts could not always be made to comport with the five days' notice required for papers brought before the Cabinet. Chamberlain was anxious that ministers be given ample opportunity to consider all papers, and he pressed the CID to conform.[215] He also reminded the Cabinet that most Cabinet and CID papers ought not be shown to minor government officials, although in some cases, ministers outside the Cabinet and senior Service advisers might be shown, at ministerial discretion, such specially secret papers as were relevant to their tasks, always under strict 'Lock and Key' protection.[216]

At this time, the Cabinet Secretariat established new guidelines for the 'Lock and Key' category; Howorth expressed pleasure that he would no longer have to 'discriminate between documents that are "Secret" and those that are "Most Secret."'[217] The latter category could be abolished, replaced by the exhortation, '*SECRET – to be kept under lock and key*,' which at least provided a functional distinction easily understood by all. Cabinet papers were placed in the 'Lock and Key' category in all cases where 'it is thought that access to them should be strictly confined to

Cabinet Ministers, their junior Ministers, and their responsible Expert Advisers.' As a matter of course, these papers were to be denied to all others, save the exceptional case noted by the Prime Minister. Ministerial responsibility was provided for through the stipulation that 'Lock and Key' papers were to be placed as well in sealed envelopes, to be opened only by the person to whom they were addressed. The Secretariat advised that more Cabinet papers would require special handling, but they strove to insure that such treatment was not commonplace; the approval of a Deputy Secretary was required for the classification.[218]

These changes, at the Prime Minister's behest, were to be included in the materials relating to Cabinet procedure which were circulated to successor governments. Of interest in that package, which we have reviewed, was the stipulation in its revised version of 1936 of the need to consult the Prime Minister prior to the circulation of a Cabinet document, although the practice was still not universally honored. Hankey also included a reference to the Cabinet decision concerning the custody of Cabinet papers, spelling out the duty of ministers to return 'all Cabinet Conclusions and Papers issued to them while in office' upon vacating office. The Cabinet Office also had a hand in defeating a proposal that junior ministers be given access to Foreign Office telegrams, 'on the ground that without such means of keeping themselves informed it was difficult for . . . those not in the Cabinet to understand and defend government policy.'[219] Although the Foreign Secretary was so inclined, Howorth looked askance at the numbers involved, more than two dozen, and he thought that their inexperience with such documents would lead to problems; Hankey was even more blunt in warning the Prime Minister: 'I think that it is a most dangerous proposal, calculated immensely to increase the risk of leakage. If it would be dangerous to-day, it would be immensely more so in the case of a new and inexperienced government.'[220] Chamberlain accepted Hankey's view, and although Halifax pressed for reconsideration, Hankey prevailed, surely a measure of the strength of his position as the custodian of Cabinet secrecy.

Under Baldwin and Chamberlain, the National Government had moved towards a more systematic organization of Cabinet committees, a method of dealing with Cabinet business which has since become commonplace. In addition to the two committees which had taken their lead from the Prime Minister, the CID and the Economic Advisory Council, the premier associated himself with the work of about a half-dozen others, which began to acquire the look of permanence. In fact, prior to MacDonald's resignation in 1935, no Cabinet committee had been continued from one administration to another, for reasons advanced by S. S. Wilson:

each administration formed its own Committee structure to meet its own problems and methods of work. The problems, in fact, were not markedly different, and each administration set up committees on subjects such as agriculture, housing, unemployment, and various aspects of foreign affairs, but the membership and terms of reference differed, no doubt with the intention that a wholly fresh approach would be made.[221]

By the latter part of the decade, among a score of Cabinet committees, five had emerged as standing bodies, whose meetings were generally presided over by the Prime Minister: the work of three – Foreign Policy, Defence Plans (Policy) and Defence Policy and Requirements (the last could report either to the Cabinet or to the CID) – was related to the threat to peace; another two – National Expenditures and General Purposes[222] – had developed for other reasons. It is probable that their standing status resulted from the continuity supplied by National Government, regardless of the premier. The role of the committee system within Cabinet government in the years before 1939 remains generally an unanswered question, except for those concerned with rearmament. No 'theory' underlay developments in these years, although in practice movement towards a permanent committee structure had occurred.

The work of the Committee of Imperial Defence we are acquainted with; as for the Economic Advisory Council, far less need be said, although its special status as a Prime Minister's committee dictates some attention to its development during the 1930s. Council committees were of three types: the two standing committees dealt with two areas for which the Council bore responsibility, namely Economic Information and Scientific Research. The former submitted, at two to three month intervals, 'a report on the economic situation,' drafted by the few civil servants attached to the Council. In the scientific area, there were specialist standing committees and ad hoc groups which investigated special problems, submitted reports, and passed out of existence. The members of the two main committees were drawn almost exclusively from the ranks of the Council, which numbered five ministers, including the premier, and fourteen 'outsiders' chosen by the Prime Minister for their expert knowledge in industry, economics, or science; others could be co-opted to sit on the specialist standing committees of the ad hoc bodies. The Economic Advisory Council remained an advisory body; any action arising from its activities was undertaken on the recommendation of the Cabinet.[223]

This fairly rigid structure dated from the re-organization of 1930, and later in the decade the recognition dawned that the reform had been misconceived: in June 1937 the Prime Minister announced his intention to review the EAC's work, and nearly a year later a Draft Report criticized the 'fixed composition' of the Council. Since a wide range of topics were discussed at its meetings, 'it inevitably happened that for any given subject only a small number of the non-Governmental members of the Council were in a position to express an informed opinion,' from which deficiency arose their disillusionment. Yet the idea itself had proved wrong:

> The change in the title of the body, and, in particular, the use of the term 'Council', appeared to imply that the body possessed more than merely advisory functions. The impression so created was definitely misleading, was harmful to the organisation in its efforts to establish and maintain close relations with the Government Departments with which its work brought it into contact.[224]

Curiously, the National Government had disengaged from the Council years earlier – for all the fact that MacDonald had presided over the reform – and that body had not met since 1931. The two standing committees and the ad hoc groups were credited with some successes, and the Draft Report did not question the potential value of a body 'specially adapted to consider and advise on economic and scientific subjects.' Yet the authors could only advise that the Council be remodelled along lines originally laid down for the Committee of Civil Research in 1925, even to the resumption of the designation, 'which has the double merit of being both accurate and descriptive.' In embracing the hoary analogy to the Committee of Imperial Defence, despite the substantial differences between military and economic organization clearly pointed out in 1930, the Draft Report must rank as one of the least imaginative government documents of the decade.

Seemingly it was greeted with an appropriate governmental yawn, and even a year later the task of re-organization had a low priority.[225] Events hung fire until the outbreak of war, at which time the position of the Economic Advisory Council was described as 'somewhat nebulous.'[226] No area of government organization for which Hankey held a measure of responsibility – the EAC remained within the Cabinet Office – had proved more 'nebulous' and generally ineffective than this body.

As Hankey had observed his sixtieth birthday in April 1937, the question of his retirement from the Cabinet Secretariat came to the fore. He was personally concerned for the financial welfare of his family and scouted about for what he characterized as 'gilt-edged directorships,' among which the principal plum was a Director's post on the Suez Canal Company, in the gift of the Prime Minister. At Easter 1938, he informed Neville Chamberlain that he would like to have it; he did not have to acknowledge that the major reason had been put by his predecessor at £5000 per annum in fees. The Prime Minister asked for some time to think the matter over,[227] whether on personal grounds or institutional: the latter involved the question of Hankey's successor, or successors, on the three bodies which he served – the Cabinet Secretariat, the

Committee of Imperial Defence, and the Privy Council. Hankey himself thought it advantageous to combine the two secretaryships, because defence matters would receive first priority at the Cabinet;[228] however, the appointment of Inskip in 1936 undercut the contention that defence matters as a whole would not gain Cabinet scrutiny without the presence of the CID Secretary. Complicating the succession was Hankey's virtual sinecure post as Clerk to the Privy Council, with the rationale that in time of grave crisis a single figure could move from Cabinet to Privy Council, there apparently to secure Orders in Council; in calmer times, Hankey relied on an assistant to tend to the Council's ceremonial work. While George V, for example, recognized Hankey's claim to combine the positions, already in 1927 the King's Private Secretary looked to a post-Hankey separation of the Clerkship from the other posts and even thought that 'if anything were to happen to Hankey it is possible that a Civil Servant would become Secretary of the Cabinet, and a Naval or Military Officer Secretary of the Defence Committee.'[229]

Such a division of labors during Hankey's absence in 1934 fueled speculation that no one individual would succeed him; a year later, a Military Assistant Secretary, Col. Henry Pownall, noted: 'I don't believe there are *insuperable* difficulties in the way of splitting Hankey's job provided that the Secretary of the CID was on a level with the Secretary to the Cabinet and charged with the *duty* of taking all Cabinet meetings at which defence, and cognate questions, were considered.'[230] With pressures mounting upon the office in subsequent years, Hankey's military deputy at the CID noted the conflict of business between that body and the Cabinet as too much for any one man; he also reflected that the two posts called for very different training and experience, and, as a result:

> It would be difficult to find a soldier who would make a good Secretary of the Cabinet, and equally difficult to find a civilian who would make a good Secretary of the Committee of Imperial Defence and the Chiefs of Staff Committee. As *The Times* put it: 'Hankey's versatility cannot become a heritable organisation.'[231]

Ismay's comments make it clear that Hankey could no longer spend most of his energies on the CID, as was his preference, although it is difficult to understand why Ismay himself could not take up the slack – assuming Hankey permitted it.

While Chamberlain deliberated, Hankey learned that others had already declared an interest in the succession, advancing a candidate, the Treasury official Edward Bridges, who was urged upon the Prime Minister by his superior, Sir Warren Fisher – as Head of the Civil Service, he had a direct interest – and by Sir Horace Wilson, nominally Chief Industrial Adviser but a close confidant of the premier. Bridges had impressed everyone, including Chamberlain, with whom he had come into contact since becoming involved in the rearmament effort in 1934;[232]

thus his candidacy appears well chosen, because of his Service experience and his undoubted grasp of the fiscal dimensions of defence problems. Confronted with a plausible nominee, Hankey's difficulties were compounded because the Cabinet Secretary could not yet advance any one individual from his own organization: Ismay didn't wish to combine the secretaryships, although he suggested a division of Cabinet labors, with the Secretary taking defence, foreign policy, imperial and colonial matters, and a deputy taking the civilian work. Hankey did not favor the idea, nor apparently did anyone else in authority.[233] Slow off the mark – unusual for Hankey – the Secretary sought to persuade his former CID associate, now Major-General Henry Pownall, to stand for the combined posts he held, appealing to Fisher to proceed no further until Pownall had time to reflect. Although reluctant to stand, the latter agreed provided that Ismay continued to decline and then 'if the position can be held for the Services only by my taking it.'[234] However, Ismay agreed to stand without re-organization, and Pownall agreed that Hankey could use his name 'as a last reserve' if Ismay's proved unacceptable.

The Cabinet Secretary prepared for battle, spelling out the qualifications of both men by way of training and service within the Secretariat so as to assure the Prime Minister 'whichever you choose I am certain that you will never regret it.'[235] He noted his own consternation that the Treasury should now contravene an understanding struck years ago that the post should go to a Service Officer, provided a suitable candidate could be found; now he offered two. There were substantive concerns which favored a combined post, including the fact that 'the manipulative services' of the Secretariat and CID were presently pooled in such a way that the Cabinet Office functioned as a team, thus making it possible for the Cabinet Secretary to render to the Prime Minister 'innumerable small and almost unnoticed services that make all the difference in the world between prompt despatch of business and dangerous delay.' Hankey also argued that a Secretary bred in the CID was better versed than a civilian counterpart for dealing with the mechanism of war government, since he spoke 'the same language' as the Service Staffs: 'They have to entrust him with their war plans – the greatest secret they possess – and with much important drafting, both in peace and war. Human nature is such that they will give their confidence more unreservedly to one who has been brought up in the same traditions and under the same system as themselves.' In summarizing his plea, Hankey reminded Chamberlain that 'the thunderclouds of war are only just over the horizon,' which heightened the need for an experienced hand in military matters. While the invocation of war may not have appealed to a man who was dedicated to its avoidance, Hankey's discussion of the issues was principled and his enumeration of priorities reasonable, with only minor barbs directed at the lack of Treasury planning for the civilian dimension of warfare, by way of contrast to the CID's 'encyclopaedic knowledge of the Government machine . . . that certainly is not equalled elsewhere.'[236]

On the following day, Chamberlain informed Hankey that he had gained the coveted directorship, an 'appointment . . . welcome in all quarters.' The Cabinet Secretary pressed the Prime Minister for a conversation on the matter of the succession, 'as there were some things easier said than written.' Although Chamberlain agreed not to take a decision until he had heard Hankey out, for the next few days Hankey was invalided – his first such absence from Whitehall in six years. Upon returning on 16 May, Hankey locked horns with Horace Wilson, who announced the premier's displeasure with his lobbying in military circles and intimated, according to Hankey, that the directorship was jeopardized: Hankey saw 'a bluff and a blackmail' in Wilson's words, and he privately rejected any notion that his agreement could be bought.[237] Thus he carried high hopes into his meeting with Chamberlain on the 18th; for an hour he spoke to the premier along lines which he had formulated in advance. Although he may not have used all the arguments with which he had, on paper, primed himself, the general tenor of his remarks was rather more assertive than his earlier memorandum.[238] He contended that the only departmental 'experience' that mattered came from within the Cabinet Office, because the work was *sui generis* and bore 'no resemblance to the work of an ordinary Government Department.' More personalized was his remark that 'a Treasury appointment would be a *terrible slap in the face for me*,' because he had been assured that his post was viewed as 'one of the blue ribands of the Services' and would be retained by the military. For this he claimed the authority of the Head of the Civil Service and, as a result, 'if a Civil Servant is appointed I shall rightly be considered in the Services as having "sold the pass."' Yet Fisher too had a high stake in the choice, since earlier in the year he had failed to prevail upon the Prime Minister to pass over Sir Alexander Cadogan as Vansittart's successor at the Foreign Office; Fisher had gone so far as to volunteer himself for the post, with a reduction in rank and loss of pay.[239]

Whether or not Hankey was aware that the Head of the Civil Service had recently lost a personnel recommendation, he did not forget Fisher's earlier 'grab' at his own position, as he reminded Chamberlain of that episode. Less tactfully, he criticized the Treasury, even if his remarks were limited to the period since Chamberlain had moved to No. 10: 'The CID and Cabinet Office have always been regarded as neutral ground. It would be a great mistake just now, when all the Services are rather resentful of Treasury activities during the past year, to give any impression that it has become a mere Annex to the Treasury.' The Prime Minister replied that he would carefully consider Hankey's remarks, although he added that he had in mind 'a compromise solution' but would require time to work it out. For his part, Hankey had done all in his power to secure the succession for Ismay or Pownall – and for the Services; the exchange had not been a pleasant one for Hankey, who took great pride in the operation which he had helped to create, because he described the business to his son as 'a frightful row.'[240] Chamberlain soon announced his 'compromise,' and Hankey recorded the results in his diary on 23 May:

> *Bridges* – Secretary to Cabinet and Cabinet Office, which includes C.I.D. and Economic Advisory Council.
> *Ismay* – Secretary to C.I.D. and Secretary C.O.S. Ctee which Bridges would attend only by invitation.
> *Howorth* – Remains Deputy Secy. to Cabinet and becomes Clerk of the Privy Council.
>
> I at once expressed satisfaction and gratitude that Ismay becomes definitely Secretary C.I.D. with improved status. Ismay is delighted. So is Howorth.

The origins of this 'compromise' are unknown, but the idea of divided labors within the Cabinet Office had surfaced in a note Hankey had sent to Warren Fisher on 10 May, in which Hankey had suggested his deputy, Howorth, as Cabinet Secretary and Ismay as Secretary to the CID, with an agreed succession to the Cabinet post, given Howorth's not too distant retirement.[241] Hankey subsequently had resisted such a division of responsibilities, but he may possibly have given Fisher room to maneuver in advancing Bridges' name.

A 'compromise' the arrangement may well have been, but there seems no doubt that Warren Fisher had gained the upper hand, although Hankey had preserved a military presence at the CID. The two positions were sundered – Hankey's warning notwithstanding – and the 'blue riband' was lost to the Fighting Services; yet Ismay held full responsibilities for the CID, and Howorth had been better treated than Hankey had foreseen.[242] That there was give-and-take in the three appointments is altogether clear, but Hankey must still have feared the possibility of excessive Treasury influence within the Cabinet Office. Nonetheless, he put his best face to the changes, which in any case would have been difficult to resist in view of the Prime Minister's accomodation. To his son Robin he insisted that the major point at issue was military leadership at the CID: 'The Treasury was fighting for Bridges to be Secretary to the Cabinet *&* *C.I.D.* So I have got my point . . . The Prime Minister has met me very handsomely by this compromise.'[243] In a reflective vein – though the process of rationalization must not be forgotten – Hankey penned a valedictory to his own system:

> I shall leave without any regret. For a long time I have been deliberately building up a system which should replace *me* and the considerable (and excessive)

authority I wielded – C.O.S. Ctee, J.P. [Joint Planning] Ctee, Minister for Co-ordination &c &c. It all works admirably, but involves the head of the office in an immense work of directing other people and reading their stuff, thus leaving less time for the personal contributions I used to make so freely. It is a seven days a week job to run the three jobs myself as I do – even with the considerable measure of decentralisation I have already introduced . . .

Altogether the job is not quite what it was. I feel I have had the best of it, a long innings and a unique experience that no-one else has ever had or ever will have again. Moreover, everything that I have set out to do has been done – except that the programmes are not yet complete owing to circumstances beyond my control, though well under weigh.

Though this description of a near-unmanageable job ill comports with Hankey's desire that Ismay should combine the two most daunting functions, there does not seem to be any reason to question Hankey's heavy load of responsibilities, which after all had taken its toll.

The timing of his resignation, now scheduled for the end of July, possessed a symbolic importance, since it corresponded to the Cabinet Office's evacuation of Whitehall Gardens and the demolition of the very site on the 1st of August: the elegant buildings were ripped down to make space for what proved to be the massive but barren façade of the Main Building of the Ministry of Defence. Henry Pownall, who had no doubts that Hankey had lost his struggle with Warren Fisher, commenting that Ismay 'will find himself in reality more *under* Bridges than he will like,' saw the significance of the end of an era:

It is time he [Hankey] went and that others took his place. But his departure is the turning over of a page of history on which his name is writ very large . . . the old building and he go together. He always said he would not see the move. Its disappearance, too, is sad for it has many and great associations. We won our greatest war in history with Hankey's room as the seat of British and Empire effort.[244]

If there be an element of exaggeration in Pownall's tribute, there is no more fit time for the words than the occasion of Hankey's retirement from a position in which he had distinguished himself for nearly twenty-two years. Although the departing Cabinet Secretary might not personally have valued a remark made by Beatrice Webb in connection with her own labors at the London School of Economics, surely it is applicable to his career: 'To be outgrown by the organisation you create is the ultimate test of victory.'[245]

When Neville Chamberlain announced Hankey's retirement and the re-organization of the Cabinet Offices on 1 June 1938, he spelled out the rationale: the Prime Minister thought it essential that the 'Permanent Secretary to the Cabinet Offices' should function as Secretary to the entire operation, including the Minister for the Co-ordination of Defence, the CID and EAC, providing 'a link between the Cabinet and the CID [on which he would sit ex-officio] which could not be divided.' In this basic sense, Hankey's argument had prevailed, although not with the results he had hoped for. Ismay would assume the actual secretarial burdens of the CID and conduct the work of the COS Committee, 'a purely military committee' whose business had lately increased markedly; Howorth would continue as Deputy Secretary to the Cabinet in addition to his duties at the Privy Council.[246] The CID continued Britain's preparations for war while Chamberlain pursued his chimera of peace to Munich and beyond to bitter disappointment. As in the First World War, the CID lost its standing with the advent of war and Churchill's later becoming Minister of Defence; 'Pug' Ismay went on to greater responsibilities which, for most observers, fully justified Hankey's confidence. Yet for the structural change, there was no lack of continuity between the peace-time military organization and the war regime, whose organizational foundations had long been laid: 'When Churchill at last achieved power he inherited a well-trained and, on the whole, a smooth running system – largely devised by Hankey; and it was Hankey's heir Ismay who persuaded him to leave well alone.'[247]

To preside over the Cabinet Office, Chamberlain announced his choice of Edward Bridges, whose work at the Treasury he praised; he reported that 'very careful soundings' had satisfied him that the re-organization would receive the enthusiastic support of all concerned; his Chancellor of the Exchequer observed that only the Treasury would be the poorer for the change, since it would suffer the loss of Bridges' services.[248] Bridges attended his first Cabinet meeting as Secretary-Designate on 20 July, in company with Hankey in order to achieve 'continuity of practice in Secretarial arrangements.'[249] After taking his first minutes, he commented to Hankey that his prior attendance at Cabinet had 'made all the difference in the world.' Hankey had also taken great pains to acquaint his successor with the fabled War Book, now passed into Bridges' custody: 'I am very grateful to you for your tip that it might be necessary to do a lot of work in stirring up Departments to do their side of the business.'[250] One wonders if Hankey singled out the Treasury for particular attention.

In the meantime, Hankey had taken his own farewell: at the last Cabinet meeting he attended as Secretary, Chamberlain paid generous but not excessive tribute to the man who he thought could 'fairly be called the creator of the modern Cabinet.' Hankey responded in an understated fashion that 'he was so unused to speaking in the Cabinet Room that he hardly knew the sound of his own voice there,' but – ever the man of records – he recalled that he had taken the minutes of some 1100 Cabinet meetings, 1700 including the War Cabinet. Serving the Cabinet he regarded as 'the greatest privilege' ever afforded him, and he confessed 'admiration' and 'affection' for the present government.[251] On a subsequent occasion, a dinner given in his behalf, he showed more humor than was his wont in countering the myth of his indispensability: 'Prime Minister, I tell you that round about the Horse Guards Parade, there are a hundred men who could take my place at a moment's notice, but in Mr. Bridges, Colonel Ismay, Sir Rupert Howorth you have chosen a perfect trinity.'[252] Nor could one deny that this 'trinity' served HMG well in the grim years ahead.

The occasion was no time for Hankey to attempt to measure the unprecedented influence which he wielded over a quarter-century, as the link – institutionally and himself an institution – between Britain's military leaders and their civilian counterparts. Yet such had been one of his principal roles, which he himself had characterized only a few months earlier, in words which ring true:

> I cannot too strongly stress that my aim throughout has been not any advantage to myself, but the public interest, and I believe that this is fully recognized by the Chiefs of Staff and by Ministers. If the Chiefs of Staff saw in me a person who, by his position and long experience, must have the ear of Ministers and who was running policies contrary to their own or thwarting their policies, my relations with them would be impossible. As it is, every Chief of Staff since the creation of the Sub-Committee has treated me as a friend and confidant and has remained my friend after his retirement.
>
> That is the position you have got to get into over a term of years. You have got to establish your position at both ends: that is to say, with your successive Ministers and with your successive Chiefs of Staffs [sic]. You must get yourself regarded and treated as one who is never out for himself or for his own policies, or for anything but the public interest. As Secretary you will, of course, not have the right of putting in a Minority Report, or of dissenting from what the Chiefs of Staff advise: but, especially as time goes on, you will find your influence constantly increasing. They will turn to you for advice, and as the draftsman of their Reports . . . your influence must be considerable.[253]

Though there has been reason in this account to question, on occasion, the wisdom of Hankey's calculation of the public interest, there is no room to doubt the integrity of his efforts in that cause.

In his administrative capacity, Hankey had observed from the outbreak of the First World War until the very eve of the Second the workings of Cabinet government more closely than had any other man: nor was he only a chronicler of Cabinet proceedings, because it was he who had forged the administrative machinery by which the modern Cabinet works. Beyond the establishment of the Cabinet Secretariat, Sir Maurice Hankey played a commanding role in the development of the modern British Cabinet: the patterns of present-day Cabinet government emerged during his tenure of office; some are only dimly recognizable – and others simply cannot be found – in the Cabinets of the Victorian and Edwardian periods. If to characterize Hankey as the creator of modern Cabinet government is to exaggerate, to deny that he was 'present at the creation' and for decades after is impossible.

Yet Cabinet government continues to unfold, and in that sense Hankey's departure from Whitehall Gardens serves only to demarcate a lengthy albeit important chapter in its history. There is no doubt that his tenure of office constitutes the decisive period in the history of the Cabinet Secretariat. Because of Hankey's unique melding of the roles of record keeper, administrator, confidant, and military adviser, no other civil servant could follow fully in his footsteps as Secretary to the Cabinet: indeed, two of his successors sought to obliterate Hankey's historical tracks, in the form of his own war memoirs; in so acting, they sought to preserve that secrecy of Cabinet proceedings which Hankey himself had done so much to bolster. Fortunately for those who value the 'better book,' Bridges and Brook ultimately failed in that particular attempt and, with Hankey, in the desire to hold Cabinet records inviolate.

Though Cabinet documents now are open for public scrutiny after a period of thirty years, we can rest assured that Hankey's successors will not leave behind the type of private materials which he collected, most important a diary. Present-day accounts hold to a depiction of the Cabinet Secretary as a quintessential civil servant, though likely possessed of his own views and prejudices, yet in future we are likely to learn nothing from that privileged source about the workings of Cabinet government, because Hankey's successors feel differently about the propriety of their recording such views. For this informed but unofficial dimension, we will surely turn to ministerial accounts, by a strange twist of fate now increasingly free of the fetters which Hankey's Secretariat laid upon such accounts.

7

The custody of Cabinet secrecy

No informed account of the post-war Cabinet Secretariat can yet be written, although it is clear that Hankey's successors have not followed in all the footsteps of the man; it is as well apparent that there was a substantial measure of continuity between his operation of the Secretariat mechanism and that of his immediate successor, Sir Edward Bridges. Nor is there direct evidence of far-reaching organizational change since that time, although questions have been posed about the contemporary Cabinet Office which deserve mention in this account. And the question of the influence of the Cabinet Secretary upon the Prime Minister and the Cabinet will remain, but it is not a matter that even the release of Cabinet records in due time can answer fully. It is certain that whatever the degree of influence of Hankey's successors, none brought to bear anything approaching his suasion in defence matters.

All Cabinet Secretaries have agreed upon the need to protect the deliberations of the Cabinet from outside scrutiny, and each has administered and enforced Cabinet secrecy with whatever devices he judged efficacious. In Hankey's time, there was no certainty that Cabinet records would eventually pass into the public domain, but the Public Records Act of 1958 made it probable that they would be released, although the legislation did not specify that Cabinet papers would be made available. In short order the probability became a certainty, and in 1967 the period of closure for most government records, including Cabinet papers, was shortened to thirty years. These developments were not foreseen when Hankey himself was ensnared by the same Official Secrets Act to which he had had recourse in 1934, although ultimately the government informally acquiesced in the publication of his memoirs of the Great War. His successors scrutinized the publication of ministerial memoirs, until in 1975 the courts intervened: new patterns have emerged, but the 'confidentiality' of Cabinet discussions has lately won legal standing. While the records of any Cabinet will not be opened for thirty years, former ministers will be free to discuss most aspects of Cabinet proceedings following the end of that Cabinet's tenure – as they have been able to do, in effect, since the end of the Second World War. Subject to certain restrictions, which in the main will lapse after fifteen years, former ministers will continue to retain a formidable advantage in depicting their own views of affairs of state before any other. That 'outsiders' should operate at a remove of thirty years from events is consistent with the role which the Cabinet Office plays as the protector of Cabinet secrecy.

Even following his own departure from Whitehall Gardens in 1938, Hankey serves to focus a discussion of the custody of Cabinet secrecy: for more than two decades, he remained hoist with the petard fashioned in his own time, and his encounters with the Cabinet Office reveal the precepts which his successors strove to enforce. In the long run, however, those men did not prove as successful as Hankey in proscribing informed ministerial accounts, and they had also to come to terms with the public's claim of access to Cabinet records. Concurrently, the growing disrepair of the Official Secrets Act handicapped their efforts to administer Cabinet secrecy through its provisions. The matter of Cabinet secrecy remains a contentious one, and our examination of the application of principles of 'closed' and 'open government' to Cabinet secrecy leads directly to the present day; suffice it to remark here that the Cabinet Office has throughout labored for the former.

Before engaging with that question, a few summary comments ought to be offered about the administrative pattern developed after Bridges' succession in August 1938. His tenure of office fell mainly within the war years, during which time the volume of Cabinet Office work, the speed with which it was conducted, and the size of the staff all increased significantly, although there was 'no basic change in the organisation of the Office as a committee machine.' Until the outbreak of war in September 1939, Bridges made no changes in the basic procedures of the Secretariat; he is credited with initiating moves to give the Cabinet Office 'a more professional appearance,'[1] but continuity characterized the transition and survived even the shock of war.

Yet it ought not escape notice that the successive moves of the Cabinet Office, first to private houses in Richmond Terrace and, after German air attacks in 1940, to government buildings in Great George Street, represent the attachment of the Secretariat to the greater governmental bureaucracy centered in the Treasury. Its independence was not at issue, but Bridges had risen to the post through the Civil Service, replacing a man – an institution – who was versed in ministerial as well as bureaucratic ways. Bridges could not assume Hankey's own commitments along with his official responsibilities: he had yielded any direct role in military affairs by agreeing to the division of Hankey's labors, but he nonetheless inherited an advisory role in other matters which had long been an aspect of the Cabinet Secretary's position.[2] Nor did Bridges shed an advisory role with the succession of Winston Churchill, although fragmentary evidence suggests that he was initially troubled in his dealings with the new premier; confidence between the two soon strengthened.[3]

When Bridges stepped down in 1946, he was succeeded by his deputy, Norman Brook, and during the latter years of his tenure the Cabinet Office was most closely connected to the Treasury: from 1956 until Brook's retirement six years later, the office was subsumed, and the Cabinet Secretary served as a Joint Permanent Secretary at the Treasury and as Head of the Civil Service. Apparently the purpose of this odd arrangement was ad hominem, designed 'to keep Sir Norman Brook as Secretary of the Cabinet, where the Government found his services invaluable, while not denying him the position of Head of the Civil Service which is accorded to the Permanent Secretary of the Treasury.'[4] As a result of pressures within the Treasury, in 1962 the association of the Secretary to the Cabinet with that central department was terminated. Presently the Cabinet Office stands institutionally independent, and the Cabinet Secretary is commonly viewed as one of the two or three most important civil servants, although the extent of his influence is heavily veiled.[5]

As to the style of operation of the Cabinet Secretariat, Bridges' major design was to simplify the very complex structure over which Hankey had presided. Ismay also contributed to the particular effort directed at the defence domain, although he resisted Churchill's more radical approach. Already at the outset of war, the CID had been absorbed into the War Cabinet and its Secretariat transformed into the Military Section of the Cabinet Secretariat.[6] Bridges himself allegedly remarked early in the course of the war that the abolition of some two dozen CID committees was the biggest blow which the enemy had to that date endured.[7] As a corollary, Bridges sought to reduce paper work, particularly in connection with the minutes of the War Cabinet and its various sub-committees; although the recollections of Lawrence Burgis on this point somewhat distort Hankey's intention, a difference in style is apparent. In Hankey's time, Burgis recalled,

> we attributed remarks and arguments to individuals, which was not too difficult, but the method was altered in World War II. The pros and cons of a problem were stated in general terms and the conclusion or decision put in at the end. There were exceptions to this, of course . . .
>
> Bridges' instructions regarding minutes were as follows: – (a) brief (b) self-contained (c) in the main, impersonal, and (d) to the full extent the discussion allows – decisive.[8]

Sir Edward Bridges himself maintained the minutes, limited to the War Cabinet conclusion coupled with 'a brief explanatory summary.' These were to be circulated to each member of the War Cabinet, to every minister holding an office which immediately prior to the war was a Cabinet post, to the Permanent Secretary to the Treasury and the Permanent Under-Secretary at the Foreign Office; Bridges thought a proposal to disseminate these materials more widely an 'elaboration . . . likely to cause mistakes and oversights,' instead opting for a straightforward model.[9] In the early months of the war, some adjustments were made, but the War Cabinet Secretariat certainly acted on well-prepared lines in facilitating the flow of government business. During that conflict, the War Cabinet Secretariat undertook a widening range of war-related responsibilities, the product of 'the interdepartmental organisation which it serves.' Such tasks account for the growth of staff from a handful more than 200 in 1939 to nearly 600 by its end.[10]

In functional terms, the abolition of the CID and the division of Secretariat business into civil and military had led to a closer integration of effort, Bridges observed in 1944:

> Taking a broad view, the main duties performed by the Cabinet Secretariat may be grouped into the following three classes:—
> (1) normal secretarial duties for the Cabinet and its Committees;
> (2) preparation of material and collation of information on matters affecting several departments;
> (3) duties involving correspondence.
> This classification errs on the side of over-simplification, and each group of duties tends to merge into the others.[11]

The performance of duties in the first category Bridges thought justified 'by experience'; the second function was related to the war, although Bridges cautiously foresaw that the Secretariat might increasingly be used in 'the central preparation of memoranda on matters affecting a number of Departments' in the domestic sphere. In words which echoed what Hankey had long insisted upon in order to protect the Cabinet Secretariat against departmental suspicions, Bridges advised that 'where it is a question of work which is preparatory to the formulation of policy, it is not enough for Departments to regard the Cabinet Secretariat as a body which acts impartially between Departments. They must feel that their own officers are taking their due share in the work.' For that reason, a post-1939 innovation had witnessed the seconding of some thirty-one permanent civil servants from their Departments to administrative positions within the Secretariat, for periods of six months or longer. Previously, only one Treasury official had been seconded at a time. Yet it had not been possible to provide for 'the whole of the war expansion' through the loan of permanent civil servants, and in the war years a number of temporary appointments had been made at the Cabinet Office.

Bridges' third category represented another innovation, and the Cabinet Secretary was especially cautious about its implications, because during the war the Secretariat had acted on behalf of various committees – which had consulted with concerned Departments – in corresponding 'with persons or bodies, either in this country or overseas, who are not responsible to (or the concern of) a single Departmental Minister.' Care had to be taken, because constitutional doctrine held that responsibility 'must be through Ministers, and cannot be shifted to the Cabinet Committee system.' In other words, the exigencies of war had produced a constitutional anomaly, and Bridges concluded that it would be undesirable that the Secretariat 'should at any time handle more than a small volume of work of this character.' In exercising such restraint, Bridges followed in his predecessor's cautious ways: his description of Secretariat functions contained nothing of substance inconsistent with the past organization of responsibilities in serving the Cabinet. If the Cabinet Office had several times been physically relocated since Hankey's retirement, the instutitional edifice which he had built remained intact: the support structure for Cabinet government during war stood in place.

Hankey himself accepted a War Cabinet post under Chamberlain and continued as a minister in the Churchill coalition: his dismissal from office at the latter's hands in 1942 impresses as an ungenerous act, but his dissent from Churchill's conduct of the war ensured a rupture.[12] Their several disagreements are not at issue here; what matters for our account is that Hankey's dismissal freed his energies to be applied to the long-delayed completion of his First World War memoirs: by September 1943 he had written his successor to arrange an official 'vetting' of the manuscript so that it might be published when the opportunity arose. Soliciting any personal comments which Bridges might wish to offer, Hankey sought 'approval for its publication subject to any amendments that are necessary for the public interest.' Although the Cabinet Secretary promised an expeditious response, five months passed until he suggested that they talk over certain matters relating to Hankey's memoirs.[13] Precisely what happened at that meeting appears to have gone unrecorded – an odd failure on Hankey's part – but it is clear that the brunt of Bridges' concern was with what he later described as the 'effect it [the memoirs] would have on the confidential relationship between Ministers and their official advisers.'[14] Since the door was not closed entirely, Hankey spent some months in revising his memoirs in order to meet the criticisms voiced by his successor: he noted that he had made perhaps a hundred changes, although 'it is impossible to conceal the intimate relations with my Chiefs, which are well known from their own Memoirs and many other publications.'[15] Hankey reminded Bridges that the Great War period had long been treated *sui generis*, with greater latitude given to informed accounts.[16]

Yet the Cabinet Secretary informed his predecessor that the omissions and alterations had failed to remove 'in any way' the central objection to publication, concluding that the publication of such a memoir would not be in the public interest:

> Your book exposes, often in great detail, the working of this relationship [between Ministers and official advisers], and the extent and degree to which Ministers were dependent on particular occasions on the help given by their officials. I fear that publication of all this material would have a very unfortunate effect on the relationship to Ministers, not only of your successors as Secretary of the Cabinet, but also of the Permanent Heads of the great Departments, and also of the Civil Servants who, in other capacities, stand in a specially trusted relationship to Ministers.

On a second reading of the manuscript, Bridges had been troubled by the use which Hankey had made of his diary: 'You extract from it the inner histories of the formation of the Government and of strains and stresses between Ministers and the Cabinet, besides of course a good deal of operational and political information which was highly secret at the time.' The existence of such a record, he argued, would impair the contemporary relationship between civil servants and ministers:

> if your book were published it would make me personally self-conscious in my dealings with the Cabinet, and it would make Ministers generally much more chary of speaking freely to members of the Cabinet Secretariat, unless and until, as might well be the case, it was decided to promulgate some general rule against the keeping of diaries by members of this Office.[17]

In effect Bridges stood the *sui generis* argument on its head, insisting that Hankey's memoirs were unique in his perspective upon the inner workings of government, which would suffer through their publication. *The Supreme Command*, it is fair to say, appeared to Edward Bridges not another memoir about the First World War but rather a singular revelation of the influence wielded by civil servants, the depiction of which could undermine public confidence in the doctrine of ministerial responsibility.

The second Cabinet Secretary thus supplemented the 1934 limitations which the first had brought to bear upon ministerial memoirs with an even far more wide-ranging stricture against civil servants commenting upon the relationship to ministers. In seeking to proscribe such revelations about the inner workings of government Bridges might well have used Hankey's own words to deny the request: 'Unfortunately the practice of doing so started immediately after the war, with the result that much secret material had been used which, in the public interest, it would have been far better not to have published.'[18] The interpretation of the public interest, whether affected by official materials or memoirs, now lay in the hands of Sir Edward Bridges. Hankey pursued the matter with the Prime Minister, who was ultimately responsible, although he informed Bridges that they must agree to disagree: 'I believe on a very long experience that your fears are wholly groundless. So much has been said already . . . that my own relationship to Ministers is very generally known already. I had apprehensions at one time that this might have some effect on the office, but it had none.'[19] In pitting his own experience against his successor's timidity, Hankey either failed to see or ignored the fact that Bridges had based his case upon the principle that civil servants ought not to pass retrospective judgment upon ministers or their policies.

In communicating with Churchill, Hankey assembled the justification for publication of his memoirs: the events were now more than a quarter-century distant, and other war memoirs had addressed the point of the relations between ministers and advisers. In pointing to memoirs written by the latter, Hankey enumerated military figures only, but he insisted that his status during the conflict 'resembled that of a high Service Staff Officer more than that of a Civil Servant.'[20] He noted that a number of statesmen, including Asquith, Bonar Law, Balfour, Lloyd George, and Smuts, had urged the eventual publication of his memoirs, and he reminded the premier that Churchill's own memoirs constituted a rebuttal of Bridges' fears: 'Much good and no harm resulted from their publication. They did not affect the relations of Ministers and their advisers detrimentally; rather the contrary.' The appeal proved in vain, and Bridges' hand is apparent in Churchill's informing Hankey that 'the War Cabinet have reached the conclusion that the publication of the book would not be in the public interest,' specifying the concern felt for the protection of the 'special relationship' between ministers and their chief advisers, which would be subverted by 'keep[ing] – still more to reveal – a private record of the many secret and confidential matters which come before him [the adviser] in the course of his official duties.'[21]

As if unable to believe the War Cabinet's decision, Hankey inquired testily whether his personal and confidential letter to Churchill had been brought to the War Cabinet's attention, and Bridges assured him such had been the case.[22] As the shock registered, Hankey refused to accept at face value such an explanation, advancing to Tom Jones a different explanation:

> It is astonishing that Churchill, who was practically the first to publish all the inner secrets of his rows with Fisher, and so many intimate and confidential letters, should now have the effrontery to turn me down – but I have little doubt that the reason is that the historian who studies my book will sometimes find that

Churchill was wrong. Probably also the large Civil Service element – John Anderson, Grigg and Bridges – who have always been against the Cabinet Office and generally obscurantist – have had something to say.[23]

While Hankey lamented to Jones, who had maintained a diary while at the Secretariat, that 'an immense number of public servants from Prime Ministers to bottlewashers have not only kept diaries but they were used afterwards to describe the same sort of incidents that I described' – he itemized Asquith, Haig, Henry Wilson, John French, and Ian Hamilton – he simply could not conceive that his role was different in kind from the activities of those whom he specified. Nor is there any reason to think that Hankey was aware of the fact that other civil servants, whose service had overlapped his last years at Whitehall Gardens, had kept diaries which would later lay bare the relationship between ministers and advisers. Only with the eventual failure of Bridges and Norman Brook to prevail in proscribing diaries as the basis for such accounts did the private diaries maintained by Hankey's former associates Jones and Henry Pownall emerge; the latter had begun a diary upon entering the CID Secretariat in 1933, with no eye on publication but a purpose limited to 'a harmless outlet for his irascible feelings about individuals.'[24]

In that same year, a senior Foreign Office official, Sir Alexander Cadogan, also started a diary, which assumes crucial importance with his appointment as Permanent Under-Secretary in 1938. Although he had no interest to publish the diary, its existence was known to the Foreign Secretary, Lord Halifax, as early as 1939, when he used portions of the diary to outline the events which had led to the outbreak of the war.[25] The episode demonstrates the utility of such a private record as a supplement to official accounts, but Bridges a few years later could see only the deleterious effects of publishing diary extracts. Had the second Cabinet Secretary known the contents of Cadogan's record, his fears likely would have been strengthened, precisely because 'the Diary provided a place for Cadogan to express himself without restraint, a comforting outlet in a life of excessive burden and business.' In a sense, Cadogan continued Hankey's record of the inner workings of government – Hankey's diary extended well beyond the end of the First World War – although the perspectives were quite different, and Cadogan's interest in the process of government rather less. Yet with the possible exception of Bridges for a portion of the period, no one stood closer to the center of power for the whole of the years between 1938 and 1950.[26]

Yet another perspective on foreign affairs in the crucial years before and after Munich is supplied in the diaries of Oliver Harvey, who served as Private Secretary to Eden and Halifax; his acid comments on the moral cowardice of the Chamberlain Cabinet reveal the frustration so often sublimated by advisers in their diary entries.[27] A third perspective from within the Foreign Office can be found in the diary of the war period by Sir Robert Bruce Lockhart; the editor of that diary, Kenneth Young, has remarked of Lockhart's disposition that he was 'a diplomat by nature, but fortunately indiscreet in his diaries, a fault, if such it is, that must endear him to succeeding generations.'[28] Without the element of indiscretion – to record what otherwise might have gone unnoted – the diaries maintained by such officials would lose a good part of their unique value. Obviously, diaries must be used with caution and a sense of proportion – not only is the diarist likely to loom larger than life, but on occasion he may record impressions based upon incomplete or erroneous perceptions of events[29] – but diaries do convey 'the immediate impression and atmosphere'[30] in which decisions must be taken and thus afford insights about the workings of government and the formulation of policy.[31] Yet another explanation for the existence of such private records may be hazarded, arising from the fact that civil servants and diplomats were denied access to any official records of their activities. Prior to the Public Records Act of 1958 advisers had no way of protecting themselves from ministerial criticism, by official documentation. To be sure, the Cabinet Office sought to provide against such prejudicial treatment, but highly placed advisers had reason – beyond placing themselves at the center of events – to maintain a record of their activities and ministerial foibles.

While Hankey prepared an appeal of the War Cabinet's decision, Tom Jones cautioned him that while the proscription came as a 'bombshell,' the timing of publication of diary extracts represented a legitimate concern; he thought there was no question about the propriety of a civil servant's keeping a diary.[32] Spurred by his former deputy's sympathies, Hankey pressed him to read the memoirs, from which he was excising 'many of the more flippant passages that Churchill would not like, but of course I cannot alter history.'[33] Hankey reiterated the justice of his case in asserting to Jones that 'if I cannot publish with permission I propose to publish without permission.'[34] The 'man of secrets' found himself in an odd position.

Yet upon a close reading of Hankey's manuscript Jones drew back from his initial advice that Hankey should have no hesitation in arranging for publication:

> I am not surprised that the Cabinet should hesitate to pass these volumes for publication at this comparatively early stage. It is bound to have a profound effect on the habits of future Secretaries to the Cabinet and Ministers, and the financial temptations for revelations will be great. There are other repercussions one can imagine.[35]

Hankey admitted to being 'shaken' by Jones' remarks, but he nonetheless adhered to the position that his diary had been singled out for suppression. Despite the flood of war memoirs and biographies, many based on diaries, Hankey still insisted that the relationship between ministers and their advisers had not been compromised. This observation strengthened his appeal, sent to Bridges on 29 March, in which he stressed the legitimacy of his diary, which had served a functional purpose during the war years: 'My own diary aimed at describing the numerous "off the record" decisions, conversations and events bearing on policy, of which no other record existed, and which I found absolutely essential to the work of co-ordination with which Mr. Asquith charged me at the outset of the war.'[36] Citing the lack of official records in those years, Hankey stressed the need for such a compilation of events. Hankey's appeal broke no new ground: insofar as he narrowed the issue, he argued that 'to make a new rule *ad hoc*, applying to a single individual, whose status differs little from that of some previous writers, involves a discrimination that is untenable.' He reported progress as a result of his meeting again with Bridges: 'I have now agreed everything . . . except the question of principle as to using diary extracts, on which he is very obstinate. I fancy he wants to find a way out which will not hurt his *amour propre.*'[37] Towards such an avenue, Hankey agreed to discussions with two ministers, but Churchill's government fell from office; a new Labour Cabinet inherited – among more pressing problems – the question of Hankey's war memoirs.

While Churchill withdrew to Chartwell to prepare his massively documented *Second World War*, for which he had secured official license, Hankey renewed his unsuccessful quest for sanction to publish his account of the British role in the last war but one. Attlee agreed to Bridges' suggestion that two Labour ministers talk to Hankey about his memoirs, but they subsequently informed Hankey that two types of revision were required: extracts from the diary would have to be omitted, and Hankey would also have to delete 'detailed records about your day to day relations with Ministers and the relations between Ministers'; these revisions would then have to be submitted to the Prime Minister before the amended version could be approved.[38] Hankey professed his willingness to comply with the first condition and to comply with 'a reasonable interpretation of the second,' although he claimed to reserve the right 'to make unrestricted use of material already published, notwithstanding that it may have a bearing on my relations with Ministers . . . The fact is that the whole story has been told in fragments, although it has never been put together.' But he drew the line at the third condition, in a fashion which suggested that his *amour propre* was no less involved than Bridges': yet there was merit in his claim that he had been co-operative in all particulars, with the result that eighteen months had already passed.[39] For that reason, the former Cabinet Secretary resolved to use 'his own discretion' in the matter.

The Labour government held fast to the view that the third condition contained no affront to Hankey but remained a prerequisite to publication: consultation with the government of the day was required of 'persons who have accepted high office under the Crown . . . in regard to the publication of any confidential matter of which they have acquired official knowledge,' who had further to secure formal permission in 'doubtful cases.'[40] Such a stance was consistent with the 1934 precedent, although the post-war Secretariat likely had concluded that civil servants were otherwise not covered by any formal convention; thus Hankey's account had to be viewed as precedent-setting, however removed the events of the First World War. Hankey was reminded that the responsibility for 'vetting' was vested in the Cabinet Office: 'If we were now to agree that you should publish your book without resubmitting it you would be, in marginal cases, the judge of what could or could not be published.' For his part, Hankey took counsel with Field-Marshal Smuts, who pressed him to write 'first-class history' above all else. The former Cabinet Secretary concluded that the hundreds of excisions and the loss of the whole of the diary extracts undertaken 'to try and meet the timidity of the official censorship' had compromised the historical standing which he sought for his book. Thus Hankey decided 'to withdraw all my concessions and to bide my time. I am not sure that it will be very long. A strong feeling is growing up inside and outside the Service about the Government's obscurantist attitude in recent years towards the publication of memoirs, etc.'[41] Whether Hankey had any other evidence to that effect is problematic, since his book was the only one so questioned, at a time when the government had become deliberately permissive about memoirs of the Second World War; further he erred in thinking that his time would soon come: some fifteen years were to pass before a shortened version appeared, even then without official permission.

Hankey's decision not 'to publish and be damned' in fact constituted a precedent which Tom Jones, for one, had recognized would tell against the publication of his own diaries.[42] Unlike Hankey, he did not live to witness that event, as far as those portions of his diary dealing with the Cabinet Secretariat were concerned: he made the attempt in 1954, at which time he published *Diary with Letters, 1931–1950*, but he withdrew the earlier portions when asked to make substantial excisions by Bridges, by this time Head of the Civil Service, and his successor at the Cabinet Office, Sir Norman Brook.[43] According to one interview which Jones gave at this time, he denied that official pressure had been exerted and acknowledged that he had 'doubts' about publishing diaries based on his years in the Civil Service at this time; Jones tacitly recognized that advisers could not justify their accounts on the same grounds used by ministers, and he admitted that 'it was "only right" that former civil servants should submit any projected publication for examination.'[44] His experience paralleled Hankey's although it appears that Tom Jones was more reconciled to delay in publication.

There is no indication that in these years Hankey and his former deputy were threatened with the Official Secrets Act as a bar to publication, although Hankey inferred a connection because of Addison's reference to 'official knowledge.' He was sufficiently concerned to prepare a memorandum dealing with the 'Legal Aspects' of publication; Hankey contended that the Official Secrets Act had no bearing upon his memoirs, but he did not press the point because he had decided to withdraw his request for authority to publish.[45] Since he later contested the application of the Act to his case, we will take up that protest in due course.

Here, however, we need inquire about the utilization of the Official Secrets Act in the years following upon the widened purview given it in the 1930s. Insofar as the protection of Cabinet business is concerned, its long shadow seemed to suffice, and the thrust of its application lay elsewhere, perhaps in an even more arbitrary fashion. In mid-1938 section 6 was brought to bear upon a journalist in an attempt to secure information concerning another journalist's proposing a bribe to a police officer to forewarn a criminal of his impending arrest; its terms served to protect whatever was classified as an official secret, 'the principle being that it is the duty of every citizen, irrespective of his status or official position, to assist the authorities by giving any information in his possession as to the commission of offences against the Official Secrets Act.'[46] The press had immediately raised questions concerning the wisdom of directing the Official Secrets Act at rather ordinary criminal proceedings, and the Home Secretary, Sir Samuel Hoare, informed the Cabinet that interrogation under the provisions of section 6 should be limited to what impressed the Attorney-General and the Home Secretary as exceptional cases involving disclosures of military, naval, or state secrets. Cautioned by the Minister for the Co-ordination of Defence that they ought to avoid the impression that 'the Government had weakened in this matter as a result of . . . agitation' in the press, the Cabinet approved the general lines of Hoare's proposal,[47] although there is no indication that any substantive changes followed. To the contrary, section 6 was soon invoked, directed this time at what HMG regarded as an exceptional case, involving a Member of Parliament, Duncan Sandys, who was Churchill's son-in-law.

In the view of the government, Sandys implicitly threatened to reveal the parlous condition of London's anti-aircraft defences in a parliamentary question directed to the Secretary of State for War, Leslie

Hore-Belisha, who had assured the Commons that no critical gaps existed. Although Sandys subsequently denied that such was his intention, Hore-Belisha regarded his possession of secret information a breach of military security and turned the matter over to the Attorney-General, after which, according to Churchill's account,

> He [Sandys] . . . was informed, first, that his letter revealed a knowledge of matters covered by the Official Secrets Act: secondly, that he was under an obligation to reveal the sources of his information: and thirdly, after some conversation and in reply to his request to know what would be the consequences of a refusal to reveal the sources of his information, the Attorney-General confronted him with the text of the Statute, and informed him that this might render him liable to a term of imprisonment not exceeding two years.[48]

Upon consulting the Speaker and the Clerk of the House of Commons, Sandys learned that a *prima facie* breach of privilege of the rights of a Member of Parliament had occurred. The Attorney-General quickly assured Sandys that 'there is no question of seeking to exercise against you now or hereafter the police powers of interrogation under the Official Secrets Act,'[49] but Sandys took his case to the floor of the House, because 'the general question of the rights and position of Members of the House of Commons, and the discharge of their duties, in relation to the Official Secrets Act' remained unsettled. As Churchill commented in the memorandum which he may have circulated to others besides Lloyd George, the issues were of great moment:

> First, does the Official Secrets Act enable the Government to institute a criminal proceeding against any Member for refusing to disclose the source of any information which he may use in the course of his Parliamentary duties; and are the Government going to use these powers? Secondly, should a Government use the Official Secrets Act, which was devised to secure the defence of the country, in order to prevent the exposure of Ministers who have neglected their duty? Thirdly, is not Parliamentary privilege in the larger sense involved in attempts by the Government legal authorities to intimidate Members by threats of prosecution?

After Sandys raised his point of privilege on 27 June, the Cabinet considered both the particular incident, in which the Home Secretary thought the Attorney-General's interview of Sandys 'difficult to defend,' and the implications, in which he voiced the fear that 'if M.P.s were exempt, the Press would insist on exemptions and the Act would soon become a dead letter.' However, the Cabinet could take no action, because Sandys' complaint had brought the matter *sub judice*. Nonetheless, the Cabinet's discussion betrayed an awareness that the rigors of section 6 had been pursued in the wrong place. The Cabinet's concern was nonetheless genuine, as Inskip reminded them that 'it was notorious that information had been leaking to members of Parliament for some time, particularly from the Air Force.'[50] Nor could there be doubt that Sandys, who had served in a Territorial Army regiment responsible for London's air defences, possessed military secrets of some magnitude. Hankey's former assistant Henry Pownall, now Director of Military Operations and Information at the War Office, noted the extent of Sandys' knowledge and lamented his behavior:

> the fact is that Sandys having seduced an officer from his allegiance then shelters under the umbrella of privilege – not in order to withhold the name of the officer – he must know perfectly well that we have got that – but to save himself. If that works there is no room for M.P.s in the T.A. – they cannot be allowed two loyalties which run counter to each other.

Nor was Sandys' second 'loyalty' difficult to discern: Pownall viewed him as a cat's paw, 'a slippery young gentleman who is certainly backed up by Winston.'[51]

Whether the Sandys investigation was intended partly as a shot across Churchill's bow is unknown, but Churchill himself had consistently received information which put him in violation of the Official Secrets Act.[52] In that sense, the judgment of the Clerk of the House of Commons – 'a person who communicates official information to a person to whom he is not authorised to communicate it, commits no offence if the person to whom he discloses it is a person to whom it is his duty in the interests of the State to communicate it'[53] – strengthened Churchill's practice. Certainly he must have noticed the irony that opposition to an absolutist interpretation of the Official Secrets Act had been legitimized by the government's inept disclosure of the dangers vested in section 6.

In the meantime, a Cabinet committee sought to honor the government's belief that parliamentary immunity from the powers of interrogation vested in the Act ought not to be absolute: 'it would be quite wrong to provide in section 6 that Members of Parliament should be the only class of the community who have no duty to assist the Government in detecting traitors.'[54] Recognizing that only the most serious matters ought to call forth this power, the committee nonetheless rejected a suggestion that judicial authority should be required to initiate the use of section 6; these ministers concluded that the essential interests could be protected by limiting the use of interrogation to offences falling within the scope of section 1 of the 1911 Act. Thus the Committee on the Official Secrets Act differentiated between the felony offence of disclosing information which could be useful to an enemy, under section 1, and the misdemeanor offence of disclosing other official secrets, provided for in section 2.[55] Here is the first official recognition that reliance on the law of official secrets had become excessive, and that a limitation of the powers of interrogation could be safely accepted; an obscure and infrequently used section was revised as a means of 'satisfying the critics,' but the vastly widened use of section 2 in non-espionage matters survived unscathed.

While the government introduced a bill to revise section 6 in this fashion, the House of Commons pursued the alleged breach of privilege. The Prime Minister admitted to a Select Committee that the Sandys case had been poorly handled, although he preferred to think that 'a most extraordinary catalogue of misunderstandings' had been primarily responsible.[56] The Select Committee reported in June 1939, concluding that disclosures made during debates or parliamentary proceedings were not subject to legal action under the Official Secrets Act; similar protection was claimed for confidences shared by MPs in matters related to the business of the House. The report left no doubt that Parliament, in direct response to the Sandys case, protected its proceedings from the scope of the 1911 and 1920 legislation; in broader terms, the executive's power to dictate co-operation with the Official Secrets Act had been limited to espionage-related activities. The reform was noteworthy, although an attempt made in the House of Lords to amend section 2 by restricting its use to disclosures made for a purpose prejudicial to the safety or interests of the state failed.[57] In sum, section 6 was modified, and thus the ever-widening use of the Official Secrets Act curtailed for the first time; section 2 stood intact – for many years to come.

The long shadow which the Official Secrets Act had cast over Cabinet proceedings assumed a more definite form in 1954, when it was first specifically mentioned as a deterrent; in a fitting fashion, Hankey's former deputy, Sir Rupert Howorth, long retired from the public service, insisted upon the connection. Before his intervention, the question of the secrecy of past Cabinet deliberations had been raised by Aneurin Bevan in the House of Commons, but in short order the correspondence columns of *The Times* became the forum within which the larger question of the place of such secrecy within a free society was heatedly debated. On 30 July, Bevan raked the ashes of a dispute within the late Labour government, from which he had resigned. Although his disclosures were general, the former premier, Attlee, refused to be drawn out by the allegations, remarking instead that 'there is, of course, a well established rule inhibiting members of a Government from revealing what passes either in Cabinet or in confidential discussion. The reason for this is obvious. Unless it is observed, confidence between colleagues is impossible.'[58] Bevan returned to the fray, arguing that the issue was not the doctrine of collective responsibility but the limits of its applicability:

> collective Cabinet responsibility breaks down at the point that the collectivity breaks down, and that is when a Minister resigns . . . If it did not do so, no resigning Minister could say why he resigned, and if any hon. Member likes to look up the constitutional precedents he will see that that is absolutely clear.[59]

Nonetheless, Bevan cited only one precedent, which was less than compelling because it stemmed from the extraordinary circumstances centering on the collapse of the Labour government in 1931; since that time, the rules protecting Cabinet secrecy had been considerably tightened, and as a result the search for precedents would not have been one-sided, as Bevan suggested. Indeed, when in 1932 Lloyd George desired to publish a decade-old Cabinet Minute, his request had been denied and a government spokesman had rejected as mistaken the notion that

> a Cabinet Minister, or former Cabinet Minister, could exercise his own discretion in deciding when he was released from his obligation of secrecy, or as if . . . for example, it was necessary, in order to defend themselves [sic] against a charge or to convict an opponent of inaccuracy in debate, to disclose Cabinet documents or information, then they were at liberty to do so . . . The only person who can release a Privy Councillor from his obligation of secrecy is His Majesty the King, and His Majesty, acting as always in this constitutional country, on the advice of his Ministers, is in that matter guided by the advice given by the Prime Minister of the day.[60]

Bevan, it appears, exalted his view of the doctrine of collective responsibility and ignored the individual obligations of the Privy Counsellor's Oath; the point remains that his invocation of precedent was decidedly weak.

In commenting in the pages of *The Times* upon the parliamentary exchange, the Oxford historian A. J. P. Taylor granted the obvious, namely that Bevan had no right to refer to Cabinet discussions without the Sovereign's permission secured through the Prime Minister. However, Taylor was much troubled by the implications of another statement which Attlee had made, because 'constitutional precedents are made by politicians dogmatizing about them.' In Taylor's words, the former premier had asserted that 'secrecy applied not only to an existing Cabinet but covered a previous Cabinet'; for his own part, he insisted that there was no precedent for the stance 'except as Mr. Attlee himself attempted to provide during his period of office. Former Cabinet Ministers have always been free to air their differences once the Cabinet was dissolved.'[61] As an example, Taylor cited the widespread discussion of the events which had led to Cabinet resignations in the wake of Britain's going to war in 1914, but he had no way of taking into account the precedents which had been forged since those distant events. Yet he did lament the fact that Cabinet secrecy appeared to be strengthening, which he regretted all the more as the product of the views of a 'democratic' party.

In replying to Taylor's criticism, Attlee rejected the contention that Cabinet ministers had always been free to air their differences once a Cabinet had been dissolved: 'To accept this doctrine would be destructive of the collective responsibility of the Cabinet and of the confidence which must exist among colleagues in Government.'[62] The former premier thus developed a historical dimension for the convention which served to bind the Cabinet together as a political entity: what once had been accomplished as a joint responsibility, he seemed to say, must long or always be so treated.

Attlee also commented that the doctrine of Cabinet secrecy represented no innovation on his government's part: 'the rule as to the inspection of Cabinet documents' dated to the MacDonald regime two decades earlier. He admitted that at some future, unspecified, time Cabinet records might yield to history's claim upon them, but in the short run acceptance of Taylor's doctrine would 'strike a blow at democratic government.'

On the same day, Sir Rupert Howorth stirred from retirement to lament 'the considerable mis-understanding, in Oxford and elsewhere, on the subject of Cabinet secrecy.' Disclosures of Cabinet proceedings were proscribed by the Privy Counsellor's Oath to reveal nothing said or done in Council save with the express consent of the Sovereign, in a fashion stipulated as long ago as 1878; further, the Official Secrets Act bore upon the matter, although its writ ran to all persons alike, whether or not Ministers of the Crown – he noted the successful prosecution of George Lansbury's biographer under the statute.[63] His approach to the Oath and the Act could fairly be described as absolutist, although he recognized that both had on occasion been broken; these exceptions he refused to accept as evidence that the dissolution of a Cabinet freed its members to discuss Cabinet proceedings. Responding to such authoritative commentaries, *The Times* joined in the fray on 8 August, commenting in a leading article that Bevan had invoked 'a non-existent right of a resigning Minister to reveal such Cabinet discussions as he may consider relevant to the reasons for his resignation.'[64] Taylor's search for precedents was characterized as inadequate, and the relevant comments of the nineteenth-century statesman, Lord Melbourne, had been neglected: 'If the arguments in the Cabinet are not to be protected by an impenetrable veil of secrecy, there will be no place left in the public counsels for the free investigation of truth and the unshackled exercise of the understanding.' *The Times* admitted the claims of history, but added: 'It is not easy to decide when Cabinet proceedings cease to belong to contemporary political debate and pass into history.' Were an error to be made, *The Times* thought it ought to be on the side of caution, because the alternative was the risk of sacrificing that mutual confidence and confidentiality among ministers which provided the basis for effective Cabinet government.

In response to *The Times' obiter dictum*, several correspondents questioned the assertion that Cabinet secrecy had, with well-known exceptions, been preserved inviolate: one cited a number of resignation speeches over the past thirty years which had offended in this regard, without reference to the Sovereign's permission;[65] another cited a revealing parliamentary exchange dating to 1949 between Churchill and Ernest Bevin, which no one – *The Times* included – had complained about in terms of breach of secrecy. The second correspondent insisted that recent practices carried greater weight than Victorian precepts:

> the rule has in recent times been interpreted, both in regard to resignation speeches from a Government in being and generally in regard to former administrations, as still precluding the publication without permission of Cabinet papers . . . but not as extending to statements by former Ministers indicating their degree of personal responsibility for some particular matter of policy.[66]

Such a distinction was particularly valid in light of the exchange between Lloyd George and the National Government in 1932; it also afforded the government a reasonable means of preserving the secrecy of Cabinet papers, while conceding to former ministers a freedom of discussion which a number of them had already claimed, whether in resignation speeches or thereafter.

Howorth remained unimpressed with the arguments advanced by the 'moderns,' reiterating the strictures of the Privy Counsellor's Oath and the 'very sharp and penetrating teeth' of the Official Secrets Act. Nor could he credit the concessions made in the name of history both by Attlee and *The Times*: 'The documents of each administration are domestic to that Administration and it is open to a Cabinet on vacating office to direct that all its documents should be destroyed without exception.'[67] Indeed, such a concern had contributed to the National Government's decision to recover all Cabinet papers, an action taken 'by way of compromise of this difficult problem.' While Howorth regarded destruction as 'deplorable,' there exists no evidence to indicate that such an alternative had at any time been brought to the attention of MacDonald's Cabinet.

The discussion of Cabinet secrecy took on additional legalistic trappings when another correspondent contended that no earlier 'statements' of resignation had any weight at law in determining whether Bevan had any 'right' to contravene an Act of Parliament – presumably the Official Secrets Act.[68] In dismissing that accumulation of conventions which is referred to as precedent, such a posture appears all the more misplaced since the leading authority on Cabinet government, Ivor Jennings, had held that the 'efficient sanction' in maintaining Cabinet secrecy was neither the Oath nor the Official Secrets Act but rather in the main a rule of 'practice.'[69] Thus, the practice of resignation speeches was as established a doctrine as that of collective responsibility, although the weight of tradition supporting the latter was greater. Where rules of 'practice' are in a state of evolution, as clearly is the case with Cabinet government, flexibility and change are part of the system: absolutism is misguided.

The significance of this entire exchange lies, of course, in the greater concern which forms the backdrop to the Bevan disclosures, namely the place of Cabinet secrecy within a democratic society. This matter too had been commented upon: 'The ordinary citizen, whose right and duty it is to judge the policies of his leaders, should have the freest possible means of knowing what is decided in his name.' This correspondent acknowledged the need for the preservation of strategic secrets, but he viewed secrecy as in itself an 'evil,' and he characterized as dangerous the argument that most disclosures were contrary to the public interest: the exposure to truth was a vital ingredient of a democracy, which was not defenceless against improper disclosures. Among its weapons was the Official Secrets Act, 'undoubted and dangerous breaches' of which he was prepared to entrust to a British jury.[70] Vital concerns these, involving what has come to be known as the public's 'right to know,' which in a democracy must nonetheless be balanced against the need for administrative secrecy: no Cabinet government based on the useful convention of collective responsibility can afford consistently to ventilate its differences. Immediate access to the records of government in the name of the 'right to know' could destroy any Cabinet effectiveness, for all the fact that the political aspects of contemporary Cabinet government seem to require deliberate leakage of portions of its business in a variety of ways. In contentious matters particularly, leading ministers and senior civil servants on occasion disregard, to a degree, the principles of secrecy; their critics within the government may be even more pressed to ensure that their dissent from some misguided policy is recognized.[71] Thus the galaxy of 'informed sources,' 'highly placed officials,' and 'confidants' contradict within the political process what is upheld as the rule of Cabinet secrecy. Yet such deliberate leakages do not pose the problem for Cabinet government that a systematic deference to the public's 'right to know' would entail.

Nor should this routine hypocrisy, designed to vent the pressures of politics, excuse the post-Second World War expansion of the scope of administrative secrecy – Cabinet secrecy is but a part – which has spread far beyond those matters which need to be cloaked, for instance Cabinet proceedings, diplomatic relations, and national defence. A persuasive study of such executive secrecy[72] documents the spread of the practice, intended for the most part to serve governmental convenience and enforced by resort to section 2 of the Official Secrets Act. Sufficient adverse reaction eventually led to the appointment in April 1971 of the Franks Departmental Committee; its investigation of the operation of section 2 came little more than a year later, concluding that 'a section which has been described as an ancient blunderbuss, scattering shot in all directions, needs replacement by a modern weapon.' The Franks

Committee advised that section 2 should be repealed and replaced by the narrower and more specific provisions of an Official Information Act, directing criminal sanctions only at the most important official information, which the committee proceeded to itemize.[73] What is most relevant here is that the Franks Committee provided for the protection of Cabinet documents, including all papers submitted to the Cabinet or the committees composed of ministers, and all records of Cabinet proceedings. In the context of Cabinet secrecy within a democratic society their rationale is worth recording:

> The operation of our entire system of government turns on the proper functioning of the Cabinet. Unauthorised publication of Cabinet documents could undermine public confidence to the point where the Government would find it difficult to perform the essential functions of government . . . The Cabinet works on the doctrine of collective responsibility. Whatever the individual views of its members, when the Cabinet reaches a decision it is the decision of them all. Each shares in the collective responsibility of that decision. Anything that damages the collective unity and integrity of the Cabinet damages the government of this country.[74]

Although this formulation ignores several of the ways in which collective responsibility as a theory is compromised in practice, the Franks Committee acknowledged the presence of political gossip in Westminster – 'it is unreasonable to expect the silence of the monastery in a modern centre of government' – while differentiating such 'small coin' from publications which would impair the governmental process. In 1979 HMG resolved to remove criminal sanctions from the disclosures of information related to Cabinet documents, unless those documents fall into one of the categories which would still be protected. Apparently the government is now reasonably confident that other devices, discussed below, will serve to protect an appropriate measure of secrecy for Cabinet proceedings. The 'blunderbuss' of section 2 was not a weapon well-designed to bolster the secrecy in which the modern Cabinet must function; yet such secrecy will be preserved for the foreseeable future.[75]

The deficiencies of section 2 have become clear over the years, but its writ loomed considerable for those of the inter-war generation who sought to record their observations about the policies and statesmen of that era. The restrictions upon ministerial memoirs forged in 1934 remained in place; civil servants and diplomats were barred from use of any official documents. Yet from time to time, the curtains of secrecy had parted, particularly for fleeting glances at the way in which British foreign policy had been conducted: one such outspoken revelation came from the pen of the former British Ambassador in Vienna, Sir Walford Selby, a long-time critic of Sir Warren Fisher's alleged undue interference in matters of policy and of senior diplomatic appointments.[76] Selby's ill feelings gained an even wider audience with his 1953 memoir, *Diplomatic Twilight*, in which he castigated Fisher's role specifically and called into question Vansittart's tenure as Permanent Under-Secretary. Although the Foreign Office objected to these strictures in its official review of Selby's account, he refused to amend what amounted to an *idée fixe*, and he was permitted to proceed. Since Vansittart's rejoinder was uncharacteristically restrained and less than compelling,[77] Selby's parting of the pre-war diplomatic curtains attracted some attention.

Almost certainly Vansittart's response would have been stronger had he been permitted to cite official documents, but such was not the case: already his *Lessons of My Life*, published in 1943, was not so informed, and he subsequently was denied authority to quote from his own official papers, 'on the grounds that no civil servant, whether serving or retired, "may be permitted to publish privately memoranda written in his official capacity."'[78] Although Vansittart protested a situation in which 'there should be one law for those who give their whole life to the Service of the State and another for politicians,'[79] HMG did not budge, and Vansittart was obliged to use his papers in a circumspect fashion, which his latest biographer contends contributed to the much-remarked upon 'abstruseness' of his incomplete memoirs, *The Mist Procession*, published in 1958. His near-contemporary Ivone Kirkpatrick brought out his memoirs in 1959, only a few years after his retirement from a career that had led to the Permanent Under-Secretaryship, but he took care so far as recent events were concerned 'to give no account of conversations or transactions with men who are still active in the fields of politics or diplomacy,' from a sense of respect for their confidences. Kirkpatrick's account traversed post-war events, but in such an anodyne fashion that one cannot imagine its provoking official indignation. Ultimately diplomats were granted access to documents which they had prepared, although the right to quote from such materials is subject to temporal limitations.[80] Vansittart's difficulties establish that the separation of the Foreign Service from the Civil Service was not responsible for such a change in attitude.

In an official climate which was hostile to the discussion of ministerial–adviser relationships, fittingly Lord Hankey seized the opportunity afforded him in 1957 by congratulations sent his way from Prime Minister Macmillan on the occasion of his eightieth birthday. The premier had paid him the compliment of writing that 'it must give you great satisfaction to reflect that the system which you introduced forty years ago is still in force to-day,' which encouraged Hankey to approach the new incumbent in Downing Street, not least because of Macmillan's own background in publishing.[81] In writing Macmillan, Hankey sought to avoid the past controversy by stressing the importance of 'three new factors,' namely the passage of forty years since the Armistice of 1918, the deaths of all principal characters in his memoirs save Churchill, and the recent 'signs of a more tolerant attitude towards quotations from private diaries in recently published memoirs, e.g. Field Marshal Viscount Alanbrooke's Diaries, and some others.' The last point was particularly significant, he noted, because on two past occasions his negotiations with the government had broken down due to their insistence that he eliminate all quotations from his own diary.[82] And surely the war-time CIGS's diary shed light upon the relationships between ministers and advisers, but Macmillan – and of course the Cabinet Office – were not persuaded, since such accounts of the Second World War had been given great latitude. Even if the military had not been awarded the preferential treatment given ministers, the official view would not concede to Hankey the military analogy, as Macmillan informed him: 'The basis of the earlier decisions was that publication of the book, by laying bare the inner workings of the Central Government machine, would be likely to impair for the present and the future the relations between Ministers and their most intimate official advisers.'[83] Noting that the force of such an objection had not lessened since 1946, Macmillan held out no hope of official approval, and carefully he narrowed the issue to Hankey's past position as Secretary to the Cabinet, commenting that 'if I thought that the present holder of this office was keeping a private diary . . . my official relations with him would be very different from what they are today.' Macmillan left no doubt that he spoke on behalf of Sir Edward Bridges and Sir Norman Brook, Hankey's successors at the Cabinet Office, who shared the Prime Minister's notion that the nature of their position barred the keeping of a diary.[84] Confronted with the bitter truth that his memoirs had become the object of a unique prohibition, Hankey replied intemperately to Macmillan: 'All I need say at the moment is that I do not accept your decision to maintain the ban.'[85]

Wisely, Hankey took counsel before proceeding; his former assistant, 'Pug' Ismay, who had served as an official adviser to Churchill during the war, was appalled to learn of the renewed prohibition: 'I should have thought that considering the time that has elapsed since they were written, they could have been published verbatim. But I should have thought that at the very worst they might ask you to omit certain passages which seemed to them objectionable.'[86] Hankey and his agent next sought the legal advice of the former Conservative Attorney-General, Sir Lionel Heald, who advised him to run no risk of violating the Official Secrets Act, 'a most unsatisfactory and indefinite statute.'[87] In due course he raised the matter with the Prime Minister, who offered to seek the advice of Lord Salisbury, although Hankey refused the idea of what amounted to binding arbitration. It was as well that he did, because Salisbury did not even examine the manuscript, as the principle was clear: 'He would personally regard it as entirely wrong for anybody who has held the position as Secretary to the Cabinet to publish within his own lifetime and that of others concerned a book containing information which he acquired in that capacity.'[88]

Unwisely but perhaps unwittingly, Hankey continued his correspondence with Downing Street in a fashion which brought yet another factor into play. In assuring Macmillan that 'whatever else might be the effect of the Official Secrets Act, it certainly does not empower the executive to veto the publication of a book without regard to its contents,' Hankey opened himself to a withering reply grounded on that very statute. The Prime Minister dismissed Hankey's contention that HMG's veto was unrelated to the 'actual contents' of his war memoirs:

> On the contrary, it is because of its contents that we have objected to its publication . . . I enclose an extract from Section 2 of the Act: you will not, I think, need a lawyer's interpretation to realise that this makes it an offence for any person who has held an official position to publish any information which he has acquired by virtue of holding that position. And it cannot be contested that in your book you would be publishing such information.[89]

Macmillan tempered this warning with an appeal to Hankey's sense of the public interest, pointing out that official opinion had run unanimously against publication; further, he strove to convince by differentiating between the memoirs of civil servants and those written by members of the Foreign Service or Armed Forces, because the latter were exposed to 'public comment and criticism,' while the former were not, 'least of all, perhaps, the Secretary of the Cabinet . . . closest to the Prime Minister and . . . furthest removed from the public eye.' In his turn, Hankey reiterated the technical point that he had not been a civil servant during the war, and again observed 'how fundamentally your conception of the Cabinet Secretary differs from that of your predecessors from 1911 to 1938 . . . given the totally different conditions in which I served from those of my successors to-day, no harm whatever would result to my present successor.'[90] The Prime Minister and the Cabinet Secretary simply would not grant this point, and Hankey had keenly to feel the weight of the Official Secrets Act, which his office had first invoked to protect the secrecy of the inner workings of government. Though one may regard his plight as apposite, it is difficult not to sympathize with an old man, possessed of a unique perspective, who felt that rules had been changed in order to deny him an opportunity to relate his account of distant war years.

Nor could he anticipate at this point that the worst was past, although in fact he had to compromise his account in order to publish while he lived. In the meantime, he was disappointed in his prospective publisher, Cassells, which decided in 1957 that the passing years had destroyed public interest in his book; other publishers declined the manuscript, completed a decade-and-half earlier. Comments at Hutchinson's were negative but reflected an entirely different view from HMG's about the content of the memoirs and the timing of their publication: one reported that 'the book has been written about 40 years too late' – so much for historical accounts – and the other judged that Hankey had been prevented 'from taking sides and blowing gaffes, but, by that very token . . . precluded from writing a good, readable, fascinating book.'[91] However, Allen and Unwin expressed interest in publishing, and Hankey was persuaded to agree to an abridged version in two volumes, edited to that end by the journalist R. T. Clark, who received no credit when the memoirs were finally published. Better news yet came from Heald in December 1959: he reported Macmillan's view that Hankey had behaved well about the book and now concluded that although he was not prepared to authorise publication, he suggested, in Hankey's words, that 'we should not be interfered with if we adopted the present plan of publishing the abbreviated version without asking authority.'[92] Benign neglect seemed the most the former Cabinet Secretary could hope for, and his publishers proceeded in the midst of official silence.[93] *The Supreme Command, 1914–1918* appeared in 1961, and Hankey sent copies to two of his prime ministerial antagonists, Churchill and Macmillan, rather churlishly commenting to the latter that he had 'not emulated the much wider license accorded to the published memoirs and diaries of the Second World War.'[94]

Yet the publication even of an abridged, expurgated version of Hankey's memoirs stood as an important exception to the post-war insistence that retired civil servants not publish accounts based upon officially acquired information. Whether Hankey's plea that he had not been a civil servant during the Great War had contributed to HMG's willingness to look the other way is open to doubt, because Hankey by virtue of his post would be viewed as a civil servant. Nor was the official stance against the prohibition weakening, as new regulations promulgated in 1957 by Sir Norman Brook made clear: 'The aim of these procedures . . . is to ensure that Crown Servants and former Crown Servants and in some cases persons outside the government service are aware that the publication of *any* official information which has not already officially been made public renders them liable to prosecution under the Official Secrets Act.'[95] These regulations applied to all information officially acquired, not merely secret information, and the directive has since been reissued on several occasions, with only minor amendments. Shortly after its issuance, however, Parliament passed the Public Records Act of 1958: although not stipulated in the legislation, and despite objections from the Cabinet Office,[96] Cabinet papers were shortly made accessible at a fifty-year remove; thus the eventual emergence of 'official information' relating to Cabinet business, including the relations between ministers and their advisers, was assured. Although there is some evidence that suggests the Cabinet Office brought pressure to bear upon biographers to eschew any discussion of the work of civil servants, at least for the post-war period,[97] the publication of Hankey's memoirs indicates that his successors had at last yielded the struggle over the ultimate historical depiction of the confidential relationship. In 1961 a former civil servant, Lord Salter, published memoirs in which he recalled meeting 'on terms of official intimacy the leading political figures of the day,' including Lloyd George, Lord Robert Cecil, and C. F. G. Masterman.[98] At a considerable remove in time, Hankey and Salter illumed that relationship. Following upon their accounts, books from the likes of Cadogan, Harvey, and Lockhart on the Foreign Office side and, on the civil, the memoirs of George Mallaby,[99] in addition to the Thomas Jones *Whitehall Diary* and Roskill's extensive citation of the Hankey diaries, have established the freedom for civil servants to disclose 'official information' after a suitable period, now apparently thirty years. Where diaries have been kept, eventually they will emerge, however great Cabinet Office distaste for the genre.

As this pattern gradually changed, so too did that which assured public access to governmental records, at a considerable remove in time from the actual proceedings. Even the small-scale tempest of August 1952 contributed to the public awareness that history was not being well served, and in 1958 public access to the most important records of government after the passing of a half-century was attained. Dissatisfaction with inaccessibility of such records was hardly a post-war phenomenon, because the point had been made as long ago as 1899 that 'on the general question of keeping documents secret there is no country in Europe which is so scrupulous and old-fashioned in imposing secrecy on its documents as is this country.'[100] In some cases access was granted to historians who were thought to be impartial, which may account for the fact that the Chief Secretary for Ireland proved particularly unyielding in denying access to papers dealing with Ireland after the time of the rebellion of 1798.[101] At the end of the Victorian period, the Home Office enforced a prohibition on access to records post-dating 1800; on the other hand, the Foreign Office had decided in 1924 to open its records through the end of 1878, yielding to historians' entreaties to permit a realistic evaluation of British foreign policy.[102] The Colonial Office had freed many of its nineteenth-century documents, yet even in the second half of the twentieth the Home Office had retained all its records post-dating 1800 and a good many from earlier; only a small portion of Home Office records had been transferred to the Public Record Office.[103] In short, since the Public Records Act had been written in 1838, arrangements for the transfer of departmental records varied widely, and the departments determined the closed period, selecting a suitable date to open collections 'as nearly as possible without reserve.'[104] In 1954 a Committee on Departmental Records, chaired by Sir James Grigg, had recommended that the custody and public utilization of government records should be systematized and regularized; they stressed the importance of protecting the quality of 'unself-consciousness' on the part of those who originally prepared the documents, contending that the public interest would suffer 'if an official knew that what he wrote would be available for public inspection during his life time.'[105] With no haste, the Conservative regime determined that both government records and legal records should be subject to the same general system, under the supervision of the Lord Chancellor.

Macmillan's government subsequently decided to accept the recommendation of the Grigg Committee that the government records – transferred to the Public Record Office after review and winnowing – should be made available for inspection after fifty years, or such other period, whether longer or shorter, as the Lord Chancellor might prescribe. Defending such exceptions, the Solicitor-General, Sir Harry Hylton-Foster, commented: 'The object is to withhold from public inspection, should it be necessary, documents the publication of which after so long a period as fifty years might be harmful,'[106] which as the law came to be implemented fell into four categories: documents containing information about individuals whose disclosure could cause distress or embarrassment to living persons or their immediate descendants, such as criminal, prison, or certain police records; those containing information obtained with a pledge of confidence, such as census returns; certain papers relating to Irish affairs – seemingly a constant exception to any rule; and sensitive papers which affect the security of the state, including intelligence activities.[107] For other records the government specified as a 'general rule' the passage of fifty years before public access, which would afford statutory form to a slowly developing custom. In setting such a period, they accepted the Grigg Committee's assumption that fifty years represented a 'normal period in relation to the life of a man' and so would assure 'the preservation of unself-consciousness in the writing of records.'[108] Some parliamentary critics thought such a scheme inadequate, and one commented that while fifty years may have been appropriate for the Victorian period, in the twentieth century history had accelerated and moved forward 'in bursts,' which access to public records ought to recognize. The Solicitor-General reminded the government's critics that the Lord Chancellor was empowered to grant exceptions, and the decision was sustained by a partisan vote in a thin Friday sitting of the House of Commons.[109]

In a sense parliamentary debate was perfunctory, but several concerns were raised which serve to indicate the confusion in which the question of the custody of Cabinet documents had become enveloped. One MP argued that 'the genuine student of history' was discriminated against, because Cabinet ministers had retained Cabinet Minutes and memoranda since the time such records had been maintained on a scientific basis.[110] As no government spokesman took the trouble to correct his allegation, he must be forgiven his confusion, because the massive exception provided for ministerial retention of self-authored memoranda for the Second World War could easily be mistaken for license to retain official documents on an even more comprehensive scale. To be sure, ministerial memoirs and those of their service advisers remained outside the scope of the fifty-year rule, and the Cabinet Office at this time remained hopeful that Cabinet papers would not be made available under the terms of the new legislation; the situation was a complex one.

If this official attitude were generally known in Westminster, the fact would explain another odd feature of the debate, namely the fear that certain categories of documents might be destroyed as a result of the 1958 legislation. Such fears proved to be groundless, but the words of the Solicitor-General in introducing the Public Records Act – to the effect that it would authorise the destruction of those records which ought not be preserved – fueled such concerns. Indeed, Hylton-Foster had to assure the House that 'no one is destroying Cabinet papers.'[111] Acknowledging that these represented 'the most important and informative of all State papers,' he cautioned that the several political parties had yet to resolve certain problems concerning Cabinet documents, and royal assent also had to be secured. Nonetheless, his words mark the first official assurance that HMG had agreed to the principle of public access to a category of official documents which had to this time been rigorously closed to all save ministers and, in theory, their vindicators.

In light of this development, then, Macmillan's reversal of position concerning the publication of Hankey's memoirs can properly be understood. Despite the fact that the Prime Minister threatened Hankey with the use of the Official Secrets Act a week after Parliament had approved the Public Records Act, surely the implications of the 1958 legislation led Macmillan tacitly to suggest that Hankey publish his memoirs without seeking official approval.[112] Likely Hankey would have been able to publish his fuller, three volume account, but the decision to abridge had been his publisher's. The advent of the fifty-year rule meant that the full range of Cabinet documents for the First World War would be released within a decade's time; governmental acquiescence merely advanced by a few years what was inevitable. One would like to think that the Prime Minister acted in such a way in order to pay tribute to a man who had served his country well; nonetheless, official non-recognition did not serve to commit HMG to the propriety of the Cabinet Secretary's keeping a private diary of public affairs – a measure of consolation for Hankey's successors. To be sure, the Lord Chancellor retained the power to proscribe access to Cabinet papers, for a period exceeding fifty years, but to have done so with the single most important collection of government records, the Cabinet papers, would have compromised the fifty-year rule.

More recently, the closed period for records of criminal investigations and allied matters in the custody of the Director of Public Prosecutions was reduced from a century to seventy-five years;[113] apparently some other records remain closed for the full hundred years. In Hankey's own case, his ministerial labors in connection with the organization of British intelligence and his efforts to further research in bacteriological warfare fall into a category of record which may never be made available.[114] Yet some light now has been shed even in the dark corners of intelligence, although HMG, in accepting the legitimacy of public inspection of records relating to war-time British intelligence, drew a distinction between those of the Service directorates, which have been opened, and the domestic files of the intelligence-collecting bodies, which in the words of the Official History are 'unlikely ever to be opened for such inspection.'[115] Yet the fact of access marks a turnabout in the government's attitude, both in terms of sanctioning publication of such contemporary 'official' works as Sir John Masterman's *The Double Cross System*[116] and commissioning an Official History of the influence of intelligence upon strategy and operations, in the Hinsley collaborative venture. Nor did the government discourage the publication of books dealing with the most prized long-term secret of the entire war, the Ultra operation housed at Bletchley Park, although the initial account by F. W. Winterbotham – who was not given access to official records in writing his book – was written under official constraints, as for example the details of cryptographic manipulations were barred. Nonetheless Winterbotham's partial and misleading account[117] led to a ministerial decision in 1974 to release to the Public Record Office a variety of materials, which were opened in 1977: intelligence techniques and sources remain beyond the pale, but in other regards war-time intelligence staff as well were freed from their undertakings of 'reticence' in view of the release of official materials.[118] Yet HMG decided against extending the disclosure of materials from intelligence sources into the post-war period, contending that governments do not publicly acknowledge peace-time espionage activities.[119] Against that disingenuous plea one might set the claim of

Chapman Pincher, an informed defence journalist, that the Ultra techniques continued to yield secrets of state in Africa, the Middle East, South America and elsewhere to the British and American operators for yet another thirty years after the end of the war![120]

Insofar as the closed period for post-war British documents is concerned, it has been suggested that any dealing with the country's involvement in the Suez expedition will be sealed for a full century.[121] Others have indicated that records involving discussions with France and Israel prior to Suez were either not kept, or had a circulation far less than that of the full Cabinet and were subsequently burned.[122] If surviving records are closed for a full century, they will share that restriction with records related to the Abdication crisis of 1936.[123] However, in the case of the Suez papers, one might hope for a reconsideration of such an inordinate proscription, which otherwise serves to indicate that the British government has a blot on the record worth hiding.

Macmillan's acquiescence in Hankey's publication may also have been influenced by the knowledge that his predecessor, Anthony Eden, intended to publish a volume of memoirs dealing with his years as Foreign Secretary from 1951 to 1955 and his short unhappy term as premier: governmental approval of these memoirs had to precede their serialization in February 1960. It is noteworthy that Eden had chosen to treat the last years of his career before reverting to the more distant pre-war and war-time periods, precisely because of their contemporary significance: 'This book will expose wounds; by doing so it could help to heal them.'[124] Eden acknowledged that he had drawn upon official materials, specifying personal minutes which he had written to Churchill or to colleagues when he had become leading minister – apparently applying the war-time test of authorship of a document – notes dictated as the basis for messages sent either to England from abroad or directed to foreign statesmen or British embassies, and occasional notes jotted down as the opportunity arose. He did not add that since 1954 he had employed research assistants who had been given access to Cabinet Office records, which in one striking instance included the 'rough notes' which Hankey had preserved for the meetings of the Foreign Policy Committee's meetings in early 1938.[125] Such access to persons other than former ministers[126] represents a significant if unannounced departure in policy concerning the preparation of ministerial memoirs: former ministers – or perhaps former premiers – had secured privileged access for those acting in their behalf to documents of recent date. Thus an individual with good reason to plead a special case in a highly politicized event had assured access to government records long before any of his critics were so armed. Not surprisingly, the public reaction to Eden's apologia was not long in coming.

When queried in Parliament about Eden's use in his memoirs of extracts from Cabinet Minutes, Foreign Office telegrams and other government documents, Macmillan replied that such a usage was sanctioned by precedent, specifically those which Churchill had forged; the Leader of the Opposition, Hugh Gaitskell, protested that 'the way in which these conventions have been administered lately has been increasingly lax' and rejected – properly, it appears, given the relaxation of the convention only for the war years – the Churchill case as a binding precedent. The Prime Minister observed laconically: 'Perhaps we ought to treat the war and immediate postwar as something different. It would be a novel procedure, but it was that kind of thing I had in mind when I said that we ought perhaps to consider establishing new conventions for what one might call different times.'[127] For all this professed sympathy for new ways, Macmillan rejected an Opposition suggestion that the government issue a White Paper dealing with the use of secret state documents by former ministers, taking his stand by the Morrison statement of 1946 which events had, in Eden's case, outpaced. The point remains that HMG's stance was not one which would entitle them to look severely upon Hankey's memoirs of distant times and abated passions: the invocation of section 2 was legally possible, but arbitrary, even absurd. One can only speculate whether Macmillan's disposition was colored by his own diary-keeping, a principal source for his own memoirs in years to come.

Another indication of a more latitudinarian governmental attitude towards the use of officially derived materials also involved Macmillan directly, upon the occasion of his providing for the 'emergence' of his Tory successor as premier – the last such 'emergence' because of the controversial nature of Macmillan's arrangements. In defence of his actions, Macmillan acquainted Randolph Churchill with the contents of a Cabinet paper dealing with the matter; Churchill did not quote the memorandum directly, but his account leaves little doubt that he had access to it, as he summarized its procedural contents in some detail.[128] The government of his successor, Sir Alec Douglas-Home, expressed no interest in the possibilities of a prosecution under the Official Secrets Act.

Since the furor surrounding the privileged publication of Eden's *Full Circle* did not dent HMG's attitude towards ministerial memoirs, its most significant consequence was the emergence of a group of academics concerned with the prejudice shown against public access to the records of recent history. Individual complaints were lodged in the correspondence column of *The Times* and echoed on Opposition benches in the House of Commons, but official orthodoxy countered that the release of Cabinet papers at a lesser remove than fifty years would handicap governmental proceedings. Most frustrating was Macmillan's continued insistence that 'there is no great demand' for a revision of the closed period. Officially viewed as 'a small body of disgruntled academics, complaining with infantile petulance that Lord Avon [Eden] was being unfairly accorded privileges denied to them,'[129] a number of these scholars took advantage of the review mechanism built into the Public Records Act of 1958 to organize on behalf of a revision of its terms. Bolstered by the inclusion of some senior figures who had been involved with the Official Histories, academics from the Universities of Oxford, Cambridge, and London met in 1963 to concert their efforts:

> They were concerned with the whole question of the flow of governmental information to the world of scholarship; and they saw themselves confronted with a threefold task: to persuade government to reduce the closed period; to improve the provision of information by the continuation of the Cabinet Office histories or some similar enterprise within the closed period; and to improve the flow of information given to the public on the immediate issues of politics.[130]

The Cabinet Office received a deputation, but the Foreign Office and Service Ministries resisted proposals to grant access within the closed period in exchange for an official review of the manuscript. Although on occasion the motives of the Oxford–Cambridge–London group were questioned,[131] Macmillan's retirement weakened official resistance to revision of the fifty-year rule. An important victory was won when the British Museum agreed to abandon its own enforcement of such a fifty-year closed period for the private papers under its control.[132] As the campaign gained headway, the Society of Authors in 1966 undertook efforts to secure revision of the fifty-year rule.[133]

When the governmental innings of the Conservatives ran out in 1964, a Labour government led by Harold Wilson attempted to come to terms with the post-war widening scope of ministerial memoirs and the mounting pressures to grant earlier public access to government records. Although the Wilson regime took a major step forward in the latter regard, they were unable fully to resolve the former, which to the present day continues to defy a legally binding settlement. With the Official Secrets Act widely discredited, a later Wilson administration failed to sustain a legal objection to the 1975 publication of Richard Crossman's *Cabinet Diaries*, discussed below; from HMG's point of view, the problem became more acute, because the Lord Chief Justice decided that in this case the public interest would not be damaged by the publication of a highly detailed record of Cabinet proceedings at about a decade's remove. Concurrently, a Committee of Privy Counsellors conducted an inquiry concerning the principles which should govern the publication of ministerial memoirs and other officially informed accounts. That committee advised the proscription of certain aspects of Cabinet proceedings for a period of fifteen years, a period half again as long as what the Lord

Chief Justice judged in a particular case would serve to protect free discussion within the Cabinet. With this conclusion of the Privy Counsellors, the matter of ministerial memoirs rests for the moment.

Public access to government records is an entirely different matter, and the government's decision to reduce the closed period from fifty to thirty years, announced by Harold Wilson in August 1966, owed something to the efforts of the Prime Minister himself, as well as to those who set the stage for the reform. The sole account to date of the Cabinet's reaction is contained in the Crossman diary: in his view, Wilson strategically introduced the proposal as 'a filler' in the last Cabinet meeting prior to Parliament's summer recess, and he carried the case with minimal support from three ministers, against substantial opposition voiced by the Chancellor and the Foreign Secretary. Taking our source at his word, the recent disclosures of affairs of state by former ministers logically dictated earlier access to records by non-official persons:

> I [Crossman] pointed out that the present ban, quite apart from all its other drawbacks, was rendered intolerable by the permission which a Cabinet Minister, particularly a Prime Minister, can obtain to use official documents denied to academic and objective historians for writing his memoirs. If we are going to go on exercising the right to turn out memoirs which are often nothing but powerful *plaidoyers*, there is a powerful case for letting the historians get at the documents as soon as possible.[134]

Wilson sought the Cabinet's agreement to this 'modest reform' only after he had secured the support of the Leader of the Opposition and the leader of the Liberal Party; the matter had already been considered by a parliamentary Advisory Committee on Public Records, which had reported in favor of a forty-year rule.[135]

In his own quest for a twenty-five year rule, Wilson sought to counter the criticism of any reduction in the closed period, namely the dangers of premature revelation: 'Speaking for myself, I said I would rather be alive to hit back at all who would in the seventies wish to savage my infant documents of 1947–51.'[136] Characteristically taking a personal position on a much-debated matter, Wilson agreed to compromise upon a thirty-year rule, although he had to threaten to 'thresh out' the matter with the electorate if the Opposition refused to agree. His account of the Cabinet's reaction to his proposals eschews the actual discussion – as his memoirs generally mask such proceedings – and thus fails to reveal that a number of his own colleagues were not enthusiastic about the reform. For his part, the Opposition Leader, Edward Heath, attacked the government's unwillingness to grant the press freer access to the Cabinet's on-going discussion of various options in the conduct of foreign, defence, and domestic policies.[137] To raise the matter is one thing, to settle it another; since 1966 governments have honored the principle that more can responsibly be done to inform the public, but little progress is apparent in practice: the need for administrative secrecy – not simply at the Cabinet level – conflicts with the 'right to know'. At that time, Wilson also announced the government's intention to commission official Cabinet Office histories for the post-war period and to extend *Documents on British Foreign Policy*[138] into that era, but he cautioned that such works 'would not necessarily be suitable for publication before the expiry of the closed period.'[139] Nonetheless, the Labour premier stressed the importance of 'personal recollection' of those involved in the post-war events, which indicates a disparity in viewpoint from those who saw the major importance of such publications the provision of official information at a time when the records themselves were closed.[140] Thus frustrated with regard to several of its goals, the Oxford–Cambridge–London group could take satisfaction in Wilson's amendment of the Public Records Act of 1958, which reduced the closed period to thirty years.

Wilson's remarks to the House of Commons establish his own belief that the balance of conflicting claims had at last been righted, because the reform 'would let some light and air into our public records without in any way weakening the conventions which regulate the conduct of public affairs in this country.'[141] He was pressed from his own back benches to admit that such a measure carried 'political mercy to extravagant lengths':[142] though Suez remained a sore point, a 'thirty-year rule' would exclude from inspection documents relating to Munich! The premier retorted that a two-year wait was worth the general protection that the rule afforded those who joined the Cabinet early in their political lives. As for Suez, he had on the previous day personally characterized the British intervention as a 'put-up job,' but Wilson acknowledged that his suspicions were not based on official information: 'In accordance with the accepted convention in these matters, the Government can have no knowledge of any engagement of this kind which may have been made by a previous administration but which, in the nature of things, can no longer be valid or operative.'[143]

The historical and journalistic world generally viewed Wilson's measure as progressive, although several criticisms were offered. One commentary centered on the relationship between what the Wilson government had given and what had been held back: 'The price of twenty years relaxation is to be apparently a resolute denial of all access within the closed period,' as individual scholars would be denied special authority to work on current topics.[144] This anonymous correspondent lamented the government's implicit refusal to engage in the selection of such scholars, but he did not advance criteria by which the process might fairly work. As well, he contended that HMG had burked a basic issue: 'the onus is on officialdom to show reason for its secrecy, that other things being equal the public has a right to know.' Much more was to be heard along these lines in years to come. Similar sentiments were expressed by Hugh Thomas, who objected to a 'thirty-year rule' as a binding measure of the relationship between administrative secrecy and scholarly inquiry: that period could safely be halved, he argued, except for certain exceptions in which a burden of proof would be put upon HMG to sustain restriction for a period longer than fifteen years; he suggested that a tribunal be established to hear the Cabinet's plea for an extension of closure, or an individual's petition to see documents within the closed period, 'once action upon a particular matter was complete.'[145] He saw the immediate effect as entirely beneficial, for the Civil Service and HMG:

> It would somewhat damage the old concept of the silent, neutral and politically uncommitted machine. But it would nevertheless admit the reality that public servants are in fact men like the rest of us, with prejudices and policies no less real if not always overt or realised: for and against the Common Market, for Israel and against the Arabs as the case may be.

While the likes of Hankey and Tom Jones – or for that matter, Fisher and Vansittart – underscore the validity of Thomas' point, his proposal defied both the reality of the Cabinet Office's intention to protect the ministerial–adviser relationship and its determination to maintain the impartial reputation of the Civil Service. Curiously, Thomas had himself discovered evidence pointing to that preoccupation with the image of a 'silent, neutral and politically uncommitted machine.'

Such an observation had arisen in connection with the 1967 publication of memoirs in the form of an insider's account of the Suez debacle. Anthony Nutting, a Minister of State for Foreign Affairs at that time, had broken ten years of silence to castigate Eden's government for collusion with France and Israel in those events. Although Nutting had resigned both from the government and the House of Commons, he had declined in 1956 to make a statement concerning the former, despite established practices which enabled him to secure permission to do so. A decade later, he explained: 'Either I had to tell the whole story as I saw it, or say nothing at all,' adding that only the latter course was open as long as any of the major protagonists continued to hold high public office. Yet it was essential that he contribute his version:

> Due to the intense security provisions taken at the time, only some half a dozen people in Britain today knew the story as I know it and of this 'select' group all but myself were so involved in the venture that for them to reveal the truth now would involve an act of confession too mortifying for any man to volunteer.

Coupled with the fact that no British records were kept of the discussions among Britain, France, and Israel which led to the Israeli attack, Nutting noted that the result would be that 'the historian will find no enlightenment in the archives of the Foreign Office when the official history of these times comes to be written.'[146] In sum, the time had come for him to record the truth, as he saw it, lest history be denied an informed perspective.

Yet Nutting's assertion that he had 'concealed nothing, added nothing and subtracted nothing, from what [he knew] to have happened'[147] cannot go unchallenged, because of Hugh Thomas' discovery that Nutting had deliberately masked some details of the British role, responding to a Cabinet Office *diktat*. The implications of this insistence are important for an understanding of practices involving ministerial memoirs, provided Thomas' information is correct:

> Scorning the usual procedure . . . he [Nutting] neither asked for access to documents which he worked with or prepared at the time, nor submitted his manuscript to the Cabinet Office (the normal procedure in instances such as this). He did, however, eventually submit the book in the form of page proof to the Cabinet Office. The text turned out to have a number of descriptions of Cabinet and other ministerial meetings, conversations between himself and the then Foreign Secretary and some mention of the Foreign Office telegrams. The substantial section of the book was published. The Cabinet Office did however remove the names of the civil servants involved, the exact definition of whether such a piece of information was conveyed by word of mouth or by telegram. The Cabinet Office machine looked after the Civil Service and the structure of Government, while the politicians concerned, Lord Avon and Mr. Selwyn Lloyd, in particular, were permitted to be castigated mercilessly.

Of course, these men were themselves free to account for their own actions, as Eden long since had; civil servants were not. Yet such ministerial disclosures confounded the Official Secrets Act, unless former ministers were free to determine when and to whom they may communicate official information. As Hugh Thomas doubted that license, he concluded that 'the Acts are not made to apply to politicians, *providing they accept the strictures of the Civil Service by the channel of the Cabinet Office*.'[148] Thus Hankey's successors had narrowed their sights in 'vetting' ministerial memoirs: their concern for the 'structure of government' had already been evidenced by the Cabinet Office's professed hope to review John Mackintosh's historical survey of modern Cabinet government.[149] Resident abroad at the time, Mackintosh – who had been given access to official materials which he thought worthless – resisted official importuning and published without review, although he recognized Cabinet Office objections to his listing the Cabinet's standing committees.[150]

Such a *modus operandi* left the way open to the former leaders of Britain's post-war governments to recount their experiences for posterity – and for profit, however deserved.[151] Despite the outcries from Labour back-benchers that the 'thirty-year rule' ought to apply to the use of public records by former ministers,[152] Harold Wilson – far from eschewing a 'double standard' – used the leisure of imposed absence from Downing Street to write a massive one volume account of his 1964–70 administration, surely drawing upon official records but veiled as *A Personal Record.* Obviously Wilson did not lack precedents, as Harold Macmillan had already followed in the multi-volume tradition of his Tory predecessors Churchill, who wrote only of the war years, and Anthony Eden. Among erstwhile premiers reconciled to life elsewhere than at No. 10 only Edward Heath and James Callaghan remain yet to be heard from; certainly Clement Attlee and Sir Alec Douglas-Home avoided detailed records, although the former sat for interviews which contain information on Cabinet controversies and criticisms of colleagues.[153] Nor have most former ministers shied from reflecting upon 'a job well done' at whatever departments they have headed: a procession of ministerial memoirs have revealed in varying degrees the inner workings of Cabinet government. Until recently, the leading contributor was Hugh Dalton, whose account of the Labour Cabinet from 1945 to 1950 drew heavily upon a diary – although with caution because of what could be generously described as his outspokenness in the diary. In publishing that volume in 1962, Dalton advised his readers that he intended to write frankly about colleagues and policies: 'When in doubt, publish.'[154]

Though few former ministers have written with Dalton's information and verve, generally the 'structure of government' has come into clearer focus, although the distortion of personality is difficult to disengage. It appears that only disinclination or an early death, as is the case on the one hand with Aneurin Bevan,[155] or on the other hand Iain Macleod or Anthony Crosland, inhibits the practice. While the Cabinet Office has sought to discourage discussion of the roles of civil servants, the Wilson regime grappled with the greater question of premature or excessive disclosure in ministerial memoirs: we are told that a Cabinet committee discussed the possibility of some form of mandatory censorship, although these discussions 'came to nothing.'[156] Clearly the leading figures of that regime took no self-denying ordinance, as the Prime Minister and his Foreign Secretary, George Brown, proved quick off the memoirist's mark.[157] Confidants of the Wilson administration soon brought 'inside,' if not official, knowledge to the public. Harold Wilson's long-term Private Secretary, Marcia Williams, penned memoirs sympathetic from the perspective of *Inside Number 10*; her account is revealing of the strife between Wilson's political staff and the civil servants, a dimension of the 'structure of government' otherwise in the shadows.[158] As the Williams book suggests, information concerning policies as well as personalities need not wait upon the publication of ministerial memoirs: active politicians can co-operate with biographers – whether or not the designation 'authorised' is attached – to ensure that their view of recent controversies, well within the closed period, is advanced. Thus no official documents appear to inform the biography of Denis Healey written by Bruce Reed and Geoffrey Williams, but Healey spoke his mind to them about the defence issues which the Wilson government confronted: divisions within the Cabinet over such a matter as the cancellation of the F–111, in which Healey fought a losing battle with the Prime Minister, were frankly discussed.[159]

Similar disclosures about the divisiveness of that government were found in the diary of the publishing magnate, Cecil King, who described his position as 'a seat in the front row of the political stalls.'[160] Yet King was more than an idle observer, as he freely offered his opinions to the Prime Minister, his colleagues, civil servants, and other highly placed officials.[161] The confidences were seemingly mutual, as King was made privy to insider sources: it has been alleged that the anonymous informants masked in his published diaries were Sir William Armstrong, Head of the Civil Service, and Sir Burke Trend, Secretary to the Cabinet.[162] If such confidences are irresponsibly given, the widespread suspicion that the advocates of 'closed government' manipulate secrecy to serve their own ends is reinforced.

Of course the latter type of memoir does not command the field in the fashion of ministerial memoirs. Thus the Cabinet Office has taken an interest mainly in the memoirs of former Cabinet ministers, informed military memoirs, those written by former diplomats and members of the Foreign Service, and memoirs written by former members of the Home Civil Service. Military memoirs were relatively full, in large measure because the war period had been treated specially at Churchill's insistence; although HMG had initially favored ministerial disclosures about the war to those penned by their military advisers, the latter had nonetheless related their cases, but as had been the case once before, military memoirs were a 'dying class' in the 1970s. Diplomatic memoirs had assumed a greater scope since the 1950s, when Vansittart, for instance, had worked with restrictions: a number of diaries kept in the inter-war and war period began to see the light of day, and acid observations about contemporaries often color these less-than-diplomatic accounts. Oliver Harvey's *War Diaries* extended criticism of contemporaries even to the King and Queen, published in her case while she lived.[163] Diplomats are free to review the documents which they had prepared, but they are unable to quote from such documents as fall within the closed period.[164] Treatment of personality is more restrained in memoirs than in diaries; such private records do not fall within the scope of the 'thirty-year rule,' but they are subject to the restrictions enumerated in the Radcliffe report.[165] Whatever the limitations of diplomatic memoirs, we have learned much more from them than from any counterpart records kept within the Home Civil Service, where Cabinet Office influence is strongest. Following upon Jones' revealing *Whitehall Diary* and Mallaby's *From My Level* a dearth has ensued, not surprisingly to be sure. Only the future will reveal if any of the functionaries since that time have kept diaries or wish to publish informed memoirs.

Among these several categories of memoirs, the major assault upon the maintenance of Cabinet secrecy came from within the Cabinet itself. The quarter ought not have been unexpected, because Richard Crossman, Minister of Housing in Wilson's first administration, had proclaimed – to one and all, it seems – his intention: 'All my colleagues knew of the diary I was keeping and of my determination to publish it as soon as possible. Apart from the lawyers, who feather their nests in other ways [than writing memoirs], none of them had any moral objection.'[166] Nonetheless the diary format itself represented a departure from form: ministers had kept diaries, but, as had been the case with Dalton (who, like Hankey, occasionally inserted retrospective commentary) or Macmillan,[167] the diary had been melded into a narrative, and the rougher edges of description could be smoothed either in rewriting or by Cabinet Office review. In addition, diaries had proved consistently more controversial, from the efforts of Hankey and Tom Jones to the disclosures of Alanbrooke on the one hand, and Cadogan and Harvey on the other. Surely it was the intimacy of Crossman's diary which attracted Cabinet Office attention, because his concern with events at the distance of less than a decade was hardly unprecedented. As well, Crossman's diaries included accounts of Cabinet discussions which others had handled obliquely. These aspects led both Harold Wilson and James Callaghan to implore Crossman not to publish his volume for the years 1964–6 until after the next general election. Heath's decision to go to the country in February 1974 thus set the scene for Wilson's return to Downing Street and Crossman's now-posthumous emergence as a diarist. His executors knew that Crossman had been unimpressed with the case against publication: 'Since ex-Cabinet Ministers are entitled to access to secret documents when they publish their memoirs, and rely for their accounts of Cabinet proceedings mainly on memory, how much to publish is not a matter of Government ruling, far less of the Official Secrets Act, but a concern of personal taste and personal conscience.'[168] Possibly the growing hostility towards the Official Secrets Act strengthened Crossman's resolve; personally, he appeared to view the statue with contempt.[169] By the same token, Crossman's attitude had to occasion distaste in Whitehall, since the Cabinet Office was resolved to protect the 'structure of government' from premature exposure. On two occasions during the Wilson administration, the Prime Minister had issued a confidential document detailing procedures prior to the publication of such memoirs which asserted that 'the principle of collective responsibility and the obligation not to disclose information acquired whilst holding ministerial office apply to former ministers who are contemplating the publication of material based upon their recollections of the conduct of Cabinet and Cabinet committee business in which they took part.'[170]

When Lord Chief Justice Widgery heard the government's case to enjoin the publication of Crossman's *Cabinet Diaries*, he concluded that ministerial understanding of the protection of such information varied and that no legal precedents existed 'to define the extent to which Cabinet proceedings should be treated as secret or confidential.'[171] Widgery noted that the practice of 'vetting,' initiated in Hankey's time, was 'almost always' followed a half-century later, and the Cabinet Office in effect waived the 'thirty-year rule' for former ministers, provided that their memoirs passed official muster. Even on such a controversial subject as the Suez expedition, partisan accounts had soon appeared: Eden to the fore, and Macmillan as well; Nutting had registered a dissenting report, under terms laid down by the Cabinet Office. Subsequently Pierson Dixon, Ambassador to the United Nations in 1956, recorded his view that 'we intervened by virtue of no clear and defensible principle, but, what was worse, gave a reason which was generally considered at best a lame excuse, at worst a conspiracy.'[172] Finally, the Foreign Secretary, Selwyn Lloyd, published his defence of British policy centering on Suez: while he defended Britain's motivation and denied knowledge of Israeli military planning, Lloyd's discussion of the intricacies of 'collusion' reveals the embarrassment which Britain reaped in its professed design to 'separate the combatants.'[173] Lloyd reported that convention dictated that only he could have access to the documents during the closed period;[174] thus the preferential treatment granted to Eden appears to have lapsed. It would seem idle to deny that these several accounts contained 'official' information on an event well within the closed period.

In a letter addressed to Crossman's literary executors, the Cabinet Secretary, Sir John Hunt, coupled this exemption granted in recognition of 'the personal responsibility of individual ministers' with the 'complimentary principle' of collective responsibility:

> the convention which permits former ministers to publish their memoirs is a logical and proper consequence of the second principle [collective responsibility]. It reflects a long and honourable tradition of British public life that individuals who have been publicly accountable in their own persons for their acts and

> policies are entitled to put their own versions of events on record. But they are expected to submit their texts to the authorities for clearance. This is not just to safeguard national security but to ensure that they do not indulge their right to defend the way in which they have discharged their responsibility to the point at which they endanger good government and the preservation of the confidentiality which is necessary to maintain collective responsibility and mutual trust.[175]

In his own mind, the Cabinet Secretary – who had been sent the 'text' in question – had no doubt that 'the volume as a whole is in conflict with the obligation to collective discussion.' Hunt specified the 'very detailed account of Cabinet and Cabinet committee meetings,' but he objected also to the diary's recounting 'many other conversations where the other party would clearly have been reasonably entitled to assume that confidentiality would be preserved in the public interest.' Such conversations, we have noted, had been routine in many memoirs, but Sir John was particularly concerned, it appears, with protecting the confidentiality of Crossman's dealings with civil servants, which he feared could seriously affect the whole basis of that relationship.

Nor is Hunt's point a specious one, because the temptation to opt for a cautious course in advising ministers on policy or personnel matters would be strong for senior civil servants, if their advice were to be subjected to criticism in diaries or memoirs published only a few years later. Equity too has long been a problem, because civil servants are disbarred from commenting on ministerial actions either within the closed period or as long as they remain in the Service. Given the doctrine of ministerial responsibility, one can conclude that it would be in the interest of the Civil Service if discussion of the relationship were altogether proscribed. Yet while the point tells in favor of such silence for a period of time, ultimately the public interest dictates an acknowledgment of the realities of that relationship.

The Lord Chief Justice paid close attention to concerns raised on behalf of the Civil Service; he concluded that proscriptions should apply to the disclosure of discussions relating to the promotion or transfer of senior civil servants.[176] He was also acquainted with the fact that the post-war generation of memoirists had by and large protected the anonymity of civil servants – not surprisingly, if such was (as alleged) the price of Cabinet Office approval. Crossman, however, refused to accept the view that civil servants were 'silent, neutral and politically uncommitted,' and he judged that no accurate description of his work as a Cabinet Minister was possible without an account of their role. His very first diary entry dealt with his impressions of the higher civil servants within the ministry and in the minister's Private Office. One of the linchpins of his first volume is a detailed record of his relationship with the Permanent Secretary, Dame Evelyn Sharp, whom he recognized as a formidable, accomplished, and opinionated civil servant:

She is rather like Beatrice Webb in her attitude to life, to the Left in the sense of wanting improvement and social justice quite passionately and yet a tremendous patrician and utterly contemptuous and arrogant, regarding local authorities as children which she has to examine and rebuke for their failures. She sees the ordinary human being as incapable of making a sensible decision.[177]

Obviously Sir John Hunt had not to read far in the *Cabinet Diaries* to discover the shattering of the confidential relationship between minister and adviser.

Although *The Sunday Times* was willing to delete all critical references to specific civil servants, save the most senior, in the serialized treatment of the memoirs which preceded publication, the Cabinet Secretary refused his sanction. The editors proceeded, claiming that Hunt's rules were unduly restrictive in view of the comments which his predecessor, Sir Burke Trend, had voiced to the Franks Committee, where he had treated the Secretary's role in 'vetting' as the exercise of suasion if a former minister abused collective responsibility: 'if he insists on telling his story in the way that he wants to tell it, there is no more that one could, or I think, should try to do.'[178] Sir John Hunt did not regard that comment as authoritative,[179] but his protagonists reciprocated: the first extract from the *Cabinet Diaries* was published in *The Sunday Times* of 26 January 1975.

In the furor which followed publication, several aspects of the case merit attention. The *New Statesman* proclaimed a view that Crossman's effort was no different in kind from other ministerial memoirs: the journal succinctly compared Crossman's account of the first Cabinet meeting of the Labour government with Wilson's earlier account, and it found a parallel also in the former's treatment of his Permanent Secretary and the Prime Minister's caustic observations on the role of the Governor of the Bank of England, Lord Cromer, in that regime's early days: 'Both authors may have been right or both may have been wrong: what no one – not even the cabinet secretary . . . can plausibly assert is that one was within the rules and the other not.'[180] Clearly there were surface similarities, although the Cabinet Office particularly objected to Crossman's diary format, for reasons discussed above; on the other count, Cromer was certainly freer to defend policies of the Bank of England, and his own role, than were the civil heads of the departments. Nonetheless, according to the *New Statesman*'s view, the precedent of informed ministerial memoirs was such that Crossman's account gained its protection thereby.

Such 'precedents' are, however, weak relative to statute law, and in the past HMG had threatened prosecution under statutory provisions if memoirs were disruptive of established doctrines. Yet another interesting aspect of the Crossman case is that the government did not initiate prosecution under the Official Secrets Act, informing the publishers that 'this is not a matter which depends on the Official Secrets Act (though sometimes this will be relevant).'[181] Instead, the Attorney-General sought to enjoin publication in a proceeding at common law, an action which impressed as odd, although *The Times* discerned a rationale: 'there was a perfectly clear if utterly ridiculous statute dealing with the matter. The Attorney General for fear of involving himself in greater difficulties did not choose to proceed under the relevant statute . . . it is a pity to substitute the Common Law for the will of Parliament; it is even more a pity in a matter vital to the conduct of political life.'[182] In other words, the Official Secrets Act had fallen into such disrepute that HMG feared for the success of a prosecution brought under its aegis; although section 2 had already outlived its usefulness, the Crossman case stands as the *coup de grâce*. Nor did the government place any stock in the Privy Counsellor's Oath, as the Lord Chief Justice commented that it was not 'seriously relied upon.' Despite their deep differences, *The Sunday Times* and the Cabinet Secretary co-operated in the serialization of the diaries, although the journal regarded the latter's judgment as advisory: while they accepted a number of suggested excisions, the editors were 'clearly asserting their right to be their own judges of what matter was eventually included for publication.'[183] Such was one of the setbacks suffered by the Cabinet Secretary, who had no choice but to bide his time; in the meantime, the publications continued and, in the words of a Crossman partisan, Hunt 'has simply had to watch all the ground rules he laid down for publication . . . being steadily eroded by a sustained campaign of attrition.'[184]

Crossman's literary executors were intent upon publication of the *Cabinet Diaries* without reference to Cabinet Office rules.[185] Their refusal to accommodate Sir John Hunt met with the government's determination to resolve the question in the courts. In judging the case, the Lord Chief Justice provided some satisfaction for both camps: most immediate was his refusal of an injunction to restrain publication of the first volume; yet as a general rule, Widgery opined, the publication of Cabinet discussions could be restrained in the courts. We need not here restate the precedents which his opinion drew upon in extending the principle of 'confidentiality' into affairs of state, but it is germane to note that he recognized and strove to balance two conflicting views of the public interest. In the first place, there exists an interest in preserving the secrecy of discussions among Cabinet ministers, and between them and civil servants, so that all may speak their minds freely without fearing that controversial opinions would soon be published; in the second, an interest resides in opening the processes of government so that the governed were fully aware of the decisions taken in their name. Certainly the recognition of a concept of the public interest different from that which HMG had traditionally invoked to mask the 'structure of government' represented progress for those who looked to a more 'open' model of government. For Widgery the question remained: how to balance the two principles?

Yet the *Cabinet Diaries* did not pose a daunting problem: 'I am far from convinced,' he wrote, 'that he [the Attorney-General] has made out a case that the public interest requires such a Draconian remedy when due regard is had to another public interest, such as freedom of speech.' Sympathetic to the need for 'confidentiality' within the Cabinet, the Lord Chief Justice saw Cabinet secrecy not as an absolute but a relative matter: 'Some secrets require a high degree of protection for a short time. Others may require protection until a new political generation has taken over.' Thus there could be no 'single rule of thumb' for Cabinet papers and discussions alike. The Crossman case, or any other, required settlement with respect both to general principles and specific impact. Those principles he intertwined with the discussion of his findings in the Crossman case:

1. In my judgment the Attorney General has made out his claim that the expression of individual opinions by Cabinet ministers in the course of Cabinet discussion are matters of confidence, the publication of which can be restrained by the court when this is clearly necessary in the public interest.
2. The maintenance of the doctrine of joint [collective] responsibility within the Cabinet is in the public interest, and the application of that doctrine might be prejudiced by premature disclosure of the views of individual ministers.
3. There must, however, be a limit in time after which the confidential character of the information, and the duty of the court to restrain publication, will lapse . . . It may, of course, be difficult, in a particular case, to say at what point the material loses its confidential character, on the ground that publication will no longer undermine the doctrine of joint Cabinet responsibility. It is this difficulty which prompts some to argue that Cabinet discussions should retain their confidential character for a long and arbitrary period such as 30 years, or even for all time, but this seems to be excessively restrictive. The court should intervene only in the clearest of cases where the continuing confidentiality of the material can be demonstrated. In less clear cases reliance must be placed on the good sense and good taste of the minister or ex-minister concerned.
4. . . . A minister is, no doubt, responsible for his department and accountable for its errors even though the individual fault is to be found in his subordinates. In these circumstances to disclose the fault of the subordinate may amount to cowardice or bad taste, but I can find no ground for saying that either the Crown or the individual civil servant has an enforceable right to have the advice which he gives treated as confidential for all time.[186]

In the Crossman case, the 'limit in time' had been reached and passed, Widgery concluded: ten years and three general elections had intervened, and the weight of the evidence 'had not satisfied me that publication would in any way inhibit free and open discussion in Cabinet hereafter.'

The way lay open for the publication in full of the first volume of Crossman's *Cabinet Diaries*.

As the decision had both given something to and taken something from both camps, a divided opinion on its merits was to be expected. In any event, the question of ministerial and civil service accounts subsequently reverted to a political settlement, with the report of the Radcliffe Committee charged to investigate the genre. The results of that inquiry are discussed below, but the residue of the legal settlement of the Crossman case cannot be forgotten: the Lord Chief Justice had enunciated a concept of the public interest which was not shared by the government or its senior civil servants. Since the Radcliffe Committee in its turn did not find legal sanctions appropriate as a means of proscribing ministerial memoirs which compromised the doctrine of 'confidentiality,' HMG will have to assume the burden of proof if they seek to stem some future breach; Widgery suggested that such an onus could only be assumed in the 'clearest of cases.' Similarly, his ruling specified a time limit for the breaching of the doctrine, and the precedent of a decade in the Crossman case cannot be ignored. On the other hand, he gave legal standing to the principle of 'confidentiality' in public affairs, and the privileged status of civil servants had been confirmed – though the protection was to be temporally limited.[187]

With the publication in full of the first volume of the *Cabinet Diaries* in December 1975, a number of senior civil servants whose paths had crossed with the former Minister of Housing felt the stings of his criticism; in their behalf, the Tory peer, Lord Hailsham, protested most tellingly that the volume recorded Crossman's 'constant warfare with, and distrust of, the Civil Servants who seek to save all Ministers from their worst faults with varying degrees of success.'[188] The initial reactions to the *Cabinet Diaries* are interesting, as reviewer after reviewer shared with A. J. P. Taylor a disappointment that 'there is not a single line from Cabinet papers and no revelations of Cabinet secrets other than those known at the time.'[189] While some Cabinet 'secrets' may be known to journalists and other informants of the government, surely Crossman revealed confidences in a degree of specificity which was by no means common knowledge. Nor were Cabinet secrets the only concern of the authorities: 'confidentiality' had been upheld in Widgery's opinion, although he ruled that the need for its protection had lapsed in this case. Thus a comment of Michael Ratcliffe best depicts Crossman's contribution in this regard rather than as a purveyor of Cabinet 'secrets': 'They [the *Diaries*] will embarrass to greater or lesser degree Crossman's ex-colleagues in the ministry and every member of the first two Wilson Cabinets. But they will not tell them anything they did not know at the time or the rest of us anything that we have not a right to know now.'[190]

It may well be argued that Crossman thought his *Cabinet Diaries* a blow on behalf of 'open government,' as well as against undue Cabinet secrecy. To be sure Sir John Hunt viewed it as offensive in both regards, since it exposed the ministerial–adviser relationship and thus compromised the 'structure of government.' Yet Crossman's purpose ought to be noted: 'My ambition,' he had written only two months before his death, 'was to write a book which fulfilled for our generation the functions of Bagehot's *English Constitution* a hundred years ago by disclosing the secret operations of government, which are concealed by the thick masses of foliage which we call the myth of democracy.'[191] Prior to 1964 Crossman had no practical experience in the business of Cabinet government, and some of his diary observations impress as much for their naiveté as their detail.[192] Both qualities contributed to a day-to-day revelation of the 'structure of government' quite unlike Bagehot's approach: Crossman claimed to find evidence to confirm his notion that Cabinet authority had declined – a Cabinet member, he was not privy to the workings of inner Cabinet government.[193] With concerns almost exclusively departmental, Crossman contended that for the duration of the first Wilson regime, he shared only nominally the Cabinet's collective responsibility. He noted that the basic decisions were made in Cabinet committees, although he came to question whether ministerial committees were themselves decisive, since counterpart committees of permanent officials appeared to form a 'rival administration' of civil servants.[194] The care which contemporary government takes to mask the committee system[195] indicates the intrusion upon the 'structure of government' which Crossman's account posed to the Cabinet Office and HMG.

Sir John Hunt had to be concerned with Crossman's commentary on yet another portion of that structure, namely the role of the Cabinet Secretary: his advisory capacity captured Crossman's attention in the aftermath of Wilson's successful appeal to the country in 1966, as Cabinet members awaited the decision whether they would be asked to join in the next government. In contrast, Hunt's predecessor, Sir Burke Trend, sat with the Prime Minister at 'the centre of power:' 'I wrote in my Introduction to *The English Constitution* that the Prime Minister shares his power with the head of the Civil Service. Certainly, Helsby doesn't play that kind of role. It's Burke Trend who shares power with Harold, not the head of the Treasury.'[196] Crossman also challenged the secretarial role played by Trend, in recording his dissatisfaction with the accuracy of the minutes kept of Cabinet deliberations; in regard to the Prime Minister's initiative in revising the 'fifty-year rule,' which it is safe to infer the Cabinet Office disliked, Crossman alleged that the Secretary's minute revealed only 'what we should have said if we had done as they had wished.'[197]

Several years later, at a time when Crossman indicated the tenor of his criticism of such practices, Harold Wilson protested the thesis that 'Cabinet was controlled by a conspiracy between the prime minister and the secretary of the Cabinet, who sat down the day after the meeting virtually to cook the Cabinet Conclusions,' insisting that he personally had never seen them before circulation and rarely consulted them at all.[198] Crossman freed the premier from the charge of collusion, but he insisted that the development of 'the decision-drafting technique' possibly constituted 'the great secret of [contemporary] Cabinet Government,' explaining: 'Sometimes as a member of the Cabinet you don't realise that you lost the battle; it is not your impression of what happened. But once it is there, written in the minutes, it *has* been decided – against you.' Crossman recognized that minutes were taken not in a verbatim fashion but instead to depict 'the sense of the discussions and of the decisions,' enabling the Secretariat to alter the substance of decisions in the course of preparing directives.[199] The problem, as we have seen, is a perennial one, because clarity of directive is likely to be at odds with the deliberative process, a point remarked upon in 1953 by Harold Macmillan, who made light of Cabinet Minutes depicting a group 'so intellectually disciplined that they argued each issue methodically and logically through to a set of neat and precise conclusions.'[200] Because the problem is inherent in the system of recording Conclusions which the Cabinet has traditionally followed, Crossman's 'discovery' may be routine, although his allegations of transformation and suppression cut much deeper than the impact of the practice which we have traced. Ultimately the Cabinet Minutes of the 1960s and 1970s will have to be tested against the various ministerial accounts in order to test the validity of Crossman's allegations.

Questioning the role of the Cabinet Secretary – Wilson remarked ruefully of Crossman's continuing belief that 'the Cabinet secretary was capable of doing the necessary cooking of the Minutes without my help'[201] – was a means for Crossman to inquire generally about the role of leading civil servants: in a sense, he posed the question, to whom do their loyalties belong?[202] There is implicit in his work another vital question, who – after all – governs Britain? Above all else, these questions explain the hostility which Hankey's latter-day successor showed towards the publication of *Cabinet Diaries*.

Crossman's volumes must be viewed as a defeat of the Cabinet Office's excessive claim to defend Cabinet secrecy; however, the faltering in its control of ministerial memoirs proved to be of short duration, as the political process restored to the Cabinet Secretary the central role which Widgery's judicial ruling had compromised. The custodians of Cabinet secrecy had not been idle while the *Cabinet Diaries* were *sub judice*: HMG opened a second front through the appointment of a Committee of Privy Counsellors on Ministerial Memoirs, chaired by Lord Radcliffe. Charged with considering the general principles of memoirs written by former ministers and the means by which these might be implemented, the seven-man committee, which included a former head of the Home Civil Service, Lord Armstrong, and Lord Franks, who had chaired the inquiry into section 2 of the Official Secrets Act, proceeded with unusual dispatch to complete its report in eight months. In short order, after scrutiny by a Cabinet committee and the Cabinet, the Prime Minister announced his government's full acceptance of the report on the day of its publication.[203] Since the announcement came by way of a written reply to a parliamentary question, Wilson's government did not solicit any comprehensive discussion of the report. The Radcliffe Committee advised that a special standing be given to ministerial memoirs, subject to certain conditions; in such a spirit Wilson remarked that the new conventions 'should properly be regarded as concessions made to the [memoir's] author rather than restrictions imposed upon him.'[204]

Certainly the diary of a former Minister of Housing was in the Radcliffe Committee's mind when they concluded that a prohibition upon keeping a diary of public affairs would be wrong as well as unrealistic, because such accounts served legitimate purposes:

> The reasons for making them are various and individual: as the mnemonics of future compositions, as personal experience only to be made public at some indeterminate future date, and even as an immediate private discharge of the psychological tensions generated by public office.
>
> It is not the making of a diary which matters; it is the timing of its publication, particularly when on his death the text is handed in the raw to a man's executors with the overriding duty of exploiting its value as an asset of his estate.[205]

The Radcliffe Committee also concluded that published diaries ought not to impair the confidential relationships among ministers and between them and their advisers, despite 'all the pressures of the day in favour of openness of government and public participation in the formation of public policies.' Repeatedly they concluded that 'the principle . . . [of] confidentiality in all that goes to the internal formulation of Government policy' was necessary, most compelling of all in the relationship between statesmen and civil servants:

> Indeed the case of the departmental adviser is stronger than any other since it is his professional duty to tender his advice when so required, and in our view it is critically important that he should be free to do so in the assurance that the confidence that he has given will be respected . . . the minister must observe a scrupulous reticence with regard to the attitudes and personalities of those who have served him in office . . . It seems to us wholly repugnant that he should at a later date regard himself as free to record this material and discuss it in the course of a public account of his Ministerial experience.[206]

Reticence thus became a 'public duty' for ministers preparing their memoirs in regard to attitudes expressed by advisers or ministerial colleagues on matters of government business and also in assessing civil servants who had served under the minister or whose suitability for other posts had fallen to him for evaluation: Dame Evelyn Sharp and Sir Burke Trend had not been pilloried in vain, after all.

Tempting though it is to see in these recommendations a Civil Service placed beyond criticism, on balance the Radcliffe Committee protected a legitimate concern which serves the public interest. To legitimize criticism of senior civil servants, particularly those still active, is to place them in an invidious position, because they are not free to defend themselves from the charges brought by former ministers who may themselves be arrogant, unprincipled, insensitive, or incompetent. Yet the grant of the freedom of reply to the Civil Service is nowhere seriously entertained, and thus some other alternative is needed. In the long run, that alternative is well served by such memoirs as Hankey's, which incorporated a view of ministerial foibles and fallacies long after the nature of his relationship with them ceased to matter as a political force. In the shorter run, the alternative is the type of temporal compromise incorporated in Widgery's opinion: at some point, the protection afforded to civil servants must yield to the public's 'right to know' how government is carried on. Both ministers and advisers must then stand scrutiny, in their recommendations no less than in their interaction. The problem, of course, is where to draw the line.

Before offering an opinion, the Radcliffe Committee pointed to other justified restrictions upon ministerial accounts, which ought not endanger national security nor damage Britain's relations with other countries. As no former minister was competent to judge these matters at the time of proposed publication, there re-emerged the Cabinet Secretary as custodian of those vital interests; ex-ministers were expected to submit any manuscript to the Secretary, with a right of appeal to the Prime Minister. The Radcliffe Committee freed the Cabinet Secretary to approve such memoirs at any time, provided that national security, diplomatic relations and the bounds of reticence were not breached.[207] If confidential relations were exposed, fifteen years would have to pass prior to publication, although concerns for security and diplomacy might in some cases merit protection for an even longer period. 'Confidentiality' would lapse after such a period, except with regard to individuals still in the public service.[208]

Whether or not justifiably, historical concern with the 'structure of government' was curtly dismissed in the assertion that 'government is not to be conducted in the interests of history.'[209] Few historians would dispute a literal reading of such a precept, but such an attitude will do nothing to resolve the anomaly in the form of a 'double standard': while ministers may range across recent history at the remove of fifteen years, and in many cases far less, historians will continue to work with official documents at the distance of thirty years. As a result, 'insider' accounts will continue to color recent British history. While some historians may press for a contraction of the closed period, not all are confident that such access would facilitate the conduct of government business, which remains the prime concern. In this vein, D. C. Watt has written: 'There is a body of historical opinion who feel that access at dates of less than 25 years may be purchased too dearly if it results in a distortion or decrease in completeness of the official record as experience suggests may have been the case with some American records.'[210] Since ministerial memoirs within the closed period are now sanctioned by government policy, little is likely to be gained by protesting the 'double standard'; historians would do better to weigh carefully whether the 'thirty-year rule' serves best to balance availability of full and complete records against quicker access. Yet this dilemma ought not deter them from pressing for a fuller flow of information from the government to the public on contemporary issues, although the selection of such materials will remain in the hands of HMG. The two concerns must be differentiated: the public's 'right to know' is separable from the historian's right to investigate the ways in which government policies are made – at a time consistent with the effective functioning of government.

The Radcliffe Committee, composed predominantly of 'insiders,' did not attempt to portray this conflict of legitimate interests; instead, they chose to regard 'open government' as no more than a descriptive phrase and took refuge in the meaningless assertion that no one seriously thought that every incident in the processes of government ought to be conducted in the open. Perhaps they found solace in the *reductio ad absurdum*, but the Lord Chief Justice concurrently acknowledged the legitimacy of the 'right to know.' To deny 'open government' a role within the British political process is hardly to serve the ends of twentieth-century government. In accepting the Radcliffe report, HMG struck a particular balance between the contending claims to 'open' and 'closed' models of government: clearly the bias runs towards the latter. Such a preference is defended in the name of effective government and in the implicit recognition that senior civil servants serve as advisers as well as executors of official policy, however hallowed the notion of ministerial responsibility. It is precisely in this context that the need for 'confidentiality' has lately won independent standing. The counterclaim of the public's 'right to know' is not about to disappear, and the pressure for earlier release of official documents is likely to persist, since principle is involved no less than timing. The point was well put by a leading article, critical of the

Radcliffe report, published in *New Law Journal*: 'Anyone who claims to accept that public discussion about the major matters of national importance has a place in political life at all is being totally insincere if he suggests that material that is relevant to such discussion should be kept from the public until it is no longer a matter of contemporary interest.'[211] Of course, HMG need not breach 'confidentiality' in order to improve public access to materials which would inform the contemporary debate. For that reason, the balance between opposing concepts of the public interest deserves a more careful evaluation than it received at the hands of the Radcliffe Committee.

In fact, it is another ministerial publication which has called into question the official hope that discussion of the role of civil servants could be virtually eschewed. In the quest for 'confidentiality,' the Privy Counsellors concluded that a fifteen year period would serve to protect all ministerial relations save that with their advisers, who needed such protection as long as they remained in the Civil Service. Indeed, they characterized these 'obligations of reticence' as 'public duties' binding upon all former ministers. They acknowledged that legal mechanisms were inappropriate for the protection of 'confidentiality'; here, at least, the lesson of the Crossman case was clear. Thus the obligation was cast in moral terms, although it was to be reinforced by a rule that upon or leaving office a minister should have his attention explicitly called to this duty. Ministers also would be instructed to leave testamentary instructions that any posthumous publication of their private records of Cabinet business ought not flout the understanding which they had thus accepted. Even if the undertaking were not universally honored, the Radcliffe Committee concluded that the new obligation could withstand an occasional breach.

Such a breach is much in evidence in the recent publication by Crossman's colleague and friend, Barbara Castle, who published her own Cabinet diary at a remove of but a half-decade from the events described in copious detail. Her account gives every appearance of lifting the curtains of 'confidentiality' from her dealings alike with civil servants and ministers, within and without the Cabinet room. By no means as critical of civil servants as Crossman – indeed she is protective of the reputations of her own departmental advisers – Castle's description of the views of her associates shattered the bounds of reticence proposed by the Radcliffe Committee, whose report she viewed from the first with scorn.[212]

Time is required to test the hope that those who accepted the new convention upon entering the Cabinet will honor its terms, but it is difficult to conclude that those who feel that the public interest is served by bringing the processes of late twentieth-century government into clearer focus through such accounts will be either impressed or restrained by the claims made in the name of 'confidentiality.' Agreement even among 'men or women who *ex hypothesi* have held high office under the Crown and responsible positions in public life'[213] may not prevail if ministers conclude that higher principles are at stake. Nor is the convention likely to deter those few former ministers alert to exploit the value of such accounts while issues are fresh in the public mind. The recommendations of the Privy Counsellors, experienced men all, will undergo the test of practice in years to come.

In the meantime, HMG derived satisfaction from the report of official memoirs: the Attorney-General who had witnessed Widgery's rejection of portions of his argument concluded that 'if the Lord Chief Justice had taken the 15-year period which Radcliffe has taken, the action [to enjoin publication] would have succeeded in toto instead of merely, as now, establishing the principle I was contending for.'[214] Whatever the degree of the present disposition to 'closed government' on the part of those who govern Britain – politicians and civil servants alike – portions of the public are not about to yield their 'right to know' more about the government carried on in their behalf.

To this point, then, the study of a man and an institution has brought us: the career of Sir Maurice Hankey has served as connective tissue, linking his role as first Cabinet Secretary to the development of that agency of Cabinet government, and relating the systematized procedures for the maintenance of its records to the question of the right of public access to those materials. By a strange irony, Hankey's own difficulties in securing governmental assent for the publication of his war memoirs were rooted in the restrictive decisions taken twenty years earlier by the National Government, at Hankey's own urging. In the conflict between administrative concern for 'closed government' and the public's claim to the 'right to know,' the relevant historical context is Hankey's manipulation of the Official Secrets Act and, in turn, the barrier which that legislation posed to his own memoirs and those of others. In tracing the Cabinet Office's role as custodian of Cabinet records, and in noting the license given to former Cabinet ministers to write about their experiences in office before the records were made available, we have moved well beyond Hankey's retirement in 1938. Thereafter his efforts to obtain HMG's approval for the publication of *The Supreme Command, 1914–1918* shed a unique light upon the question of the 'confidential' relationship between ministers and their civil service advisers. The custody of Cabinet secrecy has proved to be a complex task, in which the Cabinet Office has, understandably, opted for precepts of 'closed government.' Yet progress towards a more 'open' model has been reflected in the legislative initiatives of 1958 and 1967, which have served to secure public access to Cabinet records on a systematic basis; judicial intervention in the process has lately played a part as well.

We have attempted here no characterization of the role of the present-day Cabinet Office, save in its capacity as watch-dog of Cabinet secrecy, in which regard some information – though not the records themselves – has fortuitously become available. What has been related, for the first time in a comprehensive political and institutional setting, is the development of the Cabinet Secretariat between 1916 and 1938, as that body assumed a number of functions related to the business of the modern Cabinet. Though one moves into the post-Second World War era with less confidence, one can infer a substantial measure of continuity in the operations of the Cabinet Office, an institutional continuity, bridged to be sure by the War Cabinet Secretariat, which is likely to be confirmed as the relevant documents are released. Nonetheless, Hankey's own departure from Whitehall Gardens, barely a year before the outbreak of that war, serves to demarcate a lengthy, indeed decisive, period in the development of the Secretariat: decisive precisely because the roots planted by the Lloyd George regime proved deeper and more enduring than most of his war-time reforms.

Where his successors differed from Hankey lay in the type and style of the undoubted influence which the first Cabinet Secretary exerted in dealing with his political masters. Though Hankey typically resorted to an 'indirect approach' his influence has been assessed in this account, because he left a personal record in the form of a diary which supplements the official papers which his office was charged with collecting. In view of the stated opposition of his successors to the maintenance of such a personal record, it is unlikely that 'insider' accounts will in future emanate from the Cabinet Office. Insofar as the valuable private diaries of Hankey and Tom Jones are concerned, the precedent is now that such diaries ought not be kept by the confidants of ministers. Even if the contention that since Hankey's time the work of the Cabinet Office has been regularized is ultimately sustained by Cabinet records, the loss of such informed sources will prove a matter for historical regret: the development of a prime ministerial personal *cabinet* within No. 10 Downing Street, initiated by Harold Wilson in 1974 and continued by his successors, Labour and Conservative alike, is an aspect of modern Cabinet government which would be well served by such unofficial commentary.[215]

Another significant question concerns the particular role of the Secretary to the Cabinet, especially the manner and import of his influence; without a personal record, his manner of exerting influence will not yield readily to analysis. Yet the question of his influence among ministers and upon the form of the Cabinet Minutes remains a vital one. Because of the alleged utilization of the Cabinet Office as an agency of prime ministerial government – the charge is not a new one, but Crossman's account demands historical scrutiny – the question is relevant. If in fact a basic change has occurred in the responsibilities of the Cabinet Secretary – whether in heading once more the Civil Service or in providing institutional shelter for the secret services[216] – arguably contemporary Britain has a 'right to know' the range of Sir Robert Armstrong's responsibilities and the manner of his accountability. Perhaps all the more so than in the past, since it is doubtful that his influence will answer to future historical scrutiny in a similar way to that of his former predecessor, Sir Maurice Hankey.

Notes

INTRODUCTION

1 For that argument, Michael Davie, 'Notebook,' *The Observer*, 14 November 1976.
2 The suggestion that, with one possible exception, the 'Cabinet diary' approach of Crossman and Barbara Castle has exhausted itself within the ranks of the several Labour regimes led by Harold Wilson is implicit in a review of Castle's volume for 1974–6 by Michael Foot ('"To set diary against diary is to spread endless misapprehension,"' *The Listener*, 104: 386–8; 25 September 1980), who himself takes a decidedly negative view of the practice. What the future will bring from former Conservative ministers only time, and the suasion of 'confidentiality,' will tell.
3 S. S. Wilson, *The Cabinet Office to 1945* (London, 1975), p. 6.
4 Harold Wilson, *The Governance of Britain* (New York, 1976), pp. 96–7.

I. THE ORIGINS OF THE CABINET SECRETARIAT

1 David Lloyd George, *War Memoirs*, vol. II (Boston, 1933), p. 369.
2 Hankey Papers (Churchill College, Cambridge), Hankey Diary, 16 November 1916, which may be less complete than Lloyd George's recollection. According to Hankey, he had acquainted Prime Minister Asquith of his discussions with Lloyd George concerning reform of the system of government. (Lord Hankey, *Diplomacy by Conference* (London, 1946), p. 58.)
3 Cameron Hazlehurst, *Politicians at War: July 1914 to May 1915* (London, 1971), p. 16, for Lloyd George's priority.
4 Quoted by Basil Collier, *Brasshat: A Biography of Field-Marshal Sir Henry Wilson, 1864–1922* (London, 1961), p. 208.
5 Quoted by John Evelyn Wrench, *Alfred Lord Milner: The Man of No Illusions, 1854–1925* (London, 1958), p. 300.
6 Quoted by P. A. Lockwood, 'Milner's Entry into the War Cabinet, December 1916,' *Historical Journal*, 7: 120 (no. 1, 1964).
7 Leo Amery, *My Political Life*, vol. II, *1914–1929* (London, 1953), pp. 81–2. Dawson, more properly Robinson until his change of name in 1917, was editor of *The Times* and had served under Milner in South Africa.
8 Quoted by A. M. Gollin, *Proconsul in Politics: A Study of Lord Milner in Opposition and Power* (New York, 1964), p. 308.

9 Hankey's description: *The Supreme Command, 1914–1918* (2 vols., London, 1961), vol. I, pp. 238–9.

10 Quoted by Sir Llewellyn Woodward, *Great Britain and the War of 1914–1918* (London, 1967), p. 48. That those gentlemen's ladies were involved is clear in Kitchener's remark to Hankey: 'If only they will divorce their wives, I will gladly tell them everything.' (Hankey Diary, 11 September 1915.)

11 Quoted by Peter Fraser, *Lord Esher: A Political Biography* (London, 1973), p. 265.

12 Woodward, *Great Britain and the War*, p. 49.

13 For the setting of this 'very stormy meeting' of the Cabinet on 15 April 1915, see Edward David, ed., *Inside Asquith's Cabinet: From the Diaries of Charles Hobhouse* (New York, 1977), pp. 235–7. (Hereafter cited as *Hobhouse Diaries.*) Hobhouse was Postmaster-General at this time.

14 Christopher Addison, *Four and a Half Years* (2 vols., London, 1934), vol. I, p. 194; 17 April 1916.

15 John Barnes and David Nicholson, eds., *The Leo Amery Diaries*, vol. I, *1896–1929* (London, 1980), p. 123; 21 July 1915.

16 Quoted, Randolph Churchill, *Lord Derby: King of Lancashire* (New York, 1960), p. 215. Balfour allegedly characterized Lloyd George as 'the only man in the Cabinet who can do anything – the others just talk' more than a year earlier. Frances Stevenson, *Lloyd George: A Diary*, ed. A. J. P. Taylor (New York, 1971), p. 35; 25 March 1915.

17 For Balfour's recognition, Kenneth Young, *Arthur James Balfour* (London, 1963), pp. 368–9.

18 Kenneth O. Morgan, *The Age of Lloyd George* (New York, 1971), p. 55, who adds that Lloyd George's gain was 'sedulously fostered by his allies in the press.'

19 *Journals and Letters of Reginald, Viscount Esher*, vol. IV, *1916–1930*, ed. Oliver, Viscount Esher (London, 1938), p. 39.

20 Lord Riddell, *Lord Riddell's War Diary, 1914–1918* (London, n.d. [1933]), p. 234, reporting a conversation of 4 May 1919.

21 Hans Daalder, *Cabinet Reform in Britain, 1914–1963* (Stanford, 1963), p. 27.

22 In the crisis of December 1916, Hankey's diary, printed in full by Stephen Roskill, *Hankey: Man of Secrets*, vol. I, *1877–1918* (London, 1970), pp. 323–30, reveals a considerable distrust of Lloyd George's associations, particularly with the press.

23 Quoted in *The Political Diaries of C. P. Scott, 1911–1928*, ed. Trevor Wilson (Ithaca, NY, 1970), p. 215; 6–8 June 1916.

24 Hankey Diary, 7 December 1915.

25 *Ibid.*, 10 November 1916. Roskill (*Hankey*, vol. I, pp. 317–18) prints portions of the outburst, but he omits Hankey's account of the extraordinary casual behavior of ministers in a crucial phase of the war.

26 Quoted by Roy Jenkins, *Asquith* (London, 1963), p. 429; Asquith to Lloyd George, 1 December 1916. The premier's claim to 'excellent work' despite these structural defects impresses as disingenuous.

27 Frances Stevenson, *The Years that are Past* (London, 1967), p. 84, illustrates from a partisan recollection of the last Cabinet prior to Asquith's resignation: 'There are three different versions, so Ministers said, of what had been the decision upon a debate (in the Cabinet) on the Air Ministry. And nothing was definitely decided.'

28 Accounts by Hazlehurst and Peter Lowe, 'The Rise to the Premiership, 1914–1916,' in *Lloyd George: Twelve Essays*, ed. A. J. P. Taylor (New York, 1971), serve to convince that, in Lowe's words, 'paradoxically, Lloyd George achieved the office of prime minister, long the ultimate object of his ambition, at a time when he did not want or expect to achieve it' (p. 95).
29 Hankey Diary, 9 November 1916. Hankey put Law's words in direct quotation, because they indicated a 'very precarious' political situation.
30 Quoted by Lloyd George, *War Memoirs*, vol. I (Boston, 1933), p. 587; memorandum submitted by Lloyd George, Bonar Law, Sir Edward Carson and Sir Max Aitken, 1 December 1916.
31 Lowe, 'Rise to the Premiership,' p. 124.
32 The alternative is only fleetingly suggested in Lloyd George's response to a suggestion voiced on 25 November by Frances Stevenson, expressing her preference for a 'smash-up': 'D[avid] says that Derby is of the same opinion. I think D. has his doubts about it too.' (*Lloyd George: A Diary*, p. 128.)
33 *Scott Diaries*, p. 245; 4 December 1916. Fisher's judgment was proved incorrect, as Hankey was to 'transfer' his loyalties on eight occasions involving six premiers; Fisher thought that Hankey had on an earlier occasion 'sold him out' in order to protect Asquith. Scott conveyed the sentiment to Lloyd George.
34 Hankey Diary, respectively 3 and 2 December 1916; yet only weeks earlier Hankey had thought that a dictatorship might be Britain's only way out.
35 For a succinct description of Asquith's reversal of position, see Morgan, *Age of Lloyd George*, p. 66. The article in question did not differ in kind from the press campaign mounted against Asquith's policy of 'drift'; see Churchill, *Derby*, p. 222.
36 The phrase is adapted from R. Rhodes James, who concluded his Tory-derived view of these events: 'It was Asquith who deposed Asquith.' (*Memoirs of a Conservative:. J. C. C. Davidson's Memoirs and Papers, 1910–1937*, ed. R. Rhodes James (London, 1969), p. 43.)
37 Quoted by Lockwood, 'Milner's Entry,' p. 129; the underscoring is likely Milner's.
38 Hankey Diary, 10 December 1916. Unfortunately, if understandably, Hankey's diary had lapsed after 4 December 'owing to the great pressure of work' and the entry of 10 December is of a summary nature.
39 Respectively 23 *HL Debates*, 10 December 1916, col. 922 and 30 *HL Debates*, 19 June 1918, col. 265. The latter comment certainly exaggerated the immediacy of change, which came very hard indeed.
40 Hankey Diary, 3 December 1917.
41 *Ibid.*, 10 December 1916. Milner's surprising appointment may be partly explained by Lloyd George's desire to exclude Sir Edward Carson, but the once-bitter political opponents had come to share a number of ideas about the war effort.
42 Thomas Jones Papers (National Library of Wales, Aberystwyth), Class Z: Printed Diaries, 1899–1937, 10 December 1916. The unsuccessful aspirant was David Davies, a mine-owner and Liberal MP, who served instead as Parliamentary Private Secretary to the Prime Minister, 1916–17.
43 Richard Crossman, 'Introduction' to Walter Bagehot, *The English Constitution* (London, pb. edn, 1963), p. 48, noting that 'Cabinet government of the classical type lasted far longer into this century than the parliamentary system to which it was linked.' Cf. the dissenting view, not shared here, of

John Turner that the 'War Cabinet system was neither so different, nor so much better than Asquith's.' 'Cabinets, Committees and Secretariats: The Higher Direction of War,' in Kathleen Burk, ed., *War and the State* (London, 1982).

44 John Fortescue, 'The George III Papers,' *The Times*, 4 November 1925; the other two parts were published on 3 and 6 November.

45 Quoted by Hankey, *Diplomacy by Conference*, p. 47.

46 *Ibid.*, p. 51; Lord Blake apparently follows Hankey in asserting that the keeping of formal minutes incorporated 'the revival of an old usage not the establishment of a new one' (*The Office of Prime Minister* (London, 1975), p. 48); yet the practices were so divergent as to render comparisons meaningless.

47 The contention of A. B. Cooke and J. R. Vincent, eds., *Lord Carlingford's Journal . . . 1885* (Oxford, 1971) – 'the Cabinet is the least understood institution in British politics' (p. 1) – applies with particular force to the Victorian period.

48 The editors of *Carlingford's Journal* use the phrase in contrasting his account with previously published diaries and records, none of which gave 'a continuous view of what went on in Cabinet meetings.'

49 *The Cabinet Journal of Dudley Ryder, Viscount Sandon*, ed. Christopher Howard and Peter Gordon, published as Special Supplement no. 10 of the *Bulletin of the Institute of Historical Research* (November 1974), p. 11. By no means were all 'Cabinet Papers' destroyed as a matter of course, and those retained in private ministerial collections were assembled by the Public Record Office in 1962; about 3300 papers for the years 1880–1914 were catalogued in their *List of Cabinet Papers, 1880–1914* (London, HMSO, 1964).

50 Hankey, *Diplomacy by Conference*, pp. 51–2; Wilson, *Cabinet Office*, corroborates the latter attribution to Melbourne's letter of 27 December 1837, 'a kindly act on his part to initiate the young queen in the art and mystery of government' (p. 25).

51 This collection, housed in the Royal Archives, was microfilmed by the Public Record Office as CAB 41; a descriptive list of some 1700 letters, 1868–1916, has been issued by the List and Index Society, vol. V (1965).

52 *The Diary of Sir Edward Walter Hamilton, 1880–1885*, vol. I, *1880–1882*, ed. Dudley Bahlman (London, 1972), p. 79; 19 November 1880.

53 For the monarch's feelings, John Wilson, *CB: A Life of Campbell-Bannerman* (London, 1973), p. 506, comments which the biographer accepts as justified.

54 Esher's suggestion to Edward VII: 'the main reason he writes so meagerly to Your Majesty is that he has very little to tell.' (*Journals and Letters of Reginald, Viscount Esher*, vol. II, *1903–1910*, ed. Maurice V. Brett (London, 1934), pp. 160–1; 20 April 1906.)

55 Wilson, *CB*, pp. 15 and 572; in contrast, Wilson describes his private letters as 'cogent and entertaining, and peppered with characteristic turns of phrase' (p. 506).

56 HNKY (the Hankey Papers, Churchill College, Cambridge University) 13/7, Aide Memoire of 15 November 1949. George V's comments were retrospective, but presumably they did not take into account how much less information Asquith's predecessors generally had conveyed.

57 Quoted by Hankey, *Diplomacy by Conference*, pp. 66–7, from the *Manchester*

Guardian, 15 June 1922; Private Secretary of Lord Hartington to Sir Edward Hamilton, 6 July 1882. Although Bright withheld his threatened resignation another ten days, Hamilton's diary for 7 July confirms the Cabinet's deep disagreements: 'We have been living at the mouth of volcanoes again this week. Crises on Egypt. Crises on Ireland.' (*Hamilton Diary*, vol. I, p. 298.) Yet his entry is clear on the Cabinet deliberations and likely he straightened out the confusion from his own record.

58 Philip Snowden, *An Autobiography* (2 vols., London, 1934), vol. II, p. 620; the 1882 episode had been cited in the House of Lords as recently as 21 December 1932.

59 Quoted by Zara S. Steiner, *The Foreign Office and Foreign Policy, 1898–1914* (Cambridge, 1969), p. 25; Lansdowne to Balfour, 24 April 1900. Curiously, Devonshire, then the Marquess of Hartington, had been involved in the 1882 episode.

60 Quoted by Hankey, *Diplomacy by Conference*, pp. 63–4; Lord John Manners to Queen Victoria, 4 December 1877. He cites nearly a dozen instances to reinforce Derby's observation; for the unnecessary resignations, see pp. 68–9.

61 British Museum Add. MSS. 49703, the Balfour Papers, vol. XXI; Hankey to Balfour, 4 December 1914. He compared the administrative practices of the Cabinet unfavorably to those of the CID.

62 For the context of this episode, Hazlehurst, *Politicians at War*, pp. 143–5.

63 Hankey, *Supreme Command*, vol. I, pp. 156–7: as the War Office was prompt in acting, its warning was received in some departments long before the Cabinet minister in charge of the department had taken the trouble to inform his subordinates.

64 30 *HL Debates*, 19 June 1918, col. 253; cf. the recollections of two defenders of the old ways, which fail to sustain Wilson's contention that 'Curzon may have been over-stressing the weaknesses' (*Cabinet Office*, p. 27 and Annex 1).

65 CAB 21/793, Hankey to Prime Minister, 4 October 1924, a cover-letter to CP (Cabinet Paper) 30 (24).

66 HNKY 13/7, enclosure, 'Cabinet Procedure before 1916,' August 1949, in Norman Brook to Hankey, 24 October 1949. The inquiry, undertaken at Brook's request by N. H. Gibbs, had proved less than conclusive and the Cabinet Secretary had appealed to Hankey 'to fill in the gaps'; Hankey retorted that such could not be done, because the old ways were shot through with gaps. (*Ibid.*, Aide Memoire.)

67 Quoted by Fraser, *Esher*, p. 169, from the Royal Archives, R 26/41, 23 June 1905– an extraordinary comment on the old system. Austen Chamberlain was Chancellor of the Exchequer at the time.

68 *Hobhouse Diaries*, p. 106; 30 October 1912: the note-taker was 'Loulou' Harcourt.

69 N. H. Gibbs, *The Origins of Imperial Defence* (Oxford, 1955), pp. 15–16. The predecessor body was the Joint Naval and Ministerial Committee on Defence, set up in 1891 as an inter-departmental rather than a ministerial group.

70 *Ibid.*, p. 16.

71 John P. Mackintosh, 'The Role of the Committee of Imperial Defence before 1914.' *English Historical Review*, 77: 492 (July 1962). Only Devonshire and Lansdowne sought the expansion and regularization of the Defence Committee's role.

72 *Ibid.*, p. 493.
73 Gibbs, *Origins*, p. 20. In 1904 Balfour asserted that no one save the Prime Minister attended the CID meetings as a matter of right, a position which preserved its independent status from the Service ministers.
74 That part-timer, William Tyrrell, subsequently became Permanent Under-Secretary at the Foreign Office, 1925–8.
75 Gibbs, *Origins*, p. 20.
76 Nicholas d'Ombrain, *War Machinery and High Policy: Defence Administration in Peacetime Britain, 1902–1914* (London, 1973), p. 40. In 1904 two Assistant Secretaries, military and naval, were appointed.
77 Balfour once more moved very cautiously: d'Ombrain (*ibid.*, pp. 40–5) remarks that the title 'Secretariat' was 'calculated to give the least offence and maximum assurance to those who feared for the constitution and the continued responsibility of the military departments of state.'
78 Quoted by Gibbs, *Origins*, p. 22; see also Fraser, *Esher*, p. 176.
79 Quoted by Fraser, *ibid.*, p. 23.
80 Steiner, *Foreign Office*, pp. 76–82, for a description of the reforms which 'did push the office into the twentieth century.'
81 Mackintosh, 'Imperial Defence,' pp. 494–5.
82 *Ibid.*, p. 496, a conclusion stated in stronger terms by d'Ombrain: 'There was no agreement between the departments over policy, and throughout these years the CID was wholly ignored by both the naval and military planners.' (*War Machinery*, p. 90.)
83 One CID sub-committee 'heard the only mention of the "conversations" ever made to any organ of the CID made prior to 1911.' (*Ibid*, p. 96.) Of course only a handful in the Cabinet were aware of the 'conversations' prior to that time.
84 Quoted by Mackintosh, 'Imperial Defence,' p. 500; Haldane to Spender.
85 d'Ombrain, *War Machinery*, pp. 22–3, adds that the CID's existence served to mask 'the crucial divergence between the military policy of a "Continental strategy" and the contradictory one based on the amphibious capability that was inherent in the small professional army of an island empire built upon sea power.'
86 On the War Book, see Hankey, *Supreme Command*, vol. I, pp. 118–23, 155–7 and also Roskill, *Hankey*, vol. I, pp. 107–8 and 136–8. Hankey reflected in 1918: 'I built up, almost entirely by my own initiative, the system of preparation incorporated in the War Book, by which I would be willing to stand or fall before any tribunal on earth or in heaven.' (Diary, 19 July.)
87 Mackintosh, 'Imperial Defence,' p. 500. Cf. views that the question of sending an expeditionary force to the continent was an open one, including Hankey's own, and that of Hazlehurst, *Politicians at War*, p. 80.
88 The two views are recounted by Mackintosh, 'Imperial Defence,' p. 502.
89 Fraser, *Esher*, p. 260.
90 Asquith's method was 'to run the war by compartments, and by holding scratch conventions of available ministers at moments of crisis.' (*Ibid.*, p. 266.)
91 Thus Mackintosh's characterization of the 'relative failure' of the pre-war CID ('Imperial Defence,' p. 503) is more convincing than d'Ombrain's concept of 'the true measure of the failure of the Committee of Imperial Defence.' (*War Machinery*, p. 273.) Any 'true measure' must be applied at the highest level, namely the Cabinet.

92 d'Ombrain, *War Machinery*, pp. 14–15, for a description of Ottley's tenure: 'He was there to appease the dissenters [in strategic concerns] and to smooth ruffled feathers, while at the same time endeavouring to keep the CID ticking over.'

93 These phrases are used, *ibid.*, pp. 14–22; yet d'Ombrain does not convince that these activities transformed the criteria by which Ottley had steered the CID into 'a religion of detachment.'

94 Such a description, derived from Hankey's assertions, is applied to this period by Franklyn Johnson, *Defence by Committee: The British Committee of Imperial Defence, 1885–1959* (London, 1960). A pioneering effort, the book is handicapped both by a lack of official papers for the years after 1902 and by Hankey's spoon-feeding; it must be regarded as obsolete.

95 After his government's resignation in 1905, Balfour did not sit with the CID but he did co-operate with its staff and sit on one of its sub-committees. (d'Ombrain, *War Machinery*, p. 129.) On several extraordinary occasions in the inter-war period, Opposition leaders attended CID meetings. (Wilson, *Cabinet Office*, p. 69.)

96 Roskill, *Hankey*, vol. I, pp. 84–6; one must now treat as apocryphal Lord Ismay's recounting of a letter which Fisher wrote in 1906, extolling Hankey's virtues (*The Memoirs of General Lord Ismay* (New York, 1960), p. 43), although from 1911 his enthusiasm knew no bounds, e.g. 'He is Napoleonic in his ideas and Cromwellian in his thoroughness!' (Hankey Diary, 19 July 1918, printed by Roskill, *Hankey*, vol. I, p. 578; Fisher to Col. Seeley, 27 February 1912.)

97 Quoted, Roskill, *Hankey*, vol. I, p. 112; Hankey to Adeline Hankey, 19 February 1912. This contemporary description differs from his recollections incorporated in *Supreme Command*, vol. I, pp. 54–5, in which he wrote that his reference to Haldane's achievements was 'a shot in the dark, for I did not know the facts.' The contemporary version is preferable.

98 For the range of reactions, Roskill, *Hankey*, vol. I, p. 116; for the standing of his predecessors, d'Ombrain, *War Machinery*, pp. 187–202.

99 See below, pp. 46–7. d'Ombrain (*ibid.*, p. ix) does not exaggerate in commenting that 'CID's failure to entrench itself as the decision-maker of the defence establishment was the basis of his rise to power.'

100 CAB 21/128, Hankey's Speech to the Secretariat, 19 November 1918.

101 War Cabinet Minute (hereafter WC) 1, 2 of 9 December 1916 (CAB 23/1).

102 For a strange exception, dating to 1882, to the otherwise strict rule prohibiting 'outsiders' at Cabinet meetings, see below, p. 45.

103 Quoted by John Evelyn Wrench, *Geoffrey Dawson and Our Times* (London, 1955), p. 145. Not a member of the War Cabinet, Carson had been invited to attend in his capacity as First Lord; his comparison was to the work of the War Committee.

104 *Scott Diaries*, p. 277; 19–21 April 1917.

105 As summarized in Public Record Office Handbook, *The Records of the Cabinet Office to 1922* (London, 1966), p. 4; the revised 'Rules of Procedure' are printed as Appendix B, pp. 51–2. For the discussion of the draft 'Rules,' which produced slight amendment, WC 3, 6 of 12 December 1916 (CAB 23/1).

106 *Scott Diaries*, pp. 277–8; 19–21 April 1917.

107 They joined an equal number of hold-overs: Lt-Col. W. Dally Jones, Lt-Col. E. D. Swinton, Lt-Col. L. Storr, and Cyril Longhurst, who at this time

was created 'Establishment Officer,' responsible for the administration of the office.

108 Lloyd George Papers, F/21/1/2, Hankey to Prime Minister, 14 December 1916. Earlier in the year, Hankey, hearing of Amery's intrigues against the Asquith government, suggested to the Prime Minister that he should be sent 'to Salonica or somewhere equally salubrious.' (Quoted by Roskill, *Hankey*, vol. I, p. 270). Whatever the cause, in May 1916 the CIGS attached Amery to the staff of the Salonica army. His return to Whitehall thus came as a particular irony to Hankey.

109 *Amery Diaries*, vol. I, pp. 135–6 (editor's commentary).

110 Thomas Jones, *A Diary with Letters, 1931–1950* (London, 1954), p. xxiv.

111 Thomas Jones, *Whitehall Diary*, ed. Keith Middlemas (3 vols., London, 1969–71), vol. I, *1916–1925* (London, 1969), p. 15. In short order, Jones discharged liaison tasks with those departments which dealt with industrial questions and served as secretary to several Cabinet committees.

112 *Ibid.*, pp. 20 and 22; Jones to Eirene Jones, 12 and ? January 1917.

113 For the latter point, Hankey Diary, 12 December 1916; for the former, Jones, *Diary with Letters*, p. xviii, although it is unlikely that the term 'Bolshevik' enjoyed much currency in England prior to November 1917.

114 Hankey Diary, 12 December 1917. Hankey's habit of judging character on the basis of physical characteristics is among his least attractive idiosyncracies.

115 Though Roskill (*Hankey*, vol. I, p. 339) comments that the two never became 'intimate friends,' such is a misleading measure of their close professional relationship.

116 Thomas Jones Papers, Class B: 'Memorandum on the Organisation of the War Cabinet, 1916–1917.'

117 While Jones was closer to the premier than were his colleagues, his description of the process of 'cutting in' a post-Cabinet discussion is illustrative. (*Whitehall Diary*, vol. I, p. 20; letter to Eirene Jones, 12 January 1917.)

118 *Ibid.*, p. 22; Jones to Eirene Jones, 11 February 1917; for Hankey's complaints with Lloyd George's habits, see below, p. 51.

119 *Amery Diaries*, vol. I, p. 138; Amery to Prime Minister Hughes, 8 January 1917.

120 That Lloyd George had little if any hope upon assuming office that the soldiers would change their views is clear in Hankey's noting on 10 December that the premier was 'awfully down on Robertson.' (Hankey Diary.) Perhaps it was this recognition which led Lloyd George to comment to Hankey about his new post: 'You are shaking the hand of the unhappiest man on earth.' (HNKY 8/35, undated.)

121 Fraser, *Esher*, pp. 345–6.

122 John Terraine, *Douglas Haig: The Educated Soldier* (London, 1963), p. 241.

123 Hankey Diary. 'Salonica' was of course the current version of the 'Easterner' strategy.

124 *The History of The Times*, vol. IV, pt 2 (New York, 1952), p. 1068, exaggerates in placing Milner in 'second position' under the Crown; Bonar Law claimed that distinction for the war's duration. And Roskill (*Hankey*, vol. I, p. 337) misconstrued the situation in claiming that Lloyd George delegated to Milner the responsibility of 'handling' the Secretariat's problems on behalf of the War Cabinet; at most he asked that body 'to think

of men for the Civil Side of the Staff.' (Quoted by Gollin, *Proconsul*, p. 377; Milner to Prime Minister, 14 December 1916.)

125 In the words of a moderate pro-Milnerite: Gollin, *Proconsul*, p. 375.

126 Quoted, *ibid.*, pp. 377–8; Milner to Prime Minister, 14 December 1916.

127 To clinch his case, Hankey remarked that the Under Secretary for the Colonies was nowhere popular, including the House of Commons, and 'a tactless man in my office is grit in the machine.' Exercising tact, he recommended either Edwin Montagu or Mark Sykes in lieu of Steel Maitland. (Lloyd George Papers, F/21/2/2, Hankey to Prime Minister, 14 December 1916.)

128 Quoted by Roskill, *Hankey*, vol. I, p. 345; Hankey to Adeline Hankey, 13 December 1916.

129 Hankey Diary, 12 January 1917.

130 While at Versailles, Amery remained on Hankey's staff. Cf. his account of direct responsibility to Lloyd George and Milner (*Political Life*, vol. II, pp. 126–9) with Hankey's assertion that 'I and my Secretariat (Storr and Amery) took charge.' (*Supreme Command*, vol. II, p. 733.) Amery does acknowledge that 'nobody, indeed, could have been more helpful than Hankey.'

131 Quoted by Walter Nimocks, *Milner's Young Men: The 'Kindergarten' in Edwardian Imperial Affairs* (London, 1968), p. 11; Milner to George Perkin, 15 December 1893.

132 CAB 21/101, 'Note on the composition of the Secretariat of the War Cabinet,' 13 December 1916. According to Hankey's diary entry for the previous day, his first conversation with Tom Jones had been responsible: 'I caught on to a scheme of organisation of the the office into two groups – machinery and ideas.'

133 Hankey, *Supreme Command*, vol. II, pp. 589–90; yet another interim organizational scheme, outlined by Hankey on 16 December 1916 (quoted by Roskill, *Hankey*, vol. I, p. 345) also proved abortive.

134 Beaverbrook's ironic phrase, quoted by Gollin, *Proconsul*, p. 379.

135 John Turner, *Lloyd George's Secretariat* (Cambridge, 1980), p. 3.

136 For a discussion of the duties and influence of the Prime Minister's Private Secretaries during the period of Gladstone's second administration, see *Hamilton Diary*, vol. I, pp. xviii–xxv.

137 Quoted by Joseph Davies, *The Prime Minister's Secretariat* (Newport, Mon., 1951), p. xvii.

138 Turner, *Lloyd George's Secretariat*, p. 35.

139 Hankey Diary, 6 February 1917; Tom Jones had accompanied Hankey.

140 Turner, *Lloyd George's Secretariat*, pp. 10–15, for an informed description of the 'social-imperial' school and its connection to the 'Garden Suburb'; for the 'collegiate' fallacy, pp. 123–6 and 190–5. In fact, Hankey had offered Kerr a position on his staff, but the latter declined. (Lockwood, 'Milner's Entry,' p. 133.)

141 Hankey Diary, 15 August 1917, explaining his 'instinctive feeling that it is better to avoid committing myself in directions which might prove embarrassing with a change of Government.'

142 See below, pp. 51, 90–2. Hankey's determination to separate functions is confirmed in Wilson, *Cabinet Office*, p. 38.

143 See my review of Turner's *Lloyd George's Secretariat*, in the *Journal of Modern History*, 53: 720–1 (no. 4, December 1981).

144 Two such examples: Sydney Zebel, *Balfour: A Political Biography* (Cambridge, 1973), p. 231, and Michael Kinnear, *The Fall of Lloyd George* (London, 1973), p. 6.

145 HNKY 8/40, 'Whitehall Gardens: The History of the Site,' undated but 1938. Disraeli's tenancy had been brief, but Peel lived in No. 4 from 1824 to his death. For a full provenance, Wilson, *Cabinet Office*, pp. 21–3.

146 CAB 21/128, Hankey's Speech.

147 Hankey, *Supreme Command*, vol. I, p. 57; see also his description of the larger room on the first floor of No. 2, where the CID met and his Secretary worked, 'a room with an atmosphere' second to none.

148 Montagu H. Cox and Philip Norman, eds., *Survey of London*, vol. XXI, pt 2, *The Parish of St. Margaret, Westminster* (London, 1930), p. 209n.

149 Or as a hedge against political hostility to the CID ascribed in some quarters to Campbell-Bannerman; see above p. 22.

150 E.g. the account of Churchill's views on the German fleet, at the meeting of 4 July 1912 (CAB 2/2/117).

151 The phrase is Hankey's, dating to 1952, quoted by Johnson, *Defence*, p. 56.

152 CAB 2/1/13, 13 May 1903.

153 HNKY 13/7, Aide Memoire of 15 November 1949.

154 Minutes of the three committees are collected in CAB 22 and are rearranged in CAB 42; Wilson (*Cabinet Office*, p. 36) expresses reservations both about the clarity and organization of the records for the War Committee, February–December 1916.

155 CAB 42/26/6; for Lloyd George's request, Lloyd George Papers, E/2/15/4–6, 22 November 1916ff.

156 For the exchange, *ibid.*, D/17/3/12, 13 and 19, respectively 28 January, 1 and 23 February 1916; Roskill (*Hankey*, vol. I, pp. 252–3) can offer no explanation for the 'whole succession of difficulties' between the two.

157 *Ibid.*, pp. 635–6 for a specimen of the original notes taken for a Cabinet meeting, which reflects such a style. His colleague Sir Edward Spears noted in his description of Hankey (quoted, *ibid.*, p. 634) that at Cabinet meetings he 'took down everything in longhand.'

158 For the latter point I am indebted to Prof. D. C. Watt for his observation concerning the rough form and the final minutes of an Imperial War Cabinet meeting of 1918; both survive in the Borden Papers in Ottawa.

159 Roskill, *Hankey*, vol. I, p. 117.

160 Vansittart's description, quoted, *ibid.*, p. 334; Tom Jones referred to Hankey's 'prodigious memory' as well as his 'gift for distilling circumambient conversations into well-ordered memoranda.' (*Ibid.*, p. 339.) These estimable qualities did not mean that Hankey himself was without biases in his new duties.

161 CAB 21/18, Hankey to Curzon, 4 September 1917.

162 CAB 21/97, Hankey to Austen Chamberlain, 10 July 1918.

163 CAB 21/18, Hankey to Curzon, 4 September 1917.

164 *Ibid.* The point is an important one, because of the contrary, misleading assertion of an anonymous reviewer of Jones' *Whitehall Diary*, to the effect that the new system 'encouraged ministers to strike attitudes.' ('A fluid person,' *Times Literary Supplement*, 17 July 1969, p. 765.)

165 *Amery Diaries*, vol. I, p. 150; 20 April 1917.

166 CAB 21/18, Curzon to Hankey, September 1917, a reply which will amuse those acquainted with Curzon's bombast: 'I do happen to be an expert on

Museums being a trustee of the British Museum, National Portrait Gallery, having founded . . . myself one of the greatest museums in the world the Victoria Memorial Hall in Calcutta and having more to do with collections and museums than any other member of the Govt.'

167 CAB 23/8, *passim*.

168 Hankey Diary, 26 November 1917; in Hankey's defence, one might comment that his concern was administrative, but such confidence in his own judgment was considerable.

169 Whether or not apocryphal, the anecdote is that of Frederick Leith-Ross, *Money Talks: Fifty Years of International Finance* (London, 1968), p. 54.

170 See above, pp. 10–13. See also D. N. Chester and F. M. C. Willson, *The Organization of British Central Government, 1914–1956* (London, 1957), p. 286; on occasion Asquith authorized the Secretary to circulate War Committee Conclusions to the Cabinet.

171 Lloyd George Papers, F/23/1/1, Stamfordham to Hankey, 10 December 1916 and Hankey's minute of 11 December; Stamfordham had to some extent been misled, however.

172 Tom Jones twenty years later recalled: 'When Winston remarked to C.-B: "I've got a letter from L.G.," C.-B retorted: "Keep it – it is the only one extant."' Nor did his family fare much better (*Diary with Letters*, p. 262; 13 September 1936), although a collection of Lloyd George's family correspondence has been edited by Kenneth O. Morgan, *Lloyd George: Family Letters, 1885–1936* (Cardiff and Oxford, 1973).

173 *Davidson's Memoirs*, p. 92 n. 1.

174 CAB 21/100, 'The Circulation of War Cabinet Documents,' 25 September 1918.

175 For a description of the separate classification of these 'A' Minutes and those of the very few War Cabinet Minutes classified as 'especially secret' – with minutes kept in manuscript – see *Records of the Cabinet Office*, pp. 13–14.

176 Usefully described, *ibid.*, p. 6.

177 HNKY 13/7, 'Cabinet Procedures in 1916,' which dates to 1949.

178 Lloyd George Papers, F/32/4/1, Walter Long to Prime Minister, 7 December 1916; he subsequently obtained from Lloyd George permission to receive all War Cabinet memoranda dealing with military subjects. (CAB 21/100, 'Circulation'.)

179 Hankey, *Supreme Command*, vol. I, p. 325.

180 CAB 21/100, 'Office Notice,' 4 April 1918; as a rule, the assistant Secretary in whose sphere of concern the paper fell decided upon circulation; the informational papers acquired a standardized circulation.

181 *Ibid.*, 'Circulation of Cabinet Documents.'

182 Hankey Diary, 14 October 1918, supplying the answer to the question posed by the authors of *Records of the Cabinet Office* (p. 8), as to why Hankey's memorandum was not circulated to the War Cabinet.

183 CAB 21/100, 'Office Note,' 16 November 1918. Six months earlier, the rule had been otherwise: if the Assistant Secretary held 'the slightest doubt,' he was to refer the matter to Col. Dally Jones or Hankey himself. (*Ibid.*, 'Office Note,' 4 April 1918.)

184 Hankey Diary, 16 October 1918. The Foreign Secretary, Balfour, scorned the premier's exclusionary bent: 'The whole system is (in my opinion) absurd.' (FO 800/207, Balfour to Montagu, 11 August 1917.) On several occasions, the Foreign Office handled the circulation of these documents.

185 FO 800/207, Hankey to A. J. Balfour, 14 February 1917: 'Mr Asquith shall have the same telegrams as are sent to certain members of the Government who are not in the Cabinet.'
186 Jones Diary, Long to Jones, 1 February 1919.
187 For an account of this obscure incident, Jonathan Aitken, *Officially Secret* (London, 1971), pp. 7–14; according to Balfour, the prosecution failed 'not because there was any doubt of what he had done but because what he had done was no crime in the eyes of the law.'
188 *Sandon Cabinet Journal*, pp. 33–4; 29 June 1878.
189 Aitken, *Officially Secret*, pp. 15–17; for further discussion of the 1889 legislation, see below, pp. 123–4.
190 For these incidents, *Carlingford's Journal*, pp. 105–6 and 111; 23 May and 5 June 1885. The contentious issues were three pieces of Irish legislation, the dissidents were Chamberlain and Dilke, and the paper was the *Birmingham Daily Post*.
191 For a description of Grey's practices – in some cases he sent copies only to the King, Prime Minister, Ripon, and sometimes Morley and Haldane – see Steiner, *Foreign Office*, p. 87.
192 *Hobhouse Diaries*, p. 150; 18 November 1913. A number of ministers immediately disclaimed any responsibility.
193 Hazlehurst, *Politicians at War*, p. 78, with specific reference to the events of July 1914.
194 *The Times*, 28 January 1963; while his biographer settled for the less grandiose title, *Hankey: Man of Secrets*, he thought the other description 'no exaggeration.'
195 R. L. Schuyler, 'The British War Cabinet,' *Political Science Quarterly*, 33: 386 (September 1918); Schuyler was an informed and respected American scholar of British government.
196 CAB 21/69, Hankey to Prime Minister, 20 September 1916, echoing his diary entry of four days earlier.
197 *Ibid.* Hankey's statement probably derives from Lord Salisbury's well-known assertion that the first rule of Cabinet conduct was that 'no member should ever "Hansardise" another – compare his present contribution to the common fund of counsel with a previously expressed opinion.' (Paraphrased by Gwendolyn Cecil, *Life of Robert, Marquess of Salisbury*, vol. II, *1868–1880* (London, 1921), pp. 223–4.
198 CAB 42/20/8, 25 September 1916; Hankey had himself proposed a similar compromise to the War Committee five days earlier. (CAB 21/69, Hankey to Prime Minister.)
199 Roskill, *Hankey*, vol. I, pp. 291–304.
200 *Ibid.*, p. 341, for extracts of Hankey to Asquith, 12 December 1916.
201 Lloyd George Papers, F/23/1/11, 7 June 1917. For Hankey's exclusion – 'at the evening Cabinet meeting the psychological atmosphere was very sultry, and I still felt that he [Lloyd George] mistrusted me' – Hankey Diary, 7 June 1917.
202 Lloyd George Papers, F/23/2/27, Hankey to Prime Minister, 7 June 1918; Hankey assured that he strove to keep the Cabinet Secretariat 'like Caesar's wife "above reproach."' For details of his slip, see Hankey Diary, 9, 10 and 17 June 1918.
203 Hankey Diary, 17 June 1918.

204 Edward L. Spears, *Prelude to Victory* (London, 1939), p. 137. As Cabinet Secretary, Hankey's performance bears out the judgment; as adviser, he was not free from some such 'foolishness.'
205 For Hankey's precautions, Roskill, *Hankey*, vol. I, pp. 24–5; I concur with the biographer's judgment of its high degree of technical accuracy.
206 Hankey Diary, dated 5 March 1915; the first entry dates to the previous day.
207 I have found no written evidence to document Hankey's claim – which dates to 1945 – of Asquith's knowledge; on the other hand, Asquith may have given no thought to Hankey's activities, as his own correspondence forms a record of sorts.
208 For Lloyd George's awareness of the utility of Hankey's Diary, see below, p. 64.
209 Nor does his biographer remark upon this element of release, although he recognizes that Hankey confided 'his innermost thoughts and feelings at the time of any entry.' (Roskill, *Hankey*, vol. I, p. 24.)
210 *Ibid.*, p. 24; he maintained the diary in an irregular form until 1942.
211 *Ibid.*, p. 25; stripped away were 'his more candid and critical comments.'
212 *Hamilton Diary*, vol. I, p. xii; for this reason Hankey's unofficial record of Cabinet proceedings is closer to Hamilton's diary than to the participant accounts authored for shorter periods of time by Sandon and Carlingford.
213 *Ibid.*, p. 367; 26 November 1882: he attended the meeting 'with special reference to the prorogation and reassembling of Parliament.'
214 Quoted by Roskill, *Hankey*, vol. I, p. 211, from a memorandum of 2 September 1915.
215 For Hankey's truly decisive role, *ibid.*, pp. 107–8; nonetheless he shared the credit with others on his staff. (*Supreme Command*, vol. I, pp. 118–23.)
216 Quoted by Roskill, *Hankey*, vol. I, p. 136; within the War Book, he found complaint with the 'belated and unsatisfactory . . . jejune and inadequate' chapter prepared by the Treasury. (Quoted, *ibid.*, pp. 137–8.) Nor did he ever forget the Treasury performance.
217 *Ibid.*, pp. 149 and 152; for Hankey's general view of war strategy in this period, see chs. 6–8. Hankey has long been numbered among the leading 'Easterners.'
218 The phrase is R. Rhodes James', *Gallipoli* (London, 1965), p. 94; Roskill (*Hankey*, vol. I, pp. 163–4) prints Hankey's memorandum of 16 March 1915.
219 Alan Moorehead, *Gallipoli* (London, pb. edn, 1959), p. 210, confirmed by Rhodes James, *Gallipoli*, p. 249.
220 See below, p. 53.
221 *The Private Papers of Douglas Haig, 1914–1919*, ed. Robert Blake (London, 1952), pp. 90, 164, and 333.
222 Hankey Diary, 14 March and 2 May 1916. In the former entry, Hankey explained the rottenness in terms of 'this meticulous clinging to our obsolete undemocratic standard of what they [the leaders] are pleased to call discipline – saluting etc.'
223 Hankey Diary, 27 February 1917; when abroad, Hankey maintained his diary on loose sheets of paper which were subsequently collected, although they remain separate from his bound diary volumes.
224 See below, pp. 51–2.
225 Hankey Diary, 16 December 1917.
226 Hankey, *Supreme Command*, vol. II, p. 580.

2. THE LLOYD GEORGE REGIME

1 88 *HC Debates*, 19 December 1916, col. 1343.

2 A. J. P. Taylor, *Politics in Wartime and Other Essays* (London, 1954), p. 34. Among the innovations were the Prime Minister's infrequent appearances at the House of Commons; the submission of *War Cabinet Reports* not to Parliament but to the nation; and the failure of one commoner minister, Sir Joseph Maclay, even to enter the House of Commons.

3 88 *HC Debates*, 19 December 1916, col. 1343. Christopher Addison, who supported Lloyd George, remarked upon the 'wholesale freedom from recrimination.' (*Four and a Half Years*, vol. I, p. 286.)

4 91 *HC Debates*, 8 March 1917, col. 607 (Hogge). The Cabinet Secretariat numbered thirty-six at this point.

5 'The New Bureaucracy,' *The Nation*, 20: 696–7 (24 February 1917).

6 'Government without a Cabinet,' *New Statesman*, 8: 460–1 (17 February 1917).

7 Quoted by J. R. M. Butler, *Lord Lothian (Philip Kerr), 1882–1940* (London, 1960), p. 64. Hankey also stressed that the Prime Minister's Secretariat had 'press contacts,' unlike his own; for those contacts, see Turner, *Lloyd George's Secretariat*, pp. 168–9.

8 'The Organisation of the War Cabinet,' *The Spectator*, 120: 311–12 (23 March 1918); the assertion was made with the *War Cabinet Report* for 1917 in hand.

9 See above pp. 46–7.

10 John Mackintosh, *The Government and Politics of Britain* (London, 1970), p. 14.

11 Quoted by Roberta Warman, 'The Erosion of Foreign Office Influence in the Making of Foreign Policy, 1916–1919,' *Historical Journal*, 15: 156 (no. 2, 1972).

12 Hankey Diary, 18 March 1917.

13 *Ibid.*, 11 and 12 April 1917. Lloyd George's irregular ways were clear even in his days at the Treasury, when his associate Hobhouse had commented: 'Lloyd George can never concentrate his attention on anything for more than 5 min. together, [but] he is wonderfully quick at picking up an argument as he goes.' (*Hobhouse Diaries*, p. 82; 21 November 1909.)

14 Hankey Diary, 30 May 1917.

15 *Ibid.*, 2 August 1917.

16 E.g. he suggested to the premier that 'the best plan would be for you to allow the War Cabinet to meet without you to consider these . . . [domestic] questions which arise from day to day, in order that the Government machine may not become too congested.' (Lloyd George Papers, F/23/2/20, Hankey to Prime Minister, 1 April 1918.)

17 107 *HC Debates*, 19 June 1918, col. 394. In so speaking on behalf of HMG, Law served to remind the Commons that one of its leading grievances was the oft-extended absence of the Prime Minister from its deliberations.

18 30 *HL Debates*, 19 June 1918, col. 251. Critics had also attacked the government's proliferating bureaucracy.

19 *Ibid.*, cols. 265–82.

20 Hankey Diary, 17 June 1918; for portions of that speech, which Hankey frequently cited as a major indictment of past practices, see above pp. 15, 20.

21 *Haig Papers*, p. 355; 12 February 1919. Hankey's role had been to persuade Milner on a particular point.

22 Lloyd George Papers, F/23/4/39, Hankey to Prime Minister, 19 March 1919; the premier had returned temporarily to London.

23 Quoted by Hazlehurst, *Politicians at War*, vol. I, p. 188. In all fairness, the War Council Minutes record Lloyd George's acceptance of both ideas, while Churchill saw no objection to the former proposal.

24 CAB 63/19, 'Some Suggestions for Anti-Submarine Warfare,' 12 February 1917; the historical importance of this document is evident in the exhibition of the original first page in the Public Record Office Museum. See Hankey, *Supreme Command*, vol. I, p. 228 and vol. II, pp. 646–7; Roskill, *Hankey*, vol. I, pp. 146–8 and 356–8.

25 HNKY 4/24, copy of Hankey to Swinton, 5 May 1932.

26 Hankey Diary, 17 June 1918.

27 Anthony Verrier, review of *The Supreme Command; Political Quarterly*, 32: 291 (July–September 1961). Hankey himself recorded the ego-boosting remark in his diary entry for 31 October 1918.

28 Lloyd George Papers, F/38/3/23, Milner to Lloyd George, 13 April 1918. Although Hankey knew from Lloyd George that he was also considering Milner for the post, there is no evidence that Hankey thought of him as a rival. Amery thought Hankey handicapped by his lack of 'necessary authority with the public and the Army, more particularly if it was a question of shifting Haig and making other drastic reforms'; he and Henry Wilson agreed that the latter would advise the premier to appoint Milner, should his advice be sought. Both viewed Hankey 'indispensable where he is.' (*Amery Diaries*, p. 216; 14 April 1918.)

29 Hankey Diary, 30 June 1917; Hankey noted that accepting the post would constitute a 'fearful gamble' for him, since it would involve his exchanging a suitable position 'with good future prospects' for a 'rather rocky Ministry in the most criticized post with a rather doubtful staff.'

30 Quoted by Roskill, *Hankey*, vol. II, p. 183; Esher to Hankey, 7 September 1920. If Esher's description is accurate, George V's remarks were prophetic: '[He] said that you were the most important and useful public servant of the Crown and State, that you were the only possible link between this Government and any possible successor Government, and the Guardian of the traditions of Government.'

31 Riddell, *War Diary, 1914–1918*, p. 351.

32 Young, *Arthur James Balfour* (London, 1963), p. 397; source unattributed. For additional contemporary testimony, see Amery, *Political Life*, vol. II, pp. 172–3, and Gollin, *Proconsul*, p. 407 n. 1.

33 Hankey Diary, 23 November 1918; such a bias against Lloyd George calls for a corrective comment from Henry Wilson to the premier: 'you more than any other man living or dead, you almost alone, won this war. That is the bare truth and the whole truth.' (Lloyd George Papers, F/47/8/30, Wilson to Prime Minister, 6 August 1919).

34 Jones, *Diary with Letters*, p. 470, 5 September 1940.

35 HNKY 4/46, Hankey to W. W. Hadley, 18 December 1954. As George V was prejudiced against Lloyd Geroge, so was Hankey towards Churchill; for the context of that latter prejudice see below, pp. 251–2 and 270.

36 Lloyd George Papers, F/8/3/65, Churchill to Prime Minister, 23 June 1919.

37 Hankey Diary, 30 July 1919. Roskill (*Hankey*, vol. II, pp. 108–9) prints only a few excerpts, misdating the entry to 25 August 1919.
38 For a full discussion of the proceedings and records of the Imperial War Cabinet and the Supreme War Council, see Wilson, *Cabinet Office*, pp. 41–2.
39 *Records of the Cabinet Office*, p. 21; Amery's role is discussed above, p. 31.
40 The point is asserted in CAB 21/128, Hankey's speech of 19 November 1918.
41 *Ibid.*
42 *Records of the Cabinet Office*, p. 21.
43 Roskill, *Hankey*, vol. II, pp. 48–9, uncharacteristically without documentation.
44 *Ibid.*, pp. 82–3, related how Hankey was able subsequently to show that former President Wilson's claim that he had never agreed to the Yap mandate was in error; Roskill remarks that the incident 'provides an interesting example of the essential need to keep and circulate precise records of high-level discussions . . . [enabling] the British government to refute . . . a very unpleasant insinuation made against themselves and their servant [Hankey].'
45 *Records of the Cabinet Office*, p. 22.
46 Lord Riddell, *Intimate Diary of the Peace Conference and After, 1918–1923* (New York, 1934), p. 38.
47 Amery, *Political Life*, vol. II, pp. 178–9; more generally, Amery credited Hankey with an 'unobtrusive but effective part . . . in shaping the mechanism of the Conference [and] the perfect mutual co-operation between him and his chief.' Such a role is confirmed by Harold Nicolson, *Peacemaking 1919* (New York, 1939), pp. 108–9.
48 Quoted by Roskill, *Hankey*, vol. II, p. 92.
49 CAB 63/51, Hankey's untitled memorandum of 21 July 1936, recollects five reasons for his decision.
50 Quoted, Roskill, *Hankey*, vol. II, p. 79; Hankey to Lord Robert Cecil, 18 April 1919.
51 Thomas Jones Papers, Class Z, vol. IV; Hankey to Milner, 4 January 1919.
52 Jones, *Whitehall Diary*, vol. I, p. 72; Hankey to Jones, 18 January 1919.
53 For a description of their exchange of correspondence, Roskill, *Hankey*, vol. II, pp. 73–4; for two letters from Jones to Hankey, *Whitehall Diary*, vol. I, pp. 81–2.
54 *The War Cabinet: Report for the Year 1918* (Cmnd 325, 1919), p. 1; for a list of the Cabinet committees appointed during the Lloyd George regime, see Wilson, *Cabinet Office*, Annex 11, Part 1.
55 From such a perspective, the War Cabinet may be viewed as 'precisely the sort of executive council that had all along [since the Boer War] been envisaged by many members of the "efficiency group"' whose *Quest for National Efficiency* has been studied by G. R. Searle (Berkeley, 1971).
56 Turner, *Lloyd George's Secretariat*, p. 141, acknowledges that 'the result was a tendentious and selective history of the war's achievements.'
57 Lloyd George Papers, F/75/3/1, Corbett's note of 22 January 1919; Sir Julian was a well-known historian and member of the Historical Section of the Cabinet Office. Turner discusses the more important 1917 Report in some detail (*Lloyd George's Secretariat*, pp. 169–72) but he regards its successor as 'pedestrian.'
58 Hankey Diary, 27 October 1917; the 'school-master' overtones are obvious.

59 Lloyd George Papers, F/23/3/25, Hankey to Prime Minister, 13 December 1918.
60 Hankey Diary, 28 October 1918.
61 Lloyd George Papers, F/23/3/34, Esher to Hankey, 29 December 1918.
62 *Ibid.*, F/76/11/2, undated but likely the memorandum Amery notes his dictating on 6 January 1919 (*Amery Diaries*, p. 250.)
63 *Amery Diaries*, p. 250; 7 January 1919.
64 For a discussion of 'prime ministerial government,' see below, pp. 95–7.
65 The irregular incident is most fully recounted in Austen Chamberlain, *Down the Years* (London, 1935), pp. 134–42. Chamberlain insisted that the Chancellor should be a member of that body, but Lloyd George countered that making an exception for that position would lead to claims by other ministers for inclusion.
66 Robert Blake, *Unrepentant Tory* (New York, 1956), p. 398.
67 120 *HC Debates*, 23 October 1919, col. 242.
68 Ministry of Reconstruction, *Report of the Machinery of Government Committee* (Cd 9230, 1918), p. 5.
69 Hankey Diary, 26 October and 9 November 1919; the latter comment is particularly interesting in the latitude accorded to the Secretary.
70 *Machinery of Government Committee Report*, p. 6.
71 CAB 21/1084, 'Functions of the Cabinet Secretariat: Memorandum by the Secretary of the War Cabinet [Sir Edward Bridges],' 14 September 1944.
72 Lloyd George Papers, F/74/10/4, proposed statement of 7 March 1918.
73 Turner, *Lloyd George's Secretariat*, p. 197.
74 Adams contended that such a staff 'should be more than a mere recording body, or a body which circulates information. It should itself be an investigative and intelligence organ, and this is its primary function.' In the very long run, Adams' ideas were in a sense sustained in the creation of the Central Policy Review Staff by the Heath government in 1970, although it was 'designed to act for the Cabinet as a whole, to produce analyses to help Ministers make independent policy decisions and to keep a close watch on Government strategy.' Nonetheless, its depiction as 'a Prime Minister's Department' in all but name (James Fox, 'The brains behind the throne,' *Sunday Times*, 25 May 1973) does not convince, both because of its location within the Cabinet Office and because premiers have since 1974 utilized an obviously 'political' body to serve their own needs (see below, Ch. 7, n. 215). The CPRS' activities in the Heath–Wilson years are described in Frank Stacey, *British Government, 1966 to 1975: Years of Reform* (London, 1975), pp. 89–95.
75 CAB 21/221, 'The Cabinet Office: Note by the Secretary of the Cabinet,' 10 June 1922.
76 Leith-Ross, *Money Talks*, p. 52; although his comments appear in a chapter entitled '1913–18,' they clearly refer to the post-war period. Leith-Ross was briefly seconded to the Cabinet Office from the Treasury in 1920.
77 The phrase is, appropriately, that of G. M. Young, late of the Secretariat, offered in the context of the growing influence of the nineteenth-century Benthamites.
78 121 *HC Debates*, 13 November 1919, col. 500.
79 Hankey Diary, 16 November 1919.
80 CAB 63/30, Hankey to Prime Minister, 18 November 1920.

81 'The New Cabinet,' *The Spectator*, 123: 568 (1 November 1919).

82 CAB 24/92, 'Cabinet Procedure,' 5 November 1919 (reproduced as Plate IV of *Records of the Cabinet Office*).

83 CAB 21/100, Hankey to Prime Minister, 15 August 1919.

84 WC 616A, 15 August 1919 (CAB 23/15); when fuller minutes were on occasion kept, they were recorded as 'Secretary's Notes,' e.g. WC 624A, 25 September 1919.

85 Hankey Diary, 9 November 1919. Provision was made for a single copy of a fuller record, whenever explicitly specified by the Cabinet.

86 CAB 21/1084, 'Functions of the Cabinet Secretariat'; however, the rule was not regularly enforced until late 1922.

87 Lawrence Burgis Memoirs, unpublished typescript (ACC 146 in the Archives Centre, Churchill College, Cambridge University).

88 Jones, *Whitehall Diary*, vol. I, p. 76; 10 February 1919: the Cabinet Secretariat used the Foreign Office printer. Contrary to Wilson's assertion that the Cabinet Conclusions exist 'in typescript only' for the period March–October 1922, the change in format dates to November 1919; the circulation of these typewritten conclusions was restricted in these last months of Lloyd George's regime.

89 Roskill, *Hankey*, vol. II, pp. 27–8.

90 CAB 24/92, 'Cabinet Procedure,' 5 November 1919. The Secretary was required to inform affected departments; thereafter, the minister was responsible.

91 The War Cabinet Secretariat had maintained three distinct circulation lists; its practices are reviewed in CAB 21/761, Burgis to Howorth, 14 July 1939.

92 CAB 21/391, Howorth's untitled memorandum of 14 March 1934; for a description of the mechanics of distribution, see Wilson, *Cabinet Office*, pp. 18–19.

93 Jones Diary, 18 July 1922, enclosure of Austen Chamberlain to Hankey; according to Chamberlain, fuller notes were kept for the Unemployment Committee also. At this time he was Lord Privy Seal and Leader of the House of Commons.

94 As noted above, the real change did not come in October 1919, although Hankey's diary confirms the Cabinet's intention. Only with the change in regimes did a single unassisted Secretary take the Cabinet Minutes. Cf. Wilson (*Cabinet Office*, p. 7) who assumes that the practice followed upon the intent.

95 Jones, *Whitehall Diary*, vol. I, pp. 123–4; letter to Sir Maurice Powicke, 21 December 1920.

96 E.g. Jones, *ibid.*, pp. 77, 89; for some alleged examples of more recent evasion of Cabinet discussion through the Prime Minister's control of the Agenda, see Mackintosh, *Government and Politics of Britain*, pp. 61–2.

97 CAB 21/222, 'Procedure with Regard to Cabinet Minutes,' Hankey to Churchill, 10 March 1922.

98 C (Cabinet) 1 (19) 3, 4 November 1919 (CAB 23/18). The deleted paragraph Hankey cited in CAB 27/213, 'Experience in the Cabinet Office: Memorandum by the Secretary,' 24 February 1923. His attempt to recover Cabinet papers was consistent with his war-time belief that 'to allow national secrets to pass beyond the control of the Government is seriously to impair the value of these precautions [taken by his Office].' (CAB 63/22, 'The

Custody of War Cabinet Documents: Note by the Secretary,' 14 August 1917.)

99 Hankey stated his conviction that publication of Cabinet Minutes was not a possibility: 'There is, of course, no question of these [Imperial War Cabinet] minutes ever being published. The principle of the collective responsibility of the Cabinet for Cabinet decisions has been held to rule against this.' (CAB 21/198, Hankey to Prime Minister Hughes of Australia, 23 December 1918.) Whether at this time he felt the same way about Cabinet papers is nowhere apparent.

100 'The [CID] Secretariat have always done their utmost to recover Papers from Ministers on leaving Office. On the whole, their efforts have met with a considerable degree of success.' (CAB 27/213, 'Experience in the Cabinet Office'.) Until 1908, Ministers had retained copies of CID papers, while the military members had passed their files to their successors. (d'Ombrain, *War Machinery*, p. 138.)

101 CAB 63/22, 'Custody of War Cabinet Documents.'

102 CAB 27/213, 'Experience,' from WC 217 (17 August 1917). The Secretary pointed to the problem which would arise if Cabinet papers passed into the hands of the executors of deceased former ministers; in any case, if the documents were taken out of the country, they were beyond the government's control.

103 CAB 27/213, 'Experience.'

104 Lloyd George Papers, F/26/1/18, Hankey to Prime Minister, 20 March 1922; Hankey thought the incident proved the soundness of his appeal to the Cabinet to surrender their papers upon leaving office.

105 Stevenson, *Lloyd George: A Diary*, p. 243; 26 June 1922.

106 Stevenson, *The Years that Are Past*, p. 191.

107 CAB 27/313, 'Experience.'

108 For the Official Histories, see below, pp. 120–3.

109 Since Lloyd George had retained his War Cabinet records, the use of a researcher – an Army officer who had served with the CID before and during the war – likely indicated his interest in the papers of the three Cabinet committees which had influenced war policy under Asquith; also Hankey's indices were useful.

110 CAB 27/213, 'Composition and Terms of Reference,' 24 February 1923.

111 *Ibid.*, 'Note by the Secretary,' 27 February 1923, quoting the language of section 1 of the Official Secrets Act. For discussion of that legislation, see below, pp. 123–6 and 210–14.

112 *Ibid.*, 'Memorandum by the Permanent Secretary to the Admiralty,' 23 February 1923.

113 H. R. G. Greaves, *The Civil Service in the Changing State* (London, 1947), pp. 146–9.

114 Sir H. P. Hamilton, 'Sir Warren Fisher and the Public Service,' *Public Administration*, 29: 9–15 (Spring 1951); Fisher had no hand in the reorganization. For the increase of Treasury powers during the war, see Kathleen Burk, 'The Treasury: From Impotence to Power,' in Burk, ed., *War and the State*, pp. 96–102.

115 Greaves, *Civil Service*, p. 185.

116 Hamilton, 'Sir Warren Fisher,' pp. 22–5; Geoffrey Fry, *Statesmen in Disguise* (London, 1969), p. 55. Henry Roseveare comments that the re-

organization 'consolidated the Treasury's position at the head of a reshaped Civil Service, in line with the recommendations of the Machinery of Government Committee.' (*The Treasury: The Evolution of a British Institution* (London, 1969), pp. 244 and 249.)

117 D. C. Watt, *Personalities and Policies* (Notre Dame, 1965), p. 104; G. C. Peden, 'Sir Warren Fisher and British Rearmament against Germany,' *English Historical Review*, 94: 31 (no. 371, January 1979).

118 Crossman, 'Introduction' to Bagehot, *The English Constitution*, p. 48.

119 CAB 24/95, CP 332, 'Representation to the Treasury on the Secretariat of the Cabinet: Memorandum by the Chancellor . . .,' 22 December 1919.

120 C 1 (20) 2, 6 January 1920 (CAB 23/20). Leith-Ross first held the post.

121 The proposal was first made by the Financial Secretary to the Treasury, Stanley Baldwin, in a letter to Hankey on 27 January 1921, quoted in CAB 63/33, 'The Status of the Secretariat of the Cabinet . . .,' 7 November 1922.

122 *Ibid.*, quoting Hankey to Fisher, 3 March 1921.

123 Jones, *Whitehall Diary*, vol. I, p. 78; Jones to Hankey, 18 February 1919. Lloyd George Papers, F/23/4/16, Hankey to Prime Minister, 14 February 1919.

124 *Records of the Cabinet Office*, p. 24.

125 Roskill, *Hankey*, vol. II, p. 155.

126 HNKY 8/24, Hankey's memorandum, 'The Future of the Cabinet and CID Secretariats,' 11 July 1919.

127 CAB 27/213, 'Experience.' The Historical Section is treated below, pp. 120-3.

128 *Ibid.*, enclosed in 'Note by the Secretary,' 26 March 1923.

129 Quoted in Young, *Arthur James Balfour*, p. 412. Here is a piece of evidence that Hankey foresaw that some official materials would be made available to the public, but of course these were histories, not documents.

130 HNKY 8/17, 'Draft Memorandum on the Organisation of the Cabinet,' 12 July 1919; Lloyd George Papers, F/24/3/13, Hankey to Prime Minister, 27 September 1920.

131 Hankey Diary, 22 October 1920.

132 Treasury, Blue Notes, T/165/49/2; as of 1 March 1920, Hankey's salary was £3000.

133 138 *HC Debates*, 2 March 1921, col. 1904. The speaker, Ormsby-Gore, later Lord Harlech, had served as an Assistant Secretary from 1917. Numbers of staff for the inter-war years are given in Wilson, *Cabinet Office*, Annex 7 (a).

134 138 *HC Debates*, 2 March 1921, col. 1906.

135 Steiner, *Foreign Office*, p. 168.

136 Warman, 'Erosion of Foreign Office Influence,' pp. 135–6 and 149. A continuation of such decline is apparent in Alan J. Sharp, 'The Foreign Office in Eclipse, 1919–1922,' *History*, 61: 198–218 (June 1976). Zara Steiner and M. L. Dockrill, 'The Foreign Office Reforms, 1919–1921,' *Historical Journal*, 17: 131–56 (no. 1, 1974), agree that 'no administrative change could have prevented the shattering of its former monopoly over foreign affairs.'

137 Steiner and Dockrill, 'Foreign Office Reforms,' p. 139.

138 Doreen Collins, *Aspects of British Politics, 1904–1919* (Oxford, 1965), p. 133.

139 CAB 21/221, 'Note by the Secretary.'

140 Hankey Diary, 20 July 1920, where he left his impression of a 'ridiculous and vague mission.'

141 *Ibid.*, 18 September 1920; for the mission, Roskill, *Hankey*, vol. II, pp. 180–7.
142 Norman Davies, 'Sir Maurice Hankey and the Inter-Allied Mission to Poland, July–August 1920,' *Historical Journal*, 15: 560 (no. 3, 1972).
143 *Ibid.*, p. 556.
144 *Ibid.*, p. 554.
145 Lloyd George, *War Memoirs*, vol. I, pp. 44–5.
146 For an illuminating account which is somewhat critical of the Cabinet Secretariat's involvement, see Gordon Craig, 'The British Foreign Office from Grey to Chamberlain,' in *The Diplomats*, ed. Craig and Felix Gilbert (Princeton, 1953), pp. 15–25.
147 Davies, 'Hankey,' p. 561.
148 Hankey thought Curzon's character deficient in the heroic element: 'I can't form a very high opinion of Curzon . . . "No man is a hero to his valet!" I have been "intellectual valet" to many; Asquith, Balfour, Lloyd George remain heroes; Curzon does not.' (Thomas Jones, *Whitehall Diary*, ed. Keith Middlemas, vol. II, *1926–1930* (London, 1969), p. 100; Hankey to Jones, 10 May 1927.)
149 In the event of his resignation, Curzon perceived 'a great national peril' in the succession. (Quoted by the Earl of Ronaldshay, *The Life of Lord Curzon*, vol. III (London, 1928), p. 256.)
150 E.g. Allenby to Curzon, quoted by Harold Nicolson, *Curzon: The Last Phase, 1919–1925* (New York, 1939), p. 23.
151 *Ibid.*, p. 59.
152 Hankey Diary, 16 November 1920 and 13 January 1921.
153 Significantly, the title of Hankey's collection of essays on public affairs.
154 Quoted by Nicolson, *Curzon*, p. 245. Cf. Hankey's explanation of the premier's involvement in such conferences: 'foreign policy was so much a continuation of the work of the Supreme War Council and of the Peace Conference that it can be no matter for surprise that Mr. Lloyd George was not in a position to let go entirely.' (CAB 63/39, 'Lord Curzon,' 19 May 1927.)
155 Quoted by Nicolson, *Curzon*, p. 274.
156 Winston S. Churchill, *The Aftermath* (London, 1929), p. 429.
157 Robert Boothby, *I Fight to Live* (London, 1947), p. 28.
158 *Amery Diaries*, p. 294; 13 October 1922.
159 In making the comment, Lloyd George likely had his audience in mind: *Scott Diaries*, p. 423; 31 May 1922.
160 Stevenson, *Lloyd George: A Diary*, p. 230; 20 July 1920.
161 Jones, *Whitehall Diary*, vol. II, p. 23; 26 April 1926. Although the comment was retrospective, there is no room to doubt Baldwin's sentiment four years earlier.
162 On the last point, Jones noted (*Whitehall Diary*, vol. I, p. 197; 28 March 1922); 'The P.M. went off to Criccieth for three weeks . . . and the King first heard of his departure in the newspapers and sent a hot message to Chamberlain . . . to ask "Have I a Prime Minister or not?"'
163 David Walder, *The Chanak Affair* (London, 1969), pp. 186–7.
164 A. E. Montgomery, 'Lloyd George and the Greek Question, 1918–1922,' in *Lloyd George: Twelve Essays*, ed. A. J. P. Taylor (New York, 1971), pp. 257–8 and 283–4. Montgomery writes little about the Chanak crisis, and

his account makes no reference to the domestic political factors developed below.

165 Maurice Cowling contends that the decisive factor was the determination of Chamberlain, Balfour, and Birkenhead 'to push their [Unionist] critics into a corner and . . . the refusal of the under-secretaries, M.P.s and leading Conservatives to be pushed.' (*The Impact of Labour, 1920–1924* (Cambridge, 1971), p. 194.)

166 *Scott Diaries*, p. 427; letter of 4 October 1922.

167 Walder, *Chanak*, p. 214.

168 Quoted, *ibid.*, p. 230.

169 'Correspondence,' *The Times*, 26 September 1922; and CAB 21/221, 'Cabinet Secretariat Again,' *Yorkshire Post*, 4 October 1922.

170 C 49 (22) a, 15 September 1922 (CAB 23/31).

171 Churchill (*Aftermath*, pp. 426–7 and p. 421) prints the communiqué and describes his own reaction.

172 Lloyd George Papers, F/26/2/37, Hankey to Prime Minister, 26 September 1922; the occasion was the publication of a critical letter in *The Times* of that date.

173 Hankey Diary, 4 October 1922. As a result of what Nicolson describes as his 'inexcusable departure' for his country seat, Curzon did not read the communiqué until forty-eight hours had elapsed. (*Curzon*, p. 271.) Lloyd George's attack upon the Foreign Office's inability to conduct work prior to 11:30 am is reminiscent of Disraeli's 1878 description of it as 'a sleepy place.' (*Sandon Cabinet Journal*, p. 20; 7 June.)

174 Quoted in Hankey Diary, 24 October 1922; Curzon to Hankey, 23 October.

175 Quoted in Ronaldshay, *Curzon*, vol. III, p. 316.

176 Nicolson, *Curzon*, p. 56; Lloyd George's goals he views as 'impenetrably closed.'

177 Amery (*Political Life*, vol. II, p. 95) describes the 'price' paid by the premier: 'he often created an impression of clever unscrupulousness and intrigue which did not do justice to the underlying sincerity of his purpose.'

178 *Davidson's Memoirs*, p. 86.

179 For a discussion of political factors, Morgan, *Age of Lloyd George*, p. 84.

180 Trevor Wilson, *The Downfall of the Liberal Party, 1914–1935* (London, 1966), p. 222.

181 Keith Middlemas and John Barnes, *Baldwin: A Biography* (London, 1969), p. 97.

182 Morgan, *Age of Lloyd George*, p. 90.

183 Wilson, *Downfall of Liberal Party*, p. 222, confirmed in Michael Kinnear, whose thorough investigation of constituency and national politics (*Fall of Lloyd George*, p. 25) leads him to assert that from the Tory perspective the premier 'did not even seem to be an electoral asset, which may have been what told against him in the end.'

184 Lord Beaverbrook, *The Decline and Fall of Lloyd George* (New York, 1963), pp. 140–1.

185 Nicolson, *Curzon*, p. 275; subsequent actions of the Cabinet Nicolson finds irresponsible, and he credits the actions of two British representatives on the scene, Rumbold the High Commissioner and Harington, the British officer in command, with averting a 'wholly unnecessary war.'

186 Cowling, *Impact of Labour*, p. 194; see above, n. 165. Kinnear (*Fall of*

Lloyd George, p. 91) places the major responsibility upon the vacillating leadership of Austen Chamberlain.

187 Apparently this phrase was first used by Winston Churchill in criticizing Amery's organizing this particular Unionist group (Amery, *Political Life*, vol. II, pp. 235–45). Morgan (*Age of Lloyd George*, p. 92) misquotes the proper phrase.

188 Quoted by Blake, *Unrepentant Tory*, pp. 439–40. Of course the premier's advisers attempted to relate 'the truth' to him in some substantive matters, e.g. on the advisability of issuing the Balfour note in the summer of 1922, in this case in vain. (Roberta Dayer, 'The British War Debts to the United States and the Anglo-Japanese Alliance, 1920–1923,' *Pacific Historical Review*, 45: 569–95 (no. 4, November 1976).)

3. CRISIS 1922

1 Roskill, *Hankey*, vol. II, pp. 276–7.

2 Lloyd George Papers, F/16/1/30, 29 June 1922.

3 Thomas Jones Papers, Class Z, vol. V, 13 March 1920; Esher was grieved that Hankey had failed to secure a permanent post at Whitehall Gardens for none other than T. E. Lawrence. Cf. Esher's fulsome praise for Hankey, expressed in a letter to him only six months later; quoted by Roskill, *Hankey*, vol. II, pp. 182–3. Either Esher had had a change of heart, or, as do many courtiers, he walked both sides of the street.

4 155 *HC Debates*, 13 June 1922, col. 215.

5 *Ibid.*, cols. 232–8.

6 *Ibid.*, cols. 252–5 (Lieut-Col. Guinness).

7 *Ibid.*, cols. 219, 223, and 225.

8 *Ibid.*, col. 230; Asquith did pay tribute to Hankey, nonetheless.

9 *Ibid.*, cols. 263–76; Lord Eustace Percy had praised 'the good old dignified ways.'

10 Hankey was also troubled by Asquith's criticism, for all its ineffectiveness; see Roskill, *Hankey*, vol. II, p. 280.

11 CAB 21/221, 'The Cabinet Office: Note by the Secretary of the Cabinet,' 10 June 1922. Hankey was provoked into a careful review of the antecedents and functions of the Secretariat, copies of which he included in the registry of Cabinet-related materials, CAB 21, and in his own 'Magnum Opus' file. (See 'The Cabinet Secretariat: Part I, The Principle,' 7 November 1922, the major part of which he published as chapter 3 of his *Diplomacy by Conference*, in 1946; Part II, 'The Status of the Secretariat of the Cabinet and the Committee of Imperial Defence,' 7 November 1922, dealt with the alleged 'wrong and extravagant' application of the principle; CAB 63/33.)

12 'The Cabinet Secretariat,' *The Spectator*, 128: 740 (17 June 1922).

13 Sir Henry Craik, 'The Cabinet Secretariat,' *The Nineteenth Century and After*, 91: 914 (June 1922), utilized a historical analogy: 'at a much earlier period, the Secretaries, who were held to be of little account in the old days when the Privy Council exercised large executive powers, gradually became the great functionaries of State, instead of mere channels for promulgating orders. May not the new Secretariat develop along the same lines?' (p. 920). Of course the Secretariat did not come to replace the Cabinet, but the Secretary became a major figure of state.

14 *Ibid.*, pp. 922–3.
15 CAB 21/221, 'The Cabinet Secretariat,' *Law Times*, 24 June 1922; Sir William Anson's 1907 view was cited, but surely the regular attendance of 'outsiders' at War Cabinet meetings had undermined such an absolutionist interpretation.
16 CAB 21/221, 'Back Garden Beauties,' *The Sunday Pictorial*, 18 June 1922.
17 *Ibid.*, *The Weekly Dispatch*, 18 June 1922.
18 *Ibid.*, Stamfordham to Austen Chamberlain, 15 June 1922. The Treasury had stated in June 1922 that 'the staff is not in numbers or in quality [rank?] in excess of the requirements of the work.' (*Ibid.*, 'Note by the Treasury,' 9 June 1922.) As well, the Geddes Committee had chosen not to wield its 'axe' in Whitehall Gardens.
19 Wilson, *Cabinet Office*, p. 21; yet the size of the staff is less justified in view of the decline in the number of memoranda circulated from 3400 in 1918 to 800 in 1922.
20 Jones, *Diary with Letters*, p. xxi. It must be remarked that both Hankey and Jones violated an absolute prescription, but certainly less so after 1922.
21 Unfortunately, Turner (*Lloyd George's Secretariat*, p. 197) concludes his study with the end of the war, although the institution continued into the post-war years.
22 Lloyd George Papers, F/90/1/37, Hankey to Kerr, 1 February 1921.
23 So my examination of the relevant file in the Lloyd George Papers leads me to conclude; e.g. F/90/1/18, Kerr's memorandum of 2 September 1920.
24 *Ibid.*, F/90/1/35, Kerr to Prime Minister, 19 January 1921.
25 *Ibid.*, F/34/2/1–15, 18 May 1921–4 March 1922.
26 Stevenson, *The Years that are Past*, p. 100.
27 Collins, *Aspects*, p. 198; the latter phrase is quoted from Vansittart.
28 Lloyd George Papers F/86/3 and F/86/2/20, Grigg to Prime Minister, 25 May 1921 and 29 September 1922.
29 One commentator reported adversely: 'An unimportant Minister may see them, and spare the time of their chief; and they will report back a decision founded upon such evidence as they choose to deliver.' (Harold J. Laski, 'Mr. George and the Constitution: II – The Prime Minister and the Cabinet,' *The Nation*, 28: 124–5 (23 October 1920).)
30 Chester and Willson, *British Central Government*, p. 290.
31 CAB 21/221, 'Premier's Web of Secretaries,' *The Star*, 13 June 1922. Alas, the same mistake has been repeated for fifty years by some misguided historians; see above, Ch. 1 n. 144.
32 CAB 21/221, 'Downing-Street Army,' *Daily Express*, 14 June 1922.
33 *Ibid.*, 'The Tradition of the Cabinet,' *Glasgow Herald*, 16 June 1922.
34 *Field-Marshal Sir Henry Wilson: His Life and Diaries*, ed. Sir C. E. Callwell (2 vols., London, 1927), vol. II, pp. 343–4; 13 June 1922. That Wilson would not press an advantage surprises in light of his capacity for intrigue.
35 C 55 (20) 6, 14 October 1920 (CAB 23/22); CAB 63/30, Hankey to Walter Long, 8 December 1920.
36 CAB 63/33, Hankey to Prime Minister, 13 October 1922. On one occasion during the war, Hankey talked to the editor of *The Spectator*, St Loe Strachey, who had written a 'violent article' about Lloyd George. (Hankey, *Supreme Command*, vol. II, p. 728; 15 November 1917.)
37 C 62 (20) 1–2, 18 November 1920 (CAB 23/22). There exists in the Cabinet Conclusions a rare example of a verbatim 'Minute Sheet' for this discussion,

showing a sharp division and acrimonious feelings voiced in the Cabinet on the previous day (C 61 (20), 17 November 1920). By comparing this to the newspaper accounts, e.g. 'The Question at Issue,' *The Times*, 18 November, it is clear that the Cabinet opponents of the trade agreement with Russia, including Curzon and Churchill, stood to strengthen their opposition by such a public ventilation.

38 C 16 (22) 3, 8 March 1922 (CAB 23/29).

39 *Records of the Cabinet Office*, p. 9; see below, p. 109.

40 CAB 21/222, Hankey to Churchill, 10 March 1922. These personal letters contrast with the specific 'Conclusions' sent to departments under Hankey's 1919 instructions.

41 C 42 (22) 4, 25 July 1922 (CAB 23/30).

42 In 1964 Harold Wilson refused to accept any such record of dissent in the Cabinet Minutes, suggesting instead that such views be included in an official minute submitted to the Prime Minister. (*The Governance of Britain* (New York, 1976), pp. 58–9.)

43 Thomas Jones, *Lloyd George* (Cambridge, Mass., 1951), p. 268; the project was in fact delayed a decade, and even then not without repercussions.

44 Stevenson, *Lloyd George: A Diary*, p. 215; 9 May 1921. Initially, he hoped to write his memoirs during the autumn recess! Both Tom Jones and Esher advised against publication while in office, although Balfour saw no objection. (Jones, *Whitehall Diary*, vol. I, p. 204; 31 July 1922.)

45 Craik, 'Cabinet Secretariat,' p. 921.

46 CAB 21/221, 'Downing Street's Garden Suburb,' *Westminster Gazette*, 14 June 1922.

47 Even putting 'departmentalism' to the side, 'it is difficult to see how it [the Cabinet Secretariat] strengthens the Prime Minister against his colleagues who share its advantages.' (Byrum E. Carter, *The Office of the Prime Minister* (Princeton, 1956), p. 205.) Blake (*Prime Minister*, pp. 48–50) makes much the same point.

48 Respectively, Daalder, *Cabinet Reform*, p. 58, and Hankey, *Diplomacy by Conference*, p. 21.

49 Ian Gilmour, *The Body Politic* (London, 1969), pp. 179, 206, and 241.

50 Patrick Gordon Walker, *The Cabinet* (London, 1970), pp. 86–91. The terms 'presidential government' and 'prime ministerial government' have been used interchangeably to infer a departure from 'Cabinet government,' although contemporary usage favors the latter.

51 Gordon Walker, *The Cabinet*, p. 96.

52 Frank Stacey, *The Government of Modern Britain* (Oxford, 1968); John P. Mackintosh, *The British Cabinet* (2nd edn, London, 1968); Humphrey Berkeley, *The Power of the Prime Minister* (New York, 1969); Crossman, 'Introduction' to Bagehot, *The English Constitution*; Richard Crossman, *The Myths of Cabinet Government* (Cambridge, Mass., 1972). Cf. the defence of Crossman's chief Harold Wilson: 'it is the Cabinet not the Prime Minister who decides.' (*Governance of Britain*, pp. 4–11.)

53 Stacey, *Government of Modern Britain*, pp. 279 and 262. In view of the events described in this chapter, it is startling that Stacey should assert that 'the existence of the Cabinet Secretariat has not been a matter of controversy since 1918' (p. 263).

54 Berkeley, *Power of the Prime Minister*, p. 47.

55 Cf. Berkeley, who sees the latter-day process strengthened by the growth of

an 'official hierarchy of unparalleled magnitude' for which he finds a counterpart body in Lloyd George's time, although in fact renewed growth in size and influence of that 'hierarchy' came after the Treasury reorganization of 1919-20.

56 Mackintosh admits the movement away from the Cabinet as the only decision-making body with which the premier shared power but qualifies that judgment for the period to 1922: 'In these years the pattern was more that of a cone with the Premier at the apex, depending on and supported by widening rings of advisers. By far the most important of these rings was the Cabinet, as it was the only one which had a definite publicly announced membership, and the right to complain if it was not consulted.' (*British Cabinet*, p. 388.)

57 In Chamberlain's words, 'His Majesty's Government are unable to reconcile the publication of the telegram of the Government of India on the sole responsibility of the Cabinet' (151 *HC Debates*, 9 March 1922, col. 1490); he specified that Montagu had consulted no other member of the Cabinet.

58 Montagu to his constituents, quoted in *The Times*, 13 March 1922.

59 Quoted by S. D. Waley, *Edwin Montagu: A Memoir* (Bombay, 1964), p. 278.

60 Mackintosh (*British Cabinet*, p. 389) is mistaken in referring to the discussion as having taken place 'in the Cabinet'; as that meeting was in suspension, no official record of the discussion was kept.

61 Lloyd George Papers, F/26/1/13, Hankey to Prime Minister, 14 March 1922.

62 Jones, *Whitehall Diary*, vol. I, p. 211; 19 October 1922. In such ways Hankey hoped to pare expenditures from £34,000 to £15,000.

63 Hankey Diary, 19 and 20 October 1922.

64 Lloyd George Papers, G/18/8/1, 12 December 1922.

65 Jones, *Whitehall Diary*, vol. I, p. 243; 30 September 1923.

66 Roskill's description (*Hankey*, vol. II, p. 302) provides a clue, even in its exaggeration: '[Hankey] was enkindled, sometimes perhaps dazzled, by the sheer brilliance of intellect and imagination, which almost daily flashed and scintillated before him like an Aurora Borealis.'

67 WC (War Cabinet) 3, 6 of 12 December 1919 (CAB 23/1).

68 Hankey Diary, 21 October 1922.

69 *Ibid.*; Hankey had foreseen the eventual absorption of the League branch by the Foreign Office (CAB 63/33, 'Experience in the Cabinet Office,' quoting Hankey to Fisher, 5 March 1921), but he had done nothing to facilitate that transfer.

70 Hankey Diary, 21 October 1922.

71 The exception was an Assistant Secretary, Sir John Chancellor, whom Hankey judged 'rather a misfit. . . who cannot get on with his subordinates'; even so the Cabinet Secretary sought to find a colonial governorship for him, and Chancellor served in such a post in Southern Rhodesia from 1923 to 1928.

72 Hankey did not attach that account to his diary, but a copy was included in his 'Magnum Opus' file, which eventually found its way into the Public Record Office as CAB 63/1–191; Roskill wrote the first and second volume of his biography in the absence of this file, although many of the documents which Hankey retained in this file turn up in other Cabinet papers as well.

73 Apparently Hankey did not record the details of that first conversation, an unusual lapse on his part which compounded the subsequent confusion.

74 CAB 63/33, 'Notes of Conversations with Mr. Bonar Law and Sir Warren Fisher, on Wednesday, 25 October 1922,' a document which is the source for the following description.

75 In other words, Fisher had not mentioned the scheme at their first meeting, which – if Hankey's account is correct – gave him good reason for anger.

76 See above, pp. 71–2. It is ironic that 'semi-autonomous' status came as a sub-department of the Treasury, but such a relationship applied only for purposes of the parliamentary vote.

77 'Premier Opens Campaign,' *The Times*, 27 October 1922; the full text of the address is printed in Jones, *Whitehall Diary*, vol. I, p. 218.

78 Hankey Diary, 27 October 1922.

79 Fisher acknowledged that 'soldiers and sailors are constantly given inquiries,' and thus he understood Hankey's proposal.

80 Hankey Diary, 27 October 1922. Nearly a quarter-century Clerk of the Privy Council, Fitzroy had only recently been charged, convicted and fined £5 for 'wilfully . . . annoying' women in Hyde Park. As Hankey foresaw, his appeal succeeded – on a technicality. ('Sir A. Fitzroy's Appeal,' *The Times*, 11 November 1922.) Nonetheless, his behavior had been erratic, according to police testimony, and the post came Hankey's way on 31 May 1923. (Roskill, *Hankey*, vol. II, p. 314 n. 1.)

81 Hankey Diary, 27 October 1922.

82 A comparison of Hankey's own account with what he subsequently related to Tom Jones is instructive, although the former is consistently fuller. However, there is no mention in Jones' account (*Whitehall Diary*, vol. I, pp. 218–19) of Hankey's accusations directed at Treasury performance; instead we find a justification of the Secretariat's role in the Chanak imbroglio, which Hankey does not mention in his own account.

83 If such a 'cabal' existed, would Fisher have sought to add to his wide range of responsibilities? Roskill (*Hankey*, vol. II, p. 313 n. 2) thinks it unlikely, and, with the lack of any evidence, he certainly deserves the benefit of the doubt.

84 Jones Diary, dated 26 October, although the events described took place on the following day, when Bonar Law's electoral address was printed. *Whitehall Diary*, vol. I, p. 219, does not print the passage explaining Hankey's interest in the post.

85 CAB 63/53, Hankey's Memorandum of 9 May 1938. The point had recently been raised by the editors of the *Law Times*; see above, p. 89. For the impact of the Oath upon Hankey's keeping a diary, see below, pp. 133–4.

86 'The Prime Minister's Manifesto,' *The Times*, 27 October 1922.

87 Hankey had cited security reasons for dismissing Peter Wright from his Paris staff in 1918; see Roskill, *Hankey*, vol. I, p. 491 n. 1.

88 Hankey Diary, 29 October 1922.

89 *Ibid.*; to Fisher, Hankey more diplomatically spelled out 'reasons of discipline and efficiency.' *Ibid.*, 30 October 1922; extracts from the memoranda of the two combatants are printed by Wilson, *Cabinet Office*, pp. 47–8.

90 Roskill (*Hankey*, vol. II, p. 316) does not print this portion of the diary on the grounds that 'his oft-used and vehement attack on the Treasury's failure to prepare for war in 1914' is well known; while this is true, one senses that another reason for the exclusion is that Hankey's bitterness about the Treasury's indifference to the War Book verged on monomania, revealing an intense quirk of character.

91 Hankey Diary, 30 October 1922.
92 CAB 63/33, 'Notes of Conversations.'
93 Quoted, 'The Middle Course,' *The Times*, 30 October 1922.
94 Hankey Diary, 30 October 1922.
95 For Fisher's final submission of 7 November 1922, Wilson, *Cabinet Office*, pp. 48–9.
96 The latter is a suggestion of Sir Horace Wilson, whose observations are printed by Roskill, *Hankey*, vol. II, p. 320.
97 Roseveare, *The Treasury*, p. 248; the key reform item is discussed above, pp. 70–1.
98 PREM 1/53, Fisher to Prime Minister, 16 February 1926, and extract from 192 *HC Debates*, 24 February 1926, cols. 519–20; Fisher underscored the point that the dual responsibility did not confer 'independent authority'; only status was involved.
99 Lord Bridges, *The Treasury* (London, 1964), pp. 173 and 180; he prints a copy of the minute of 1867 in Appendix VII.
100 Quoted, Hamilton, 'Sir Warren Fisher,' pp. 27–9.
101 Watt, *Personalities and Policies*, p. 104. Until the 'Eden reforms' of 1943, the Foreign Office was still regarded as part of the Home Civil Service, but Fisher intended an even closer relationship.
102 Thomas Balogh, 'The Apotheosis of the Dilettante: The Establishment of Mandarins,' in *The Establishment*, ed. Hugh Thomas (London, 1969), pp. 119–120.
103 Hamilton, 'Sir Warren Fisher,' p. 14. As well, Fisher offended a number of his fellow 'mandarins' by his outspoken criticism of those who failed to meet his high standards for the Civil Service; see above, p. 71.
104 Along such lines Mackintosh assesses the role of the Secretariat in a fashion reminiscent of Hankey: 'While this office is not simply at the service of the Prime Minister, the Chief Secretary to the Cabinet has often acted as personal adviser and the effect of the Secretariat is to warn the Prime Mininster of the issues and problems that are coming up from the departments.' (*Government and Politics of Britain*, p. 64.)
105 CAB 21/223, 'Procedure in the Cabinet Office,' 30 October 1922.
106 *Ibid.*, 'Draft Instructions to the Secretary of the Cabinet,' 31 October 1922; Roskill's assertion (*Hankey*, vol. II, p. 317) that this document was 'apparently never circulated' is belied by its appearance in the Cabinet Minutes of 1 November 1922, where it is found, largely intact, as Annex III of C 64 (22), in CAB 23/32. Its 'provisional' nature proved long-term.
107 Hankey Diary, 2 November 1922. From this time, the Agenda Papers were collected with the Conclusions in the Cabinet Minutes.
108 C 66 (22), Annex III (CAB 23/32).
109 For the fairly recent restrictions, see p. 93.
110 Quoted, 'Mr Bonar Law's Policy,' *The Times*, 2 November 1922.
111 Hankey Diary, 10 November 1922. This particular offending phrase was not printed in *The Times*' account of Curzon's speech, Hankey speculated because the Foreign Secretary had himself asked for its removal on the evening of 8 November, i.e. prior to Hankey's remonstration.
112 Hankey Diary, 8 November 1922.
113 *Ibid.*, 10 November 1922. If Hankey's diary entry accurately reflects the conversation, the aristocratic Curzon can hardly ever have been humbled so thoroughly.

114 Quoted in Roskill, *Hankey*, vol. II, p. 321; Curzon to Hankey, 9 November 1922.
115 Burgis Memoirs, which are retrospective.
116 Thomas Jones Diary, 15 November 1922; Balfour he leagued with Lloyd George.
117 'Polling Day,' *The Times*, 15 November 1922. Hankey may well have had this article in mind in referring to Law's 'tepid' defence.
118 Cf. Crossman, 'Introduction,' to Bagehot, *The English Constitution*, p. 48, who maintains that 'old-fashioned Cabinet government was re-established in the 1920's in a form not very different from that described in *The English Constitution*.' Crossman exaggerates the admittedly different styles of government as between Lloyd George and his immediate successors; the work of the Cabinet Secretariat incorporated substantial continuity.
119 159 *HC Debates*, col. 281. Neither Bonar Law's nor Baldwin's statement appears much like the parliamentary 'whitewash' which Hankey had sought, but both served to confer institutional legitimacy.
120 *Ibid.*, 30 November 1922, col. 891.
121 *Ibid.*, col. 892.
122 Balfour Papers, Balfour to Hankey, 1 December 1928; Hankey had produced records which effectively routed an American interpretation of the deliberations concerning cruiser policy at the Washington Naval Conference.
123 Along these lines, Roskill (*Hankey*, vol. II, p. 258) describes Hankey's role at Washington as 'surely considerable, since it was he who got the initially gritty machinery of the conference to run smoothly, who was friendly and tactful to everyone, and who often saw the best road to compromise.'
124 159 *HC Debates*, 7 December 1922, col. 1983.
125 As well, he had drawn a distinction between his recording 'only the decisions of the Cabinet' and maintaining a record of 'Cabinet proceedings'; Bonar Law sought to put a quietus to the notion that the Cabinet Secretary was in fact 'the repository of the opinions of each member of preceding Cabinets.' (*Ibid.*, 30 November 1922, col. 891.)
126 Hankey Diary, 30 November 1922.
127 *Ibid.*, 12 December 1922.
128 Jones, *Whitehall Diary*, vol. I, pp. 219–21; 30 and 31 October and 11 and 12 November 1922.
129 Oddly, Hankey did not note what Burgis recollected, namely that at this time the Cabinet Secretary was no longer permitted to take an assistant along to help him to take the Cabinet Minutes. Possibly Hankey did not regard this as anything new, since it had been proscribed in Lloyd George's peace-time regime, although the regulation had not been enforced. See above, pp. 65–6.
130 Hankey Diary, 26 November 1922.
131 The phrase is Daalder's (*Cabinet Reform*, p. 60). Wilson (*Cabinet Office*, pp. 86–7) lists twenty-two such conferences for which the Cabinet Office 'either alone or in association with other departments, provided the secretariat for the United Kingdom delegation, and for which the Office maintained a full record of the proceedings.'
132 HNKY 4/29, G. M. Trevelyan to Hankey, 21 May 1937; Trevelyan was revising his *History of England*, and Hankey, characteristically, prevailed upon him to limit the description of the secretarial innovation to a single footnote, while treating the CID at paragraph length! (G. M. Trevelyan, *History of England*, vol. III (London, pb. edn, 1953), pp. 261–2.)

4. THE SECRETARIAT IN THE 1920S: POLICIES AND PROCEDURES

1 Hankey Diary, 12 December 1922.

2 Gounaris had cited the correspondence in his own defence at the 'show trial' which preceded his execution. (Walder, *Chanak*, p. 246.) Although A. J. P. Taylor (*Beaverbrook* (New York, 1972), pp. 195–6) does not indicate how Beaverbrook had come into possession of this particular letter, he does show that half-a-dozen members of the Coalition Cabinet, including Lloyd George, shared his belief that the document had never been circulated.

3 52 *HC Debates*, 7 December 1922, cols. 343–4.

4 PREM 1/18, Hankey to Prime Minister, 8 December 1922, found Hankey misdating the Gounaris letter to 1921, a rare slip on his part. Although Curzon protested his innocence of any such wrong-doing in a telegram on the following day, Hankey had already resolved the matter in Curzon's favor; thus Montgomery ('Lloyd George and the Greek Question,' pp. 256–8) errs in asserting that the Foreign Office refuted Birkenhead's allegations.

5 52 *HC Debates*, 11 December 1922, cols. 355–6, responding to Salisbury's recital (col. 352) of those facts, based upon Hankey's records.

6 The situation eased in 1924, when Ramsay MacDonald abandoned the practice whereby the Prime Minister's Private Secretary and others within the Private Office resigned with a change in the party complexion of the government. While the Civil Service took over the Private Office, the Political Office is staffed by partisan appointees. (Wilson, *Governance of Britain*, pp. 79–80 and 91.)

7 Churchill had earlier assumed that such official documents as his Admiralty telegrams would be published only in the Official Histories. (Martin S. Gilbert, *Winston S. Churchill*, vol. IV, *The Stricken World, 1916–1922* (Boston, 1975), pp. 751–9, an account of the gestation of Churchill's war memoirs.) For the Official Histories, see below, pp. 120–3.

8 For that decision, which Hankey continued to question until he secured repeal in 1934, see above, pp. 67–8.

9 Lloyd George Papers, G/4/4/4, draft letter to the Editor of *The Times*, which Churchill at this time (28 February 1923) 'deferred' from sending. Churchill concluded that the doctrine of Cabinet secrecy was less than absolute: 'It must be and always has been construed in conjunction with the time, the character and the purpose of the reference.'

10 160 *HC Debates*, 15 February 1923, col. 315. The King had a figurehead role, as is apparent in Hankey's comment to Churchill three years later, concerning the third volume of his *World Crisis*: 'I do not know if it has occurred to you, as a Privy Counsellor, to ask the leave of the King. I am not sure that it is necessary, and in any event the King could only refer the matter back to the Prime Minister. I have a feeling at the back of my mind that the King will take it rather well if you ask him.' (CAB 63/38, Hankey to Churchill, 10 December 1926.)

11 160 *HC Debates*, 19 February 1923, col. 593.

12 Churchill commented that Bonar Law's handling of the matter was 'very unfriendly,' and his remark about the breach of the Privy Counsellor's Oath 'crude and uncalled for.' (Lloyd George Papers, G/4/4/4, Churchill to Lloyd George, 28 February 1923.)

13 For this important episode, see the letters – printed in full, respectively Churchill and Hankey to Prime Minister, 3 and 8 March 1923, pp. 32–9, in

Winston S. Churchill, *Companion* to vol. V, Part 1, *The Exchequer Years, 1922–1929*, ed. Martin S. Gilbert (Boston, 1981).

14 Lloyd George Papers, G/4/4/20, Churchill to Lloyd George, 1 January 1929.

15 *Ibid.*, G/212, Hankey to Lloyd George, 8 January 1933.

16 *Ibid.*, G/212, Hankey to Lloyd George, 16 April 1934. Although the former premier agreed to modify the criticism, he ventured the same defence of his frankness that Churchill had earlier advanced, namely that the 'whole truth' was owed to himself, the public and posterity. (*Ibid.*, G/212, copy of Lloyd George to Hankey, 18 April 1934.)

17 CAB 63/38, Hankey to Churchill, 8 December 1926.

18 Martin S. Gilbert, *Winston S. Churchill*, vol. V, *The Prophet of Truth, 1922–1939* (Boston, 1977), p. 318 n. 1.

19 Churchill, *The Aftermath*, p. vii.

20 For a description of the structural relationship and guidelines drawn up for the contents of the Official Histories, see above, p. 73.

21 CAB 103/83, recounted in CID 238-B: 'Official Histories: Memorandum by the Secretary of the Historical Section of the CID [E. Y. Daniel],' 3 September 1919.

22 *Ibid.*; CAB 103/82, as recounted by E. Y. Daniel in a draft, 'Historical Section of the CID: Memorandum by the Secretary,' 12 July 1922.

23 Hankey's action stands in marked contrast to d'Ombrain's reference to his inaction in face of a cut of roughly half in the Historical Section's budget early in 1914, at Asquith's behest: 'To this Hankey raised not the slightest objection. "To live is to outlive" had become his bon mot.' (*War Machinery*, p. 217.)

24 CAB 103/83, 'Official Histories,' 3 September 1919. For the full range of the series, see below, p. 226 and Ch. 6 n. 67.

25 CAB 103/82, 'Historical Section of the CID,' 12 July 1922.

26 Thus Hankey stipulated the virtue of producing 'one account which is based on a review of all the facts and gives the authentic considerations by which those officially responsible were actuated.' (CAB 63/40, untitled memorandum by Hankey, 12 June 1928.) For Churchill's objection to Corbett's version of 'an absolutely reliable and impartial account,' see above p. 73.

27 CAB 103/83, copy of Hankey to Fortescue, 28 October 1919. Already in August of that year, Fortescue indicated his preference not to continue his investigations, but he remained attached to the Section until the review appeared.

28 CAB 103/82, 'Historical Section of the CID,' 12 July 1922.

29 The exchange of views continued even beyond the time of Corbett's death in 1922; see above, p. 73.

30 CAB 103/83, CP 9 (19), 'Cabinet Official Histories: Note by the Secretary,' 28 October 1919.

31 C 12 (19), Appendix V (4), 10 December 1919 (CAB 23/18).

32 At that Conference opinions were evenly divided concerning Corbett's volume – 'a casting vote clinched it [publication]' – but sentiments overwhelmingly favored the publication of Walter Raleigh's 'War in the Air.' (CAB 103/83, Daniel to Raleigh, 13 December 1919.)

33 *Ibid.*, Hankey Minute on Corbett to Daniel, 14 December 1919. Corbett had entered the strongest protest: 'Publication was an essential condition of my contract and I must beg that it will be understood that I cannot accept the repudiation of the Government's commitments as in any way modifying my position.'

34 Hankey used Daniel's memorandum virtually verbatim in drafting CP 1034 (20), 'Official History of the War,' 8 April 1920; Cabinet action is found in C 20 (20) 4, 15 April 1920 and C 15 (21) 7, 24 March 1921 (CAB 23/24).
35 C 33 (21) 9, 5 May 1921 (CAB 23/25).
36 H. Montgomery-Hyde, *British Air Policy Between the Wars, 1918–1939* (London, 1976), pp. 196–8, demonstrates the Cabinet Secretary's veto power; in the case of the successor to Raleigh, author only of the first volume, Montgomery-Hyde characterized the result as 'accurate historiography but unexciting prose.'
37 CAB 103/83, CP 2790 (21), 'The Official History of the War,' 1 April 1921. For the specific guidelines, see above, p. 73.
38 CAB 103/83, Hankey to Eyre Crowe, 23 May 1921.
39 Wilson, *Cabinet Office*, p. 126.
40 CAB 103/83, Hankey to Prime Minister, 1 August 1923, a minute on Daniel to Hankey, 30 July 1923.
41 *Ibid.*, Fisher to Chancellor of the Exchequer and Prime Minister, 7 November 1922, cited by Wilson, *Cabinet Office*, p. 49.
42 *Ibid.*, p. 122; the last qualification likely stems from the deliberate exclusion of all materials relating to Allied deception in warfare and all cryptanalytical practices, with whatever distortions or falsifications of the historical record only time, and the use of these sources, will tell; see below, p. 293.
43 Austen Chamberlain, 'Correspondence,' *The Times*, 3 December 1924.
44 R. W. Seton-Watson, 'Correspondence,' *ibid.*, his letter of 25 November 1924 to the Foreign Secretary. In commenting on the exchange, *The Times* noted that since Sir Edward Grey's White Paper of August 1914, Britain had fallen behind and paid a price: 'The facts, reports or points of view which make their way into the public mind first have always an advantage over those which follow later.' ('Publishing the Archives,' *ibid.*)
45 *The War Diaries of Oliver Harvey*, ed. John Harvey (London, 1978), p. 42; 15 September 1941. Halifax was opposed, but Vansittart acidly commented that 'our Ministers were fools, but not knaves.'
46 In view of this recognition, the halting progress of the entire series is difficult to fathom. For a discussion of the public's 'right to know' – Harvey made precisely this point in 1941 – see below, Ch. 7.
47 For these actions, see David Williams, *Not in the Public Interest* (London, 1965), pp. 16–24.
48 The text is cited, p. 112, and the judgment made in a commentary, p. 113, of the Franks Committee. (*Report of the Departmental Committee on Section 2 of the Official Secrets Act 1911* (Cmnd 5104, 1972) (hereafter cited as *Franks Committee Report*).)
49 In this case, the defendant was a War Office clerk who had passed information concerning contracts for army officer's clothing to the director of a firm of tailors. (*Ibid.*, p. 116, Appendix II.)
50 Hugh Thomas, 'Towards a Revision of the Official Secrets Act,' in his anthology, *Crisis in the Civil Service* (London, 1968), p. 111.
51 *Franks Committee Report*, p. 123.
52 Williams, *Public Interest*, p. 45; for war-time violations of secrecy, see above, pp. 10–11, 41.
53 Noted by Hugh Thomas, who comments aptly: 'the fact that it should be Asquith . . . who explained that ministers were bound by the Official Secrets Act becomes exquisitely entertaining.' ('Towards a Revision,' p. 115.)

54 *Franks Committee Report*, p. 123, judged 'obviously erroneous' the conclusion implicit in the 1920 remarks of the Attorney-General, Sir Gordon Hewart, that the whole of the 1911 Act, including section 2, was concerned only with spying. Certainly the 1919 court case did not concern espionage. Hewart's remarks served only to cloud the issue, as the Franks Committee recognized.

55 For the privileged status, D. C. Watt, 'Foreign Affairs, the Public Interest and the Right to Know,' *Political Quarterly*, 34: 127–80 (no. 2, April–June 1963), who adds that officials thus stand as judges of what may be published.

56 135 *HC Debates*, 2 December 1920, cols. 1537–8 and 1578.

57 *Franks Committee Report*, p. 37.

58 160 *HC Debates*, 19 February 1923, col. 591 (Lieut-Col. Arthur Murray).

59 On the latter point, Frances Stevenson (*The Years that are Past*, p. 210) errs in asserting that her former colleague A. J. Sylvester 'remained at Downing Street in Mr. Bonar Law's Secretariat.' Sylvester remained on his staff.

60 Hankey Diary, 11 November 1923.

61 Roskill, *Hankey*, vol. II, p. 343.

62 Burgis Memoirs. As Burgis prepared his memoirs late in a long life, he had been exposed to the many memoirs of the period.

63 Middlemas and Barnes, *Baldwin*, p. 177. Of the relations between the Secretary and his deputy, Roskill (*Hankey*, vol. II, p. 344) comments that 'Jones and Hankey continued to work together as a team, and no harsh words seem ever to have passed between them.'

64 Jones, *Whitehall Diary*, vol. I, p. 250. Roskill (*Hankey*, vol. I, p. 350 n. 4) misread this entry in writing that Hankey was not wanted 'at a discussion with M.P.s at the House of Commons,' when in fact Jones had noted that 'the House of Commons members [of the Cabinet] remained behind.'

65 Gordon Walker, *The Cabinet*, p. 54: 'On one occasion, in 1924, Baldwin asked the Cabinet Secretary to withdraw during a sharp dispute on protection.'

66 Hankey Diary, 18 January and 7 July 1917. In view of the complete confidence in which Lloyd George held the Cabinet Secretariat, Blake's 'possible' explanation for the Prime Minister's annexation of the decision to request a dissolution – prior to the war, the decision had rested with the Cabinet – namely that 'so very "political" a matter . . . came to be regarded as an awkward matter to discuss in Cabinet in front of officials' (*Prime Minister*, p. 59) fails to persuade. However, contemporary practices may well differ.

67 Gordon Walker, *The Cabinet*, p. 54, assuming that his sources are well-informed.

68 Wilson, *Governance of Britain*, pp. 56–7.

69 Jones, *Whitehall Diary*, vol. I, p. 262; 22 December 1923.

70 *Amery Diaries*, pp. 342–3 and 349; 14 October 1923.

71 Jones, *Whitehall Diary*, vol. I, p. 262; 22 December 1923.

72 Baldwin's attraction to Jones is imaginatively reconstructed by Roskill, *Hankey*, vol. II, p. 344.

73 Jones Diary, 30 October 1922 (unprinted); on 19 October Jones had confided to Hankey and to his diary that the Tory 'Die Hards might force him [Bonar Law] to throw me out because of my close association with L.G. whose nominee I was when I joined the Secretariat.' (Jones Diary, unprinted.)

74 Hankey Diary, 9 December 1923.

75 See above, p. 52. Roskill (*Hankey*, vol. II, p. 352 n. 1) acknowledges 'the enormous amount of material' which Hankey had prepared for political speeches.
76 This particular grievance – Jones' salary was half Hankey's – is spelled out in *Whitehall Diary*, vol. II, p. 267; 24 January 1924; the discord apparently vanished when Hankey secured his deputy a £300 increment. (Jones Diary, unprinted, enclosure in Hankey to Warren Fisher, 29 January and 24 March 1924.)
77 *Davidson's Memoirs*, p. 144.
78 Middlemas and Barnes, *Baldwin*, p. 172.
79 Roskill, *Hankey*, vol. II, p. 154, quoting Hankey to Lloyd George, 17 March 1920; the following paragraph is based upon Roskill's account.
80 Roskill, *ibid.*, pp. 337–40, and Montgomery-Hyde, *British Air Policy*, pp. 119–20 and 134–50, provide a concise introduction to the work of the Salisbury Sub-Committee, sometimes known as the Salisbury Main Committee to differentiate its level from that of the Balfour Sub-Committee on the Fleet Air Arm.
81 Quoted, Montgomery-Hyde, *British Air Policy*, p. 144.
82 The latest word in the debate inclines to the Admiralty case against the Air Ministry, not surprisingly in view of the source, the diaries kept by the-then First Lord; *Amery Diaries*, pp. 316–17 and 334–5.
83 HNKY 4/46, Hankey to Trenchard, 5 February 1954, quoting Cmd 1938 (1922).
84 Trenchard admitted to Hankey that he coveted 'an official ring where I can face Wilson and Beatty as an equal. If they intend to destroy me, they'd have to do so under Queensberry rules,' according to Andrew Boyle's sympathetic if imaginative biography, *Trenchard* (London, 1962), p. 348.
85 Hankey traced the embryonic form of the COS Committee to the Chanak crisis, at which time the three met together to concert their advice, without a Secretary; the tentative arrangement persisted after the crisis eased. (HNKY 4/46, Hankey to Trenchard, 5 February 1954, based upon Hankey's 'Magnum Opus' file, now CAB 63.) Trenchard deferred to Hankey's account: 'We [the RAF] owed a lot to you in those days, and we also owed a lot to the Salisbury Committee, for whose report you were responsible.' (*Ibid.*, Trenchard to Hankey, 8 February 1954.)
86 Roskill, *Hankey*, vol. II, p. 340.
87 Middlemas and Barnes, *Baldwin*, p. 318; cf. Roskill's view of the relations between the two, quoted above, p. 127.
88 CAB 21/469, 'Existing Methods of Co-ordination in Defence Matters,' 3 April 1923.
89 CAB 63/38, draft of Hankey to Esher, 11 February 1926; the letter was not sent because Esher did not forward his proposal to the Editor of *The Times*, as he had initially intended. In that draft, Hankey struck through the last sentence quoted here, but he could well have voiced the depth of his sentiment when he met with Esher a few days later.
90 Quoted by Roskill, *Hankey*, vol. II, p. 345; Hankey to Trenchard, 31 December 1923.
91 Relatively full minutes were more likely to provide retorts from ministers who had missed a particular meeting, especially when remarks 'not really intended for the record but simply for general reflection by members of the committee' were in fact quoted. N. H. Gibbs cites as an example a minute,

dating to 1934, for the Chiefs of Staff Committee in his *Grand Strategy*, vol. I, *Rearmament Policy* (London, 1976), pp. 306–7 (*History of the Second World War: United Kingdom Military Series*).

92 The COS Committee Minutes for 1923–January 1927 are in CAB 53/1. Hankey traced a decline in the inter-service relations at the COS level to the actions of the Air COS, Trenchard, who circulated to the Cabinet his outspoken 'swan song' upon resigning that post in 1929; he gave his counterparts only a day's notice. For the exchange between Hankey and Trenchard, see Montgomery-Hyde, *British Air Policy*, pp. 245–7, and for the renewed conflict between the two in 1935, see below, p. 243.

93 In claiming MacDonald's sanction for the resumption of his diary (see Roskill, *Hankey*, vol. I, p. 24) the Clerk of the Privy Council paid little heed to that Oath.

94 Hankey Diary, 11 October 1924.

95 Lawrence Burgis recalled: 'Little Hankey was all a-twit setting off [to see MacDonald]. Not unnaturally, he was nervous regarding his new master's reactions to defence, which was all Hankey really cared about.' (Burgis Memoirs.)

96 CAB 2/4, 180 CID, 4 February 1924.

97 HNKY 4/16, copy of Hankey to Haldane, 4 August 1924. While such sentiments were fulsome, there is no reason to doubt Hankey's sincerity.

98 Roskill, *Hankey*, vol. II, p. 354.

99 Hankey Diary, 11 October 1924. In fairness to those 'Colonels and Admirals' one should note that the very same evening the Club Committee posted an invitation to MacDonald to become an honorary member, and several members commended Hankey for his initiative.

100 Jones was no mere contributor: in Baldwin's wide-ranging speech at the opening of the Imperial Conference in October 1923, Jones had written all but one paragraph. (*Whitehall Diary*, vol. I, pp. 243–4.)

101 *Ibid.*, pp. 255–7; Jones had asked for the photograph 'as a private souvenir not for publication,' which was agreed to '"unless it makes a very nice picture."'

102 Cf. Hankey's action when the new Labour ministers left Buckingham Palace after kissing hands: 'they wanted me to be photographed with them, but I resisted this.' (Diary, 11 October 1924.) Yet his recent counterpart, Sir John Hunt, feels differently, as he posed, 'a sentinel guarding the corridor linking the Cabinet Office and Number 10 Downing Street,' for a dramatic photograph accompanying Peter Hennessy's article, 'A magnificent piece of powerful bureaucratic machinery,' *The Times*, 8 March 1976.

103 Jones, *Whitehall Diary*, vol. I, pp. 266–7; 23 and 24 January 1924.

104 'Sidney was chuckling over a hitch in the solemn ceremony in which he had been right and Hankey wrong.' (*Beatrice Webb's Diaries, 1924–1932*, ed. Margaret Cole (London, 1956), pp. 1–2. Cf. Philip Snowden's recollection: 'Everything, however, passed off without a hitch, greatly to Sir Maurice Hankey's relief.' (Philip, Viscount Snowden, *An Autobiography* (2 vols., London, 1934), vol. II, p. 606.)

105 *Webb Diaries*, p. 77; 10 November 1925.

106 HNKY 3/37, Hankey to Adeline Hankey, 4 January 1930.

107 *Webb Diaries*, p. 142; 8 May 1927.

108 C 7 (24) 1, 23 January 1924 (CAB 23/47). Draft copies of the Conclusions circulated to all Cabinet ministers for correction, and a final draft copy went

to the Prime Minister for his approval before circulation and filing of the record copy.

109 C 9 (24) 21, 4 February 1924 (*ibid.*) Beatrice Webb's assertion (*Webb Diaries*, p. 1) that the press communiqué issued after the first meeting of the Labour Cabinet was an innovation which was thereafter discontinued is incorrect.

110 Quoted by Roskill, *Hankey*, vol. II, p. 358; Hankey's Aide-Memoire, 10 November 1949. A variant of the story is quoted by Dudley Sommer, *Haldane of Cloan: His Life and Times, 1856–1928* (London, 1960), p. 401 n. 2. Yet the matter was not settled forevermore: Edward Heath banned the practice, as Attlee had before him, but Harold Wilson announced in 1974: 'Smoking is not compulsory.' (*Governance of Britain*, p. 62.)

111 C 17 (24) 1, 28 February 1924 and C 19 (24) 7, 12 March 1924 (CAB 23/47).

112 C 25 (24) 3, 7 April 1924 (*ibid.*), and CAB 21/443, 'Publicity – Unauthorised Publications. Leakage of Information.'

113 CAB 21/793, Hankey to Prime Minister, 4 October 1924.

114 *Ibid.* The cover letter was attached to CP 30 (24), 'Custody of Cabinet Minutes.'

115 *Ibid.*, Hankey to Prime Minister, 13 November 1924; Baldwin did not object. MacDonald had received two sets, because he held two offices in his administration.

116 *Ibid.*, Hankey to Prime Minister, 1 December 1927; again, Baldwin agreed.

117 Thus he sharply turned down a request from Viscount Cecil: 'You talk of this merely being red-tape, but I do not think that I agree . . . That there is some risk of divulgence of secrecy in foreign hotels I know from personal experience . . . Present company always excepted, Cabinet Ministers are too busy to be really careful about papers, and in foreign hotels their staffs are usually both small and over-worked.' (*Ibid.*, Hankey to Cecil, 7 April 1927.)

118 Colin Seymour-Ure, *The Press, Politics, and the Public* (London, 1968), p. 194; see also Williams, *Public Interest*, p. 52.

119 C 27 (24) 4, 13 April 1924 (CAB 23/48). Earlier, Lloyd George had addressed the problem by bringing the Attorney General, Gordon Hewart, into the Cabinet in late 1921.

120 *Ibid.* Hankey had initially asked for an interval of seven days. (CAB 21/294, 'Cabinet Procedure'.)

121 *Ibid.*, copy of Treasury Note No. 22B/24; as we have seen, the scrutiny of the Cabinet's Home Affairs Committee was also involved.

122 HNKY 4/16, copy of Hankey to Smuts, 1 April 1924.

123 Beatrice Webb (*Webb Diaries*, p. 4) advanced a similar explanation: 'The peculiar characteristic of this Government is, in fact, that every member, except perhaps Wheatley, has been a public servant and not a profiteer . . . Whether its policy is right or wrong, Labour will prove itself emphatically fit for *administration.*'

124 HNKY 4/16, copy of Hankey to Smuts, 1 April 1924.

125 Roskill, *Hankey*, vol. I, p. 24 asserts that MacDonald 'asked Hankey whether he was still keeping a diary, and on receiving a qualified negative in reply he instructed him to restart it for the benefit of himself and other Ministers.'

126 Jones, 'Introduction' to *Diary with Letters*, p. xiii; whether such a rationale or his own desire for a private record was decisive, on at least one occasion Jones made a rather full diary entry concerning a meeting of the Cabinet's Coal Committee, despite the Prime Minister's instruction to circulate no minutes. (Gilbert, *Churchill*, vol. V, p. 201 n. 1.)

127 Thomas Jones Papers, Class Y, vol. II, no. 2; Hankey to Jones, 28 February 1945; relevant portions of this letter are quoted by Middlemas, 'Introduction,' p. xiv (Jones, *Whitehall Diary*, vol. I.) For the origins of Hankey's diary, see above, p. 44.
128 Hankey Diary, 11 October 1924.
129 Thus Roskill, *Hankey*, vol. II, p. 369 n. 1: 'he had worked hard to achieve the position of "principal adviser and counsellor" since the day MacDonald achieved power'; he insists nonetheless that Hankey desired 'not to usurp the Foreign Office's prerogatives at the conference.'
130 *Webb Diaries*, p. 44.
131 Quoted, 'By Whose Representation?' in *The Times*, 15 August 1924.
132 Only recently has the author of the letter been identified as Harry Pollitt, then a member of the CPGB and later its Secretary. Of course the authorities had no means of determining more than nominal responsibility. See N. D. Siederer, 'The Campbell Case,' *Journal of Contemporary History*, 9: 143 (April 1974).
133 176 *HC Debates*, 30 July 1924, col. 2061 (G. S. Rentoul).
134 Sir Patrick Hastings, *Autobiography* (London, 1948), pp. 236–8; alone among the Law Officers Hastings was a Member of the House of Commons, and insufficient attention has been given his claim that 'nothing that I began was I ever allowed to finish, and nothing was ever finished until something else was begun.' Most difficult to accept is his claim that he put in a 'working day' of twenty-two hours!
135 MacDonald objected to prosecution on the grounds that the CPGB was 'a miserable lot of creatures, out for notoriety and mischief'; quoted by Harold Nicolson, *King George V*, pb. edn (London, 1952), pp. 514–15; MacDonald to Stamfordham, 22 August 1924. Such an attitude to prosecution is confirmed in his remarks to the Cabinet, quoted below, p. 142.
136 C 48 (24) 5, 6 August 1924 (CAB 23/48).
137 The authoritative account of F. H. Newark, 'The Campbell Case and the First Labour Government,' *Northern Ireland Legal Quarterly*, 20: 19–42 (March 1969) asserts on the basis of Jones' notes that note-taking was not among his abilities, but Middlemas ('Introduction,' Jones, *Whitehall Diary*, vol. I, p. xiv) has pointed to the fact that Jones used a system of speed-writing and a system of key words which, coupled to his powerful memory, made for Conclusions in no way inferior to Hankey's.
138 The full text of Jones' notes is published in *Whitehall Diary*, vol. I, pp. 287–90, although Roskill (*Hankey*, vol. II, p. 377 n. 5) complains that Middlemas added several errors in printing these notes.
139 David Marquand, *Ramsay MacDonald* (London, 1977), p. 369, points to the discrepancy, although he cautions: 'The discrepancy was not large, and it is not particularly surprising that Jones did not spot it.'
140 It is in this regard that Hastings' explanation is questionable, because incomplete. In his parliamentary remarks, Hastings asserted his desire to tell the Commons 'every word that was said by everyone' at the Cabinet meeting on 6 August, but he had been told 'I am not entitled to say what happened in the Cabinet.' (177 *HC Debates*, 8 October 1924, col. 606). Nonetheless, if the existence of such a letter had been alleged to him, surely he could have made reference to it, independent of the Cabinet discussions.
141 PREM 1/45, Henderson to Stamfordham, 26 August 1924.
142 Newark, 'Campbell Case,' p. 40.
143 Siederer, 'Campbell Case,' pp. 151–2.

144 *Ibid.* The CPGB allegation was tactically well chosen; at the same time, Campbell and the party declared that they stood by the article and had themselves made no 'representations' concerning its meaning.

145 'By Whose Representation?' *The Times*, 15 August 1924.

146 PREM 1/45, respectively H. R. Doyel to Sir Patrick Gower (MacDonald's secretary), 18 August 1924; MacDonald to Hastings, 13 September 1924; and MacDonald's minute on Doyel to Gower, 20 August 1924; there is no evidence that his staff followed through in the interim.

147 *Ibid.*, Hastings to Prime Minister, September 1924, n.d., but not later than 15 September.

148 Neither MacDonald, in his own diary, nor his biographer Marquand make what could be a telling exculpatory point in his behalf.

149 Note by Hankey, attached to C 48 (24), 6 August 1924 (CAB 23/48).

150 It is nowhere clear why Hankey took no action other than to record MacDonald's challenge, although he may have concluded that the Prime Minister wished only to make a statement for the record.

151 Marquand, *MacDonald*, p. 273, stresses the premier's 'rattling' in handling the affair, although he views HMG's behavior as 'inept' rather than unconstitutional. Even in its most favorable construction, MacDonald's parliamentary answer is viewed as an 'appalling blunder,' although the Prime Minister himself construed these events in a way more favorable to his own conduct. (Quoted, p. 373.)

152 177 *HC Debates*, 30 September 1924, col. 16. His subsequent attempt to explain away such an unqualified assertion, based upon a distinction between his personal and official roles, is altogether unconvincing; the parliamentary explanation is printed by Marquand, *MacDonald*, pp. 375–6.

153 Jones, *Whitehall Diary*, vol. I, p. 296; 15 October 1924, noting his own reaction as well: 'When I heard it, as I did, in the House, a shiver ran down my spine.'

154 *Ibid.* Hankey's practice guarded against what he thought Gladstone's fear of the risk of one Cabinet minister 'Hansardising' another, through references to individual views expressed in Cabinet. (CAB 21/297, 'Notes on Lord Cecil's speech in the House of Lords on the 16th November, 1927,' undated.)

155 Note by Hankey, attached to C 48 (24). According to Jones, he 'pointed out to Hankey how damaging a procedure this was – to correct a Minute on the 22 September which had been approved on the 7 August and to do so after a public agitation had begun.' He also pressed Hankey 'that if such a statement was to be put on our records the Prime Minister should indicate precisely in what respect the Minute was inaccurate.' (Jones, *Whitehall Diary*, vol. I, pp. 296–7; 15 October 1924.) In fact the Cabinet Secretary did not correct anything; he added a statement.

156 *Ibid.*, pp. 291–2, copy of Hankey to Prime Minister, 2 October 1924. Although Richard Crossman (*Myths of Cabinet Government*, p. 35) used this incident to document his belief that 'the Cabinet Secretary can browbeat a Prime Minister,' in my reading Hankey was seeking to set the record straight, a proper function of his position.

157 MacDonald made precisely the same point in his diary entry, following upon his conversation with Hankey. (Quoted, Marquand, *Macdonald*, pp. 373–4.) Marquand does not credit Hankey's veiled attempt to give the Prime Minister grounds to plead 'nolo contendere,' although such an effort balances against his apparent inaction when MacDonald first challenged the accuracy of the Cabinet Minute.

158 Cowling, *Impact of Labour*, p. 381, asserts that the Conservative leaders were by this time prepared to bring down the minority government, whatever the occasion.
159 *Scott Diaries*, pp. 475–6; 4 March 1925.
160 In view of MacDonald's attitude, from the perspective of Whitehall Gardens it was fortuitous that the rough notes existed; in their absence the premier could have argued that the Conclusion had been incorrectly drawn up, perhaps securing a memorandum from the Attorney-General accepting full responsibility. The credibility of the Cabinet Secretariat would surely have suffered.
161 Jones, *Whitehall Diary*, vol. I, p. 293; 6 October 1924. In discussing the circulation of the minute, the Cabinet ignored the real issue – its substance. In fact, very little summary of the discussion appeared in the minute. In view of the faulty memories of the Cabinet's discussion of the Campbell prosecution, the prospect of ministerial paraphrasing of Cabinet Conclusions ought to have given someone cause for concern.
162 *Scott Diaries*, p. 476.
163 Roskill, *Hankey*, vol. II, p. 382, quoting Jones to Hankey, 8 October 1924; he gives full marks to Jones' arguing against a dissolution, since the likely return of Baldwin would restore the Deputy Secretary 'to his former privileged position.'
164 For the monarch's personal minute, Nicolson, *George V*, pp. 516–17.
165 Jones, *Whitehall Diary*, vol. I, p. 297; 15 October 1924.
166 C 51 (24), 22 September 1924 (CAB 23/48). With Parliament in recess, there were nine absentees.
167 The narrative in this paragraph draws upon L. Chester, S. Fay and H. Young, *The Zinoviev Letter* (London, 1967). For other analyses of what transpired see Christopher Andrew, 'The British Secret Service and Anglo-Soviet Relations in the 1920s,' Part I, *Historical Journal*, 20: 673–706 (no. 3, 1977) along with E. H. Carr 'Communications: The Zinoviev Letter,' *ibid.*, 22: 209–10 (no. 1, 1979) and C. Andrew, 'More on the Zinoviev Letter,' *ibid.*, 22: 211–14 (no. 1, 1979), and also Gabriel Gorodetsky, *The Precarious Truce: Anglo-Soviet Relations, 1924–27* (Cambridge, 1977), pp. 35–52. The delay may well be explained by a fact about which there is no dispute, namely that other, similar 'Zinoviev letters' had come to the Foreign Office's attention in 1924; the latest incorporated nothing new or unusual.
168 Quoted by Sommer, *Haldane*, p. 409.
169 Although Crowe's role is sympathetically examined in Andrew, 'The British Secret Service,' pp. 699–703, A. J. P. Taylor's explanation impresses: 'Crowe always thought that he knew better than his political superiors.' (*English History, 1914–1945* (Oxford, 1965), p. 226.)
170 Quoted, Marquand, *MacDonald*, pp. 384–5.
171 Jones, *Whitehall Diary*, vol. I, pp. 299–300; 31 October 1924. Cf. the Foreign Office's own version, quoted by Andrew, 'British Secret Service,' p. 703. Yet at the very least MacDonald ought to have been informed of the course of events.
172 His political support from Labour party headquarters was 'hopelessly inadequate' throughout the campaign (Marquand, *MacDonald*, p. 379), but the Foreign Office's official support was no better.
173 Though rationalization likely entered, the Labour Cabinet, in J. H. Thomas' words, 'agreed that up to Friday night all was going well with the Party prospects; but with the publication on Saturday morning of the Zinoviev

letter there was a slump, "the people lost confidence in us; the women felt frightened; speakers were paralyzed."' (Jones, *Whitehall Diary*, vol. I, p. 299; 31 October 1924.) Although Macdonald's own explanation, offered on the 27th, did not succeed in clarifying the matter, Marquand (*MacDonald*, pp. 285–6) rightly observes that it is difficult to see what else he could have said, sorely beset as he was on all sides.

174 Jones, *Whitehall Diary*, vol. I, pp. 300–1; 31 October 1924.

175 179 *HC Debates*, 15 December 1924, col. 674. Chamberlain's smugness reads ironically in the light of past Foreign Office and Secret Intelligence service debacles in dealing with forged intercepts; Andrew does, however, point to a tightening of procedures which had taken hold well before the events of 1924. (Andrew, 'British Secret Service,' pp. 688–95.)

176 C 17 (27) 4, 17 March 1927 (CAB 23/90B); while he informed the Cabinet that the source of information had in the past proved trustworthy, Andrew's recent account points to several such sources, all confirming authenticity. Hankey, who knew the intelligence community well, accepted the 'Zinoviev letter' as genuine throughout his life. (Andrew, 'More on the Zinoviev Letter,' *Historical Journal*, 22: 213.)

177 Andrew, 'British Secret Service,' p. 705; he contends that the 'genuineness' of the document is, in light of extant evidence, a more compelling hypothesis than its forgery. Cf. Chester, Fay and Young, *Zinoviev Letter*, passim; Gorodetsky, *Precarious Truce*, pp. 41–6; and E. H. Carr (who was a Foreign Office official in 1924), 'Zinoviev Letter.'

178 The amount of the payment from Conservative funds has been variously given as between £5000 and £10,000, but in any case constitutes an enormous sum, especially if compared to the probable annual estimate for the whole of the Secret Service in March 1921, £65,000! (Andrew, 'British Secret Service,' p. 706.)

179 *Davidson's Memoirs*, p. 179 (undated); the following paragraph is based upon this source.

180 *Ibid.*, quoting Storr's memorandum of 10 December 1923; Col. Lancelot Storr was Davidson's secretary and a former associate of Hankey; Davidson was assisted in drawing up the plans by the then civil servant, John Anderson.

181 *Ibid.*, p. 180.

182 C 58 (24) 3, 4 November 1924 (CAB 23/48).

183 CAB 21/283, 'Peace Conference Records: Supply of Documents to the Foreign Office,' Hankey to Headlam-Morley, 1 April 1924; Hankey opined that publication in this instance would be 'inexpedient, or at least of doubtful expediency.'

184 Marquand, *MacDonald*, p. 324.

185 Quoted in Sommer, *Haldane*, p. 401 (undated).

186 Sidney Webb, 'The First Labour Government,' *Political Quarterly*, 32: 19–20 (January–March 1961).

187 C 59 (24) 1, 12 November 1924 (CAB 23/49).

188 CAB 21/294, 'Cabinet Procedure,' Hankey to Prime Minister, 6 November 1924.

189 C 3 (23) 7, 26 January 1923 (CAB 23/45).

190 C 28 (24) 4, 29 April 1924 (CAB 23/48), which the Cabinet accepted as a response to a parliamentary question concerning its willingness to abide by the precedent set by Bonar Law's Cabinet.

191 Earl of Birkenhead, *The Life of F.E. Smith, First Earl of Birkenhead* (London, 1965 edn), p. 544.
192 *Davidson's Memoirs*, pp. 276–7, quoting an undated memorandum by the party Chairman, F. S. Jackson, and Baldwin to Jackson, 21 May 1926; the Prime Minister sought to retain Birkenhead's 'great legal knowledge and long Parliamentary experience.'
193 Birkenhead, *F.E. Smith*, pp. 544–5; the biographer regards the violation of the agreement 'unpardonable.'
194 C 52 (28) 3, 21 November 1928 (CAB 23/49).
195 Thomas Jones Papers, Class B, no. 34; August 1927.
196 C 65 (24) 8, 3 December 1924 (CAB 23/49).
197 733 *HC Debates*, 9 August 1966, col. 1393. Michael Foot has pointed to one occasion in which Churchill 'brilliantly and scandalously revealed – in defiance of the rule which the Civil Service is normally supposed to enforce on incoming administrations about the activities of their predecessors' that the late Labour government had accepted the idea of an enlarged Korean war, directed against China, in certain eventualities. Churchill proceeded to chide the Labour Opposition for moving a vote of censure against his administration because of a similar design. (*Aneurin Bevan*, vol. II, *1945–1960* (New York, 1973), p. 361.) At the time, Bevan drew attention to Churchill's constitutional impropriety; see 496 *HC Debates*, 26 February 1952, col. 593. For the Suez controversy, see below, pp. 298–300.
198 C 48 (24), Hankey's Note of 3 December 1924. In so acting, he had reference to Macdonald's request of 3 November that 'if ever the Cabinet Minute . . . should be called for, I should also bring to notice the attached transcript of the notes made at the meeting by Mr. T. Jones.' (*Ibid.*, Hankey Note of 3 November.)
199 C 65 (24) 8c, 3 December 1924 (CAB 23/49).
200 179 *HC Debates*, 11 December 1924, cols. 354–5.
201 J. Ll. J. Edwards, *The Law Officers of the Crown* (London, 1964), p. 233, recognizes the role of the Campbell case in establishing that position, but he points out that in the context of 1924 'the Ramsey MacDonald Cabinet and its Attorney-General, although bitterly criticised by former Law Officers at the time, did not violate any well-established constitutional principles.' For the Campbell case as precedent, see p. 178 n. 6.
202 *Franks Committee Report*, p. 91.
203 Roskill, *Hankey*, vol. II, p. 387, who characterizes the four and a half years of Baldwin's second administration as the unhappiest period of Hankey's tenure.
204 Baldwin Papers, vol. 65, pp. 50–2. Roskill (*Hankey*, vol. II, pp. 388–9) exaggerates in claiming that Hankey 'often' received such instructions, when only several such requests can be documented. Party matters were the major concern, and it is unlikely that Baldwin would speak freely with the Cabinet Secretary about such business.
205 Middlemas and Barnes, *Baldwin*, p. 389.
206 Roskill so judges (*Hankey*, vol. II, p. 424); for the Supply and Transport Committee, see above, pp. 152–3.
207 C 21–3 (26), in CAB 23/52.
208 Quoted by Roskill, *Hankey*, vol. II, p. 425; Hankey to Adeline Hankey, 3 May 1926; see also his moderate views, expressed to Stamfordham on 31 July 1925, quoted, *ibid.*, p. 412.

209 Jones, *Whitehall Diary*, vol. II, p. 45; 10 May 1926.
210 *Ibid.*
211 *Ibid.*, pp. 10–11; 14 April 1926.
212 C 46 (26) 5, 14 July 1926 (CAB 23/53).
213 CAB 21/443, 'Publicity: Authorised Publications,' Hankey to Cunliffe-Lister, 23 February 1926.
214 CAB 21/297, Hankey to Balfour, 26 August 1927. For a fuller account of Hankey's actions, see Roskill, *Hankey*, vol. II, pp. 441–2.
215 CAB 21/297, Hankey to Prime Minister, 30 August 1927. Austen Chamberlain served as Hankey's ministerial counterpart in securing an acceptable explanation of Cecil's resignation.
216 Quoted by Roskill, *Hankey*, vol. II, p. 422; Austen Chamberlain to Neville Chamberlain, 29 August 1927.
217 CAB 63/39, Hankey's memorandum of 30 August 1927.
218 Quoted by Roskill, *Hankey*, vol. II, p. 444; Baldwin to Hankey, 3 September 1927.
219 CAB 21/298, 'Organisation of the Cabinet Office: Memorandum on the British Cabinet Office,' 17 July 1925; Chamberlain's minute, 20 July.
220 *Ibid.*, press clipping; M. Painleve was premier at the time.
221 Thomas Jones Papers, Class B, vol. I, no. 32, 'Correspondence, J. Burgon Bickersteth-W. Mackenzie King, August–September 1927.'
222 Quoted in Jones, *Whitehall Diary*, vol. II, p. 106; Bickersteth to Jones, 14 July 1927. Mackenzie King was not intent upon an imitation of the Cabinet Secretariat system in Canada at this time; cf. Roskill, *Hankey*, vol. II, p. 431.
223 Quoted, Jones, *Whitehall Diary*, vol. II, p. 108; Bickersteth to Jones, 12 August 1927.
224 Thomas Jones Papers, Class B, vol. I, no. 33, copy of Bickersteth to Mackenzie King, 22 August 1927, undated marginalia.
225 Hankey's inference, in British Museum Add MSS. 49704, 'The Balfour Papers,' vol. XXII, Hankey to Balfour, 22 May 1925.
226 Wilson, *Cabinet Office*, Annex 7 (a), p. 174.
227 'The Balfour Papers,' Hankey to Balfour, 22 May 1925.
228 *Ibid.*; and CAB 63/37, 'Memorandum on the British Cabinet Office,' by Sir Maurice Hankey, 24 July 1925, Appendix II. The Historical Section remained a separate operation within the Cabinet Office, to be sure.
229 See Wilson, *Cabinet Office*, Annex 7 (a), p. 174.
230 CAB 63/37, 'The British Cabinet Office.'
231 A. J. Balfour's comment on the scheme, quoted by Roy M. MacLeod and E. Kay Andrews, 'The Committee of Civil Research: Scientific Advice for Economic Development, 1925–30,' *Minerva*, 7: (no. 27, Summer 1969).
232 Quoted CAB 24/204, CP 53 (29).
233 Jones, *Whitehall Diary*, vol. I, p. 286; 22 July 1924; for a fuller account of the origins and initial work of the Committee of Civil Research, see Susan Howson and Donald Winch, *The Economic Advisory Council, 1930–1939* (Cambridge, 1977), pp. 5–16.
234 MacLeod and Andrews, 'Civil Research,' pp. 680–1; for Haldane's disappointment, see Jones, *Whitehall Diary*, vol. I, p. 286.
235 Quoted by Roskill, *Hankey*, vol. II, p. 392; Balfour to Hankey, 19 February 1926. For Balfour as patron of science, see MacLeod and Andrews, 'Civil Research,' pp. 681–2.
236 CAB 24/204, CP 53 (29); a convenient listing of the topics of inquiry for the

main committee and the technical sub-committees is in Middlemas, 'Introduction,' to Jones, *Whitehall Diary*, vol. II, p. xi n. 1.

237 The re-organization is treated below, pp. 184–5; at this time Jones criticized the CID analogy. (*Whitehall Diary*, vol. II, p. 218; 28 November 1929.)

238 MacLeod and Andrews, 'Civil Research,' p. 704. Such a 'research department' existed from 1970 to mid-1983 and is briefly described, above, Ch. 2 n. 74.

239 Roskill, *Hankey*, vol. II, p. 391, whose citation of an exchange of correspondence with Balfour can as easily be read as reassurance to an elder statesman whom Hankey greatly respected as a reflection of such an interest in the work of the CCR. The Cabinet Secretary's limited hopes for the Committee is clear in CAB 63/37, Hankey to Balfour, 22 May 1925.

240 He advised Baldwin to include in his remarks to the opening session of the Imperial Conference of 1926 a reference to the CCR as an example of the machinery for continuous contact between the dominions and Great Britain (Roskill, *Hankey*, vol. II, pp. 427–8).

5. TWIN INSTITUTIONS

1 Thomas Jones Papers, Class B, vol. I, no. 36; Hankey to Bickersteth, 30 September 1927 and HNKY 3/36, Hankey to Robin Hankey, 3 April 1929.

2 Between 1924 and 1929, the Cabinet averaged fully a score fewer yearly meetings than in the peace-time Lloyd George coalition (Wilson, *Cabinet Office*, Annex 7 (a)). The 1924–9 average of nearly fifty-six meetings contrasts to the figure of approximately forty which has been given for the years 1900–14 (HNKY 13/7, enclosure, 'Cabinet Procedure before 1916,' August 1949).

3 CAB 2/4, 180 CID, 4 February 1924.

4 At this first meeting, both MacDonald and Haldane rejected the notion of a Sub-Committee on National and Imperial Defence that certain ministers and officials should be CID members as 'a matter of right' rather than practice, which would have altered the nature of the committee.

5 Quoted in Stephen Roskill, *Naval Policy between the Wars*, vol. I (New York, 1968), pp. 419–22, a fuller account than in his *Hankey*, vol. II, pp. 360–2.

6 171 *HC Debates*, 18 March 1924, cols. 322–3.

7 CAB 21/469, 'Committee of Imperial Defence: Constitution and Functions, 1922–1927,' Hankey to Prime Minister, 22 March 1924, and MacDonald's minute of 23 March.

8 Roskill, *Hankey*, vol. II, p. 363.

9 Quoted, *ibid.*, p. 390. During the Labour regime, Haldane had shown a strong hand at the CID, and, according to Hankey, he reported to Curzon that real progress had been made in the few months of that regime. (National Library of Scotland, Haldane Papers: Hankey to Haldane, 10 November 1924.)

10 CAB 63/38, Hankey to Esher, 3 March 1926.

11 Walter Bagehot, *The English Constitution* (London, 1867), pp. 111, 118 in the Fontana pb. edn, 1963. Richard Crossman's 'Introduction' (p. 18) serves to strengthen this comparison by examining the role assigned to the monarch by Bagehot *vis-à-vis* that of the present-day permanent head of a government department.

12 Thomas Dillon, 'British Strategic Bombing Doctrine and Policy,

1914–1939' (unpublished doctoral dissertation, State University of New York at Buffalo, 1975), passim.

13 Roskill's speculation is more extreme: had it not been for Hankey, 'a stage might have been reached, as was the case with the German armed services, where inter-service co-operation was totally frustrated – with fatal results.' (*Hankey*, vol. II, p. 449.) Roskill (p. 345) correctly remarks upon the vague generalities and unsatisfactory compromises found in the 'joint appreciations.'

14 C 64 (24) 3, 26 November 1924 (CAB 23/49); for the sub-committee's interim Conclusions, CID 243-C, 'The Singapore Base,' 27 February 1925 (CAB 5/5). For the Singapore base generally, Roskill, *Naval Policy*, vol. I, passim.

15 CAB 63/37, 'Limitation of Armaments and Unemployment,' 9 February 1925. Hankey was aware that the 'subsidy' might be shown to be 'artificial and economically unsound,' but his main concern was the maintenance of heavy industry.

16 *Ibid.*, Thomas Jones, 'Limitation of Armaments,' 11 February 1925, and Hankey's marginalia. It is clear that Hankey read Jones' contribution closely before it was sent to the Prime Minister, which invalidates Roskill's assertion (*Hankey*, vol. II, p. 404) that the deputy had gone behind the back of his 'Chief.'

17 CAB 21/469, enclosure of [Labour Party] Advisory Committee on International Questions Memorandum 336-B in 'Note on the Committee of Imperial Defence,' February 1926.

18 *Ibid.*, MacDonald to Hankey, 17 February 1926, and Hankey to MacDonald, 25 February 1926.

19 CAB 21/289, Cecil to Hankey, 8 December 1924, and Hankey to Cecil, 9 December 1924. Cecil remained unconvinced, although he avoided Hankey's practical point by continuing to return to the actual drafting of the Covenant.

20 CAB 63/37, Hankey's memorandum, 'Geneva Protocol and Anglo-French-Belgo Pact,' 23 January 1925.

21 Hankey Diary, 22 March 1925.

22 Cf. Roskill (*Hankey*, vol. II, pp. 393–6), who writes that Hankey did not share 'Curzon's outright opposition to a Security Pact . . . and greatly preferred that alternative . . . to the Protocol.' As Hankey's diary for 22 March conveys little enthusiasm for any security pact, his position was closer to Curzon's than to Austen Chamberlain's, although he did come round to support the idea of a guarantee pact. For a Foreign Office appreciation of the sole reason in favor of such a pact, CAB 4/12, CID 540-B, 'A Review of the Protocol for the Pacific Settlement of International Disputes.'

23 Hankey Diary, 22 March 1925.

24 Yet Hankey admitted to Chamberlain that he was concerned with the decline of 'the military spirit in this country.' (Austen Chamberlain Papers, University of Birmingham Library, AC 24/7/16, 21 August 1925.)

25 Quoted by Roskill, *Hankey*, vol. II, p. 415; Hankey to Austen Chamberlain, 19 October 1925.

26 Roskill, *Hankey*, vol. II, p. 415.

27 For these exchanges, see *ibid.*, pp. 438–40.

28 CAB 21/297, 'Notes on Lord Robert Cecil's Speech . . . on the Subject of his Resignation,' unsigned and undated, but Hankey's work; Cecil's speech may

be found in 69 *HL Debates*, 16 November 1927, cols. 84–100.
29 CAB 63/37, Hankey to Cecil, 18 August 1925.
30 CAB 21/469, Hankey to Churchill, 19 March 1926.
31 215 *HC Debates*, 27 March 1928, col. 1050.
32 CAB 63/40, Hankey to Prime Minister, 26 March 1928.
33 Marquand, *MacDonald*, p. 317.
34 CAB 63/36, 'Some Observations on the Channel Tunnel . . .,' 24 June 1924, and 'Channel Tunnel: Statement in Parliament Prepared for the Prime Minister by Secretary [CID],' 7 July 1924. For Hankey's long-standing opposition to the project, see the collection of relevant materials in CAB 63/25.
35 Quoted, Marquand, *MacDonald*, p. 318.
36 HNKY 3/37, Hankey to Robin Hankey, 1 June 1930.
37 Extracts from this minute of 25 February 1915 are quoted in Hankey, *Supreme Command*, vol. I, pp. 366–7.
38 Roskill, *Hankey*, vol. II, pp. 451–9, for a full description of Hankey's reaction – and actions – from the re-emergence of the issue to the end of the Baldwin regime in 1929.
39 Jones, *Whitehall Diary*, vol. II, p. 116; Hankey to Jones, 19 November 1927.
40 He had on an earlier occasion thought of informing Esher that he would not 'hesitate to go' if the defence organization underwent 'considerable change,' but that sentiment he had likely not communicated ever to Esher, let alone the Prime Minister. See above, pp. 132–3.
41 Jones, *Whitehall Diary*, vol. II, pp. 116–17.
42 Roskill, *Hankey*, vol. II, p. 452.
43 The activities of Sir Warren Fisher at the Treasury and Sir Robert Vansittart at the Foreign Office also serve to undermine the notion of neutrality, at least at this level of the Civil Service; cf. the claim advanced on behalf of the doctrine by C. K. Munro, *The Fountains of Trafalgar Square* (London, 1952), pp. 201–2.
44 E.g. Hankey to Esher, 21 December 1927, quoted by Roskill, *Hankey*, vol. II, pp. 452–3.
45 'In presenting the facts,' read the waiver; CAB 63/40, 'Anglo-American Relations. Belligerent Rights at Sea: Memorandum by Secretary, CID,' 13 December 1928.
46 *Ibid.*, 'Belligerent Rights at Sea: Suggested Policy. Note by the Secretary CID,' January 1928.
47 This exchange is in Jones, *Whitehall Diary*, vol. II, pp. 144, 146 and 147–9, respectively Hankey to Jones, 2 October 1928, Jones to Hankey, 9 October 1928, and Hankey to Jones, 11 October 1928.
48 *Ibid.*, p. 157, diary of 14 November 1928. The expression may have been voiced to Jones by Sir Arthur Salter – in context the point is uncertain – but Jones certainly agreed with the sentiment.
49 HNKY 3/37, Hankey to Robin Hankey, 17 September 1929. Not without irony, Jones accompanied MacDonald as a speech-writer, the Campbell case apparently by this time only history.
50 Hankey Diary, 18 October 1929 (possibly misdated, more likely 6 or 7 October).
51 *Ibid.*, 8 October 1929.
52 *Ibid.*, 10 October 1929.
53 *Ibid.*, 15 November 1929; Hankey's assertion cannot go unqualified; for his

previous limited contacts with the press, see above p. 93 and Ch. 4 n. 102.
54 'Mr. Hoover's Confidence,' *The Times*, 12 November 1929.
55 Enunciated as recently as August 1927, in Thomas Jones Papers, Class B, vol. I, no. 34, 'Memorandum on the Introduction of Certain Features of the British Cabinet Office into Canada.'
56 Hankey Diary, 15 November 1929.
57 For that confidence, Stamfordham to Hankey, 15 January 1928, quoted by Roskill, *Hankey*, vol. II, p. 455.
58 Middlemas and Barnes (*Baldwin*, p. 496) recognize that Hankey, in defence matters, 'was prepared to go further than now would be thought proper in a civil servant,' but otherwise played 'an impeccably constitutional hand.' Despite this major exception, they nonetheless characterize Tom Jones' relations with premiers 'unique in the history of the Civil Service.' Given Hankey's activities, one cannot validate that claim.
59 C 23 (29) 3, 21 June 1929 (CAB 23/61).
60 C 28 (29) 1, 10 July 1929 (CAB 23/61).
61 These procedural decisions are found in C 22 (29), 10 June 1929 (CAB 23/61), although the heading for this meeting still bore the term 'Conclusions.'
62 In Hankey's absence at The Hague Conference in August 1929, Jones kept the minutes for meetings of ministers, since MacDonald spent several weeks away from London and a full Cabinet could not be convened.
63 Roskill, *Hankey*, vol. II, p. 477, who does not specify the departure from the 1929 mandate by Jones or, in August 1931, by Howorth.
64 For the collapse of the doctrine proper, see below, pp. 195–6.
65 Collected in CAB 23/90B.
66 Most at point is Crossman's allegation that the Cabinet Secretariat, during Harold Wilson's first administration of 1964–6, regularly suppressed entire sections of Cabinet Minutes on the grounds that they were too secret to circulate. The result: 'By eliminating whole sections from the discussion and reporting others in full the Secretariat can greatly affect the way a decision is interpreted in Whitehall.' (Richard Crossman, *The Diaries of a Cabinet Minister*, vol. I, *1964–66* (London 1975), p. 590; 28 July 1966. Hereafter cited as Crossman, *Cabinet Diaries*.) For a discussion of Crossman's charge, see below, pp. 310–11.
67 *Ibid.*, p. 90; 7 December 1964. A feature common to the two systems is shown in Trend's claim that the Secretariat did not give verbatim what ministers said but instead 'precis the sense and give the substance of what they say.' In this specific instance, however, Crossman rejected such an explanation.
68 The claim must be somewhat qualified: Hankey's own diary yields evidence of 'a small alteration proposed to the Cabinet Minutes' (4 March 1933). Wilson, *Cabinet Office*, p. 10, prints in facsimile a more important instance of Austen Chamberlain's amendment of Hankey's draft of a Cabinet Minute, dating to 1922. And apparently MacDonald's questioning of Tom Jones' minute bearing on the Campbell case in 1924 altogether slipped Burgis' mind. Churchill had once challenged the accuracy of Hankey's record of 'the opinions expressed,' though in this case a Conference of Ministers was the setting. (Gilbert, *Churchill*, vol. IV, p. 503; 2 December 1920.)
69 CAB 24/204, CP 153 (29), 10 June 1928.
70 Howson and Winch, *Economic Advisory Council*, p. 12. Cf. the claim, otherwise unsupported, by Middlemas, 'Introduction,' to Jones, *Whitehall Diary*, vol. II, p. xi.

71 Middlemas, *ibid.*, admits that the CCR 'represented an advance in piecemeal rather than synoptic planning.'
72 Jones, *Whitehall Diary*, vol. II, p. 223, Minutes to Prime Minister's Conference on the Industrial Situation and 'Economic General Staff,' 2 December 1929.
73 Its deficiencies are spelled out by MacLeod and Andrews, 'Civil Research,' pp. 703–4, in its particular impact on scientific research, and, in a general administrative context, by Robert Skidelsky, *Politicians and the Slump: The Labour Government of 1929–31* (London, 1967), p. 157, in addition to the comprehensive review of Howson and Winch, *Economic Advisory Council*, pp. 14–15.
74 CAB 24/104, CP 153 (29).
75 *Webb Diaries*, p. 231; 2 December 1929.
76 CAB 24/104, CP 152 (29); when Hankey subsequently reported on the CID, his description tallied exactly with past discussion of the CID's origins, constitutional position, and procedures. (CAB 63/41, 'The Committee of Imperial Defence: Memorandum by the Prime Minister,' 14 June 1929.)
77 Wilson, *Cabinet Office*, p. 12; for his list of inter-war Cabinet committees, *ibid.*, Annex 11, part 2. See also CAB 21/1084, 'Functions of the Cabinet Secretariat: Memorandum by the Secretary of the War Cabinet,' 14 September 1944.
78 230 *HC Debates*, 24 July 1929, cols. 1292–3. Roskill (*Hankey*, vol. II, p. 476) cites an article in the *Morning Post* on 18 July, but he does not connect MacDonald's assertion to this article and thus cannot fathom 'the evasiveness, not to say untruth, of MacDonald's answer.'
79 E.g. C 51 (29) 3, 3 December 1929 (CAB 23/62).
80 CAB 21/597, Hankey to Prime Minister, 13 February 1931; the Cabinet Secretary assigned responsibility for the 'oversight' to the Treasury.
81 C 15 (31) 4, 25 February 1931 (CAB 23/66).
82 Jones, *Whitehall Diary*, vol. II, p. 235; 14 January 1930.
83 *Ibid.*, pp. 255–6; May 1930; the proprietor is quoted in Seymour-Ure, *The Press*, p. 152.
84 Jones, *Whitehall Diary*, vol. II, p. 256; 7 May 1930.
85 CAB 63/44, 'Leakage of Information,' 9 December 1931. Roskill (*Hankey*, vol. II, p. 364) cites other aphorisms, but mistakenly he links the memorandum to the late Labour government rather than to the coalition regime headed by MacDonald.
86 HNKY 3/36, Hankey to Robin Hankey, 3 July 1929.
87 HNKY 8/27, Hankey to Robin Hankey, 5 September 1929.
88 Though the recall of the deputy to the Cabinet Office in the Secretary's absence was understandable (Hankey explained to Jones that the Cabinet had insisted 'on my going to this Reparations Conference – a most unpleasant [task]'; Hankey to Jones, 1 August 1929, in *Whitehall Diary*, vol. II, pp. 196–7) Hankey no doubt was aware of the rapport between Jones and the Prime Minister.
89 HNKY 3/36 and 8/27, Hankey to Robin Hankey, 7 August and 5 September 1929. In the former file, Hankey's letters to his wife, although episodic, reveal much about the workings of the Conference and substitute quite well for the lack of any diary materials.
90 E.g. Hankey to Jones, 24 August 1929, in *Whitehall Diary*, vol. II, p. 199.
91 For Hankey's sentiment, HNKY 3/36, Hankey to Adeline Hankey, 28 August 1929.

92 Jones, *Whitehall Diary*, vol. II, p. 198; Hankey to Jones, 11 August 1929. Lloyd George used the telephone technique at the Paris Peace Conference, but he first devised the practice in writing to his wife Margaret from the Law Courts in London, in order to protect his privacy. (John Grigg, *The Young Lloyd George* (London, 1973), p. 62.)
93 HNKY 8/27, Hankey to Robin Hankey, 5 September 1929, which he claimed to be 'the only true and unvarnished account of the Hague Conference,' and HNKY 3/36; Hankey's letters were appallingly indiscreet, nonetheless.
94 Jones, *Whitehall Diary*, vol. II, p. 218; Jones to Prof. Henry Clay, 28 November 1929.
95 *Ibid.*, p. 219; Hankey to Jones, 28 November 1929.
96 *Ibid.*, pp. 224–8; minutes of a luncheon, 16 December 1929.
97 Howson and Winch, *Economic Advisory Council*, p. 24: see their fuller description of the establishment of the EAC, pp. 17–25.
98 Jones, *Whitehall Diary*, vol. II, pp. 228–30; Jones to Bickersteth, 23 December 1929. Jones' reference to a group of ministers is incorrect, as the Prime Minister initially sat with five permanent officials, with the balance 'outsiders.'
99 Quoted by Skidelsky, *Politicians*, p. 158. The description applies to its first months; subsequently, it came more to the fore, as the government turned to it for a reappraisal of unemployment policy.
100 Jones, *Whitehall Diary*, vol. II, p. 266; 23 June 1930.
101 E.g. his record of a conversation, dating to 1929, with the Baldwins, *ibid.*, p. 192; 20 June 1929.
102 *Ibid.*, pp. 273–4; 13 September 1929.
103 Roskill, *Hankey*, vol. II, p. 523.
104 There are very few and unimportant letters from Jones to Hankey in HNKY 4, and only one of any import from Hankey for this period.
105 CAB 4/18, CID 955-B, 'Committee of Imperial Defence: Policy Regarding Naval Construction Programme and Singapore. Statement by Prime Minister,' 25 July 1929. In citing only a portion of these remarks, Roskill (*Hankey*, vol. II, p. 496) protests that 'he gave no clue as to how or why this was so,' but the balance of his comments addresses relevant international conditions.
106 However, the COS Annual Review for 1930 maintained that the London Treaty introduced no new factors 'tending to diminish the strategic importance of the Singapore base.' (Quoted in Stephen Roskill, *Naval Policy between the Wars*, vol. II, *1930–1939* (Annapolis, 1976), p. 77.)
107 Roskill, *Hankey*, vol. II, pp. 496–7.
108 PREM 1/152, MacDonald to Ottawa, Canberra, etc., undated but dispatched 19 June 1930, attached to CID 346-C of 4 June.
109 The Secretary to the Overseas Defence Committee, G. N. Macready, bore direct responsibility for the preparation of the document, but there is a strong probability that the Secretary to the parent committee examined it.
110 PREM 1/152, respectively Duff memorandum for Prime Minister, 20 June 1930; Duff to Hankey, 23 June 1930; Hankey to Duff, 25 June 1930.
111 *Ibid.*, Duff to Prime Minister, 26 June 1930, and MacDonald's minute, 27 June.
112 The Board of Admiralty view is quoted by Roskill, *Hankey*, vol. II, p. 520; see his account of the exchanges among the interested parties in *Naval Policy*, vol. II, pp. 52–5.

113 These LNC records, series B, C, E, and F, can be found in CAB 29/117–34; CAB 29/135 contains notes for the informal meetings.
114 Quoted by Roskill, *Hankey*, vol. II, p. 520; MacDonald to Hankey, 22 April 1930.
115 Quoted, *ibid.*, p. 520; the relative reduction in strength referred to 'paper' as well as actual ships.
116 238 *HC Debates*, 15 May 1930, cols. 2107–8.
117 Roskill (*Hankey*, vol. II, p. 520) does not specify the greater responsibilities borne by others: the First Lord of the Admiralty, A. V. Alexander, judged British interests well served by the pact's facilitating a much needed cruiser construction program. (Information from Prof. D. C. Watt.) Whether Hankey was so influenced is nowhere apparent.
118 For Roskill's curious criticism, *ibid.*, pp. 519–21. Hankey's sensitivity to the Japanese threat is consistent with his priority given the defence of the British Empire.
119 CAB 21/372, 'Note of a Conversation with Sir Robert Vansittart on November 21, 1930.'
120 CAB 63/44, 'The Basis of Service Estimates: The "Ten-Year" Assumption: Memorandum by Sir Maurice Hankey,' 9 January 1931, and Fry to Hankey, 28 January 1931. The 1928 reformulation of the rule is quoted by Wilson, *Cabinet Office*, p. 73.
121 Gibbs, *Rearmament*, p. 80.
122 *Ibid.*, pp. 80–2, for a discussion of these deterrent factors.
123 For Hankey's frustrated efforts in this period, Roskill, *Hankey*, vol. II, p. 537.
124 CAB 63/46, Hankey to Neville Chamberlain, 2 March 1933, a little more than a month after Hitler's succession.
125 Peden, 'Fisher and Rearmament.' For the background to this seminal change of policy, see Gibbs, *Rearmament*, ch. 3.
126 CAB 63/44, 'A Ministry of Defence: Notes by Sir Maurice Hankey,' 2 July 1931.
127 Respectively, C 41 (31) 1, 19 August 1931, and C 43 (31) 1, 21 August 1931 (CAB 23/67).
128 Marquand, *MacDonald*, pp. 640–1.
129 The Cabinet Minutes understandably fail to convey the breach in ideology which divided MacDonald from those, like Arthur Henderson, who came from the trade union side of the movement, a breach which is depicted on MacDonald's behalf by Marquand, *MacDonald*, pp. 676–7. For the general reaction to the Prime Minister's announcement, see John F. Naylor, *Labour's International Policy: The Labour Party in the 1930s* (London and Boston, 1969), pp. 16–19.
130 Hankey Diary, 6 September 1931.
131 CAB 63/43, 'Unemployment: A Challenge to Defeatism,' 19 September 1930.
132 Photocopy of the original, drafted and with corrections in Hankey's hand, printed in Roskill, *Hankey*, vol. II, p. 549.
133 Among those ministers not in the Cabinet participating in the Conference were Austen Chamberlain, Maclean, Londonderry, Amulree, Sinclair, Winterton, and Lothian.
134 C 48 (31), Appendix 3, 26 August 1931 (CAB 23/68).
135 CAB 21/778, CP 205 (31), 'Cabinet Procedure: Memorandum by the Secretary,' 27 August 1931. In a 1936 version, these historical sanctions were

omitted; the discoveries are discussed above, pp. 16–17.

136 C 47 (31) 2, 24 August 1931 (CAB 23/68). The two memoranda were CP 203 (31) and CP 203 Revised (31).

137 C 81 (31) 6, 25 November 1931 (CAB 23/68). Cf. the established practice, dating to 1922, of accepting a record of dissent, described above, p. 94.

138 No capsule of the 'doctor's mandate' improves on Hankey's own, offered to the Prime Minister during a Cabinet meeting: '*Conservatives* to be free to say "We believe tariffs are essential, but we will keep an open mind." *Liberals* to be free to say "We believe Free Trade will stand, but we will keep an open mind." [National] *Labour* according as they are Tariff Reformers or Free Traders.' Although MacDonald pencilled out this illustration, Hankey remarked in his diary on 7 October 1931 that his outline proved to be 'substantially the ultimate settlement.'

139 Foot, *Bevan*, vol. II, p. 308 records this instance of Bevan's 'doubt and dissent.' Harold Wilson's 1964 ruling (see above, Ch. 3 n. 42) appears to qualify this outright refusal to record the existence of dissent with the Cabinet.

140 He confided in his diary on 3 October: 'there are occasions when it is wise to be slow in circulating, just as there are times when one cannot be too quick. In a crisis like this Minutes are a delicate business.'

141 C 7 (32) 1–3, 22 January 1932 (CAB 23/70).

142 The parliamentary exchange had been initiated by MacDonald's assertion: 'a Cabinet works as a whole and not in sections. [An hon. Member: "Does this one?"] I hope so. When it ceases to do so, we will cease to exist.' (256 *HC Debates*, 11 September 1931, col. 433.)

143 261 *HC Debates*, 8 February 1932, cols. 518–19. By an odd twist of fate, Lansbury was dislodged from his position as Leader in 1935 following an attack by Ernest Bevin cast precisely along these lines. (Naylor, *Labour's International Policy*, p. 107.)

144 In 1975, the Labour government stuck an 'agreement to differ' concerning Britain's continued membership in the European Economic Community; although Harold Wilson concluded that the 1932 'precedent' was not an exact one – there were substantive and procedural differences – he considered it a sound one. (*Governance of Britain*, pp. 55 and 196–7.)

145 HNKY 3/38, Hankey to Adeline Hankey, 25 August 1931; he added in uncharacteristically strong language, 'and I shall be having a hell of a time.'

146 CAB 21/350, Hankey to Prime Minister, 28 August 1931. By dating this letter a week later, Roskill (*Hankey*, vol. II, p. 550) does not recognize the speed with which he put this independently conceived project into operation, since Hankey had already canvassed a half-dozen leading civil servants.

147 256 *HC Debates*, 11 September 1931, cols. 489–90.

148 *Ibid.*, col. 486.

149 Hankey Diary, 13 September 1931.

150 *Ibid.*, 6 September 1931. Hankey's comments were consistent with his own hopes for the National Government; he judged the insistence on maintaining the 'standard of living' 'the most potent cause of mistrust [in financial quarters] of our position.' (CAB 63/44, 'Draft Programme of the National Government,' 2 October 1931.)

151 Roskill, *Hankey*, vol. II, pp. 572–3.

152 *Chief of Staff: The Diaries of Lieutenant-General Sir Henry Pownall*, vol. I, *1933–1940*, ed. Brian Bond (Hamden, Conn., 1973), p. 14; 20 March 1933. (Hereafter cited as *Pownall Diaries.*)

153 *Ibid.*, p. 17; 22 May 1933. Pownall, a Military Assistant Secretary at this time, subsequently commented that Hankey 'likes to handle the big things himself, de-centralisation . . . is outside him' (p. 19; 12 June 1933). At the same time, Pownall judged him 'a strange character, and not lovable.'
154 F. H. Hinsley *et al.*, *British Intelligence in the Second World War*, vol. I (Cambridge, 1979), p. 34, fn. (*History of the Second World War: United Kingdom Military Series*).
155 Hankey Diary, 6 September 1931.
156 HNKY 3/38, Hankey to Henry Hankey, 31 October 1931, underscores the impropriety of the request: 'By the way, this is not a story to repeat, as the Labour Party would not like the King to canvas for the National Party [sic], and would be capable of using the story if they got hold of it.'
157 Jones, *Diary with Letters*, p. 20; 28 October 1931.
158 Hankey Diary, 28 October 1931.
159 *Ibid.*, 28 and 30 October 1931.
160 E.g. C 21 (32) 1, 13 April 1932 (CAB 23/71); C 56 (32) 2, 31 October 1932 (CAB 23/72).
161 C 63 (33) 4, 16 November 1933 (CAB 23/77); CAB 21/597, 'Preparation of Cabinet Agenda Papers' (by Rupert Howorth), 21 October 1936. The practice was revised to suit the Prime Minister's convenience; his vision was worsening.
162 Both the Admiralty and the War Office protested such an exercise of 'Treasury control,' but in vain. (Peden, 'Fisher and Rearmament,' p. 35.)
163 CAB 21/793, Hankey to C. P. Duff, 15 March 1932. Hankey was correct as the long-term trend was downward; however, 1930 and 1932 were exceptions to that trend. (See Wilson, *Cabinet Office*, Annex 8, p. 175.)
164 Jones, *Diary with Letters*, p. 69; 10 November 1932.
165 CAB 24/261, CP 88 (36), 'Cabinet Procedure: Note by the Secretary, Cabinet,' 2 April 1936, Appendix I.
166 C 13 (34) 1, 28 March 1934 (CAB 23/78).
167 CAB 21/391, according to Howorth, as reported in 'Cabinet Secrets in a Book,' *Daily Telegraph*, 21 March 1934.
168 *Ibid.*, untitled memorandum by Howorth, 14 March 1934.
169 C 8 (33) 1, 13 February 1933 (CAB 23/75).
170 C 22 (32) 1, 18 April 1932 (CAB 23/71).
171 273 *HC Debates*, 14 December 1932, cols. 405–10. Clearly Lloyd George's intention was to embarrass Baldwin as well as Horne, because the former, as Chancellor during Bonar Law's administration, had run against the grain of the Balfour Note in completing Horne's mission in Washington. In routing Horne and entangling Baldwin, Lloyd George was master of the situation.
172 Such is the direct thrust of Lloyd George to Baldwin, 15 December 1932, 'unless I hear from you to the contrary.' (CAB 21/372.)
173 *Ibid.*, Hankey's memorandum, 'The Publication of Cabinet Minutes,' which is the source of this account. Nonetheless, the King's permission was taken for granted – if HMG were prepared to give it – until 1934; see below, p. 207.
174 273 *HC Debates*, 15 December 1932, cols. 526–7; MacDonald was indisposed.
175 CAB 21/372, 'Publication of Cabinet Minutes.'
176 86 *HL Debates*, 21 December 1932, cols. 529, 524.
177 *Ibid.*, col. 526.
178 *Ibid.*, cols. 531–2.

179 273 *HC Debates*, 22 December 1932, col. 1301.
180 According to Hankey, 'Publication of Cabinet Minutes,' CAB 21/372.
181 Stevenson, *The Years that are Past*, p. 225. Lloyd George's private secretary, A. J. Sylvester, was given access to the Whitehall archives in researching the *War Memoirs*. (*Life with Lloyd George: The Diary of A.J. Sylvester*, ed. Colin Cross) (New York, 1975), 'Introduction,' p. 13.)
182 Lloyd George Papers, G/212, copy of Lloyd George to Hankey, 18 April 1934.
183 E.g. *ibid.*, Hankey to Lloyd George, 1 October 1936.
184 *Ibid.*, memorandum of Sylvester to Lloyd George, 10 April 1934, adding: 'Hankey, as always, has read your Ms. in the most thorough fashion.'
185 For Hankey's disavowal of official responsibility, see above, pp. 118–19.
186 Jones, *Diary with Letters*, p. 105; Baldwin to Jones, 20 April 1933; for Baldwin's being 'very much in Hankey's hands,' *Sylvester Diary*, p. 107; 10 April 1934.
187 Jones, *Diary with Letters*, p. 129; 28 April 1934.
188 *Ibid.*, p. 191; 30 April 1936.
189 Basil Liddell Hart, *Memoirs* (London, 1965), vol. I, p. 361.
190 Stevenson, *Lloyd George: A Diary*, p. 264; 29 March 1934. Frances Stevenson saw both a connection and an 'awkward precedent' in the prosecution of Lansbury's son and reflected: 'I am not sure it was not done deliberately.' See below, pp. 212–14.
191 PREM 1/171, Howorth to H. G. Vincent, 26 October 1934. Such a linkage apparently countered the complaint voiced as long ago as 1922 by the King's Private Secretary that disclosure of Cabinet proceedings without prior sanction from the Sovereign infringed the Privy Counsellor's Oath. (See C 68 (22) 9, 29 November 1922, in CAB 23/32.)
192 PREM 1/171, Howorth to Sir Clive Wigram, 2 November 1934; both Howorth and Vincent, in conversation with Wigram, agreed that 'in future the consent of the King should be obtained, wherever practicable, before Secret Cabinet material is published.' (CAB 21/444, Howorth to Secretary, 31 December 1934.)
193 *Sylvester Diary*, p. 93; 4 April 1933. Hankey offered the suggestion both because he thought George V deserved such recognition and he reasoned that the King might be less critical of Lloyd George's hostile treatment of the military figures.
194 Stevenson, *Lloyd George: A Diary*, p. 269; 24 April 1934.
195 E.g. John M. Cooper, Jr, 'The British Response to the House Grey Memorandum: New Evidence and New Questions,' *Journal of American History*, 59: 958–71 (March 1973).
196 Liddell Hart, *Memoirs*, vol. I, p. 361; of course Liddell Hart, like Lloyd George, was a convinced 'Westerner' and so was sympathetic to the latter's 'great decisions.'
197 CAB 21/444, Keynes to Hankey, 19 October 1933. The extracts were printed in Lloyd George's *War Memoirs*, vol. II, pp. 134–6, coupled with a bitter attack on the civil servant, concluding 'now not even his friends – least of all his friends – have any longer the slightest faith in his judgments on finance.'
198 CAB 21/444, Hankey to Keynes, 20 October 1933.
199 Keynes' reference was to documents published in G. P. Gooch and Harold Temperley, eds., *British Documents on the Origins of the War, 1898–1914* (11 vols. in 13, London, 1926–38), discussed above, p. 123.

200 'Correspondence,' *The Times*, 28 November 1933.
201 CAB 63/53, Hankey to Lloyd George, 11 July 1938. These comments can be found in David Lloyd George, *Memoirs of the Peace Conference*, vol II (New Haven, 1939), pp. 294, 296, 301, and 335–8, although these strictures are relatively mild in comparison to his attack on Keynes in 1933.

6. HANKEY'S LAST YEARS

1 Peter Singleton-Gates, 'But the Act Remains,' *Spectator*, 196: 816–17 (15 June 1956); also see the commentary, 'Shady Secrets?' by Robert Blake, *ibid.*, pp. 817–18.
2 Quoted by Williams, *Public Interest*, p. 70. In such a spirit, even the marginal notes to section 1, written by the draftsmen in 1911, were dismissed as 'mere catch-words' in a 1962 House of Lords judicial opinion, when section 1 was extended to provide against acts of sabotage. (*Ibid.*, p. 107.)
3 *Ibid.*, p. 113.
4 Compton Mackenzie, *My Life and Times: Octave 7, 1931–1938* (London, 1968), pp. 306, 60. Ultimately, the volume in question, *Greek Memories*, was published in 1939, in an edition which Mackenzie claimed had not been censored.
5 *Ibid.*, pp. 84, 102. Mackenzie added: 'Four or five years later Winston Churchill told me that when my trial came on he did burn a lot of papers he afterwards regretted burning.' One wonders if any such damage is evident in the Churchill Papers at Chartwell.
6 The lack of any materials in Cabinet Secretariat files bearing on the Mackenzie case reinforces his belief that the initiative lay with the Secret Service.
7 Compton Mackenzie, *Greek Memories* (London, 1939), p. xiii. His anger was fueled by a fine of £100 and a like sum in court costs; his legal fees were £2500.
8 CAB 21/444, Hankey to H. G. Vincent, 15 September 1933, and Hankey to Lloyd George, 17 October 1933. It appears that Lansdowne was given permission to publish at least one memorandum but that he was denied permission for several other requests.
9 CAB 21/391, from the *Manchester Guardian*, 6 March 1934. This copy of the article is marked with references to the paragraphs in the documents which Edgar Lansbury had drawn directly from.
10 *Ibid.*, Howorth to Secretary, 6 March 1934: the two documents were the specially secret CP 145 (30), 'Unemployment Policy (1930) Committee: Memorandum by the First Commissioner of Works,' 6 May 1930, and UP (30) 61, 'Panel of Ministers on Unemployment: Unemployment Insurance, Memorandum by the First Commissioner of Works,' 6 February 1931; Lansbury was the author of both. *Ibid.*, *Daily Telegraph*, 21 March 1934, contains Edgar Lansbury's assertion: 'I did not know it was an offence at the time,' but the presiding magistrate rejected the defendant's explanation.
11 *Ibid.*, Howorth to Secretary, 'Biography of Mr. George Lansbury,' 5 March 1934; while Howorth mentioned 'the consent of the Sovereign' as a further requirement for publication, he admitted that there had been no such case since the war. Only subsequently was the Monarch's involvement specified by HMG. (See above, pp. 117 and 207.)
12 Quoted, *Report of the Committee of Privy Counsellors on Ministerial Memoirs*

(Cmnd 6386, 1976), p. 2. (Hereafter cited as *Radcliffe Committee Report.*) For Churchill's earlier role, see above, pp. 117–20.

13 CAB 21/391, Howorth to Secretary, 'Biography.' In Howorth's view, the *Guardian*, 'by reproducing the secret extracts verbatim, would also seem to have infringed the Official Secrets Act, and to have done so with their eyes open.'

14 *Ibid.*, Fuce to Howorth, 19 March 1934.

15 CAB 21/443, Howorth to Secretary, 3 November 1931.

16 CAB 21/391, quoted from 'Cabinet Secrets in a Book,' *Daily Telegraph*, 21 March 1934.

17 *Ibid.*

18 For this observation, I am indebted to Prof. D. C. Watt. Edgar Lansbury's summons had charged that he had 'unlawfully received certain information . . . having reasonable ground to believe that the said information had been communicated in contravention of the Official Secrets Act.'

19 The implication is that Cabinet Ministers are 'more equal than others' under the statute of Official Secrets. (Aitken, *Officially Secret*, p. 56.)

20 CAB 21/448, CP 69 (34), 'Cabinet Procedure: The Retention by Cabinet Ministers of their Cabinet Papers on Leaving Office,' 9 March 1934. The seminal impact of the Lansbury case is treated in a cursory fashion in Wilson, *Cabinet Office*, pp. 52–4.

21 Not coincidentally, in 1966 the first War Cabinet papers were about to escape the restrictions of the fifty year rule; they were transferred to the Public Record Office. See below, pp. 289–93.

22 C 11 (34) 5, 21 March 1934 (CAB 23/78).

23 Hankey could not resist noting that 'it is unfortunate that the first *post*-war Cabinet did not adopt my suggestion to continue the procedure of the War Cabinet.' (CAB 24/448, 'Note by the Secretary,' 12 March 1934, attached to CP 29 (34).)

24 This heading had been taken from pre-war Cabinet memoranda, which had borne exactly this statement, along with the notation: 'Printed for the use of the Cabinet.' (CAB 21/391, 'The Property in Cabinet Documents,' undated but 21 or 22 March 1934; Howorth is the likely author.)

25 Quoted, *ibid.*, 'Property.' It is interesting that the Law Officers had at this time linked the Official Secrets Act to Cabinet documents.

26 CAB 21/462, Hankey to Howorth, 9 July 1931.

27 E.g. C 37 (38), in CAB 23/95, the first Cabinet meeting after his retirement.

28 CAB 21/457, 'Cabinet Papers: Opinions of the Law Officers of the Crown,' 18 June 1934.

29 Quoted by Raymond Postgate, *The Life of George Lansbury* (London, 1951), p. ix.

30 Howorth had communicated directly with Baldwin; the Secretariat was well aware of the legal position, e.g. Howorth's memorandum of 23 July 1934: 'The right of retention springs from the formula used at the last meeting of each Cabinet since the war.' (CAB 21/457.)

31 *Ibid.*, circular letter from Acting Secretary to the Cabinet, September 1934.

32 CAB 21/444, Howorth to Secretary, 31 December 1934.

33 Lloyd George Papers, G/1/4/3, Addison to Lloyd George, 29 September 1934.

34 Lord Randolph Churchill had executed a deed specifying departmental approval for his India Office and Foreign Office documents, a precedent

which his son applied to his own collection of Cabinet papers, noting that he had 'invariably obtained . . . prior sanction' for publication. (*Winston S. Churchill: Companion* to vol. V, Part 2, *The Wilderness Years, 1929–1935*, ed. Martin S. Gilbert (Boston, 1981), p. 925; Churchill to Howorth, 19 November 1934.)

35 Lloyd George Papers, G/1/4/4, Lloyd George to Addison, 3 October 1934.

36 CAB 21/457, 'Secrets and Safe Keeping,' *Evening News*, 5 October 1934.

37 CAB 21/457, Howorth to C. V. Vincent, 5 October 1934, with Howorth's claim that the text of his letter had been distorted.

38 CAB 21/457, 'Attack on Publication of Memoirs,' *News Chronicle*, 5 October 1934. Other newspaper articles referred to below are collected in this file.

39 For the first two, see above, Ch. 3 n. 36 and p. 176; in August 1934, under different circumstances, Hankey had given the *Evening Standard* an interview concerning his imperial tour. (Roskill, *Hankey*, vol. III, *1931–1963* (London, 1974), p. 118.)

40 CAB 21/457, 'Secrets and Safe Keeping,' quoting from an 'informant' at Whitehall Gardens. Churchill had not yet replied, to be sure.

41 Possibly Howorth preferred the quiet purchase of such papers to legal confiscation, but he did not specify any such instances; nor have I found reference to such commercial transactions in any other source.

42 CAB 21/457, 'Ex Ministers and Secrets,' *Daily Telegraph*, 6 October 1934. Howorth apparently concluded that the *Times*' article, 'Cabinet Documents,' of that date, was not worth retaining in his files.

43 *Ibid.*, 'Ex Ministers Demand an Explanation from the Premier,' *News Chronicle*, 6 October 1934, and 'Ex Ministers and Secrets.'

44 Quoted, *ibid.*, '100 Demands Sent Out from No. 10,' *Daily Express*, 6 October 1934.

45 Taylor, *English History*, p. 603, advances the claim without source attribution, but the source is likely Postgate, *Lansbury*, pp. vii–ix. Such correspondence does not survive in the Lansbury Papers at the London School of Economics; further doubt is thrown by Lloyd George's lack of sympathy for the Lansburys in their recent travail (e.g. HNKY 4/26, Lloyd George to Hankey, 19 April 1934).

46 For that pairing, Lloyd George Papers, G/4/5, Miss Pearman to Miss Stevenson, 21 September 1934, and vice versa, 24 September.

47 See above, p. 68.

48 For this information, I am grateful to A. J. P. Taylor.

49 HNKY 5/1, 'Note of a Conversation with Mr. Winston Churchill on Sunday, 19th April 1936.' For the 1935 exchange of letters between the two, see *Winston S. Churchill: Companion* to vol. V, Part 2, pp. 1195–7, 1198–9 and 1203–4. Of most interest was Hankey's response to Churchill's obfuscatory query at what point a draft written by a Minister became a Cabinet paper: 'once a draft has been initialled for an official purpose it becomes an official document,' whatever its ultimate disposition.

50 Burgis Memoirs, Churchill College, Cambridge.

51 CAB 24/257, CP 218 (35), 'Cabinet Procedure . . . Recovery of Cabinet Papers: Report,' 29 November 1935. The conclusion concerning the Curzon collection is puzzling since Lord Ronaldshay, in his *Life of Curzon*, which had not been submitted to the Cabinet Office, published materials which compromised the secrecy of post-war Cabinet discussions, particularly at the time of the Chanak crisis. For this point about the biography I am indebted

to Prof. Keith Middlemas. How many of the seven in fact delivered their collections is not known.

52 C 51 (35) 10, 4 December 1935 (CAB 23/82).

53 CAB 21/790, 'Reconstruction of the Government: Arrangements made by Individual Ministers. . . ,' 14 June 1935, and Note by A. J. Banks, 2 June 1937.

54 CAB 21/598, 'Cabinet Procedure: Note by the Secretary, Cabinet,' Appendix III, 2 April 1936; Howorth noted that in some cases CID papers had been retained by individual ministers as long as they continued in office.

55 CAB 21/443, Howorth to Secretary, 27 April 1934.

56 See above, pp. 85 and 91–2.

57 Lloyd George, *War Memoirs*, vol. II, p. 468. As was his wont, Lloyd George commented acerbically concerning Milner and other members of the British deputation: 'Having regard to the warnings which were blaring at them in every direction, it is incomprehensible that they should have been so deaf and blind.'

58 C 35 (34) 4, 17 October 1934 (CAB 23/80). The detail of the minute is surely no accident, although one wonders if it is greater than the actual discussion.

59 In the last regard, Howorth mentioned 'instances where, in order to save the expense of reprinting, a document containing facts and figures has, with the necessary consents [the present and past premiers] been shown to a later administration which was considering the same subject.' Such a practice had followed only two or three times since the war, he added. (CAB 21/444, 'Publication of Cabinet Documents,' 26 November 1934.)

60 CAB 24/161, CP 381 (23), 'Cabinet: Committee on the Historical Section of the CID, Report,' 9 August 1923. For its earlier activities, see above, pp. 120–3.

61 Ruled against was the publication of a one volume abridged history of the Ministry of Munitions, which had been prepared, in twelve volumes, for official use, because of 'highly secret matters . . . which would be undesirable to issue to the public.' (CAB 24/161, 'Committee on the Historical Section.') A copy of the twelve volume set is now available at the Public Record Office as MUN 5/321A.

62 For the committee's composition and its suspension, CAB 16/52, COH 1; for the vesting of the Chair, CAB 103/102, Bridges to Prime Minister, 31 January 1939.

63 The committee met annually to review the progress of the Official Histories and to consider the estimate for the forthcoming year; the Reports for 1915–39 are collected in CAB 103/1–16.

64 CAB 103/103, C. V. O. Owens' description, attached to Bridges to Earl de la Warr, 3 July 1939; Daniel's anonymity was shed only in his contribution of a signed 'Preface' to the revised second edition of Sir Julian Corbett's *Naval Operations*, vols. I and III. He spent nearly thirty years in the Section.

65 The former expression is Owens' (CAB 103/103); Hankey quotes Thucydides in CAB 63/40, 'Note on Official Histories,' 12 June 1928.

66 Sales are listed through 31 December 1938 in CAB 103/103, COH 45, Appendix II; in the major series, sales declined by roughly two-thirds from first to last.

67 The staff was fast becoming superannuated. (CAB 103/102, Howorth's Note, 'The Historical Section,' 20 January 1939.) The last volume was ultimately published in 1949; for a list of the First World War publications, see Wilson, *Cabinet Office*, Annex 10, p. 178.

68 CAB 103/102, Minutes of Bridges to Cyril Longhurst, 25 November 1938.
69 CAB 21/444, Howorth's Note, 'My England. By George Lansbury,' 1 October 1934.
70 Except for 'very exceptional cases,' Lansbury maintained that 'it would be very good indeed if all Cabinet records, conclusions, and minutes were published.' (261 *HC Debates*, 8 February 1932, cols. 523–4.)
71 George Lansbury, *My England* (London, n.d. [1934]), pp. 123–30.
72 Wilson (*Cabinet Office*, p. 120) bases the suspicion on an occasional Personal Minute 'demanding action on some matter which was already well in hand for the purpose of having a record of his intervention and inspiration.'
73 PREM 4/7/6, Churchill to Edward Bridges, 30 April 1945. Of course, Churchill had published documents which he had 'written and signed' in his memoirs of the First World War; no doubt he would have cited the precedent, had he been pressed by the Cabinet Office.
74 *Ibid.*, J.R.C. [olville] to Bridges, 23 May 1945.
75 *Ibid.*, 'Return of Cabinet Documents,' 22 May 1945; the Note, WP (45) 320, 'War Cabinet Documents,' 23 May 1945, was published over Churchill's initials.
76 The bar upon publication without authority had been reiterated in 1942 by the Deputy Prime Minister, Attlee. (Quoted, *Radcliffe Committee Report*, p. 4; the Privy Counsellors ignored Churchill's role in dictating the rules for the war period.) Bridges' memorandum, circulated to the Labour Cabinet on 10 May 1946, is published in full, *ibid.*, pp. 5–8.
77 426 *HC Debates*, 1 August 1946, cols. 1207–8. The dispensation for pre-war 'defence themes' Bridges had insisted upon because 'the opening date can hardly be the 3rd September, 1939.'
78 Thomas Jones Papers, Class W, vol. IX, no. 152, Hankey to Jones, 19 March 1935. There is no evidence of a reply in the Hankey Papers.
79 Lloyd George Papers, G/8/16/15, Hankey to Lloyd George, 2 December 1930.
80 *Ibid.*, G/8/18/16, 11 December 1930; Roskill (*Hankey*, vol. II, p. 532) missed evidence of a telephone call in concluding that 'rather oddly no reply from Lloyd George has survived.' Hankey's altered feelings are spelled out in Lloyd George Papers, G/8/18/22, Hankey to Sylvester, 26 January 1935.
81 CAB 21/445, Hankey to Sir Eric Geddes, 17 April 1936.
82 CAB 21/446, Memorandum, Howorth to Secretary, 7 July 1936. Thomas' troubled financial condition – the former trade unionist and Labour leader accepted funds from Tory coffers (*Davidson's Memoirs*, p. 410) – may have been general knowledge in Whitehall and raised fears that his memoirs would be replete with profitable revelations; the point remains speculative.
83 The Labour Opposition had pressed for a prosecution under the Official Secrets Act, because a judicial inquiry had found that Thomas had made certain unauthorized disclosures, which had led to rumored speculation on the Stock Exchange: Attlee had pointed to the disparity between the Lansbury case and Thomas' offence, which he claimed was far more serious. (For the legal technicalities, Williams, *Public Interest*, pp. 46–7.)
84 CAB 24/263, CP 198 (36), 'Cabinet Procedure: Use of Post-War Cabinet Papers in Autobiographies,' 17 July 1936.
85 MacDonald thought Thomas' mind 'not quite normal' owing to his recent reversal of fortune. (CAB 21/446, MacDonald to Hankey, undated but likely 23 July 1936.)
86 C 35 (34) 4, 17 October 1934 (CAB 23/80) is the precedent Hankey cited.

87 C 54 (36) 10, 22 July 1936, and C 55 (36) 1, 29 July (CAB 23/85). Although Wilson (*Cabinet Office*, pp. 54–5) notes that the procedure followed in the Thomas case became standard, he does not specify Hankey's transformation of the 1934 ruling into this form.

88 For MacDonald's humanitarian suggestion, CAB 21/446, MacDonald to Hankey, undated but likely 23 July 1936; Hankey's letter to Thomas of 24 July (*ibid.*) stated his belief that any exception to the rules would cause the whole position to 'go west.'

89 *Ibid.*, Hankey to Thomas, 10 November 1936.

90 See above, pp. 197–8.

91 Colin Cross, *Philip Snowden* (London, 1966), p. 334.

92 For the language of section 2, see *Franks Committee Report*, pp. 112–15; for the suggestion that Hankey had this provision in mind, I am indebted to Prof. D. C. Watt.

93 'In many respects the guts have been knocked out of the chapter . . .,' wrote Thomas to Hankey, 16 November 1936 (CAB 21/446).

94 CAB 21/444, Howorth to Petrie, 17 February 1936, and Howorth to Secretary, 24 February; Howorth acknowledged that Long's draft memorandum had been 'inadvertently preserved,' which makes the summons to Petrie verge on the outrageous.

95 PREM 4/6/14, Notes of J.R.C. [olville], 17 January 1945, reporting to the Prime Minister the views of Sir Edward Bridges, Sir Alex Cadogan, and Sir Gilbert Laithwaite; Bridges to Keith Feiling (*ibid.*), 13 March 1945; to be sure, the Milner case defined 'vindication' in a technical fashion which Chamberlain's misfortunes did not meet. Feiling was given access to certain departmental records, but no doubt these preceded Chamberlain's tenure as premier.

96 *Ibid.*, Bridges to Prime Minister, 15 October 1945, and Attlee's note of the following day. Earlier, a delay of three or four years had been mentioned.

97 Thomas Jones Papers, Class A, vol. VI, no. 216, copy of Stanley Baldwin (drafted by Jones) to Prime Minister, undated but 1944 or 1945.

98 A. E. B. Owen, 'Handlist of the Political Papers of Stanley Baldwin . . .,' in the University Library, Cambridge.

99 G. M. Young, *Stanley Baldwin* (London, 1952), passim, with particular regard to matters of foreign policy.

100 Lloyd George Papers, G/8/18/39, Hankey to Lloyd George, 11 July 1938. Lloyd George's two volume *Memoirs of the Peace Conference* reached well into the early post-war years and dealt with topics of current interest.

101 HNKY 3/43, Hankey to Robin Hankey, 1 March 1938.

102 Viscount Simon, *Retrospect* (London, 1952); Viscount Halifax, *Fulness of Days* (London, 1957); Viscount Samuel, *Memoirs* (London, 1945).

103 Duff Cooper, *Old Men Forget* (London, 1953), pp. 210–11 and ch. 14; for information concerning the reaction, I am indebted to Prof. D. C. Watt.

104 Sir Samuel Hoare (Viscount Templewood), *Nine Troubled Years* (London, 1954).

105 Lord Chatfield, *It Might Happen Again* (London, 1947); Marquess of Londonderry, *Wings of Destiny* (London, 1942). For information, derived from Cabinet records, concerning these memoirs, I am indebted to Prof. Keith Middlemas.

106 Postgate, *Lansbury*, p. vii.

107 *Ibid.*, pp. vii–ix; additional information from Prof. D. C. Watt.

108 Postgate, *Lansbury*, pp. viii–ix; see above, n. 45.
109 Postgate, *Lansbury*, p. viii.
110 The files CAB 21/457 and CAB 21/790, dealing with the recovery of Cabinet documents, are continued in a file referred to in the Cabinet Office system as 'Part 3,' but that particular file had not been transferred to the Public Record Office with them, surely because some of its contents considerably post-date 1945.
111 Richard Ullman, *Anglo-Soviet Relations, 1917–1921*, vol. I, *Intervention and the War* (Princeton, 1961).
112 It is unlikely that the Milner heirs resisted the request, but some Cabinet papers obviously were not returned to Whitehall Gardens.
113 Information from Prof. D. C. Watt; for the 1958 legislation, see below, pp. 289–93.
114 Wilson (*Cabinet Office*, p. 81) conveys official anxiety even forty years after the fact: 'The visit appears to have given rise to a good deal of misunderstanding both at home and overseas as to why, when on what was ostensibly a private visit, he was engaged in official conversations, which if they were to be entered in at all should be at ministerial level.' Cf. Roskill, *Hankey*, vol. III, ch. 3.
115 Roskill, *Hankey*, vol. III, p. 142; Roskill's assertion that Howorth's performance left something to be desired is based upon fragmentary information; certainly his success in regaining custody of Cabinet papers Hankey weighed heavily in his favor.
116 Gibbs, *Rearmament*; G. C. Peden, *British Rearmament and the Treasury, 1932–1939* (Edinburgh, 1979) and 'Fisher and Rearmament'; Robert Paul Shay, Jr, *British Rearmament in the Thirties: Politics and Profits* (Princeton, 1977). The first two authors are major sources for the account below.
117 Inskip, a lawyer-politician with no experience in defence matters, was selected because he would improve the government's debating strength in the House of Commons; Hankey's candidate had been Halifax, who of course was a peer. (Peden, 'Fisher and Rearmament,' p. 41.)
118 Watt, *Personalities and Policies*, p. 116.
119 The verdict of the leading scholar of rearmament: Gibbs, *Rearmament*, p. 772.
120 Montgomery Hyde, *British Air Policy*, pp. 280–1.
121 The DRC proposals had been examined in some detail by the Ministerial Committee on Disarmament (DC(M)) prior to the Cabinet's action.
122 For an informative account of the discussions between February and June 1934, Peden, 'Fisher and Rearmament,' pp. 35–7; Ann Trotter, *Britain and East Asia, 1933–1937* (Cambridge, 1975), makes the point that Chamberlain failed to get his way concerning Naval expenditure at the time (pp. 88–92), but Gibbs (*Rearmament*, p. 125) depicts Chamberlain as quite pleased with his efforts.
123 The phrase is Norman Rose's, in his *Vansittart: Study of a Diplomat* (New York, 1978), p. 134.
124 E.g. Henry Pownall, quoted, *ibid.*, p. 132; Vansittart and Fisher (Watt, *Personalities and Policies*, p. 115) were both outspoken on the point.
125 D. C. Watt, *Too Serious a Business* (London, 1975), p. 98. Fisher and Vansittart insisted on a corollary, namely that the most strenuous efforts were required to reach an agreement with Japan.
126 Trotter, *Britain and East Asia*, pp. 94–109, supplies an institutional account

of the tour; for the biographical details, Roskill, *Hankey*, vol. III, ch. 3.

127 Hankey to Lord Templewood, cited, Roskill, *Hankey*, vol. III, p. 141.

128 Gibbs, *Rearmament*, pp. 170–1.

129 For Hankey's draft, dated 25 January 1934, with emendations in MacDonald's hand, see PREM 1/175; the final version is CP 38 (35), Cmd 4827, *Statement Relating to Defence*, 4 March 1935, whose contents are discussed in Gibbs, *Rearmament*, pp. 170–2.

130 For Fisher's disappointment, Peden, 'Fisher and Rearmament,' p. 40.

131 Diary, 5 March, quoted by Marquand, *MacDonald*, p. 771; Roskill, noting that this feature had not appeared in Hankey's draft, reviews press commentary. (*Hankey*, vol. III, p. 150 and n. 3.)

132 For the intelligence, Peden, 'Fisher and Rearmament,' p. 40; for the subsequent developments, Gibbs, *Rearmament*, pp. 177–80.

133 Gibbs, *Rearmament*, p. 255.

134 Yet not even this scheme ought to obscure the fact that the diversity of threats to Britain and her Empire meant that defence planning for the next several years centered on what has been called 'a war of limited liability.' (Watt, *Too Serious a Business*, pp. 99–103.)

135 Specifically, in the form of the 'Peace Ballot' of 1935; see Naylor, *Labour's International Policy*, pp. 61–7, for the general misunderstanding.

136 '"An act of bad faith,"' Hankey commented. (Quoted by Rose, *Vansittart*, p. 142.) Hankey had long since abandoned the idea of a convention, which he had backed in 1932.

137 *Pownall Diaries*, vol. I, p. 36; 15 February 1934. Hankey's comment that Fisher was 'rather mad' likely reflects in part Hankey's frustration with the Treasury's scaling down of the first DRC report: yet Hankey specified a 'nerve disorder,' and Fisher had only returned to Whitehall in September 1933, following upon a long illness.

138 Watt, *Personalities and Policies*, pp. 100–1.

139 125 *HL Debates*, 25 November 1942, cols. 267–9.

140 HNKY 13/7, Hankey to Sir Alan Barlow, 28 October 1943.

141 Peden, 'Fisher and Rearmament,' p. 35.

142 *Ibid.*, pp. 46–7; Peden insists that 'if any one man dictated the course of British defence policy in the years 1933–9 that man was Chamberlain.'

143 N. H. Gibbs argues persuasively that to assume all would have been well without 'Treasury control' is 'to diagnose a complicated disease by considering only one of its many symptoms.' (*Rearmament*, pp. 316–19). Cf. Shay, *British Rearmament*, passim, which while not monocausal makes a strong case against the actions of the National Government.

144 Peden, *British Rearmament*, pp. 181–4.

145 Such a statement does not dispute the deep-seated financial limits to rearmament described by Peden, *ibid.*, ch. 3, but it does draw the overall balance differently.

146 Peden, 'Fisher and Rearmament,' pp. 34–5.

147 For the persistent criticisms led by the Tory MP, Wing-Commander Archibald James, Roskill, *Hankey*, vol. III, pp. 52–3.

148 Liddell Hart, *Memoirs*, vol. I, p. 313; D. C. Watt suggests that Liddell Hart's vanity makes him a poor judge of the strength of the call for this appointment.

149 Liddell Hart, *Memoirs*, vol. I, p. 313.

150 'Correspondence,' *The Times*, 16 December 1935; Hankey's reply was

private, and he rejected Trenchard's suggestion on the grounds of past experiences with Salisbury, Haldane, and Curzon. The exchange of views is excerpted in Montgomery-Hyde, *British Air Policy*, pp. 245–7.

151 CAB 63/51, CP 30 (36), 'Defence Co-ordination,' 7 February 1936. In the midst of advancing ten arguments against any such proposal, Hankey recalled that 'dual control was the rock on which Mr. Asquith and Mr. Lloyd George split in December 1916.'

152 *Pownall Diaries*, vol. I, p. 102; 17 February 1936. Hankey's latest objections to such a scheme are contained in his 'Notes for the Lord President of the Council, in connection with his speech in the Parliamentary Debates on May 22, 1935,' 17 May 1935 (CAB 63/50).

153 Whatever the other abilities of the former Attorney-General. Cf. Roskill, *Hankey*, vol. III, p. 208.

154 *Pownall Diaries*, vol. I, p. 100; 3 February 1936: Hankey proposed the appointment to Ismay in April.

155 Ismay, *Memoirs*, p. 76; for the latter point, I am indebted to Prof. D. C. Watt.

156 Gibbs, *Rearmament*, p. 772; see his discussion of the defence machinery of government in ch. 20.

157 For this reason, A. J. P. Taylor's incisive description of the new post – 'Inskip had one room, two secretaries and no powers' (*English History*, p. 390) – is misleading, although Inskip in fact had no power of decision.

158 Diary, 11 March 1936, quoted by Iain Macleod, *Neville Chamberlain* (New York, 1962), p. 173.

159 The words are attributed to Ismay by the official historians, Sir Charles Webster and Noble Frankland, *The Strategic Air Offensive Against Germany, 1939–1945*, vol. I, *Preparation* (London, 1961), pp. 76–7. (*History of the Second World War: United Kingdom Military Series.*) They add that the Cabinet also recognized that fighters were cheaper and easier to build.

160 Quoted, Peden, 'Fisher and Rearmament,' p. 43.

161 Peden, *British Rearmament*, pp. 149–50, 113–15.

162 Thus Gibbs (*Rearmament*, p. 772) who assigns to Inskip no original role but notes his acting as an 'able second' to the Prime Minister and as 'virtually a deputy to the Chancellor . . . for defence expenditure.'

163 HNKY 3/43, Hankey to Robin Hankey, respectively 21 May and 3 April 1938.

164 Hankey Diary, 25 November 1935.

165 CAB 63/51, 'Foreign Policy and Imperial Defence: A Memorandum by the Secretary, Committee of Imperial Defence,' 8 June 1936.

166 Gibbs, *Rearmament*, pp. 212–17, and the fullest account, Arthur Marder, 'The Royal Navy and the Ethiopian Crisis of 1935–36,' *American Historical Review*, 75: 1327–56 (June 1970).

167 Quoted by Marder, *ibid.*, p. 1355.

168 Hankey Diary, 25 November 1935. For the General Election of 1935, see Tom Stannage, *Baldwin Thwarts the Opposition* (London, 1980).

169 For these electoral commitments, see Stannage, *ibid.*, passim, and Naylor, *Labour's International Policy*, pp. 113–18, 124–5.

170 Daniel Waley, *British Public Opinion and the Abyssinian War, 1935–6* (London, 1975), pp. 68–9.

171 Of course, Hankey shared these views with a number of others, most important among them the COS. (Gibbs, *Rearmament*, pp. 793–5.)

172 CAB 63/51, Hankey to Richard Casey, 20 April 1936.

173 Not least by his biographer: Roskill, *Hankey*, vol. III, pp. 178–9 and 288–9.
174 CAB 63/53, Note of 27 May 1938, in response to Churchill's charge that CID committees were too numerous and too deliberative.
175 Gibbs, *Rearmament*, pp. 767–71 for a summary of the CID machinery.
176 A verdict shared by the official historian of rearmament, *ibid.*, p. 809; cf. the views of Lawrence R. Pratt, *East of Malta, West of Suez: Britain's Mediterranean Policy, 1936–1939* (Cambridge, 1975), pp. 104–5, that Chamberlain's 'real failing lay in his willingness to be guided by mediocre advice . . . the fallible opinion of very fallible men.' It is difficult to see this relationship other than in terms of near-identity of strategic thought, however.
177 CAB 63/52, 'Role of the British Army: Note by the Secretary,' 18 January 1937: 'without haste but without rest.'
178 Both views are quoted by Michael Howard, *The Continental Commitment* (London, 1972), pp. 118–19. 1939 had emerged from the deliberations of the DRC, whose second, interim, report looked to 1 January 1939 as the date beyond which it would not be safe to postpone readiness for war, although, on balance, the DRC concluded that German aggression ought not to eventuate before 1942. (Gibbs, *Rearmament*, pp. 178–80.) Hankey subscribed to the prospect of Britain's readiness by 1939. (Roskill, *Hankey*, vol. III, pp. 236–8.)
179 That the Foreign Office encouraged the 'buying [of] time until British rearmament had reached the stage of defensive impregnability in 1939' is shown in W. N. Medlicott, *Britain and Germany: The Search for Agreement, 1930–1937* (London, 1969), pp. 27–31. Vansittart, who supported the project, dubbed those who held this view 'The Thirty-Niners,' although he personally saw no certainty that Hitler would wait until that time.
180 Quoted by Pratt, *East of Malta*, p. 95.
181 Quoted, *ibid.*, p. 96; Pratt's account establishes Hankey's centrality in the formulation of Mediterranean strategy and diplomacy, not least because Chamberlain had enlisted him to lobby for the policy of accommodation.
182 *Ibid.*, pp. 94–100. Frustration within the Foreign Office felt with the policy of accommodation is typified in Oliver Harvey's comment – 'The attitude of the Service departments is most disturbing. Whenever ANY action is proposed they produce nothing but difficulties.' (*The Diplomatic Diaries of Oliver Harvey, 1937–1940*, ed. John Harvey (New York, 1970), p. 87; 8 February 1938 (hereafter cited as *Harvey Diplomatic Diaries*).)
183 Pratt, *East of Malta*, p. 94; Pratt minces no words about Hankey's 'emotional approval of Fascism,' and it must be remarked that his 'Italy, Some Notes of a Holiday Visit,' 27 September 1937 (CAB 21/563) lend themselves to such a characterization; cf. Roskill, *Hankey*, vol. III, pp. 269–70.
184 Quoted, Roskill, *Hankey*, vol. III, p. 306; Hankey to Vansittart, 18 February 1938.
185 Both points are made by Pratt, *East of Malta*, pp. 104–5, but they are quite distinct: the one is acceptable, the other not.
186 In 1935 Hankey had prodded MacDonald to resign but had urged Baldwin not to defer to Chamberlain; Balfour's opinion dated to 1929. (Hankey Diary, 24 February 1935.)
187 CAB 23/52, 'Role of the British Army.'
188 Both a CID sub-committee and the Treasury remarked upon these developments, and the latter linked the prospects for radar with Britain's defence needs. (Peden, *British Rearmament*, pp. 129–30.)

189 Quoted, *ibid.*, p. 131.
190 *Ibid.*, p. 131; cf. Roskill, *Hankey*, vol. III, p. 285.
191 Peden, *British Rearmament*, pp. 131–3; Fisher opined in July 1938 that '"Parity" in the sense of exact equality with Germany is unobtainable in peace conditions.'
192 CAB 63/53, copy of Hankey to Sir Eric Phipps [Roskill's attribution], 21 February 1938. Hankey's peaceful repose contrasts distinctly to Winston Churchill's turmoil and 'vision of Death.' (*The Gathering Storm* (Boston, 1948), pp. 257–8.)
193 Although the term 'appeaser' has developed a loose historical connotation (see Naylor, *Labour's International Policy*, pp. 214–23), it is well to differentiate Chamberlain's purpose (*ibid.*, pp. 237–49) from those of others, Hankey included.
194 Gibbs, *Rearmament*, p. 782.
195 Roskill, *Hankey*, vol. III, pp. 218–19.
196 For the substantive issues which had divided the two, Roskill, *Hankey*, vol. II, pp. 402–5, 417–18.
197 CAB 63/51, Hankey to Prime Minister, 24 July 1936. In 1949, Hankey reiterated his criticism of Churchill's involvement (162 *HL Debates*, 5 May 1949, col. 404).
198 Gilbert, *Churchill*, vol. V, pp. 756–7; Swinton to Hankey, 26 June 1936.
199 Quoted, *ibid.*, p. 758; Hankey to Prime Minister, 29 June 1936.
200 Morton's actions have long been recognized, although challenged by Montgomery-Hyde (*British Air Policy*, p. 462 n. 9). Gilbert's *Churchill* leaves no doubt of Morton's involvement.
201 In January 1936 Hankey had asked the same of Churchill, receiving the assurance that nothing save his own experienced judgment was involved. (Gilbert, *Churchill*, vol. V, pp. 701–2.)
202 Montgomery-Hyde, *British Air Policy*, pp. 394–5; on the other hand, Swinton took very seriously Milch's reference during the visit to a possible doubling in size of the Luftwaffe. (Quoted, Gibbs, *Rearmament*, pp. 568–9.)
203 Quoted, Gilbert, *Churchill*, vol. V, pp. 875–6; MacLean to Wing-Cmdr Anderson.
204 Fuller quotations from the exchange between the two are found, *ibid.*, pp. 877–81, than in Roskill.
205 Cf. Gilbert's use (*ibid.*, pp. 881–4) of contemporary records to prove Churchill's case with Roskill's reliance (*Hankey*, vol. III, pp. 263 and 664–5) on reconstructed German sources.
206 See the colorful account, based upon a conversation with Hankey, of C. P. Snow, who marveled: 'It would have been untypical for Hankey to say unnecessary rude words in a conversation: to do it on paper (a civil servant's major sin) seemed beyond belief.' (*Variety of Men* (New York, 1966), p. 158.)
207 See Roskill, *Hankey*, vol. III, pp. 315–17.
208 Burgis Papers, Pownall to Burgis, 30 March 1938; see also Ismay to Burgis and Howorth to Burgis, respectively 22 and 23 March 1938.
209 Roskill, *Hankey*, vol. III, p. 307. In May 1938 Hankey noted accurately that the rearmament programs were not complete, 'owing to circumstances beyond my control, though well under weigh.' (HNKY 3/43, Hankey to Robin Hankey, 21 May.)
210 Ismay, *Memoirs*, p. 84.
211 C 56 (35), 18 December 1935 (CAB 23/90B), including Hankey to Prime Minister, 8 January 1936.

212 John W. Wheeler-Bennett, *King George VI: His Life and Reign* (New York, 1958), p. 233.
213 Frances Donaldson, *Edward VIII* (pb. edn, New York, 1974), p. 263.
214 CAB 21/778, including Hardinge to Hankey, 21 February 1938, and vice versa, 25 February and 4 March 1938; Hardinge to Hankey, 7 March 1938; and Cleverly to Hankey, 7 March 1938.
215 CAB 21/474, Ismay to Assistant Secretaries CID, 17 February 1938; CAB 21/598, cover letter by Prime Minister, 22 June 1937, attached to CP 88 (36), 'Cabinet Procedure.'
216 CAB 24/273, CP 285 (37), 'Cabinet Procedure: Note by the Prime Minister,' 25 November 1937. The most recent documents relating to such procedural matters were collected in CP 88 (36), 'Cabinet Procedure,' 2 April 1936, Appendix I (CAB 24/261). 'Lock and Key' protection is discussed above, p. 202.
217 CAB 21/792, Howorth to Col. Ismay, 30 November 1937; as Hankey had drafted the Prime Minister's 'note,' such changes hardly came by way of a surprise.
218 *Ibid.*, 'Office Notice: Custody and Distribution of Secret Documents,' 14 December 1937.
219 PREM 1/302, Halifax to Prime Minister, 7 May 1938.
220 *Ibid.*, Memorandum, Howorth to Secretary, 9 May 1938; Hankey to Prime Minister of the same date.
221 Wilson, *Cabinet Office*, p. 56.
222 *Ibid.*, pp. 56–7, for a description of the activities of a half-dozen standing committees; Wilson concludes that the India Committee had in fact finished its work in 1935.
223 CAB 24/261, CP 88 (36), 'Cabinet Procedure,' Appendix IV. For a particular perspective, namely its contribution of 'economic advice during depression and recovery,' see Howson and Winch, *Economic Advisory Council*, passim.
224 CAB 21/482, Draft Report, with Sir Warren Fisher's cover letter of 23 May 1938; Fisher served as Chair of the review committee.
225 The lowest of low, seemingly, since the Secretary of the EAC claimed greater involvement in the work of the 'International committee for the application of the agreement regarding non-intervention in Spain' (for which see Wilson, *Cabinet Office*, p. 85) – in May 1939! (CAB 21/482, A. F. Hemming to Secretary, 22 May 1939.)
226 *Ibid.*, Hemming to Eastwood, 8 November 1939.
227 HNKY 3/43, Hankey to Robin Hankey, 22 April 1938. Until April 1937, Hankey had had an informal understanding with Warren Fisher to stay on until 1940, but at that time Hankey had been released from that agreement if a suitable position opened. (Hankey Diary, 6 April 1937.) Although Roskill (*Hankey*, vol. III, p. 279) records Hankey's interest in the Suez Canal Company in June 1937, he does not establish the Cabinet Secretary's direct approach to Chamberlain some months later.
228 As long ago as 1927, Hankey had foreseen the possibility that the CID Secretary might serve as a Deputy Secretary to the Cabinet. (Quoted, Roskill, *Hankey*, vol. II, p. 445; Hankey to Esher, 29 September 1927.)
229 Quoted, *ibid.*, Stamfordham to Esher, 3 October 1927.
230 *Pownall Diaries*, vol. I, p. 60; 14 January 1935.
231 Ismay, *Memoirs*, p. 89; the comment is retrospective.

232 Peden, *British Rearmament*, pp. 24–5.
233 Hankey Diary, 6 May 1938; Hankey noted that he had spoken well of Bridges, but 'I didn't think him the best man for the job.'
234 *Pownall Diaries*, vol. I, pp. 144–5; mistakenly dated 2 May 1938, with a *cri de coeur* certainly not shared with Hankey: '"I don't want to be anybody's Secretary – it's not a man's job."'
235 CAB 63/53, Hankey to Prime Minister, 9 May 1938.
236 *Ibid.*, Hankey's Memorandum, 9 May 1938.
237 Hankey Diary, 10 and 16 May 1938. Hankey was buoyed to learn that Ismay thought that he could handle the combined posts 'as well as anyone else' (9 May 1938).
238 CAB 63/53, 'Reasons for Appointing . . .,' dates to 17 May; Roskill (*Hankey*, vol. III, p. 357 n. 1) errs in referring instead to Hankey's cover letter and memorandum of 9 May as the basis for his conversation with the Prime Minister.
239 For this odd offer, Peden, 'Fisher and Rearmament,' p. 42. The Treasury official had not yet lost Chamberlain's confidence, which followed upon Fisher's resolute criticism of the Munich arrangements.
240 HNKY 3/43, Hankey to Robin Hankey, 21 May 1938, continued three days later.
241 CAB 63/53, Hankey to Fisher, 10 May 1938; Howorth was aged fifty-eight at this time.
242 *Ibid.*, Hankey to Prime Minister, 9 May 1938, in which he asked only that 'in making the new appointment, it would be advisable, so far as is possible, to avoid anything in the nature of an affront to him [Howorth].'
243 HNKY 3/43, Hankey to Robin Hankey, 24 May 1938; he described Warren Fisher as 'rather sore' at the turn of events.
244 *Pownall Diaries*, vol. I, pp. 149 and 154; 30 May and 24 July 1938.
245 *Webb Diaries*, p. 12; 6 March 1924.
246 C 27 (38) 1, 1 June 1938 (CAB 23/93). In fact, the Prime Minister did not have the gift of the Clerkship, and Hankey and Fisher both were involved in straightening out the *faux pas* and securing the post for Howorth. (CAB 21/454, 'Privy Council: Appointment to the Clerkship.')
247 Roskill, *Hankey*, vol. III, p. 362. Burgis' direct observation is apt: 'What he [Churchill] wanted to do was to jettison our organisation . . . and replace it by some contraption of his own. Pug Ismay, to his everlasting credit, fought this revolutionary idea tooth and nail. What is more, he won. Considering that Ismay scarcely knew Churchill in those days, this was something of a feat and a notable contribution to ultimate victory.' (Burgis Memoirs.)
248 C 27 (38) 1, 1 June 1938 (CAB 23/93).
249 C 33 (38) 1, 20 July 1938 (CAB 23/94).
250 HNKY 4/30, Bridges to Hankey, 7 August 1938.
251 C 36 (38) 8, 28 July 1938 (CAB 23/94).
252 HNKY 8/37, 'Notes for a Speech,' 19 June 1938.
253 CAB 63/53, Hankey to F.F. Sheddon, 10 January 1938. If 'Boom' Trenchard was such a friend, Hankey was in no need of enemies.

7. THE CUSTODY OF CABINET SECRECY

1 Wilson, *Cabinet Office*, pp. 90, 115; ch. 9 describes the relationship between the Cabinet Office and the War Cabinet. Cf. Hennessy, 'A magnificent

piece,' who maintains that the war 'transformed the Cabinet Office as it did the entire structure of central government'; the operation was conducted, however, along well-established lines, and the contribution of the inter-war Cabinet Secretariat is under-valued, however 'rudimentary' the operation may appear.

2 An early example is his involvement in a meeting with the Foreign Secretary, the Chancellor, the Home Secretary, and the Permanent Under-Secretary to the Foreign Office, at which the possibilities of a plebiscite as a means of settling the Sudeten dispute were discussed; Vansittart was 'deliberately excluded.' (*The Diaries of Sir Alexander Cadogan, 1938–45*, ed. David Dilks (New York, 1972), p. 98; 15 September 1938.)

3 Lawrence Burgis, once again in the office, described the Cabinet Secretary as 'all at sea' with the new premier; Burgis Memoirs.

4 Stacey, *Government of Modern Britain*, p. 361. From 1968 until recently, the post of Head of the Civil Service carried with it a Civil Service Department. Following upon its abolition, since the spring of 1983 the Cabinet Secretary, Sir Robert Armstrong, has also served as Head of the Civil Service, although some of the former department's functions were assigned to the Treasury.

5 For descriptions of the role and influence, Stacey, *British Government, 1966 to 1975*, pp. 86–95; G. W. Jones, 'The Development of the Cabinet,' in William Thornhill, ed., *The Modernization of British Government* (London, 1975), pp. 50–3; Hennessy, 'A magnificent piece.' The best-known description (Anthony Sampson, *The New Anatomy of Britain* (London, 1971), pp. 69–73 and 249–64) is also the most controversial.

6 With the merger, Howorth was appointed Deputy Secretary (Civil) and Ismay Deputy Secretary (Military). For Ismay's resistance to Churchill's scheme, see above Ch. 6 n. 247.

7 A recollection of Ronald Wells, quoted by Roskill, *Hankey*, vol. III, p. 366 n. 1; Churchill expressed strong misgivings about the extant committee system in a minute of 24 May 1940; re-organization followed in June. (Wilson, *Cabinet Office*, pp. 94–5.)

8 Burgis Memoirs. The judgment fails to take into account Hankey's deferring to the wishes of successive premiers with regard to the fullness of minutes.

9 CAB 21/1341, WP (G) (39) 1, 'Institution of the War Cabinet: Note by the Secretary,' 5 September 1939. In such a fashion the invidious distinctions about which ministers should receive which minutes was avoided. Surely, the King continued to receive the Cabinet Minutes, as he had from the first.

10 Wilson, *Cabinet Office*, p. 113; in 1976 the staff numbered 681, although nearly half were employed in the Central Statistical Office. The responsibilities are sketched in CAB 21/778, Howorth's Office Note, 11 September 1939.

11 CAB 21/1084, 'Functions of the Cabinet Secretariat: Memorandum by the Secretary of the War Cabinet,' 14 September 1944. Bridges' claim that this document was the first-ever formal statement of Secretariat functions impresses as disingenuous.

12 For the disagreements with Churchill and an evaluation of Hankey's ministerial contributions, see Roskill, *Hankey*, vol. III, chs. 12–15. Perhaps their ministerial relationship was flawed from the first, as Hankey judged that his 'main job' in the Chamberlain War Cabinet was 'to keep an eye on Winston!' (Quoted, Gilbert, *Churchill*, vol. V, p. 1108; Hankey to Adeline Hankey, 3 September 1939.)

13 HNKY 25/1, Bridges to Hankey, 28 September 1943 and 3 March 1944; Hankey had yet to approach a publisher.

14 *Ibid.*, Bridges to Hankey, 30 November 1944, referred to this as 'the main issue' which he had raised with Hankey at their March meeting.

15 *Ibid.*, Hankey to Bridges, 27 October 1944.

16 Given this argument, it is altogether odd that Hankey's appeal did not specify the distinction 'formalised in a decision taken by the Prime Minister in June 1938 that information relating to the period from the beginning of the war to the 1st November, 1919 . . . should be treated on a different and more lenient basis than information relating to the period after that date.' (Memorandum of Sir Edward Bridges, May 1946, printed in *Radcliffe Committee Report*, p. 6.) Hankey had of course been Cabinet Secretary at the time.

17 HNKY 25/1, Bridges to Hankey, 30 November 1944.

18 CAB 21/445, Hankey to Sir Eric Geddes, 17 April 1936; for the context, see above, pp. 230–1.

19 HNKY 25/1, Hankey to Bridges, 3 December 1944.

20 *Ibid.*, Hankey to Prime Minister, 8 December 1944. Hankey cited an analogy to Ismay's position, although it better approximates his serving as Secretary to the CID than as Secretary to the Cabinet.

21 *Ibid.*, Bridges to Hankey, 23 February 1945.

22 *Ibid.*, Hankey to Bridges, 24 February 1945, and vice versa, 28 February. My review of the War Cabinet records for the period reveals no reference to the matter.

23 Thomas Jones Papers, Class Y, vol. II, no. 2, Hankey to Jones, 28 February 1945.

24 In the judgment of Brian Bond, editor of the *Pownall Diaries*, vol. I, p. xx. Each of the individual diaries was prefaced: '*Private and Confidential*. This is a private diary, to read only by myself or my wife. It can however be made available to the eventual student of the War, if he wishes – provided that he makes no *quotations* from it and, in making use of it, does not refer to its existence.' Eventually he relented and held no objection to its publication after his death.

25 Dilks, 'Introduction' to *Cadogan Diaries*, p. 17. Halifax's effort was the last of the diplomatic 'blue books' published in this century, a development indicative of the restricted flow of information given the public about the conduct of British foreign policy. (Watt 'Foreign Affairs.' pp. 123–4.) Yet something of the practice survived in the 1965 publication of a collection dealing with post-war events in Southeast Asia, *Documents relating to British Involvement in the Indo-China conflict, 1945–1965*, Cmnd 2834.

26 Dilks, 'Introduction' to *Cadogan Diaries*, p. 16.

27 E.g. Oliver Harvey in *Harvey Diplomatic Diaries* (pp. 50–1; 15 October 1937) on the personnel of the Chamberlain Cabinet: 'The worst ones are Hoare and Swinton: the first is consumed with ambition to be P.M., though God knows he'd land his party on the rocks in six months, and has never forgiven A.E.[den] for succeeding him. Swinton is anyway a very second-rate politician. Simon is slippery and evasive, a moral coward; yet incredible as it seems, he also believes that he can become P.M.' And so on, in a lesser key, for most of the others, save Eden.

28 *The Diaries of Sir Robert Bruce Lockhart*, vol. I, *1915–1939*, ed. Kenneth Young (London, 1973), 'Introduction,' p. 8.

29 For an instance of the latter, Cooper, *Old Men Forget*, p. 211, citing an instance from his own diary of 13 February 1938.
30 The words of a compulsive diarist, Oliver Harvey, who underscores the point: 'This is how we saw things at the time.' (Quoted, *Harvey War Diaries*, p. 12; May 1958.)
31 For a compelling example, dating to an earlier era, see *Hobhouse Diaries*, 'Introduction,' pp. 10–11.
32 Thomas Jones Papers, Class Y, vol. II, no. 3, Jones to Hankey, 1 March 1945.
33 *Ibid.*, nos. 4 and 6, Hankey to Jones, 6 March and 11 April 1945.
34 *Ibid.*, no. 6. At the same time, Hankey continued his correspondence with Bridges, without resorting to such a threat. (HNKY 25/1, 10 April 1945.)
35 Thomas Jones Papers, Class Y, vol. II, no. 11, Jones to Hankey, 19 April 1945. Curiously, Jones had assured Hankey that his own diaries had recorded 'nothing comparable with your diary. My notes are very irregular' (*ibid.*, no. 9, Jones to Hankey, 12 April 1945). Readers of *Whitehall Diary* will not likely agree.
36 HNKY 25/1, 'The Supreme Command, 1914–1918: Memorandum by Lord Hankey,' 28 March 1945.
37 Thomas Jones Papers, Class Y, vol. II, no. 13, Hankey to Jones, 20 June 1945.
38 HNKY 25/1, Addison to Hankey, 5 April 1946. Attlee had refused to return his official papers at the behest of the National Government in 1934, as had Churchill, and yet another irony, Addison; the other Labour minister involved was the Home Secretary, Chuter Ede, who alone had played no part in those proceedings.
39 *Ibid.*, Hankey to Addison, 13 April 1946.
40 *Ibid.*, Addison to Hankey, 13 May 1946.
41 *Ibid.*, Hankey to Addison, 29 May 1946: one man's 'vetting' had become another's 'censorship.' Three years later, Hankey asserted that the Labour ministers had not acted in an independent fashion: 'I had the impression that they funked giving a decision adverse to Winston.' (*Ibid.*, Hankey to Trenchard, 6 April 1949.)
42 Thomas Jones Papers, Class Y, vol. II, nos. 11 and 9; Jones' conclusion accompanied his assertion that their efforts were not comparable.
43 Jones' own comments, which were the basis for 'Cabinet Diary Withheld,' *Daily Telegraph*, 8 September 1954, and an untitled article in the *Evening Standard* of the previous day. (*Ibid.*, no. 16.) The Jones Papers appear to contain no exchange of correspondence either with Bridges or Brook.
44 *Ibid.*, no. 16, 'Cabinet Diary Withheld.' The untitled article in the *Evening Standard* nonetheless claimed that Jones decided not to proceed only after 'so many alterations and deletions were made when he submitted the manuscript.' Perhaps he did not consider these a form of official pressure.
45 Roskill, *Hankey*, vol. III, p. 613. To a prospective publisher Hankey commented ruefully: 'I had hoped that the new Government would have been more reasonable, and that it was the reference to a certain person which made the late Government so severe.' (HNKY 25/2, Hankey to Sir Newman Flowers, 22 June 1946.)
46 PREM 1/283, 'Home Office Note on Section 6 of the Official Secrets Act,' 30 June 1938. Curiously, the report on the incident compiled by the Home Secretary has been removed from the Cabinet paper collection at the Public Records Office (CAB 24/276, CP 105 (28), 29 April 1938), perhaps because

judicial proceedings are protected for a longer period than Cabinet papers; the incident can be reconstructed, however, from C 22 (38) 13, 4 May 1938 (CAB 23/93).

47 C 22 (38) 13, 4 May 1938 (CAB 23/93).

48 Lloyd George Papers, G/4/5/27, memorandum by Churchill, undated but sent to Lloyd George on 25 June 1938; the meeting had been two days earlier.

49 *Ibid.*, copy of letter from the Attorney-General to Sandys, oddly undated but 24 or 25 June 1938.

50 C 30 (38) 11, 29 June 1938 (CAB 23/94). For Sandys' point of privilege, see 337 *HC Debates*, 27 June 1938, cols. 1534–6.

51 *Pownall Diaries*, vol. I, pp. 151 and 152; 20 and 27 June 1938. Aitken, *Officially Secret*, p. 63, identifies the officer as Capt. Hogan, adjutant of the regiment.

52 Aitken, *Officially Secret*, p. 65, and Thomas, 'Towards a Revision,' pp. 120–1, the latter adding that Churchill's role was 'to the general profit of the nation.' For Churchill's involvement, see above, pp. 251–2.

53 Quoted, Aitken, *Officially Secret*, p. 65, and misdated to 15 March 1938, from his comments to a Select Committee of the House of Commons. Nor need the information be broadcast to all members; a select process, even a single MP, was consistent with a sense of duty to communicate the information.

54 PREM 1/283, 'Home Office Note on Section 6 of the Official Secrets Act,' 30 June 1938. The Cabinet Committee on the Official Secrets Act entertained the views of a Committee of Heads of Departments, accepting this conclusion but rejecting a further suggestion.

55 CAB 16/195, CP 16 (39), 'Report of the Committee on the Official Secrets Act,' 20 January 1939. The Attorney-General had admitted from the first that section 6 was 'too wide and . . . a source of embarrassment to everyone.'

56 342 *HC Debates*, 5 December 1938, col. 892.

57 *Franks Committee Report*, p. 124 (Appendix III). Churchill made much the same point in commenting that 'the Official Secrets Act was intended for spies, crooks, traitors and traffickers in official information, and should never be invoked unless there is a prima facie case on these lines.' (Quoted by Gilbert, *Churchill*, vol. V, p. 953 n. 1.)

58 For this reason, Attlee refused to commit 'the same error' as had Bevan, adding: 'I make this statement lest my silence should be misconstrued.' (504 *HC Debates*, 31 July 1954, col. 1692.) Bevan's disclosures were all but routine; Michael Foot (*Bevan*, vol. II, p. 377) demonstrates that Bevan had referred to the controversial matter on many previous occasions.

59 504 *HC Debates*, 1 August 1954, cols. 1867–8.

60 86 *HL Debates*, 21 December 1932, cols. 530–1 (Hailsham). For the Lloyd George incident, see above pp. 202–5; the precedent was not exact, as no resignation was at issue.

61 A. J. P. Taylor, 'Correspondence,' *The Times*, 6 August 1952.

62 Clement Attlee, 'Correspondence,' *The Times*, 8 August 1952.

63 Rupert Howorth, *ibid.* In placing such weight upon the Privy Counsellor's Oath, Howorth ignored the authoritative views of Sir Frederick Pollack, who had held as long ago as 1909 that the Oath was not an 'indispensable obligation of secrecy,' but instead 'a mere case of historical survival.' ('Government by Committee in England,' *The Law Quarterly Review*, 25: 60–2; January 1909.)

64 'Cabinet Secrecy,' *The Times*, 8 August 1952.

65 Michael Foot, 'Correspondence,' *The Times*, 11 August 1952; he ignored the opinion of Ivor Jennings' *Cabinet Government* (Cambridge, 1947), p. 208, that the King's consent must be secured through the Prime Minister.
66 Geoffrey Bing, 'Correspondence,' *The Times*, 13 August 1952.
67 Rupert Howorth, 'Correspondence,' *The Times*, 14 August 1952.
68 Anthony Barber, 'Correspondence,' *The Times*, 15 August 1952.
69 Jennings, *Cabinet Government*, p. 208, acknowledged the need for Cabinet secrecy but noted that 'there comes a time when Cabinet proceedings pass into history.'
70 W. Harvey Moore, 'Correspondence,' *The Times*, 16 August 1952.
71 Such a reality had long confounded Hankey's attempts to administer Cabinet secrecy.
72 Williams, *Public Interest*, especially pp. 194–7.
73 *Franks Committee Report*, pp. 40–4 and, for the categories, pp. 102–5. Six years later, HMG moved to implement the bulk of these proposals: the test of criminal sanctions would be the causing of 'serious injury' to the interests of the nation. (*Reform of Section 2 of the Official Secrets Act 1911* (Cmnd 7285, 1978).) Parliamentary approval remains to be sought.
74 *Franks Committee Report*, pp. 67–8.
75 In the words of the Labour Home Secretary, Roy Jenkins: 'it was not in dispute that there were areas where full, constant and immediate disclosure was against the public interest.' (Quoted in *The Times*, 11 March 1975.)
76 In a letter to *The Times* of 28 August 1942, Selby did not specifically name Fisher, but the inference was clear. Medlicott, *Britain and Germany*, pp. 4–5, and Rose, *Vansittart*, pp. 266–8, cite other published critiques of these actions, but neither accepts the notion of undue interference. Fisher's role was a legitimate function of his heading the Civil Service at this time.
77 Information that the Foreign Office reviewed and objected (while ultimately yielding) to Selby's account from Prof. D. C. Watt; for Vansittart's response, Rose, *Vansittart*, p. 268. The Foreign Office of course reviews diplomatic accounts.
78 Quoted, *ibid.*, p. 285; Sir Orme Sargent to Vansittart, 30 October 1946.
79 Quoted, *ibid.*; Vansittart to Sargent, 2 November 1946; he was especially critical of the large sums which leading politicians raised for their memoirs.
80 See below, pp. 313–15; Ivone Kirkpatrick, *The Inner Circle* (London, 1959), p. ix.
81 HNKY 25/3, Macmillan to Hankey, 31 March 1957; the latter connection had been suggested to Hankey by his literary agent. (HNKY 25/2, Higham to Hankey, 2 April 1957.)
82 HNKY 25/3, Hankey to Prime Minister, 1 May 1957. Arthur Bryant, the author of *The Turn of the Tide* (New York, 1957), had described Alanbrooke's diary as 'the jewel for which this book is the setting.'
83 HNKY 25/3, Macmillan to Hankey, 23 May 1957.
84 *Ibid.*, Macmillan to Hankey, 11 July 1958, in words which echo those of Bridges thirteen years earlier. Consistent with the objections to such records, neither Bridges nor Brook retained any official documents, nor is there any evidence of a diary. (Chris Cook, ed., *Sources in British Political History, 1900–1951*, vol. II (London, 1975), pp. 28, 182.)
85 HNKY 25/3, Hankey to Prime Minister, 25 May 1957.
86 HNKY 25/5, Ismay to Hankey, 6 June 1957.
87 HNKY 25/3, Heald to Hankey, 13 January 1958.
88 *Ibid.*, Macmillan to Heald, 30 April 1958.

89 *Ibid.*, Hankey to Prime Minister, 16 June, and Macmillan to Hankey, 11 July 1958. In view of Hankey's protestation, his claim that Macmillan's rejoinder contained 'the first mention of a possible infringement of the Official Secrets Act' (note on Macmillan's letter) is simplified if not misleading; it stands as the first explicit threat of prosecution, which is Hankey's real point.
90 *Ibid.*, Hankey to Prime Minister, 15 August 1958.
91 HNKY 25/4, Hutchinson's Reports Nos. 1 and 2, included in Paul Scott to Hankey, 11 August 1958. The allegation that Hankey's memoirs, even in the revised version, failed to take sides and to 'blow' gaffes cannot be sustained.
92 HNKY 25/6, Hankey's Note, 'The Supreme Command, 1914–1918. Sir Lionel Heald,' 16 December 1959.
93 *Ibid.*, Hankey to Heald, 14 May 1960.
94 HNKY 25/3, draft letter to Macmillan, undated. Churchill's warm response – whether he actually wrote or for that matter read Hankey's book is problematic – is quoted by Roskill, *Hankey*, vol. III, p. 619.
95 Quoted by Aitken, *Officially Secret*, p. 69; Establishment Circular No. 40/57, 10 September 1957.
96 Information from Prof. D. C. Watt.
97 E.g. Lord Birkenhead, who prepared his account of Lord Cherwell's role in the 1951–4 Churchill government with extreme restrictions placed upon his use of the latter's papers; see *The Professor and the Prime Minister* (Boston, 1961), chs. 10–12. Information from Prof. D. C. Watt.
98 Lord Salter, *Memoirs of a Public Servant* (London, 1961), ch. 3.
99 George Mallaby, *From My Level* (London, 1965), provoked hostile official reaction.
100 Quoted by Williams, *Public Interest*, p. 65, the most informative account of the imposition of such secrecy.
101 At an earlier date both Lecky and Froude – neither an 'impartial' historian – had been given access to some Irish papers.
102 Austen Chamberlain, 'Correspondence,' *The Times*, 3 December 1924; at the same time, the Foreign Secretary authorized the publication of what became *British Documents on the Origins of the War*; see above, p. 123. In contrast to the practices of other Foreign Offices, official policy remained timid, with harmful effects discussed by Watt in 'Foreign Affairs,' pp. 129–30.
103 As characterized by Montgomery-Hyde, basing his remarks upon the Grigg Committee report. (585 *HC Debates*, 26 March 1958, cols. 527–8.)
104 As characterized by the Attorney-General, Sir Elwyn Jones, in 1967. (749 *HC Debates*, 26 June 1967, col. 26.)
105 Quoted by Watt, 'Foreign Affairs,' p. 129.
106 585 *HC Debates*, 26 March 1958, cols. 499–500.
107 The categories were retrospectively outlined in 1967 (749 *HC Debates*, 26 June 1967, col. 28) by Sir Elwyn Jones; in 1958 only records of criminal investigations or business statistics submitted to the Board of Trade had been offered as 'specimens.' (585 *HC Debates*, 26 March 1958, col. 505.)
108 590 *HC Debates*, 4 July 1958, col. 1797 (Hylton-Foster).
109 *Ibid.*, cols. 1784–5 and 1797; the vote was 38–22.
110 *Ibid.*, col. 1778.
111 585 *HC Debates*, 26 March 1958, cols. 515 and 540.
112 Roskill, *Hankey*, vol. III, p. 619, finds Macmillan's reversal 'puzzling' because he did not look to these developments; to this point, the sole source

for Macmillan's views is Hankey's second-hand account, but the Prime Minister's attitude is proved out by the government's inaction.

113 For one result of the decision to open papers relating to criminal investigations after seventy-five years, see the account of a purulent Victorian scandal involving criminal homosexual offences within the 'Establishment' and touching the royal family, dating to 1882–9, in 'Victorian Scandal Recalled,' *The Times*, 11 March 1975.

114 The suggestion is Roskill's – an experienced intelligence hand – implicit in a remark about one such report: 'Even if copies have survived they are not likely to be released to historians.' (*Hankey*, vol. III, p. 447.)

115 Hinsley *et al.*, *British Intelligence*, vol. I, p. vii. These Official Historians were given access to the files, although in the interests of security they were not permitted to make precise reference to those sources.

116 New Haven, 1971. Although unwilling to comment on the negotiations which led to the publication of Masterman's work in America, the Yale University Press notes that the lengthy process served to acquaint HMG with the fact of impending publication, which the authorities could not prevent. (Edward Tripp to the author, 30 December 1982.)

117 F. W. Winterbotham, *The Ultra Secret* (New York, 1974). Cf. the corrections specified by the Official Historians (Hinsley *et al.*, *British Intelligence*, vol. I, Appendix 1, 'The Polish, French and British Contributions to the Breaking of the Enigma').

118 Hinsley *et al.*, *British Intelligence*, vol. I, p. viii; Peter Hennessy, 'History will be changed by Enigma disclosures,' *The Times*, 13 October 1977.

119 Hennessy, *ibid.*

120 Chapman Pincher, *Inside Story* (pb. edn, London, 1978), pp. 220–1.

121 Roskill, *Hankey*, vol. III, p. 638; such an action would require the Lord Chancellor's sanction.

122 The first point is made by a former minister, Anthony Nutting, *No End of a Lesson: The Story of Suez* (New York, 1967), p. 13; the latter by Hugh Thomas, in *Suez* (New York, 1967), p. 102, who specifies as sources 'a critically placed Minister' and a 'senior official.' See below, n. 146.

123 For restrictions placed upon relevant minutes of eight Cabinet meetings dealing with the Abdication, see Donaldson, *Edward VIII*, p. 284.

124 Anthony Eden (Earl of Avon), *Full Circle* (Boston, 1960), p. vii.

125 As a rule, Hankey destroyed such notes upon receiving approval for the formal minutes; the lapse is inexplicable. Roskill notes (*Hankey*, vol. III, p. 299) that since the 1950s 'the original documents have . . . been destroyed, though the notes taken by Avon's research assistant have survived.'

126 Eden's research assistant for the volume dealing with events to his resignation in 1938, published in 1962, was David Dilks.

127 618 *HC Debates*, 25 February 1960, cols. 570–3. Whatever the reason, Macmillan erred, because only the war period had been regarded as 'something different'; the exception had been granted precisely because 'during the war much information that would ordinarily have been published had to be kept secret for reasons of military security.' (426 *HC Debates*, 1 August 1946, cols. 1207–8.) Nonetheless, post-war governments generally accepted the 'precedent.' (*Radcliffe Committee Report*, p. 17.)

128 Randolph S. Churchill, *The Fight for the Tory Leadership* (Boston, 1964), p. 126; he reported that the Cabinet had unanimously approved Macmillan's proposals.

129 Macmillan is quoted, as is one concerned academic, by Watt, 'Foreign Affairs,' pp. 121–2.

130 D. C. Watt, 'Contemporary History in Britain: Problems and Perspectives,' *Journal of the Society of Archivists* (1969).

131 Something of the tone of exasperation felt in official circles with 'jackals fighting for carcass-scraps' is present in the comments of Robert Rhodes James, 'The Fifty-Year Rule,' *The Spectator*, 213: 233–4 (21 August 1964), whose proposals were soon outpaced by events; similarly, his fear that the maintenance of Cabinet Minutes had compromised the integrity of Cabinet discussions was belied by the availability of those minutes. Rhodes James was at this time Senior Clerk of the House of Commons, and thus a public servant.

132 Watt, 'Contemporary History.' The Balfour and Cecil papers were released directly.

133 The Society claims responsibility for persuading HMG to reduce the period of closure, but I am persuaded by D. C. Watt's evidence that the Oxford–Cambridge–London group had already made substantial progress, particularly at the Cabinet Office. Certainly the presence of leading academics who had served in the Cabinet Office Historical Section on the civil and military sides of the Second World War series was an important asset in the group's endeavors.

134 Crossman, *Cabinet Diaries*, vol. I, pp. 303–4; 5 August 1966. Bolstering his constant complaint that the Cabinet Minutes failed to reflect accurately the actual course of the deliberations, Crossman noted: 'This formed the main discussion but I wasn't surprised to find not a word of my arguments was retained in the Cabinet minutes.'

135 According to Harold Wilson, who pointed out that his government had 'gone beyond the advice which we have received, which was for a period of 40 years.' (733 *HC Debates*, 10 August 1966, col. 1708.)

136 Harold Wilson, *A Personal Record: The Labour Government, 1964–1970* (Boston, 1971), pp. 203–4.

137 Quoted in Thomas, 'Towards a Revision,' p. 124; 8 February 1967. Yet when Heath came to power in 1970, his government took no steps to implement the Franks Committee's proposal to reduce the scope of the Official Secrets Act in the cause of such access.

138 The years 1945–50 were proposed; editorial problems have delayed publication. (Information from Prof. D. C. Watt.)

139 Quoted, Watt, 'Contemporary History.' Certainly precedent existed for such a delay in publication, as the multi-volume version of Sir Llewellyn Woodward's *British Foreign Policy in the Second World War* (5 vols., 1970–6) (*History of the Second World War: United Kingdom Military Series*), written for official use between 1942 and 1950, was long held back and has only recently been published in its entirety.

140 At some point after 1966 policies concerning the Official Histories were relaxed, thus enabling Norman Gibbs, for example, 'to assign to individuals by name the view expressed by them in Cabinet and also to give specific references to sources' in his account of the defence plans of the 1930s. (*Rearmament*, 'Editor's Preface,' by J. R. M. B[utler], p. xix.) The change is of course consistent with the availability of the records themselves.

141 733 *HC Debates*, 10 August 1966, cols. 1706–8, quoting his own remarks of 9 March of that year.

142 *Ibid.*, col. 1708; the phrase is Michael Foot's.

143 *Ibid.*, 9 August 1966, col. 1393. Probably his remarks on the previous day concerning Suez were anything but coincidental, as he had then fueled the Labour left in its persistent criticisms of the Tory begetters of Suez.

144 'Thirty Years On,' *The Economist*, 218: 1133 (19 March 1966). The correspondent was in fact D. C. Watt.

145 Thomas, 'Towards a Revision,' pp. 123–4.

146 Nutting, *No End of a Lesson*, pp. 13–14; the view is reinforced by the recent assertion made by the-then public relations adviser to Eden, William Clark, that 'the official documents of the time "if not destroyed totally" were confined "in a way that will not make them available for a very long time."' (Quoted, 'Briton Divulges Steps to '56 Decision to Seize Suez,' *New York Times*, 25 November 1979.) Cf. Selwyn Lloyd, *Suez, 1956: A Personal Account* (London, 1978), who claimed to have had access to Cabinet and Foreign Office papers 'affecting his time in office.'

147 The comment is attributed to Nutting's 'Preface' on the dust jacket of the book, but the comment cannot be found there; perhaps one may speculate that Nutting rewrote the 'Preface' which is identical in the English and American editions, eliminating the claim which his publishers nonetheless featured.

148 Thomas, 'Towards a Revision,' p. 121; the italics are his.

149 John P. Mackintosh, *The British Cabinet* (London, 1962; 2nd edn, 1968).

150 For this information, I am indebted to Una Maclean Mackintosh.

151 J. K. Galbraith, 'The Downing Street Papers,' *New Statesman*, 90: 759 (12 December 1975), who remarks on ministerial memoirs that they are 'rightly or wrongly, a recognized part of the personal estate of politicians, a delayed compensation, perhaps, for long hours at modest pay.'

152 E.g. J. M. Dickens' querying the 'double standard' whereby former ministers used documents 'to substantiate their points of view and to justify their positions before other historians can get all the facts.' (749 *HC Debates*, 3 July 1967, col. 1212.)

153 Sir Alec Douglas-Home, *The Way the Wind Blows* (New York, 1976). Francis Williams, *A Prime Minister Remembers: The War and Post-War Memoirs of the Rt Hon Earl Attlee* (London, 1961); e.g. Attlee's description of his differences with Cabinet colleagues over Middle Eastern policy in 1946 (pp. 179–81) and again in 1951 (pp. 254–5).

154 Hugh Dalton, *High Tide and After: Memoirs, 1945–1960* (London, 1962), p. xiv. Dalton did not indicate that he discussed portions of his memoirs on a passage by passage basis with the Cabinet Secretary. (Information from Prof. D. C. Watt.)

155 Late in his life, nearly a decade after leaving office, Bevan directed his wit against the practice: 'I strongly disapprove of people in active public life writing their memoirs. They do nothing but mischief. If they tell the truth it is hurtful, but usually they don't tell the truth.' (Foot, *Bevan*, vol. II, p. 655.)

156 Aitken, *Officially Secret*, p. 68. Clearly, a proscription applies to incumbent ministers publishing accounts relating to recent policy-making: for an example of a junior minister who left the Wilson government for this reason, see Sampson, *New Anatomy*, p. 71.

157 Wilson, *A Personal Record*; George Brown, *In My Way* (New York, 1971), went so far as to recapitulate discussions of key appointments within the Foreign Office and to several embassies, made in part to avoid his becoming 'the purveyor of views already formed within the Office' (p. 129).

158 Marcia Williams, *Inside Number 10* (New York, 1972).
159 *Denis Healey and the Politics of Power* (London, 1971), pp. 238–41.
160 *The Cecil King Diary*, vol. I, *1965–1970* (London, 1972), p. 9.
161 *Ibid.*, e.g. pp. 71–4 for a letter addressed to the Prime Minister, and pp. 75–8 for a follow-up conversation.
162 'London Diary,' *New Statesman*, 90: 640 (21 November 1975). The figures of 'A.B.' and 'C.D.' made their appearances in *The Cecil King Diary*, vol. II, *1970–1974* (London, 1975). Whatever their identities – neither responded to the allegations, but surely regulations prevented any comment – the fact that leading civil servants consorted with the discredited figure of King provided for Anthony Howard (*New Statesman*, 90: 476; 17 October 1975) 'a telling answer to those . . . who even today insist on equating civil servants with Vestal Virgins.'
163 *Harvey War Diaries*, p. 275; 14 July 1943.
164 *The Memoirs of Lord Gladwyn* (London, 1972), p. ix. The *Radcliffe Committee Report* (p. 33) proposed that 'the principles that we have enunciated concerning publication by ex-Ministers, the obligations which we have suggested should rest upon them, and the periods for which those obligations should be maintained' apply as well to all former members of the public services.
165 Diary insights concerning the conduct of diplomacy may well be limited in the process of official review, but see the curious blend produced by the use of Pierson Dixon's diary in the biography written by his son, Piers Dixon, *Double Diploma: The Life of Sir Pierson Dixon* (London, 1968).
166 Crossman, *Cabinet Diaries*, vol. I, p. 13; nonetheless, the finding dismissed this argument: 'It is not enough to show that his colleagues accepted the keeping of the diary. It was vital to show that they accepted Mr. Crossman's intention to use the diary whether it passed the scrutiny of the Secretary of the Cabinet or not.' Quoted from the opinion of Lord Chief Justice Widgery, printed in 'Law Report,' *The Times*, 2 October 1975. (Hereafter cited as Widgery, 'Law Report'.) Particularly for the legal aspects of the case, see R. K. Middlemas, 'Cabinet Secrecy and the Crossman Diaries,' *Political Quarterly*, 47: 39–51 (1976).
167 Harold Macmillan, *At the End of the Day, 1961–1963* (New York, 1973). In one case it is now possible to compare a full memoir account written in accord with the 1934 conventions, Amery, *My Political Life*, and based upon private diaries, with the diaries proper: *The Leo Amery Diaries*, ed. John Barnes and David Nicholson, of which vol. I, *1896–1929* (London, 1980) has been published.
168 Crossman, *Cabinet Diaries*, vol I, p. 13.
169 Cited by Aitken, *Officially Secret*, p. 68, from the *Daily Telegraph* of 27 September 1970. Queried by two former Law Officers whether the *New Statesman*, which he edited at this time, was going to continue to breach the Official Secrets Act, Crossman contended that he would continue to do so – at the rate of a secret each week!
170 Quoted by Widgery, 'Law Report.'
171 Quoted, *ibid.*; Widgery remarked that he was not surprised that 'different views on this subject are contained in the evidence.' Cabinet papers, of course, were not at issue.
172 Dixon, *Double Diploma*, p. 278; diary, 3 November 1957.
173 Lloyd, *Suez, 1956*, passim, but particularly ch. 15.
174 *Ibid.*, p. xiii; see above p. 294.

175 Quoted, Widgery, 'Law Report'; Sir John Hunt to Graham C. Greene of Jonathan Cape, 22 June 1974. As contemporary practices are not a matter of public record, the statement is particularly valuable.

176 Widgery, 'Law Report.' Crossman extended no protection to the 'confidential' relationship, to be sure, but George Brown's memoirs had certainly breached this particular point; see above, n. 157.

177 Crossman, *Cabinet Diaries*, vol. I, p. 24; 22 October 1964. *The Sunday Times* deleted all critical references to identified civil servants with the exception of Dame Evelyn and the-then Cabinet Secretary, Sir Burke Trend. Prior to the court decision, Anthony Howard ('Crossman: Bagehot or Creevy?' *New Statesman*, 89: 330; 14 March 1975) claimed such deletions made for 'an important imbalance' and contended that Crossman deserved 'the same freedom of expression that Lady Falkenden [Marcia Williams] exercised in her 1964–70 memoirs, *Inside Number 10*.'

178 Quoted by Corina Adam, 'Rules for Gentlemen,' *New Statesman*, 90: 132 (1 August 1975). Trend's reference had been directed to 'what passed between him and his colleagues on a particular occasion,' and thus it is unlikely that Sir Burke intended such license for the ministerial-adviser relationship.

179 Adam, 'Rules for Gentlemen,' p. 132. Hunt argued that Trend had made the statement '"at the end of a very long day of oral evidence,"' as if to signal a weakness in his predecessor's resolve.

180 'Double Standards at Number 10?' *New Statesman*, 89: 125 (31 January 1975).

181 Quoted, Widgery, 'Law Report'; Hunt to Greene, 22 June 1974.

182 'Clear and Necessary,' *The Times*, 2 October 1975. Obviously the leader was not written on behalf of the Official Secrets Act, but in preference for parliamentary legislation to judicial interpretation where freedom of speech was at issue.

183 Quoted, Widgery, 'Law Report.'

184 Howard, 'Crossman,' p. 329; not quite all, e.g. the masking of the identities of all but the most senior civil servants.

185 Some suspect that the entire matter would have been handled differently had Crossman lived; it has even been suggested that HMG would not have taken any action to bar publication were he alive. (Private information.) His executors seemingly viewed any passage by passage review, along the lines agreed to by Hugh Dalton (see above, n. 154), as a breach of their obligation to preserve the text of Crossman's diary as he had prepared it. (Information from Prof. D. C. Watt.)

186 Widgery, 'Law Report.'

187 *The Spectator* was quite critical of the protection afforded the Civil Service: 'A more open system of government in the civil service would both help to expose those who have consistently been wrong in terms of government policy but consistently successful in terms of bureaucratic warfare, and might even help to ventilate conflicting views within the bureaucracy which are otherwise stifled.' ('A Judgement for More Open Government,' 235: 459; 11 October 1975.)

188 Lord Hailsham, 'Gossip, not History,' *The Spectator*: 235: 760 (13 December 1975).

189 A. J. P. Taylor, review in *The Observer*, 7 December 1975. For roughly similar disappointment: *The Economist*, 13 December; W. F. Deedes in *The Daily Telegraph*, 8 December; Michael Ratcliffe in *The Times*, 8 December;

Woodrow Wyatt in *The Sunday Times*, 7 December; Peregrine Worsthorne in *The Sunday Telegraph*, 7 December.

190 *The Times*, 8 December.

191 Crossman, *Cabinet Diaries*, vol. I, p. 11; Middlemas' comment ('Cabinet Secrecy,' p. 50) is apt: 'For the first time in the post-war years, we have had a broad and yet intricate picture of modern Cabinet government, impressive as much for its accumulation of detail as for its critique of the political process.'

192 Testified to by his associate in editing the diaries for publication: Janet Morgan, 'The Making of the Crossman Diary,' *New Statesman*, 90: 702 (5 December 1975).

193 E.g. Crossman, *Cabinet Diaries*, vol. I. p. 132 (17 January 1965) and p. 433 (23 January 1966).

194 Howard, 'Crossman,' p. 330, uses the term 'rival administration' in describing this as Crossman's most important discovery; Woodrow Wyatt makes much the same point in his review, remarking that 'inter-departmental committees of civil servants . . . with the blessing of the prime minister, make many of the decisions that matter without most ministers understanding what is going on.' For an earlier recognition, see above, p. 63.

195 Such secrecy is not new: with the exception of the Second World War years, 'it was not the usual practice to give information to Parliament or the public about the existence, terms, or membership of Cabinet committees.' (Wilson, *Cabinet Office*, p. 15.) Their present role is highly protected, even if in a maladroit fashion criticized by Michael Davie in a three-part 'Notebook' (*The Observer*, 7, 14, and 21 November 1976).

196 Crossman, *Cabinet Diaries*, vol. I, p. 491; 3 April 1966.

197 Crossman's assertion is quoted more fully, above, p. 179. Barbara Castle recorded several similar assertions for the Wilson regime of 1974–6, commenting that 'it is almost impossible to get them altered afterwards, particularly if the PM has a vested interest in the official version.' (*The Castle Diaries, 1974–1976* (New York, 1980), pp. 251–2; 14 December 1974 and p. 711; 31 March 1976.)

198 Wilson, *Governance of Britain*, p. 56. Yet Wilson supplied an example of such inventiveness, dating to his service in the Cabinet Office in 1940. Provided a set of inconclusive notes, he was told by Sir Edward Bridges to summarize a Cabinet discussion which he had not himself heard: '"This is your subject. You know what they ought to have decided, presumably. Write the Minutes on those lines, and no one will ever question it."' (*Ibid.*, p. 53.) Nor could Wilson resist drafting a minute at the time of his stepping down in 1976, in his Cabinet Secretary's words, '"the first time he has undertaken such a task (despite some stories to the contrary) since he served in the Cabinet Secretariat during the war."' (*Castle Diaries, 1974–1976*, p. 693; 18 March 1976.)

199 Crossman, *Myths of Cabinet Government* (Cambridge, Mass., 1972), pp. 33–4.

200 Mallaby, *From My Level*; Macmillan added that 'historians reading this fifty or a hundred years hence will get a totally false picture.'

201 Wilson, *Governance of Britain*, p. 56, adding tongue-in-cheek: 'The Cabinet minutes are immaculately conceived.'

202 A. J. P. Taylor (review) proposed a 'historian's' answer which merits consideration: 'Crossman never grasped that in the British system civil servants are loyal to their department, to the Treasury which determines

their promotion and to the general principles of the service. They are not loyal to the Minister except in a conventional way. For civil servants the Minister is a transient phenomenon, satisfactory only if he has no ideas of his own. Crossman had ideas of his own . . . There seems no remedy short of sacking the entire Civil Service and starting again.'

203 Unaware of the work of the Cabinet committee, Barbara Castle recorded the tenor of objections raised within the Cabinet, including her own, adding that Wilson had 'little difficulty in getting acceptance of the report through that supine Cabinet.' (*Castle Diaries, 1974–1976*, pp. 626–8; 21 January 1976.) The chronology of events is given in Peter Hennessy, 'The eternal fireman who always answers the call to duty,' *The Times*, 30 January 1976; he contrasts the urgent reception to that of 'many other reports, like that of the Franks committee on Official Secrecy published in 1972, still languishing, their recommendations not yet implemented.'

204 Quoted, 'Conventions upheld on ministerial disclosures,' *The Times*, 23 January 1976.

205 *Radcliffe Committee Report*, p. 35. It is difficult not to view the second paragraph as a commentary on the Crossman proceedings, and the prejudice against Cabinet diaries, among ministerial accounts, follows directly. Likely such suspicions fuel official resentment, which is colored as well by the assertion, voiced by Harold Wilson, that portions of the diary were historically inaccurate. (Quoted, 'Mr. Wilson's View of Crossman Diaries,' *The Times*, 3 March 1976.) D. C. Watt has commented that those who knew Crossman recognized that 'his version of events . . . was not only idiosyncratic . . . but apt to change according to his audience and the nature of the point he was trying to illustrate at the time.' (Letter to the author, August, 1979.)

206 *Radcliffe Committee Report*, pp. 19–20: anonymity had been given civil servants in the Official Histories written about the Second World War.

207 *Ibid.*, p. 31.

208 *Ibid.*, pp. 30–1; the editors of *The Times* pointed out that the other concerns 'should not be difficult to enforce so long as there is an Official Secrets Act or something like it.' ('Rules for Reticence,' *The Times*, 23 January 1976.) HMG has recently exhibited no interest in repealing section 2.

209 Yet the Radcliffe Committee presumed to speak in behalf of the historians' best interests, contending that historical knowledge must in any event accrue over a lengthy period of time: 'There is no sudden flash of light that illumines the whole landscape: we should be surprised if historians would wish that there were. We do not therefore regard our proposals as presenting any impediment to historical scholarship.' (*Radcliffe Committee Report*, p. 35.) The condescension is obvious.

210 Prof. D. C. Watt to the author, August 1979. Watt had discussed American attitudes to the release of documents dealing with foreign policy in 'Restrictions on Research: The Fifty-Year Rule and British Foreign Policy,' *International Affairs*, 41: 89–95 (January 1965); the last point has emerged since that time.

211 Quoted, 'Lawyers Criticize Report on Memoirs,' *The Times*, 29 January 1976. For observations from an experienced observer sympathetic to the need for 'more open government on the Cabinet level,' see Stacey, *British Government*, pp. 94 and 104–5.

212 *Castle Diaries, 1974–1976*, pp. 626–8; 21 January 1976. Castle added that she

did not intend to sign any agreement subscribing to the terms of the Radcliffe report: 'I don't intend to sign anything which prevents me putting distorted records straight.' Shades of Lloyd George!

213 The phrase is used in the *Radcliffe Committee Report*, p. 25, as a means of discounting the relevance of criminal law in such cases. In the wake of the publication of the *Castle Diaries*, there are signs of a burgeoning impatience that such responsible individuals should have recourse to 'instant books'; see Michael Foot, '"To set diary against diary is to spread endless misapprehension,"' *The Listener*, 104: 386–8 (25 September 1980) and David Wood, 'Spare Us the Political Diaries,' *The Times*, 29 September 1980.

214 Quoted, 'Court Action on Memoirs . . .,' *The Times*, 27 January 1976.

215 The group was headed by Dr Bernard Donoughue of the London School of Economics; its political coloration is confirmed by Donoughue's retirement upon Margaret Thatcher's succession. Although civil servants are seconded to this body, preserved by the Tory regime, it is wholly distinct from the Central Policy Review Staff disbanded by the Thatcher government in mid-1983. Barbara Castle has retrospectively claimed that in the years 1974–6 she 'never found that the CPRS or Dr Donoghue's [sic] unit had any noticeable effect on the decisions we took.' (*Castle Diaries, 1974–1976*, p. 49 n. 1.) Yet that diary demonstrates that Mrs Castle was not involved in the inner workings of the Wilson regime.

216 Anthony Sampson (*The Changing Anatomy of Britain* (London, 1982), pp. 240–5) locates 'the heart of the secrecy world' in the Joint Intelligence Committee, lodged in the Cabinet Office, where its head works alongside the Cabinet Secretary, although directly responsible to the Prime Minister.

Bibliography

I. DOCUMENTARY COLLECTIONS AND RELATED WORKS

Documentary collections comprise the core of the historical materials upon which this study has been based; were it not for the existence of such collections, accumulated in official and private hands, any attempt to depict the interaction of institutional and political factors contributing to the development of the Cabinet Secretariat would be futile. It is the peculiar admixture of Cabinet records with the private accounts and correspondence of the men who brought order from chaos in the maintenance of Cabinet records that enables us to take the measure of their contributions to the establishment of an institution and to the development of modern Cabinet government.

My own debt to Cabinet records – the term is used in a comprehensive fashion – is apparent throughout my work; fortunate for those who have used these records in Chancery Lane and now in Kew, several publications prepared by the staff of the Public Record Office serve as a valuable guide to the invaluable collection. The first, *The Records of the Cabinet Office to 1922*, written principally by A. W. Mabbs, was published in 1966 to accompany the release of the first Cabinet records, originating in the Lloyd George war-time coalition and extending through the demise of its peace-time counterpart in 1922. Three categories of Cabinet records particularly informed my account of these formative years, namely CAB 23, Cabinet Minutes; CAB 24, Memoranda and other papers circulated to the Cabinet (often referred to as Cabinet Papers); and CAB 21, a collection of Registered Files dealing topically with a variegated range of issues brought to the Cabinet or, in some cases, concerned with the work of the Cabinet Secretariat. The contents of CAB 21 have been winnowed to remove materials duplicated elsewhere, e.g. in CAB 24, but there remains much evidence otherwise unavailable about the workings of the Cabinet Secretariat. *Records of the Cabinet Office to 1922* describes other categories of Cabinet records less frequently used here but occasionally of considerable significance, e.g. records maintained prior to 1916 for the Committee of Imperial Defence and during the early years of the war for the War Council, the Dardanelles Committee and the War Committee. To be sure, Cabinet papers exist for the years prior to 1916, although no system guided their maintenance; as a result, the Public Record Office mounted an effort to collect such documents for the years from 1880 to 1916, drawing upon private as well as government collections. In 1964 and 1966, *Lists of Cabinet Papers* for

1880–1914 and 1915–16 were published by the PRO, with the contents of each item specified; thus the papers of the three war committees alluded to above are described, as now collected within CAB 42. In a similar fashion, CAB 41 contains photographic copies of the Prime Minister's Letters to the Sovereign from 1867 to 1916; the List and Index Society published a descriptive list of the contents of these items in 1965.

A second Public Record Office Handbook extended the description of the Secretariat, known from 1921 as the Cabinet Office; published in 1975 under the title of *The Cabinet Office to 1945*, S. S. Wilson's institutional treatment describes both the activities of the operation and the one hundred and twenty-seven CAB categories developed to the end of the Second World War; Wilson appends a useful set of twelve annexes, including a valuable set of recollections of Cabinet procedures prior to the Lloyd George reforms. Also noteworthy are several chapters dealing with the Committee of Imperial Defence and with the Historical Section of the Cabinet Office. The volume impresses as a model of the way in which the Public Record Office discharges its obligation to inform the public concerning the Cabinet records which it maintains and to guide scholars in their utilization of the collection. For the Cabinet records to the time of Hankey's departure in 1938, the triad of CAB 21, 23, and 24 continues to account for the institutional dimension of the work of the Cabinet and its secretariat. One other category deserves mention, namely CAB 63, a collection of Sir Maurice Hankey's own devising, including copies of official papers which he had written or dealing with topics in which he took a strong interest (thus duplicating a number of documents found in other places). Designed to provide for Hankey's long-planned 'Magnum Opus,' in several instances Hankey himself drew upon the collection; yet his biographer, Captain Roskill, lacked access to the file while engaged upon the first two volumes of his work. Discovered and thereafter transferred to the Public Record Office, the collection was fittingly included among the other Cabinet records which Hankey had provided and maintained. Certain other categories of Cabinet records, e.g. CAB 101–3, which deal with the work of the Historical Section, are cited in this study, but, given the thorough review of all classes contained in *The Cabinet Office to 1945*, review of their contents here would serve no real purpose.

Albeit not a class of Cabinet records, PREM 1 affords some limited insights about the workings of the Prime Minister's own office in the years to 1939; with the advent of war, and of Winston Churchill, the staff work done for him in his capacity as Minister of Defence can be found in PREM 3 and PREM 4, known popularly as 'the PM files' and 'the Churchill papers.' A number of government publications over the years assume a documentary importance in the activities of the Cabinet Office; indeed, several recent items shed light on aspects of the custody of Cabinet secrecy which could not otherwise be discerned within the dark shadows of the thirty-year rule. In particular, the *Report of the Departmental Committee on Section 2 of the Official Secrets Act 1911* (Cmnd 5104, 1972), cited as the *Franks Committee Report*; the *Reform of Section 2 of the Official Secrets Act 1911* (Cmnd 7285, 1978); and the *Report of the Committee of Privy Counsellors on Ministerial Memoirs* (Cmnd 6386, 1976) are essential in tracing through present-day patterns stemming from the designs initiated or developed by the first Secretary to the Cabinet. Linked to the last of these reports is the judicial opinion of Lord Chief Justice Widgery, by way of comment upon the propriety of ministerial memoirs; including discussion of matters which the contemporary Cabinet Office would not otherwise comment upon, Widgery's finding, printed in the 'Law Report' column of *The Times* on 2 October 1975, cleared the way for the publication of Richard Crossman's provocative *Cabinet Diaries*.

To revert to the early years of Hankey's own tenure of office, the two *War Cabinet Reports* for 1917 and 1918 (respectively Cd 9005, 1918 and Cmd 325, 1919) are useful, although they must be used with caution, prepared as they were by those who had an interest in sustaining the Lloyd George reforms; also useful, and in this case written by the advocates of a future order, is the *Report of the Machinery of Government Committee* (Cd 9230, 1918). A publication of a different sort, and indispensable, is the Parliamentary Debates, which occasionally raises issues which inform this work, from the first days of the Cabinet Secretariat to the recent discussions of the parameters of official secrecy in a free society: both the *House of Commons Debates* and the *House of Lords Debates* proved significant in limning the political context in which the Cabinet Office has operated.

Precisely because the office itself and the Cabinet Secretary in his own right are adjuncts to modern Cabinet government, neither official sources nor the useful institutional accounts contained in the PRO Handbooks suffice for a comprehensive account of the development of the Secretariat. Nor do they attempt to raise the question of the influence which the founding generation of the Cabinet Secretariat exercised upon their political 'masters.' Yet the influence of such highly placed civil servants as Maurice Hankey and Thomas Jones is a topic well worth the attention of students of British government. For this reason, private paper collections are vital if such an assessment is to be undertaken. Not surprisingly, the most important of such collections is the Hankey Papers, housed in the Churchill College Archives Centre of Cambridge University. In addition to an extensive assemblage of Hankey's correspondence, spanning the years from his service with the Committee of Imperial Defence to his lengthy struggle with latter-day Cabinet Secretaries to secure official sanction for the publication of his memoirs of the First World War, Hankey's diary, kept, albeit with lapses, until August 1942, is of utmost importance, for reasons adduced above. For all the excellence of Roskill's biography, *Hankey: Man of Secrets* (3 vols., London, 1970–4) – I have addressed the specifics of that excellence in the *Historical Journal*, 13 (no. 4, 1970); 16 (no. 3, 1973); and 18 (no. 2, 1975) – the student of 'the man and the institution' must have recourse to the Hankey Papers. While Roskill prints lengthy extracts from the diary in dealing with important episodes, in many cases he limits himself to phrases or sentences; for that reason, references in this work are to the diary proper, although much of this material perforce can be found in the biography. In addition to the Cabinet Secretary's correspondence with many of the leading political and military figures of his time, his letters to his family, particularly to his wife while abroad, are replete with comments upon the proceedings at international conferences and the like; in fact this correspondence ultimately outpaces in detail and incisiveness the private record which Hankey intended to attach to his diary upon returning to England. Hankey himself used the diaries, albeit in a veiled fashion which was dictated by his successors at the Cabinet Office, in preparing his memoirs of the war, *The Supreme Command, 1914–1918* (2 vols., London, 1961), and of Versailles, *The Supreme Control at the Paris Peace Conference, 1919* (London, 1963). In addition to several published lectures, Hankey drew upon his 'Magnum Opus' file in collecting a number of essays under the title of *Diplomacy by Conference* (London, 1946). Whatever the keenness of his observations expressed in these forums, his own participation in nearly all of the events he described ought not be forgotten.

Yet another participant-observer of the Cabinet Secretariat from its first days until well past the time of its acceptance as a permanent part of the scene was Hankey's deputy, Thomas Jones, whose diary has seen light of print in a more systematic way than has that of his chief. Edited by Keith Middlemas, Jones' record, *Whitehall Diary* (3 vols., London, 1969–71) is most germane to this inquiry in its first two volumes, dealing with the Cabinet Office from 1916 to his own retirement in 1930. Middlemas' selections incline towards lengthy and self-contained extracts, usefully framed by connective and explanatory materials. The result is a greater sense of the diary proper, although the process of selection mandates examination of the diary itself (which Jones had privately printed), at the National Library of Wales, Aberystwyth. Also included in the Thomas Jones Papers is his correspondence with a wide range of public figures; Jones himself published *A Diary with Letters, 1931–1950* (London, 1954), which drew upon his experiences after he left government service. Yet a third Secretariat functionary, of lesser significance, was Lawrence Burgis, who late in his life prepared memoirs, which are now available at the Churchill College Archives Centre, Cambridge.

Among other collections of private papers the most useful proved to be the Lloyd George Papers, once a part of the much-lamented Beaverbrook Library and now available in the House of Lords Record Office; sharing a similar fate and facilities, but of much less import, are the Bonar Law Papers. In addition, I have found the following collections useful, although I have utilized some only on a very selective basis:

Asquith Papers, Bodleian Library, Oxford University
Baldwin Papers, University Library, Cambridge
Balfour Papers, British Museum (now Library)
Campbell-Bannerman Papers, British Museum
Austen Chamberlain Papers, University of Birmingham Library
Esher Archives, Churchill College Archives Centre
Haldane Papers, National Library of Scotland, Edinburgh
Lansbury Papers, London School of Economics Library

II. PRINTED SOURCES

Only printed sources cited in the text are listed here, primarily to serve as a guide to those who wish to pursue further the matters raised in this book; towards that end I have classified several types of printed sources. The first category is organized by the author of the collection, rather than by the latter-day editor. Several of the most important printed sources have been discussed above, in conjunction with the major documentary collection upon which they are based. A last point: English editions of works cited in an American edition exist in many cases.

Edited diaries, journals, or collections of correspondence

The Leo Amery Diaries, vol. I, *1896–1929*, ed. John Barnes and David Nicholson (London, 1980)

The Diaries of Sir Alexander Cadogan, 1938–1945, ed. David Dilks (New York, 1972)

Lord Carlingford's Journal: Reflections of a Cabinet Minister, 1885, ed. A.B. Cooke and J.R. Vincent (Oxford, 1971)

Castle, Barbara, *The Castle Diaries, 1974–1976* (New York, 1980)

Winston S. Churchill: Companion, vol. V, part 1, *The Exchequer Years*,

1922–1929, and Part 2, *The Wilderness Years, 1929–1939*, ed. Martin S. Gilbert (Boston, 1981)

Crossman, Richard, *The Diaries of a Cabinet Minister* (3 vols., London, 1975–7)

Memoirs of a Conservative: J. C. C. Davidson's Memoirs and Papers, 1910–1937, ed. R. Rhodes James (London, 1969)

Journals and Letters of Reginald, Viscount Esher, vol. II, *1903–1910*, ed. Maurice V. Brett (London, 1934) and vol. IV, *1916–1930*, ed. Oliver, Viscount Esher (London, 1938)

The Private Papers of Douglas Haig, 1914–1919, ed. Robert Blake (London, 1952)

The Diary of Sir Edward Walter Hamilton, 1880–1885, vol. I, *1880–1882*, ed. Dudley Bahlman (London, 1972)

The Diplomatic Diaries of Oliver Harvey, 1937–1940, ed. John Harvey (New York, 1970)

The War Diaries of Oliver Harvey, ed. John Harvey (London, 1978)

Inside Asquith's Cabinet: From the Diaries of Charles Hobhouse, ed. Edward David (New York, 1977)

Jones, Thomas, *A Diary with Letters, 1931–1950* (London, 1954) *Whitehall Diary*, ed. Keith Middlemas (3 vols., London, 1969–71)

King, Cecil, *The Cecil King Diaries* (2 vols., London, 1972–5)

The Diaries of Sir Robert Bruce Lockhart, vol. I, *1915–1939*, ed. Kenneth Young (London, 1973)

Chief of Staff: The Diaries of Lieutenant-General Sir Henry Pownall, vol. I, *1933–1940*, ed. Brian Bond (Hamden, Conn., 1973)

Riddell, Lord, *Intimate Diary of the Peace Conference and After, 1918–1923* (New York, 1934)

Lord Riddell's War Diary, 1914–1918 (London, n.d. [1933])

The Cabinet Journal of Dudley Ryder, Viscount Sandon, ed. Christopher Howard and Peter Gordon (published as Special Supplement no. 10 of the *Bulletin of the Institute of Historical Research*, London, 1974)

The Political Diaries of C. P. Scott, 1911–1928, ed. Trevor Wilson (Ithaca, NY, 1970)

Stevenson, Frances (Countess Lloyd George), *Lloyd George: A Diary*, ed. A. J. P. Taylor (New York, 1971)

Life with Lloyd George: The Diary of A. J. Sylvester, ed. Colin Cross (New York, 1975)

Beatrice Webb's Diaries, 1924–1932, ed. Margaret Cole (London, 1956)

Field-Marshal Sir Henry Wilson: His Life and Diaries, ed. Sir C. E. Callwell (2 vols., London, 1927)

Autobiographies, memoirs

Addison, Christopher, *Four and a Half Years* (2 vols., London, 1934)

Amery, Leo, *My Political Life* (3 vols., London, 1953–5)

Beaverbrook, Lord, *The Decline and Fall of Lloyd George* (New York, 1963)

Men and Power, 1917–1918 (London, 1956)

Politicians and the War (London, 1928; 1932)

Boothby, Robert, *I Fight to Live* (London, 1947)

Brown, George, *In My Way* (New York, 1971)

Chamberlain, Austen, *Down the Years* (London, 1935)

Chatfield, Lord, *It Might Happen Again* (London, 1947)

Churchill, Winston S., *The Aftermath* (London, 1929)

The Gathering Storm (Boston, 1948)

Cooper, Duff, *Old Men Forget* (London, 1953)
Dalton, Hugh, *High Tide and After: Memoirs, 1945–1960* (London, 1962)
Douglas-Home, Sir Alec, *The Way the Wind Blows* (New York, 1976)
Eden, Anthony (Earl of Avon), *Full Circle* (Boston, 1960)
Gladwyn, Lord, *The Memoirs of Lord Gladwyn* (London, 1972)
Halifax, Viscount, *Fulness of Days* (London, 1957)
Hankey, Lord, *The Supreme Command, 1914–1918* (2 vols., London, 1961)
The Supreme Control at the Paris Peace Conference, 1919 (London, 1963)
Hastings, Sir Patrick, *Autobiography* (London, 1948)
Hoare, Sir Samuel (Viscount Templewood), *Nine Troubled Years* (London, 1954)
Ismay, Lord, *The Memoirs of General Lord Ismay* (New York, 1960)
Kirkpatrick, Ivone, *The Inner Circle* (London, 1959)
Lansbury, George, *My England* (London, n.d. [1934])
Leith-Ross, Frederick, *Money Talks: Fifty years of International Finance* (London, 1968)
Liddell Hart, Basil, *Memoirs* (2 vols., London, 1965)
Lloyd, Selwyn, *Suez, 1956: A Personal Account* (London, 1978)
Lloyd George, David, *Memoirs of the Peace Conference* (New Haven, 1939)
War Memoirs, vols. I–II (Boston, 1933)
Londonderry, Marquess of, *Wings of Destiny* (London, 1942)
Mackenzie, Compton, *Greek Memories* (London, 1939)
My Life and Times: Octave 7, 1931–1938 (London, 1968)
Macmillan, Harold, *At the End of the Day, 1961–1963* (New York, 1973)
Mallaby, George, *From My Level* (London, 1965)
Nutting, Anthony, *No End of a Lesson: The Story of Suez* (New York, 1967)
Salter, Lord, *Memoirs of a Public Servant* (London, 1961)
Samuel, Viscount, *Memoirs* (London, 1945)
Simon, Viscount, *Retrospect* (London, 1952)
Snowden, Philip, *An Autobiography* (2 vols., London, 1934)
Spears, Edward L., *Prelude to Victory* (London, 1939)
Stevenson, Frances (Countess Lloyd George), *The Years that are Past* (London, 1967)
Thomas, James Henry, *My Story* (London, 1937)
Williams, Francis, *A Prime Minister Remembers: The War and Post-War Memoirs of the Rt Hon Earl Attlee* (London, 1961)
Williams, Marcia, *Inside Number 10* (New York, 1972)
Wilson, Harold, *A Personal Record: The Labour Government, 1964–1970* (Boston, 1971)

Biographies

Birkenhead, Earl of, *The Life of F. E. Smith, First Earl of Birkenhead* (London, 1965 edn)
The Professor and the Prime Minister (Boston, 1961)
Blake, Robert, *Unrepentant Tory* (New York, 1956)
Boyle, Andrew, *Trenchard* (London, 1962)
Bryant, Arthur, *The Turn of the Tide: A History of the War Years Based on the Diaries of Field-Marshal Lord Alanbrooke, Chief of the Imperial General Staff* (New York, 1957)
Butler, J. R. M., *Lord Lothian (Philip Kerr), 1882–1940* (London, 1960)
Cecil, Gwendolyn, *Life of Robert, Marquess of Salisbury*, vol. II, *1868–1880* (London, 1921)

Churchill, Randolph, *Lord Derby: King of Lancashire* (New York, 1960)
Collier, Basil, *Brasshat: A Biography of Field-Marshal Sir Henry Wilson, 1864–1922* (London, 1961)
Cross, Colin, *Philip Snowden* (London, 1966)
Dixon, Piers, *Double Diploma: The Life of Sir Pierson Dixon* (London, 1968)
Donaldson, Frances, *Edward VIII* (pb. edn, New York, 1974)
Foot, Michael, *Aneurin Bevan*, vol. II, *1945–1960* (New York, 1973)
Fraser, Peter, *Lord Esher: A Political Biography* (London, 1973)
Gilbert, Martin S., *Winston S. Churchill*, vol. IV, *The Stricken World, 1916–1922* (Boston, 1975) and vol. V, *The Prophet of Truth, 1922–1939* (Boston, 1977)
Gollin, A. M., *Proconsul in Politics: A Study of Lord Milner in Opposition and Power* (New York, 1964)
Grigg, John, *The Young Lloyd George* (London, 1973)
Jenkins, Roy, *Asquith* (London, 1963)
Jones, Thomas, *Lloyd George* (Cambridge, Mass., 1951)
Macleod, Iain, *Neville Chamberlain* (New York, 1962)
Marquand, David, *Ramsay MacDonald* (London, 1977)
Middlemas, Keith, and Barnes, John, *Baldwin: A Biography* (London, 1969)
Nicolson, Harold, *Curzon: The Last Phase, 1919–1925* (New York, 1939)
King George V (pb. edn, London, 1952)
Postgate, Raymond, *The Life of George Lansbury* (London, 1951)
Reed, Bruce, and Williams, Geoffrey, *Denis Healey and the Politics of Power* (London, 1971)
Ronaldshay, Earl of, *The Life of Lord Curzon*, vol. III (London, 1928)
Rose, Norman, *Vansittart: Study of a Diplomat* (New York, 1978)
Roskill, Stephen, *Hankey: Man of Secrets* (3 vols., London, 1970–4)
Sommer, Dudley, *Haldane of Cloan: His Life and Times, 1856–1928* (London, 1960)
Taylor, A. J. P., *Beaverbrook* (New York, 1972)
Terraine, John, *Douglas Haig: The Educated Soldier* (London, 1963)
Waley, S. D., *Edwin Montagu: A Memoir* (Bombay, 1964)
Wheeler-Bennett, John W., *King George VI: His Life and Reign* (New York, 1958)
Wilson, John, *CB: A Life of Campbell-Bannerman* (London, 1972)
Wrench, John Evelyn, *Alfred Lord Milner: The Man of No Illusions, 1854–1925* (London, 1958)
Geoffrey Dawson and Our Times (London, 1955)
Young, G. M., *Stanley Baldwin* (London, 1952)
Young, Kenneth, *Arthur James Balfour* (London, 1963)
Zebel, Sydney, *Balfour: A Political Biography* (Cambridge, 1973)

Books

Aitken, Jonathan, *Officially Secret* (London, 1971)
Bagehot, Walter, *The English Constitution* (London, 1867; 1963 pb. edn)
Berkeley, Humphrey, *The Power of the Prime Minister* (New York, 1969)
Blake, Lord, *The Office of Prime Minister* (London, 1975)
Bridges, Lord, *The Treasury* (London, 1964)
Carter, Byrum E., *The Office of Prime Minister* (Princeton, 1956)
Chester, D. N., and Willson, F. M. C., *The Organization of British Central Government, 1914–1956* (London, 1957)

Chester, L., Fay, S., and Young, H., *The Zinoviev Letter* (London, 1967)
Churchill, Randolph S., *The Fight for the Tory Leadership* (Boston, 1964)
Collins, Doreen, *Aspects of British Politics, 1904–1919* (Oxford, 1965)
Cook, Chris, ed., *Sources in British Political History, 1900–1951*, vol. II (London, 1975)
Cowling, Maurice, *The Impact of Labour, 1920–1924* (Cambridge, 1971)
Cox, Montagu H., and Norman, Philip, eds., *Survey of London*, vol. XXI, Part 2, *The Parish of St. Margaret, Westminster* (London, 1930)
Crossman, Richard, *The Myths of Cabinet Government* (Cambridge, Mass., 1972)
Daalder, Hans, *Cabinet Reform in Britain, 1914–1963* (Stanford, 1963)
Davies, Joseph, *The Prime Minister's Secretariat* (Newport, Mon., 1951)
Edwards, J. Ll. J., *The Law Officers of the Crown* (London, 1964)
Fry, Geoffrey, *Statesmen in Disguise* (London, 1969)
Gibbs, N. H., *Grand Strategy*, vol. I, *Rearmament Policy* (London, 1976) (*History of the Second World War: United Kingdom Military Series*)
The Origins of Imperial Defence (Oxford, 1955)
Gilmour, Ian, *The Body Politic* (London, 1969)
Gorodetsky, Gabriel, *The Precarious Truce: Anglo-Soviet Relations, 1924–1927* (Cambridge, 1977)
Greaves, H. R. G., *The Civil Service in the Changing State* (London, 1947)
Hankey, Lord, *Diplomacy by Conference* (London, 1946)
Hazelhurst, Cameron, *Politicians at War: July 1914 to May 1915* (London, 1971)
Hinsley, F. H., *et al.*, *British Intelligence in the Second World War*, vol. I (Cambridge, 1979) (*History of the Second World War: United Kingdom Military Series*)
Howard, Michael, *The Continental Commitment* (London, 1972)
Howson, Susan, and Winch, Donald, *The Economic Advisory Council, 1930–1939* (Cambridge, 1977)
Jennings, Ivor, *Cabinet Government* (Cambridge, 1947 edn)
Johnson, Franklyn, *Defence by Committee: The British Committee of Imperial Defence, 1885–1959* (London, 1960)
Kinnear, Michael, *The Fall of Lloyd George* (London, 1973)
Mackintosh, John P., *The British Cabinet* (2nd edn, London, 1968)
The Government and Politics of Britain (London, 1970)
Masterman, J. C., *The Double Cross System* (New Haven, 1971)
Medlicott, W. N., *Britain and Germany: The Search for Agreement, 1930–1937* (London, 1969)
Montgomery-Hyde, H., *British Air Policy Between the Wars, 1919–1939* (London, 1976)
Moorehead, Alan, *Gallipoli* (London, 1959 pb. edn)
Morgan, Kenneth O., *The Age of Lloyd George* (New York, 1971)
Mowat, Charles L., *Great Britain since 1914* (Ithaca, NY, 1971)
Munro, C. K., *The Fountains of Trafalgar Square* (London, 1952)
Naylor, John F., *Labour's International Policy: The Labour Party in the 1930s* (Boston, 1969)
Nicolson, Harold, *Peacemaking 1919* (New York, 1939)
Nimocks, Walter, *Milner's Young Men: The 'Kindergarten' in Edwardian Imperial Affairs* (London, 1968)
d'Ombrain, Nicholas, *War Machinery and High Policy: Defence Administration in Peacetime Britain, 1902–1914* (London, 1973)
Peden, G. C., *British Rearmament and the Treasury, 1932–1939* (Edinburgh, 1979)

Pincher, Chapman, *Inside Story* (London, 1978 pb. edn)
Pratt, Lawrence R., *East of Malta, West of Suez: Britain's Mediterranean Policy, 1936–1939* (Cambridge, 1975)
Rhodes James, R., *Gallipoli* (London, 1965)
Roseveare, Henry, *The Treasury: The Evolution of a British Institution* (London, 1969)
Roskill, Stephen, *Naval Policy between the Wars* (2 vols., New York and Annapolis, 1968–76)
Sampson, Anthony, *The Changing Anatomy of Britain* (London, 1982)
The New Anatomy of Britain (London, 1971)
Searle, G. R., *The Quest for National Efficiency* (Berkeley, 1971)
Seymour-Ure, Colin, *The Press, Politics and the Public* (London, 1968)
Shay, Robert Paul, Jr, *British Rearmament in the Thirties: Politics and Profits* (Princeton, 1977)
Skidelsky, Robert, *Politicians and the Slump: The Labour Government of 1929–1931* (London, 1967)
Snow, C. P., *Variety of Men* (New York, 1966)
Stacey, Frank, *British Government, 1966 to 1975: Years of Reform* (London, 1975)
The Government of Modern Britain (Oxford, 1968)
Stannage, Tom, *Baldwin Thwarts the Opposition* (London, 1980)
Steiner, Zara S., *The Foreign Office and Foreign Policy, 1898–1914* (Cambridge, 1969)
Taylor, A. J. P., *English History, 1914–1945* (Oxford, 1965)
Politics in Wartime and Other Essays (London, 1954)
Thomas, Hugh, *Suez* (New York, 1967)
The History of The Times, vol. IV, Part 2 (New York, 1952)
Trevelyan, G. M., *History of England*, vol. III (London, 1953 pb. edn)
Trotter, Ann, *Britain and East Asia, 1933–1937* (Cambridge, 1975)
Turner, John, *Lloyd George's Secretariat* (Cambridge, 1980)
Ullman, Richard H., *Anglo-Soviet Relations, 1917–1921*, vol. I, *Intervention and the War* (Princeton, 1961)
Walder, David, *The Chanak Affair* (London, 1969)
Waley, Daniel, *British Public Opinion and the Abyssinian War, 1935–6* (London, 1975)
Walker, Patrick Gordon, *The Cabinet* (London, 1970)
Watt, D. C., *Personalities and Policies* (Notre Dame, 1965)
Too Serious a Business (London, 1975)
Webster, Sir Charles, and Frankland, Noble, *The Strategic Air Offensive against Germany, 1939–1945*, vol. I, *Preparation* (London, 1961) (*History of the Second World War: United Kingdom Military Series*)
Williams, David, *Not in the Public Interest* (London, 1965)
Wilson, Harold, *The Governance of Britain* (New York, 1976)
Wilson, Trevor, *The Downfall of the Liberal Party, 1914–1935* (London, 1966)
Wilson, S. S., *The Cabinet Office to 1945* (London, 1975)
Winterbotham, F. W., *The Ultra Secret* (New York, 1974)
Woodward, Sir Llewellyn, *British Foreign Policy in the Second World War* (5 vols., London, 1970–6) (*History of the Second World War: United Kingdom Civil Series*)
Great Britain and the War of 1914–1918 (London, 1967)

Articles and book chapters

Andrew, Christopher, 'The British Secret Service and Anglo-Soviet Relations in the 1920s,' Part I, *Historical Journal*, 20 (1977)
'Whitehall, Washington and the Intelligence Services,' *International Affairs*, 53 (1977)
Balogh, Thomas, 'The Apotheosis of the Dilettante: The Establishment of Mandarins,' in Hugh Thomas, ed., *The Establishment* (London, 1969)
Burk, Kathleen, 'The Treasury: From Impotence to Power,' in Burk, ed., *War and the State* (London, 1982)
Cooper, John M., Jr, 'The British Response to the House Grey Memorandum: New Evidence and New Questions,' *Journal of American History*, 59 (1973)
Craig, Gordon, 'The British Foreign Office from Grey to Chamberlain,' in Craig and Felix Gilbert, eds., *The Diplomats* (Princeton, 1953)
Crossman, Richard, 'Introduction' to Walter Bagehot, *The English Constitution* (London, 1963 pb. edn)
Davie, Michael, 'Notebook,' *The Observer* (7, 14, and 21 November 1976)
Davies, Norman, 'Sir Maurice Hankey and the Inter-Allied Mission to Poland, July–August 1920,' *Historical Journal*, 15 (1972)
Dayer, Roberta, 'The British War Debts to the United States and the Anglo-Japanese Alliance, 1920–1923,' *Pacific Historical Review*, 45 (1976)
Fortescue, John, 'The George III Papers,' *The Times* (3, 4, and 6 November 1925)
Fox, James, 'The brains behind the throne,' *The Sunday Times* (25 May 1973)
Hamilton, Sir H.P., 'Sir Warren Fisher and the Public Service,' *Public Administration*, 29 (1951)
Hennessy, Peter, 'The eternal fireman [Lord Radcliffe] who always answers the call to duty,' *The Times* (30 January 1976)
'A magnificent piece of powerful bureaucratic machinery,' *The Times* (8 March 1976)
Jones, G. W., 'The Development of the Cabinet,' in William Thornhill, ed., *The Modernization of British Government* (London, 1975)
Lockwood, P.A., 'Milner's Entry into the War Cabinet, December 1916,' *Historical Journal*, 7 (1964)
Lowe, Peter, 'The Rise to the Premiership,' in A. J. P. Taylor, ed., *Lloyd George: Twelve Essays* (New York, 1971)
Mackintosh, John P., 'The Role of the Committee of Imperial Defence before 1914,' *English Historical Review*, 77 (1962)
MacLeod, Roy M., and Andrews, E. Kay, 'The Committee of Civil Research: Scientific Advice for Economic Development, 1925–1930,' *Minerva*, 7 (1969)
Marder, Arthur, 'The Royal Navy and the Ethiopian Crisis of 1935–36,' *American Historical Review*, 75 (1970)
Middlemas, R.K., 'Cabinet Secrecy and the Crossman Diaries,' *Political Quarterly*, 47 (1976)
Montgomery, A.E., 'Lloyd George and the Greek Question, 1918–1922,' in Taylor, ed., *Lloyd George*
Naylor, John F., 'The Establishment of the Cabinet Secretariat,' *Historical Journal*, 14 (1971)
Newark, F.H., 'The Campbell Case and the First Labour Government,' *Northern Ireland Legal Quarterly*, 20 (1969)

Peden, G. C., 'Sir Warren Fisher and British Rearmament against Germany,' *English Historical Review*, 94 (1979)
Schuyler, R. L., 'The British War Cabinet,' *Political Science Quarterly*, 33 (1918)
Sharp, Alan J., 'The Foreign Office in Eclipse, 1919–1922,' *History*, 61 (1976)
Siederer, N. D., 'The Campbell Case,' *Journal of Contemporary History*, 9 (1974)
Steiner, Zara, and Dockrill, M. L., 'The Foreign Office Reforms, 1919–1921,' *Historical Journal*, 17 (1974)
Thomas, Hugh, 'Towards a Revision of the Official Secrets Act,' in Thomas, ed., *Crisis in the Civil Service* (London, 1968)
Turner, John, 'Cabinets, Committees and Secretariats: The Higher Direction of War,' in Burk, ed., *War and the State*
Warman, Roberta, 'The Erosion of Foreign Office Influence in the Making of Foreign Policy, 1916–1919,' *Historical Journal*, 15 (1972)
Watt, D. C., 'Contemporary History in Britain: Problems and Perspectives,' *Journal of the Society of Archivists* (1969)
'Foreign Affairs, the Public Interest and the Right to Know,' *Political Quarterly*, 34 (1963)
'Restrictions on Research: The Fifty-Year Rule and British Foreign Policy,' *International Affairs*, 41 (1965)
Webb, Sidney, 'The First Labour Government,' *Political Quarterly*, 32 (1961)

Thesis

Dillon, Thomas, 'British Strategic Bombing Doctrine and Policy, 1914–1939,' unpublished doctoral dissertation, State University of New York at Buffalo (1975)

Newspapers and Journals

Some journal articles of lesser importance to this study are not listed above, but each is fully referenced in the Notes. In a similar fashion, far more newspapers have been drawn upon than are here cited, courtesy of the copious file of press clippings kept by the Cabinet Secretariat, which subsequently found their way into a CAB 21 file. The newspapers and journals cited below have been used independently of that convenient source of press opinion. Among newspapers I would specify *The Daily Telegraph, The Observer, The Sunday Telegraph, The Sunday Times* and, indispensably, *The Times*; among journals *The Economist, Law Quarterly Review, The Listener, The Nation, The New Statesman, The Nineteenth Century and After, The Spectator*, and *The Times Literary Supplement*.

Index

Made in the USA
Middletown, DE
01 September 2025

13428779R00262